THE AMERICAN PEACE MOVEMENT
AND SOCIAL REFORM 1898-1918

THE AMERICAN PEACE MOVEMENT AND SOCIAL REFORM, 1898-1918

by C. Roland Marchand

PRINCETON UNIVERSITY PRESS · NEW JERSEY

COPYRIGHT © 1972 BY PRINCETON UNIVERSITY PRESS. ALL RIGHTS
RESERVED. No part of this book may be reproduced in any form or by any
electronic or mechanical means including information storage and retrieval
systems without permission in writing from the publisher, except by a re-
viewer who may quote brief passages in a review. Printed in the United
States of America, by Princeton University Press, Princeton, New Jersey.

L.C. Card: 70-166382   ISBN: 0-691-04609-3

To Betsy

Contents

Preface

In the mid 1890s the peace movement in the United States consisted of a small handful of provincial, impoverished societies with little claim to power or influence. The leaders of these societies had largely reconciled themselves to playing the role of semimartyred visionaries calling for reforms that were too "advanced" to gain current respectability.

By 1912 the movement had become relatively affluent and eminently respectable. Participation in the movement by an impressive number of the nation's political, business, religious, and academic leaders gave promise of influence upon national policy and a kind of "establishment" status.

Yet only five years later, the active portion of the movement was once again weak, financially destitute, and largely excluded from any access to the formulators of national policy. This mercurial rise and fall of the peace movement entailed several substantial changes of leadership and purpose. Underlying the pattern of rise and fall was one of progressive development from genteel mugwumpery to practical conservatism to progressive humanitarianism to social radicalism.

The peace movement between 1898 and 1918 thus offers fascinating opportunities for the study of shifting coalitions of leadership in a reform movement and of the complex organizational expressions of shifting purposes and goals. But the history of the peace movement in this period is far from a self-contained story. No account of its history in terms simply of successive organizations, methods, goals, and day-by-day activities can reveal more than a part of the movement's meaning and function. Its development from 1898 to 1918 was not the mere working out of some inner logic. The dramatic changes of content and purpose reflected not so much a logical progression of ideas, or even the impact of international events, as they did the motives of various groups which successively joined and came to dominate the movement.

Those who participated in the peace movement in these years

cannot be understood simply as "pacifists" or as "peace advocates." Even the officers of the organizations and the most active supporters were often men and women for whom the peace movement was just one among a number of reform and professional concerns. In many cases it was the desire to promote another reform program, to advance the interests of their profession, to exercise social and civic leadership, or to find a safe outlet for philanthropic or reform impulses that brought individuals into peace organizations. Throughout the period the percentage of those in the movement who adhered to a philosophy of nonresistance to violence and war remained infinitesimal. Among the great majority, who were not absolute pacifists, few found the rather abstract idea of world peace capable of commanding their total devotion. Most of the supporters of the movement were absorbed in the pursuit of other reform, professional, or status objectives. It was these other concerns, often supplemented by some particular international experience—through business, travel, or participation in some international organization—that first led them into the peace movement and then determined the purposes to which they sought to direct it.

In tracing the course of the peace movement between 1898 and 1918, therefore, I have not sought to give a complete year-by-year or event-by-event account. Rather, I have tried to emphasize the interconnections of this reform movement with other contemporary social movements and concerns. By analyzing the motives, assumptions, and effects of several distinguishable reform or occupational groups as they successively came to play a significant role in peace organizations, I have come to view the story of the peace movement in these years as a part of innumerable other stories—the campaign for woman suffrage, the movement toward Anglo-American rapprochement, the increase of specialization in the legal profession and the law schools, the impact of Jewish immigration from Eastern Europe upon New York City labor organization, the struggle over judicial recall, the search for industrial harmony, the professionalization of social work, the movements for a social gospel and church unity, the failure of the Socialist Party of America to gain significant political power, and countless others. In nearly every case, the connecting link between these multifarious stories and the peace movement was the perception by some new group of how certain configurations of international politics or attitudes toward international affairs would affect its crucial domestic concerns.

Thus the peace movement, particularly in the period before

1914, provided a kind of superficial overlay that could only partially conceal the fact that different groups and individuals saw in various programs for peace the fulfillment of other more immediately important goals—goals such as the extension and solidification of social reform, the enhancement of the prestige of the courts, the emancipation of women, or the preservation of social stability. Many Americans at the turn of the century, particularly those from older elite groups, shared a central concern about the widening social divisions within the nation—the increasing evidences of industrial upheaval, class antagonism, and declining social homogeneity. Both conservatives and liberals shared these anxieties, although their solutions for the problems of social disharmony often differed. These fears and anxieties about domestic disharmony were projected outward into the realm of foreign affairs, often by analogy. Peace programs were replete with discussions of how to establish law and order in place of international anarchy, how to establish direct democracy internationally, how to control international monopolies or create an international harmony of interests. Leading figures in the peace movement explored the parallels between international relations and such domestic matters as labor disputes or the relations among immigrant groups in American cities.

For some, frustrated in the face of threatening domestic problems, the peace movement may have offered an outlet for ceremonial reform action in a way that would not disturb social arrangements at home. Those who dominated the peace movement in the prewar period were largely moderates or social conservatives. Their plans for peace predictably reflected a longing for order, for stability, for regularity, for the channeling of change into slow processes. Their visions of a triumph of the forces of restraint and order over those of unrest and violence reflected hopes and fears that were as much domestic as foreign in origin. Similarly, at a later stage in the movement, when radical leaders attacked the alleged interventionist and warmongering activities of Wall Street, demanded referendums and people's representatives in future international conferences, and enthusiastically endorsed the peace program of the Petrograd Soviet, they exemplified an outlook shaped largely by the exigencies of domestic radicalism.

Yet the peace movement was not merely an abstracted projection of domestic problems. With international contacts of all varieties increasing, the size of the "attentive public" for discussions of foreign affairs expanded steadily. In the absence of other organizations specifically suited to the public discussion of foreign affairs, the peace organizations assumed the position of foreign policy forums. This was particularly true of the national peace and arbitration congresses and of the yearly conferences at Lake Mohonk, New York. The organizers, speakers, and regular participants in these conferences and organizations formed the first publicly organized elite groups in the United States for the regular dissemination of information about broad issues of foreign affairs and the theoretical discussion of foreign policy.[1]

After about 1905 these conferences and the closely allied peace organizations attracted increasing numbers of national political figures, prominent businessmen and philanthropists, and leading journalists and academicians. Soon most of the policy-making positions in the State Department were held by men who were also members of peace organizations. The peace societies and foundations, and the closely allied international law organizations, served as forums for a national elite engaged in laying the groundwork for popular support of a foreign policy that would meet the needs of a new age of greater international involvement. Prominent clergymen, journalists, and others among the civic elites who held themselves responsible for molding public opinion on a wide range of issues utilized the same occasions for informing themselves on international affairs, developing their own views to pass on to their "constituencies," and inserting their demands for the recognition of certain underlying moral or political assumptions in the formulation of foreign policy.

What resulted from the influx of political and other "influentials" into the peace organizations was a focusing of attention upon what seemed to be the most practical program of the peace movement—international arbitration and an international court. This program rapidly won acceptance as a modification of long-range United States foreign policy toward Europe. As a mildly internationalist appendage to traditional isolationism the program was not without a persuasive logic. Contacts with Europe were increasing. Such changes were both exciting and worrisome. Europe was still looked upon as dangerously unstable; its diplomacy and militarism were distrusted as potentially contaminating. Those political and civic leaders who participated in the peace or-

---

[1] The concept of the "attentive public" is taken from Gabriel Almond, *The American People and Foreign Policy* (New York 1950), pp. 139-43, 150-52, 233, which discusses the role of elite groups in foreign policy formulation. A fruitful application of these and other recent approaches to the role of public-opinion leaders in foreign policy appears in Ernest R. May, *American Imperialism: A Speculative Essay* (New York 1968).

ganizations agreed that balance of power politics, particularly as practiced by European diplomats, was basically immoral and constantly provocative of war.

The question then arose: How could America enjoy the advantages of its more prominent international role without becoming contaminated, or worse yet, becoming involved in the wars that such an alien diplomatic system could produce? How could American economic well-being be protected from the presumed ill effects of war in Europe? The answer was to hold the European system, if possible, at arms distance, while gradually reforming it to conform with a more rational American model, with arbitration tribunals and eventually an international Supreme Court. World organization on judicial lines would not involve the United States in European diplomacy and power politics. Rather, it would settle European quarrels before they flared into wars and endangered American interests or sucked America into the maelstrom.

The gradual emergence of the peace movement as a kind of "establishment" movement in the prewar years, evidenced both by establishment participation in the movement and the adoption of the arbitration and court program as a basic element in official foreign policy toward Europe, helps explain some curious problems that arise when one attempts to analyze the peace movement as a "reform" movement. Most reform movements have had some distinctive antiestablishment qualities. They have had as their goals the removal of those presently in power, or the reform of present institutions, or the promotion of a change in policy. But despite occasional and specific criticisms, the peace movement was largely satisfied with American political leadership and with American foreign policy. Most of the spokesmen for the prewar peace movement were almost ecstatic over American political institutions and proposed them unreservedly for models abroad. The State Department was presumably the agency of the government which peace interests would most wish to influence, but such influence required no reform. A large number of the significant posts in the department between 1905 and 1914 were held by men who were active in peace organizations. Presidents Taft and Wilson were both members of peace societies, as were Secretaries of State Root, Bacon, Knox, Bryan, and Lansing.

What, then, did the "reformers" in this reform movement seek to reform? The answer to this question for different factions of the peace movement, or for the most active leaders in any given period, again reveals the importance of the other preoccupations and goals of the members of peace organizations. The changes that various peace groups sought in international relations were never divorced from considerations, overt or latent, of what would make the world safe for woman suffrage, the labor movement, domestic law and order, social welfare reforms, or international commerce. Although nearly all supporters of peace organizations could agree upon the desirability of preventing major outbreaks of international violence, shifting leadership groups in the movement came to quite different conclusions about "what" or "who" should be reformed to accomplish the desired ends.

In the prewar period, particularly between 1906 and 1914, the leaders of the peace movement could discover little in American leadership, institutions, or policies that required reform—except, perhaps, for an overly provincial Senate that failed to share their enthusiasm for arbitration treaties. The proper objects for reform lay elsewhere. Convinced that in foreign policy as in domestic matters the dangers of violence and turmoil came largely from the "turbulent masses," the conservatively inclined leaders of the peace movement sought to educate the populace in a respect for law and treaties, and in qualities of self-restraint that would make them less restless and warlike. But more significant than this impulse to reform the masses was the desire to reform European diplomacy. It was the secret diplomacy, militarism, and nondemocratic institutions of the major European powers that stood in the way of a peaceful world. Since the reform impulses of the prewar peace movement were thus directed largely "downward" and "outward," toward the masses and toward Europe, it was not incongruous for the movement to develop close ties with the establishment yet remain a movement for reform.

Until late in 1914, the peace movement comfortably maintained this position as a relatively uncontroversial establishment reform movement. The common animus of most Americans against the aristocratic institutions and the frankly power-oriented diplomacy of Europe afforded the basis for support by both liberals and conservatives of vague programs to replace European diplomacy with international institutions patterned after American models. Even staunch radicals could hardly protest when Andrew Carnegie championed peace and denounced militarism, power politics, and European aristocracy. During the war such organizations as the League to Enforce Peace, the World Court League, and the Carnegie Endowment for International Peace perpetuated the basic attitudes of this establishment movement and continued to find favor in official circles.

But beginning in late 1914, the peace movement gained vitality from the activity of new peace organizations led by men and women who were stirred by fears of the effect of the war upon social reform. These new organizations—epitomized by the Woman's Peace Party and the American Union Against Militarism rejected many of the assumptions and reform objectives of the prewar movement. They rejected entirely the responsibility of the masses for war and began to find faults with American diplomacy and American institutions. Eventually this segment of the movement was to conclude that fundamental changes in American society and institutions were a necessary part of any world movement toward the reform of international relations.

In tracing the changes of leadership and reform purpose in the peace movement, I have sacrificed strict chronological continuity in an attempt to analyze the motives which led particular groups to join the movement and to describe the manner in which these groups interpreted and shaped it. Therefore, I have devoted separate chapters to the development of each group's interest in the peace movement and the eventual organizational and ideological form which this interest assumed. The participation of a distinguishable new group in the movement was frequently marked by the appearance of a new peace organization, since such groups as the woman suffragists, the international lawyers, the social workers, the Socialists, and the promoters of church unity all found the existing peace societies at the time of their entrance into the movement unsatisfactory instruments for the expression of their particular ideas or programs. Thus chapters devoted to the role of particular groups in the peace movement also focus upon the origins, characteristics, and impact of a variety of peace organizations. Although obviously not every member of such groups as the international lawyers or the woman suffragists or the social workers entered the peace movement at exactly the same time, still members of most of these groups came into the movement as part of a sudden surge of interest in peace by the whole group. By discussing these groups in the order in which they came to exert an appreciable impact upon the peace movement, I have been able to preserve vestiges of a chronological survey of major phases of the movement's development.

In emphasizing the generalized ideologies of various groups and organizations within the peace movement, I recognize that I have occasionally given only partial depictions of the whole spectrum of ideas held by some of the individuals involved. Similarly, in emphasizing the fundamental changes within the movement, I have devoted relatively little attention to "peace workers" who did not participate significantly in those changes. But shifting organizational patterns and profound ideological changes were the hallmarks of the peace movement between 1898 and 1918. Within the span of these two decades, the movement embraced a membership and a body of ideas as diverse as those which had characterized any previous reform movement in the United States. This diversity was sequential rather than static, a result of the influx of new professional, reform, and special interest groups into the movement. And in an age in which most Americans were preoccupied with domestic political and social issues, the biases and programs that new groups carried over from their domestic concerns into their newer, and often more superficial, interest in international relations were crucial in determining the various configurations which the evolving peace movement assumed.

Thus I have placed my emphasis on the network of interrelationships between the peace movement and the domestic concerns of its various groups of participants. In so doing, I have not meant to suggest that individuals who joined the peace movement were inspired only by such motivations as the desire to promote woman suffrage or advance church unity or exalt the virtues of business or law or scholarship. But neither do I find it fruitful to continue to envision them as motivated solely by instincts toward "pacifism," or "internationalism," or to characterize them simply as "peace workers" or "peace advocates." The *kind* of pacifist or peace advocate that an individual became, I am convinced, was deeply influenced by his attitudes toward issues of domestic social and political reform. These attitudes, in turn, were often shaped by the professional or reform groups to which he belonged. And it was the way in which a series of these groups came to see the peace movement as an extension of their domestic attitudes or programs that brought diversity and change into the movement—which made it, in these years, truly a protean reform.

Acknowledgments

DURING nearly a decade of scholarly investigation of the peace movement in the United States, I have benefited from the support of several institutions and the assistance and scholarly advice of many individuals. Among the numerous librarians, scholars, and institutions that have given me their generous assistance, I wish to make particular mention of those to whom I owe a special indebtedness.

A thorough reevaluation and reorientation of my interpretation of the peace movement was made possible by a research fellowship at the Charles Warren Center for Studies in American History during the year 1967-1968. I am greatly indebted to the Center and to Professor Oscar Handlin, its director, for a year spent in an atmosphere of stimulating intellectual interchange and in close proximity to the voluminous manuscript sources in East Coast repositories. A summer faculty fellowship from the University of California, Davis enabled me to complete the final major chapter and make necessary revisions. The Academic Senate Committee on Research of the University of California, Davis has been both generous and patient in its support of a project that has extended well beyond its expected date of completion.

Several individuals have offered special guidance and stimulating criticism. Professor George Harmon Knoles of Stanford University first directed my attention to the research possibilities in the history of the peace movement and attempted to sharpen my standards of precision in writing and research. I was especially fortunate, not only in the guidance of my doctoral research but also in my preparation as a teacher, to learn from a dissertation adviser, Professor Otis A. Pease, whose approach to history has exemplified the most stimulating and humane qualities of teacher and scholar.

Professor Paul Goodman of the University of California, Davis read an early version of the study and offered a perceptive critique that reinforced my resolve to reapproach my topic from a new perspective. Professors Irwin Unger of New York University and Ernest May of Harvard University read substantial portions of the manuscript at different stages and made valuable suggestions. Professors William N. Chambers of Washington University, St. Louis, James Holt of the University of Auckland, David Grimsted of the University of Maryland, Valentin Rabe of State University College, Geneseo, New York, and David Brody, Daniel Calhoun, and Wilson Smith of the University of California, Davis kindly read and commented upon chapters or portions of chapters of the manuscript. Others, including Professors William R. Hutchison of the Harvard School of Divinity, Charles Chatfield of Wittenberg University, Blanche Wiesen Cook of John Jay College, City University of New York, Tamara Hareven of Clark University, Oscar Handlin, and the late Richard Hofstadter spared time to discuss with me the problems surrounding my interpretation of the peace movement of the progressive era. In the processes of final revision I have been aided by valuable advice from Mr. Sanford G. Thatcher of Princeton University Press, and have benefited greatly from his sympathy with my basic line of approach. Unfortunately I lacked the time, energy, and wisdom to respond adequately to many of the constructive criticisms and ideas these colleagues suggested. Certainly only I am responsible for the omissions, errors, or vagaries of interpretation that may still remain.

Any historian of the peace movement in the United States finds himself heavily dependent upon the manuscript sources available in the Swarthmore College Peace Collection. I am much indebted to Miss Ardith Emmons and Mrs. Bernice B. Nichols, curators of the Collection, for their many forms of assistance. Mrs. Arline Paul helpfully guided me through the David Starr Jordan Papers and other collections at the Hoover Institution on War, Revolution and Peace and Mr. Kimball B. Elkins assisted me in the use of the Lowell and Eliot Papers in the Harvard University Archives. Miss Cynthia Cheney of the University of California, Davis library bore patiently with my frequent demands on the services of interlibrary loan. The curators and librarians of the Houghton Library, Harvard University, the Harvard University Archives, the New York Public Library, the Columbia University Library, the Tamiment Institute and Library, the Rollins College Library, the Arthur and Elizabeth Schlesinger Library, the Manuscript Division of the Library of Congress and the Henry E. Huntington Library extended assistance, hospitality, and often special services. Mr. John R. Inman, vice-president of the Council on Religion and International Affairs, was most hospitable in providing me access to the papers of the Church Peace Union in the council's archives.

Among several students who aided me briefly as research assistants I wish particularly to acknowledge the efforts of Daniel Wright, Kathleen Weisker, Claudia Marson, and Frank Lortie. Miss Judy Ryerson, Miss Patricia Banks, and Mrs. Doris Craven patiently converted the tortuous pages of rough draft into a comprehensible typed manuscript. The careful copyediting and perceptive suggestions of Mrs. Polly Hanford of Princeton University Press were invaluable. I have been encouraged in my labor by many friends and relatives who have been kind enough to inquire about the progress of my work, and to continue their encouraging inquiries in the face of unpromising "progress reports." My mother, Mildred Marchand, helped sustain me with her confidence that I would surely reach the end, and my daughters Suzy and Jean accepted patiently and lovingly the absences and curtailed activities that came as part of the demands of "the book." Above all, to my wife, Betsy Ann Marchand, whose editorial wisdom and loving encouragement both stimulated and consoled me during this long process, I owe a gratitude more profound than the dedication of this book can express.

C. ROLAND MARCHAND
Davis, California
July 1972

THE AMERICAN PEACE MOVEMENT
AND SOCIAL REFORM 1898-1918

Key to Abbreviations

ACDTP	American Conference on Democracy and Terms of Peace
APS	American Peace Society
ASIL	American Society of International Law
ASJSID	American Society for the Judicial Settlement of International Disputes
AUAM	American Union Against Militarism
CEIP	Carnegie Endowment for International Peace
CPU	Church Peace Union
CRIA	Council on Religion and International Affairs, New York City
CUL	Columbia University Library
FC	Federal Council of the Churches of Christ in America
FHL	Friends' Historical Library, Swarthmore College
FOR	Fellowship of Reconciliation
HA	Harvard University Archives
HHL	Henry E. Huntington Library, San Marino, California
HI	Hoover Institution on War, Revolution and Peace, Stanford, California
HL	Houghton Library, Harvard University
LC	Library of Congress
LEP	League to Enforce Peace
NYPL	New York Public Library
NYPS	New York Peace Society
OHRO	Oral History Research Office, Columbia University
PC	People's Council of America for Democracy and Peace
SCPC	Swarthmore College Peace Collection
SL	Arthur and Elizabeth Schlesinger Library, Radcliffe College
TL	Tamiment Institute and Library, New York City
WA	World Alliance for International Friendship Through the Churches
WPF	World Peace Foundation
WPP	Woman's Peace Party
WPPNY	Woman's Peace Party, New York Branch

CHAPTER ONE

Up from Sentimentalism

THE year 1909, to the casual observer, may easily assume the appearance of a banner year for the peace movement in the United States. Statements by leaders of the movement during that year bristled with pride, expectancy, and optimism. "No congress in our land," boasted Frederick Lynch, gained so large an attendance as the recent New York Arbitration Congress of 1907. "Now we have the sight of statesmen and governors and kings of finance almost fighting each other at peace gatherings to get the rostrum to plead for the peace of the world. . . ." During the same year, Edwin D. Mead in Boston proclaimed the arrival of "the critical hour in the history of the peace movement," an hour when "decisive success . . . seems clearly within sight."[1]

From a more distant perspective, the single year 1909 retains little of this implied significance as an apogee or turning point within the peace movement in the United States. Prophecies and assessments, equally sanguine, had flowed regularly from the lips and pens of leaders of the peace movement every year since the turn of the century. Yet Lynch and Mead, both of whom were soon to gain positions as directors of endowed peace foundations, were not entirely mistaken in their perceptions. A change *had* occurred in the peace movement in recent years. Other leaders soon announced their own, corroborating discovery: that the "missionary" or "sentimental" phase of the peace movement had come to an end. A new age of practical advance had begun.

With increasing frequency, after about 1909, leaders of the peace movement emphasized how what formerly had been merely a moral reform was now becoming a "science." Idealists, necessary in their time, were giving way to practical men of affairs. As

---

[1] Lynch, "The Minister in Association with International Movements," in Charles S. Macfarland, ed., *The Christian Ministry and the Social Order* (New Haven 1909), p. 301; Mead, *The Literature of the Peace Movement* (Boston 1909), p. 14. For similar expressions of optimism about the "new" peace movement in 1909, see *Advocate of Peace*, 71 (Apr. 1909), 91; 71 (May 1909), 100; 71 (June 1909), 21; and Benjamin F. Trueblood, "The Present Position of the International Peace Movement," *Proceedings of the Second National Peace Congress* (Chicago 1909), p. 92.

the sentimental and relatively obscure apostles of peace proved ill equipped to meet the problems and take advantage of the opportunities of a new age, prominent businessmen, national religious and educational leaders, and men of political influence were taking over the leadership of the peace organizations. The day of the statesman and organizer was at hand.[2]

But this much-proclaimed transformation from ineffective idealism to influential practicality had only recently begun. At the turn of the century the peace societies at least partly deserved inclusion among those "somnolent and inactive" reform associations described by John Jay Chapman as having fine names, an "aroma of original benevolence," and a constituency of "respectable, rich, lazy and conservative people."[3] (Radicals were later to argue that, despite all the recent changes in the peace movement, Chapman's description still applied in 1914.) Having first come of age in the 1830s and 1840s, in company with such compatible moral and social reform movements as temperance, religious perfectionism, and abolitionism, the American peace movement carried forward into the twentieth century many characteristics acquired during the reform surge of half a century earlier.[4] A number of its leaders at the beginning of the twentieth century were also active in the temperance cause. Many still identified the moral reformism of the peace movement with that of the abolitionist crusade, comparing their progress with that of the abolitionists of the 1850s. Such a comparison served to stimulate their optimism and exaggerate the extent of their radicalism and mar-

[2] William I. Hull, "The New Peace Movement," *Swarthmore College Bulletin*, 7 (Sept. 1909), 6; Theodore Marburg, "Salient Thoughts of the Conference," *Proceedings of the American Society for Judicial Settlement of International Disputes, 1910*, p. ix; Elihu Root, "The Importance of Judicial Settlement," in *ibid.*, p. 9; Charles E. Beals, "The St. Louis Congress," *The Survey*, 30 (17 May 1913), 247; Fannie Fern Andrews, "The Objectives of the American School Peace League," enclosure to Andrews to William I. Hull, 5 Jan. 1909, Box 1, William I. Hull Papers, Friends' Historical Library, Swarthmore College; W. H. Short to "Dear Sir" (form letter), 23 Nov. 1909, Andrew Carnegie Papers, MS Div., Library of Congress; New York Peace Society, *Year Book 1909-1910* (New York 1910), p. 7; Frederick Lynch, *The Peace Problem: The Task of the Twentieth Century* (New York 1911), pp. 81-84.

[3] Quoted in Oswald Garrison Villard, "What is Wrong with our Pacifists?" typed speech MS, Oswald Garrison Villard Papers, Houghton Library, Harvard University, p. 6.

[4] The best monographs on the early years of the peace movement in the United States are Merle Curti, *The American Peace Crusade* (Durham, N.C. 1929) and Christina Phelps, *The Anglo-American Peace Movement in the Mid-Nineteenth Century* (New York 1930). For ties with other reform movements, see esp. Phelps, pp. 27-29, Curti, pp. 29, 51, 64; and Peter Brock, *Pacifism in the United States: From the Colonial Era to the First World War* (Princeton 1968), pp. 527-38, 541, 560, 562, 578.

tyrdom. Identification with abolitionism, a moral crusade which had triumphed despite initial unpopularity, may have helped sustain them while they were forced to acknowledge, as late as 1900, that leading newspapers still characterized their conferences as gatherings of "enthusiasts, visionaries and cranks."[5] Certainly during the first few years of the twentieth century, the structure, personnel, and literature of the peace movement reflected as much of the genteel reformism of its origins as it did of the businesslike practicality of the decade to come.

To understand the transformation that took place in the peace movement during the first decade of the century, it is necessary to look first at the composition, ideas, and leaders of the major peace organizations at the opening of the century and then at the way in which international events and new leaders were beginning to push the peace movement, by 1905, toward new prominence and popularity. The changes that had already taken place by 1905, and the new leaders who had begun to appear on the peace movement's horizon, had by then set the stage for the emergence of the organized international lawyers, the impact of endowed peace foundations, and the campaign for business support that would bring the peace movement affluence, influence, and respectability by the eve of World War I.

The largest and oldest of the peace organizations at the turn of the century was the venerable American Peace Society. Now laboring under the burden of over seven decades of accumulated Victorianism, the society had begun in 1828 as a coalition of several local peace societies. Its goals were "to illustrate the inconsistency of war with Christianity, to show its baleful influence on all the great interests of mankind, and to devise means for insuring universal and permanent peace."[6] At its founding, the society had been impoverished, provincial, and without significant influence upon national leaders or policies. Three-quarters of a century later none of these conditions had changed. In the interim the society had oscillated between modest prominence and quies-

---

[5] *Report of the Sixth Annual Meeting of the Lake Mohonk Conference on International Arbitration* (Lake Mohonk, N.Y. 1900), p. 116 (hereafter cited as *Mohonk Conference* with appropriate date); Hull, "The New Peace Movement," p. 5; *Advocate of Peace*, 71 (June 1908), 129; 75 (May 1913), 102; *Proceedings of the American Society for Judicial Settlement of International Disputes, 1911*, p. 89. For further examples of and commentary on the prediliction of leaders of the peace movement to draw analogies from the abolitionist crusade, see David Sands Patterson, "The Travail of the American Peace Movement, 1887-1914," Ph.D. diss., University of California, Berkeley, 1968, pp. 261-62.

[6] *Advocate of Peace*, 1 (June 1837), 30.

cent obscurity. It had condemned a host of minor wars; but in 1861 the abolitionist sympathies of many of its leaders had brought it to reject compromise with the South and acquiesce in a major conflict. During the 1870s and 1880s its energies had been largely absorbed in the effort simply to stay alive. In all these years the society had advanced little beyond its founders' ideas or methods.[7]

Needless to say, the American Peace Society drew certain strengths from its continuity with the New England reform tradition. The society's leaders at the turn of the century could still rely with absolute moral certainty upon those Enlightenment ideas of reason, education, and the dignity and universality of man which antebellum New England reformers had embodied in their moral crusades. The giants of New England's nineteenth century intellectual life and moral activism—Emerson, Thoreau, Channing, Alcott, Garrison, Parker, Samuel Gridley Howe, Dorothea Dix, Horace Mann—seemed to stand behind them, as well as their more direct reform ancestors—Elihu Burritt, William Ladd, and Noah Worcester. In a host of civic commitments and reform movements, from temperance and abolitionism to feminism, school reform, municipal housing, and insane asylum and prison reform, their predecessors had taught them that men, by their active efforts, could succeed in shaping their society in the image of the ideal. Edward Everett Hale, an active leader in the peace movement in 1900 and a living link with the antebellum reform tradition, succinctly described the legacy of reform optimism in *James Russell Lowell and His Friends*: "If they made a school for the blind, they made it for all the blind people in Massachusetts. They expected it to succeed. They always had succeeded. Why should they not succeed?"[8]

After the tarnished years of the late nineteenth century, of course, the heirs of the New England reform tradition were no longer so accustomed to prompt success. But they retained a deep

[7] Edson L. Whitney, *The American Peace Society: A Centennial History* (Washington, D.C. 1928), 112-13, 136-38, 148; Merle Curti, *Peace or War: The American Struggle, 1636-1936* (New York 1936), pp. 50-58; Brock, *Pacifism in the United States*, pp. 689-91, 707-9.

[8] Quoted in Martin Green, *The Problem of Boston: Some Readings in Cultural History* (New York 1966), p. 43. The following paragraphs rest upon the portraits of late nineteenth century Boston reformers presented by Green and by Arthur Mann, *Yankee Reformers in the Urban Age: Social Reform in Boston, 1880-1900* (Cambridge, Mass. 1954); Barbara Miller Solomon, *Ancestors and Immigrants: A Changing New England Tradition* (Cambridge, Mass. 1956); and Geoffrey Blodgett, *The Gentle Reformers: Massachusetts Democrats in the Cleveland Era* (Cambridge, Mass. 1966).

sense of social responsibility and the conviction that labor and self-sacrifice on behalf of a cause with moral connotations could not go unrewarded. The ultimate success of such an endeavor was inevitable. The frustrations of current defeats and the indignities of ridicule or neglect could thus be endured with fortitude, even with a complacency born of faith in eventual triumph. To a certain degree, the leaders of the peace movement "measured pleasure," as Arthur Mann remarks of other heirs of the reform tradition, "by the amount of pain they suffered in helping mankind," accepting "public indifference or hostility as a sign that their ideas were predestined to prevail in the future."[9]

The leaders of the American Peace Society, so intimately connected with the political mugwumps of the age and region, thus buttressed their optimism with a willingness to fall back upon the mugwump sense of moral grandeur in defeats suffered on behalf of principle.[10] But since the defeats suffered by the peace movement were so easily dismissed as aberrant outbreaks of violence that would reinforce public abhorrence of war, an atmosphere of hopefulness was sustained. In this movement, men who had inherited a need for a sustaining reform optimism might escape the dismaying frustrations of local politics and overwhelming urban problems by fixing their attention on a universal cause. In this new reform arena, they might rest confident that the irresistible forces of universal progress would themselves insure the triumph of world peace, a reform (like antislavery in the nineteenth century) whose time had come, if only its champions kept alive the ideas and spread the message.

The issues arising from immigration, urbanization, and industrialization had found the inheritors of the New England reform tradition politically ineffective, unable to formulate a simple, satisfactory moral response, and unwilling to contemplate fundamental economic and social reforms that might challenge continuity, harmony, and social balance. But such reform issues as the peace movement provided an attractive alternative for exercising reform propensities. Here genteel reformers might continue to satisfy their impulses toward civic responsibility and public action. Here they could apply the methods of moral suasion and intellectual leadership through education that they believed had achieved victory for abolitionism and would yet be vindicated in the temperance cause. Hence, the American Peace Society not only drew upon the same professional groups and so-

9 Mann, *Yankee Reformers*, pp. 234-35.
10 Blodgett, *Gentle Reformers*, pp. 46, 269.

cial circles for its leadership in 1900 as it had in the 1830s, but it also carried forward the same reform attitudes, by now less ardent in intensity, more "pastel" in tone, more antiquated in style, that it had developed during its period of early growth.

It was not only the inherited nineteenth century reform attitudes that gave the American Peace Society a slightly archaic cast. The average age of those who held positions as officers in the society between 1900 and 1905 was sixty-three.[11] Of the ninety officers in this period whose birthdate could be determined, twenty-nine were seventy or over. Members of the group directly responsible for the operation of the society, the board of directors, averaged a more sprightly sixty-one. Prominent Bostonians such as Julia Ward Howe, Edward Everett Hale, and Mary A. Livermore, characterized by Arthur Mann as already "old-time reformers" and "survivors in the age of newness" in the 1880s, were still active in the leadership of the American Peace Society and other peace organizations two decades later.[12]

Nor were all the octogenarians as active as this triumvirate. Occasionally one of the elder members of the board was too ill or senile to join the discussions, and the society's organ, the *Advocate of Peace*, found cause for elation in 1899 because the new members that year had managed to more than replace those lost by death. Several octogenarians were reported to have attended board meetings until a few weeks or days of their death. In 1901, when the society changed offices, its announcement of the move proclaimed the most notable improvement to be the acquisition of an elevator, making access easier to those who had difficulty climbing two flights of stairs.[13] Judged in physical terms alone, the American Peace Society of 1900-1905 did not seem a likely source of vigor for pressing the peace campaign in the century ahead.

The debilitating effects of superannuation upon the society were supplemented by the weaknesses of provinciality. Although it pretended to national scope and influence, the society drew nearly all of its active leadership from the environs of Boston.

[11] These figures and the subsequent descriptions of the leadership of the American Peace Society are based upon a survey of the 117 persons who served as its officers during any portion of the period from 1900 through 1905. In most instances the information given is confined to the 90 out of a total sample of 117 for whom dates of birth and a minimum level of other information could be obtained. Figures for average ages were computed by subtracting dates of birth from the midpoint of the period selected, 1903. Lists of the officers are given in Whitney, *American Peace Society*, pp. 320-37, and in each issue of the *Advocate of Peace*.

[12] Mann, *Yankee Reformers*, pp. 11-13.

[13] *Advocate of Peace*, 61 (May 1899), 103; 63 (July 1901), 142; 63 (Sept. 1901), 169.

All seven members of the executive committee in 1905 were from the Boston area. All nineteen directors of the society were residents of Massachusetts. Even a majority of the vice-presidents, most of whom played no direct part in the management of the society, were drawn from New England. In June of 1905, out of eighty-six officers, only two came from south of Washington, D.C. and only ten from west of Ohio.[14] An auxiliary society had been formed in Chicago in 1902 but it had expired when its president left Chicago shortly thereafter. By 1904 the *Advocate of Peace* was listing three auxiliaries outside of New England—the defunct Chicago society and two others in Kansas and Minnesota—but none of these represented an effective or growing organization. Such regional provinciality was nearly matched by the degree of racial and religious exclusiveness. In 1905, among eighty-six officers, not one blemished the purity of the society's Protestantism and only Booker T. Washington represented a minority race.[15]

The regional provinciality, in particular, seems now to have been both symbolic and appropriate, just as the emergence of New York City as the center of the peace movement of the subsequent decade and the transfer of the American Peace Society headquarters to Washington, D.C. in 1912 were symbolic of the triumph of new forces in the movement after 1905. Not only did the Boston setting reflect the continuity of the American Peace Society with the New England reform tradition, but the predominant style of the society, that of gentlemanly high-mindedness, scholarly reasonableness, and righteous but restrained moral activism could scarcely have enjoyed as congenial an environment elsewhere as it did in Boston. Here, among the sons and daughters of the Brahmins, those social amenities were instinctively observed which reflected the qualities of restraint, dignity, order, and a sense of fitness and taste that were understood to embody the characteristics of a world at peace. And here the relatively leisurely pace of the seventy-year-old peace movement's reform activities found a partial haven from the intense pressures of a wider culture dominated by the new standards of business efficiency. If the Boston of that day seemed to have undergone a cultural decline in the face of foreign immigration and the vulgarities of urban politics and business amoralism, its "better element" might compensate for being shut out of local politics and having their proffered reform leadership discounted by asserting their

14 *Ibid.*, 67 (June 1905), 138.
15 *Ibid.*, 66 (June 1904), 113; 67 (June 1905), 138; Whitney, *American Peace Society*, p. 278.

standards in a wider realm. Perhaps the violence and restlessness of immigrant and other turbulent and uneducated groups at home could be counteracted by the reeducation of the whole society in the ideas of order and restraint that would also stave off potential threats to order and stability by turbulent nations and peoples abroad.

In many ways, as we shall see, the leaders of the peace movement were eager to enter the new age; but they parted reluctantly with the amenities, the security of very slow and undisruptive progress, the sense of moral autonomy and partly imagined martyrdom that characterized their Bostonian past. Under the heading "Pleasant Days at the Peace Office in Boston," James L. Tryon, a subsequent director of the society, later recalled nostalgically the rows of the old, historic literature of the peace movement "tastefully bound" upon the secretary's shelves and the days when the Boston group *was* the peace movement, when popular interest was low, when the president and other gentlemen of the society would call at the office and invite the staff to luncheon. To such sensibilities, the success of such subsequent events as the 1907 Arbitration and Peace Congress in New York City was "bewildering." "What followed almost immediately," Tryon reminisced, "I have often likened to a tidal wave, sweeping everything before it."[16]

But in the first years of the twentieth century, the "tidal wave" that brought the movement prominence, prestige, and "establishment" status was as yet hardly visible upon the horizon. While the American Peace Society's leadership included several figures of regional and even national prominence, few of these leaders could wield political power or exercise direct influence upon foreign policy. In the early twentieth century clergymen still played a large role in the peace organizations, their presence serving to accentuate the moral and nonpolitical nature of the movement. In 1905 ministers and bishops constituted nearly one-third of the vice-presidents and directors of the American Peace Society. The same kind of moral emphasis was represented by presidents of small colleges such as Amherst, Wellesley, Bryn Mawr, Macalaster, and Western Reserve.[17] Influential university presidents such

---

[16] Tryon, "Dr. Trueblood at Work," copy of typed MS dated 1919 in Box 8, American Peace Society Papers, Swarthmore College Peace Collection.

[17] These were: Merrill Gates of Amherst, Alice Freeman Palmer of Wellesley, M. Carey Thomas of Bryn Mawr, James Wallace of Macalaster, and Charles F. Thwing of Western Reserve. Within the next three years David Starr Jordan of Stanford, Mary Woolley of Mt. Holyoke, and S. P. Brooks of Baylor became officers also.

as Charles W. Eliot of Harvard and Nicholas Murray Butler of Columbia, who were later prominent in the peace movement, had not been attracted to the society. The other officers of the society, largely lawyers, journalists, philanthropists, and assorted free-lance reformers, included several persons of national reputation such as Jane Addams, Edward Atkinson, Josephine Shaw Lowell, Moorfield Storey, and Booker T. Washington, but few who were in a position to influence national policy on international matters. Moreover, most of these prominent figures served merely in honorary positions. Except for the presence of three former Boston mayors among its vice-presidents, the society's only claim to direct political influence or even recognition by American political leadership in these first years of the century was the name of the aging Secretary of State John Sherman among its honorary officers. The absence of political "influentials" among its leadership meant that as of 1905 the American Peace Society could hope to influence national action only by shaping public opinion.

The character of the reform motives and attitudes which the leaders of the American Peace Society carried into their peace activities is probably best revealed through examination of their other reform and philanthropic interests. Many of the leaders of the society were best known for their work in other causes and most of them divided their energies among several organized reforms or philanthropies. Nineteen of the officers between 1900 and 1905 were also active participants in the cause of Indian reform, either as members of the Indian Rights Association or as participants in the Lake Mohonk Conferences of the Friends of the Indian.[18] Herbert Welsh, Phillip C. Garrett, Merrill Gates, and Lyman Abbott were among the foremost leaders of Indian reform. Temperance claimed the allegiance of another significant segment of the American Peace Society officers. Four were prominent officers in the Women's Christian Temperance Union; another was president of the National Temperance Society; and numerous others gave frequent support to the temperance cause.[19] Several of the officers, including the president of the Massachusetts Woman Suffrage Association, the editor of the *Woman's Journal*, and such assiduous women's rights advocates as Mary Livermore and Julia

[18] *Proceedings of the Lake Mohonk Conference of Friends of the Indian* (1895-1905); *Annual Reports of the Executive Committee of the Indian Rights Association* (1895-1905).
[19] Those most prominent in temperance work were: Hannah J. Bailey, Maria Freeman Gray, Mary A. Livermore, Ruth H. Spray, Mrs. L.M.N. Stevens, and Joshua Baily.

Ward Howe combined interest in the crusade for peace with that for votes for women.[20]

In view of their sympathy with various reform movements of conscious moral purpose at home, it is not surprising that leaders of the American Peace Society were also particularly attracted to causes other than the peace movement which embodied a moral or religious approach to international issues. At least thirty-two officers gave active support to anti-imperialist organizations or spoke at anti-imperialist meetings during the late 1890s, some arguing that the two movements were inseparable.[21] Several leaders in the Protestant foreign missions movement, including Samuel B. Capen, the president of the American Board of Commissioners for Foreign Missions, participated actively in the American Peace Society.

Other organizations that attracted the interest of leaders in the society often held only a single crucial characteristic in common with the peace movement. As reputable and unobjectionable philanthropies they offered safe outlets for reform impulses in ways that required no disruptive social change. One officer was editor of *Our Dumb Animals* and president of the Massachusetts Society for Prevention to Cruelty to Animals. Four others were leading officers in local animal rescue leagues. One was president of the Boston Children's Aid Society and another devoted his attentions to the "Home for Little Wanderers." Two served on the Board of Governors of the Massachusetts SPCA.[22] A number of other officers belonged to essentially charitable agencies for legal aid, housing, or employment for the poor. Edward Atkinson, a freelance economist, was the inventor of the Aladdin Oven, a stove utilizing a low-cost fuel which he promoted along with diet suggestions as a salvation for the poor, allowing them to eat better on

20 Lucia Ames Mead was president of the Massachusetts Woman Suffrage Association. Alice Stone Blackwell, daughter of Lucy Stone, edited the most prominent suffrage periodical, the *Woman's Journal*. Other officers of the society such as Hannah Bailey, Jane Addams, M. Carey Thomas, and May Wright Sewall were active supporters of woman suffrage.

21 Information on participants in anti-imperialist organizations was gathered from various pamphlets and other literature of the Anti-Imperialist League of New York, and the Anti-Imperialist League (Boston). On the interconnections between anti-imperialism and the peace movement, see also E. Berkeley Tompkins, *Anti-Imperialism in the United States: The Great Debate, 1890-1920* (Philadelphia 1970), pp. 157-58.

22 These were, in the order cited above: George T. Angell; Edward H. Clement, Julia Ward Howe, Edward Everett Hale, and Ruth H. Spray; Robert Treat Paine; Everett O. Fisk; Kate Gannett Wells and George T. Angell.

their low wages.[23] Two officers, Josephine Shaw Lowell and Robert Treat Paine, were best known as leaders of major urban charity organization societies. Several others had led organizations for prison reform, civil service reform, or municipal and civic reform.

The image that emerges from this panorama of overlapping interests is one of an impulse toward ameliorative public service, toward action on behalf of "the good," toward exercise of the moral instincts, channeled primarily into safe and conservative reforms. The peace movement with its combination of exalted goals, unblemished moral respectability, and restrained methods shared the attractions of social causes that blended reform with philanthropy. Certainly the family backgrounds, social positions, and cultural interests of the American Peace Society leaders were consonant with such genteel reformism. Representatives of old Boston families such as Robert Treat Paine, Josephine Shaw Lowell, Kate Gannett Wells, George Foster Peabody, and Julia Ward Howe lent an aura of aristocratic *noblesse oblige* to the society, while Alice Stone Blackwell, Edward Atkinson, Mary Livermore, George Dana Boardman, and numerous others represented the moral impulse of missionary and abolitionist family backgrounds.

The attitudes suggested by the composition of the American Peace Society's leadership were further reflected in the tone of its publications, the *Advocate of Peace* and the *Angel of Peace*. The latter, a peace periodical for children, was advertised as "devoted to peace, temperance, good morals and good manners" and as "free from over-exciting, sensational reading."[24] It promised to cultivate in youth the quality of personal self-restraint, the attribute of character most admired by genteel reformers and most conducive, in their opinion, to peace, temperance, and other worthy causes. The *Advocate of Peace*, the society's regular monthly periodical, exemplified the same concern on an adult level. It stressed the need for a "sensible, conservative spirit" and lauded every triumph of reason and restraint over passion and violence.[25] Editorial reviews of recent developments in interna-

[23] Among those active in such efforts were Edwin Ginn, Edwin D. Mead, Frederic Cunningham, Robert Treat Paine, Philip Garrett, and Kate Gannett Wells. On Atkinson see Robert L. Beisner, *Twelve Against Empire: The Anti-Imperialists, 1898-1900* (New York 1968), pp. 89-90 and Geoffrey T. Blodgett, "The Mind of the Boston Mugwump," *Mississippi Valley Historical Review*, 68 (Mar. 1962), 627.

[24] This advertisement appeared in every issue of the *Advocate of Peace* between 1900 and 1905.

[25] *Advocate of Peace*, 65 (Jan. 1903), 1.

tional relations were usually supplemented by original peace
poetry, extended excerpts from peace sermons, and reprints of
significant addresses at peace conferences. The emphasis of
editorial comments fluctuated from portrayals of the horrors,
cruelty, and wickedness of war to optimistic assessments of the
probability of a warless future.

In style, the *Advocate of Peace* was often heavily religious in
tone and metaphor, frequently personifying war as the devil in-
carnate who must not be allowed to carry out his infernal purposes.[26] The Bible, Benjamin Franklin, John Ruskin, Montes-
quieu, Emerson, and Grover Cleveland were variously quoted in
behalf of peace in a section of "brevities" which included brief
news items, personal notes, notices of meetings and conferences,
and pithy aphorisms on peace that ranged from the sayings of
Confucius to the dying words of John Knox.[27] In the pattern of
its attention to news of other organizations the journal indicated
which other movements it considered as its major allies in the
campaign for world peace. Activities of other peace societies received the greatest coverage, followed closely by those of the
WCTU, the United Society of Christian Endeavor, various educational, missionary, and Bible societies, and religious conventions. Although the churches were often chastised for their lukewarm support of peace and thus their infidelity to Christian duty,
the society avidly sought clergymen as adherents and obviously
viewed religious and semireligious organizations as major supporters. Its appraisal of the value of such allies was often inflated.
In 1898 it reported in apparent seriousness: "The American Humane Education Society has now established . . . thirty-four thousand and two hundred and sixty-three Bands of Mercy. War is
doomed."[28]

If the composition of its leadership and the attitudes revealed
in the *Advocate of Peace* reflected the cautious and even archaic
quality of the American Peace Society's reform stance, the state
of the society's finances revealed that even a conservative program could not be carried out with any real vigor. Throughout
its career, the society had fought frequent skirmishes with impending bankruptcy. By 1900 it had gained firmer financial foot-
ing, with a permanent fund established. Nevertheless, in June

[26] *Ibid.*, 62 (Dec. 1900), 228; 65 (Jan. 1903), 1; 65 (May 1903), 84.

[27] *Ibid.*, 61 (May 1899), 99; 61 (Nov. 1899), 239; 62 (June 1900), 128; 62 (Sept. 1900), 173; 62 (Dec. 1900), 236; 65 (May 1903), 84-85.

[28] *Ibid.*, 61 (June 1899), 126; 61 (Oct. 1899), 228; 62 (June 1900), 129; 63 (June 1901), 118; 63 (Aug. 1901), 158.

1900 it acknowledged an excess of liabilities over assets of $1,349.[29] Some of its income came from rentals on run-down buildings on Boston's Albany and Beach Streets, and it worried in 1900 and again in 1903 about the financial pinch resulting from a decline in rental values.[30] From 1900 to 1905 its expenditures averaged $5,700 a year, barely enough to support a permanent secretary, maintain an office, and subsidize a periodical and a small amount of pamphlet literature. Despite the much-lauded "opportunities" for the peace movement in the new century, the average level of expenditure through 1905 remained lower than it had been in the decade of the 1890s.[31] Such financial inertia did not promise active promotion of new and expanded programs.

Whatever potentialities existed for growth and effective action by the American Peace Society lay largely in the work of Benjamin Trueblood, secretary of the society, editor of its journal, lobbyist for peace programs, and indefatigable participant in peace conferences. While most of the other officers may have served only as expressions of the society's projected self-image, Trueblood constituted the society in action. A Quaker scholar and former college president who derived his inspiration from William Penn and Immanuel Kant as well as from the early founders of the peace movement in America, Trueblood was, in effect, the nation's first professional peace worker, employed to devote his full time to the cause of peace. A "master of old facts" and a man "very adapted" to the "gentleman" and "philanthropist" who was then president of the society, Trueblood combined the genteel style and moralistic temper of the American Peace Society's background with a more practical interest in the details of programs for international arbitration and world federation and a more modern emphasis on the goal of a "stated" (or periodic) international congress. Under his editorship, the *Advocate of Peace* substantially increased its circulation and became, for a time, the leading disseminator of information on peace activities and new programs of internationalism in the United States and abroad.[32]

Within the American Peace Society, Trueblood drew his most active direct support from its president, Robert Treat Paine, and from editor and reformer Edwin D. Mead. A prominent Boston-

[29] *Ibid.*, 62 (June 1900), 132.
[30] *Ibid.*, 65 (Jan. 1903), 5.
[31] Whitney, *American Peace Society*, pp. 190, 257.
[32] Tryon, "Dr. Trueblood at Work," Box 8, APS Papers, SCPC; Curti, *Peace or War*, pp. 138-39, 143, 158, 168, 199; Warren F. Kuehl, *Seeking World Order: The United States and International Organization to 1920* (Nashville 1969), pp. 54, 97, 100, 107; Benjamin Trueblood, *The Federation of the World* (New York 1899).

ian, Paine was president of the Associated Charities of Boston and the Boston Children's Aid Society and a leading member of the Twentieth Century Club and the Immigration Restriction League. Chosen president by "surprise" in 1894, on the basis of his "philanthropic character and work and his high standing as a citizen," Paine did manage to spare enough time from his other causes to contribute to the society's lobbying activities and participate regularly in peace conferences.[33] Edwin Mead was the editor of the reformist *New England Magazine*, president of the Massachusetts Society for Promoting Good Citizenship and the Men's Woman's Suffrage League, and founder of Boston's Twentieth Century Club, a literary-oriented club for "public-spirited citizens." A vice-president of the American Peace Society, he had resigned from the *New England Magazine* in 1901 to edit a peace journal, write peace pamphlets, and edit peace classics.[34] Mead and his wife, Lucia Ames Mead, quickly became prolific writers and promulgators of peace literature, effective associates of Trueblood, and instigators of new organizations that would take form after 1905.

Ironically, the very efforts of the society and such of its leaders as Trueblood and Mead to reinvigorate and expand the peace movement eventuated in the relative eclipse of the traditional, genteel reformism of the old peace movement and of the American Peace Society itself. The society did expand rapidly in numbers and in branch organizations after 1905, but it was soon overshadowed by more affluent and prestigious peace organizations. Trueblood sought to champion the new, more "practical" programs for international organization and Mead denounced the outmoded, "foolish, sentimental" peace societies while praising the American Peace Society's sensible and dignified emphasis on "constructive work." But the new leaders of the peace movement who began to emerge about 1905 found Trueblood, the American Peace Society, and even Mead, too sentimental and moralistic in approach, too insistent upon disarmament as an integral part of the peace movement, and too visionary and impractical.[35] From

[33] *Advocate of Peace*, 72 (Sept. 1910), 181-82; Curti, *Peace or War*, pp. 138, 143, 158, 175.

[34] Curti, *Peace or War*, pp. 143, 188, 199; Arthur Mann, "Edwin Doak Mead," *Dictionary of American Biography* (New York 1958), 442-43.

[35] [Edwin D. Mead to Andrew Carnegie, Mar. 1905], [Edwin Ginn] to Carnegie, 13 Jan. 1910 and Carnegie to Mead, n.d., Box 1, Edwin D. Mead Papers, SCPC; Carnegie to Benjamin Trueblood, 5 Feb. 1908, Box 6, APS Papers, SCPC. For criticisms of the APS (and, by implication, Trueblood), see below, chap. four, pp. 129-36. See also Nicholas Murray Butler to Andrew Carnegie, 8 Apr. 1910 and Theodore Roosevelt to Carnegie, 18 Feb. 1910, Carnegie Papers, LC. Roosevelt's remark that

the perspective of a decade later, even the most vigorous and "modern" leaders of the society at the turn of the century were to appear as embodiments of the ineffectual Victorian sentimentalism and moralism which the peace movement was rapidly renouncing.

Even with its uncertain prospects for expansion of its activities and influence, the American Peace Society clearly displayed greater promise of effective growth than the other established peace societies of the early twentieth century. Only the Universal Peace Union and the Peace Association of Friends in America made any pretense to national scope. The Universal Peace Union had been formed in 1866 as a revival of the pre-Civil War New England Non-Resistance Society and had been supported by some former members of the American Peace Society who objected to that organization's refusal to condemn the Civil War.[36] Adin Ballou, leader of the practical experiment in Christian socialism at the Hopedale Community and faithful adherent to non-resistance, was among the founders of the Union; Alfred H. Love, a nonresister of Quaker sympathies who had refused to serve in the Civil War, dominated and in a sense *was* the Union, serving as president from its founding until its demise in 1913.

By the beginning of the twentieth century, Love began to flag in his tireless peace efforts. Crushed in spirit by the bitterness of popular attacks upon him after he had tried to avert war with Spain in 1898, Love lacked the "vital enthusiasm" to rejuvenate an organization which had come to give increasing attention to obituary notices and memorial hours. After 1900, the financial condition of the Union was desperate. Love, who had earlier blasted the compromising and "selfish" attitudes of the "Boston element" was reduced by 1912 to pleading for affiliation with the American Peace Society in hopes of obtaining supporting funds. The society rejected Love's plea, its own biases against the idiosyncratic Love reinforced by advice from a trusted Pennsylvania Quaker and scholar who wrote that the Union existed "almost altogether on paper," that it was "not only inefficient but injurious" to the cause of peace because of its simultaneous efforts to reform industrial conditions, abolish capital punishment, and ban prize fighting, and that it was so weak as to "excite popular contempt."

Trueblood belonged "to the type that makes a good cause ridiculous" did not come, of course, from a leader in the peace movement. Nevertheless, many leaders in the peace movement by 1910 found Roosevelt's ideas on peace more attractive than those espoused by Trueblood, Mead, or any of the older American Peace Society men.

36 Whitney, *American Peace Society*, pp. 116-17; Curti, *Peace or War*, p. 76.

More than ever a one-man organization, the Universal Peace Union had "watched without guiding or sharing" the growth of the peace movement after 1905. Love's attempt to associate the peace movement with labor and radical movements did not reappear until after 1915.[37]

The Peace Association of Friends, also organized in 1866, exemplified the same emphasis on nonresistant pacifism. By 1900 it was an affiliate of the American Peace Society. Except for publishing a periodical, it hardly maintained a separate existence. Compared with the American Peace Society, these two organizations were even more provincial, more impecunious, and less capable of gaining any degree of national influence. Although they deserve a place in the history of nonresistance movements in America, their brand of absolute pacifism played little part in the development of the peace movement between 1900 and 1917. When their qualities of uncompromising pacifism reappeared after 1915 in the War Resisters League and the Fellowship of Reconciliation, these qualities had become associated with a far broader social radicalism than the Universal Peace Union or the Peace Association of Friends had embodied. Even the defense of conscientious objectors during World War I was mainly taken up not by these dying older organizations but by new groups stemming from the newly created peace movement of 1915 to 1917.[38]

If the smaller, nonresistant peace societies only reflected, in exaggerated form, the weaknesses of the American Peace Society, one new peace organization did manage to foreshadow the direction the movement was to take in the period after 1905. This was the Lake Mohonk Conference on International Arbitration, a series of single annual meetings begun in 1895 for the discussion and promotion of "arbitration," a topic with broad appeal to groups not previously attracted to the peace societies. Even generals and diplomats could participate in the Mohonk Conferences without feeling that they had compromised their positions.

The Mohonk Conferences met late each spring at a mountain-top resort hotel in the Catskills about one hundred miles from New York City. The proprietors of the hotel, brothers Alfred and Daniel Smiley, were Quaker reformers who had acted as hosts for

[37] Love to Benjamin Trueblood, 10 Aug. 1912 and 25 Feb. 1913, William I. Hull to Trueblood, 31 Oct. 1912, Box 6, APS Papers, SCPC; Robert Wesley Doherty, "Alfred H. Love and the Universal Peace Union," Ph.D. diss., University of Pennsylvania, 1962, pp. 142, 150-56; Curti, *Peace or War*, pp. 76-82, 133, 198-99; Brock, *Pacifism in the United States*, pp. 923-31.

[38] Brock, *Pacifism in the United States*, pp. 869, 871-76, 930-31.

a Lake Mohonk Conference of Friends of the Indian for a number of years. In 1895 Alfred Smiley had decided that the time was ripe for a similar annual conference on international peace. Formerly a nonresister, Smiley had recently been convinced by the Pullman strike and other labor upheavals that police and government militia were necessary for internal peace and stability.[39] Smiley emphasized that the conference would be primarily concerned with arbitration, not pacifism. He outlawed discussions of the horrors of war and sought to keep the conferences clear of any connection with the doctrine of "peace at all hazards."[40]

In his efforts to maintain a genteel harmony and to avoid any slackening of interest by unpacifistic businessmen, politicians, or military leaders, Smiley eventually sought to dissuade speakers from discussing the "abstract advantages of peace," from referring to any war in progress, and even from engaging in unrestricted debate on disarmament. "Every time the subject (of disarmament) has come up at Mohonk and been allowed any scope," the secretary of the conference later complained, "a few over-enthusiastic members have insisted upon dragging in concrete reference to this country and asking some action particularly aimed at this Government and its naval policy." The discussion of such divisive issues being "futile and rather unwise," the Mohonk Conference consistently applied prescriptive rules and selectivity of membership in an attempt to insure that no untoward issues, no distressing international or national realities, would disturb the conference's elevated contemplations and genteel demeanor.[41] Since the conference members came to the hotel by invitation only, Smiley could exercise control over the discussions to insure whatever range of viewpoints he desired. Transgressors of the rules might be denied future invitations.

Despite the broader appeal of emphasis on arbitration, the differences between the Mohonk Conferences and the American Peace Society at the turn of the century should not be overemphasized. In leadership, reform outlook, and style they were often hardly distinguishable. Forty-five of those who served as officers of the American Peace Society between 1900 and 1905 had also participated in the Mohonk Conferences. Seventeen of these officers had attended the Mohonk Conference at least four times between 1895 and 1904. Benjamin Trueblood was partly responsible

[39] *Mohonk Conference, 1896*, p. 51.
[40] *Ibid., 1895*, p. 5.
[41] H. C. Phillips to William I. Hull, 29 Jan. 1909 and 16 Mar. 1917, Boxes 1 and 5, Hull Papers, FHL.

for the inauguration of the Mohonk Conferences and for carrying out the details of planning. President Robert Treat Paine of the American Peace Society rarely missed a Mohonk Convention.[42] Although the Mohonk Conference, particularly after 1900, sought to achieve a larger representation of political leaders, international lawyers, and businessmen, it continued to invite many men of the same viewpoints and backgrounds as those who controlled the American Peace Society. Protestant clergymen and editors of religious periodicals played a prominent role, and their influence was augmented by several presidents of small colleges.

Like officers in the American Peace Society, members of the Mohonk Conferences displayed allegiances to a variety of genteel reforms. The role of the Smileys as hosts of the conference on Indian affairs insured that some adherents to the cause of Indian reform would be among the guests at the arbitration conferences as well. World missions, good government, and temperance interests were well represented among the Conference members. Aaron M. Powell, a member of several of the earliest conferences, was president of the American Purity Alliance, a federation of moral education societies. Wilbur Crafts, a later participant, headed the Reform Bureau, which lobbied in Washington for observance of the Sabbath, suppression of intemperance, social purity, and antigambling legislation and stood for "conscience and uprightness in politics."[43] At the 1901 Annual Conference one speaker was warmly applauded for declaring that evils stemming from intemperance surpassed those resulting from war.[44]

Although many of them sympathized with such "allied causes," a number of the regular participants at the Mohonk Conferences refused to be diverted from a central concern with the peace movement. Trueblood, Mead, Paine, Edwin Ginn, Edward Everett Hale, and Albert Smiley sought to provide continuing leadership for the peace movement, as did such newer participants as Charles Jefferson, Samuel T. Dutton, and Frederick Lynch. Others who would continue to play a role in the peace movement, such as John Bates Clark, and W.H.P. Faunce, regularly attended the conferences.

Speakers at the Mohonk Conferences displayed the same tendency as the *Advocate of Peace* to view international arbitration primarily as a moral and religious question. But despite its reliance upon religious organizations as allies, the Mohonk Confer-

42 Whitney, *American Peace Society*, p. 223; *Mohonk Conference, 1895-1905.*
43 *Advocate of Peace*, 63 (May 1901), 96.
44 *Mohonk Conference, 1901*, p. 52.

ence did begin to reach out toward "more men of large influence and means." When a speaker suggested in 1901 that more "practical politicians" should be invited to the conference, Albert Smiley replied that invitations had been extended. The politicians simply had not come.[45] Within a few years, however, more of them were beginning to attend and businessmen were being successfully courted in sizable numbers.

By 1905 the Mohonk Conference could boast among its newer participants such prominent figures as David Brewer, justice of the Supreme Court, John Bassett Moore, expert on international law, Oscar Straus, Hague Court member and future secretary of commerce, John R. Mott, noted evangelist and international religious organizer, A. B. Farquhar, a prominent national business leader, and Daniel Coit Gilman, president of the Carnegie Institution. The most recent presidents of the conference had been John W. Foster, a former secretary of state, and Judge George Gray, a member of the Hague Court. Frederick Lynch may have exaggerated the degree of change in the composition of the Mohonk Conference when he compared the "leading statesmen, jurists, clergymen, editors, college presidents and financiers of the land" who were attending by 1911 with the "members of the peace cult" who had comprised the first Mohonk Conference.[46] But the new names of relative prominence that began to appear on Mohonk programs about 1905 suggested that the peace movement was beginning to emerge from its previous condition of obscurity, imputed impracticality, and exclusion from contact with those who might directly influence national policy.

Despite its weaknesses, the American Peace Society also began to seize opportunities for expanded activity and influence. In 1904 its leaders arranged for the meeting of the annual international peace congress in Boston and obtained the cooperation of Andrew Carnegie, Andrew Dickson White, John W. Foster, and George Gray in promoting the congress. Secretary of State John Hay was persuaded to make the leading address, an epochal event according to the society, which "brought the whole peace movement into vital connection with the authorities of government and secured official, governmental recognition of the sound-

45 *Ibid., 1895,* p. 82. See also *ibid., 1900,* p. 5; *ibid., 1901,* p. 26. At the 1899 conference one speaker had declared the spread of the Christian Endeavor Society to be "one of the clearest auguries of universal peace." *Ibid., 1899,* p. 86.

46 Lynch, *The Peace Problem,* p. 82. On the changes in the peace movement reflected in the series of Mohonk Conferences, see also the discussion in Michael Arnold Lutzker, "The 'Practical' Peace Advocates: An Interpretation of the American Peace Movement, 1898-1917," Ph.D. diss., Rutgers University, 1969, pp. 102-14.

ness of its principles and the justice of its claims."[47] The society's
Annual Report for 1905 claimed six "auxiliaries," including several new ones that apparently were active. That same year the
board of directors decided that the "commanding position" which
the peace movement held as "the foremost cause before the
world" required that the society acquire a building of its own.[48]
Slowly the peace movement was effecting a transformation that
would grace the letterheads of peace organizations with prominent and powerful names, and which would make peace and arbitration organizations thoroughly respectable among the political and intellectual elite. Peace movement leaders welcomed the
changes that promised new power and practicality. Yet some of
them would later find reason to question whether they had not
lost more by the transformation than they had gained.

For all of their zealous efforts, however, the peace organizations
themselves contributed relatively little to the new opportunities
for influence and prestige that became apparent during the first
few years of the new century. External and partly fortuitous
events supplied much of the new impetus. Both the Spanish-
American War and the ensuing debate over imperialism brought
new attention to issues of international relations. The call for the
First Hague Conference, proposals for a permanent world court,
and the growth of the practice of international arbitration all
gave the peace movement an opportunity to focus upon concrete
events and programs. The gradual development of an Anglo-
American rapprochement after the Venezuela boundary dispute
of 1895 helped provide a mood, especially among the eastern social and political elite, that was conducive to musings about world
peace. Fears of a possible conflict in Europe only served to accentuate the compatibility of a program for international arbitration
with steadfast nationalism. Finally, the assumptions of the traditional peace societies about the need for restraint and social
harmony found favor with American business and civic leaders
concerned about the threats to American domestic peace and
stability. While peace movement leaders promoted conferences and
reached out for new adherents, these conditions and events
brought numbers of prominent Americans, for various reasons,
to consider the peace movement an attractive reform.

The broadest of these invigorating external influences upon the

[47] *Seventy-Seventh Annual Report of the Directors of the American Peace Society,
1905*, p. 7.
[48] *Ibid.*, pp. 13, 22, 26.

peace movement, and the least traceable in its effects, was simply the rapid intensification of American involvement in international affairs. As the degree of economic and political interaction increased, American reactions to those changes took on an ambiguous cast. Expansion of trade and investment abroad seemed essential to the continued health and growth of the American economy. Overseas missionary activity, which reached a peak of popular enthusiasm in the 1890s and early 1900s, promised the spread of cherished American ideas and values abroad. Increased political involvement with foreign powers seemed necessary to protect American economic interests and could prove flattering to American self-esteem and to aspirations for great-power status.

Some of the interest in expanding foreign involvement undoubtedly stemmed, consciously or unconsciously, from concerns about the closing of the frontier and fears of a rising tide of violence and economic discontent at home. A few leading Americans even expressed hopes that absorption in the traditional problems of acquiring and administering an empire would curtail internal turbulence by displacing American energies and aggressiveness abroad. But a wider consensus of influential American opinion rejected any explicit call for wider political dominion. Internal economic strains could be eased and the Anglo-Saxon destiny of peaceful world dominance could be achieved through the processes of increased commercial expansion. America might express her new status as a dominant international power yet avoid European patterns of imperialism through brute force by proving her superior Darwinian "fitness" in the contest for foreign markets. Here was a civilized and, hopefully, a safe and secure means of providing American industry with its necessary markets and satisfying the growing urge for the spread of American influence and ideals.[49]

But the attractions of increased international involvement were often clouded by ominous forebodings. Americans worried about the dangers that might arise from increased interaction with barbarous nations and from entanglement in the meshes of the notorious European system of balance of power diplomacy. Having apotheosized the unique features of their own political system, Americans wondered how safely the United States could enter into intimate relations with nations less pure and enlightened in ethical standards and political institutions. The veritable flood of plans for world courts, world federation, and world government

[49] For a broader discussion of these issues, see Walter LaFeber, *The New Empire: An Interpretation of American Expansion, 1860-1898* (Ithaca, N.Y. 1963), *passim*.

(nearly all of them drawing heavily upon the American political experience and American institutions as models) that poured forth from American authors after the mid-1890s may have been inspired, in part, by the desire to understand how the economically desirable and apparently inevitable increase of American international involvements might take place without subjecting the nation to un-American contagions.[50] Thus, by the turn of the century, the peace movement had begun to benefit by becoming a vehicle through which Americans could express their concerns about how the world could be made safe for the international emergence of a virtuous America.

The effects of the Spanish-American War upon the fortunes of the peace movement were complex and partly antithetical. Since the leaders of the movement had pointed proudly to the relative absence of wars between the great powers in the late nineteenth century as a sure sign of the unrelenting progress of peace, any conflict between leading nations was bound to come as an embarrassment. Moreover, spokesmen for the American peace organizations had so often offered the example of the United States as a model of peaceful federation and international decorum that America's involvement provided cause for redoubled chagrin. But the war was a short one and its effect in making Americans more conscious of the opportunities for their nation to play a leading role in world affairs redounded to the eventual benefit of the peace organizations.

In the face of this brief catastrophe, the peace movement proved remarkably resilient. The *Advocate of Peace* bemoaned the war and condemned the seizure of the Philippines without ever deflating its optimism. It confessed that little could be accomplished "when the public mind is in a state of frenzy and suspense," but it reminded its readers that the purpose of the American Peace Society was to conduct a constant and patient program of public education, not to attempt "to prevent war in times of great excitement and passion."[51] Benjamin Trueblood vigorously opposed the war, but the directors of the American Peace Society, meeting in June of 1898, prudently reported that it was "not considered best at this time" to formulate any resolution. They reported simply that they had had "an interesting and enthusiastic meeting despite the cloud of war." During the same month, the *Advocate of Peace* found solace in small victories. The quarter-

---

[50] For a discussion of a number of these plans for world federation and related programs, see Kuehl, *Seeking World Order*, pp. 43, 50-55, 58-95.

[51] *Advocate of Peace*, 60 (April 1898), 77-78; 60 (June 1898), 134.

master general, it reported, had assured the president of the Massachusetts SPCA that animals wounded in battle would be "promptly and mercifully killed."[52] By September the *Advocate of Peace* had fully recovered its confidence. "We doubt if the essentially pacific spirit of the nation has on the whole been seriously affected," it complacently concluded. Moreover, it prophesied a new surge of commitment to peace: "The war has aroused many others to a sense of their unfaithfulness in the past and to a purpose to work faithfully in the future." Surveying the year's events, the *Advocate of Peace* concluded in December 1898, "We are a year nearer, in every sense, to the beginning of the reign of universal peace. . . ."[53]

The Mohonk Conference, meeting in June 1898, preserved its optimism in a slightly different manner. In accordance with the desire of the host of the conference, Albert Smiley, the conference chairman announced that "nothing whatever should be said with reference to the present state of affairs between this country and Spain." He imposed a rule for speakers which required that "nothing which has happened since the meeting of this Conference last year, or which may be expected to happen before the meeting of next year, is to be referred to in any way."[54] With the discussion thus sufficiently elevated above the turmoil of current events, optimism was safe from misgivings and the image of a pacific America could remain unchallenged. "We rejoice at the progress which the cause of arbitration has made during the last year," declared the convention platform. The conference proclaimed its loyalty and its endorsement of service to the country and asked that the sufferings of war be mitigated, if possible.[55]

But the rule of silence could not be enforced. Some broke it to express their endorsement of the war; others could not resist the impulse to explain how God had brought good out of evil. Not one speech expressed frustration or dejection. The Reverend Theodore Cuyler pointed out such benefits of the war as the increased reconciliation of North and South and the improved relations between America and England.[56] Another clergyman was even less restrained in his optimism:

This war, as a baptism of fire, may prove a blessing. Even Spain may be better off for it! Think of the travellers who will pour

---

[52] *Ibid.*, 133-34; Devere Allen, *The Fight for Peace* (New York 1930), pp. 488-89; Curti, *Peace or War*, p. 168.

[53] *Advocate of Peace*, 60 (Aug. and Sept. 1898), 173; 60 (Dec. 1898), 246.

[54] *Mohonk Conference, 1898*, pp. 5-6.

[55] *Ibid.*, p. 99.   [56] *Ibid.*, p. 107.

into every corner of Spain, as soon as this war is safely over, and carry American money, intelligence and inventions there, until they may become as prosperous as ever, and perchance, more worthy of the name of a Christian nation. . . ."[57]

Gradually a formula emerged within the peace movement which guaranteed the triumph of optimism over any possible challenge by obstinate events. Long durations of peace were signs of progress. But occasional wars were not, on that account, a cause for discouragement. The horrors and folly of war taught "a sad lesson" and made ever-increasing converts to peace. The *Advocate of Peace* was arguing by 1900 that "men recover . . . their moral balance more quickly than formerly," and that after the recent wars in Cuba and Africa the world could expect a "great reaction." Two months later it predicted that "the tide of opposition to brute force in human affairs will go higher than ever before."[58] Thus the major peace organizations took the Spanish-American War in stride. As forums for the discussion of international affairs, they gained new stature from the increased interest in America's role abroad. The refusal of the major organizations to condemn the war, and the presence within the movement of many fervent supporters of the war, meant that the movement had avoided estranging itself from the main tide of American sentiment.

The ensuing debate over imperialism, focused largely on the problem of the Philippines, also held potential perils for the peace movement. But again the peace organizations avoided permanent and intransigent commitment to the unpopular side of the issue and reaped the further benefits of international interests awakened by American expansion.[59] As might have been expected, many peace leaders were strongly drawn to anti-imperialism. Thirty-two directors and vice-presidents of the American Peace Society between 1900 and 1905, or more than one-fourth of its officers, had been active in anti-imperialist organizations. The logical connection between the preservation of peace and the avoidance of foreign entanglements and an enlarged military establishment afforded a strong argument for support of anti-im-

[57] *Ibid.*, p. 34.

[58] *Advocate of Peace*, 62 (Oct. 1900), 187; 62 (Dec. 1900), 228; 63 (Jan. 1901), 2; *Mohonk Conference, 1900*, p. 105. See also *Advocate of Peace*, 62 (April 1900), 75.

[59] For a similar view of the effect of American overseas expansion in stimulating interest in other movements with an international scope, see Valentin Hanno Rabe, "Protestant Foreign Missions, 1880-1920," Ph.D. diss., Harvard University, 1964, p. 68.

perialism among the leaders of the peace movement. Perhaps as important was the compatibility of the two causes in terms of political mood, temperamental bent, and social outlook. The anti-imperialist leaders as a group have been described as elitist, principled and self-righteous, fearful of social instability, conservative on domestic issues, strongly Anglophile, and disdainful of belligerence or "vulgar bluster" whether by individuals or nations. Typically they were supporters of such other mugwump causes as civil service reform, good government, free trade, and sound money.[60] Nearly all of these characteristics were shared by a majority of the leaders of the peace movement. Perhaps none was shared so thoroughly as the penchant for national and personal self-restraint, discipline, moral uprightness, courtesy, and good form—an expression more of the social biases and sense of style of genteel New England gentlemen and clergymen than of the results of an analysis of foreign affairs.

But the connection between the peace movement and anti-imperialism was neither complete nor long-lasting. The American Peace Society and the Mohonk Conference included among their leaders such supporters of expansion as Lyman Abbott, editor of *The Outlook*, Samuel B. Capen, president of the American Board of Commissioners for Foreign Missions, William Hayes Ward, editor of *The Independent*, and Joseph Cook, W. S. Crowe, and Josiah Strong, all prominent religious leaders. Albert Smiley again imposed a rule of silence regarding current American policies in the Mohonk Conference of 1899, but several speakers made it clear that they had no objections to imperialism. One session of the conference adopted as its topic "The General Hopefulness of the Situation."[61] Even the strongly anti-imperialist editor of the *Advocate of Peace*, like many others in the anti-imperialist movement, made little complaint about the retention of Puerto Rico or the general handling of Cuba. Although anti-im-

---

[60] Beisner, *Twelve Against Empire*, pp. 7-17, 222, and Tompkins, *Anti-Imperialism in the United States*, pp. 140-60. See also Robert L. Beisner, "The Anti-Imperialist Impulse: The Mugwumps and the Republicans, 1898-1900," Ph.D. diss., University of Chicago, 1965, pp. 40, 71-73, 80, 83, 108, 340 and Edwin Berkeley Tompkins, "The Great Debate: Anti-Imperialism in the United States, 1880-1920," Ph.D. diss., University of Pennsylvania, 1963, pp. 299, 302, 308, 319. For additional descriptions of the "mugwump mind" or "mugwump culture," see Blodgett, *The Gentle Reformers*, pp. 19-47; Richard Hofstadter, *Anti-Intellectualism in American Life* (New York 1962), pp. 400-403; and Hofstadter, *The Age of Reform: From Bryan to F.D.R.* (New York 1955), pp. 137-43. For a description of the role of anti-imperialism in the development of mugwump politics, see Blodgett, *The Gentle Reformers*, pp. 265-69. For sources of information on the anti-imperialist activities of peace movement leaders, see above, n. 21.

[61] *Mohonk Conference, 1899*, pp. 5, 92.

perialists clearly dominated the American Peace Society and probably were in the majority at the Mohonk Conferences, those supporting the administration's policy in the Philippines and praising the accomplishments of English imperialism were neither denounced at Mohonk nor excluded from the American Peace Society. Only the belligerent stance of Lyman Abbott, who glorified imperialism and described aggressive war as "Christian duty," evoked vocal criticism.[62]

As the issue receded from national attention and the anti-imperialist organizations faded, the question of imperialism ceased to be divisive within the peace organizations. The elite groups from which both anti-imperialism and imperialism drew their intellectual champions shared the vision popularized by the Darwinist John Fiske of a civilized and peaceful world, evolving in accordance with the American model and benevolently dominated by American political ideals. The most passionate of the anti-imperialists, of course, had recoiled with dismay at what they considered the perversion of the American mission in the extension and maintenance of American influence by naked military force and arbitrary colonial rule. In rejecting the more genteel methods of extending American ideals through missionary effort, commercial contact, and education by the force of example, these crude modes of expansion threatened to lower the nation's moral tone and disturb its social stability. In contrast to the peace movement, through which the United States could simultaneously participate more fully in international affairs and elevate them to conform with American standards, imperialist expansion would bring America into the world arena by sacrificing its traditional ideals and accepting the entangling alliances, colonial jealousies and insecurities, and power-oriented diplomacy of the European powers.[63]

Once the distasteful violence of the Philippine insurrection had passed, however, most of the anti-imperialists within the peace movement happily swung their attention to the more optimistic, positive prospects for international relations. None of them opposed the spread of American influence and many looked positively upon the presumed "civilizing effects" of further American trade expansion. Former anti-imperialists lost much of their inter-

---

[62] *Advocate of Peace*, 61 (May 1899), 105; 61 (Nov. 1899), 228; 62 (Jan. 1900), 6.

[63] On Fiske's ideas and influence, see Milton Berman, *John Fiske: The Evolution of a Popularizer* (Cambridge, Mass. 1961), esp. pp. 139-40, 208, 219 and Lutzker, "The 'Practical' Peace Advocates," pp. 19, 61-64. On the fears of the anti-imperialists, see Beisner, *Twelve Against Empire*, pp. 218-25.

est in Philippine independence when it became a standard opposition issue which the Democratic Party employed to irritate the administration. Meanwhile, many of those who had supported territorial expansion now reaffirmed a position that discounted the advantages of new territories and disclaimed territorial ambitions. As former expansionists once again stressed trade expansion and the civilizing of backward areas through American moral guidance, factions within the peace movement again found themselves absorbed in the mutually agreeable vision of a world evolving with American guidance toward peaceful federation.

The peace movement, basically nationalistic and laudatory of all things American, thus avoided removing itself from the mainstream of public opinion through inflexible adherence to an unpopular position. Soon former imperialists and anti-imperialists found common ground in the peace movement in support of such programs as arbitration, a world court, federal protection of aliens, and repeal of the Panama Canal Tolls legislation. Such issues both met the requirements of the old anti-imperialists for good form, dignity, and self-restraint and provided former imperialists with the attractions of seeming practicality and positive national action toward expanded influence in world affairs. By 1912 the peace movement included among its leaders and adherents not only such prominent former spokesmen for imperialism as Albert Shaw, Nicholas Murray Butler, Theodore Marburg, A. Lawrence Lowell, and Franklin H. Giddings, but also two of the major architects of the colonial administration, Elihu Root and William Howard Taft. Thus the peace movement did not become an ideological or political heir of anti-imperialism. On the contrary, its very strength in the prewar decade derived from its focus upon programs that, in their emphasis upon the propagation of American institutional arrangements and American moral influence in world affairs, combined some of the never entirely distinct attractions of both imperialism and anti-imperialism.

If the Spanish-American War and issues of imperialism had indirectly aided the peace organizations by stimulating increased public interest in international affairs, another even more fortuitous event gave the peace movement a further impetus and an immediate cause for elation. The Spanish-American War had hardly subsided when, in August of 1898, Czar Nicholas of Russia circulated a surprise proposal for a conference of the nations to discuss disarmament. This seemingly idealistic and humanitarian proposal met with profound skepticism in many quarters, but not among the peace organizations. Subsequent historians have traced the source of the proposals to the concerns of the Czar's ministers about Russia's growing military obsolescence and financial difficulties.[64] But the leaders of the peace movement, although apparently troubled by the widespread American suspicion of the Czar's motives, searched for corroboration of the Czar's sincerity until ultimately a belief in his noble intentions became an article of faith. Many leaders in the peace movement were still preoccupied with the issue of imperialism and the attempt to reintroduce an arbitration treaty with Great Britain, but they increasingly found time, particularly after the Czar's second circular in January 1899, to extol the Czar's initiative and to envision auspicious results. Contributors to the *Advocate of Peace* invoked divine blessings upon the Czar and composed poems celebrating his sublime deed. At the Mohonk Conference the following year, Albert Smiley berated the cynics and made his declaration of faith in the Czar's good intentions. Samuel Capen detected the "finger of God" in the Czar's rescript and the *Advocate of Peace* proclaimed it "the most Christian proposition ever made in the whole history of international politics."[65]

Despite this exalted view of the origins of the First Hague Conference, the spokesmen for the peace movement did not allow themselves to become discouraged over the meager accomplishments at The Hague in 1899.[66] After all, this had been the first great peace conference of the nations to take place in time of peace. Thus the mere fact that such a conference of twenty-six nations had met could be celebrated as an unprecedented step toward improvement of international relations. Any disappointments over the failure of the conference to take concrete action toward disarmament were more than compensated for, in the opinion of the leaders of the American peace movement, by the adoption of the Convention for the Pacific Settlement of International Disputes, which created machinery for a Permanent Court

[64] Merze Tate, *The Disarmament Illusion: The Movement for a Limitation of Armaments to 1907* (New York 1942), pp. 167-96; Calvin DeArmond Davis, *The United States and the First Hague Peace Conference* (Ithaca, N.Y. 1962), pp. 36-53; Thomas K. Ford, "The Genesis of the First Hague Peace Conference," *Political Science Quarterly*, 51 (Sept. 1936), 362-77, 380-81.

[65] *Advocate of Peace*, 60 (Dec. 1898), 256; 61 (Jan. 1899), 6; 61 (Feb. 1899), 29; 61 (Oct. 1899), 227; *Mohonk Conference, 1899*, pp. 67, 117. A fuller discussion of the reaction by the peace movement to the Czar's proposal which stresses the initial reservations of the peace leaders and their gradual increase of enthusiasm appears in Patterson, "Travail of the American Peace Movement," pp. 141-51, 159.

[66] An exception was Alfred Love of the Universal Peace Union whose views found little sympathy in the major peace groups (Doherty, "Alfred Love," pp. 112-13).

of Arbitration. The practice of international arbitration had been growing rapidly over the previous three decades, but in each case the arbitral board or court had been set up on an ad hoc basis with no suggestion of continuity of judges or decisions. The idea of a "permanent" court thus seemed to represent a great step forward. Nations would more readily submit disputes to arbitration if permanent machinery was already in existence. The centralization of arbitrations in a single court would offer some hope for the selection of more prestigious and impartial judges and the achievement of greater continuity of principles and decisions.

It is true that the only permanent thing about the new court, with the exception of its administrative staff, was a large panel of arbitrators from which the disputants in any case might choose. But despite this very rudimentary organization, the newly created court did provide a visible image of practical accomplishment in the reform of international relations. It gave the peace organizations an institution toward which they could direct efforts that seemed more immediately practical than those employed in giving lessons on the immorality of war to the general public. The results of the First Hague Conference bolstered the morale of the established peace movement, which proclaimed the conference a "brilliant success" and "the greatest practical step forward" in the history of the movement.[67] Enthusiasm for a perfected international court and an appreciation of the way in which the drive for international arbitration and a central court might contribute to the goals of American foreign policy toward Europe brought new and influential men into the movement through the older organizations or through new allied ones.

Meanwhile the peace movement had been keeping step with the front ranks of American opinion on several other issues. One of these was the enthusiasm for Anglo-American rapprochement, which intensified rapidly in the wake of the peaceful settlement of the Venezuelan Crisis of 1895. The diplomatic rapprochement of 1895-1905 was accompanied by a rising wave of sentimental and theoretical Anglo-Saxonism that engulfed the intellectual and political elite of America. Leading scholars in history and the emerging social sciences such as John W. Burgess, Henry Adams, Francis Amasa Walker, and Herbert Baxter Adams had spurred on a search for the Teutonic and Anglo-Saxon roots of American political institutions. Popular philosophers and religious spokesmen such as John Fiske and Josiah Strong had popularized the

---

[67] *Advocate of Peace*, 62 (Jan. 1900), 3; *Mohonk Conference, 1900*, p. 109.

idea of the manifest destiny of the United States, as the most vigorous of the Anglo-Saxon nations, to serve as the architect, organizer, and model for world order and civilization. Implicitly racial theories drawing upon Darwinist thought stressed the superior "fitness" of the Anglo-Saxon "race" or of the "English-speaking nations" to introduce the world to the rule of law. Particularly in its New England, town-meeting origins, and during the "critical period" before the ratification of the Constitution, according to John Fiske, the United States had demonstrated its capacity to lead the world toward federative unity in accordance with republican principles. Thus, as Milton Berman epitomizes Fiske's message, "the destiny of America and the destiny of mankind were identical."[68]

In New England particularly, where the peace movement still found its center of gravity, the message of Anglo-Saxonism found an eager audience. In the face of the overwhelming tide of immigration, many of the new generation of the educated and elite of New England had turned to the worship of tradition and the anxious investigation of their personal and collective Anglo-Saxon origins as a means of coping with their feelings of political powerlessness and incipient cultural decline. Already heavily English in education, culture, and opinions, the genteel and reformist sons of the Brahmins found more and more satisfaction in their close contacts with England, past and present, and talked more often of "race" patriotism. As a call or justification for the triumph of the "Anglo-Saxon race" in an international racial struggle for Darwinian survival, this Anglo-Saxon mystique could clearly take on violent and explicitly warlike connotations. But as Richard Hofstadter has pointed out, Anglo-Saxonism could be peaceful as well as militaristic in tenor. If the genius of the Anglo-Saxon peoples lay in political wisdom, then perhaps that wisdom could be applied to a benighted world by achieving gradual dominance through commercial competition or by persuading less civilized nations to accept restraining international institutions embodying

68 Berman, *John Fiske*, p. 219. The diplomatic aspects of the turn of the century rapprochement are discussed in Charles S. Campbell, Jr., *Anglo-American Understanding, 1898-1903* (Baltimore 1957); Alexander E. Campbell, *Great Britain and the United States* (Glasgow 1960); Bradford Perkins, *The Great Rapprochement* (New York 1968); and R. G. Neale, *Great Britain and the United States Expansion, 1898-1900* (East Lansing, Mich. 1966). The backgrounds of the Anglo-Saxon mystique and its relationship to the peace movement have been discussed in numerous studies including Ernest Lee Tuveson, *Redeemer Nation: The Idea of America's Millennial Role* (Chicago 1968); Richard Hofstadter, *Social Darwinism in American Thought*, rev. ed. (Boston 1955); Lutzker, "The 'Practical' Peace Advocates"; and Patterson, "Travail of the American Peace Movement."

Anglo-Saxon principles. Insofar as the cult of Anglo-Saxonism looked toward Anglo-American cooperation for a stable and civilized world order, toward a "pax Anglo-Americana," leaders of the peace movement were second to none in their devotion to its doctrines.[69]

At the first meeting of the Mohonk Conference in 1895, the president of the American Peace Society, Robert Treat Paine, set forth one of the major goals of the peace organizations for the ensuing decade and a half—the negotiation of a general arbitration treaty between the two great English-speaking nations. This was not a new idea, but after 1895 it thoroughly captured the imagination of the peace organizations. By such a treaty the Anglo-Saxons, who were "taking the lead in everything that pertains to civilization," would set an example for the rest of the world.[70] Other speakers at the Mohonk Conferences prophesied a future for the Anglo-Saxons that would preclude any need to promote the cause of peace by mere example. "The world knows," asserted one, ". . . that the English-speaking people are soon to rule the world." Another proclaimed: ". . . the Anglo-Saxon race assimilates and is never itself assimilated. It is the dominant element; it comes to the top; it rules."[71] The subdued remarks at the conferences of the famed promoter of Anglo-Saxon expansionism, Josiah Strong, were hardly a match for the impassioned visions of Rev. R. R. Meredith:

> But I have a dream, it thrills me in the night. . . . There will be a congress of nations, and Columbia will take her seat near the head of the table! And by her side will be Britannia; and if those two say, for instance, that China shall not be divided, the matter will be settled without any war. . . . We may get . . . an alliance of two world-powers, which speak the same language, which have the same ideals, which think the same thoughts.

[69] Hofstadter, *Social Darwinism*, pp. 172, 181-84; Solomon, *Ancestors and Immigrants*, pp. 16, 59-81, 85; *Mohonk Conference, 1895*, pp. 43-44; *ibid., 1896*, pp. 13, 18, 58; *ibid., 1898*, pp. 39-40; Sondra R. Herman, *Eleven Against War: Studies in American Internationalist Thought, 1898-1921* (Stanford 1969), p. 13. On Anglophilia and the Anglo-Saxon cult among Protestant clergymen who were a mainstay of the peace movement at the turn of the century, see John Edwin Smylie, "Protestant Clergymen and America's World Role 1865-1900: A Study of Christianity, Nationality and International Relations," Th.D. diss., Princeton Theological Seminary, 1959, pp. 91, 93, 105, 117, 190, 193, 302-3, 313, 467-71.

[70] Robert Treat Paine, "Address," *Mohonk Conference, 1895*, pp. 32, 36; Walter S. Logan, "A Working Plan for a Permanent International Tribunal," *ibid., 1896*, pp. 60, 65; Clinton Rogers Woodruff, "Address," *ibid., 1900*, p. 48.

[71] James Wood, "Address," *ibid., 1895*, pp. 43-44; Philip S. Moxom, "Address," *ibid., 1897*, p. 90.

Then these two strongest and richest nations on earth will be one . . . ; and when they say "Peace," there will be peace.[72]

Others sought to soften the suggestion of mere dominance by force by urging a British-American union "not as a menace to any people, but as an assurance of peace and a benediction to all nations . . ." and by referring to the "responsibility of the English-speaking people . . . as the custodian of God's purpose. . . ."[73]

Most leaders of the peace movement did not take so power-oriented a view of Anglo-Saxon expansionism, but nearly all agreed that the future of international peace and arbitration rested with the fate of the United States and England. In 1898 the *Advocate of Peace* complained of an increase of militarism and naval armament in Britain. Such action might provoke an alliance of great European powers against Britain which America could not view with indifference. "The whole of Anglo-Saxon civilization," the editor warned, "is likely to go up or down together."[74] The *Advocate of Peace* opposed any alliance with England that might entangle America in dangerous European problems, but it urged Britain to avoid actions that might threaten Anglo-Saxon "solidarity," and avowed its faith that "these two great countries are appointed by Providence to move side by side in promoting the progress of the world."[75]

The significance of the prevalent Anglo-Saxonism of the peace movement was that it placed the movement within the mainstream of opinion among the nation's political and intellectual elite on an issue affecting foreign policy assumptions. The Anglo-Saxon cult was not highly esteemed among the western silverites nor, as peace leaders complained, among "our Celtic citizens";[76] but Anglophilic sentiments retained a healthy vestigial popularity and influence in elite circles until and after 1914. Abortive attempts were made to gain Senate approval for a general arbitration treaty with England in 1897, 1903, and 1911, and a limited treaty was ratified in 1907. Each campaign brought renewed

[72] *Ibid., 1898*, pp. 31, 70-75.

[73] W. A. Mowry, "Can America Secure the Peace of the World?" *ibid., 1896*, pp. 13, 18; John B. Garrett, "Address," *ibid.*, p. 50; Walter S. Logan, "A Working Plan for a Permanent International Tribunal," *ibid.*, pp. 64-66.

[74] *Advocate of Peace*, 60 (Jan. 1898), 6; 60 (Apr. 1898), 83. As Martin Green remarks of Bostonians generally, they "got more angry with England from time to time than with any other country. But they judged England by standards they had learned from her. They admired the real England. . . ." Green, *The Problem of Boston*, p. 58.

[75] *Advocate of Peace*, 60 (June 1898), 128-29; 62 (Jan. 1900), 7; 63 (Feb. 1901), 29.

[76] A. H. Bradford, "Remarks," *Mohonk Conference, 1896*, p. 99; Clinton Rogers Woodruff, "Address," *ibid., 1900*, pp. 47, 52, 54.

paeans to the similarity and superiority of English and American habits of thought, judicial procedures, and political institutions.[77] The peace movement gained the prestigious support of President Taft in a campaign for an Anglo-American arbitration treaty. Andrew Carnegie, long an advocate of an American-English-Canadian political alliance, endowed the peace movement with his millions as a result, he said, of Taft's advanced proposals for an arbitration treaty with England. In Carnegie's letter to his trustees, accompanying the peace movement's greatest financial windfall, he inserted a gentle reminder that the first prospect for success in achieving world peace would be an example set by "the English-speaking race."[78]

On at least two other questions the leaders of the peace movement put forward arguments that proved highly compatible with the attitudes of a majority of America's political, social, and intellectual elites. One of these, often implied if not explicitly stated, was that the movement for international arbitration and other peace-keeping machinery meant no curtailment of American sovereignty and no waning of the fervor of American nationalism. The "center of gravity" of the peace movement, according to the *Advocate of Peace*, had always been in America. "I believe in arbitration," declared one speaker at Mohonk, "because I believe in the American people." Presumably America had nothing to fear from submission of disputes to arbitration since "the American people have nearly always been right. . . ."[79] Most spokesmen for the peace movement assumed that the process of building world peace would not mean the surrender of any powers or principles or policies by the United States, but rather the gradual extension of American influence through the acceptance abroad

[77] The United States did not seek arbitration treaties *only* with Great Britain, but it was always the treaty with England that received the greatest public attention and the most enthusiastic support of peace organizations. Some peace activists like Andrew Carnegie were eager to include Germany in a series of arbitration treaties that would bring "all the branches of our Teutonic race in harmony" but Germany showed little interest in arbitration schemes. Her curt rebuffs to American overtures so antagonized American advocates of arbitration, a world court, and international law that former Secretary of State Elihu Root privately fulminated to Andrew Carnegie in 1909 that Germany was "the great disturber of the peace in the world." Germany's disinterest in arbitration served to gain her the enmity of several influential leaders in the American peace movement well before World War I (Elihu Root to Andrew Carnegie, 3 Apr. 1909, Carnegie to John Morley, Mar. and 25 Apr. 1909, David J. Hill to Carnegie, 20 Feb. 1909, Carnegie to Hill, 24 and 27 Apr. 1909, Carnegie Papers, LC.

[78] Carnegie Endowment for International Peace, *Year Book for 1913-1914* (Washington, D.C. 1914), pp. 2-3.

[79] *Advocate of Peace*, 60 (May 1898), 102; W. S. Crowe, "Trusting the People," *Mohonk Conference, 1899*, p. 82.

of American principles, habits of thought, and institutions. "The United States of America," proclaimed Edward Everett Hale at the first Mohonk Conference, "is the oldest, as it is the largest and most successful, peace society which the world has ever known." Lyman Abbott repeated this claim. The United States, the *Advocate of Peace* asserted, was "the mother of arbitration."[80] The world needed only to develop the same practices and institutions on an expanded scale. Thus the "internationalism" of the peace movement required little sacrifice of American nationalism.

On the leading American domestic concern, the peace movement also expressed ideas attractive to a disturbed national elite. Anxieties about social disorganization, class antagonism, industrial violence, and declining social homogeneity engendered both a fear and distrust of lower classes and immigrant groups and a desire to achieve reconciliation between alienated groups and to restore social harmony. Leaders of the peace movement often suggested connections between their objectives and the solution of domestic problems by labeling their programs as campaigns for stability, respect for law and order, elevation of public taste and morals, and popular restraint and conservatism.[81] Anarchy, national or international, became the enemy. The *Advocate of Peace* even argued that the spirit of anarchy arising from disordered international relations had created the anarchical thinking that led to President McKinley's assassination.[82] Peace leaders saw one of their greatest adversaries in the turbulent masses, "the waterfront, music hall crowd," "the loafers, the people who wait for something to turn up," who were the first supporters of any war craze. Identification of war with the "lower passions of men" was easily transposed in the thinking of genteel peace advocates to "the passions of lower men." The passion for war, said Edward Everett Hale, was "not a passion of . . . the really important people in the work of the world."[83] The "really important people" faced the same problem domestically and internationally—the teaching of restraint, nonviolence, and rational, conservative

---

[80] *Advocate of Peace*, 61 (Mar. 1899), 51; *Mohonk Conference, 1895*, p. 21.

[81] *Advocate of Peace*, 60 (April 1898), 77-78; 60 (June 1898), 137; 62 (Feb. 1900), 28; 65 (Nov. 1903), 191. For a similar view of the relationship between domestic political conservatism and the elitist views that dominated much of the pre-1914 peace movement, see Herman, *Eleven Against War*, pp. 23, 27-33 and Lutzker, "The 'Practical' Peace Advocates," pp. xiv, 153.

[82] *Advocate of Peace*, 63 (Aug. 1901), 163, 164; 63 (Oct. 1901), 193-94; 63 (Nov. 1901), 281. See also the discussion of war as "the great anarchist," *ibid.*, 64 (Apr. 1902), 74.

[83] *Mohonk Conference, 1895*, p. 25; *ibid., 1899*, p. 25; *ibid., 1900*, p. 31; *Advocate of Peace*, 62 (Dec. 1900), 232; 63 (Feb. 1901), 37. See also below chap. two, pp. 55-57.

habits of thought to those groups and classes whose passions were less restrained. While the peace movement reached out to endorse industrial arbitration and urge industrial peace, it attracted new adherents who envisioned it as a comfortable and morally satisfying avenue for reform action that would express their yearnings for a more harmonious, less turbulent society and world.

By 1905, the impact of recent events which had stimulated greater American interest in international affairs had begun to transform the peace movement. New leaders and new organizations were appearing with unprecedented rapidity. In 1902 and 1903 journalist Raymond Bridgman, in cooperation with the American Peace Society, began his campaign for a periodic world congress. In 1903 and 1904 Hayne Davis, a New York lawyer, wrote articles for *The Independent* advocating world federation and a world congress based upon the American model and experience. In the process, he converted the influential editor of *The Independent*, Hamilton Holt, to his vision, thus inaugurating Holt's long years of leadership in the peace movement and in campaigns for world organization.[84] The same years saw the initial founding of the Association of Cosmopolitan Clubs, an organization of student clubs devoted to improved international understanding that was soon to produce such vigorous leaders in the peace movement as George Nasmyth, Charles E. Beals, and Louis Lochner.[85]

The year 1904 brought the peace movement further gains in the form of two important conferences. The list of prominent speakers attracted to the Boston Peace Congress of 1904, the first international peace congress in the United States for a decade, brought the movement increased publicity and prestige. In the same year, the Interparliamentary Union, an organization of legislators from various nations, came to St. Louis for its first meeting in the United States since its founding in 1888. Richard Bartholdt, a congressman of German background from St. Louis, had become the first American legislator to undertake a continuing involvement in the Interparliamentary Union. He not only persuaded the Union to meet in the United States in 1904, but arranged for and publicized the meeting and persuaded the members to pass a resolution requesting President Roosevelt to issue a call for a second international conference at The Hague. Since

[84] Kuehl, *Seeking World Order*, pp. 62-70; Warren F. Kuehl, *Hamilton Holt: Journalist, Internationalist, Educator* (Gainesville, Fla. 1960), pp. 66, 68-74.
[85] Kuehl, *Seeking World Order*, p. 107.

the First Hague Conference had become a central focus of attention for the peace movement, Bartholdt's success in initiating diplomatic efforts leading to a second conference in 1907 gave the movement new cause for elation.[86]

By 1905 signs of expansion and reinvigoration within the peace movement were observable everywhere. The American Peace Society was expanding and the Mohonk Conference was reaching out for participants of greater influence and prominence. President Nicholas Murray Butler of Columbia University joined with Baron d'Estournelles de Constant of France in 1905 to found an agency for the publication of peace pamphlets known as *Conciliation Internationale*. Within two more years Butler would establish the American Association for International Conciliation to begin a pamphlet series in the United States.[87] Meanwhile, in New York City a small group, including Hamilton Holt, Samuel T. Dutton, Charles T. Jefferson, Ernst Richard, and Hayne Davis, had begun plans for what was to become one of the most important of the new peace organizations, the New York Peace Society. Andrew Carnegie, who had reaffirmed his commitment to peace activism in his rectoral address at the University of St. Andrews in October 1905, was soon persuaded to accept the presidency of the new peace organization.[88]

If Warren Kuehl is correct in suggesting that it was the anticipation of the forthcoming Second Hague Conference and the desire to influence its agenda that spurred the unprecedented activity in the peace movement between 1905 and 1907, then perhaps the efforts of those who could most directly apply their ideas and expertise to the Hague Conference—the international lawyers—deserve particular attention.[89] For it was also during 1905 that the strategically placed international lawyers took steps to organize themselves. And it was their powerful and organized impact upon the peace movement that would contribute greatly toward transforming it within a few years into a powerfully patronized establishment reform.

[86] *Ibid.*, pp. 70-74; Curti, *Peace or War*, pp. 206-7.

[87] Butler, *Across the Busy Years* (New York 1935), II, 88; Kuehl, *Seeking World Order*, p. 107.

[88] Charles Herbert Levermore, *Samuel Train Dutton: A Biography* (New York 1922), pp. 81-84; Curti, *Peace or War*, p. 200; Kuehl, *Seeking World Order*, p. 108.

[89] Kuehl, *Seeking World Order*, pp. 75-76.

CHAPTER TWO

Courts, Judges, and the Rule of Law

In 1905 a minor secession took place within the ranks of the decade-old Lake Mohonk Conference on International Arbitration. Dean George Kirchwey of the Columbia University Law School, appearing at the conference for the first time, expressed the dissatisfaction of a small but growing faction within the conference with the diffuseness and impracticality of the present organization. "I have longed," said Kirchwey on the final day of the meetings, "for some exhibition of a more definite purpose in the gathering than the threshing of the old straw of the Constitution or treading the wine press of ancient wars." It was all very well, Kirchwey continued, for the participants in the Mohonk Conference to engage in a kind of semireligious "experience-meeting" in which, by constant recitations and incantations on the same theme, they gained a new level of spiritual exaltation and went forth to preach the principles of peace with renewed faith.[1] But that was not enough.

The time had come, Kirchwey told the members of the Mohonk Conference, for the taking of "some definite step in the direction of organization of machinery for forwarding the purpose." This "purpose," as Kirchwey explained it, was not to foster vague longings for peace, but to advance such concrete programs as the development of international law and the advancement of the Hague Conferences. To meet the need for more practical, more effective work Kirchwey proposed the formation of a new organization—an American Society of International Law.[2]

It was significant that Kirchwey called for the founding of a new organization rather than a reorientation of the program of the old one. Presumably the Lake Mohonk Conference could have met his specific criticisms by taking up the campaign for "the institution of a reign of law" and the perfection and implementa-

---

[1] *Report of the Eleventh Annual Meeting of the Lake Mohonk Conference on International Arbitration* (Lake Mohonk, N.Y. 1905), p. 128 (hereafter cited as *Mohonk Conference* with appropriate date).

[2] *Ibid.*, pp. 28-30.

tion of the Hague Court as its central program.[3] Certainly it was already giving considerable attention to this approach to peace. But the dissatisfaction on the part of those for whom Kirchwey spoke was based upon the makeup of the group as well as its current ideas and programs.

A new group of lawyers, with academic or practical expertise in international law, had recently begun to play an important role in the Mohonk Conferences. While only one or two members of the Conferences of 1901 and 1902 had been involved professionally, as teachers, diplomats, or international lawyers, with international arbitration tribunals and matters of international law, in 1903 the number of such figures in attendance reached five. By 1904 the contingent of international lawyers reached nine and by 1905, thirteen.[4] These men eagerly sought a forum for the discussion of international relations but they were disappointed by the lack of expertise and the atmosphere of sentimentalism and impracticality that seemed to pervade Mohonk. The level of discussion of international law at Mohonk was far too unsophisticated, they concluded. The majority of the participants were insufficiently aware of the need for a judicial resolution of international problems. The international lawyers wanted to argue such matters with professionals of their own kind and they wanted a professional journal in which to publish their views. In promoting peace through a new, separate organization, they might also forward their own academic or professional careers.

Thus the peace movement of the early twentieth century began to transform itself. In reaching out to bring men of greater promi-

[3] *Ibid.*, p. 29.

[4] See the yearly list of "Members of the Conference," in *Mohonk Conference*, from 1901 through 1905. The numbers are derived by comparing the list of Mohonk Conference members with a list of forty-five international lawyers selected on the basis of their prominence in initiating the American Society of International Law, holding positions of leadership in the society, and participating actively in the programs, meetings, and publications of the society. It is to this core group, and to those who closely followed their lead, that I have subsequently referred when using such general terms as "the international lawyers" or "the international lawyer group." The list of forty-five includes: Chandler P. Anderson, James B. Angell, Thomas W. Balch, Simeon E. Baldwin, J. H. Beale, Edwin Borchard, David J. Brewer, Philip M. Brown, Charles Henry Butler, Joseph H. Choate, Reuben Clark, William C. Dennis, J. M. Dickinson, John W. Foster, Melville Fuller, George Gray, Charles Noble Gregory, John W. Griggs, Amos Hershey, David Jayne Hill, Charles Cheney Hyde, George Kirchwey, Robert Lansing, Theodore Marburg, A. J. Montague, John Bassett Moore, William W. Morrow, Denys P. Myers, Richard Olney, Frank Partridge, William Penfield, Jackson Ralston, Jesse Reeves, Paul S. Reinsch, Elihu Root, Leo S. Rowe, James Brown Scott, Alpheus H. Snow, Oscar S. Straus, Charles B. Warren, Everett P. Wheeler, Andrew D. White, George Grafton Wilson, Theodore Woolsey, and Eugene Wambaugh.

nence, position, and expertise in international affairs into its ranks, the Mohonk Conference had attracted a group of men who sought to inject their legal knowledge into the discussion of foreign affairs but who could not accept the attitudes and programs of the old peace societies. The international lawyers advanced specific principles for the reform of international institutions. The amorphous ideas of the older peace movement provided little resistance against the more pointed proposals of the lawyers for the development of international law and the perfection of a judicial court.

The "secession" represented by the founding of the American Society of International Law was neither a bitter nor a complete one. The Mohonk Conference gave the new organization its blessings, and the international lawyers continued to play an important role at Mohonk. As they gradually took leading positions in other peace organizations, their outlook came to dominate much of the prewar peace movement. Convinced that efforts toward the reign of law were the only true path to world peace, the international lawyers could easily conclude that activities advancing the study of international law, encouraging higher professional standards among international law experts, and promoting respect for the law and for judicial bodies were integral and necessary parts of a movement for peace.

The story of the peace movement in the decade before World War I thus becomes part of several other stories: the internal history of the legal profession and of academic legal training; the gradual rise to group self-consciousness of men with common backgrounds of experience in international adjudication; and the growing sensitivity of the legal profession to threats to the prestige and power of the judiciary on the domestic front. In its search for practicality and expertise, the early twentieth century peace movement eagerly cultivated the interest of the international lawyers and largely adopted the particular emphasis on judicial models for world peace and international organization that arose from the lawyers' experiences and preoccupations.

Kirchwey's call for a new, "practical" association to promote international law generated immediate action. Before the 1905 Mohonk Conference adjourned, Kirchwey and others had selected a committee of twenty-one members to plan the new organization. By 1906 the American Society of International Law had been established. The first issue of its periodical, *The American Journal of International Law*, appeared the following year. From the outset, attitudes of professionalism dominated the organization. At one point in the organizational process the committee apparently voted to maintain intellectual purity by excluding businessmen and others from the organization and by restricting membership to lawyers and former diplomats. Eventually it was decided that such formal exclusions were unnecessary since the very nature and purpose of the organization would insure that the lawyers remained in a controlling position. Among the initial group of vice-presidents, only Andrew Carnegie was not a lawyer, diplomat, or judge.[5]

The active leadership of the new society came almost entirely from two partially overlapping groups. The largest of these was made up of those who had taken an active part in various international commissions, boards of adjudication, or arbitration tribunals during the previous decades. Between 1860 and 1900 the United States had been a party to thirty-eight international arbitrations and had acted as umpire in five others.[6] As the new century began, the rate of arbitrations showed no signs of slackening.

The major impetus behind the growth of the arbitration movement in the late nineteenth century had come from the arbitration of the *Alabama* Claims by the Geneva Tribunal in 1872. Not only did this case represent the submission of a question involving "national honor" to arbitration by a great power and the acceptance of an adverse award, but it also offered symbolic support for advocates of the development and codification of international law. The Treaty of Washington in 1871 had delineated principles of law which subsequently formed the basis for the successful arbitration. This sequence of events was taken as "proof-positive" by many international lawyers that "the definition of international law was the natural prelude to the pacific settlement of disputes."[7]

In the wake of the *Alabama* Claims arbitration, two new international associations sprang into existence. American lawyers and peace society officers took a prominent part in the founding of the

5 *Mohonk Conference, 1905*, pp. 141-42; *Proceedings of the First Annual Meeting of the American Society of International Law* (Washington, D.C. 1907), p. 32 (hereafter cited as ASIL, *Proceedings* with appropriate date). ASIL *Proceedings, 1916*, pp. 137, 158.

6 John Bassett Moore, "A Hundred Years of American Diplomacy," *Harvard Law Review*, 14 (Nov. 1900), 182.

7 Irwin Abrams, "The Emergence of the International Law Societies," *The Review of Politics*, 19 (July 1957), 364; John Bassett Moore, *The Collected Papers of John Bassett Moore*, 7 vols. (New Haven 1944), I, 308; Jackson H. Ralston, "Some Suggestions as to the Permanent Court of Arbitration," *American Journal of International Law*, 1 (July 1907), 325.

Institute of International Law and the Association for Reform and Codification of the Law of Nations (later the International Law Association) in 1873. Although inspired by the Geneva Tribunal which had also served to focus the attention of the peace societies on arbitration, the new international law organizations did not long retain significant connections with the peace movement. The Institute of International Law took a "scientific" view of its purposes, rejecting the consideration of "utopian" plans for peace and world organization. When its central efforts toward codification seemed to reach a dead end in the absence of an international assembly and court to enact and apply any code, its influence declined. The International Law Association was more hospitable to peace society delegates and regularly passed resolutions in favor of arbitration, but commercial interests came to dominate the organization and divert its attention toward such practical matters of private international law as bills of exchange and collisions at sea.[8] The crucial role of international lawyers within the American peace movement of the decade after 1905 was not to stem from these organizations. It arose, instead, from the mutual reinforcement of the lawyers' gratifying practical experiences in international arbitration, their immediate professional aspirations, and their emerging vision of arbitration as a step toward the resolution of international conflicts by an international court and judiciary. Such a course of development would promote reverence for the law and the courts. It would embody the lessons of American legal and institutional development in a truly American foreign policy.

Meanwhile, the enthusiasm of leaders of the American peace movement for arbitration treaties and the frequent rekindling of that enthusiasm by campaigns for an arbitration treaty with Great Britain continued to stimulate that concern for the "perfection" of the arbitration process that would soon bring international lawyers into intimate relations with the peace movement once again. First in 1887 and again in 1893 the British labor leader and member of the House of Commons, Randal Cremer, with the support of Andrew Carnegie and American peace movement leaders, had initiated campaigns to bring about an arbitration treaty between Great Britain and the United States. The Interparliamentary Union, an international organization of legislators, fostered the idea of arbitration continuously from its first meeting in 1889; the Lake Mohonk Conference, originating in 1895, fo-

8 Abrams, 374-79.

cused attention on arbitration with an almost exclusive emphasis on the prospects for such arbitration among the "English-speaking" nations. In 1897 these efforts came to a temporary climax. Disturbed by the near collision with Great Britain over the Venezuela boundary dispute in 1895, many lawyers joined the large Anglophilic segments of the American elite in speaking vigorously for a general arbitration treaty with Great Britain. The move toward rapprochement which had ensued after the war scare of 1895 made the proposed Olney-Pauncefote Treaty of 1897 take on the aspect of an Anglo-American alliance in the eyes of some of those who fondly hoped for closer ties with the "mother country." Rarely in subsequent years would the idea of arbitration evoke such enthusiasm from international lawyers as it did in 1897 when it seemed so intimately connected with the first evidence of Anglo-American rapprochement and so evocative of visions of a world-regulating alliance of the bearers of Anglo-Saxon jurisprudence and civilization. Despite the defeat of the Olney-Pauncefote Treaty in the Senate, the resolutely optimistic arbitration movement went on to achieve a kind of apex in its support from the legal profession with the publication in 1898 of John Bassett Moore's monumental six-volume *History and Digest of the International Arbitrations to Which the United States Has Been a Party*.[9]

The increasing frequency of the arbitrations which Moore was busy compiling and their resulting absorption of considerable attention from the State Department had come to amount to a kind of conspiracy of events in support of a judicial conception of international relations. From the perspective of the early twentieth century, many of America's international frictions seemed to stem from disputes over boundary lines, over the rights and protection

[9] Members of the international lawyers' group like Simeon Baldwin had particularly hoped that the Olney-Pauncefote Treaty might establish the basis for a world court since two nations with similar (and exemplary) judicial systems would be laying the groundwork. See Simeon E. Baldwin, *Modern Political Institutions* (Boston 1908), pp. 348-49, 351-52. On the Anglo-American rapprochement of this period, see especially Charles S. Campbell, *Anglo-American Understanding, 1898-1903* (Baltimore 1957) and Bradford Perkins. *The Great Rapprochement: England and the United States, 1895-1914* (New York 1968). Accounts of the agitation for an Anglo-American arbitration treaty appear in Merle Curti, *Peace or War: The American Struggle, 1636-1936* (New York 1936), pp. 152-65 and David Sands Patterson, "The Travail of the American Peace Movement, 1887-1914," Ph.D. diss., University of California, Berkeley, 1968, pp. 21-65. For a pronounced example of the Anglophilia of many of the international lawyers see the comments on the "mother country" by Theodore Marburg, later the president of the American Society for the Judicial Settlement of International Disputes, in his *Expansion* (Baltimore 1900), pp. 14-16, 29.

of aliens, over the delineation of fishing and sealing rights, and over the interpretation of previous treaties and conventions. Superficially, such issues did not appear to represent deep and irreconcilable political or economic cleavages, but rather seemed to invite technical or juridical answers, or at least adjustment through arbitration based upon expertise. An increasing number of American lawyers were finding stimulating employment in the preparation of briefs, the presentations of the American case, and the performance of other official and consultive duties on arbitration tribunals. Legal presentations before international arbitration boards were often elaborate and impressive. The American case had usually fared well and great arguments for the American position were fondly remembered. Several prominent American lawyers had made their legal reputations before these tribunals.

The formation of a "Permanent Court of Arbitration" by the First Hague Conference in 1899 seemed to culminate the first phase of this movement toward international arbitration in which the American international lawyers had begun to take considerable pride. At the same time, the new court, however nominal, was eagerly interpreted by the international lawyers as symbolic of the new direction that the next phase of international adjudication must take. The pitfalls of "mere arbitration" must now be avoided by perfecting a world court which earlier peace advocates had envisioned and which Edward Everett Hale was currently promoting so untiringly at Mohonk and elsewhere. Stirred by a new sense of professionalism and provoked into exceptional adulation of courts and the judiciary by the attacks of progressive reformers on judicial supremacy at home, the international lawyers took up the old idea of an international judicial tribunal with new fervor. But if reform of international relations through a purely judicial institution was the ultimate goal, the lawyers saw no reason to disparage their own efforts in the early, and less juridically respectable, formative cases. Having acquired a "reputational stake" in arbitral and semijudicial solutions of international disputes, they took great interest in the further advance of international adjudication, the success of which would demonstrate the value and enhance the prestige of the cases which lay at the origin of a new mode of international relations.

Within the organizing committee and the early executive council of the American Society of International Law these veterans of international arbitration took a prominent position. Robert Lansing, heralded in 1914 as having "appeared more frequently before arbitral tribunals than any living lawyer," was a prime mover in the new organization. Equally active was Lansing's father-in-law, John W. Foster, a former secretary of state who prided himself on a long record of service as United States agent before international tribunals and commissions. William Penfield had been counsel for the United States in three recent arbitrations and Chandler P. Anderson had participated in three others. Jacob M. Dickinson had served as a counsel before the Alaskan Boundary Tribunal and William W. Morrow had served as United States special attorney in connection with the most famous of all arbitrations in American eyes, the *Alabama* Claims. Charles B. Warren, James B. Angell, Chief Justice Melville Fuller, Associate Justice David Brewer, Charles Henry Butler, and Secretary of State Elihu Root had all served with at least one such tribunal or commission. John Bassett Moore, former assistant secretary of state, had been secretary at innumerable international conferences and arbitrations. Andrew D. White had headed the American delegation to the First Hague Conference and George Gray, Oscar Straus and John W. Griggs were judges of the Permanent Tribunal of Arbitration set up at The Hague. Joseph Choate, a vice-president, was to earn his laurels at the Second Hague Conference in 1907.[10]

Thus, participation in these tribunals and commissions gradually produced an informal corps of international lawyers and lawyer-diplomats who came to rival the more traditional diplomats in the conduct of a substantial segment of American foreign relations. The new American Society of International Law reflected their sense of professionalism within a new, hitherto unspecialized field. The plethora of legal and technical questions surrounding the major steps toward Anglo-American rapprochement—the abortive Joint High Commission with Canada, the negotiation of the Hay-Pauncefote Treaty, the second Venezuelan dispute, and the Alaskan Boundary Commission—had seemed to place the skills of the international lawyer in the forefront of diplomatic efforts leading toward Anglo-Saxon solidarity, a commonly assumed prerequisite for a stable world peace. Such demonstrations of the pacific effects of the exercise of the lawyers' expertise, and the lawyers' emphasis on law rather than force in international relations, served to cast them in the role of heroes in the eyes of the peace societies. The American Society

---

[10] See entries for individuals concerned in *Who Was Who in America* and *Dictionary of American Biography*. The quote on Lansing is from *American Journal of International Law*, 8 (Apr. 1914), 337.

of International Law, with its origins in the peace movement, served both to express and reinforce the new sense of common experience, pride, and professionalism in international adjudication of a rising segment of participants in American foreign relations and to establish in influential and prestigious proximity to the peace movement an organization of men almost unanimously committed by background, training, and experience to a legalistic approach to the attainment of world peace.

The other main component of the leadership of the new society came from the ranks of lawyer-scholars in the field of international law. Again, their interest in the peace movement was inseparable from their other professional concerns. If peace was to come through the development and institutionalization of international law, the nation would need more experts in this field and a wider understanding of the subject by all educated men. Universities and law schools would need to improve and expand their offerings in international law. Scholars would need a publication in which to discuss issues of international law and publish their latest findings. Having thus assumed an identity between measures advancing their profession and efforts toward world peace, the leaders of the American Society of International Law acted quite consistently in proposing that peace foundation funds be used for purposes clearly professional in nature. They successfully persuaded the Carnegie Endowment for International Peace to establish lectureships and professorships in international law, to subsidize scholarly publications, to establish an Academy of International Law at The Hague, and to defray the costs of preparing collections of treaties and arbitrations and tentative codifications of international law.[11]

Most prominent among these scholars was John Bassett Moore, professor of international law at Columbia University. A former official in the State Department, he was the author not only of the six-volume *History and Digest* mentioned above but also of an eight-volume *Digest of International Law*. Moore participated in the founding of the new society at Mohonk and served as an influential member of the executive committee. James Brown

[11] ASIL, *Proceedings, 1914*, p. 5; James Brown Scott, "Rough Notes on the Organization, Scope and Purposes of the Carnegie Endowment, With Tentative Suggestions for Carrying on its Work," copy of typed MS, 7 Dec. 1910, pp. 6-7, 10, Charles W. Eliot Papers, Harvard University Archives; Carnegie Endowment for International Peace, *Yearbook for 1912* (Washington, D.C. 1913), p. 48; "Minutes of the Meeting of the Board of Trustees of the Carnegie Endowment for International Peace," 14 Nov. 1913, pp. 116-18, Carnegie Endowment for International Peace Papers, Columbia University Library (hereafter cited as CEIP, "Minutes," with appropriate date).

Scott, author of a case book on international law and soon to become solicitor of the State Department, quickly emerged as the dominant figure in the organization and became editor of the journal. Scott had taught in several law schools prior to entering the State Department and thereafter lectured intermittently on international law at George Washington University and Johns Hopkins. Other academic international lawyers on the organizing committee included George Grafton Wilson of Harvard, Theodore Woolsey of Yale, and Charles Noble Gregory of Iowa. Within a few years prominent professors of international law or closely related subjects at the University of Chicago, University of Indiana, New York University, University of Pennsylvania, University of Michigan, Northwestern University, Cornell University, and Princeton University came to play an important role in the organization.

Even more than the veterans of international arbitrations, the teachers of international law expressed the aspirations of what appeared to be an emerging subprofession. During the late nineteenth century, while such subjects as government and economics had been forced out of the law school curriculum by demands for an increase in purely professional training, international law had more than held its own.[12] Except for occasional courses in diplomatic history, international law was often the only course offered by the colleges and law schools that dealt specifically with international relations. Increased American interest in international affairs had only begun to make an impact upon academic curricula; historians and political scientists with special interests in foreign policy, such as Albert Bushnell Hart, Paul S. Reinsch, Leo S. Rowe, Jesse S. Reeves, and John H. Latané found in the American Society of International Law the best expression of their specific academic interests. The society's periodical, the *American Journal of International Law*, served as the only scholarly journal of the prewar years devoted specifically to research and criticism in the field of international relations.[13]

Professors of international law at the nation's leading law schools shared with their colleagues the urge to advance professional standards and lengthen the period of academic legal training. The bar was emerging in 1900 from what Roscoe Pound called the "deprofessionalizing" of law in the mid-nineteenth

---

[12] Alfred Z. Reed, *Training for the Public Profession of the Law* (New York 1921), pp. 299-300.

[13] Lawrence E. Gelfand, *The Inquiry: American Preparations for Peace 1917-1919* (New Haven 1963), p. 35.

century.[14] The formation of the American Bar Association in 1878, with its emphasis on high standards of legal training and practice, had been part of the late nineteenth century drive by the elite of the American bar to reestablish the prestige of their profession. International lawyers and teachers of international law had been an important part of the American Bar Association elite. Now they sought to insure that their field of specialization would develop its own "special professorships and departments" and obtain a "place of equality with other subjects in the curriculum."[15] Some may have anticipated a somewhat more elevated position. International law was particularly strong at the most prestigious university law schools and figured largely in what little advanced study of law was then being carried on. Undoubtedly some scholars in the field retained that sense of the particular dignity of international law that Timothy Walker had expressed so well a half-century earlier: "Next to religion, I know not that the human mind can employ itself in contemplations more interesting or sublime; and if the law of nations be not as practical, as the branches which follow, it certainly makes up in grandeur, what it lacks in every day utility."[16]

But in the age of the Hague Conferences, the grandeur of international law seemed to remain undiminished with the day of practical utility now at hand. With the aid of the Carnegie Endowment for International Peace, the leaders of the American Society of International Law campaigned for increased facilities for the study of international law, and requirements for a fuller knowledge of international law by candidates for advanced degrees. A survey by the Carnegie Endowment of the teaching of international law in America revealed that in 1911-1912 international law was taught in slightly over half of the nation's 122 law schools. Twenty university-connected law schools had listed it as a required course.[17] This was an impressive showing for a subject ignored by bar examinations and unlikely to be pertinent to the legal careers of most law school graduates. But the leaders of the American Society of International Law were unsatisfied.

[14] Roscoe Pound, *The Lawyers: From Antiquity to Modern Times* (St. Paul 1953), p. 233.

[15] ASIL, *Proceedings, 1914*, p. 273.

[16] Timothy Walker, "Introductory Lecture on the Dignity of the Law as a Profession," in Perry Miller, ed., *The Legal Mind in America: From Independence to the Civil War* (New York 1962), p. 243.

[17] ASIL, *Proceedings, 1914*, p. 273; Carnegie Endowment for International Peace, *Report on the Teaching of International Law in the Educational Institutions of the United States* (Washington, D.C. 1913), pp. 24-25.

Through a special conference of Teachers of International Law and Related Subjects, they sought to persuade all universities with graduate programs in law to add courses in international law and to induce state examiners to include it in the bar examinations. Although Professor Sherman of Yale expressed a common sentiment when he warned that the "teaching of international law should not be made the occasion for a universal peace propaganda," academic international lawyers saw little reason to doubt that all steps toward the improved knowledge and development of international law, however narrowly professional in scope, were advances along the surest path to the ameliorative reform of international relations.[18]

These two major groups in the leadership of the American Society of International Law, the arbitration veterans and the lawyer-scholars, partially overlapped and found their attitudes and goals in complete harmony. Aside from their semiprofessional interests, they shared many attributes of social and political outlook, which, of course, were also common to many nonlawyers of similar background and social position. A majority of the leaders were Republicans. Of the older men a significant number had shown mugwump tendencies. Several had been strong supporters of Grover Cleveland and others had taken active roles in civil service reform, tariff reform agitation, and various municipal reforms.[19] But with the exception of George Kirchwey and Oscar Straus, few were active in the political and social reforms of the progressive era; and some, such as Chief Justice Fuller, Justice Brewer, Simeon Baldwin, and Joseph Choate were associated in the public mind with extreme conservatism. Most of them exemplified that admiration for cultivated and disinterested public service that had been a hallmark of the mugwump outlook. Although less than half came from clearly upperclass backgrounds, many had come from families in the professions and had shared very similar educational experiences. Of forty-five active leaders in the organization, nineteen had studied or taught at Harvard at some time. Seven, including two of the previous nineteen, had

18 ASIL, *Proceedings, 1914*, pp. 253-54, 272.

19 Among those in the international lawyer group born before 1850, the majority, including John W. Foster, Elihu Root, Joseph Choate, Oscar Straus, Everett P. Wheeler, George Gray, and Simeon Baldwin had been involved in good government, civil service, or other mugwump reforms and had largely been Cleveland supporters or at least associated with the reform elements in the Republican Party. For the relationship between attacks on corrupt government and the organization of the legal elite in bar associations, see Willard Hurst, *The Growth of American Law: The Law Makers* (Boston 1950), pp. 268, 360.

studied at Yale, and lesser numbers had been associated with Columbia, Princeton, Johns Hopkins, and Brown.[20] Thus a similarity of immediate professional interests among the academic international lawyers and veterans of international arbitrations was reinforced by common attitudes derived from background and training.

The new American Society of International Law had high hopes for the Second Hague Conference in 1907, in which several of the society's leaders took a significant part. Although they had looked upon the First Hague Conference as a great landmark in the development of a new international system, the international lawyers were far from satisfied with the Permanent Court of Arbitration that had been established at that conference in 1899. For all their enthusiam for the recent growth of international arbitration, the lawyers could not refrain from comparing the work of these tribunals with the far higher standards of legal justice attained by the domestic judicial system of the United States. The so-called Permanent Court of Arbitration, they pointed out, was actually neither permanent nor a court. Consisting merely of a large panel of jurists, from which contending nations could select when each occasion arose, the "court" had no continuity, no true judicial independence, and little opportunity for building up by precedent a body of law that would make possible more exact and consistent decisions in the future. Arbitration had been a necessary first step, but the time had now come for a true world court which would not merely arbitrate differences, but would hand down true judicial decisions.[21]

None of the international lawyers gave more influential expression to these ideas than did the president of the American Society of International Law, Elihu Root, who, significantly, was simultaneously serving as secretary of state in Theodore Roosevelt's cabinet. Above all others, Root epitomized the international lawyers' preferred self-image. A man of exceptional intelligence and organizational ability, Root had established a wide reputation for his talented legal counsel to leading financiers and industrial trusts as a corporation lawyer, and for his reorganization of

20 Information largely derived from *Dictionary of American Biography* and *Who Was Who in America*.

21 ASIL, *Proceedings, 1910*, pp. x, xiv, 11-13; James Brown Scott, ed., *Instructions to the American Delegates to the Hague Peace Conferences and Their Official Reports* (New York 1916), pp. 132-33; James Brown Scott, *The Hague Peace Conferences of 1899 and 1907* (Baltimore 1909), I, 280-81, 311, 442-45; *American Journal of International Law*, 2 (Oct. 1908), 772-76, 787-89.

the War Department and the American military as secretary of war. His tenure as secretary of state, if less eventful and flamboyant than that of some of his predecessors, had demonstrated his capacity to gain considerable congressional cooperation.

But Root's reputation did not rest only upon these accomplishments. He was almost adulated among groups like the international lawyers for his demeanor and style. Reserved, dignified, cautious but decisive, Root exuded an air of deliberate and reasoned judgment. He seemed to have no personal political ambitions and therefore his public stands on current issues took on the appearance of studied and impartial statesmanship. To his admirers he was the exemplar of the high-mindedness, self-discipline, and resistance to unexamined change that characterized true conservatism. Leaders of the peace movement could hardly find words to express their enthusiasm in finding a man of such position and demeanor taking part in new organizations in the expanding peace movement, and the international lawyers rejoiced at having their views represented by Root and his colleague, William Howard Taft, in critical seats of power. With Root as president, the American Society of International Law represented the emerging "establishment status" of the peace movement in its purest form.[22]

It was upon Root, as secretary of state, that the responsibility fell for instructing the American delegation to the Second Hague Conference in 1907. The president of the American Society of International Law employed this conspicuous occasion to point out the weaknesses of the Permanent Court of Arbitration. Mere arbitrators, he warned, had a tendency to act as "negotiators" rather than as judges. Nations, therefore, had reason to fear that the court might not be completely impartial or truly just. Seeking a court "with the same impartial and impersonal judgment" as that rendered by the United States Supreme Court, Root instructed the delegation to attempt to convert the Hague Tribunal "into a permanent tribunal composed of judges who are judicial officers and nothing else, . . . and who will devote their entire time to the trial and decision of international cases by judicial methods and under a sense of judicial responsibility."[23]

Sharing Root's enthusiasm for a purely judicial world court,

[22] On Root's personal characteristics and his importance in early twentieth century politics, diplomacy, and government organization, see Richard W. Leopold, *Elihu Root and the Conservative Tradition* (Boston 1954), and Philip C. Jessup, *Elihu Root*, 2 vols. (New York 1938). On Root's subsequent role in the peace movement, see below, chaps. four and five.

[23] Scott, ed., *Instructions to the American Delegates*, pp. 79-80.

international lawyers found the results of the Second Hague Conference both encouraging and disappointing. The actual revisions of the convention setting up the Permanent Court of Arbitration failed completely to transform the court into the institution that Root and other leaders of the American Society of International Law desired. An International Court of Prize was created, however, as a court of appeal in cases of neutral ships captured during wartime. James Brown Scott, secretary of the American Society of International Law, lauded the Prize Court as "the first really important world judiciary."[24] Attempts to create a truly judicial court for all types of international disputes were thwarted by irreconcilable differences over the proper method of apportioning and selecting the judges. But the conference proposed the adoption of a new "Court of Arbitral Justice," and declared that such a court would be established when the signatory powers agreed upon a method of appointing the judges. Thus temporary defeat for the program of the international lawyers was partially offset by developments that they chose to interpret as auspicious signs of ultimate victory.

In this instance, as in several others, the international lawyers tended to celebrate abstract declarations of general principles, even in the absence of any steps toward practical implementation. David Jayne Hill, for instance, declared it a great victory that the Second Hague Conference had declared itself unanimously in favor of the *principle* of obligatory arbitration. The success of international conferences, Hill argued, should be judged "largely by the uncontested principles which issue from their discussions." James Brown Scott went even further. "It is of little moment," he wrote, "whether the [arbitral] court is constituted now or later, for the recognition of the idea makes the ultimate realization a certainty. The American delegation forced the idea on the Conference, and, notwithstanding bitter opposition, the idea stands." Both Scott and Elihu Root suggested that such important ideas and principles could best be established if not discussed in connection with practical considerations such as the composition of the court and the selection of judges. "The only way to secure a general agreement upon a rule of action," Root later pointed out, "is to secure consideration of it at a time when there is no concrete case calling for its application."[25] Interpreted

24 Scott, *The Hague Peace Conferences*, pp. 465-66.

25 David Jayne Hill, *World Organization as Affected by the Nature of the Modern State* (New York 1911), pp. 191-92; Elihu Root, *Addresses on International Subjects*, collected and edited by Robert Bacon and James Brown Scott (Cambridge,

in such fashion, the successes in the assertion of principles by the Second Hague Conference overshadowed the failures in practical accomplishments.

Certainly the leaders of the American Society of International Law did not allow the results of the Second Hague Conference to dampen their enthusiasm for a purely judicial international court. On the contrary, in the society's journal and at its annual meetings the attacks upon mere arbitration multiplied. Elihu Root and James Brown Scott led the attack, but other leaders enthusiastically joined in. Root insisted upon viewing "judicial settlement" as entirely distinct from what he referred to as "ordinary arbitration." He deplored the tendency of arbitrations merely "to negotiate a settlement" or effect a compromise rather than to decide "questions of fact and law."[26] John W. Foster, a participant in a number of arbitral tribunals, announced to the society, "I condemn the general results of these arbitrations." Like Root, Foster complained of the lack of impartiality and judicial character in the semidiplomatic "give and take" atmosphere of the courts of arbitration.[27]

The retention of the word "arbitral" in the title of the Court of Arbitral Justice proposed by the Second Hague Conference seemed a distasteful compromise to the lawyers. They wanted a court that would decide questions on the basis of law and the eternal principles of justice. The criticism of arbitration reached such a point that members of the older peace societies began to worry that the lawyers, in aspiring for perfection, might discredit the semijudicial institution already formed. The secretary of the American Peace Society, Benjamin Trueblood, appeared before the American Society of International Law in 1912 to plead that "our friends who are so deeply interested in the creation of an international court of justice . . . not say too much against the present Court of Arbitration."[28] But while most of the leaders of the American Society of International law argued that they did not oppose arbitration "in its place," the suggestion that the highest international tribunal would remain one that might

---

Mass. 1916), pp. 60-61; James Brown Scott to William I. Hull, 27 May 1908, Box 1, William I. Hull Papers, Friends' Historical Library, Swarthmore College.

26 ASIL, *Proceedings, 1912*, p. 12; *Proceedings of the International Conference under the Auspices of the American Society for the Judicial Settlement of International Disputes* (Washington, D.C., 1910), pp. 11-13 (hereafter cited as ASJSID, *Proceedings* with appropriate date). ASIL, *Proceedings, 1910*, p. 15.

27 ASIL, *Proceedings, 1909*, pp. 26, 32-34. See also the views of Robert Lansing in ASIL, *Proceedings, 1912*, pp. 159-61.

28 ASIL, *Proceedings, 1912*, pp. 167-68.

make arbitrated decisions, influenced by considerations of power and diplomacy, necessarily rankled in their minds.

If the idea of a purely judicial court as the central, and perhaps the only, institutional expression of a new system of international relations became a kind of fixation among the international lawyers, their zeal for this program was not an illogical or even an entirely impractical one. Such an approach was entirely consistent with the political attitudes of most of the leaders of the American Society of International Law and with the assumptions imbedded in their professional training. It required no sacrifice of even the most extreme sentiments of nationalism and required only a slight modification of traditional isolationism. Above all, it necessarily involved a glorification of law and of the judiciary that was not unwelcome in concurrent efforts to advance the repute of the legal profession and to ward off attacks upon the judiciary at home.

In political terms, the idea of an international court seemed to express both conservatism and disinterestedness. In the 1890s, as Arnold Paul has pointed out, a revolutionary expansion in the "scope of judicial supremacy" had established the judiciary "as the principal bulwark of conservative defense." Reverence for judges, courts, and the development of law through judicial precedent reached new heights in conservative circles as the judiciary came to be seen as "the only breakwater against the haste and the passions of the people."[29] Such reverence for the judiciary was easily carried over into programs for international relations by the predominantly conservative international lawyers. Both Elihu Root and Joseph Choate discussed international law and international courts as means by which to avoid hasty popular judgments and to "handle" irate American public opinion. Not only did leaders of the American Society of International Law frequently call attention to the "conservative" nature of their program and the conservative character of those who would become international judges, but the two major representatives of the "extreme conservative wing" of the Supreme Court, Chief Justice Fuller and Justice Brewer, appeared to endorse the notion of the international court as an extension of domestic conservatism by accepting vice-presidencies in the society and by endorsing its proposals.[30]

[29] Arnold N. Paul, *Conservative Crisis and the Rule of Law: Attitudes of Bar and Bench, 1887-1895* (Ithaca, N.Y. 1960), pp. 2, 64, 81, 195.

[30] *Ibid.*, pp. 42, 70; CEIP, "Minutes," 14 Nov. 1913, p. 133 and 16 Apr. 1915, p. 45, CEIP Papers, CUL; Elihu Root, "The Need of Popular Understanding of Interna-

Many of the leaders of the American Society of International Law had mugwump backgrounds or had been active in "good government" political reform movements. Their conservatism was expressed in terms of such central mugwump political values as nonpartisanship, detachment, and restraint. Self-control, John Bassett Moore proclaimed, was "the highest type of civic virtue." The great value of law, David Jayne Hill contended, was that it led to the "gradual subjection of impulse to reason"—thus fostering self-control. If restraint and self-control were virtues in the individual, they should be counted as virtues in the behavior of nations as well. The essential prerequisite for both self-government and international peace, Elihu Root insisted, was "self-restraint, self-control. . . ." Nations should cultivate the virtue of forebearance by subjecting themselves to "self-denying ordinances." Both internationally and domestically, the habits engendered by judicial tribunals would reduce popular clamor and give opportunities for exercising forebearance and self-control.[31]

In their vision of a truly judicial international court, the international lawyers emphasized the qualities of objectivity, unbiased detachment, and freedom from political pressures that they had long admired. An expanded role for the courts, both domestically and internationally, became their proposed alternative to what now appeared to them as political power struggles among groups and nations and the dangerous manipulation of restless and uneducated majorities by demagogues seeking domestic or international upheaval. Elihu Root reminded his fellow international lawyers that the rise of popular governments had opened the doors to "great abuses and great dangers, because people are subject to gusts of passion and temper and intolerance." The establishment of a system of law, and the education of the people to support that system, was necessary in order to avoid the hasty

---

tional Law," *American Journal of International Law*, 1 (Jan. 1907), 1-3. Professor Sondra R. Herman makes essentially the same observation in *Eleven Against War: Studies in American Internationalist Thought, 1898-1921* (Stanford 1969), p. 24: "Cherishing the Supreme Court as the institution best devised for protecting the American polity against disorder and egalitarian legislation, they [the conservative members of the international law societies] projected its image upon the international polity."

[31] Moore, *Collected Papers*, I, 99 and II, 25-26; David Jayne Hill, "The Net Result at the Hague," *The American Review of Reviews*, 36 (Dec. 1907), 727; Elihu Root, *Miscellaneous Addresses*, collected and edited by Robert Bacon and James Brown Scott (Cambridge, Mass. 1917), p. 101; CEIP, "Minutes," 13 Nov. 1914, p. 62, CEIP Papers, CUL; Herman, *Eleven Against War*, pp. 30, 53-54. Professor Herman describes the lawyers' vision of an international legal polity as one based on "the gentlemen's world of social privilege, judicial supremacy and international good manners."

judgments of popular government. Speakers at the society's meetings attacked the "inter-mingling of political and legal considerations" and concessions to "political expediency" and called for "juridical detachment" and "restraint upon power."[32]

The ideal of the leaders of the American Society of International Law was disinterested justice, determined and administered by a court isolated from political pressures. The opinions arrived at by men with the background, social standing, and professional training requisite to high positions on the domestic or international bench would represent, they assumed, not partisan points of view, but rather abstract justice of universal validity. Walter Lippmann was later to argue against the world court approach on the grounds that the central question in international, as in domestic, conflicts was not which group or nation was "abstractly right," but which was to "have the say-so."[33] But the suggestion that they were involved in a relatively amoral conflict over power rather than a search for justice was anathema to the international lawyers. In their glorification of disinterestedness and their unwillingness to acknowledge the role of power, the leaders of the American Society of International Law clearly revealed their political assumptions.

Enthusiasm for a purely judicial court was not only congenial to the political attitudes of most international lawyers; it also drew strength from certain biases deriving from their professional experience and legal training. Ingrained habits of thought tended to lead the lawyers to envision all international problems as specific, definable legal disputes, amenable to judicial determination. They attempted, as Sondra Herman succinctly puts it, "to convert international conflicts into cases."[34] Elihu Root, the acknowledged oracle of the international lawyers, argued that all efforts to eliminate the causes of war would have to rest upon "the peaceable decision of questions of fact and law in accordance with the rules of justice." In other words, grave international problems could and should be reduced to a series of "justiciable disputes." Determination of fact and application of law were clearly the tasks of a court. At times the urge to fit all international conflicts into the conceptual framework of "legal disputes" reached high levels of abstraction. According to Root's interpre-

---

[32] ASIL, *Proceedings, 1910*, p. 37; *ibid., 1916*, p. 152; CEIP, "Minutes," 13 Nov. 1914, pp. 61-62, CEIP Papers, CUL.

[33] Walter Lippmann, *The Stakes of Diplomacy* (New York 1915), p. 215.

[34] Herman, *Eleven Against War*, p. 24.

tation, "No demand can ever be made by one nation upon another . . . but that the demand is met by an avowed readiness to do justice . . . in accordance with the rules of international law. The only question that can arise upon such a demand is the question, 'What is just in this case?' " Since diplomacy and even arbitration tended toward compromise and negotiation rather than a strict determination of legal right and justice, only a purely judicial court could answer such a question.[35]

The tendency to view international conflicts as resulting from specific disputes rather than from the clash of broader political and economic interests, while not limited to lawyers alone, may still have been strengthened by new trends in legal education. In the 1870s Dean Langdell had introduced the case method of instruction at Harvard Law School. By the first decade of the twentieth century nearly all of the leading law schools had been converted to this method, which emphasized tracing certain principles through selected cases.[36] The first casebook for international law had appeared in 1893. In 1902 James Brown Scott brought out an influential casebook of international law, which was soon widely used and which stimulated study of international law in schools already committed to the case method.[37] A substantial number of the leaders of the American Society of International Law had received their academic legal training under the case method, or were employing it as instructors themselves.

As Willard Hurst has pointed out, the case-method approach, by focusing upon the development of principles through a series of narrow and specific court decisions, tended to remove legal cases from their wider social, political, and economic context. It cultivated the propensity to ignore the role of legislation in the creation of law and to emphasize the role of judicial precedent and the importance of "judge-made law." In encouraging the lawyer to view the law "as a self-sufficient body of learning" unrelated to wider social and political developments, the case method may have served to exaggerate tendencies among the international lawyers to perceive international conflict in terms of narrow "disputes," to ignore the role of economic conflicts,

35 ASIL, *Proceedings, 1909*, p. 19; *ibid., 1910*, p. 11.

36 Reed, *Training for the Public Profession of the Law*, p. 380; Hurst, *The Growth of American Law*, p. 265.

37 Manley O. Hudson, "Twelve Casebooks on International Law," *American Journal of International Law*, 32 (July 1938), 447-48; Manley O. Hudson, "The Teaching of International Law in America," *Proceedings of the Third Conference of Teachers of International Law* (Apr. 1928), pp. 7-8; Carnegie Endowment of International Peace, *Report on the Teaching of International Law*, pp. 43ff.

balances of power, and religious and racial tensions, and to insist that the world needed judicial rather than political organization.[38]

Their particular emphasis on the importance of "judge-made law" and on the crucial role of the judiciary also led the lawyers to offer their own special interpretation of the evolving idea of a congress, league, or federation of nations. Among American internationalists, the argument that American institutions and the American process of federation provided a perfect example for future world organization had long been popular. Like John Fiske, they speculated that the transition from anarchy to law and order among nations would follow the pattern set by the United States in its progress from disorder under the Articles of Confederation to peace and stability under the Constitution.[39] To many this analogy implied the need for an international constitution and an international government with legislative and, perhaps, administrative powers. It should also have encouraged discussion of how a pattern of shared interests and attitudes, a nation-creating social and ideological consensus, might be developed on an international plane.[40] But if such promoters of world federation within the peace movement as Benjamin Trueblood, Edwin D. Mead, and Edward Everett Hale failed to appreciate the broadest social, economic, and cultural issues involved, the international lawyers were even narrower in their approach. In countless speeches and articles they acclaimed the United States Supreme Court as the single and sufficient model for an adequate international institution. Some were content to propose the Supreme Court merely as a general prototype. But others called for a world court that would duplicate the American model down to such details as the number of judges and the method of their selection and appointment.[41]

[38] Hurst, *The Growth of American Law*, pp. 185-86, 265, 268-69.

[39] Milton Berman, *John Fiske: The Evolution of a Popularizer* (Cambridge, Mass. 1961), pp. 138-40, 208, 216. For a survey of the evolution of ideas of world federation, see Warren F. Kuehl, *Seeking World Order: The United States and International Organization to 1920* (Nashville 1969), pp. 3-21 and *passim*.

[40] Several other leaders in the peace movement proved more willing than the international lawyers to accept these implications and work out broader plans for world legislatures and executives based upon the American experience. For a survey of a number of these proposals, see Kuehl, *Seeking World Order*, pp. 64-70, 80-82, 86-91, 119-21, 148-50 and Martin David Dubin, "The Development of the Concept of Collective Security in the American Peace Movement, 1899-1917," Ph.D. diss., Indiana University, 1960, pp. 9-67.

[41] For examples, see A. J. Montague, "The Supreme Court as a Prototype of an International Court," ASJSID, *Proceedings, 1910*, pp. 210-22; Frederick N. Judson, "The Jurisdiction of the Supreme Court of the United States over the Controversies

In the international lawyers' application of the American historical analogy, the Supreme Court, from the beginning, had been "the central feature of the plan of American Union." It was the Supreme Court which had supplanted the "clumsy arbitral methods" under the Articles of Confederation. Therefore an international supreme court might now supplant the present, unsatisfactory methods of international arbitration. Moreover, the Supreme Court, which was empowered to decide cases arising between states and between "sovereign" states and the federal government and which could rule upon its own jurisdiction, suggested how an international organization might exist in conjunction with the retention of national sovereignty.[42] No legislative or administrative arms would be needed for the international court to function, many of the lawyers argued. The judges would create their own law—"judge-made law"—and public opinion would enforce the verdicts just as public opinion presumably enforced the verdicts of the Supreme Court at home. The assumptions that lay behind such thinking—the idea that public opinion naturally supported all impartial, judicial decisions, that the creation of a true judicial court in itself would have been enough to transform the original American colonies into a single, stable, peaceful legal entity, and that the same process could be accomplished among the nations—again revealed the proclivity of the international lawyers to view the growth of law and judicial institutions with little attention to the role of political power and of social and economic forces.

The substitution of international arbitration and other "strictly legal procedures" for the "conference system" in European international relations after 1880 has been interpreted by F. H. Hinsley as a reflection of an intensified nationalism. Certainly the enthusiasm of the leaders of the American Society of International Law for moving beyond arbitration to a judicial court demanded no real curtailment of sovereignty, or lessening of what Hinsley calls the lawyer's "tenderness for the independence of the state."[43] Elihu Root, James Brown Scott, and other speakers

of the States a Prototype of the International Court of Arbitral Justice," ASJSID, *Proceedings, 1910*, pp. 258-74. See also ASIL, *Proceedings*, 1909, pp. 51, 227; *ibid.*, *1912*, pp. 148-55; and James Brown Scott, *Peace Through Justice: Three Papers on International Justice and the Means of Attaining It* (New York 1917), p. 66.

42 ASIL *Proceedings, 1909*, pp. 228-30; *ibid.*, *1912*, p. 149; Scott, *The Hague Peace Conferences*, pp. 429, 461-64; *American Journal of International Law*, 2 (Oct. 1908), 776-77; Kuehl, *Seeking World Order*, p. 54.

43 F. H. Hinsley, *Power and the Pursuit of Peace: Theory and Practice in the*

before the American Society of International Law called for the enforcement of the decrees of an international court by moral force alone.[44] The absence of coercion would thus leave every state entirely independent and without obligation to join in collective actions. Such freedom of action and lack of responsibility under an international judicial system thus left unimpaired the traditional American position toward European affairs. Despite its expanded international concerns and influence, the United States would incur no necessity of forming entangling alliances or engaging in balance of power politics with European nations. Instead, it would convert other nations to a court system which might solve European disputes through judicial action. By accepting the single obligation to submit justiciable disputes to an international court, the United States could adhere to the policy of maintaining distance from Europe's troubles which the State Department had recently reaffirmed in reservations and disclaimers amended to the conventions of the First Hague Conference and the Algeciras Conference.

Once again the Supreme Court analogy was called upon to demonstrate that the United States could avoid the dangers and responsibilities of collective coercive action and still expect practical results from an international court. The international lawyers frequently argued that the United States Supreme Court relied on public respect and moral force alone for the enforcement of its decisions. No state had been so recalcitrant as to require the use of force to carry out an adverse Supreme Court decision.[45] A few protested against this interpretation, but their protests were largely ignored. Similarly, it was argued, world opinion on the international level would enforce the decrees of a purely judicial court that would command respect and hand down decisions that were "just." It was unthinkable, for instance, that the United States would refuse to accept an adverse but just decision. A few worried that an international court might arrive at decisions that would interfere with the Monroe Doctrine or American policies toward immigration and aliens. But Elihu Root discounted such objections. An international court would have no jurisdiction over internal matters like immigration. The Monroe

History of Relations Between States (Cambridge, England 1963), pp. 138, 255-59, 266-67.

[44] ASIL, Proceedings, 1908, pp. 16-17; ibid., 1912, pp. 155-56; Scott, Peace Through Justice, p. 77; ASJSID, Proceedings, 1911, p. 81; Moore, Collected Papers, II, 26.

[45] ASJSID, Proceedings, 1910, pp. xii, 258-74; ASIL, Proceedings, 1915, pp. 89, 94; ibid., 1912, pp. 155-56.

Doctrine was merely an aspect of American self-defense and, as such, not a "justiciable" question.[46]

Thus the international lawyers could advertise their proposed judicial world court as a potential political bargain for America. It would entail no risk of entanglement in European diplomacy and require no sacrifice of sovereignty. Yet if the court should succeed, it might well provide a peaceful substitute for the war-breeding, power-oriented diplomacy of Europe. Certainly no weakening of patriotism or nationalism was involved in thus renewing the sense of American mission. While assuming its full place in world affairs, the United States would simultaneously remold the world in its own image by securing the establishment of an expanded version of its own most hallowed institution, the Supreme Court, as the axis of a new international system.[47]

The appeal of the court idea to conservative political opinion, to certain professional biases, and to desires for continuing diplomatic nonentanglement was almost certainly intensified by the immediate pressures arising from the movement for domestic political reform. Reformers had become highly critical of the courts and had pressed for legislation allowing the recall of judges and of judicial decisions. The Democratic Party's attack in its 1896 platform upon "government by injunction" and upon the Supreme Court for its decision against the income tax had intensified the disfavor with which most lawyers already viewed William Jennings Bryan.[48] But Bryan's defeats did not end the anticourt agitation. The emerging progressive movement displayed a startling lack of reverence for the idea of "judicial supremacy" and for the "aristocracy of the robe." After the "reactionary" *Lochner* v. *New York* decision in 1905, the judiciary found itself uneasily on the defense in the face of progressive ire. In 1908 came the adoption of judicial recall in Oregon followed by successful campaigns for this reform in California in 1911, Arizona and Colorado in 1912, and Nevada in 1913. The growing antagonism toward the courts and the judiciary found further expression in 1912 when Theodore Roosevelt called for curbs upon the power of the courts and advocated the recall of judicial decisions on constitutional issues. In 1912 and 1913 reso-

---

[46] Root, *Addresses on International Subjects*, pp. 109-11, 120, 180-81.

[47] For examples of the argument for increased American influence through the power of its detachment, see ASIL, *Proceedings, 1907*, pp. 42, 216 and *ibid., 1910*, pp. 41-42.

[48] Kirk Harold Porter, *National Party Platforms* (New York 1924), pp. 184-85; Paul, *Conservative Crisis*, p. 225.

lutions were proposed in Congress advocating judicial recall and the veto by Congress of Supreme Court decisions.[49]

These direct attacks upon the courts were accompanied by other developments that greatly perturbed the conservative elite of the legal profession. In the formulation and administration of laws to regulate business and bring about other reforms, the judiciary was now taking a back seat to legislatures and commissions. Presidents of the American Bar Association began to complain loudly about "over-legislation," "meddlesome legislation," and "crude and ill-digested legislation."[50] Elihu Root complained about the attempt "to cure evils by making more statutory rules," thus hampering the courts "in their efforts to do justice." Roscoe Pound had warned his fellow lawyers in 1906 that the doctrine of the supremacy of law was in decline, that commissions were now the fashion, and that the nation had entered a period in which "the growing point of law has shifted to legislation."[51] Although nothing could be done immediately to reverse the trend undermining the predominance of the courts in lawmaking, by 1911 the American Bar Association had thrown its major energies into a counterattack upon the recall, the ultimate threat to judicial independence and supremacy.

It is impossible, of course, to determine the extent to which enthusiasm for a world court and international judiciary was augmented by defensiveness about domestic judicial institutions. Undoubtedly most of the international lawyers would have found the idea of a purely judicial world court attractive entirely on its own merits. But the extremes to which the "cult of the robe" was carried in some of their speeches suggest that consciously or unconsciously their devotion to the cause may have been deepened by domestic concerns. With the hallowed concept of judicial supremacy under aggressive attack, it was probably not mere coincidence that a conservative lawyer like Justice David Brewer

49 M. Louise Rutherford, "The Influence of the American Bar Association on Public Opinion and Legislation," Ph.D. diss., University of Pennsylvania, 1937, p. 142; Barbara C. Steidle, "Conservative Progressives: A Study of the Attitudes and Role of Bar and Bench, 1905-1912," Ph.D. diss., Rutgers University, 1969, pp. 3-4, 29, 318-20.

50 *Reports of the American Bar Association*, 31 (1906), Part I, pp. 309-10, 312, 386, 390 and 35 (1910), 331-33. For an extended discussion of the concern of the bar about "over-legislation," see Steidle, "Conservative Progressives," pp. 37-49, 63, 67-68.

51 Elihu Root to Nicholas Murray Butler, 19 Oct. 1910, Elihu Root Papers, MS Div., Library of Congress; Roscoe Pound, "The Causes of Popular Dissatisfaction with the Administration of Justice," *Reports of the American Bar Association*, 31 (1906), Part I, pp. 396, 415.

should be busily promoting and exalting the idea of an international court and judiciary at the same time that he was proclaiming it "of the supremest importance that the judiciary of the State and nation should be upheld in the utmost stretch and reach of their power."[52] The international lawyers' predictable interest in international judicial organizations was certainly enhanced by the desire to project their hopes for the supremacy of judge-made law into a new realm or to defend the judiciary in a new forum.

Some of the international lawyers satisfied themselves with tributes to the "discriminating sense," "moral elevation," or "trained impartiality" of the judicial mind. Others exalted "judge-made law," delivered short sermons on the need for reverence for the law, or referred grandiloquently to "the august presence of Justice," or to judges "sitting robed in the majesty of judicial right and law." Several stressed the importance of life tenure for international judges and emphasized the importance of legal training and judicial experience. Any candidate for an international judicial position should first have been a domestic judge, Judge Simeon Baldwin argued.[53]

Whether these eulogies to the judiciary were intended as defenses of the domestic courts can only be surmised. But several of the speakers before the American Society of International Law made the connection between domestic and international judicial questions quite clear. A. J. Montague proclaimed the United States Supreme Court as a model for the method of appointment since its justices were "not chosen by popular clamor . . . or through the stratagems of legislators." Albert Bushnell Hart tied his call for a world court and a wider knowledge of international law to a sharp warning about dangerous trends "toward a fluidity of law," toward overlegislation, and toward the initiative and referendum and other manifestations of a disbelief in the importance and durability of law.[54] Judge Gray emphatically denied that there could be any recall of an international award. To submit a court decision to any popular vote, he warned, "would result in an anarchy that would put us back into the barbarism of the medieval ages." Linking the question of international decisions with Roosevelt's recent advocacy of the

---

[52] Brewer is quoted in Steidle, "Conservative Progressives," p. 316.

[53] Simeon E. Baldwin, "Justice Between Nations," *Judicial Settlement of International Disputes*, No. 17 (1914), 13-14; ASIL, *Proceedings, 1908*, p. 56; *ibid., 1909*, p. 51; *ibid., 1910*, pp. 231-34; *ibid., 1911*, pp. 294, 297; *ibid., 1912*, p. 213; ASJSID, *Proceedings, 1910*, pp. x, xv, 184.

[54] ASIL, *Proceedings, 1909*, p. 231; *ibid., 1913*, p. 280.

recall of judicial decisions, Gray denounced "the popular notion that has been bruited about in some quarters" that laws announced by the Supreme Court "can be submitted to any other forum for further review."[55] The source of Gray's concern was fairly clear, since the question of the recall of the decisions of an international tribunal had hardly arisen.

Sustained by this variety of political and professional motives, the campaign for a purely judicial court easily survived the temporary disappointments of the Second Hague Conference. Elihu Root immediately initiated what Philip Jessup has characterized as a "laboratory experiment" in the efficacy of a permanent court of justice.[56] He secured from the 1907 Central American Conference a convention setting up a Central American Court of Justice. Here the world would be able to observe and copy a court established upon those principles propounded by the leaders of the American Society of International Law. The tribunal was to be genuinely judicial, composed of judges who would weigh evidence and hand down decisions strictly in accordance with international law, thus substituting "judicial action for diplomatic action."[57]

The Central American Court survived only until 1917, but meanwhile the international lawyers had expanded their campaign to bring to all of Latin America the benefits that would result from the recognition of the duties of nations under international law and from training in American legal conceptions. Steps were taken to create an American Institute of International Law as a "bond of scientific union between the international lawyers of the Western Hemisphere." With the aid of the Carnegie Endowment for International Peace, leaders of the American Society of International Law would seek to create local societies of international law in each Latin American republic and to bring Latin American students to the United States for training in international law and related subjects.[58]

[55] *Ibid., 1912*, p. 212. All of the prominent leaders of the American Society of International Law publicly denounced the recall movement and affirmed their admiration for judicial power. President Taft, a close ally of the lawyers in ideas and sympathies, argued in 1914 that the attack on the principles of absolute justice and the independence of the judiciary by the leaders of the Progressive Party had threatened conceptions crucial to a new system of international relations. William Howard Taft, *The United States and Peace* (New York 1914), pp. 143, 172-73.

[56] Jessup, *Elihu Root*, I, 512.

[57] ASIL, *Proceedings, 1908*, p. 14.

[58] *Ibid., 1913*, p. 7; *ibid., 1914*, pp. 231-32; Scott, "Rough Notes on Carnegie Endowment," pp. 5-6.

Meanwhile, some of the more sanguine international lawyers found in the International Court of Prize, set up by the Second Hague Conference, a more immediate hope for the desired international tribunal. The project of a Court of Arbitral Justice had been unable to surmount disagreements between the great powers and the smaller nations over the selection of judges. But the Prize Court had already been successfully established with great-power dominance, under the assumption that under its limited jurisdiction only the major maritime powers were likely to be frequently involved. Beginning early in 1909 the State Department began to suggest the idea of extending the jurisdiction of the Prize Court.[59]

The Prize Court, as James Brown Scott pointed out, was "not . . . a court of arbitration," but "a court in the strictly judicial sense of the word—a court composed of judges . . . who either from experience at the bar, upon the bench, or in the higher schools of learning had acquired legal habits of thought."[60] Thus this court would meet all the requirements of the international lawyers for a purely judicial court, gradually creating law by precedent. Secretary of State Philander Knox, a member of the executive council of the American Society of International Law, succeeded during 1909 in getting a number of the European nations to agree informally to a proposal to convert the Prize Court into a full-fledged tribunal. Scott, who as solicitor in the State Department may have initiated the plan, was elated over the prospects and maintained a sanguine outlook at least through 1910.[61] But Great Britain destroyed whatever promise the plan may have had. She declined to join in the establishment of a prize court until maritime law was more clearly defined, and then refused to ratify the declarations of the Naval Conference of 1909 which would have provided initial definitions.

The proponents of judicial organization for the world were little dismayed, however, by temporary setbacks and frustrations. In 1910 the indefatigable James Brown Scott joined with Theodore Marburg, a conservative Baltimore lawyer, in promoting a new organization, the American Society for the Judicial Settle-

59 On the initiation of this attempt before Philander Knox took office see David Jayne Hill to Andrew Carnegie, 30 Jan. 1910, Andrew Carnegie Papers, MS Div., LC.

60 ASIL, *Proceedings, 1908*, p. 156.

61 *The Survey*, 35 (20 Nov. 1915), 183; Herbert F. Wright, "Philander Chase Knox," in Samuel Flagg Bemis, ed., *American Secretaries of State and their Diplomacy* (New York 1928), IV, 348; Andrew Carnegie to David Jayne Hill, 18 Apr. 1910, Carnegie Papers, LC; ASIL, *Proceedings, 1908*, pp. 157-59.

ment of International Disputes. Again the leadership was drawn from the most conservative quarters of the legal profession. Prominent conservatives Simeon Baldwin and Joseph Choate served as president and vice-president. With his acceptance of the position of "honorary president" the new society gained the endorsement of President Taft, whose veneration for the "judicial mind" matched that of any of the international lawyers and who was soon to introduce the notion of "judiciable" questions into his interpretation of his 1911 arbitration treaties. Although the leaders of the American Society of International Law had made their preference for a judicial court instead of arbitration unquestionably clear, the new organization further accentuated the extreme judicial program. The society, Scott declared, was to be a single-purpose organization, "limited to a discussion of the judicial determination, as distinguished from the arbitral adjustment, of international controversies."[62] In the opening address before the first meeting of the society in 1910 Elihu Root reaffirmed Scott's call for the creation of sentiment in favor of judicial settlement rather than diplomatic compromise.[63]

While this new organization assumed some of the burdens of propagandizing the program for a judicial tribunal, the older American Society of International Law turned its attention to a persistent concern among international lawyers—codification. One of the problems foreseen by some proponents of a purely judicial world court was that such a court would have to have a body of accepted law to apply. None of them questioned that international law existed, most of them taking the positivistic view that such law consisted of the accumulated body of accepted rules arising from treaties and international conventions, and from established customs of international practice. The present need was to codify this law—to collect, harmonize, and clarify it. In 1909 the American Society of International Law boldly assumed this task. Urged on by Robert Lansing and James Brown Scott, it appointed a committee to draw up such a code for the world and submit a draft to the society by 1911.[64]

But the committee was unable to meet the 1911, or any other, deadline. The task was too monumental and the lawyers themselves differed in their degree of enthusiasm for the project and in conceptions of what the code should attempt. The very notion

---

[62] ASJSID, *Proceedings, 1910*, p. 3; *American Journal of International Law*, 4 (Oct. 1910), 932.

[63] ASJSID, *Proceedings, 1910*, pp. 11-13.

[64] ASIL, *Proceedings, 1909*, pp. 11, 261.

of codification still retained for some the unsavory odor of its background in Benthamite radicalism and utopianism. Some of these lawyers had opposed codification domestically and may have feared that both domestically and internationally it might lead to excessive emphasis upon legislation rather than upon judge-made law.[65] The committee composed vast outlines, engaged in debate over content and organization of the code, postponed its report, and then quietly ceased to function. Codification remained a common objective in the lawyers' peace programs, but its formulation was usually assigned to subsequent Hague Conferences. Codification began to regain some of its attraction when it was relegated once again to the realm of anticipation.

Despite the preoccupation of the international lawyers with their own narrow program for international reform and their own narrowly focused and semiprofessional societies, they were simultaneously coming to exert an increasing influence over the whole peace movement and over the formulation of foreign policy. Rigid adhesion to the single program of a purely judicial court had its advantages, for it resulted in the detailed development of a program that seemed concrete and practical next to the rather vague objectives of many of the established peace organizations. Although the international lawyers had amicably seceded from the Lake Mohonk Conference and although they had, in accordance with their prejudice against arbitration, given only equivocal support to the 1911 arbitration treaty with Great Britain, they continued to play an influential role in the Mohonk Conferences and other peace organizations.[66] The American Peace Society had included none of the leaders of the new American Society of International Law among its officers in 1906. By 1912 it was listing nine of the international lawyers including John W. Foster, James Brown Scott, Theodore Marburg, and

[65] "Report of Sub-Committee Upon the History and Status of Codification," *ibid.*, *1910*, pp. 209-14. On the political implications of the earlier codification movements, see Charles Warren, *A History of the American Bar* (New York 1911), pp. 513-15, 532.

[66] On the lukewarm attitude of the international lawyers toward the arbitration treaty of 1911, see John P. Campbell's perceptive article "Taft, Roosevelt and the Arbitration Treaties of 1911," *Journal of American History*, 53 (Sept. 1966), 292. On the less than whole-hearted support of the treaties by the Carnegie Endowment, with its strong leadership by international lawyers, see Michael Arnold Lutzker, "The 'Practical' Peace Advocates: An Interpretation of the American Peace Movement, 1898-1917," Ph.D. diss., Rutgers University, 1969, pp. 287-90. See also James Brown Scott to Andrew Carnegie, 8 Nov. 1910, Carnegie Papers, LC.

John Bassett Moore among its directors. The Carnegie Endowment for International Peace, founded during the surge of emphasis on a world judicial tribunal, devoted one of its three divisions strictly to the promotion of international law. Elihu Root, the acknowledged head of the international lawyers' group, became president of the Carnegie Endowment and James Brown Scott, the most active promoter of the lawyers' outlook, became director of the international law division.

Through their influential positions in these organizations and by virtue of the prestige which their technical expertise and political connections afforded them, the international lawyers were able to impress much of their program upon the major peace organizations. This is not to say that their ideas were unwelcome. Most of the peace organizations were avid for "practicality," eager to add prestigious names to their rolls, and dominated by conservative political views which were highly compatible with the campaign for a purely judicial court. Most programs for international peace came to include a plank calling for a court and codification. Many stressed the need of a Third Hague Conference to establish such a court, and even the League to Enforce Peace, the major wartime proponent of a League of Nations and collective security, adopted most of the lawyers' program and merely added the use of collective force to insure the submission of disputes to the proposed court.[67]

While the international lawyers were extending their influence over the major prewar peace organizations, they were also gaining significant representation within the State Department. The office of solicitor, the chief legal officer of the department, was a stronghold for the lawyers. James Brown Scott held this post from 1906 through 1911 and later returned as a special adviser. The work of the solicitor had been expanding rapidly and by 1909 positions had been established for three assistant solicitors.[68] All of the assistants belonged to the international-lawyer group and two had ties to other peace organizations. One of them, William C. Dennis, was a former secretary of the Mohonk Conference and another, J. Reuben Clark, was, after 1912, a director of the American Peace Society. The new office of counselor, established in 1909 as the second ranking position in the department, was held consecutively from 1910 to 1915 by Chandler P.

[67] See the League to Enforce Peace programs in Ruhl J. Bartlett, *The League to Enforce Peace* (Chapel Hill, N.C. 1944), pp. 38-39, 220-29.

[68] Graham H. Stuart, *The Department of State: A History of its Organization, Procedure, and Personnel* (New York 1949), p. 215.

Anderson, John Bassett Moore, and Robert Lansing, all members of the original executive committee of the American Society of International Law.[69] Two of the secretaries of state between 1905 and 1917, Root and Lansing, were active promoters of the international lawyers' point of view. Since the second assistant secretary, the deaf and aging Alvey Adee, confined his attention mainly to administrative matters and routine affairs, the international lawyers held effective control of the State Department. The burden of upholding the viewpoints of the professional diplomats against the lawyers often fell upon the shoulders of only a single representative among the department's leading officers—either Huntington Wilson or William Phillips.[70]

Differences between the international lawyers and the professional diplomats, although often blunted by common political assumptions or social connections, did clearly exist. A number of the professional diplomats had become members of the American Society of International Law, but only those with particular ties to the legal profession or the colleges had played any significant role in the organization.[71] Career diplomats like William Phillips, Lloyd Griscom, and Huntington Wilson bemoaned the lawyers' emphasis on details of international law, and noncareerists like Thomas Nelson Page joined in complaints about the department's "library lawyers."[72] Both Griscom and Huntington Wilson confessed to having found international law vague and dull. Huntington Wilson, in looking back upon the period, complained bitterly about "the endless procession of words" which he associated with such projects of Root's as the American proposals at the Second

[69] *Ibid.*, pp. 213, 247; F. M. Huntington Wilson, *Memoirs of an Ex-Diplomat* (Boston 1945), pp. 190-91.

[70] Stuart, *Department of State*, pp. 205-7; Huntington Wilson, *Memoirs*, pp. 154, 156; William Phillips, *Ventures in Diplomacy* (Portland, Me. 1952), p. 35.

[71] On the social backgrounds of career diplomatic officers during the period see Waldo H. Heinrichs, Jr., *American Ambassador: Joseph C. Grew and the Development of the United States Diplomatic Tradition* (Boston 1966), pp. 18, 96-97 and Warren Frederick Ilchman, *Professional Diplomacy in the United States, 1779-1939* (Chicago 1961), pp. 75-76. Several of the international lawyers were of similar social background and a larger number had attended the same eastern colleges. But on the average the international lawyers came from less elevated social backgrounds and were less a product of exclusive private prep schools.

Career diplomats Joseph Grew, Lloyd Griscom, William Phillips, and Huntington Wilson joined the society but did not play an active role. Diplomats such as Oscar Straus, David Jayne Hill, Andrew D. White, and James B. Angell who participated more actively in the society did not think of themselves as career diplomats and, except for Straus, were closely tied to universities.

[72] Stuart, *Department of State*, p. 234; Huntington Wilson, *Memoirs*, pp. 185, 238.

Hague Conference and the plan for a Central American Court.[73] Career diplomat Henry White, in discussing international conferences before the American Society of International Law, stressed all the desirable traits of the traditional diplomat without once mentioning a knowledge of international law. Herbert Peirce quietly defended diplomacy and compromise while Huntington Wilson anonymously penned a propaganda dialogue exalting traditional diplomacy and violently attacking the "peace trust."[74] Henry White refused to serve as a trustee of even so conservative an organization as the Carnegie Endowment for International Peace without assurances that the organization would not engage in dangerous diplomatic meddling.[75]

The professional diplomats' distrust of international lawyers rested upon an accurate perception of differing motives and assumptions. The diplomats, through experience and through association with their European counterparts, had come to accept many of the practices of traditional European diplomacy and the necessities of balance of power strategies. But most of the international lawyers gravely distrusted balance of power politics and sought, through a world tribunal, a thorough reform of the old and degenerate practices of international diplomacy. The lawyers took pride in their campaign as a particularly American movement to instruct Europe in more enlightened international relations. This is what the State Department had done in pressing the world court idea at the First and Second Hague Conferences, in setting up the Central American Court as a model, in urging the expansion of the Prize Court, and in pushing for compulsory arbitration to give the Hague Court an opportunity to get started. In their enthusiasm for the new judicial basis of international relations, the lawyers were apt to launch indiscriminate attacks upon diplomacy, the basis of the old system. Not only did Root and Scott constantly juxtapose the desired "judicial settlement" with the inferior "diplomatic compromise" of arbitration, but others went further in making unfavorable comparisons between the

[73] Huntington Wilson, *Memoirs*, pp. 62, 166, 172, 185, 238; Lloyd C. Griscom, *Diplomatically Speaking* (Boston 1940), p. 48.

[74] ASIL, *Proceedings, 1912*, p. 187; Herbert Peirce to Andrew Carnegie, 10 May 1909, Carnegie Papers, LC; Anonymous [F. M. Huntington Wilson] *Stultitia: A Nightmare and an Awakening* (New York 1913), pp. 42, 148.

[75] Henry White to Andrew Carnegie, 27 Nov. 1910, Carnegie Papers, LC. Rather than attempt to answer White's demands for assurances, Carnegie accepted his letter as a temporary declination to become a trustee. See Carnegie to White, 10 Dec. 1910, Carnegie Papers, LC.

diplomatic outlook and the judicial mind and in denouncing the "jealousies and suspicions of professional diplomats."[76]

Since a new international order would have to rest upon justice, the lawyers argued that judges, not diplomats, would be best equipped by training and temperament to reach the correct decisions. Thus William Dennis, in an article entitled "Compromise—The Great Defect of Arbitration," disparaged the tendency of arbitral commissions to follow diplomatic practices and "split the difference instead of doing justice though the heavens fall."[77] The lawyers argued that nations would abandon war only when other means were provided to obtain justice. A world court would provide this alternate means. An appeal to such a court should be the first resort in any international conflict. Diplomacy, an inferior method of settlement, should become a last resort to fall back upon in cases where perfect justice could not be obtained.

Career diplomats, now developing a new sense of professionalism, did not appreciate such a view of the role of their profession. But the differences between the lawyers and the diplomats were not always expressed so openly and their disagreements usually remained latent, overshadowed by basic agreement on promotion of American interests, nonentanglement, and preservation of full American freedom of action with regard to vital American interests. It remained for Admiral Alfred T. Mahan to express public concern about the tendency of the international lawyers' plans for peace and international reform. Mahan complained that the campaigns for arbitration and a court were attacks not on armament, but on diplomacy. It was fundamentally destructive of all the values of diplomacy, he argued, to "carry all cases into court instead of arranging them outside by compromise and adjustment." Such a program substituted the "rigidity of law" for the "flexibility of diplomacy." Where was the contribution to peace, he might have asked, in "doing justice though the heavens fall?" "Govern-

[76] ASIL, *Proceedings, 1909*, pp. 14, 27; *ibid., 1910*, p. 15; *ibid., 1912*, pp. 149, 172; ASJSID, *Proceedings, 1910*, pp. ix, 3, 137, 163, 165, 231. Scott was particularly given to damning the diplomats with faint praise as in remarks about how highly one might "appreciate the diplomat in his proper sphere." See Scott, *Peace Through Justice*, p. 25. Former Supreme Court Justice Henry B. Brown similarly referred to "men, however high their rank, who are distinguished only as diplomatists or politicians" (ASIL, *Proceedings, 1908*, p. 136). One leading international lawyer even argued that the idea that teachers of international law should have had diplomatic experience accounted "for the entire obscurity of Harvard in International Law as compared with . . . Yale or Columbia." Charles Noble Gregory to Oswald Garrison Villard, 1 Feb. 1907, Oswald Garrison Villard Papers, Houghton Library, Harvard University.

[77] William Cullen Dennis, "Compromise—The Great Defect of Arbitration," *Columbia Law Review*, 11 (June 1911), 494.

ment," Mahan lamented, "is everywhere in the hands of lawyers: and . . . in their eyes there is nothing like the law."[78]

The relative narrowness and inflexibility of the lawyers' program for international relations did little to hinder their influence over the pre-1914 peace movement. Under the leadership of Scott, Marburg, and Root, their semiprofessional organizations— the American Society for International Law and the American Society for the Judicial Settlement of International Disputes— quickly assumed a prominent place among the nation's peace organizations. Through Scott and Root they maintained control over most of the Carnegie Endowment for International Peace. Their expertise on matters of international law and the intricacies of the Hague Conferences won them speaking invitations before the other peace societies, and officerships and influence in those organizations. Other leaders within the peace movement sometimes argued for a more pacifist emphasis or for more ambitious programs of world government, but by 1914 few demurred from the international lawyers' objectives as a minimum program, a kind of common denominator of the peace movement.

The hegemony of the lawyers and their ideas, however, depended upon a continuing affinity of the movement with some degree of domestic conservatism and the acquiescence of other members of the peace movement in one crucial assumption. One had to acknowledge that international law truly existed and that respect for it and adherence to it were increasing among the nations. That assumption, so plausible in the early twentieth century, was to appear far more questionable after August 1914. And the increasing association of active peace efforts with domestic reform groups after 1914 eventually acted to undermine the legalistic understanding of international conflict and its proper resolution.

[78] Alfred T. Mahan, "The Deficiencies of Law as an Instrument of International Adjustments," *North American Review*, 194 (Nov. 1911), 677, 681; Alfred T. Mahan, "Diplomacy and Arbitration," *ibid.* (July 1911), 124. The final remark by Mahan is quoted in Campbell, "Taft, Roosevelt and the Arbitration Treaties of 1911," p. 295. Ironically, for all of Mahan's distrust of campaigns for arbitration and international law as veiled attacks on diplomacy, he was himself a staunch defender of international law as a subject of study at the Naval War College. It is indicative of the way that international law had implanted itself in American thinking about foreign affairs that the Naval War College had included instruction in international law since its founding in 1884. Alfred Thayer Mahan, "The Naval War College," *The North American Review*, 196 (July 1912), 84; William E. Livesey, *Mahan on Sea Power* (Norman, Okla. 1947), p. 206.

CHAPTER THREE

Businessmen and Practicality

As the peace movement of the opening years of the twentieth century began to quicken and expand, it sought desperately to cast off its reputation for utopianism, moral sentimentalism, and impractical idealism. In order to appeal to a wider audience and seize the opportunities of the new century, its leaders concluded, they must prove their movement to be effective and modern. Their zealous quest for practicality took on two forms—the search for a practical program and the campaign for the support of practical men.

The first need, that of a practical program, brought the peace movement to focus its attention upon arbitration treaties, world federation plans, the Hague Conferences, and particularly upon the concrete and seemingly practical proposals of the international lawyers. In the process the movement gained an infusion of men of national prestige and power. But, as men of action and "hard-headed practicality," the international lawyers could hardly compare with the idols of the age. From the beginning of the century, the peace movement's quest for the image of practicality found its major expression in crusades to enlist the support of businessmen.

The role that most businessmen were to play in the peace movement was quite distinct from that of the international lawyers. The lawyers had actively injected themselves into the movement, dominating it with their expertise in international affairs and seeking to enlist the older peace societies in their specific causes. In the process they had formed new semiprofessional, narrow-purpose organizations which nurtured their own specific programs and which integrated peace activities with the promotion of professional interests. Business converts, by contrast, lacked expertise and singularity of purpose. The peace movement, although perhaps morally satisfying, seemed tangential to their main occupational concerns. Although a few businessmen came to exercise great influence in the peace movement, businessmen as a group contented themselves with passive participation.

The numbers of businessmen who attended peace conferences and joined peace societies increased rapidly between 1900 and 1914, but their participation had little impact upon the peace organizations. Rather it was the appeals and arguments directed *toward* businessmen which were most significant. These appeals, and the *kinds* of businessmen who responded by identifying themselves with peace societies, reveal clearly the transformation that was taking place in the peace movement and reflect the new self-image that it was seeking to project.

It was the aging New England reformer Edward Everett Hale who, as early as 1901, pointed out the proper path from dreams to practicality for the American peace movement. In advancing their program, Hale told the members of the Lake Mohonk Conference, they should look to the "men of action" who "developed the industries which have called into being the enormous wealth of the country"—in other words, the businessmen. Since the great and honest industries of the world depended on peace for efficient and profitable operation, he argued, they would prove willing and valuable allies. Hale pressed the executive board of the conference "to open and maintain communications with all who represent the great business interests of the country. . . ." In a culminating declaration he prophesied that the major participants in the Mohonk Conference ten years hence would be the businessmen who carried through the "great practical enterprises" of the nation.[1]

Hale's proposal gained immediate support and adoption. Economist John Bates Clark had been reminding the conference for years of the relation of commerce and industry to world peace, and other speakers at the 1901 conference now discovered an important role in the movement for businessmen.[2] Millionaire publisher and businessman Edwin Ginn suggested that the conference establish a committee of men with "great organizing power" such as J. P. Morgan, John Wanamaker, and Andrew Carnegie, evidently with the thought that the peace movement could best be forwarded by minds that could organize International Harvester or Carnegie Steel. Hale had earlier claimed that the great peacemakers of the century would be the great railroad builders.

[1] *Report of the Seventh Annual Meeting of the Lake Mohonk Conference on International Arbitration* (Lake Mohonk, N.Y. 1901), pp. 16-19 (hereafter cited as *Mohonk Conference*, with appropriate date).

[2] *Ibid.*, pp. 51-55, 57, 72, 87. On Clark, see *Mohonk Conference, 1896*, pp. 37-39; *ibid., 1897*, pp. 74-76; *ibid., 1898*, pp. 91-93; *ibid., 1899*, pp. 72-74; *ibid., 1901*, pp. 46-48.

Robert Treat Paine, president of the American Peace Society, declared that enlistment of the cooperation of "the great intelligent mercantile classes, the commercial classes, the industrial classes" was "the supreme thing at which this . . . Conference ought to aim."[3]

A campaign for business support was launched immediately. Beginning in 1902 the Mohonk Conference devoted a separate session each year to the subject of business and war. Attending businessmen led the discussions. Before 1901 only a handful of businessmen, most of whom were Quakers, had attended the conferences. But by 1903 some forty businessmen were present, and for the first time they outnumbered the clergymen. In 1902 a special committee on Securing the Interest of Business Bodies had been formed to prepare special circulars for businessmen and to promote the establishment of standing committees on international arbitration in business organizations. Within a year the distribution of circulars to businessmen had already reached ten thousand. By 1908 forty-seven different national and local business organizations, including the National Association of Manufacturers and the National Board of Trade were represented by delegates at Mohonk. The Conference Report listed 166 boards of trade and chambers of commerce as "Cooperating and Corresponding Business Organizations."[4]

This surge of interest in attracting businessmen to the peace movement was matched by an enthusiasm for arguments aimed at demonstrating a state of mutual dependence between business and peace. At the Mohonk Conferences, and in other peace organizations as well, the rage for practicality put a premium upon arguments directed toward "practical" interests. The most obvious of these appeals to business interests were discussions of the economic impact of war upon commerce, industry, and the individual pocketbook. Often the same arguments characterized both the speeches of those seeking to convert the businessmen and the responses of those who claimed to speak for the business position, the necessities of peace for business or the virtues of a business approach being nearly as often set forth by clergymen and lawyers as by bona fide businessmen. What resulted was a body of theory that represented a kind of "business thought" on the subject of international relations, but which was often subscribed to as enthusiastically by economists, journalists, and clergymen as

3 *Ibid., 1901*, pp. 19, 21, 58.
4 *Ibid., 1902*, p. 23; *ibid., 1903*, pp. 5, 77; *ibid., 1908*, pp. 89-92.

by businessmen. So avid were some peace organizations to associate themselves with business efficiency and practicality that at times they seemed ready to entrust the entire future of the movement to businessmen, if the latter could only be persuaded to take it on. As early as 1902, the pacifist banker and philanthropist George Foster Peabody complained that the tendency of discussion at Mohonk was toward "adjourning the whole Conference, leaving Mr. Morgan and a few other businessmen to finish the work. . . ."[5]

The arguments which were presented to the businessman, both by business spokesmen and others in the peace movement, served to flatter him, to commend his activities, and to encourage him to calculate his economic self-interest in broad terms. Usually it was assumed that only the economic argument would have impact upon the businessman, and even this argument would have to be presented concisely as he was quite wrapped up in his own immediate concerns and could hardly be expected to give his attention to anything requiring an interruption of his single-minded concentration or the devotion of more than a few minutes of his time.[6] Occasionally a business spokesman would try to point out that businessmen, like others, often took an interest in civic responsibilities unconnected with their own immediate business gains and were no more totally absorbed in their own economic well-being than other men.[7] But the appeal to the businessman as the epitome of "economic man" largely prevailed. Ironically, however, it was just those businessmen who were least absorbed in the details of their businesses and who devoted the most time and concern to civic and cultural affairs who were most likely to participate in the peace organizations.

At the core of most of the appeals to the businessman was the argument that business prosperity depended upon stable conditions and uninterrupted trade relations. Spokesmen for the peace movement extended the oft-repeated complaint of businessmen about internal politics and reform agitation—that uncertainty was the greatest enemy of business—to the international level. Not only did war scares create financial and commercial uncertainties that affected the whole world, but war itself brought the greatest possible commercial disruption. Such disruption, one business spokesman confirmed, would be particularly dangerous to Ameri-

5 *Ibid., 1905,* p. 81.
6 *Ibid., 1902,* p. 23; *ibid., 1907,* p. 106; *ibid., 1908,* p. 96.
7 *Ibid., 1908,* p. 118.

can business, since America had "perhaps . . . the largest stake in the uninterrupted trade of the world."[8] Not only could business not afford to have the United States go to war, but it would suffer greatly if a war elsewhere should shut America off from its markets. The State Department's chief of the Bureau of Trade Relations described international commerce as a fragile plant requiring the "sunshine of peace" for growth and fruition. The Mohonk Conference businessmen reflected the same assumptions in their 1905 declaration that "the success of modern commercial enterprise depends largely upon stable conditions."[9]

The notion that traditional business concerns about stable conditions needed to be extended to cover possible disturbances to peace anywhere in the world rested upon a recognition of international economic and industrial interdependence. Speakers at businessmen's sessions of peace conferences in the early years of the twentieth century often rediscovered with elation this new fact of interdependence. The world had become an "economic organism," economist John Bates Clark explained. In yearly sermons on the miracles of industrial interdependence, Clark described to the members of the Mohonk Conferences how the natural interplay of worldwide financial and commercial forces would inevitably suppress war. "Parts of the world are already drawn into such delicate relations that war encounters new and powerful obstacles," he argued. New economic solidarities would defy disruption. "We shall multiply these solidarities," he prophesied, "we shall do much to develop a world-state, we shall make ten-fold more difficult the breaking of ties between nations."[10]

Although the argument that peace must come with international economic interdependence was most often directed toward the businessmen, it was soon to become one of the most popular weapons in the arsenal of rational arguments against war. Norman Angell, the British journalist, popularized the idea with great success beginning in 1910 with his argument that it was a "great illusion" in an economically interdependent world to continue to believe that any nation could benefit from waging war. Angell's book, *The Great Illusion*, which quickly became as popular in the United States as in England, warned that war would dislocate the

8 *Ibid., 1904*, p. 86. On the attitudes of businessmen toward economic and political uncertainty, see Edward C. Kirkland, *Dream and Thought in the Business Community, 1860-1890* (Ithaca, N. Y. 1956), pp. 9-10, 26, 115-16.

9 John Ball Osborne, "The Influence of Commerce in the Promotion of International Peace," *International Conciliation*, No. 22 (Sept. 1909), p. 4; *Mohonk Conference, 1905*, p. 86.

10 *Mohonk Conference, 1897*, pp. 76-77; *ibid., 1898*, p. 93; *ibid., 1901*, p. 47.

sensitive international credit system which linked the banks and economies of every nation. Any war would disrupt international finance and trade and thus destroy prosperity. Even for the victor, war could not pay. Angell toured the United States publicizing his views and David Starr Jordan, a director of the World Peace Foundation, further popularized Angell's ideas in his eclectic antiwar speeches and articles. Jordan warned that those seeking private gains through overseas exploitation might still manipulate governments to take the risks and invite the inevitable economic penalties of war. But a leading spokesman for the State Department gave the idea of peace through economic interdependence a new twist by arguing that American dollar diplomacy promoted peace by increasing stability, peaceful commercial intercourse, and interdependence.[11] What businessman could object to peace at that price?

Several business spokesmen, however, argued that it was the potential *dangers* stemming from the new international interdependence which necessitated a greater business interest in world peace. Samuel B. Capen, a Boston carpet manufacturer active in Protestant foreign missions, pointed out that the Boxer Rebellion, a disturbance of only three months' duration in three provinces of China, had severely interfered with some parts of the cotton goods business in the United States, forcing a number of mills to shut down. President James W. Van Cleave of the National Association of Manufacturers expressed curtly the business concern over such conflicts as the Russo-Japanese War: "Dead men buy no clothes."[12] Accounts of the losses of trade and profits resulting from wars, war scares, and financial panics in Europe, Asia, and the Balkans seemed to point to a new economic principle: "mutuality of interest." "An injury to one is an injury to all" became a frequent slogan. Businessmen congratulated themselves on discovering that, far from benefiting from the economic misfortunes of other nations in war, they would only lose when such nations no longer had commodities to exchange or money for purchases.

[11] Norman Angell, *The Great Illusion: A Study of the Relation of Military Power in Nations to Their Economic and Social Advantage* (New York 1910), *passim*; David Starr Jordan, *War and Waste: A Series of Discussions of War and War Accessories* (New York 1913), pp. 9-10, 13-14, 41-45, 48-49, 105-12, 174-78; Huntington Wilson, "Address," *Proceedings of the Second National Peace Congress* (Chicago 1909), pp. 113-16 (hereafter cited as *Chicago Peace Congress, 1909*).

[12] *Mohonk Conference, 1904*, p. 90; *Official Report of the Thirteenth Universal Peace Congress* (Boston 1904), p. 85 (hereafter cited as *Boston Peace Congress, 1904*); James W. Van Cleave, "The Importance of Peace to Industry," *Proceedings of the National Arbitration and Peace Congress* (New York 1907), pp. 139-40 (hereafter cited as *National Arbitration Congress, 1907*).

"The economics of commerce," said Secretary of Commerce
Oscar Straus, "have shown that the wealth and progress of other
lands are the direct source of wealth and progress of one's
own. . . ."[13]

But trade disruption and economic instability were not the only
dangers that businessmen were urged to recognize in the existing
system of international relations. In the absence of world confidence in an established system of international arbitration, the
constant expectation of a possible resort to war meant that nations
would continue to carry an increasing burden of armament.
American businessmen, as Edward Kirkland has pointed out, had
long believed that American industry had gained great competitive advantages because the nation had generally remained at
peace. Freed from the necessity of supporting a large standing
army, the United States had avoided wasteful expenditures on
armaments and the consequent burden of high taxes. Manpower,
unneeded for military purposes, had been available for industrial
use. Banker Frank A. Vanderlip reinforced this view in an influential series of articles in 1902 on "The American 'Commercial
Invasion' of Europe" by including freedom from military burdens
among the advantages that were contributing to American commercial supremacy.[14]

Businessmen who warned about the waste of excessive armament and high taxes resulting from military expenditures nearly
always characterized the burden of such waste and taxation as
falling particularly on the back of the businessman. Accepting it
as axiomatic that the businessman harbored a very special hatred
of waste, speakers at the peace conferences often seemed to assume that proof of the wastefulness of war would be sufficient to
convert businessmen to international arbitration. How could
these men reject arbitration when "the whole course of modern
business" had embodied the attempt "to economize expense and
waste in every direction . . ."? "Good business depends upon
sound economic conditions," the business delegates at Mohonk

13 Oscar S. Straus, "The Peace of Nations and Peace Within Nations," *National
Arbitration Congress, 1907*, p. 64. See also *Mohonk Conference, 1903*, p. 76; *ibid.,
1902*, p. 39; John Ball Osborne, "How Commerce Promotes Peace," *Proceedings of
the Third American Peace Congress* (Baltimore 1911), p. 428 (hereafter cited as
Baltimore Peace Congress, 1911).

14 Edward C. Kirkland, "Introduction," in Andrew Carnegie, *The Gospel of
Wealth and Other Timely Essays* (Cambridge, Mass. 1962), p. xvi; Frank A. Van-
derlip, "The American 'Commercial Invasion' of Europe," *Scribner's Magazine*, 31
(Jan.-Mar. 1902), 3-22, 194-213, 287-306.

stated succinctly, "and war is waste."[15] Not only was the peace movement no longer visionary and utopian; it even rested upon and reinforced sound, conservative business principles.

In appealing for wider and stronger business support, business spokesmen at the peace conferences stressed not only the value to business interests of peace and arbitration, but also the special qualifications of businessmen to contribute to the success of the peace movement. As practicality was to be the great contribution of businessmen, hardly a conference went by without several encomiums to the presumed conservative, "hard-headed," unemotional, and practical traits of the business class.[16] Organizations of businessmen, by marshaling such reserves of practicality, could drive home "sledge hammer blows of hard-headed, conservative, practical men in behalf of this great proposition. . . ." Businessmen and business organizations "act more upon facts than upon theories," proclaimed an ex-president of the Boston Chamber of Commerce; for that reason "their action procures recognition and influence." As late as 1915 Boston merchandiser Edward A. Filene was still arguing that peace programs would best succeed if left "largely, if not wholly, to a picked group of our most successful businessmen." "Great business executives," he explained, "are accustomed to succeed."[17]

Leaders of the peace movement expressed great confidence in the political power of business sentiment. "It would be difficult to exaggerate the value of the influence which they can bring to bear upon the government and upon the press . . . ," asserted a Mohonk Committee seeking to solicit the support of businessmen. "You know very well that what business men say gets into the newspapers, and is received in general society," the host of the Mohonk Conference, Albert Smiley, told his audience in 1905. "Everybody heeds what they say. . . ."[18] Businessmen were quick to agree with such characterizations of themselves as not only geniuses of organization, but also wielders of vast influence in the

15 George Foster Peabody, "Address," *Boston Peace Congress, 1904*, p. 110; *Mohonk Conference, 1914*, p. 173. See also *Mohonk Conference, 1903*, pp. 76-77; *ibid., 1904*, pp. 94, 96; *ibid., 1906*, p. 120; W. A. Mahony, "Damage and Cost of War to Commerce and Industry," *Chicago Peace Congress, 1909*, pp. 182, 186.

16 *Mohonk Conference, 1902*, p. 95; *ibid., 1903*, p. 108; *ibid., 1904*, pp. 94, 98; *ibid., 1907*, pp. 102, 105, 109, 124-25; *ibid., 1908*, pp. 96, 117; *Boston Peace Congress, 1904*, pp. 115-16; *Chicago Peace Congress, 1909*, p. 194.

17 *Mohonk Conference, 1907*, p. 105; William H. Lincoln, "Remarks," *Boston Peace Congress, 1904*, p. 102; *Mohonk Conference, 1915*, p. 135.

18 *Mohonk Conference, 1906*, p. 85; *ibid., 1905*, p. 10. See also *ibid., 1904*, p. 85.

legislative halls of the nation. This was not only because "more brain power, more thought, more muscle [was] put into the great business interests of the country than . . . into any other profession or calling," but because, it was argued, the businessman was the true representative of the average American. Political leaders recognized that the businessman was in constant contact with a variety of men and thus likely to reflect a wide range of popular sentiment. The businessman had "the ear of the government," because of his organizational strength, and because he was a practical, conservative, and representative man. Examples of previous effectiveness by business organizations in influencing foreign policy, several suggested, could be found in the campaign for consular reform. Being practical, businessmen could carry forward any "practical proposition." Great hope was possible now that the dreamers had been joined "by hard-headed men of affairs whose daily cry is for results—results!"[19]

Although the businessman was looked upon as having particular talents to lend to the cause of international peace and arbitration, he was not expected to press forward any special peace program of his own. By and large, this expectation proved correct. Business delegates to the various peace conferences often declared that they had come simply "to listen and learn," and many of those who spoke merely professed their belief in the propositions urged upon them. A number of the businessmen at Mohonk may have looked upon their brief, often platitudinous speeches mainly as proper recompense for the hospitality they had received at the pleasant resort. Occasionally a business spokesman would claim priority for business in the development of the principle of arbitration. In actuality, however, the first evidences of widespread interest in industrial arbitration in the United States came after international arbitration had been well established. If any casual influence did exist, it was probably successful international arbitrations like the *Alabama* Claims case that stimulated thinking about industrial arbitration. Given the obvious analogies, it is surprising how rarely discussions of either type of arbitration drew comparisons with or examples from the other.[20]

---

[19] *Ibid., 1903*, p. 108; *ibid., 1904*, p. 81; *ibid., 1906*, pp. 102, 104; *ibid., 1907*, p. 103; *Boston Peace Congress, 1904*, p. 111; *Chicago Peace Congress, 1909*, p. 194.

[20] *Boston Peace Congress, 1904*, p. 110; *Mohonk Conference, 1903*, p. 109; *ibid., 1907*, pp. 115, 118; *ibid., 1909*, p. 113. The suggestion of the chronological priority of international arbitration is only a very tentative and impressionistic one, based on a survey of entries in *Poole's Index to Periodical Literature* and the *Nineteenth Century Reader's Guide to Periodical Literature* for the period 1870 to 1910.

Several business representatives at the various peace and arbitration conferences largely ignored the issues of foreign relations and devoted their remarks to "boosting" the city or business organization they represented or to venting concerns about labor unrest and the need for compulsory arbitration in labor disputes. When they offered specific proposals, these tended to be narrow programs for such aids to commerce as uniform customs and port regulations, a subsidized merchant marine, or neutralized trade routes. The leading investment banker James Speyer, for instance, devoted particular attention to the need for ending certain discriminations against foreign investments and eliminating regulations that excluded foreign securities from the funds in which trustees of funds, institutions, and certain banks were allowed to invest. While such matters may have borne some relation to peace, they were obviously of more immediate importance to Speyer's considerable interests in marketing foreign securities.[21]

But a number of businessmen did discover one broader program for peace that could inspire their enthusiasm. Commerce, they agreed, had become "the paramount power in the civilized world." It had the power to serve as a promoter as well as a beneficiary of peace. Expanding upon Herbert Spencer's theory of the transformation of civilized society from militarism to industrialism, business spokesmen proclaimed their era to be the "Economic Age." Banker George E. Roberts described the new age as one of "cost-keeping" and efficiency, of "calculation and analysis" in which old sentiments of militarism had become obsolete and the wastefulness of war an abomination. Thus any further advances of commerce and the "commercial spirit" could be counted as steps toward a more rationalized and less warlike world.[22]

Peace, these businessmen argued, would find an ally not only in the broad advance of the "commercial spirit" but also in the specific and individual contacts that were being multiplied by the growth of international commerce. Such contacts made for increased friendship, understanding, and mutual trust. Those who found the major causes of modern war in trade wars and commercial rivalries were quite mistaken, according to the analysis offered by the chief of the State Department's Bureau of Trade Relations. An earlier age of "predatory commerce" had now

---

Articles on industrial arbitration suddenly proliferated in the two decades between 1890 and 1910.

21 *Baltimore Peace Congress, 1911*, p. 138; *Mohonk Conference, 1906*, pp. 91-99; *ibid., 1907*, pp. 104-5.

22 *Chicago Peace Congress, 1909*, p. 179; *Boston Peace Congress, 1904*, p. 108; *Mohonk Conference, 1907*, p. 93.

passed. Modern international commercial and financial relations, based upon mutual confidence, had created both mutual understanding and ties of economic interdependence that nations would be extremely reluctant to break. Any forces that would act to increase this international mutuality of commercial interests, including the increase of international investment and the expansion of the operations of the great corporations, should be greeted as allies in the reform of international relations. Thus, viewed correctly, international commerce was not war, but a mutual exchange of benefits. "The Golden Rule in international trade," avowed one businessman, "will be the real guiding principle that will lead us into permanent peace."[23]

Sometimes the tributes to the power of commerce and its peaceful proclivities were blended with unblushing assessments of the ethical function of businessmen. Finding themselves in the atmosphere of moral pretentiousness that characterized the peace conferences, the businessmen were apt to respond with assertions of their own claims to moral leadership. They modestly accepted encomiums for their hard-headed practicality, but were not content with the self-image of business practicality alone. Clergymen, educators, and politicians might excel in talking about such great moral and civic problems as peace, but businessmen had been the world's actual civilizers and pacificators. Commerce was essentially an ethical force; its promoters were philanthropists in a great moral cause. One businessman looked forward to the "day when directors of finance, manufactures and commerce shall vie with the philanthropist, the academician and the statesman . . ." in leading the cause of peace. But others insisted that this day had already come. "The businessmen, with their talent, manage and conduct everything that exists," proclaimed the president of the Philadelphia Board of Trade. The cause of peace might be confidently entrusted to such men, another speaker implied, since the Boston Chamber of Commerce had always been "on the right side of every great moral question."[24]

But for all their willingness to accept philanthropic credit for

23 *Mohonk Conference, 1902*, pp. 70, 77; *ibid., 1905*, p. 55; Osborne, "The Influence of Commerce in the Promotion of International Peace," pp. 3, 5; *Baltimore Peace Congress, 1911*, pp. 137-38, 426, 428; *Book of the Fourth American Peace Congress*, (St. Louis 1913), p. 522 (hereafter cited as *St. Louis Peace Congress*, 1913).

24 *Boston Peace Congress, 1904*, p. 115; *Mohonk Conference, 1906*, p. 89; *Baltimore Peace Congress, 1911*, p. 431; *Mohonk Conference, 1903*, p. 108; *Chicago Peace Congress, 1909*, p. 425. On the concern of businessmen with their larger ethical and civic role, see also Kirkland, *Dream and Thought in the Business Community*, pp. 84-85, 164-65 and Robert Wiebe, *Businessmen and Reform: A Study of the Progressive Movement* (Cambridge, Mass. 1962), p. 186.

the progress of the world toward peace, the businessmen did not, as a group, form their own peace organizations or take substantial leadership in the existing societies. Although they shared the sympathies of the international lawyers and many other conservative groups with the prewar peace movement's emphasis on order and stability, their generalized sympathies were not reinforced by specific professional interests that might coincide with or be enhanced by current peace programs. They might accept as rational and logical the arguments that stressed the mutual interdependence of commerce and peace, but they might also conclude that if commerce was so effective a promoter of peace the businessman could logically do no better for the cause than to throw his energies into his own commercial activities. Although businessmen joined the peace organizations in increasing numbers, their participation remained largely passive and their commitment superficial. And the *types* of businessmen who joined peace societies suggest that it was the aura of philanthropic respectability and civic responsibility rather than the specific arguments for business support that had attracted them.

Although the Mohonk Conference had been the first of the peace organizations to campaign vigorously for business participation, other peace organizations soon proved themselves equally avid for the aura of practicality and the enhanced prestige that business support might bring. The American Peace Society began to devote more attention to business organizations and business points of view. National peace conferences after 1907 invariably devoted special sessions to businessmen. Spokesmen for the peace movement took great satisfaction in the fact that local business and merchant groups had taken part in underwriting and making the arrangements for these conferences. The Chicago Peace Society, organized in 1909 as a branch of the American Peace Society, included several prominent bankers among its highest officers and enjoyed the support of Julius Rosenwald of Sears, Roebuck and Company.[25]

[25] *Eighty-First Annual Report of the American Peace Society* (1909), pp. 7-9; Louis P. Lochner, *Always the Unexpected* (New York 1956), p. 46; *Advocate of Peace*, 69 (Apr. 1907), 83; 69 (May 1907), 97, 99, 108; 69 (June 1907) 126, 128; 69 (Dec. 1907), 256-58; 70 (Feb. 1908), 39-43; 70 (Nov. 1908), 241-42; 71 (Mar. 1909), 63; 71 (June 1909), 122, 131; 71 (Nov. 1909), 235; 72 (Feb. 1910), 30-31; "Minutes of the Executive Committee of the American Peace Society," 23 May 1913, Box 1, William I. Hull Papers, Friends' Historical Library, Swarthmore College. For additional evidence of the increasing participation and influence in peace societies of businessmen see Thomas Sands Patterson, "The Travail of the American Peace Movement, 1887-1914," Ph.D. diss., University of California, Berkeley, 1968, pp. 248, 267, 272

A few businessmen rose to particularly influential places within the peace movement between 1900 and 1914. Most of these men, like publisher Edwin Ginn, retired steel magnate Andrew Carnegie, and the Quaker banker George Foster Peabody, were not part of a new businessman's interest in peace but had participated in the anti-imperialist movement and earlier peace activities. They did, however, often try to further the movement's search for a more businesslike image. Ginn took great pride in his own practicality and business experience, and sought to persuade Andrew Carnegie that only men like themselves could provide "a businessman's handling of a great business question." Ginn constantly lectured the trustees and directors of his foundation on the importance of the position of business manager and the need for businesslike methods. By 1911 Ginn's own endowed World Peace Foundation had established a Department of Commercial Associations and thereafter directed much attention to work with commercial organizations. What the peace movement lacked, said Ginn's director of the Department of Commercial Associations, was "the cooperation of commercial and industrial men" in a "Taylor system of efficiency engineering."[26]

Of the newer peace organizations after 1905, the one which most avidly and successfully sought the support of businessmen was the New York Peace Society. Organized early in 1906, just as the new drive for practicality and prestige was beginning to invigorate and transform the peace movement, the New York Peace Society came to exemplify the new "establishment" quality of the movement. In this society, as in all the other peace organizations, the businessmen did not provide the core of initiators and active workers. These leaders, including Samuel T. Dutton, Charles T. Jefferson, William H. Short, George Kirchwey, Hamilton Holt, Ernst Richard, and Frederick Lynch, were largely representative of such traditional groups within the peace movement as educators, journalists, and clergymen. But the New York Peace Society demonstrated an early and continuing propensity to aim primarily at the enlistment and cultivation of men of the greatest

---

and Michael Arnold Lutzker, "The 'Practical' Peace Advocates: An Interpretation of the American Peace Movement, 1898-1917," Ph.D. diss., Rutgers University, 1969, pp. 32, 111, 114, 166, 170.

[26] Edwin Ginn to Andrew Carnegie, 30 Nov. 1909 and Ginn to Carnegie, 17 Jan. 1910, Andrew Carnegie Papers, MS Div., Library of Congress; Ginn to Edwin Mead and David Starr Jordan, 29 Mar. 1912 and Ginn to Board of Trustees, World Peace Foundation, 10 Dec. 1913, World Peace Foundation Collection, A. Lawrence Lowell Papers, Harvard University Archives; *Boston Peace Congress, 1904*, p. 221; *Baltimore Peace Congress, 1911*, pp. 439-40.

prestige and influence. Not only did the society gain the adherence of much of New York City's educational and ecclesiastical elite, but it surpassed previous peace organizations in its attainment of at least passive and honorific participation by the city's legal elite and by businessmen.

The success of the New York Peace Society's efforts to recruit businessmen makes this society a useful one to investigate more closely in seeking to understand the role of businessmen in the changing peace movement. What types of businessmen were attracted to at least superficial participation in a society which reflected the new emphasis of the peace movement? What can be surmised about their probable reasons for joining? How did their participation influence this particular peace society and the peace movement as a whole?

Businessmen joined the New York Peace Society, in part, because they were actively and persistently courted by the leaders of the society. Andrew Carnegie, who became president of the New York Peace Society in 1907, made vigorous efforts to attract men of prominence, especially leading lawyers and businessmen, into the organization. Together with the society's executive secretary, William H. Short, Carnegie pushed programs to circulate free peace propaganda (mostly from Carnegie's own pen) to leading businessmen and to gain the support of business organizations for the society's resolutions. Although the clergy still ranked highest in total numbers on the mailing list for a pamphlet in 1909, the category of "leading financiers in New York" was a strong second, receiving greater attention than the press and "prominent educators" combined. Another mailing list ranked the "finance list" and members of the Bar Association as second and third in total numbers after the clergymen. By 1912 businessmen constituted a third of the New York Peace Society's vice-presidents and a third of its board of directors.[27] In the years 1913-1914, businessmen comprised 31 percent of the men who were regular members of the society and 45 percent of those whose occupations could be identified.[28]

[27] William H. Short to Andrew Carnegie, 1 Apr., 6 Aug., and 30 Dec. 1909; Carnegie to Short, 23 Aug. 1909; Short to "Dear Sir" n.d. (filed with 23 Nov. 1909), Carnegie Papers, LC; Short to John Bates Clark, 14 May 1914, Box 3, New York Peace Society Papers, Swarthmore College Peace Collection; New York Peace Society, *Yearbook 1909-1910*, p. 33.

[28] These percentages and the following data on and characterizations of the businessmen in the New York Peace Society are based upon a survey of the membership of the society for the years 1913 and 1914. During that period, the society listed 891 members, including officers. Of these, 280 were women and 611 men. Of the 430 men who could be identified by occupation, 193 were businessmen. In-

Although the argument that business needed peace and stability had sought to stimulate interest in peace on the part of all businessmen, those who actually came to participate in the peace conferences and organizations did not represent a cross-section of the nation's businessmen. Since most of the peace societies had been organized in northeastern metropolitan areas, their business adherents also reflected that sectional and urban concentration. As a group, the businessmen who joined peace societies certainly stood well above the average in wealth and prestige. This tendency stemmed partly from the specific efforts of the societies to seek out potential contributors to their treasuries and prestigious names to add to their letterheads and partly, as we shall see, from the kinds of satisfactions that membership in such societies provided for business adherents. But even beyond these initial distinctions, as a survey of the New York Peace Society reveals, business members of peace societies were not "typical" businessmen.[29]

One plausible hypothesis is that businessmen in the peace movement might have been disproportionately representative of those who had the greatest direct economic interests in stable conditions abroad—those most involved in foreign trade and foreign investments. Certainly a number of the businessmen in the New York Peace Society in 1913-1914 might reasonably be sus-

cluded as "businessmen" in the survey were mining engineers who were deeply involved in the business side of mining companies, stockbrokers, and those designated simply as capitalists. Not included were publishers (who often seemed to be more journalists than businessmen) and corporation lawyers. Although somewhat arbitrary decisions or decisions based upon sparse information were sometimes necessary in categorizing certain individuals, the data indicated no significant differences in the areas investigated between those who were clearly businessmen and those, such as publishers, corporation lawyers, and mining engineers whose varying involvements in business operations were harder to assess.

[29] The assertion that businessmen in the New York Peace Society were not "typical" businessmen rests more upon what I hope are plausible common-sense assumptions than upon comparative data. For the purposes of this study I was not able to discover a convenient method by which to arrive at a control group of "typical" New York businessmen. In several instances New York Peace Society businessmen have been cross-checked against individual members of the Merchants' Association of New York City, the New York Chamber of Commerce, and the New York Produce Exchange. These other groups were probably not perfectly representative of New York businessmen either—the Chamber of Commerce certainly over-represented businessmen and nonbusinessmen of larger interests and greater concern for civic responsibility and prominence. But such groups as the Merchants' Association and the Produce Exchange did represent wider and different segments of the New York business community. The relatively infrequent participation of their members in various civic organizations and the remarkably high participation of New York Peace Society businessmen in such organizations suggests that the atypical quality of the peace society businessmen extended well beyond the obviously disproportionate number of exceptionally prominent names in the New York Peace Society roster.

pected of having come to an interest in peace through direct concern for their own business operations. The investment banking houses of Kuhn, Loeb & Co., Speyer & Co., J. P. Morgan & Co., J. & W. Seligman & Co., and August Belmont & Co. were all represented among the members of the society. All of these houses had extensive foreign connections and considerable foreign investments. All were engaged in selling American securities abroad and in marketing foreign securities in America. Presumably they were particularly sensitive, due to their everyday business activities, to the economic importance of world peace and stability.

Other prominent business members of the New York Peace Society had been deeply involved in the kinds of overseas business operations that might have influenced them to take a narrowly self-interested concern in world peace. One of the society's directors, George W. Perkins, had been a J. P. Morgan partner until 1910 and had played a major role in the international expansion of the New York Life Insurance Company, the only one of the large insurance companies that had attempted to maintain a high level of foreign business after 1905.[30] Overseas mining interests, a major segment of American foreign investment, were reflected by the participation in the New York Peace Society of such figures as Daniel Guggenheim, Adolph Lewisohn, Cleveland Dodge, and John Hays Hammond. William P. Clyde, the president of the Clyde Steamship Lines, was a member, as were John Craig Havemeyer and several other sugar refiners. Frank Hagemeyer and E. H. Outerbridge headed import-export firms. Others who may have had a direct and immediate economic stake in international peace and stability included several importers of wines, chemicals, or silks, a marine insurance adjuster, two cotton merchants, and several leather manufacturers or dealers in hides and skins.

But even if one were to assume that these men had joined the peace movement out of a notion of their own economic self-interest in peace, one would still find that they comprised only a small fraction of the businessmen in the New York Peace Society. They were heavily outnumbered by such businessmen as insurance brokers, building contractors, brewers, promoters of domestic railroads, presidents and general managers of electric companies,

30 New York Peace Society, *Year Book, 1914*, pp. 3, 45-53; Morton Keller, *The Life Insurance Enterprise, 1885-1910: A Study in the Limits of Corporate Power* (Cambridge, Mass. 1963), p. 274; John A. Garraty, *Right-Hand Man: The Life of George W. Perkins* (New York 1957), pp. 59-60, 240. Of all the businessmen, the insurance company executives were most likely to take an exalted view of their moral role in international relations. See Keller, *op. cit.*, pp. 94, 276.

department store owners, other clothing retailers and whole-salers, restaurant owners, and scores of other businessmen who appeared to have little direct concern with international trade and investments. The vice-president of a corset company, the president of a cold storage company, the proprietor of the Hotel Astor, the owner of a chain of ice-cream parlors, and many others like them clearly did not join the peace society because they saw their own business ventures intimately involved with current pro-grams for world peace. Even among the bankers and financiers who belonged to the society, a majority were not significantly en-gaged in international operations.

Not only were those involved in international trade and finance a small minority among New York Peace Society businessmen; they also shared with the other businessmen in the society cer-tain characteristics that were probably far more important in aligning them with the peace society than any specific economic interests. Large business interests were heavily represented. So were retired and semiretired businessmen. The cosmopolitan elite of the Jewish business community of New York contributed a full quota of members.[31] Perhaps most significant of all the character-istics of the business members, however, was the extent of their common participation in civic and cultural activities. For most of them, the peace movement was no isolated civic or social activity. Membership in the New York Peace Society fitted, perhaps even off-handedly, into a broader pattern of philanthropic and civic concerns.

Almost 70 percent of the businessmen in the New York Peace So-ciety were active, often as directors or officers, in some philan-thropic organization. Eleven were leading officers in the Charity Organization Society of New York and seventy-six others had contributed to the Charity Organization Society in 1913 or 1914.

---

[31] The Jewish business community was represented by, among others, Charles L. Bernheimer, Edward Blum, Benedict J. Greenhut, Daniel Guggenheim, Selig and Sol G. Rosenbaum, Arthur Lehman, Adolph and Sam Lewisohn, Marcus Marks, Jacob Schiff, I. N. and D. W. Seligman, James Speyer, Leopold Stern, Percy S. Straus, and Felix Warburg. The Jewish financier August Belmont, whose company held a life membership in the New York Peace Society, was not part of the tight-knit business, philanthropic and social community that included most of the others. See Barry E. Supple, "A Business Elite: German Jewish Financiers in Nineteenth-Century New York," *Business History Review*, 31 (Summer 1957), 162, 166. Thirty of the business members of the New York Peace Society were retired from active business operations and at least a dozen others appear to have been heavily engaged in nonbusiness activities. Most of these men probably belonged to the category of "businessman-reformer," a group which Robert Wiebe has characterized as typically retired or semiretired and unrepresentative of their occupation group (*Businessmen and Reform*, p. ix).

Businessmen from the New York Peace Society were also well represented among the officers and contributors to the New York Association for Improving the Condition of the Poor and the New York Association for the Blind.[32] Many were directors of hospitals, invalid homes, and sanitariums. More than a score were prominent in leading Jewish and Catholic charities. Others were officers or leading financial supporters of Negro colleges, children's aid societies, anti-child labor organizations, low-interest loan societies, YMCA's, boys clubs, mental hygiene committees, and settlement houses. One businessman in the New York Peace Society was president of the American Christian Missionary Society; another was treasurer of the Layman's Missionary Movement; and at least a dozen others had served on missionary boards and societies.[33] Many of the businessmen who were officers of the society—such men as R. Fulton Cutting, Andrew Carnegie, Cleveland Dodge, Robert C. Ogden, George F. Peabody, Adolph Lewisohn, Marcus Marks, Algernon Frissell, William Jay Schiefflin, Jacob Schiff, James Speyer, Issac Seligman, John D. Crimmins, and John A. Stewart—were active supporters of a host of philanthropic activities.[34]

In forms of philanthropy other than health, charity, and religion the New York Peace Society businessmen also distinguished themselves. Twenty-nine percent were contributing members of the New York Zoological Society and 30 percent supported the New York Botanical Gardens. Slightly more than half of the New

32 Charity Organization Society of the City of New York, *Thirty-First Annual Report, 1913* and *Thirty-Second Annual Report 1914*; New York Association For Improving the Condition of the Poor, *Seventieth Annual Report, 1913* and *Seventy-First Annual Report, 1914*; The New York Association for the Blind, *Seventh Report, for the Year ending November 1, 1913*.

33 Data on philanthropic activities were derived largely from sketches of the individuals in the *Dictionary of American Biography*, *Who's Who in New York, 1914*, and *New York Times* obituaries. The mission leaders referred to are William Jay Schiefflin and Eben Olcott.

34 Cutting, Peabody, Frissell, Schiff, Speyer, and Seligman were financiers and investment bankers. Lewisohn was head of a mercantile and investment firm with large interests in copper mining and smelting. Ogden was a former partner of department store owner John Wanamaker, and Dodge came from a merchant family with large copper interests. Marks was a retired clothing manufacturer, organizer of the National Association of Clothiers, and president of the Borough of Manhattan. Schiefflin was president of a wholesale drug company, Stewart a manufacturer, and Crimmins a building contractor. Dodge, Peabody, and Schiefflin came from families with traditions of philanthropy. A list of the dozen most prominent New York philanthropists in 1912 would probably have included Andrew Carnegie, John D. Rockefeller, Mrs. Russell Sage, Robert C. Ogden, Cleveland Dodge, Robert W. DeForest, Jacob Schiff, William J. Schiefflin, Adolph Lewisohn, O. G. Villard, and James Speyer. Of these, only Rockefeller was not a member of the New York Peace Society.

York Peace Society businessmen were members of the American Museum of Natural History compared with only 3 percent of the individual members of the Merchants' Association of New York and only 1 percent of the members of the New York Produce Exchange. Almost two-thirds of the peace society businessmen supported some scientific or educational philanthropy.[35]

In cultural activities, as well, the businessmen in the New York Peace Society demonstrated their distinguishing characteristics. Again, they appear to have engaged far more often than the average businessman in philanthropic activities that would display their qualities of civic and cultural responsibility. Fifty-six percent were members of the Metropolitan Museum of Art and 25 percent were members of the Municipal Art Society. Over 60 percent were listed as contributors, members, or officers of a major organization for the promotion of art or music. Calvin Tompkins, a manufacturer of building materials, was a recent president of the Municipal Art Society. A. Augustus Healy, a retired merchant in the wholesale leather business, was a member of the Brooklyn Academy of Music, and a member of the Art Commission of New York City. William D. H. Washington, the president of a hydraulic construction company, was a director of the New York City Grand Conservatory of Music, while Frank Babbott, a "retired manufacturer," was an officer on at least four art and music academies and commissions.[36]

To a somewhat lesser extent, participation by businessmen in the New York Peace Society was related to club membership. Twenty-five percent of the businessmen were also members of the Union League Club, the fortress of conservative Republicanism.

[35] *Forty-Fifth and Forty-Sixth Annual Reports of the Trustees of the American Museum of Natural History* (New York 1913 and 1914); New York Zoological Society, *Eighteenth Annual Report, 1913* and *Nineteenth Annual Report, 1914*; New York Botanical Garden, *Bulletin*, 8 (1913), 309-23 and 9 (1914), 61-75; The Merchants' Association of New York, *Year Book, 1913; Report of the New York Produce Exchange, With the Charter, By-Laws and the Several Trade Rules Adopted by the Exchange, and a List of its Members* (July 1913-July 1914). Of the members of the New York Chamber of Commerce, 32 percent were also members of the American Museum of Natural History as compared with 51 percent of New York Peace Society businessmen and 3 percent of Merchants' Association members. This may suggest that the peace society businessmen were an even more select group in terms of predilections for civic and cultural prominence and responsibility than Chamber of Commerce members. *Fifty-Sixth Annual Report of the Corporation of the Chamber of Commerce of the State of New York 1913-1914.*

[36] Data on cultural activities were derived from the *Dictionary of American Biography, The National Cyclopedia of American Biography, Who's Who in New York, 1914*, obituaries in the *New York Times*, and other biographical sources. For membership in the Metropolitan Museum of Art, see the museum's *Forty-Fifth Annual Report of the Trustees for the Year Ended December 31, 1914.*

Fourteen percent were members of the more exclusive Metropolitan Club and 10 percent belonged to the prestigious Union Club. The less restricted Century Club claimed 13 percent of the businessmen as members, while the New York Yacht Club listed 12 percent. Of the entire group of businessmen in the New York Peace Society, almost two-thirds belonged to at least one prestigious social club. Of these, a majority belonged to two clubs or more.[37]

This pattern of significant participation in civic, cultural, philanthropic, and club activities was not, however, unique among the businessmen in the New York Peace Society. The organizational connections of lawyers or educators in the society reveal much the same pattern. This may suggest that businessmen were largely attracted to the society not out of concern for specific business interests but out of more general social concerns. For many, membership in a peace society—now that the campaign for arbitration and a court was seen as thoroughly practical and respectable—was simply part of a larger pattern of social and civic leadership. The frequency with which they supported and engaged in philanthropic and cultural activities suggests that they believed that they were, or ought to be, more than just businessmen.

For some businessmen the peace society, like other philanthropic activities, represented a form of civic duty incumbent upon those with social position and a sense of social responsibility. For others who could not count themselves among the city's civic leaders, membership in organizations such as the New York Peace Society may have represented an urge to enhance one's self-esteem by playing the role of public-minded citizen and by associating oneself with the city's social, political, and business leaders. The sedate conferences, expensive dinners, and topical discussion meetings of the New York Peace Society and similar peace societies offered ample opportunities for the enhancement of one's sense of social and civic importance. This does not mean that businessmen would have chosen to join a peace society out of a sense of social responsibility or a desire for civic prestige alone. In many cases some special form of international experience—through travel, overseas business experiences, or family

[37] Information on club memberships was derived from the biographical sources listed in n. 36 above and from *Club Men of New York, 1903*; *Club Members of New York, 1912*; *The Union League Club of New York* (New York 1913 and 1914); *Officers, Members, Constitution and Rules of the Union Club of the City of New York* (New York 1913); *Annual of the University Club: Fiftieth Year, 1914-1915* (New York 1914); and *Reports, Constitution, By-Laws and List of Members of the Century Association for the Year 1912* (New York 1913).

connections—appears to have initially awakened their interest in international relations.

But whatever the businessman's motives in joining a peace society, he was likely to find that membership offered less direct satisfaction of his narrow economic interests than it did of his desires to express broad interests in national issues, to transcend purely business concerns, and to obtain public recognition of his civic importance. If the peace organizations sought business support to enhance their prestige and image of practicality, businessmen began to find that peace societies, with new "practical" programs and the patronage of prominent politicians and international law experts, could themselves contribute to the civic prestige of their business members. The process became a dynamic one: each time the peace society gained new prominent members it was able, in turn, to confer even greater prestige upon new members who might join. So successful were the initial campaigns of the New York Peace Society for the recruitment of businessmen and other practical and prominent figures that it largely escaped association in the public mind with the crankishness and utopianism that had been attributed to peace societies in the past. In consequence, it became an organization of high social repute and one in which membership connoted responsible civic leadership in the search for answers to the loftiest and gravest issues of world affairs. No businessman need fear criticism for joining such a society. Rather, he might count on rubbing shoulders, if he chose, with the city's elite and enhancing his own image as a public figure of social vision.

The same businessmen of prominence in the New York Peace Society who were exceptionally active in philanthropic and cultural activities were also likely to belong to that segment of the business community most attracted to programs of welfare capitalism, industrial arbitration, and public relations. They were animated by what Gordon M. Jensen describes as "a new spirit of social-mindedness" and concerned with what James Weinstein has called "the promotion of social responsibility." As financiers, leaders of large corporations, or semiretired businessmen they were often free enough from the demands of daily business operations to devote considerable attention to public matters. Typically their primary interests lay in the financial and public relations side of their business rather than in production. Such interests encouraged them to take a broad view of the political and economic context in which their business operated and impressed upon them the need to create conditions of economic stability and to prevent detrimental political agitation. Alert to the dangers of class antagonism and industrial strife, they sought to meet these problems through compromise, adjustment, and public relations rather than to aggravate them through intransigence.[38] Often they came to think of themselves as society's true reformers, solving the nation's social problems through remedial yet conservative action. When Andrew Carnegie invited Britain's Earl Grey in 1909 to a quiet dinner with a select group of Americans "engaged in the social uplift of humanity," and interested in all social questions, he saw no incongruity in inviting Elihu Root, Judge Gary of U.S. Steel, financier R. Fulton Cutting, Francis Lynde Stetson of J. P. Morgan & Co., George W. Perkins, Robert C. Ogden, retired partner of John Wanamaker, and Joseph H. Choate, conservative leader of the New York bar. All of these men, plus most of the others whom Carnegie included among the social uplifters, were members of the New York Peace Society.[39]

The major organizational expression of the "socially conscious" big businessmen was the National Civic Federation.[40] Nearly half of the businessmen who were officers in the New York Peace Society—including George W. Perkins, Andrew Carnegie, John Hays Hammond, Marcus M. Marks, Issac N. Seligman, James Speyer, and John A. Stewart—also played important roles in the Civic Federation. This overlapping of leadership, which extended also to lawyers and other public figures in the two organizations, was not merely coincidental. The National Civic Federation had held at least two meetings devoted to promotion of international arbitration. The possible analogies between industrial arbitration, a primary early concern of the Civic Federation, and international arbitration were too enticing to ignore.[41] But beyond this,

[38] Weinstein, *The Corporate Ideal in the Liberal State, 1910-1918* (Boston 1968), pp. 3, 9-10, 30-31, 172; Wiebe, *Businessmen and Reform*, pp. 50, 165, 213; Gordon Maurice Jensen, "The National Civic Federation: American Business in an Age of Social Change and Social Reform, 1900-1919," Ph.D. diss., Princeton University, 1956, pp. 27, 52-54, 61.

[39] Andrew Carnegie to Joseph H. Choate, 25 Mar. and Carnegie to Elbert H. Gary, 25 Mar. 1909, Carnegie Papers, LC. Carnegie's idea of "business trusteeship," which coincided so closely with the impulses which brought business leaders into the peace movement and with Carnegie's selection of "uplifters," is discussed in Robert Green McCloskey, *American Conservatism in the Age of Enterprise, 1865-1910* (Cambridge, Mass. 1951), pp. 163-66. The emphasis of the "public spirited" businessmen on "conservative" action as reflected in the literature of the National Civic Federation is described in Jensen, "The National Civic Federation," pp. 71-75.

[40] Jensen, "The National Civic Federation," pp. 49-51, 56-61; Weinstein, *The Corporate Ideal in the Liberal State*, p. 6.

[41] *New York Times*, 27 Sept. 1904, 6:1 and 6 Apr. 1907, 1:7; *The National Civic Federation Review*, 1 (Oct. 1904), 1-5; 3 (Sept. 1907), 1-2. The obvious analogies

the two organizations both represented an attempt by business-men as well as other public leaders to take a long-range view and foresee possible threats to economic and social stability. Concerned less with tomorrow's profits and losses than with fundamental threats to the larger economic and social system, the businessmen in both organizations sought to avoid disruptive conflict through programs of arbitration or conciliation.[42]

The National Association of Manufacturers, the spokesman for smaller businessmen, supported the movement for international arbitration. But peace organizations like the New York Peace Society attuned themselves more clearly to the attitudes of the larger and more politically sophisticated businessmen.[43] Representatives of smaller business interests continued to play a role in the Mohonk Conferences. But businessmen of the Civic Federation variety came to exercise greater influence upon the peace movement as a whole. Such businessmen added prestige and power to the prewar peace movement. Envisaging the movement as an arena for broad action which would promote long-range economic stability and advance such ideas as the nondisruptive and lawful resolution of conflict, they reinforced its conservative tendencies. The more respectable and practical the peace movement became, and the more it drew even passive and superficial support from the socially conscious businessmen of high repute, the less likely it became that the peace organizations would take disreputable or highly controversial stands in any international crisis that might erupt.

Having joined the peace organizations for other than narrow business concerns, the businessmen brought with them few orig-

---

between industrial and international arbitration received surprisingly little public attention. Even within the Civic Federation such analogies were explored only intermittently.

[42] Leroy A. Goodard, a prominent banker and president of the Chicago Peace Society, even complained that the "busy businessmen, those who are deeply immersed in the mad chase for money . . . are the hardest men to . . . influence toward taking . . . personal interest in this work." Both civic federation and peace society businessmen liked to think of themselves as standing above the "mad chase for money," as fulfilling the role of industrial or financial statesmen (*St. Louis Peace Congress, 1913*, p. 506). For the striking similarities between the business participants in the National Civic Federation and the New York Peace Society, compare the foregoing description with the description of NCF businessmen in Jensen, "The National Civic Federation," pp. 52-64.

[43] On NAM support, see *Proceedings of the Fifteenth Annual Convention of the National Association of Manufacturers of the United States of America* (New York 1910), pp. 295-96; *NAM Convention Proceedings, 1911*, p. 229. On the relationships between the new trends in the peace movement and men who were "at home in large-scale organizations" see Sondra R. Herman, *Eleven Against War: Studies in American Internationalist Thought, 1898-1921* (Stanford 1969), pp. 16, 19.

inal or "business-oriented" programs for the peace movement. Except for the promotion of peaceful contact through commerce they offered few proposals. In the New York Peace Society, it was such leaders as Professor Samuel T. Dutton of Columbia Teachers' College, Hamilton Holt, editor of the *Independent*, the Reverend Charles T. Jefferson, and Secretary William H. Short, a former clergyman, who made the plans, published the literature, and set policy. The president of the society, Andrew Carnegie, had retired from business to assume the roles of social philanthropist and world statesman. Except for pressing for the recruitment of businessmen and financiers to the society, he made no effort to give it a businessman's outlook.

By 1914, the numbers of businessmen associated with the peace movement seemed to attest to the validity of the movement's new claims to practicality. Lacking the specific professional or occupational interests in the movement of the international lawyers, they perfunctorily endorsed the major outlines of the proposals for arbitration, a permanent court, and further Hague conferences. Moreover, they found highly agreeable the undemanding and nationalistic assumptions of the movement: American institutions would be copied at an international level; American sovereignty need not be circumscribed; opportunities for American commercial operations and investments abroad would be increased through international stability; no economic or political limitations upon, or sacrifices by, the United States would be required. A reform movement so undemanding, so lofty in aim, and so intent upon proving itself pragmatic and scientific found businessmen increasingly willing, even eager, to lend it their names and the aura of practicality that went with them.

But with no common peace programs of their own, with no common moral commitment or professional stake in particular pacifist doctrines or international programs, the businessmen had little to hold them to a predictable course should the peace movement face a time of crisis. The movement had diverted their attention spasmodically to issues of international law and politics. It had not, however, induced them to arrive at firm common convictions about issues of military preparedness, the efficacy of war in defending neutral rights, neutral mediation to end wars, or other questions that would later become tests of one's adherence to an ongoing peace movement. Attracted to the peace movement partly because of its unobjectionable aims, its emphasis on order and stability, and its image of civic respectability (to which they, in turn, greatly contributed), the businessmen could hardly have been expected to join the new peace organizations which arose during and after 1915. By then, the major organizations opposing war were stressing social reform, rather than paternalism, political change rather than stability. Businessmen found peace less respectable and attractive when it became associated with proponents of domestic reform and social activism.

CHAPTER FOUR

Peace through Research: The Great Foundations

By 1910 efficiency had become the new watchword of the peace movement in the United States. With the international lawyers equating the peace movement with expedient American foreign policy and the businessmen describing it in terms of "hard-headed practicality," the movement had largely effaced the taint of utopianism. The new "establishment" status of the movement was epitomized by the New York Peace Society, with its successful enlistment of men of wealth, influence, and prestige. "A New York Peace Society dinner looks like a banquet of the Chamber of Commerce," wrote Frederick Lynch in 1911. In describing the composition of the New York Peace Society, its secretary, William H. Short, stressed the role of jurists, captains of industry, kings of finance, and women of social prominence.[1]

Power and prestige brought to the peace movement a heightened sense of expectation, a sense of being on the verge of an era of great advance. As opportunities for real effectiveness seemed to beckon, old organizations bestirred themselves and new ones emerged. The new, more prominent leaders of the movement began to demand a consolidation of peace forces and other efficiencies of method appropriate to a realistic reform that had forsaken impractical idealism and had now arrived at its appointed time.

New leaders in the peace movement agreed that fundamental to the reshaping of the movement for efficiency was the adoption of a "scientific" approach. To some of them, "scientific" meant merely "businesslike" or "unsentimental." But others defined their objective more specifically as the search for the causes and cures of war through research based upon the model of the natural sciences and the emerging social sciences. The prevention of war,

---

[1] Frederick Lynch, *The Peace Problem: The Task of the Twentieth Century* (New York 1911), pp. 81-82; Frederick Lynch, "The Minister in Association with International Movements," in Charles S. Macfarland, ed., *The Christian Ministry and the Social Order* (New Haven 1909), p. 301; *Proceedings of the Second National Peace Congress* (Chicago 1909), p. 365 (hereafter cited as *Chicago Peace Congress*, 1909).

they argued, was like the prevention of disease. Complete knowledge of the disease, gained through research and observation, was necessary before a remedy or immunizing process could be found.[2] The older peace societies, many of the new recruits believed, had largely wasted their efforts in the attempt to stimulate a moral repudiation of war. It was time to replace sermons on the horrors and evils of war with the kind of propaganda that would offer specific, practical proposals based upon a systematic, scientific study of war and international relations.

The sense of unprecedented opportunity for success also stimulated a drive for consolidation within the peace movement. The more "practical" men now joining the movement were often appalled at the lack of coordination among the rapidly proliferating peace societies. Andrew Carnegie, already a generous supporter of peace organizations, quietly let it be known as early as 1908 that he might be even more openhanded if presented with a concrete and efficient overall plan for the peace movement. Even earlier, Boston publisher Edwin Ginn had stressed the need for a well-financed organization to carry out a massive plan. In 1907 the peace movement took a small step toward unity by organizing a series of biennial National Peace Congresses bringing together at least momentarily all the major organizations.[3]

Beginning in 1909 the drive for consolidation intensified. In that year the Mohonk Conference authorized its president, Nicholas Murray Butler, to appoint a Commmittee of Ten "to consider the advisability of a National Council of Peace and Arbitration." Several weeks earlier Edwin Ginn had set forth a program for an International School of Peace to serve as the "nucleus . . . of a great endowment" and a clearing house for "receiving and disbursing contributions."[4] Organizers of the National Peace

[2] For an example of the use of this analogy, see Carnegie Endowment for International Peace, "Minutes—Meeting of Trustees," 9 Mar. 1911, p. 60, Box 19, Carnegie Endowment for International Peace Papers, Columbia University Library.

[3] Nicholas Murray Butler to Andrew Carnegie, 8 Jan. and 16 Apr. 1909, Carnegie to Butler, 11 Jan. 1909, Hamilton Holt to Butler, 14 Jan. 1909, Andrew Carnegie Papers, MS Div., Library of Congress; *Report of the Seventh Annual Meeting of the Lake Mohonk Conference on International Arbitration* (Lake Mohonk, N.Y. 1910), pp. 19-22 (hereafter cited as *Mohonk Conference*, with appropriate date). In connection with the following discussion of the drive for consolidation and the appearance of large-scale organizations within the peace movement, see Sondra Herman's description of those leading figures whom she sees as favoring "political internationalism" over "community internationalism" in *Eleven Against War: Studies in American Internationalist Thought, 1898-1921* (Stanford 1969), pp. 6-7, 16-19.

[4] *Mohonk Conference, 1909*, pp. 185-86; *Chicago Peace Congress, 1909*, pp. 322-25. For further evidence of the development of plans of coordination, see "National

Congress in 1911 again sought integration and coordination of the peace forces, this time with the added urging of no less a figure than President Taft. Meanwhile the secretary of the American Peace Society had proposed to move his organization's headquarters from Boston to Washington so that the board of directors of the largest peace society could become a "general National Peace Council." On several occasions the urge for consolidation and full official acceptability and influence even led leaders in the movement to propose that a coordinating peace council be given official status, perhaps as a cabinet-level department, in the federal government.[5]

Plans for a national council or clearing house did not immediately materialize. Although the American Peace Society was eventually to gain apparent recognition of its board of directors as "essentially a National Peace Council" differing viewpoints and personal jealousies continued to thwart perfect consolidation.[6] But after 1910, within a large part of the movement, a restive unity did come. Rivalries and provincialisms that had resisted all other attempts at integration gave way finally before the consolidating power of money. To an impecunious reform movement it was the centripetal effect of available funds—in the form of large endowments by Ginn and Carnegie—that brought a kind of effective unity that no clearing house or national council could have achieved alone.

The new endowed peace foundations—Edwin Ginn's International School of Peace (which became the World Peace Foundation in 1911) with an endowment of $1 million and the Carnegie Endowment for International Peace, endowed late in 1910 with $10 million, transformed certain aspects of the peace movement and consolidated its recent tendencies. With Elihu Root heading the Carnegie Endowment and James Brown Scott holding high positions in both foundations, the role of the international lawyers

---

Council for Arbitration and Peace" (typed sheets at end of 1910 Correspondence), Carnegie Papers, LC.

[5] *Proceedings of the Third American Peace Congress* (Baltimore 1911), pp. 15, 389, 391; Hamilton Holt to Theodore Marburg, 7 May 1911, Marburg to Holt, 9 May 1911, Hamilton Holt Papers, Rollins College, Winter Park, Fla.; Benjamin Trueblood to Andrew Carnegie, 29 Oct. 1910, Carnegie Papers, LC; William I. Hull to Edwin Ginn, 19 Oct. 1908, Box 1, William I. Hull Papers, Friends' Historical Library, Swarthmore College.

[6] "Minutes of the meeting of the Board of Directors of the American Peace Society," 5 Dec. 1913, Box 1, Hull Papers, FHL; George Kirchwey to Benjamin Trueblood, 23 Oct. 1911, Box 6, American Peace Society Papers, Swarthmore College Peace Collection. On the details of the eventual consolidation, see below, pp. 129-35.

was enhanced. The peace movement's recent success in attracting men of prestige and influence was hardly dimmed by the appointment of two prestigious new boards of trustees. The foundations reinforced growing sentiments for a more practical and more scientific approach. The Carnegie Endowment, in particular, devoted far more energy to research than to exhortation. With this emphasis came a more prominent role for academicians, particularly those with some claim to a scientific approach.

Power over the purse strings of the foundations, particularly over those of the Carnegie Endowment, gave a few men great power over the policies, personnel, and even the effective existence of many small and medium-sized organizations. A unity arising out of the economic necessities of the small organizations led to a considerable interlocking of directorates and a state of dependence even for the venerable American Peace Society. The veritable avalanche of money represented by the foundations certainly did nothing to retard the trend of the movement toward establishment status. Some veteran leaders in the peace movement distrusted the excessive "practicality" of the new foundations and bemoaned their neglect of the moral and religious approach to peace. Chronically in need of funds, they greeted the new affluence with a mixture of enthusiasm and apprehension. After all, it was Andrew Carnegie himself who had warned in 1900: "There is nothing that robs a righteous cause of its strength more than a millionaire's money."[7]

The two foundations did not ally forces or even follow the same course of development. They differed both in the nature of their early leadership and in their wartime positions on programs for a postwar league of nations. Ginn and Carnegie harbored mutual jealousies. Each lectured the other on the principles of philanthropy and the need for cooperation for common ends. Ginn chided Carnegie on his failure to select personally "the most intelligent, young, active men to help carry on this work," and expressed privately his sorrow that the Carnegie Endowment "was not anchored more upon principle than upon personality." To the director of his own foundation Ginn wrote in exasperation, "Let them [the Carnegie Endowment] go and hire old men seventy or so to do their economic work." He had always suspected that his foundation "should never get one dollar of Carnegie's money for our work, for that dear good man feels so satisfied with his trus-

7 Quoted in Burton J. Hendrick, *The Life of Andrew Carnegie* (Garden City, N.Y. 1932), II, 337.

tees and the work they are planning that he prefers to keep his money to continue that work, ignoring us wholly."[8]

In this judgment, Ginn was entirely correct. Carnegie replied to Ginn's proposal of "cooperation" (apparently a suggestion that some of the Carnegie money should find its way into the World Peace Foundation) by chiding him for failing to "merge personal considerations" and to "efface" himself in the operation of his foundation. In seeking to continue to control and administer his gift, Carnegie implied, Ginn was interfering with the experts in the peace movement and failing to "sink the personal equation." Carnegie refused to consider turning over any of his funds to the leaders of the World Peace Foundation in whose selection Ginn took such satisfaction. Each of the two philanthropists remained convinced that the other had sacrificed cooperation for personal promotion. Mutual suspicions persisted and no real cooperation between the Carnegie Endowment and the World Peace Foundation ever took place.[9]

A tenfold disparity in wealth between the two foundations served to give the Carnegie Endowment a far more commanding influence over the whole peace movement and to minimize mutual competition. The World Peace Foundation undertook the support of the American School Peace League under Fannie Fern Andrews and devoted a substantial part of its attention to the popularization of the peace cause. Its activities assumed a less integrated, less academic, and slightly more popular pattern than those of the Carnegie Endowment. Still, the two foundations exhibited a number of the same characteristics. Each of the foundations modeled its structure upon that of a university. Both disdained the work of the older peace societies and saw their own function as bringing the peace movement to a new level of effectiveness through a more scientific approach. The founders of both were successful businessmen seeking to imbue the peace movement with business efficiency and to obtain immediate results. But in both organizations, those who became the actual directors

[8] Edwin Ginn to Andrew Carnegie, 30 Nov. 1909 and 17 Jan. 1910, Carnegie to Ginn, 9 Nov., 8 Dec. 1909, and 19 Jan. 1910, Carnegie Papers, LC. Ginn to Carnegie, 2 Mar. and 28 Mar. 1911, Carnegie to Ginn, 22 Mar. 1911, Ginn to Edwin D. Mead, 7 Jan., 27 Jan., 8 Mar. 1911, and 1 Nov. 1912, Boxes 2 and 5, World Peace Foundation Papers, SCPC.

[9] Edwin Ginn to Andrew Carnegie, 13 Jan. 1910, Carnegie to Ginn, 19 Jan. 1910, [Edwin D. Mead] to [Samuel Dutton], 14 Feb. 1910, Edwin D. Mead Papers, SCPC; Carnegie to Benjamin Trueblood, 20 Dec. 1909, Mead to Trueblood, 13 Oct. 1911, Box 6, APS Papers, SCPC.

were primarily scholarly men with penchants for writing and research rather than for popular organization and salesmanship. And in both foundations, the principal directors believed that the peace movement could best be advanced by the work of a small elite. Although their lines of development can best be examined separately, these basic similarities between the two foundations should be kept clearly in mind.

The World Peace Foundation originated not in a particular plan for world peace but in a wealthy businessman's demand that the peace movement be organized for real effectiveness along business lines. As early as 1901 Edwin Ginn had begun to emphasize the movement's need for better organization. The "war power," he argued, had "unlimited resources of wealth and men" and "the most complete system of organization that has ever been known." The peace movement could not cope with this power without a powerful organization of its own, headed by men "of great ability in organization and financeering." To be effective, the peace enterprise would need a committee of executives, statesmen, and educators of "great organizating power" (Ginn suggested such men as Carnegie, John Wanamaker, J. P. Morgan, and Presidents Eliot of Harvard and Low of Columbia). It would need a strong financier and a fund of at least a million dollars as a beginning. At the 1901 Mohonk Conference Ginn pledged $100,000 for the purpose himself and called for nine others to join him.[10]

Although Ginn's appeal found no immediate response he continued his interest in the cause. Throughout the next decade he pondered the "great peace problem" from a "business standpoint," searching for a means by which the movement could be conducted "in the way that all great business enterprises are carried on." After 1901 he contributed up to $10,000 a year to the peace movement and created an International Library to provide peace literature at low prices. Still he grumbled that the American Peace Society was not "getting things done." In 1909 he appealed again for fellow millionaires to join him in financing a new peace institution. This time he had worked out a more specific plan for what he termed an "International School of Peace." When no others responded, Ginn proceeded immediately to set up his organization alone—with an initial income of $50,000 a year and an endowment of $1 million upon his death.[11]

[10] *Mohonk Conference, 1901*, pp. 21-22.

[11] Edwin D. Mead, *The World Peace Foundation—Its Present Activities* (Boston 1912), p. 2; Edwin Ginn to George Foster Peabody, 8 July 1902 and Ginn to W. T.

The model for the International School of Peace, or World Peace Foundation as it was soon renamed, was that of a college or university.[12] A board of trustees would govern the organization; a group of directors or faculty members would carry out the programs of investigation and education; and the unconverted populace would be the student body. Educators dominated the organization. Five of the ten trustees and thirty-three of the sixty-six members of the advisory council were professors, deans, or college presidents.[13] Ginn declared the education of the people in the evils of war to be the central purpose of the foundation, but the question of the proper method of achieving such education elicited differing opinions within the organization. Leaders of the foundation never concurred in a single approach. They poured their energies intermittently into research and investigation, the distribution of peace documents and propaganda, the introduction of peace materials into the schools, the enlightenment of businessmen's organizations, and grass roots lecturing and organizing.

In its early years the organization was dominated by three men: Ginn and the two most active directors, Edwin D. Mead and David Starr Jordan. Jordan, a noted ichthyologist and president of Stanford University, labored hardest for a scientific approach. Jordan had entered the peace movement by way of anti-imperialism, having become concerned in 1898 and 1899 about the threats to American democracy posed by the nation's new penchant for imperialism. Once involved in the peace movement, he sought to bring his scientific background to bear upon issues of peace and war. His first two books on peace, *The Blood of the Nation* and *The Human Harvest*, both decried war primarily for its detrimental effects upon the biological evolution of the human

---

Stead, 18 Mar. 1911, Boxes 1 and 2, WPF Papers, SCPC; Ginn to Andrew Carnegie, 13 Jan. 1910, Box 1, E. D. Mead Papers, SCPC.

[12] Edwin Ginn, "World Peace Foundation," *World Peace Foundation Pamphlet Series*, No. 1, Part III (Apr. 1911), p. 1; David Starr Jordan to Albert E. Pillsbury, 31 July 1916, World Peace Foundation Collection, A. Lawrence Lowell Papers, Harvard University Archives; Edwin D. Mead to Pillsbury, Box 1, E. D. Mead Papers, SCPC; "Additional Standing Orders" (24 Nov. 1914), Box 1A, WPF Papers, SCPC. In this and subsequent paragraphs I have drawn upon certain aspects of Peter A. Filene's interpretation of the World Peace Foundation in his "The World Peace Foundation and Progressivism: 1910-1918," *The New England Quarterly*, 36 (Dec. 1963), 478-501. Another description of the World Peace Foundation with emphases similar to my own appears in Thomas Sands Patterson, "The Travail of the American Peace Movement, 1887-1914," Ph.D. diss., University of California, Berkeley, 1968, pp. 292-301.

[13] For lists of trustees and members of the advisory council see Ginn, "World Peace Foundation," pp. 1-3.

race. As Jordan came to lecture more and more frequently on behalf of peace, he adopted a more eclectic approach, combining his biological arguments with expanded attacks upon war as undemocratic in origin and result.[14] The effectiveness of his lectures, he remained convinced, lay in their reliance on rational argument and proof rather than mere moral suasion. Jordan saw his speeches and articles as expressions of the new emphasis in the peace movement upon factual material and a scientific approach.

Another academician, Professor William Hull of Swarthmore College, had urged Ginn at the outset to establish a bureau of investigation "to procure the actual facts," and Jordan continued to press this approach. The molding of public opinion was important, Jordan recognized, but it was even more important to carry on continuing research to provide the facts upon which the propaganda would rest. The peace movement had advanced from sentimentality to rationality. The present need was not for popular peace societies, but for a small core of capable men to assemble the knowledge upon which to base the arguments that would bring rational men "to think straight and act rightly." Jordan traveled and lectured widely, but he devoted much of his energy to research and investigation.[15]

Edwin Mead, the other leading director, played a more continuously influential but less innovative role within the World Peace Foundation. Mead was well known in New England as a former editor of the *New England Magazine*, founder of the Twentieth Century Club, and supporter of numerous reforms. He had edited Ginn's International Library since 1901 and had sought to have Andrew Carnegie establish him in control of a "literary bureau" for peace. "I believe more and more in *printer's ink*," he had written to Carnegie in an appeal for funds for his "literary bureau" in 1905. The spread of sound information was crucial, "for the mass of people who go 'wrong' do it not through 'cussedness' but through ignorance." Mead had been staunchly anti-imperialist and remained uncompromisingly opposed to war and militarism, but he preferred genteel and refined forms of agi-

14 Edward McNall Burns, *David Starr Jordan: Prophet of Freedom* (Stanford, 1953), pp. 23, 89-96, 123-26; David Starr Jordan, *The Blood of the Nation* (Boston 1902), *The Human Harvest* (Boston 1907), and *The Days of a Man* (New York 1922), I, 618-19. For examples of Jordan's later, more eclectic approach see his *War and Waste* (New York 1913), *passim*.

15 William Hull to Edwin Ginn, 19 Oct. 1908, Box 1, Hull Papers, FHL; David Starr Jordan to Ginn, 3 Feb. 1912, David Starr Jordan Papers, Hoover Institution on War, Revolution and Peace; Jordan to Andrew Dickson White, 24 Dec. 1910, Carnegie Papers, LC; Jordan to Ginn, 5 Feb. 1912, Box 3, WPF Papers, SCPC.

tation. His reform style and his emphasis on education had developed during a long career as an outspoken but moderate reformer in such causes as good government, slum clearance and beautification, housing for the poor, and missionary work in the Americanization of immigrants through education in American history, traditions, and values. Like Jordan, Mead sought to advance the cause of peace by reaching men of reason with the best, most rationally persuasive arguments. And like Jordan, he stressed the primacy in the peace movement of the work of an intellectual elite.[16]

A "bookish man," Mead drew his inspiration from the intellectuals of Emerson's generation who had provided examples of "the scholar in reform." He was less interested in scientific investigation than in the "literary bureau" mode of approach—the publication of great works on peace and the wide distribution of effective pamphlet literature. An editor by background and "a Puritan and a Bostonian by conviction and choice," Mead joined with Jordan in seeking to prevent the foundation from emphasizing popular recruiting and organization. "My effort here," Mead wrote in 1912, ". . . has been to keep Mr. Ginn from spreading into too varied activities. What I want is to concentrate on educational work, broadly defined, leaving to the Peace Societies the more popular forms of propaganda." Even when the foundation began to take on multiple activities, Mead continued to insist that his work, as principal director, was to deal with "general editorial and publicity work" in detail.[17]

Edwin Ginn, who retained ultimate control of the purse strings of the foundation and withheld the full endowment until his death, continued to take a paternalistic interest in his institutional progeny. Through frequent proddings, compliments, and criticisms he sought to keep the organization keyed to the pitch of zealous devotion and efficient operation that he desired. Ginn craved tangible results and was not content with a quiet, academic program. He wanted a "bureaucracy of zealots," he told his trustees, and criticized the Carnegie Endowment for its lack of a

16 [Edwin D. Mead] to Andrew Carnegie [Mar. 1905], Box 1, E. D. Mead Papers, SCPC; Barbara Miller Solomon, *Ancestors and Immigrants: A Changing New England Tradition* (Cambridge, Mass. 1954), pp. 85-86; Patterson, "Travail of the American Peace Movement," pp. 98-99, 101, 297-98.

17 Arthur Mann, *Yankee Reformers in the Urban Age* (Cambridge, Mass. 1954), pp. 159-63, 172-73; Edwin D. Mead to Benjamin Trueblood, 23 Feb. 1912, Box 6, APS Papers, SCPC; Mead to Edwin Ginn, 18 Nov. 1912, Box 3, WPF Papers, SCPC; [Mead to Andrew Carnegie, Mar. 1905], Box 1, Hull Papers, FHL; Filene, "The World Peace Foundation," p. 485.

"practical live-wire" and its "work among the fossils and economists" which would only bear fruit in the next millennium.[18]

Ginn's passion was for activity and efficiency. He continually
stressed the need for a "far-seeing business man" to act as financier, administrator, and organizer of the foundation. Finally in
late 1913, Ginn dispatched Albert G. Bryant, a recent appointee
as business manager of the foundation, upon an intensive campaign to establish "centers of activity" for the promotion of peace
propaganda among influential civic leaders and businessmen in
cities of the South and Midwest. Only then did Ginn seem fully
satisfied with the course the foundation was following. The deaths
of Ginn in 1914 and Bryant in 1915 cut short this drive to expand
the foundation's base by creating local organizations.[19]

Part of the foundation's delay in implementing Ginn's proposals
to involve the wider public in the peace movement through centers of activity undoubtedly stemmed from the differences of
viewpoint among its three principal leaders. Mead and Jordan
shared Ginn's desire to arouse public support for the peace movement. But while Ginn called for the effective promulgation of
available propaganda by dynamic business methods and sought
to enlist the multitudes in active participation in the movement,
Mead and Jordan emphasized the need for better arguments,
more convincing data, and better-informed experts. For models
for his centers of activity, Ginn looked to such organizations as
Dr. Francis Clark's Christian Endeavor Societies, which had stimulated volunteer work in religious evangelism. What was needed
in the peace movement, Ginn argued, was a self-help philosophy.
He feared that large donations, like his own, might actually undermine the movement by inviting complacency and inaction. To
prevent such a development, his money should be used to mount
a dynamic effort—evangelistic, but businesslike and efficient—
which would educate the people and persuade them "to put their
shoulders to the wheel and contribute money. . . ." But Jordan
denied that such evangelical approaches which asked men "to

[18] Edwin Ginn to Edwin D. Mead and David Starr Jordan, 29 Mar. 1912, Ginn
to Ralph (Norman Angell) Lane, 30 Apr. 1912, Ginn to Trustees of the World
Peace Foundation, 16 Dec. 1913, WPF Collection, Lowell Papers, HA.

[19] Edwin Ginn to Edwin D. Mead and David Starr Jordan, 29 Mar. 1912, Ginn
to Trustees of the World Peace Foundation, 10 Dec. and 16 Dec. 1913, WPF Collection, Lowell Papers, HA; Albert G. Bryant to Ginn, 3 Nov. and 7 Nov. 1913,
Jordan Papers, HI. On Ginn's enthusiasm for Bryant's work, see also Ginn to Mead,
30 Sept., 28 Oct., and 7 Nov. 1913, Box 5, WPF Papers, SCPC; Bryant to Ginn, 14
Nov. 1913, Ginn to Directors, World Peace Foundation, 17 Nov. 1913, Hull Papers,
FHL. See also Filene, *loc. cit.*

keep busy with religious and social effort" were appropriate to the new organization. The job of a peace foundation, he argued, should be to teach people the facts about the social, economic, and biological consequences of war. Such a task did not need local, popular participation and donations nearly as much as it needed the development of arguments and scientific data for the use of "a few great men who have shown their power to mould and to guide public opinion."[20]

Predictably, Ginn and his major directors did not agree on the value of research to the peace movement. Ginn sneered at the Carnegie Endowment for "collecting data that may be useful a thousand years hence." The Carnegie Endowment would certainly not interfere with the work of the World Peace Foundation, Ginn wrote Mead, because the Endowment was merely "working on paper." "Getting all the economists in the world together will have very little effect on the peace cause," he continued, "even if they should put out a hundred volumes."[21] Ginn acknowledged the importance of experts in the peace movement, but assumed that such men would be specialists in organization and efficient propagandizing rather than experts in research. But while Ginn constantly emphasized the application of salesmanship and business efficiency to the peace movement, Jordan and Mead preferred to hold tenaciously to the university as model for the World Peace Foundation. "We must always remember that the analogy for our Foundation is a school rather than a shop," Mead wrote Ginn. He reminded Ginn that the colleges and universities were "the field which we have expressly undertaken to look after," and reported to Jordan that "our university constituencies are riper for our cause than almost any other." Jordan urged Ginn to "come back to the ideal of intensive work . . ." and sought to convince him that increased knowledge was the key to effective public impact. While Ginn pleaded for organizational and evangelical work, Mead replied with letters of praise for new reference works on arbitration and Jordan called for a corps of "stu-

20 Edwin Ginn to John R. Mott, 13 Feb. 1912, Ginn to Ralph (Norman Angell) Lane, 30 Apr. 1912, Ginn to Samuel T. Dutton, 16 May 1912, David Starr Jordan to Ginn, 3 Feb. 1912, Box 3, WPF Papers, SCPC. Jordan had served twice on Joint International Commissions. His experiences had given him a high regard for the arbitration of international disputes by scientific experts who would carefully investigate the facts outside the glare of publicity and away from the heat of nationalistic emotions.

21 Edwin Ginn to Edwin D. Mead, 1 Nov. and 5 Dec. 1912, Ginn to Mead and David Starr Jordan, 29 Mar. 1912, Boxes 3 and 5, WPF Papers, SCPC.

dents and investigators adding constantly original material to the subject. . . ." By 1912 Ginn was complaining that "not one of my co-workers appreciates my point of view. . . ."[22]

Despite the diffuseness of its program and the penchant of its founder for organization-building, field work, and a crusading effort to reach the "unconverted," the World Peace Foundation did reflect some newer tendencies that would become dominant in the larger Carnegie Endowment for International Peace. In both organizations the wealthy founders had hoped for dramatic activity and quick results. In both, such hopes were frustrated by the more deliberate, more academic approaches adopted by the scholars and editors who assumed effective control. Both organizations sought to enhance the role of the expert in the peace movement and to establish the movement on a more scientific basis. And both of the great foundations found that academic research or expert investigation was necessary, or at least justified, in developing a scientific approach. These tendencies clearly characterized nearly every aspect of the Carnegie Endowment's program. In the World Peace Foundation the same tendencies were far more intermittent, far less characteristic of the organization's work as a whole. But such tendencies did begin to appear early as a minor theme within the World Peace Foundation, particularly in the work of David Starr Jordan.

Between 1912 and 1914 the World Peace Foundation found funds to support two projects which partook of the academic and scientific approach to peace. One of these was Jordan's research into the biological effects of war. As a biologist, Jordan was a fervent Darwinist. But he was also a major popularizer of the ideas of Kropotkin and Novicow, who argued for the importance of cooperation rather than struggle within species. Jordan argued that many, under the spell of evolutionary doctrines, had mistakenly interpreted war as a positive agent in promoting the desirable process of natural selection. But modern warfare, in Jordan's view, was not a natural process. It was an unnatural struggle in which the strong were killed and the weak survived. War, therefore, was actually the agent of reverse selection.[23]

During trips for the foundation to England and France Jordan

22 Edwin Ginn to Samuel T. Dutton, 16 May 1912, Edwin D. Mead to Ginn, 14 Oct. 1911, 31 May, and 20 June 1912, Mead to David Starr Jordan, 20 Feb. 1911, Jordan to Ginn, 3 Feb., 5 Feb., and 3 June 1912, Boxes 3 and 5, WPF Papers, SCPC; Jordan to Andrew Dickson White, 24 Dec. 1910, Carnegie Papers, LC; Mead to Benjamin Trueblood, 23 Feb. 1912, Box 6, APS Papers, SCPC.

23 For Jordan's theories, see his, *Blood of the Nation* and *The Human Harvest*.

took time to seek further support for his theories in the records of war casualties. But his main effort in these years was a study of the eugenic effects of the American Civil War. Sponsored by the World Peace Foundation, Jordan, his cousin Harvey Jordan of the University of Virginia, and Professor Benjamin Krehbiel of Stanford sought to substantiate Jordan's theories through intensive population studies of several southern counties. Working through county records and questionnaires the investigators sought proof that the war had been disproportionately destructive of the healthier, stronger, biologically superior men. Jordan planned to extend the investigation into the North and other regions for comparisons and eventually to make similar studies of Alsace-Lorraine and Spain.[24]

Jordan also sought the support of the wealthier Carnegie Endowment for a protracted ten-year research program into the biological effects of war. Although it rejected Jordan's extensive proposal, the Carnegie Endowment was sufficiently attracted by this scientific approach to peace to support investigations of the same nature in Europe by biologist Vernon Kellogg, Jordan's close associate at Stanford. The findings of both Jordan and Kellogg were inconclusive and their methods open to question. But the interest of both organizations in the development of evidence to support scientific arguments against war revealed how the foundations served to emphasize new investigational and academic tendencies within the peace movement.[25]

The World Peace Foundation's other main venture into peace research was its sponsorship of trips by Jordan to Europe in 1913 and to the Balkans in the spring of 1914 to investigate the causes of war. The Balkan trip, in particular, was envisioned as an exercise in scientific investigation. It was true that Jordan did noth-

[24] David Starr Jordan to Edwin Ginn, 29 Oct. 1912, Jordan to David D. Barrow, 11 Apr. and 30 Apr. 1912, Edward B. Krehbiel to Jordan, 1 June, 8 June, and 7 July 1912, Jordan Papers, HI. For the findings of the study, see David Starr Jordan and Harvey Ernest Jordan, *War's Aftermath* (Boston 1914).

[25] David Starr Jordan to Board of Trustees, Carnegie Peace Endowment, n.d., Jordan to Nicholas Murray Butler, 23 Apr. 1915, Jordan Papers, HI. For Kellogg's findings see Vernon Lyman Kellogg, *Beyond War: A Chapter in the Natural History of War* (New York 1912) and *Military Selection and Race Deterioration* (Oxford 1916). Both Jordan and Kellogg were occasionally apt to treat acquired physical defects (i.e., physically crippled, maimed, etc.) or moral characteristics (bravery, etc.) as genetically inheritable. Jordan's method of argument in *War's Aftermath* went as follows: "In brief the theoretical argument for reversed selection seems beyond question. The actual facts concerning our Civil War and the events which followed yield no direct countervailing evidence. We must, therefore, decide that the war has seriously impoverished this country of its best human values." See *War's Aftermath*, p. 79.

ing more systematic than merely travel and observe, but observing the immediate effects of a small war at first hand seemed an appropriate way of collecting useful data. The Carnegie Endowment also established a commission to study the Balkans and Jordan praised this commission for the use of the "laboratory method" in studying war as a physician would study a disease.[26] Again in Jordan's study of war in the Balkans, the World Peace Foundation gave partial attention to an approach to peace through research.

But Jordan's approach, which anticipated the emphasis of the more influential Carnegie Endowment, never became the dominant one within the World Peace Foundation. Under the leadership of Ginn, Mead, and Jordan, the foundation never focused its energies on any single, distinctive program. Jordan himself was too much the activist and popular lecturer to insist upon a thorough-going research emphasis. The foundation directors— who also included two journalists, Hamilton Holt and James A. Macdonald, two international lawyers, James Brown Scott and Denys P. Myers, and two clergymen, Charles R. Brown and John R. Mott—participated in varying degrees and operated largely as free-lance associates who chose their own activities and drew upon the foundation for occasional support. They engaged intermittently in lecturing, foreign travel, research, organization-building, and the editing and writing of peace literature, rarely coordinating their efforts.

For all of Ginn's enthusiasm for efficiency and dedication, he contributed to the inefficiency and confused purposes of his own organization by his choice of trustees and his failure to create clear lines of authority and responsibility among the directors. From 1912 until 1915 the leaders of the organization wrangled continuously over the question of who was the chief director. Mead claimed that Ginn had given full responsibility to him; Jordan later made the same claim for himself. Some of the trustees insisted after Ginn's death that a chief director had never been appointed and that Ginn had died still searching for the right man.[27]

[26] David Starr Jordan, "The Balkan Investigation," *The Independent*, 75 (4 Sept. 1913), 531 and "War's Aftermath in Macedonia," in *War's Aftermath*, pp. 84-104; David Starr Jordan to Edwin Ginn, 10 Dec. 1912, Box 3, WPF Papers, SCPC. See also Carnegie Endowment for International Peace, *Report of the International Commission to Inquire into the Causes and Conduct of the Balkan Wars* (Washington, D.C. 1914).

[27] "Minutes of the Meeting of the Board of Trustees," 22 Dec. 1910, Edwin Mead to Edwin Ginn, 14 Oct. 1911, Boxes 1a and 5, WPF Papers, SCPC; Edwin D. Mead

In his choice of trustees, Ginn exhibited the penchant for prestige and prominence that had come to characterize the peace movement. Most of the trustees were more noted for their civic prominence than for their dedication to the cause. At least half of them had displayed no previous commitment to the peace movement. President A. Lawrence Lowell of Harvard University, one of the original trustees, had given little indication of interest and stood opposed to a major objective of most of the peace organizations—the negotiation of arbitration treaties. Yet when Lowell attempted to resign, Ginn begged him to remain. "Your name alone will have great influence in our work," Ginn pleaded, "and it may be that next year you can give us an hour of your time at the [annual] meeting. . . ." Another prewar trustee of the foundation was looked upon even by moderates in the peace movement as an "out and out militarist."[28] Ginn's tendency to value prominence and influence above dedication to well-defined purposes in choosing trustees was hardly unusual in such organizations. But it did contribute further to internal divisions within the foundation.

The outbreak of World War I, six months after Ginn's death, found the World Peace Foundation disorganized and incapable of action. Mead's position was challenged and he responded with passion. Lowell and other trustees remained skeptical of the value of the organization and distrustful or critical of its directors. Disputes about Ginn's true intentions arose and a power struggle within the organization loomed. The foundation had developed no clear program, academic or otherwise, capable of responding to the challenges presented by the war. It reacted with indecision and inaction.[29]

---

to Arthur E. Pillsbury, 12 Dec. 1914, George W. Anderson to Mead, 2 Jan. 1915, Anderson to A. Lawrence Lowell, 11 Aug. 1916, WPF Collection, Lowell Papers, HA; David Starr Jordan to George A. Plimpton, 1 Mar. 1916, Jordan Papers, HI.

[28] A. Lawrence Lowell to Edward Cummings, 22 June 1912 and 12 Nov. 1913, Edwin Ginn to Lowell, 7 Dec. 1912, WPF Collection, Lowell Papers; Lowell to Ginn, 26 Nov. 1915, WPF Papers, SCPC. The "out and out militarist" was President Arthur Hadley of Yale University. See Frederick Lynch to W.H.P. Faunce, 11 Dec. 1914, Church Peace Union Papers, Council on Religion and International Affairs, New York City. Of the ten original trustees, only George A. Plimpton, an executive in Ginn and Co., Professor Samuel T. Dutton of Columbia University, President W.H.P. Faunce of Brown University, and Ginn himself had previously participated to any significant extent in the peace movement.

[29] Edwin D. Mead to Arthur E. Pillsbury, 12 Dec. 1914, George W. Anderson to Mead, 2 Jan. 1915, W.H.P. Faunce to A. Lawrence Lowell, 4 Nov. 1915, Lowell to Edward Cummings, 22 June 1912, WPF Collection, Lowell Papers, HA; W.H.P. Faunce to David Starr Jordan, 31 Oct. 1916, Jordan Papers, HI. See also Filene, "The World Peace Foundation," p. 491.

The World Peace Foundation had reinforced certain trends in the peace movement through its solicitation of business organizations on behalf of peace, its publication of a number of works by the international lawyers, and its founder's enthusiasm for practicality, prominent names, and expertise. It had also ventured tentatively into peace research. The founding of the affluent Carnegie Endowment for International Peace in December 1910 gave further impetus to these trends—particularly those toward an emphasis on international law and upon scholarly research. The differences in emphasis between the two organizations were primarily related to the much larger size of the Carnegie Fund, the more completely academic orientation of the Carnegie directors, and the absence of ties between the directors of the Carnegie Endowment and older peace organizations such as the American Peace Society. While Ginn and Edwin Mead of the World Peace Foundation had long been active members of the older peace societies and had brought some of the attitudes and goals of those organizations into the foundation, the directors of the Carnegie Endowment were largely disdainful of the work of the older societies and more determined to employ an entirely different, wholly scientific approach.

The Carnegie Endowment did not emphasize research because Carnegie was more scientific than Ginn in outlook. Carnegie did not hold greater faith in the creation of a scientific international law than did Ginn, nor was he more attracted to the idea of a long-range approach to peace through painstaking scholarly research. Quite the contrary, Carnegie was impatient of temper, eager for dramatic action, undisciplined and erratic in his advocacy of various peace programs, and attracted by moral arguments. But despite Carnegie's often vigorous attempts to promote specific peace programs of his own invention, the character of his endowment was determined less by his personal whims than by the attitudes of those prominent figures whose social favor and confidential friendship he coveted, whose superior urbanity, intellectual sophistication, and social polish he admired, and whose direct access to political power and influence he enjoyed sharing. Carnegie approved of a "scientific" approach, but it was the influence of Elihu Root and President Nicholas Murray Butler of Columbia University, and the men they chose to work with them, that counted most in making scholarly research and international law the primary concerns of the Carnegie Endowment.

By the time that Andrew Carnegie decided to establish a $10

million peace fund in the fall of 1910, his interest in the peace movement had already spanned more than two decades. As early as 1886, Carnegie had discussed antidotes for war and imperialism in his *Triumphant Democracy*. In the following year he had introduced to President Cleveland a Committee of Members of the British Parliament seeking to promote a treaty of arbitration between the two nations. Between 1898 and 1900 Carnegie had emerged as one of the most vociferous critics of American imperialism, although his inconsistencies, the restriction of his criticism to American policy toward the Philippines, and his failure to carry out his threats to break with the Republican Party over the issue have led Robert Beisner to describe him as "something of a tinsel anti-imperialist."[30]

In the succeeding years Carnegie had given steadily increasing support and attention to the peace movement. He had participated in the recurrent campaigns for arbitration treaties and had pursued the search for moral equivalents for war by establishing a Hero Fund for nonmilitary heroes and their survivors. A number of his speeches and pamphlets for peace had achieved wide circulation. He had donated a million and a half dollars for a permanent headquarters for the Hague Court, $100,000 for a building for Elihu Root's Central American Court of Justice, and nearly a million dollars for a Pan-American building in Washington, D.C. In 1907 he accepted the presidency of the New York Peace Society and in 1909 organized a drive to obtain the Nobel Peace Prize for Elihu Root. Carnegie's contributions kept nearly a dozen peace societies alive and defrayed the costs of several major peace conferences. By 1910, when he created the Carnegie Endowment, he estimated that he was contributing $50,000 a year to peace societies and was helping to support at least sixteen such organizations.[31]

[30] Andrew Carnegie, *Triumphant Democracy* (New York 1886), pp. 112, 209-10, 265-67, 398-413; Andrew Carnegie, *Autobiography* (Boston 1920), p. 283; Robert L. Beisner, *Twelve Against Empire: The Anti-Imperialists, 1898-1900* (New York 1968), p. 184. Within a few years Carnegie would be looking upon three of the major architects of American colonial policy in the Philippines, Elihu Root, William Howard Taft, and Theodore Roosevelt, as his major allies in the peace movement.

[31] Hendrick, *Carnegie*, II, 332-35; Carnegie Endowment for International Peace, *A Manual of the Public Benefactions of Andrew Carnegie* (Washington, D.C. 1919), pp. 273, 281, 285-86; Carnegie, *Autobiography*, p. 273; Carnegie to Nobel Committee of the Norwegian Parliament, 16 Jan. 1909, Carnegie to John W. Griggs, Carnegie to George Gray, Carnegie to Melville W. Fuller, 12 Jan. 1909, Carnegie Papers, LC. The estimate of Carnegie's yearly contributions comes from Carnegie Endowment for International Peace, "Minutes—Meeting of Trustees," 9 Mar. 1911, pp. 57, 69, Box 19, CEIP Papers, CUL. See also Edwin D. Mead to Carnegie, 21 Dec. 1910, Carnegie Papers, LC.

Although he contributed to a great variety of peace societies and programs, several dominant themes frequently recurred in Carnegie's own writings and private peace activities. Foremost among these was Anglo-Saxon unity. A Scotsman by birth, Carnegie usually spent his summers after 1898 at his castle, Skibo, in Scotland. He delighted in his chosen dual allegiance to the United States and Great Britain and dramatized his passion for Anglo-American unity by flying at Skibo a unique flag composed of the Stars and Stripes and the Union Jack sewn together. Proposed treaties of arbitration between the United States and Great Britain always awakened Carnegie's hopes for further steps toward Anglo-American political unity. In the late nineteenth century he had predicted an inevitable fusion of Canada and the United States and had sought to extend this to a union of all the "English-speaking countries."[32] Avowedly anti-imperialist with respect to unilateral expansionist actions by America or Britain, Carnegie had unabashedly advocated a benevolent "race imperialism" on the part of the English-speaking nations. Among his various plans for peace, one of his fondest was the vision of an Anglo-Saxon alliance so powerful that "by raising its arm [it] could compel peace." By 1909 he was urging a limited mutual defense pact with Britain and even the merging of the British and American fleets as a step toward peace through the unity of the most pacific nations.[33]

Although he talked much about the need to impress upon the popular mind the wastefulness, foolishness, and immorality of war, Carnegie's own greatest enthusiasm was for immediate peace agreements and alliances through high-level private diplomatic action. For all his concern about the popular mind, Carnegie enjoyed most the energies he expended on schemes for diplomatic coups for peace to be carried out by Elihu Root or Theodore Roosevelt with his own aid and advice. In the forceful action of great national leaders, particularly when these leaders drew moral strength from a democratic society, Carnegie placed his greatest hope for peace.

Of several schemes for high-level negotiations, Carnegie threw his greatest energies into his plan in 1910 to bring the combined talents of Root and Roosevelt to bear in persuading Kaiser Wil-

[32] Hendrick, *Carnegie*, I, 421-24; II, 150, 193; Andrew Carnegie, "A Look Ahead," *North American Review*, 156 (June 1893), 685-86, 691-94.

[33] Hendrick, *Carnegie*, I, 421-22; Carnegie to John Morley, 24 Feb. 1909, Carnegie to W. H. Taft, 14 Mar. 1909, Carnegie to "Editor," *New York Tribune* (draft copy), 12 Mar. 1909, Carnegie Papers, LC.

helm of Germany to join in a League of Peace. Such a league, composed of Great Britain, Germany, and the United States, would be assured of a preponderance of power to enforce peace. If Germany failed to join, the rest of the Western powers would know who the foe of peace was and would form an Anglo-American–dominated League of Peace to isolate her. Root and Roosevelt were reluctant to push the idea too far and Roosevelt's meeting with the Kaiser in Berlin in 1909 proved a disappointment. But Carnegie never wavered in his faith in Roosevelt and Root. In 1909 and 1910 he sought to throw his financial support behind first one and then the other if they would take the leadership in a new peace movement.[34]

Carnegie's overtures to Roosevelt and Root were not his first intimations that he might endow the peace movement with a large fund. In early 1908 he had invited Nicholas Murray Butler to suggest how "a large sum of money could wisely be used," but had taken no action on Butler's reply. Later that year, perhaps having heard of Carnegie's invitation, the editor of the *Independent*, Hamilton Holt, approached Butler about seeking an endowment for peace modeled upon the research-supporting Carnegie Institution at Washington. Early in 1909 Butler probed Carnegie on Holt's new proposal, whose coauthors were such veterans in the movement as Edward Everett Hale, vice-president of the American Peace Society and frequent speaker at Mohonk, Albert Smiley, host of the Mohonk Conference, Samuel T. Dutton, secretary of the New York Peace Society, and Edwin Mead. The new proposal was endorsed by Butler and Elihu Root. Again Carnegie rejected the plan as lacking in concrete proposals and "too much in the air."[35] But Holt, Butler, and the others refused to be discouraged. Butler tried a new plan on Carnegie in April of 1909 which added to the usual catalog of peace society programs a provision for scholarly study of technical questions of international organization. When the Mohonk Conference of 1909 authorized Butler to appoint a Committee of Ten to explore the possibilities of setting up a national coordinating council for

[34] Carnegie to Theodore Roosevelt, 26 June and 7 Nov. 1909 (draft), 31 Jan. and 18 Apr. 1910, Roosevelt to Carnegie, 18 Feb. and 22 Apr. 1910, Carnegie to David Jayne Hill, 24 Dec. 1909, Elihu Root to Carnegie, 11 Feb. 1910, Carnegie Papers, LC.

[35] Nicholas Murray Butler to Carnegie, 8 Jan. 1909, Carnegie to Butler, 11 Jan. 1909, Carnegie Papers, LC; Warren F. Kuehl, *Hamilton Holt: Journalist, Internationalist, Educator* (Gainesville, Fla. 1960), p. 98. Additional details on the preliminary steps leading to the founding of the Carnegie Endowment can be found in Patterson, "Travail of the American Peace Movement," pp. 224-26.

the peace movement, Butler quickly appointed Carnegie to the committee.[36]

Meanwhile, Carnegie's attention had been partly distracted from the proposals for a new organization by the prospects of a dramatic step toward peace through personal diplomacy that Roosevelt's prospective visit to Berlin seemed to offer. Roosevelt had embarked on an extended safari in Africa shortly after Taft's inauguration and was due to visit Berlin on his return in the spring of 1910. Carnegie lectured Roosevelt by letter on his responsibilities to peace, indulged in exaggerated visions of Roosevelt converting the Kaiser into a prince of peace, and attempted to goad Roosevelt into action with fulsome references to his greatness and destiny. It was Roosevelt's destined role, Carnegie wrote, to be the "Moses" of his people and, potentially, of the world. Twice Carnegie offered to act as Roosevelt's "treasurer" if Roosevelt would assume leadership of a peace initiative. Carnegie sought to persuade Root to go to Berlin as well and hoped that he and Butler would be asked to join in the historic meetings in which a League of Peace would be agreed upon.[37]

By the time that Carnegie's hopes for maneuvering the Kaiser into a League of Peace collapsed in mid-1910, other events had begun to fix his attention once again on the idea of a peace fund. Edwin Ginn had endowed his foundation the preceding fall. Carnegie had refused Ginn's plea for additional financial aid, suggesting that he had something of his own in mind.[38] Undoubtedly Carnegie had no intention of allowing himself to be outbid in generosity to a cause to which he was now giving much of his attention. Moreover the presence of Ginn's new foundation in Boston was precipitating new efforts to consolidate the peace forces. The American Peace Society, after seventy years in Boston, had begun to consider a move to Washington in order to place itself symbolically and politically in a position to act as coordinator for peace organizations throughout the nation. When Ginn's new foundation installed itself only two doors away from the American Peace Society headquarters in Boston, threatening to overshadow the older organization and duplicate certain lines

[36] Hamilton Holt to Nicholas Murray Butler, 11 Jan. 1909, Samuel T. Dutton to Butler, 18 Feb. 1909, Butler to Andrew Carnegie, 6 Apr. and 24 Dec. 1909, Carnegie Papers, LC.

[37] Andrew Carnegie to Theodore Roosevelt, Mar. 1909 (draft), 26 June and 7 Nov. 1909 (draft), 22 Apr. 1910, Carnegie to David Jayne Hill, 24 Dec. 1909, Carnegie Papers, LC.

[38] Andrew Carnegie to Edwin Ginn, 9 Nov. and 8 Dec. 1909, 19 Jan. 1910, Carnegie Papers, LC.

of its work, the directors of the American Peace Society accelerated their decision to relocate. Since Carnegie was contributing $6,000 per year, or over one-third of its annual budget, the society sought Carnegie's advice. As might have been expected, the request for advice was accompanied by a plea for more funds. When the society relocated, Secretary Trueblood wrote in October 1910, it would need a guarantee of $50,000 a year for five years.[39] The peace movement seemed about to undergo some kind of reorganization. If Carnegie intended to put his financial power behind an efficient consolidation and a program and men of his choosing, he would obviously have to act soon.

Butler's Committee of Ten to consolidate the peace movement had continued to meet. By 1910 it seems to have settled upon a single approach—the submission of a plan to Carnegie for his financial support. As early as February 1910, Elihu Root had begun to refer to the group as a "Committee to provide for a Peace Trust."[40] Carnegie, himself, appears to have narrowed his circle of advisers on the question to Butler and Root. When President Taft announced late in 1910 his advocacy of an unlimited arbitration treaty with England the impatient Carnegie seized upon this declaration as a new electrifying step toward peace. With Root's help Carnegie drew up a specific plan for his peace trust and sought Taft's advice and approval. He praised the president as another Abraham Lincoln, and gave Taft's proposed arbitration treaty special commendation in his instructions to his trustees when he finally announced his $10 million endowment for peace at the end of 1910.[41]

To the peace movement, only recently beginning to emerge from dire impoverishment, Carnegie's gift seemed a stroke of good fortune and a confirmation that the movement was destined for imminent success. Even the more skeptical, and those who felt Carnegie had ignored them, acknowledged the great "potential" of so affluent an organization. But more important for the future direction of the movement than the money itself was the question

[39] Benjamin Trueblood to Andrew Carnegie, 15 Dec. 1909 and 29 Oct. 1910, Nicholas Murray Butler to Carnegie, 8 Apr. 1910, Carnegie Papers, LC. American Peace Society, *Eighty-Third Annual Report of the Directors of the American Peace Society, 1911*, p. 17.

[40] Nicholas Murray Butler to Andrew Carnegie, 7 Mar. 1910, Elihu Root to Carnegie, 11 Feb. 1910, Carnegie Papers, LC.

[41] Andrew Carnegie to Theodore Roosevelt, 24 Dec. and 24 Nov. 1909, Carnegie to William H. Taft, 26 Mar. 1910, Carnegie Papers, LC; Carnegie Endowment for International Peace, *Year Book for 1911* (Washington, D.C., 1912), pp. 1-3.

of who would control this huge fund and how it would be used. Although Carnegie acted out of immediate enthusiasm for a particular program, out of desire for efficiency in the peace movement, and perhaps with latent partisan political intention, his immediate motives of this nature counted for far less than his choices of directors and trustees.[42] In these choices, Carnegie placed prime value upon qualities of prominence, respectability, political influence, and experience in other foundations. Elihu Root was designated as the president of the new organization and Nicholas Murray Butler and James Brown Scott, secretary of the American Society of International Law, were guaranteed positions of control. Thus Carnegie entrusted the initial direction of the Carnegie Endowment to a triumvirate composed of two politically active, conservative Republicans (Root and Butler), two leaders of the international lawyer group (Root and Scott), and two academicians (Butler and Scott). All three were temperamentally, politically, and professionally committed to a cautious, slow, undramatic, scholarly approach to peace. All were secure members of the "establishment," and partisans of the Taft administration. None held much sympathy for the older peace societies or their leaders. When John Bates Clark, an economist and academician, became a division head in 1911 the leadership that would control the endowment through the war years was complete.

Of the twenty-eight trustees of the endowment (which included Root, Butler, and Scott) only two had actively participated in peace organizations before 1905. None of the principal leaders of the American Peace Society were included and only three of the trustees held any office in this oldest and largest peace organization. Only Albert Smiley was chosen from the group that had submitted one of the main early proposals in 1909.[43] The inter-

---

[42] The extent of Carnegie's partisan political motives is obscure. Probably they were merely incidental. Carnegie did, however, frankly discuss in private letters how the arbitration treaty with Britain, which he intended his new endowment to back, would bring political advantages to the Republicans and insure Taft the second term that he deserved. Early drafts of Carnegie's letter to his trustees contained a disclaimer of "sectarian or party purposes" which was absent from the final document. Carnegie to William Howard Taft, 10 Dec. 1910, Carnegie to Philander C. Knox, 11 Nov. 1910, Carnegie, "Manuscript of letters to Trustees," 9 Nov. 1910, and "Final draft of letter to Trustees," 14 Nov. 1910, Carnegie Papers, LC.

[43] The two trustees who had participated early in the peace societies were Albert Smiley and John W. Foster. Smiley, Foster, and James Brown Scott were vice-presidents in the American Peace Society. Of the group submitting the 1909 proposal to Carnegie, Samuel T. Dutton, Edwin D. Mead, and Hamilton Holt were ignored by Carnegie in choosing his trustees. Edward Everett Hale, also a signer of the early proposal, had died in 1909. Dutton commented to Edwin Ginn, "Mr.

national lawyers were well represented with seven trustees. Two trustees were Wall Street lawyers and six were active or retired financiers and businessmen. Twelve were already serving as trustees of some other Carnegie-endowed institution. Four had been, or still were, presidents of major universities. For balance the group included a sprinkling of southerners and westerners. The inclusion of several former Cleveland Democrats served to establish the foundation's nonpartisan position. Carnegie's private financial secretary and three potentially useful members of Congress filled out the remainder of the board.[44]

Thus the announcement of the directors and trustees of the new endowment served notice that the influence of the Carnegie millions would be thrown behind those new tendencies in the peace movement represented by the influx of international lawyers, businessmen, and others of social and political prominence. The selection as trustees of a group of "eminences,"[45] a number of whom could almost qualify as "professional trustees," insured that the new endowment would draw upon so much experience in older benevolent institutions that it would be very unlikely to take any radical departures. During early meetings, leading members of the trustees made plain their distaste for any "general scheme for the education and redemption of mankind," and noted how their "influence" had already increased "because of the con-

---

Carnegie evidently thought that he would not put any of us who were active in the work on the Board, although he intimated to me that he should do so. I think the lawyers rather turned the scale." Samuel T. Dutton to Edwin Ginn, 15 Feb. 1911, Box 2, WPF Papers, SCPC; Edson L. Whitney, *The American Peace Society: A Centennial History* (Washington, D.C. 1928), pp. 332-37; Nicholas Murray Butler to Andrew Carnegie, 8 Jan. 1909, Carnegie Papers, LC.

44 The international lawyers were represented by Joseph H. Choate, John W. Foster, Andrew J. Montague, Elihu Root, James Brown Scott, Oscar S. Straus, and Andrew D. White. (See above, chap. II, n. 4.) Austin G. Fox and John L. Cadwalader were Wall Street lawyers, as was Joseph Choate, listed above. Thomas Burke, now a judge, was a former railroad lawyer and promoter. Active and retired businessmen included Robert S. Brookings, Cleveland H. Dodge, Samuel Mather, George W. Perkins, Jacob G. Schmidlapp, Charles L. Taylor, and Charlemagne Tower. Nicholas Murray Butler was President of Columbia University and Andrew D. White, Henry S. Pritchett, and Charles W. Eliot were retired from the presidencies of Cornell, M.I.T., and Harvard respectively. Robert A. Franks was Carnegie's financial secretary. Senator John Sharp Williams and Representatives William M. Howard and James L. Slayden were Democrats. Robert S. Woodward was president of the Carnegie Institution of Washington. Root, Montague, Brookings, Butler, Franks, Pritchett, Taylor, Cadwalader, Dodge, Eliot, and White had all served as trustees of the Carnegie Institution or some other Carnegie philanthropy.

45 The description is Norman Angell's in "The Reminiscences of Norman Angell," p. 130, Oral History Research Office, Columbia University. Carnegie himself referred to "the list of illustrious names" which were to control his foundation (Andrew Carnegie to Nicholas Murray Butler, 14 Jan. 1911, Carnegie Papers, LC).

servatism with which this Board has proceeded. . . ." Nicholas Murray Butler particularly stressed the necessity of avoiding any actions that would interfere "with our influence with the real important personalities in Europe" or with "the sympathy which we now have in high places. . . ." "We make a mistake," warned one trustee, "whenever we touch a political question or a diplomatic question."[46] Clearly the endowment would look with little favor upon political radicals or revolutionary methods.

If the eminence of the trustees did not sufficiently indicate the Endowment's "establishment" status, Carnegie gained official sanction by consulting frequently with the president and secretary of state during the preliminary drafting of the organization. He obtained Taft's endorsement, and his acceptance of an honorary presidency, and invited Secretary of State Philander Knox to make suggestions and become a trustee. Root and Knox eventually decided that it would be better for the secretary of state not to be on the board of the endowment, but Carnegie arranged for Taft and Knox to appear at the ceremonies announcing the great benefaction. Carnegie and his officers had no intention of embarrassing the administration on any point, and Carnegie was not reluctant to point out to Knox and Taft how the arbitration treaty, which the endowment would back with all its resources, could be used as a political weapon against the Democrats.[47]

Carnegie attempted to imbue the officers of his new endowment with his own enthusiasm for an instant peace program to "render war impossible" by proceeding from an Anglo-American arbitration treaty to a consolidation of the "English-Speaking race." Exuberant predictions of the "reunion of the race," and "the abolition of war within the side boundaries of the English-Speaking race" appeared frequently in Carnegie's private letters during 1911. He referred to President Taft, Ambassador Bryce,

[46] "Minutes of the Annual Meeting of the Board of Trustees," 12 Dec. 1912, pp. 5-10, 80, 14 Nov. 1913, p. 42, 17 Apr. 1914, pp. 56, 69, 75, CEIP Papers, CUL. A convincing assessment of Butler's conservative ideology, his role in the endowment, and his biases toward converting peace organizations into unofficial agencies of the federal government appears in Michael Arnold Lutzker, "The 'Practical' Peace Advocates: An Interpretation of the American Peace Movement, 1898-1917," Ph.D. diss., Rutgers University, 1969, pp. 134-52, 236, 242, 246-47.

[47] William Howard Taft to Andrew Carnegie, 11 Nov. and 11 Dec. 1910, Carnegie to Taft (draft) 10 Dec. 1910, Carnegie to Philander C. Knox, 11 Nov. and 30 Nov. 1910, Knox to Carnegie, 28 Nov. and 4 Dec. 1910, Elihu Root to Carnegie, 7 Dec. 1910, R. S. Woodward to Carnegie, 4 Dec. 1910, Carnegie Papers, LC. See also Lutzker, "The 'Practical' Peace Advocates," pp. 137-38 on Butler's previous search for "establishment" status for the American Association for International Conciliation.

and Secretary of State Knox, the three principal negotiators of the treaty, as "the trinity engaged in the holy work . . . ," and promised Knox that "immortality is yours if your name be signed to the treaty which is to banish war. . . ."[48] But Carnegie's appointed leaders worked from the outset to structure the organization along the lines of their own preferences for a slow-but-sure, scholarly, and scientific approach. One of the three divisions within the endowment, the Division of Intercourse and Education headed by President Butler, would coordinate and finance the worthiest of the older peace societies, those who could "prove themselves something more than societies for the propagation of useless sentimentalism." It would push forward the "judicious spread of judiciously chosen literature" and take charge of public campaigns in support of such projects as the arbitration treaty. But the other two divisions—the Division of International Law under James Brown Scott and the Division of Economics and History under John Bates Clark—would concentrate on research and investigation. "We must do what the scientific men do," Root told the trustees at the endowment's first meeting. The endowment, he argued, should be different from all peace organizations that had existed before. It should be practical and should "base its action upon a careful, scientific and thorough study of the causes of war . . ." seeking "that deeper insight . . . attained only by long and faithful and continuous study. . . ."[49]

As the planning for the new endowment progressed, its scientific and academic bent became even more apparent. It patterned itself after the older Carnegie Institution of Washington, an organization devoted to the promotion of scientific research, and even scheduled its annual meeting to coincide with that of the Carnegie Institution.[50] Eight trustees of the endowment were

[48] Carnegie Endowment for International Peace, *Year Book, 1911*, pp. 3-6; Andrew Carnegie to William H. Taft, 25 Mar. 1911, Carnegie to Alton B. Parker, 21 Mar. 1911, Carnegie to W. T. Stead, 21 Feb. 1911, Carnegie to Philander C. Knox, 21 Mar. 1911, Carnegie to James Bryce, 8 Feb. 1911, Carnegie to John Morley, 30 Dec. 1910, Carnegie Papers, LC. So strong were the suggestions of Carnegie and others involved with his plans that only the United States and Great Britain were "ripe" for the newest step in international relations through comprehensive arbitration treaties that a leading American diplomat had to remind Carnegie that "we have to be very careful not to give the impression that our arrangements are merely of the nature of an old-fashioned alliance. . . ." David J. Hill to Carnegie, 31 Jan. 1911, Carnegie Papers, LC.

[49] Carnegie Peace Fund, "Stenographic Report of Proceedings, First Meeting of the Board of Trustees," 14 Dec. 1910, p. 21, Box 19, CEIP Papers, CUL; The *Times* (London), 7 Jan. 1911, 6:1.

[50] James Brown Scott, "Rough Notes of the Organization, Scope and Purposes

also officers of the Carnegie Institution. The endowment's Division of International Law assumed the responsibility for a program of publishing classics in international law previously undertaken by the Carnegie Institution. James Brown Scott edited the publications under both institutions. To this inherited project, the Division of International Law added such scholarly programs as the preparation and publication of international law digests, collections of arbitration treaties and arbitral decisions, treaties and bibliographies of international law, and collections of decisions of national courts that involved principles of international law.[51]

One of the earliest arguments over tactics in the new endowment concerned the proposal of James Brown Scott, director of the Division of International Law, to appropriate $30,000 for the work of the Institute of International Law, a small but prestigious international organization of specialists in the field. As on other occasions, Scott pressed home his case, with Root's support, by stressing the institute's scientific role in contributing to a "gradual scientific codification. . . ." From the beginning, Scott had emphasized the superiority of "scientific bodies" over peace societies, and he continued to justify the projects of the Division of International Law as contributions to the scientific building and application of international law.[52]

Thus, through emphasizing their commitment to a scientific approach and the application of expertise to the problem of peace, the international lawyers gained the backing of the endowment for their distinctive projects. James Brown Scott reiterated the argument that the endowment should be "scientific in character" rather than "a peace agency, pure and simple," as a preface to his proposal to utilize endowment funds for subventions to international law journals. Later, Scott urged further efforts by the endowment to encourage expansion of academic programs in international law, to call the attention of bar examiners to the importance of international law, and to sponsor scholarly publica-

of the Carnegie Endowment, With Tentative Suggestions for Carrying On its Work" (typed MS, 7 Dec. 1910), p. 2, Charles W. Eliot Papers, HA; John L. Cadwalader to Elihu Root, 6 Jan. 1911, Elihu Root Papers, MS Div., LC; "Minutes, Meeting of Trustees," 9 Mar. 1911, pp. 13, 19, 24, 36, 45, 48, 53, 61, 63, Box 19, CEIP Papers, CUL.

51 Carnegie Endowment for International Peace, *Year Book for 1913-1914*, pp. 99-187. On Scott's role in the publishing of international law classics see Elihu Root to Electors of Oxford, 6 Oct. 1910, Root Papers, LC.

52 Carnegie Endowment for International Peace, "Proceedings of a Meeting of the Board of Trustees," 14 Dec. 1911, pp. 36-47, Box 19, CEIP Papers, CUL; Scott, "Rough Notes on the Organization, Scope and Purposes of the Carnegie Endowment," pp. 5, 9-11, Eliot Papers, HA.

tions and works of codification. Andrew D. White urged the organization to throw its efforts into the promotion of wider instruction in international law in the colleges through lectureships and fellowships. All such projects, Scott continually pointed out, should be scientific. They should "commend themselves not merely to public opinion, but to experts in the domain of international law." So persistent were the arguments of Scott and Elihu Root on behalf of the international lawyers' programs that Carnegie himself acknowledged that his "frequent interviews with the wise man, Elihu Root," had convinced him of the importance of codifying international law. Even at that, Carnegie never accepted the scientific approach as thoroughly as Scott, Root, and the other directors wished. In 1915 Root remarked with a mixture of vexation and condescension that Carnegie was "somewhat disappointed because we are so humdrum, plodding along with uninteresting methods, trying to teach people about law which he thinks very little of."[53]

The Division of Economics and History, under John Bates Clark, surpassed even the International Law Division in its fervor for the scientific approach. Clark's division devoted itself entirely to the scholarly study of the causes of war and designated the preparation of a complete bibliography as its first task. A conference of experts or "quasi-faculty" assembled at Berne, Switzerland in 1911 to compile a list of topics to be investigated and set up a Committee of Research. Clark saw economic research as the greatest hope for peace. Under his guidance the committee adopted a program which reflected his emphasis on such economic topics as tariffs, loans, investments, customs policies, the economic effects of war, and the attitudes of trade unionists and socialists toward war. Other topics for study included armaments and armament industries, the biological effects of war, and epidemics resulting from war. All these subjects, Clark reported, were to be "discussed scientifically, and as far as possible without prejudice either for or against war."[54]

Clark's demand for scientific neutrality on the question of the desirability of peace or war reflected both a commitment by the

[53] "Annual Meeting of the Board of Trustees," 12 Dec. 1912, pp. 29-35, 14 Nov. 1913, pp. 51-52, 116-18, 16 Apr. 1915, p. 67, CEIP Papers, CUL; Scott, "Rough Notes on the Organization, Scope and Purposes of the Carnegie Endowment," pp. 6-7, 10, Eliot Papers, HA; Andrew Carnegie to David J. Hill, 5 Jan. 1911, Carnegie Papers, LC.

[54] Carnegie Endowment, *Year Book, 1911*, pp. 80, 93; Carnegie Endowment, *Year Book for 1913-1914*, pp. 91-94.

organization to the scholarly ideal of an unprejudiced search for truth and Clark's assumption that the true economic facts would always support the case for peace. Works which revealed the consequences of war, Clark argued, would furnish a basis for judgments upon its "reasonableness." If scholarly studies of wars showed that the "evils are in reality larger and the benefits smaller" than commonly believed, then a scientific basis would have been provided for "enlightened policy." Clark even proposed the "tabulation of all the costs and gains of a selected list of modern wars" as the basis for a statistical "profit-and-loss account."[55] Although the account would be calculated with scientific objectivity, Clark was apparently confident that the final balance would not favor war. Almost no consideration was given to the use of the completed studies as weapons in campaigns for changes of economic or other policies. The intention, rather, seems to have been primarily to assemble evidence in support of *arguments* against war. Elihu Root expressed the rationale perfectly in 1911. The subjects selected for examination by the Division of Economics and History, he announced, "include a great number of subjects upon which definite and certain information, prepared by competent scientific investigators, will be of the very greatest value in order to convert mere talk about peace into argument that can be addressed to reasonable and practical men."[56]

The idea of peace through scholarship, upon which much of the work of the new endowment was based, imposed certain limitations and even inner contradictions upon the organization. The limitations, however, were principally those of excessive caution, a tendency to seek slow, long-range progress rather than immediate action, and a rejection of extensive popular agitation—none of which conflicted with the inclinations of the directors and trustees. The emphasis upon scholarly investigation gave the endowment a certain stability in the face of events; for whatever happens, one can always study it. The "brick-building" conception of developing scientific truths about international relations through the slow piling of monograph upon monograph conditioned the endowment to take the long view.

---

[55] Carnegie Endowment, *Year Book, 1911*, pp. 87-88. [John Bates Clark] "Conference at Berne in 1911 under the auspices of the Division of Economics and History of the Carnegie Endowment for International Peace," Division of Economics and History, 1914, CEIP Papers, CUL.

[56] Carnegie Endowment, "Proceedings of a Meeting of the Board of Trustees," 14 Dec. 1911, p. 59, Box 19, CEIP Papers, CUL. On Root's views see also American Society of International Law, *Proceedings, 1912*, p. 3.

Neither the organization of the endowment nor its commitment to the long-range viewpoint gave much promise of action to prevent or curtail immediate wars or war scares. Nor were the men employed by the International Law and Economics and History Divisions inclined toward resolute action along any particular line. The endowment's provision of liberal funds for travel and study and its subsidized publication of scholarly works attracted many who had little direct interest in peace. An academic "slush-fund" had been created and scholars hastened to seek support for economic and other studies only marginally related to peace. One critic complained in 1914, with some justification, that at least one-third of the proposed studies simply amounted to the support of students writing theses on subjects of general economics. If the endowment was going to support such studies as "The Industrial Effects of the Hundred Years' War on the Population and Industry of Paraguay," then it was in danger of becoming "simply another school of economics and statistics" and not a force for peace.[57]

A more perplexing problem was that of reconciling the demands of scientific objectivity and those of peaceful international relations. Even before the outbreak of World War I, the endowment began to discover that the publication of unpleasant truths about other nations did not necessarily create better international relations. By the fall of 1914 the problem had become critical. One book awaiting publication by the endowment contained "indiscreet" sections that might "compromise the usefulness of the institution," by seeming to endorse the Allies. Another, *The Law of Prize*, was rejected for publication out of fear that it might "show up unfavorably the English practice in the present war."[58] Soon Clark was questioning whether the endowment could continue to be a peace society and a publishing agency at the same time. The endowment's scientific pretensions were weakened further when a prominent trustee began to protest any further "dallying" with German and Austrian authors. In 1915 Clark questioned whether the endowment could make the full facts known about Chinese-Japanese diplomatic correspondence and

57 F. W. Hirst to John Bates Clark, 22 July 1914, in "Report of the Director of the Division of Economics and History," 17 Mar. 1915, Division of Economics and History, General Correspondence 1915, Vol. II, CEIP Papers, CUL.

58 John Bates Clark to James Brown Scott, 19 Jan. 1914, Clark to S.N.D. North, 10 Feb. and 17 Feb. 1914, Alvin S. Johnson to S.N.D. North, 30 Sept. 1914, James Brown Scott to Elihu Root, 7 Nov. 1914, Division of Economics and History, General Correspondence, 1914, Vol. II, CEIP Papers, CUL.

still hope to promote good relations.[59] It began to seem that scientific truth and scholarly frankness were not identical, at least in the short run, with the promotion of peaceful relations. In general the endowment solved the problem of the conflicting demands of scholarship and peace by indefinitely suspending many of its publications.

The third division of the Carnegie Endowment, the Division of Intercourse and Education, was intended as the propaganda arm of the organization. But even this division found ways of employing the scientific approach. It established a commission to make a scientific investigation of the Balkan War and heralded the resulting report as "an epoch-making document" in its freedom of bias or partisanship. "We merely ascertained facts," reported the director of the division, Nicholas Murray Butler. Because the Division of Intercourse and Education sought to maintain its detached, scientific stance, Butler assured his fellow trustees it "would never dream of interfering with a matter of politics." It would simply acquire information. For instance, it would not assign any representative of the organization to the Balkan peninsula so as not to interfere with relations between the "great powers and their subordinate and dependent nationalities." Thus, adherence to scientific detachment and noninterference in politics would also enable the endowment to maintain "the sympathy which we now have in high places" in Europe.[60]

As a further demonstration of its scientific approach, the Division of Intercourse and Education sent President-emeritus Charles W. Eliot of Harvard on a trip to the Orient that was conceived of more as a fact-finding expedition than a goodwill tour. Eliot defined his report on the trip as a treatise on the causes of war and later suggested fact-finding studies by the division that would publish facts "without comment or inference" on the pattern of reports by the Rockefeller Social Hygiene Bureau. Eliot's report also stimulated the endowment to engage briefly in the exportation of "scientific expertise" in the field of government. On Eliot's recommendation the endowment sent a political scientist

[59] John Bates Clark to S.N.D. North, 9 Nov. 1914, Division of Economics and History, General Correspondence, 1914, Vol. II, Joseph H. Choate to James Brown Scott, 14 Apr. 1915, John Bates Clark to George A. Finch, 24 June 1915, [Clark], "Report of the Director of the Division of Economics and History," General Correspondence, 1915, Vol. II, CEIP Papers, CUL.

[60] "Minutes of the Annual Meeting of the Board of Trustees," 12 Dec. 1912, pp. 5-6, 10-11, and 17 Apr. 1914, pp. 32, 44, CEIP Papers, CUL. "Sympathy . . . in high places" might well have been the motto of the endowment. Certainly it typified the goal which most of the peace movement, under the endowment's new leadership, was increasingly seeking.

to serve as constitutional adviser to the new republic under Yüan Shih-k'ai in China.[61]

One of the primary responsibilities of the Division of Intercourse and Education was the support and consolidation of the various peace societies. Centralized coordination of the work of the various peace organizations had been a major objective of the early plans submitted to Carnegie and the passion for efficiency had given rise to the conception of a "peace trust." Although peace organizations continued to proliferate after 1910, the Carnegie Endowment quickly gained partial control over most of the larger ones. Carnegie's private donations had previously kept many of these peace societies solvent. Upon setting up his peace endowment, Carnegie turned over to the new organization the responsibility for dealing with these societies and deciding which were deserving of future support. As Carnegie rather ominously described the new conditions to the secretary of the American Peace Society, "the idea is that payments will be made upon results." Thus he effectively granted his new endowment life or death powers over the societies and insured their subordination.[62]

Meanwhile, discussions of a move to Washington, D.C. by the directors of the American Peace Society had precipitated a minor power struggle among the peace societies. Benjamin Trueblood seemed determined to maintain the position of his American Peace Society at the head of the "popular" peace movement by transferring its headquarters from their historic Boston home to the national capital. Such a relocation would place the society where it might easily become the "national council" which the Mohonk Conference had recently proposed, and would insure, at the least, that it would not be bypassed in the reorganization of the movement that was obviously underway. But other new and vigorous leaders in the peace movement, particularly in the New York Peace Society, looked askance at such a plan, regarding the American Peace Society as too provincial, old-fashioned, and impractical to represent adequately the new tendencies in the peace movement. This apparently unilateral decision of the

[61] Charles W. Eliot to Nicholas Murray Butler, 30 Jan. 1913, 11 Feb. 1913, 5 July 1913, and 29 Apr. 1914, Philander C. Knox to Eliot, 13 Jan. 1913, Eliot to Chang Yin Tang, 21 Feb. 1913, Eliot Papers, HA; "Minutes of the Annual Meeting of the Board of Trustees," 14 Nov. 1913, p. 55, CEIP Papers, CUL.

[62] Andrew Carnegie to Nicholas Murray Butler, 11 Dec. 1910, Carnegie to Benjamin Trueblood, 19 Dec. 1910, Carnegie to William H. Short, 19 Dec. 1910, Unsigned [Carnegie] to Frederick Lynch, 23 Dec. 1910, Carnegie Papers, LC; Carnegie to Trueblood, 21 Dec. 1910, Box 6, APS Papers, SCPC.

American Peace Society to set itself up in Washington looked a bit like an "end run" which would ignore the new forces represented by the New York group. "To put it in a nutshell," Samuel Dutton of the New York Peace Society wrote to Trueblood, "if you were going to Washington with the idea of standing before the country as a national organization, you would have to have the support of the peace workers of the country in order to be successful. As it looks now, I believe you will be criticized if you do not first take into conference those who would naturally be the members of a national advisory council." George Kirchwey of the New York Peace Society seconded Dutton's warning. The American Peace Society was ill-suited to become a national council. Certainly it should not go either to Washington or New York "without full and free conference with the representative men in the peace movement."[63]

At this point, Edwin Mead, who was a vice-president of the American Peace Society as well as a director of the World Peace Foundation and whose wife was a director of the American Peace Society, attempted to reconcile the bickering factions with a flurry of telegrams, letters, and personal contacts. It may be that Mead saw future possibilities for the World Peace Foundation in establishing himself in a strategic position as intermediary between Trueblood's American Peace Society and the prominent personages of the New York Peace Society and the Carnegie Endowment. But Mead also had a quicker and clearer instinct than Trueblood for the new power realities within the peace movement. Mead was probably already aware of Carnegie's desire to oust Trueblood on a pension and certainly perceived the influential connections with the Carnegie Endowment of the New York Peace Society men, "who are so influential at the source of supplies. . . ." Only "generous financial support," he wrote to Trueblood, should be an adequate inducement to removal to Washington by the American Peace Society. It would be dangerous, perhaps "disastrous," to make such a move without consultation with and the approval of the New York Peace Society men with whom Root, the president of the Carnegie Endowment, "is in much closer conference about this whole business than you know."[64]

Accused by Trueblood of encouraging the New York forces to

[63] Samuel T. Dutton to Benjamin Trueblood, 16 Mar. and 20 Mar. 1911, George Kirchwey to Trueblood, 20 Mar. 1911, Hamilton Holt to Trueblood, 16 Apr. 1910, Box 6, APS Papers, SCPC.

[64] Edwin D. Mead to Benjamin Trueblood, 23 Mar. 1911, Box 6, APS Papers, SCPC; Andrew Carnegie to Mead, n.d., Box 1, E. D. Mead Papers, SCPC.

oppose the plans of the American Peace Society, Mead replied
that many of the officers of the society failed to realize that, with
the new foundations and the move toward reorganization, the
peace movement was now proceeding "under conditions which
have suddenly become utterly changed." The New York men, he
cautioned Trueblood, were "in hand and glove relations" with
Root, Butler, and Carnegie. "We must never forget this," Mead
continued, "and never forget that any failure on our part to pro-
pitiate these men, to make them our firm and influential friends,
is the worst 'business' conceivable." He proposed seeking an
early informal conference with the leaders of the New York Peace
Society. If the American Peace Society moved to Washington
without their "good understanding and cooperation," Mead
warned, "and especially if we did it in a sort of defiance of them,
we should be in the suds."[65] He had heard, he concluded, of talk
among the American Peace Society officers that if the Carnegie
money was withheld from the American Peace Society (presumably on account of New York opposition) it should go to Washington anyway and "appeal to the country." "I hope indeed," Mead
wrote,

> that the American Peace Society is not, and never will be, de-
> pendent upon Andrew Carnegie or any other Croesus for its
> existence; but our efficiency for the years just ahead certainly
> does depend upon our keeping all the Carnegie favor we now
> have, and in my judgment in getting vastly more of it. I believe
> we can get vastly more. I am confident we can in good time se-
> cure most generous treatment from Mr. Root and Dr. Butler,
> especially, if we are conciliatory, cooperative and wise. But any
> superficial or foolish criticism of the Carnegie people, especial-
> ly any air of seeming defiance or even indifference . . . at this
> time of all times, must be most carefully suppressed.
>
> Even as concerns our World Peace Foundation's future, I
> am most scrupulous to keep in the right touch with New York.
> How doubly important is this for the Peace Society.[66]

Although Mead's warning may have encouraged a more flexible
attitude by the American Peace Society, it was the naked financial
power of the Carnegie Endowment's purse, wielded with rigor
by Butler and Root, that eventually quieted the bickering and

[65] Edwin D. Mead to Benjamin Trueblood, 23 Mar., 28 Mar., and 29 Mar. 1911,
Box 6, APS Papers, SCPC.
[66] Edwin D. Mead to Benjamin Trueblood, 29 Mar. 1911, Box 6, APS Papers,
SCPC.

"consolidated" the "popular" peace organizations. Keeping "in the right touch," as Mead had advised, proved to be a simple matter of complying with the endowment's demands or losing its subventions. Butler, declaring himself "very reluctant to make suggestions . . . because it would easily be made to appear that . . . the support of the Carnegie Endowment was being used as a club," proceeded to dictate the terms of consolidation to the American Peace Society. The board of directors of the American Peace Society would become the new "National Council," but in so doing the board would have to reconstitute itself to become "national in character" and "representative of the local Societies." The constitution of the society was to be revised, the headquarters moved to Washington, and a new "expert, high-class organizing secretary" appointed to carry on the propaganda work of the organization. Trueblood would remain as editor of the *Advocate of Peace*. The relationship of authority between Trueblood and the new executive secretary was left rather ambiguous, the endowment leaders evidently counting on gradually pushing the aging Trueblood out of effective control.[67]

In one sense the venerable American Peace Society had emerged victorious in its effort to maintain itself as the leader of the "popular" peace movement. The endowment offered it the opportunity of remaining the major open-membership peace society and of increasing its influence over the smaller societies if it would meet the endowment's demands. The American Peace Society quickly reorganized itself along the required lines. Of the twenty members of the society's board of directors in 1910, only three remained by 1912. The Boston monopoly was abruptly broken, and the new directors were men of greater national prestige, wider political connections, and more sympathy with the new "practical" directions of the peace movement. The international lawyers, previously unrepresented on the board, now held three positions. The New York Peace Society became a partly subordinate affiliate of the American Peace Society.[68] But the new tendencies represented by the New York Peace Society

[67] Nicholas Murray Butler to Benjamin Trueblood, 11 and 17 Oct. 1911, 15, 16, and 28 Dec. 1911, Box 6, APS Papers, SCPC; American Peace Society, *Eighty-Fourth Annual Report of the Directors, 1912*, pp. 8-9; Carnegie Endowment for International Peace, *Yearbook for 1911*, p. 68; "Proceedings of a Meeting of the Board of Trustees," 14 Dec. 1911, pp. 66-67, Box 19, CEIP Papers, CUL.

[68] American Peace Society, *Eighty-Second Annual Report of the Directors, 1910*, p. 3, and, *Eighty-Fourth Annual Report of the Directors, 1912*, p. 4. International lawyers among the directors and representative directors included Jackson Ralston, George W. Kirchwey, and Theodore Marburg.

gained in the reorganization and the "New York men" maintained their own special pipeline to the endowment's leaders until late in the war period.

Upon meeting the Carnegie Endowment's requirements, the American Peace Society was granted an annual subvention of $31,000 and delegated the responsibility for distributing a portion of this sum among the other peace societies. Thus the endowment forced unification of the smaller peace societies by making them dependent upon the American Peace Society for their funds. Each society was required to submit a detailed account of its use of the subvention. The endowment engaged a professional statistician to compile the data necessary for the evaluation of the various peace organizations, works, and publications in terms of such criteria as their "weight," "standing," and "practicality." The endowment would reassess its subventions yearly and could effectively force the American Peace Society to curtail or terminate support of "unwise, improper or unnecessary work."[69]

The price of the American Peace Society's superficial triumph as the effective "national council" was the loss of independent status. Hamilton Holt had warned early in 1912 that the American Peace Society "must henceforth not only be the master but the servant of the peace movement" representing "the movement as a whole." But it soon became apparent that the American Peace Society would have little opportunity to exercise the role of "master." Employing the proposed subvention as both threat and promise, Butler "advised" Trueblood on every step of the reorganization, praising his initiatives in carrying out the endowment proposals and, on appropriations, continually warning him of the prerequisites for support by the endowment. It was understood that the endowment would exercise at least a decisive veto power over the appointment of the new executive secretary, and Trueblood was frequently reminded that the year-by-year subvention must be "justified" and that some elements of the endowment leadership thought that allotments to peace societies should be reduced.[70] Whereas Carnegie's 1910 donation of $6,000 (constituting about one-third of the American Peace Society's income) had made the society solicitous of Carnegie's favor,

[69] Nicholas Murray Butler to Charles W. Eliot, 8 Apr. 1913, Box 395, Eliot Papers, HA; Carnegie Endowment for International Peace, *Yearbook for 1911*, pp. 32, 35, 37; "Proceedings of a Meeting of the Board of Trustees," 14 Dec. 1911, p. 66, Box 19, CEIP Papers, CUL.

[70] Hamilton Holt to Benjamin Trueblood, 29 Feb. 1912, Nicholas Murray Butler to Trueblood, 11 and 17 Oct. 1911, 16 and 28 Dec. 1911, 12 Feb. 1912, 8 Nov. 1912, Box 6, APS Papers, SCPC.

after 1912 the society received over 70 per cent of its income from the endowment and fell into a position of almost total dependency. Within three years the endowment-approved executive secretary was commenting privately to Trueblood that "Mammon" (in the form of Butler) would likely control even the selection of a new president for the society. As Charles W. Eliot of the Carnegie Endowment remarked in April 1914, the American Peace Society ". . . is absolutely today a creation of this Board, and nothing else."[71]

The Carnegie Endowment's work of unification among the peace societies was not a service of love. Butler, the director of the Division of Intercourse and Education, was contemptuous of the societies and disapproved of organizations within the movement which included the word "peace" in their names. Elihu Root, James Brown Scott, and Charles W. Eliot, who were influential in determining the division's policy, held similar views. Eliot regularly entreated the various division directors to cut down their subventions. Peace societies, he warned, were "wholly ineffectual." They were likely to do more harm than good. They had already "hindered" the cause of peace and their advocacy of disarmament was "irritating to those in power." Instead of supporting peace societies, Eliot argued, the endowment should sponsor an "inductive" approach to peace; it should reject popular lecturing and seek "real, scientific gains."[72]

Scott, Root, and Butler all agreed that the peace societies were too visionary, too impractical, too crankish. Butler contrasted the peace societies with "the effective, scientific part of our organization." Scott, in his initial recommendations for organization of the endowment, had portrayed the endowment as giving dignity and "much needed sanity" to the peace movement. A scientific body was needed, he had argued, to replace the societies whose "visionary plans often retard the movement." Eliot was adamant on

71 Arthur D. Call to Benjamin Trueblood, 30 Oct. 1915, Box 8, APS Papers, SCPC; "Minutes of the Annual Meeting of the Board of Trustees," 17 Apr. 1914, p. 54, CEIP Papers, CUL. For the fiscal year 1 May 1912 to 30 Apr. 1913, the endowment supplied $31,000 out of the American Peace Society's income of $46,700. For the fiscal year 1913-1914 the endowment supplied $31,000 out of a total income of $39,632. American Peace Society, *Eighty-Fifth Annual Report of the Directors, 1913*, p. 27, and *Eighty-Sixth Annual Report of the Directors, 1914*, pp. 41-42.

72 Nicholas Murray Butler to Samuel T. Dutton, 21 Jan. 1908, Box 2, New York Peace Society Papers, SCPC; Charles W. Eliot to James Brown Scott, 15 Apr. 1911, and 27 Mar. 1913, Eliot to John Bates Clark, 26 Dec. 1912, Box 395, Eliot Papers, HA; "Minutes of the Annual Meeting of the Board of Trustees," 12 Dec. 1912, pp. 5, 12-15, 17-18, 26, 14 Nov. 1913, pp. 127, 132, 17 Apr. 1914, pp. 48, 56, 66, and 16 Apr. 1915, pp. 64-66, CEIP Papers, CUL; Scott to Benjamin Trueblood, Box 7, APS Papers, SCPC.

this point. "I am clear," he wrote to Scott, "that there is nothing whatever which can be properly called *visionary* about the peace movement as you and I and Senator Root understand it."[73]

Despite the private contempt of its leaders for the peace societies, the endowment continued to give them unenthusiastic financial support. Although they were wasteful, the societies were occasionally useful as propaganda agencies. The endowment could "do certain things through the American Peace Society. . . ."[74] Also Carnegie continued to urge support of certain individuals or societies upon the endowment despite his claim that he never interfered with the administration of his philanthropic organizations. Butler argued that although much of the work of the societies was useless or even mischievous, the "organized pacifists" should not be antagonized. They did constitute a link with one section of the public. "We must face the fact," Butler wrote to Eliot, "that our rather scientific and intellectual program is on too high a plane to be understood and sympathized with by large numbers of persons."[75]

To the directors of the Carnegie Endowment, the task of supporting, coordinating, and controlling the peace societies seemed of minor importance. But to the veteran leaders of the societies, the centripetal force exerted by the financial resources of the endowment was overwhelming. They were happy to have an unearned increment of income—indeed, could hardly have survived without it—but they disliked their loss of independence and pro-

[73] Scott, "Rough Notes on the Organization, Scope and Purposes of the Carnegie Endowment," pp. 4, 9-10, Charles W. Eliot to James Brown Scott, 15 Apr. 1911, Box 395, Eliot Papers, HA; "Minutes of the Annual Meeting of the Board of Trustees," 12 Dec. 1912, pp. 12-13, 26, CEIP Papers, CUL.

[74] "Proceedings of a Meeting of the Board of Trustees," 14 Dec. 1911, p. 21, Box 19, CEIP Papers, CUL.

[75] Nicholas Murray Butler to Charles W. Eliot, 8 Apr. 1913, Box 395, Eliot Papers, CUL. Like Butler, Elihu Root was reluctant to move too abruptly in cutting off the peace societies, partly out of a desire to placate Carnegie. The endowment's disdain for popular work, he pointed out, had been partly responsible for Carnegie's unscientific donation of $2 million for a Church Peace Union. It would be better for the endowment to spend a few thousands on the peace societies than incur Carnegie's displeasure for inaction on the sentimental front and inspire him to rash actions in support of impractical peace organizations like the Church Peace Union ("Minutes of the Annual Meeting of the Board of Trustees," 12 Dec. 1912, p. 26, and 16 Apr. 1915, p. 67, CEIP Papers, CUL). On Carnegie's interference in the administration of the endowment, see "Minutes of the Annual Meeting of the Board of Trustees," 17 Apr. 1914, p. 52, CEIP Papers, CUL. Carnegie even sought to induce the directors to promote his enthusiasm for "Simplified Spelling" within their organization. But the directors protested that such a step would ruin their reputation in academic and scientific circles and resolutely demurred. See Andrew Carnegie to J. B. Scott, 9 May 1911, Carnegie to R. S. Woodward, 9 May 1911, Henry Pritchett to Carnegie, 11 May 1911, Carnegie Papers, LC.

tested against the rejection of their tried and true methods. Long-established leaders resented their exclusion from the leadership of the rich new organization.

A few individuals had complained almost at once about the conservative composition of the trustees of the endowment and the inclusion of several big-armament and Navy League men. Hamilton Holt's *Independent* praised Carnegie's action, but noted with disappointment that the trustees were conservative and that many of them were new to the peace movement. Holt privately cautioned Trueblood not to "shape our policies so as to meet their rather conservative ideals," and suggested publicly two years later that "some of the trustees prefer peace but are not much averse to war." *The Nation* remarked more pointedly: "Not a single radical opponent of war is on the list. . . ." Elihu Root, it continued, had reached the age when "the forces of conservatism are at their height" and six other trustees averaged a decidedly unradical seventy-seven. Norman Angell, an English journalist and author of *The Great Illusion*, a popular treatise on the economic futility of war, later recalled that he had urged Carnegie in 1912 not to rely on such "conservatively minded" men but to establish ties with the younger generation.[76]

Most newspapers and periodicals, however, were inclined to praise rather than criticize the endowment's putative conservatism. The *New York Times* found nothing to criticize and much to commend in the fact that its activities would fall under the "direction of men of world-known-eminence." It praised the ability and experience of Root and Butler and the careful selection of trustees, and rejoiced that the promotion of peace had now "passed to the hands of practical men." The London *Times* remarked approvingly that the work of the endowment would be undertaken "in the most practical spirit," establishing the endowment as a "sober and steady force," rather than encouraging "pacifists of the sentimental order." *The World's Work* marvelled that it would employ "all the resources of modern scientific methods" in the first "concentrated scientific endeavor" to combat war,

76 Angell, "The Reminiscences of Norman Angell," pp. 112, 130; Hamilton Holt to Benjamin Trueblood, 2 Mar. 1912, Box 6, APS Papers, SCPC; *Independent*, 69 (15 Dec. 1910), 1339-41 and 77 (16 Feb. 1914), 219; *The Nation*, 91 (22 Dec. 1910), 598. Had critics of Carnegie's choice of trustees known of his notion, apparently not acted upon, to offer Theodore Roosevelt an open invitation to become a trustee at any time, they might have been even more disturbed. See Carnegie to Theodore Roosevelt (draft) 16 Nov. 1910, especially deleted portion. Carnegie omitted from the trustees Benjamin Trueblood, secretary of the American Peace Society and a logical appointee, but one to whom Roosevelt had previously objected. Roosevelt to Carnegie, 18 Feb. 1910, Carnegie Papers, LC.

"not by rhetoric, but by exhaustive research." Paul S. Reinsch in the *North American Review* praised the selection of "men of wide practical experience" as trustees, and applauded the endowment's decision to emphasize "careful scientific study of the field of action." It was commendable, Reinsch added, that Carnegie had appointed trustees who, owing to their own practical background as men of action, might easily organize peace sentiment among "the leaders of the financial and industrial world."[77]

In the light of the subsequent changes in the peace movement of the wartime period, one of the most interesting reactions to the Carnegie grant came from Paul Kellogg, a reform-minded editor of the *Survey* who took no direct interest in the peace movement until it took on a more liberal coloring after 1914. The United States, Kellogg warned, would be "judged by its slums" not by its foreign philanthropies and missions. The Carnegie money would be much better spent in advancing "the human side of the steel industry." Peace was too safe a cause. For Carnegie "to live a month in poverty in the Monongahela mill towns" would "take more courage than to fight war." But the majority of veteran peace leaders could hardly have been expected to share such a view of reform priorities. Although disappointed at having been ignored in Carnegie's appointments, they, like Mead and Trueblood, concerned themselves initially with attempts at least to get ample subventions from the endowment.[78]

However, the vexations of their new situation of relative dependence and unimportance kept the veteran peace movement leaders alert to emergent signs of apostasy on the part of the endowment and other new forces in the peace movement. Even Edwin Mead, who had advocated the solicitous and uncritical cultivating of the new endowment and who, as late as May, 1913, was still cautioning Trueblood about an issue that had disturbed Joseph Choate and other Carnegie trustees and "might make trouble when the matter of appropriations came up again," could not remain complacent. He could not escape moments of panic during which he feared that the endowment leaders had persuaded Trueblood to drop his campaigns against armaments and could not refrain from private criticisms of new tendencies in

---

[77] *New York Times*, 15 Dec. 1910, 8:1; the *Times* (London), 7 Jan. 1911, 6:1; *The World's Work*, 22 (July 1911), 14559; Paul S. Reinsch, "The Carnegie Peace Fund," *North American Review*, 193 (Feb. 1911), 181, 183, 189-90.

[78] Paul Kellogg, "Of Peace and Good Will," *American Magazine*, 71 (Apr. 1911), 739-45. The mixture of bitter resentment and hopeful solicitation by the veteran peace leaders is clearly expressed in Benjamin Trueblood to Andrew Carnegie, 20 Dec. 1910, Carnegie Papers, LC.

the peace movement. While he denied hotly that Carnegie sub-
sidies had changed the principles or weakened the will of the
American Peace Society, he did confess that "timidity and a mere
legalism" had increased in some circles since "the movement has
become big and fashionable." The new "timid and conservative
folk" in the national council of the American Peace Society, Mead
predicted, would try "to clip the wings of courage and water the
stock." "A lot of us have got to be very wise," he warned William
Hull, to save the principles of the movement from destruction at
the hands of "a lot of these half-baked 'new' pacifists." Hull himself complained of a "strange hesitancy" and lack of "frank and
outspoken expression" among the "nominal peace leaders," and
David Starr Jordan declared himself skeptical of the efforts of
Taft and his intimates and disappointed in the Carnegie Endowment's failure to oppose big armaments. Benjamin Trueblood
took up the defense of the "old pacifism" of those "not addicted
to 'high finance.' " The new practical movement still needed the
"vitalizing power of moral and humanitarian considerations." At
least the old pacifism had not been so compromising. "Our 'new
pacifists,' " Trueblood concluded, "strong and wise as we recognize them to be, cannot afford in any way to speak with reproach
of the older peace workers."[79]

But such criticism arising from those whom the new endowment had neglected, subordinated, or disparaged fell far short
of the attacks upon the endowment's "academic," "aristocratic,"
and "exclusive" policies that more radical recruits to the peace
movement would soon launch.[80] By the time that the troubling
questions of 1914-17 came upon them, the leaders of the American Peace Society and its subordinate organizations had largely

[79] Edwin D. Mead to Benjamin Trueblood, 29 Feb., 14 June, 19 Dec. 1912, and
28 May 1913, Mead to Erving Winslow, 4 Mar. 1912, William I. Hull to Trueblood,
25 Feb. 1914, Box 6, APS Papers, SCPC; Mead to Hull, 13 Dec. 1913, Box 1, Hull
Papers, FHL; Mead to Samuel T. Dutton, 6 May 1914 and Trueblood to Hull, 5
Feb. 1914, Box 2, Hull Papers, FHL; [David Starr Jordan] to Mead, 12 Feb. 1913,
Box 1, E. D. Mead Papers, SCPC; *Advocate of Peace* 75 (Nov. 1913), 221-22. For
other evidence of the restiveness of older peace workers, see New York Peace Society,
Yearbook, 1913, p. 25 and *Advocate of Peace* 75 (Aug. and Sept. 1913), 173.

[80] For examples of some early attacks, see John Haynes Holmes, "Democratize the
Peace Movement," *The Survey*, 30 (12 Apr. 1913), 65; Oswald Garrison Villard,
"What's Wrong with our Pacifists?" typed speech MS, n.d., Oswald Garrison Villard
Papers, Houghton Library, Harvard University; Anna Garlin Spencer, "Laid Up
in a Napkin," *The Survey*, 35 (4 Dec. 1915), 235-36; Louis Lochner to Benjamin
Trueblood, 15 May and 9 Nov. 1914, Box 8, APS Papers, SCPC; Lars P. Nelson
to Dr. Anna Howard Shaw, 18 Jan. 1915, Woman's Peace Party Correspondence,
SCPC; and David Starr Jordan to Dr. Henry S. Pritchett (draft), 23 Nov. 1915 and
Jordan to R. L. Wilber, 1 Feb. 1916, Jordan Papers, HI.

accepted their satellite position. They quietly followed the endowment's course of inaction.[81]

The basic assumptions that underlay the Carnegie Endowment's detached, academic approach and its attitudes toward peace societies were also revealed in its propaganda activities during the prewar years. Although most of the energies of the endowment leaders were absorbed by the work of internal organization, the initiation of scholarly programs in economics and international law, and the establishment of "centers of influence and constructive policy" in Europe,[82] the endowment did involve itself in several domestic propaganda campaigns. After the failure of Carnegie's pet project, the arbitration treaty with Britain, the endowment devoted its attention to such matters as agitation for preparations for a Third Hague Conference, planning for a 1915 celebration of one hundred years of peace between Britain and the United States, and opposition to racial exclusion laws in California. Its major propaganda expenditures, after 1911, were devoted to the support of Elihu Root's campaign to repeal the exemption of United States coastal vessels from Panama Canal Tolls. All of these campaigns conformed to and reinforced the endowment leaders' basic convictions.

The Panama Canal Tolls issue arose out of the disputed interpretation of a treaty. The United States had chosen to interpret the Hay-Pauncefote Treaty of 1901 as not prohibiting the United States from exempting its own coastwise shipping from canal tolls. Great Britain denied the accuracy of this interpretation. According to an arbitration treaty existing between the two na-

[81] The major exception was Louis Lochner who had moved into a position as secretary of the Chicago Peace Society, a branch of the American Peace Society, in early 1914. A young idealist who had won his early laurels in the peace movement through leadership of the cosmopolitan clubs in the colleges, Lochner quickly found himself at odds with the "bosses" of his own executive committee and with "the whole policy of the Carnegie Foundation." His energetic peace activities brought pressure from the new executive secretary of the American Peace Society to force him out of the organization in 1915. Lochner was to figure prominently in the promotion of the Woman's Peace Party, the Ford peace ship and neutral conference committee venture, and the People's Council. See below, chaps. six and eight. Louis Lochner to Benjamin Trueblood, 16 Feb., 15 May, and 9 Nov. 1914, Box 6, APS Papers, SCPC; Lochner to Mrs. Benjamin F. Trueblood, 13 Apr. 1915, Lochner to Arthur D. Call, 28 Nov. 1915, Call to Trueblood, 9 Dec. 1915, Box 8, APS Papers, SCPC.

[82] Nicholas Murray Butler, the director of the Division of Intercourse and Education, employed this phrase to emphasize the distinction between practical peace organizations and propaganda supported by the Carnegie Endowment and "those aspects of peace propaganda that are primarily rhetorical and fleeting in character" (Carnegie Endowment for International Peace, *Year Book for 1913-1914*, p. 57).

tions, such a dispute over the interpretation of a treaty should have been submitted to international arbitration. When the Taft administration and the Senate refused to do this, various groups, including Root and most of the international lawyers, sought to avoid the embarrassment of disregarding treaty obligations by obtaining the repeal of the controversial American exemptions. In March 1913 twenty-two of the endowment's twenty-eight trustees signed a statement written by President Eliot which put the endowment squarely behind the effort to repeal the exemptions. The endowment's Division of Intercourse and Education printed and distributed over a million copies of the statement. A Senate speech by Root on behalf of repeal was also widely distributed at the endowment's expense.[83]

The lesson of the Panama Canal Tolls issue, as the endowment's leaders saw it, was that the United States should not sacrifice a reputation for international probity for the minor commercial advantages that might be gained by a tortured unilateral interpretation of the treaty. American advocates of international courts and arbitration would invite charges of hypocrisy if they did not face up to what was simply "a question of the efficacy and force of treaties." High-minded gentlemanliness, meticulous adherence to the intention of treaties, and the establishment of certain international legal principles marked the proper path to peace. Moreover, the United States, as exemplar for the world, must maintain her moral dignity. In her own interest, she must try to establish an unblemished record of respect for developing principles of international law. By surrendering some unimportant interests in this case, the United States might teach the nations a lesson in national forbearance and the willing surrender of interests in the name of principle. In Root's view, the establishment of certain principles internationally was fundamental to peace. It would be insane not to try to establish the principles of respect for treaties and recourse to arbitration in cases like this when self-denial cost so little.[84]

[83] *Ibid.*, pp. 37-38, 79-81; "Statement Showing the Endowment's Activities in Connection with the Panama Canal Toll Questions," typed copy, and James Brown Scott to Charles W. Eliot, 20 Feb. and 1 Mar. 1913, Box 396, Eliot Papers, HA.

[84] Elihu Root, *Addresses on International Subjects*, collected and edited by Robert Bacon and James Brown Scott (Cambridge, Mass. 1916), pp. 178, 209, 232, 239-40, 308, 311; "Minutes of the Annual Meeting of the Board of Trustees," 12 Dec. 1912, pp. 75, 80-81, 84, 97, CEIP Papers, CUL. A more thorough description of the role of the Carnegie Peace Endowment in the Panama Tolls controversy appears in Lutzker, "The 'Practical' Peace Advocates," pp. 291-97.

From the phenomena of the California antialien laws and agitation, leaders of the endowment drew another lesson that reinforced their previous assumptions. The dangerous and insulting actions that invited war came not from men at the top, but from "the unrestrained impulses of the great democracy." Elihu Root particularly stressed the threat of war rising from popular intolerance and popular passions. The "one great obstacle to peaceful settlement of international differences," Root later commented, "is that the people will not back up the negotiator." This was the danger of democracies, where diplomats and other leaders were subject to powerful influences from a populace that made hasty judgments, was ignorant and intolerant, and did not recognize its legal obligations. Popular frenzy could only be restrained, another trustee remarked, through a knowledge of international law. Since the "educated classes," as James Brown Scott pointed out, did not need converting, the task of the peace worker was to educate the masses. Peace leaders should teach the common man his nation's responsibilities and the virtues of restraint.[85]

The endowment's other prewar campaigns—to stimulate preparations for a Third Hague Conference and for a celebration of the centennial of peace between Britain and the United States—were both aborted. In each of these efforts, the endowment leaders again exhibited aspects of their basic attitudes. The endowment promoted the appointment of an arrangements committee in Washington, D.C. for the Centenary of One Hundred Years of Peace between English-Speaking Peoples and secured the appointment of James Brown Scott as chairman of this committee. The endowment provided full clerical services and meeting space for the citizens committee.[86] Although the One Hundred Years' celebration appealed to all segments of the peace movement, preparations for the event seemed to fall particularly

[85] American Society of International Law, *Proceedings, 1914*, pp. 252, 326; Scott, "Rough Notes on the Organization, Scope and Purposes of the Carnegie Endowment," p. 4, Box 396, Eliot Papers, HA; Elihu Root, "The Need of Popular Understanding of International Law," *American Journal of International Law*, 1 (Jan. 1907), 2-3; Root, *Addresses on International Subjects*, pp. 147, 163-64; "Minutes of the Annual Meeting of the Board of Trustees," 14 Nov. 1913, p. 133 and 16 Apr. 1915, pp. 45, 46, CEIP Papers, CUL. For a discussion of the intellectual background of the elitist view of the causes of war and its relation to domestic conservatism, see the analysis of Butler and Root in Herman, *Eleven Against War*, pp. 23, 28-33. The elitist assumptions of the prewar peace movement are also suggested, with greater attention to historical background and development in Patterson, "The Travail of the American Peace Movement, 1887-1914," and given more explicit interpretation in Lutzker, "The 'Practical' Peace Advocates," both *passim*.

[86] Carnegie Endowment, *Year Book for 1913-1914*, pp. 43-44.

within the province of the Carnegie Endowment and the New York Peace Society because of their intimate connections with men of wealth, political power, and social prestige. Perhaps the anticipated celebration, soon to be thwarted by the war, also held particular appeal for some of the more anglophilic trustees of the Carnegie Endowment. Certainly the celebration would again accentuate the presumed superior capabilities of the Anglo-Saxon nations for peace under law.

The efforts of the Carnegie Endowment to stimulate initiatives and preparations leading to a Third Hague Conference also failed to achieve the desired result. But here, especially, the endowment leaders expressed again their fundamental preferences for a certain mode of approach to the reform of international relations. Since the interval between the First Hague Conference in 1899 and the Second Hague Conference in 1907 had been eight years, it had been assumed that a Third Hague Conference might be expected to meet eight years later, in 1915. By late 1913, the leaders of the endowment had become so concerned about the lack of international action to prepare for a third conference that they instructed Root to communicate directly with the secretary of state on the issue and directed Scott to prepare a report on the status of preparations and the further steps which the endowment might take.[87] The Hague Conferences were particularly treasured by the international lawyers, who looked upon them as the formulators of principles of international law and hoped that the next conference would finally complete the creation of a permanent court of international justice. It was along these lines —the creation of a court and the gradual development of law— that Root and Scott, the two most powerful leaders of the endowment, had projected their fondest aspirations.

While the World Peace Foundation had remained diffuse in its efforts, thus reflecting the occasional cross-purposes of its leaders, the Carnegie Endowment had clearly established itself by 1914 as a purposeful and powerful agent of new methods and attitudes within the peace movement. Shunning the cultivation of "ephemeral manifestations of sentiment" in favor of peace,[88] the endowment had opted for a thoroughly scientific approach, one that stressed research, the scholarly compilation of materials, the development of expertise, and the expansion of education in international law. While the World Peace Foundation searched

[87] *Ibid.*, pp. 26, 121-24; Warren F. Kuehl, *Seeking World Order: The United States and International Organization to 1920* (Nashville 1969), pp. 157-59, 161.
[88] Carnegie Endowment, *Year Book for 1913-1914*, p. 57.

confusedly for a program after August 1914, the Carnegie Endowment's commitment to scholarship and the biases of the international lawyers would give greater stability and consistency to its wartime programs.

CHAPTER FIVE

Responses to the War Crisis

THE outbreak of war in Europe in August 1914 burst like a bombshell upon the sanguine and unsuspecting peace organizations in the United States. Fears of a conflagration in Europe had been almost forgotten in the rising crescendo of optimistic rhetoric proclaiming the rapid progress of the peace movement. Benjamin Trueblood had recently described the movement as on the threshold of its "final stage" and the Quaker internationalist William I. Hull had compared the movement to a ship nearing the end of its voyage. "Its advocates," he wrote, "have seen it sail so swiftly within the past dozen years, over such notable leagues of progress, that its haven already looms ahead and the lower lights are seen upon the shore."[1]

With war in Europe now a reality, leaders of the peace movement were forced to abandon the optimistic confidence of the previous decade and face thorny immediate questions. The peace movement had come to identify itself with actual American foreign policy and had now successfully recruited many leaders and supporters from among the nation's social, professional, and business elites. Could the movement, with its new composition and leadership, take a position apart from and, if necessary, critical of official American policy? Should the American peace organizations encourage and support all efforts to bring the war to an early, negotiated settlement? Should they seek to initiate mediation efforts? Should they support efforts to restrict the flow of munitions and loans to the belligerents? Should they oppose expansion of American military strength; and should they, if the issue of American intervention loomed, insist that their own nation remain at peace?

In responding to these and similar questions, the peace organizations soon revealed a bifurcation of basic attitudes that would increase as the peace movement continued to transform itself

---

[1] Benjamin F. Trueblood, "The Present Demands of the Peace Movement," *Book of the Fourth American Peace Congress* (St. Louis 1913), pp. 106-9; William I. Hull, *The New Peace Movement* (Boston 1912), p. 46.

144

between 1914 and 1917. One group of organizations, largely of post-1914 origin, insisted upon maintaining a "peace posture" and working actively for peace in the *present circumstances* and with respect to the *present war*. They worked for an early peace, mediation, firm limits on military increases, and no American intervention. The other group of peace societies and foundations concluded that nothing could or should be done to halt the present war. Many of them actively supported military preparedness and, eventually, participation in the war; others simply refused to mount a vigorous opposition to these actions. Refusing to talk peace under the present circumstances, they looked ahead to what might be done in the realm of international organization and international law after the war.

The first of these groups became what might appropriately be called the "peace movement" between 1914 and 1917. For whatever reasons, leaders of these organizations sought peace as an immediate goal. The organizations of the second group, however internationalist in outlook and however "realistic" in their assessment of current possibilities, were only marginally connected with the active peace movement of the war years. The period 1914-1915 thus became a new turning point within the peace movement: it was during this period that most of the affluent and prestigious prewar peace societies and foundations decided to eschew peace activities directed against the current war, while new groups arose to fill the vacuum created by their inaction.

For many of the older peace organizations, the war in Europe came at a time of internal reorganization. Several of them had recently lost older leaders who were a degree more pacifist and less compromising than the newer, more "practical" men. The faltering Universal Peace Union had collapsed upon the death of Alfred Love in 1913. Albert Smiley, the founder and host of the Mohonk Conferences on International Arbitration had died in December 1912, and Edwin Ginn, founder of the World Peace Foundation, had died early in 1914, leaving that organization in confusion. Edwin Mead, another of the seasoned peace workers, attempted to hold the World Peace Foundation to a firm antipreparedness stance, only to be undercut by the trustees and to suffer a nervous breakdown in early 1915. Within the American Peace Society the aging Benjamin Trueblood had recently, at the insistence of the Carnegie Endowment, been forced to share his authority with a new endowment-approved executive director. Trueblood suffered a physical collapse late in 1913, recovered sufficiently to edit the *Advocate of Peace* during most of 1914, and then resigned as of mid-1915.[2]

But the loss of several venerable leaders cannot be judged responsible for the withdrawal of the older peace organizations from active leadership in the 1914-1917 peace movement. Few of the older leaders had shown a tendency to favor the more flamboyant and activist methods that newer antiwar organizations were to employ. An instinctive preference for gentlemanly respectability, genteel manners, and favor in high places unfitted most of these older leaders for the bolder projects and more radical outlook of the peace movement after 1914. Even had some of the older leaders been able and willing to take a bolder course, they would have faced the formidable obstacle of the conservatism of the leading lawyers, businessmen, and other prestigious figures that they had successfully recruited into influential positions in their organizations during the previous decade. Edwin Mead, for instance, remained active for over six months after the outbreak of war. But he could not block the trustees from moving to withdraw the World Peace Foundation from peace activity for the war's duration.

When the war began, in August of 1914, the American Peace Society with its thirty-one constituent branches, remained the nation's largest peace organization. Initially stunned by the war, its leaders quickly recovered to claim that they had prophesied the catastrophe. Their message was particularly urgent now, they argued, to reinforce the lesson in the necessity of peaceful world organization that the war was teaching.[3] But the national leaders of the society exerted little initiative in the period of crisis. They supported the initiatives of other groups in calling for a national day of prayer and in sending to the president a resolution asking

[2] *Advocate of Peace*, 76 (June 1914), 134, 136 and 77 (June 1915), 137, 139. On Mead and the World Peace Foundation, see below pp. 154-56. Trueblood and the executive director, Arthur D. Call, soon found themselves at odds over several issues and filled their correspondence with mutual recriminations and protestations. Trueblood evidently believed he was being surreptitiously "ousted." See Arthur D. Call to Benjamin Trueblood, 28 July 1914, 16 Aug. 1914, and 9 Dec. 1915, Call to Lyra D. Trueblood, 7 Aug. 1914 and n.d. [1914], Trueblood to Call, 7 Aug. 1914 and 27 July 1915, Box 8, American Peace Society Papers, Swarthmore College Peace Collection. Thomas Patterson characterizes the illnesses of Mead, Trueblood, and Andrew Carnegie after mid-1914 as largely psychosomatic responses to the destruction of their sustaining visions by the war. In the cases of Mead and Trueblood, the strains of internal conflict in their organizations may have been equally important. See Thomas Sands Patterson, "The Travail of the American Peace Movement, 1887-1914," Ph.D. diss., University of California, Berkeley, 1968, pp. 380-82.

[3] *Advocate of Peace*, 76 (June 1914), 145 and (Oct. 1914), 197.

for a conference of neutrals. But they were unable to agree upon a proposed declaration of principles that would have opposed increases in American military or naval strength and the private manufacture of armament. The society's main response to the war by late 1914 had been primarily a reassertion of optimism in its traditional methods and programs. A "remarkable opportunity" for a wider public hearing now existed if money could be raised to carry out these traditional efforts on an expanded scale.[4]

Although the *Advocate of Peace* still supported a conference of neutrals in January of 1915 and opposed military preparedness throughout the year, a decided trend toward disengagement from immediate peace efforts soon emerged. In April 1915 the *Advocate of Peace* commented resignedly that "the European War will end sometime" and directed its attention to problems after peace would be restored. In May it intimated that it had lost interest in proposals to stop the war, remarking that "much can be said in favor of not discussing the precise terms of peace at this moment." Arthur Deerin Call, the executive secretary of the society, reflected the mood of withdrawal from immediate agitation by devoting his attention to the society's glorious past. His report in June 1915 made no comment on the present war, except to say that the society's aims had not been "materially changed."[5] Privately, Call commented in June that his hope was "to deepen and extend the influence of the *Advocate of Peace* along conservative lines. . . ." In keeping with the growing distaste for the word "peace" among many of the new men in the established peace organizations, Call proposed that the name of the American Peace Society journal be changed from *Advocate of Peace* to *American Internationalist*. The *Advocate of Peace* soon disclaimed any attempt "to guide and to preach," seeking only an "impersonal and dignified" editorial policy that would be "conservatively in advance of the age." Its immediate responsibility, it argued, was to "study," "interpret," and encourage the "reflective habit." It should also "reincarnate the international principles" of its founders. There were those, the *Advocate of Peace* noted in October 1915, who said they should try to stop the war. From such a program, the American Peace Society de-

---

[4] *Ibid.* (Oct. 1914), 204; 76 (Nov. 1914), 221, 224-25; 77 (June 1915), 139; *New York Times*, 13 Sept. 1914, II, 5:5.

[5] *Advocate of Peace*, 77 (Jan. 1915), 10-13; 77 (April 1915), 77; 77 (May 1915), 105; 77 (June 1915), 143-44; 77 (Oct. 1915), 222-23; Arthur Deerin Call, "A Hundred Years of Organized Peace Work," *Proceedings of the Fifth American Peace Congress* (San Francisco 1915), p. 190.

murred. It would plead, instead, for "a Congress and High Court of Nations."[6]

Meanwhile a struggle was taking place within one of the potentially most vigorous of the American Peace Society branches, the Chicago Peace Society. The youthful new secretary of the Chicago branch, Louis Lochner, who had criticized the attitude of the Carnegie Endowment even before the war, now sought to mobilize the Chicago Peace Society for peace initiatives and to use his position as a platform from which to make statements in support of mediation and against preparedness. In December 1914 Lochner had taken the lead with Jane Addams in organizing an Emergency Federation of Peace Forces in Chicago on the basis of recent peace agitation by leading woman-suffrage leaders from Europe. In 1915 Lochner was to identify himself even further with the most active and dramatic segments of the peace movement, eventually taking a leading part in the Henry Ford Peace Ship venture and the campaign for a neutral conference to bring a mediated conclusion to the war. But Lochner's efforts were increasingly undertaken without the aegis of the Chicago Peace Society and its parent body. In November 1914 Lochner had already found "great skepticism in my board as to the advisability of doing anything at this time." The "bosses" of the society's executive committee objected to Lochner's letters to the press, opposed a candidate he had proposed to fill a vacancy on the executive committe because "he was all together too much of a pacifist!" and had shown a "lack of enthusiasm" for any meetings of the society. Before long the executive director of the American Peace Society was also frowning on Lochner's activities. Warning Lochner that his programs were "utterly absurd and impossible" and that his activities were harming the American Peace Society, Call eventually pressured Lochner to resign.[7]

Despite this trend toward withdrawal on the part of the American Peace Society, the *Advocate of Peace* did occasionally give evidence during 1915 of sympathy with more energetic peace activities. It invited contributions of "radical views of an intelligent order" and printed speeches and articles by active peace workers such as Jane Addams, George Nasmyth, and Louis Lochner. It praised the Emergency Peace Federation in Chicago for bringing Socialists and trade unionists into the organized peace

[6] *Advocate of Peace*, 77 (June 1915), 138; 77 (Aug. 1915), 185, 187-88; 77 (Oct. 1915), 211-12; Arthur D. Call to Benjamin Trueblood, 30 June and 30 July 1915, Trueblood to Call, 27 July 1915, Box 6, APS Papers, SCPC.

[7] Louis Lochner to Benjamin Trueblood, 20 June and 9 Nov. 1914, Lochner to Arthur D. Call, 28 Nov. 1915, Box 8, APS Papers, SCPC.

movement and even sought, with scant justification, to claim credit for the American Peace Society in the work of more dynamic organizations like the Woman's Peace Party and the Emergency Peace Federation. Editorials and articles which opposed military preparedness continued to appear.[8]

By the end of 1915, however, the American Peace Society had largely ceased even to show sympathy with the active peace movement. The Carnegie Endowment, the financial mainstay of the society, effectively extended its policy of inaction and opposition to current peace activities to its dependent and satellite organizations. In the November 1915 issue of the *Advocate of Peace* there appeared the full text of a letter dated 16 June 1915 from James Brown Scott to Jackson Ralston, a prominent international lawyer and a director of the American Peace Society. This letter, coming from the secretary of the Carnegie Endowment with control over nearly three-fourths of the society's yearly income, was ominously entitled "The Future of the American Peace Society."

Scott "hesitated," he said, to make any suggestions regarding the "very delicate and difficult questions" of reorganizing the society or making changes in the *Advocate of Peace*. But he did not entirely conceal his disappointment with certain aspects of the society's propaganda. It might be inviting, he remarked, "to take up the cudgels against the partisans of increased armament." But the American Peace Society would do better to stick to "constructive work" in the tradition of its founders. Personally, Scott confided, he favored a "larger army and a more efficient navy." At any rate, since there was no danger of militarism in the United States, the American Peace Society should cease its criticism of preparedness. It would achieve better results by campaigning for its traditional program of a world court and world organization than by "indulging in the denunciation of concrete abuses. . . ." It should read the works of its founders on a world court, which Scott was going to edit and reprint through the Carnegie Endowment, and "consider carefully its traditions." Those traditions involved "constructive measures" that would "win the confidence of men of affairs" and increase the society's "standing in the community." "The wisest course, for the American Peace Society," Scott emphasized, "is to withdraw itself, as it were, during the present war, to consider carefully what can best be done in the

---

[8] *Advocate of Peace*, 77 (Feb. 1915), 36-38, 42; 77 (Apr. 1915), 78, 95-96; 77 (June 1915), 142; 77 (July 1915), 173-75; 77 (Aug. 1915), 194-97; 77 (Nov. 1915), 236-37; 76 (Dec. 1914), 266.

future, to limit its program consciously, and, having so limited it, endeavor to carry it into effect when the conclusion of peace will give the Society a hearing."[9]

Scott's letter was printed without reply in the *Advocate of Peace*, prefaced laconically by the remark that the letter was "vitally pertinent to the work of the American Peace Society," and "self-explanatory." Certainly the American Peace Society did not ignore advice from so significant a source. In the same issue, the editors criticized a continuous mediation proposal recommended by the Fifth American Peace Congress and recommended the *Year Book* of the Carnegie Endowment to "those who do not know" and who therefore remained critics of the endowment. In response to the complaint by Secretary Trueblood, now incapacitated and near death, that the American Peace Society had so diluted its principles through the attempt "to be conciliatory and to keep in with everybody" that it had destroyed its "reason for existence," Call replied rather complacently that the society was "in excellent condition to accomplish great things when once a hearing can be had." The American Peace Society could pride itself, he suggested, on avoiding "being swept off our feet by . . . various wild-cat schemes. . . ." The society, he wrote subsequently, was returning to the "promotion of our ancient program," a program which Scott was "rewriting . . . in his own language to be sure."[10]

Actually, Scott's letter in 1915 had encouraged the leaders of the American Peace Society to recognize their real position. Their society was now the propaganda "agent" of the endowment, and they gradually sought more complete endowment censorship of their propaganda. Characterized as "moribund" and "hardly fit to live" and charged with "cowardice" and "incompetence" by a few of its old adherents, the society drifted away from any significant connection with the active peace movement. In 1917 it even sought to outdo the Carnegie Endowment in its support of American intervention.[11]

[9] James Brown Scott, "The Future of the American Peace Society," *Advocate of Peace*, 77 (Nov. 1915), 235-36.

[10] *Advocate of Peace*, 77 (Nov. 1915), 235-36, 239, 256; Arthur D. Call to Benjamin Trueblood, 9 Dec. 1915 and 1 Mar. 1916, Box 8, APS Papers, SCPC; Call to William I. Hull, 9 Dec. 1916, Box 1, APS Papers, SCPC; John Mez to David Starr Jordan, 9 Dec. 1915, David Starr Jordan Papers.

[11] American Peace Society, *Eighty-Ninth Annual Report of the Directors, 1917*, pp. 8, 12, 15, 19; Merle Curti, *Peace or War: The American Struggle, 1636-1936* (New York 1936), pp. 254-55. For examples of pointed criticism of the American Peace Society and the Carnegie Endowment, see Louis Lochner to Mrs. Benjamin F. True-

The Lake Mohonk Conference on International Arbitration, the other major peace organization of nineteenth century origin, had no occasion to react immediately to the war. A yearly conference with no interim agency to undertake action or establish policy, the Mohonk Conference did not meet until more than nine months after the war began. Even after this period, Daniel Smiley, the new host of the Conference since 1913, felt it necessary to request that there be no "discussion of the causes and conduct of the war in the form of direct criticism of specific policies or acts. . . ." Smiley also made a point of insisting that "this is not, nor has it ever been, a peace conference, so-called." "It is rather," he continued, "a conference of experts on a scientific problem, a company of experts addressing itself to an uninformed populace."[12]

So effective was the Mohonk Conference's insistence that it was no unscientific, sentimental peace organization that the *New York Times* reported its opening session under the headline, "Peace Conference Talks Mostly War."[13] Although Smiley's restrictions on criticism of the belligerents restrained the expression of pro-Allied sentiments, he and other conference leaders had insured that the opponents of military increases in the United States would have no monopoly of the conference's attention. The secretary of war, the editor of the *Army and Navy Journal*, General Leonard Wood, Rear-Admiral Colby Chester, and President John Greer Hibben of Princeton University, a leading champion of "preparedness," had all been invited to speak.[14] Much of the time not consumed by their appeals for preparedness was given over to presentations by Theodore Marburg, Hamilton Holt, and John Bates Clark of the program proposed by the embryonic League to Enforce Peace. Here, too, more traditional pacifists were likely to be startled by the emphasis upon the use of force. The program included the lawyers' "true court of Justice" and regular conferences to codify international law; but it also called for members of the proposed league to use force to require nations to submit their disputes to the world court.

blood, 13 Apr. 1917, Box 8, APS Papers, SCPC; David Starr Jordan to Henry S. Pritchett, 23 Nov. 1915, Jordan Papers, HI; William I. Hull to Arthur D. Call, 18 Dec. 1916, Box 1, APS Papers, SCPC; and Patterson, "The Travail of the American Peace Movement," pp. 388-93.

12 *Report of the Twenty-First Lake Mohonk Conference on International Arbitration* (Mohonk Lake, N.Y. 1915), pp. 11-12 (hereafter cited as *Mohonk Conference* with appropriate date).

13 *New York Times*, 20 May 1915, 4:2.

14 *Mohonk Conference, 1915*, pp. 73-91, 94-98, 166-70.

International lawyers were present in sufficient numbers to insure that the conference platform eliminated the provisions for the use of force from the League to Enforce Peace proposal and preparedness sentiment was not yet widespread enough among Mohonk delegates to write the demands of Secretary of War Garrison and General Wood into the conference resolutions. But the business delegates did pass a declaration calling for the "strengthening of the military and naval forces" for protection.[15] Nothing was heard at the conference of the proposals of the more radical peace groups or of efforts toward mediation and an early end to the war. So little was heard of peace activism at the conference that the *New York Times* and other papers concluded elatedly that the militarists had come out in the lead. Even the *Advocate of Peace* felt itself obliged to defend the conference, despite its "vagaries," as having been "no joke" upon the peace movement.[16]

If the actions of the American Peace Society and the Lake Mohonk Conference promised little in the way of dynamic antiwar activity after 1914, the activities and policies of such newer, and presumably more effective organizations as the New York Peace Society, the World Peace Foundation, the American Society of International Law, the American Society for Judicial

[15] *Ibid.*, pp. 9-10, 129-30.

[16] *New York Times*, 21 May 1915, 12:4 and 22 May 1915, 10:2; *Advocate of Peace*, 77 (June 1915), 129-30. See also Lucia Ames Mead to David Starr Jordan, 2 June 1915, Jordan Papers, HI. By early 1917 the secretary of the Mohonk Conference was considering postponement of that year's conference because "only 'pacifists' will have time or inclination to attend" and "the holding of the conference might be considered unpatriotic. . . ." After contemplating the alternative of further limiting permissible topics "to exclude discussion of purely national interests, policies or acts of the United States in connection with the European conflict" the conference administration decided upon postponement. The conferences were never resumed. See H. C. Phillips to William I. Hull, 16 Mar. and 12 Apr. 1917, Box 5, William I. Hull Papers, Friends' Historical Library, Swarthmore College. Of course, it was not only the larger organizations within the older peace movement which found themselves adrift in 1914 and 1915, unable to agree upon the continuation of old policies or the proper new programs to adopt. One intriguing case is that of the small International Peace Arbitration Committee of the Daughters of the American Revolution. Its chairman, despairing over the "diametrically opposed" policies offered for approval by the national organizations, sought diligently to unite her committee behind some least common denominator. "Will you . . . tell me," she wrote her local leaders, "of anything you may know of movements or measures in your state for the preservation and conservation of human life—such as 'Sane Fourth' celebrations; restriction of the sale of firearms and fireworks; 'safety first' and prevention of infant mortality crusades, etc.?" Mrs. Henry L. Cook to State Chairman and Members at Large, 16 Feb. 1915 and Cook to Lucia Ames Mead, 19 Feb. 1915, Box 6, Lucia Ames Mead Papers, SCPC.

Settlement of International Disputes, and the Carnegie Endowment offered even less encouragement to those still seeking to hasten the end of the war, limit American armament, and avoid American intervention. The responses of these organizations to the challenges of the years 1914-1917 can best be described in two segments. The reactions of the law societies and the Carnegie Endowment fell into one general pattern. The New York Peace Society and the World Peace Foundation expended their resources, in quite different ways, to advance the program carried on by a new organization, the League to Enforce Peace. Both sets of organizations—the ones dominated by the international lawyers and the ones drawn upon by the League to Enforce Peace—effectively withdrew from all immediate peace action.

As the most vigorous of the newer peace societies, the New York Peace Society took the lead in early appeals to the president to offer mediation. A "plan of action" committee was formed in October 1914 which initially recommended that the society endorse a call for a conference of neutrals and belligerents. But objections were raised against such a policy and by December the committee had overwhelmingly rejected its previous proposal for an immediate conference of the powers to resolve the crisis and had instead fastened its hopes upon a postwar league of nations.[17] In January 1915 the society let it be known publicly that it believed it unwise for the government "to take steps toward peace other than those it has already taken." At the same time it announced that it advocated "a powerful navy" and an extension of the militia system as long as the military forces did not make "extraordinary additions." It refused to promote "spectacular and popular appeals," to issue protests that would "only serve to make the Society ridiculous," or to "lead the Society into controversy." It made no appeal for restrictions upon war loans, declined further to urge any mediation actions upon the government, moved steadily away from any opposition to preparedness, and, in September of 1915, protested strongly against any embargo on American exports of munitions.[18]

Although the New York Peace Society was decisively backing away from all immediate peace activities, the main leaders of the

17 *Advocate of Peace*, 76 (Oct. 1914), 204; 77 (Mar. 1915), 54; Warren F. Kuehl, *Hamilton Holt: Journalist, Internationalist, Educator* (Gainesville, Fla. 1960), p. 125; Ruhl J. Bartlett, *The League to Enforce Peace* (Chapel Hill, N.C. 1944), pp. 31-32.

18 *New York Times*, 7 Jan. 1915, 7:1 and 8 Jan. 1915, 10:8; New York Peace Society, *Year Book, 1914*, pp. 16, 19 and *Year Book, 1915 and 1916*, pp. 10-12; *Advocate of Peace*, 77 (Oct. 1915), 230; William H. Short to Joseph Choate, 13 Sept. 1915, John Bates Clark to Short, 27 Sept. 1916, Box 3, New York Peace Society Papers, SCPC.

plan of action committee, Hamilton Holt and Theodore Marburg, still concluded that it would be best to promote their league of peace plan through a new organization that would have more aggressive leadership and a more clearly defined single purpose. During a series of dinner meetings they developed their plan for a league of peace with the aid of a select group composed largely of other New York Peace Society leaders. The focus of the league would be a true world court on the lawyers' model. Provisions were also made for a court of conciliation for nonjusticiable controversies and for regular meetings of league members to develop and codify international law. But the plan went beyond the international lawyers' program in calling for an international police force to compel nations to submit their disputes to the international court. The introduction of the element of collective force into the plan produced controversy, but at a final dinner meeting, early in 1915, prestigious allies, including former President Taft and A. Lawrence Lowell, president of Harvard University, endorsed the plan. Taft became president and Lowell became chairman of the executive committee of the new League to Enforce Peace.[19]

Meanwhile, A. Lawrence Lowell had been working to redirect the activities and funds of the World Peace Foundation along more "constructive" and less pacifistic lines. The death of the organization's founder, Edwin Ginn, in early 1914 had left the World Peace Foundation in confusion. Edwin Mead fought off early challenges to his position as chief director and promulgated statements offensive to Lowell and several other trustees in which he denounced militarism and any increase of armaments, opposed private loans to the belligerents, and called for the nationalization of arms and munitions manufacture. His friend, Samuel Dutton, sought to embellish a report of the foundation's Committee on Organization in such a way as to indicate support for Mead's position. Lowell, meantime, was marshaling his forces on the board of trustees, warning that "our friend Mead is liable to get

19 Bartlett, *The League to Enforce Peace*, pp. 30-37, 39, 43; Kuehl, *Hamilton Holt*, pp. 125-29. The most detailed account of the formation of the League appears in Martin David Dubin, "The Development of the Concept of Collective Security in the American Peace Movement, 1899-1917," Ph.D. diss., Indiana University, 1960, pp. 107ff. For lists of guests at the various dinners at which the league was planned, see Bartlett, *op. cit.*, pp. 34-35, a statement entitled "From Theodore Marburg," 25 Jan. 1915, Box 1, Franklin Giddings Papers, Columbia University Library, and Hamilton Holt to Jeremiah Jenks, 12 Jan. 1915, Hamilton Holt Papers, Rollins College.

out publications on the war which we shall not approve, unless we restrain him. . . ."[20]

A majority of the board of trustees, controlled and led by Lowell, moved quickly to demand a veto power over Mead. By the early spring of 1915, the trustees had imposed a new policy which stipulated that no manifesto, platform, or program, including Mead's earlier statement, could be issued by the foundation without the approval of both the full board of directors and the board of trustees. Similar restrictions were placed on the publication of any books or pamphlets in the name of the foundation. The new policy hamstrung the chief director. In March 1915 the period of internal struggle and public inaction by the foundation culminated in Edwin Mead's nervous breakdown.[21]

Lowell's dedication to the League to Enforce Peace coincided with Mead's breakdown. With Mead gone, the drifting World Peace Foundation had become more than ever a foundation without a program. In late 1914, its finance committee had already moved to conserve its resources "until the wisdom and expediency of certain lines of activity may be more clearly seen than at present." Lowell now moved quickly to tap the foundation's idle treasury for the League to Enforce Peace. Employing a threat of resignation he swung a majority of the trustees behind his position. At the meeting of 12 July 1915 the trustees voted to commit the foundation to the support of the League to Enforce Peace. By the beginning of 1916 it had approved a $10,000 yearly contribution to the League and had narrowed its own work to the publication of pamphlets and work in schools and colleges.[22]

20 "World Peace Foundation" (untitled sheet dated 1 Oct. 1914), Edwin Mead to "Dear Sir," 22 Dec. 1914, Box 6, World Peace Foundation Papers, SCPC; "Minutes of the Annual Meeting of the Board of Trustees," 24 Nov. 1914, pp. 60-62, Box 1A, WPF Papers, SCPC; A. Lawrence Lowell to George W. Anderson, 12 Dec. and 19 Dec. 1914, World Peace Foundation Collection, A. Lawrence Lowell Papers, Harvard University Archives; Edwin Mead to William I. Hull, 4 Nov. 1914, Box 2, Hull Papers, FHL.

21 "Minutes of a Special Meeting of the Board of Trustees," 17 Apr. 1915, pp. 80, 83-84, Box 1A, WPF Papers, SCPC; George W. Anderson to Edwin Mead, 2 Jan. 1915, A. Lawrence Lowell to Anderson, 19 Dec. 1914, WPF Collection, Lowell Papers, HA; *Advocate of Peace*, 76 (May 1915), 110.

22 A. Lawrence Lowell to William H. Short, 13 July 1915, Hamilton Holt to Lowell, 9 July 1915, League to Enforce Peace Collection, Lowell Papers, HA; Edward Cummings to Lowell, 14 Mar. 1917, Lowell to George W. Anderson, 17 July 1923, "Annual Report of Dr. Charles H. Levermore to the Board of Trustees of the World Peace Foundation," 30 Nov. 1915, WPF Collection, Lowell Papers, HA; "Minutes of the Annual Meeting of the Board of Trustees," 24 Nov. 1914, p. 69, "Minutes of the Meeting of the Board of Trustees," 12 July 1915, p. 92, Box 1A, WPF Papers, SCPC.

Lowell, who was now chairman of the executive committees of both organizations, secured the appointment as director of the World Peace Foundation of the "safe and sane" Edward Cummings, who obediently took his instructions from Lowell. Among Cummings' major problems as director was the task of meeting the league's increasing financial demands.[23] David Starr Jordan, now an inactive director, attacked the transfer of the foundation's funds as a subversion of Ginn's intentions and one trustee chided the foundation for its spineless refusal to combat preparedness propaganda; but most of the trustees willingly acquiesced in Lowell's coup. President W.H.P. Faunce of Brown University, a leading trustee, explained: "Our World Peace Foundation found itself . . . practically paralyzed. We dissented from the work that Dr. Mead was doing and yet had no work to propose. . . . The work of the League to Enforce Peace did seem a practical measure on which men of various minds might unite."[24]

Having drawn its impetus from the New York Peace Society and a portion of its financial support from the World Peace Foundation, the League to Enforce Peace carried forward the newer trends in the peace movement toward practicality and the solicitation of business support. Its supporters included many of those whose names had recently contributed to the rising prestige of the prewar peace movement. The league sought and partially obtained close ties with the administration. Several of its major leaders were strongly pro-Allied from the outset and were early proponents of both expanded military programs and American intervention.[25]

The League to Enforce Peace attempted to make its plan the official postwar program of the United States government. In its search for broad-based, mainstream support the league sought to avoid unnecessary controversy and alienate as few influential groups as possible. It avoided all discussion of proposals for ending the present war and adjusted its policy on military preparedness and American intervention to a point midway between that

[23] Edward Cummings to A. Lawrence Lowell, 27 June and 29 June 1917, Cummings to William H. Short, 17 Oct. 1917, Cummings to Members of the Executive Committee, 5 July 1917, W.H.P. Faunce to Lowell, 23 Dec. 1921, WPF Collection, Lowell Papers, HA.

[24] David Starr Jordan to Albert E. Pillsbury, 31 July 1916, Charles H. Levermore to A. Lawrence Lowell, 27 July 1915, Jordan to Lowell, 14 Aug. 1916, WPF Collection, Lowell Papers, HA; W.H.P. Faunce to Jordan, 31 Oct. 1916, Jordan Papers, HI.

[25] This was particularly true of Lowell and Theodore Marburg. For example see Marburg to Lowell, 28 Oct. 1916, LEP Collection, Lowell Papers, HA.

of the Wilson administration and that of its more belligerent backers. By the fall of 1916 it was including on its letterhead the explicit statement, "The League to Enforce Peace does *not* seek to end the present war." While the league hoped to retain the backing of the old peace forces, its desire to enlist widespread and influential support made it even more anxious not to offend the propreparedness men. The league's secretary acknowledged that it welcomed even those with the most extreme views on military preparedness. The league's goal, it bluntly avowed, was not peace agitation, but a postwar league.[26]

In seeking to erase any stigma it might carry on account of its peace society origins, the league even allowed itself to be used, on occasion, by the preparedness advocates. One leader stated frankly to his colleagues that his only interest in the league was that propaganda for a league was the only way to induce people to accept increased military expenditures. In consultation with preparedness groups on the possibilities of mutual cooperation, the league's representative explained carefully how their program could be employed as an argument for increased armaments. In mid-1916 one member reported in some dismay that when one of the league's representatives spoke in outlying towns, "the newspapers there thought he was merely talking about preparedness and did not discover that he had any plan for peace at all."[27]

The league's prominent leadership and aggressive program of propaganda made it the major organization in the United States seeking a postwar league of nations. Ruhl J. Bartlett, in his history of the League to Enforce Peace, has concluded that the league "greatly influenced American thought" and that its success until 1919 "was almost incredible."[28] That success was due, in part, to the vigor with which the league had dissociated itself from the increasingly unpopular peace organizations. Not only did the league seek cooperation with preparedness groups and attempt to court enthusiasts for military action by printing the word "enforce" on its stationery in "blood red letters"; it also demanded,

[26] William H. Short to David Starr Jordan, 31 Aug. 1915, Jordan Papers, HI; A. Lawrence Lowell to Short, 4 Dec. 1916, Short to Lowell, 1 Mar., 15 Oct., and 27 Dec. 1916, *LEP* Collection, Lowell Papers, HA.

[27] "Minutes of the Executive Committee of the League to Enforce Peace," 12 July 1916, "In Re Conference with Preparedness Group," 1 Apr. 1916 (typed enclosure to Short to Members of Executive Committee, 28 Mar. 1916), Charles C. Jackson to A. Lawrence Lowell, 5 Apr. 1916, and William H. Short to Lowell, 8 Jan. 1917, LEP Collection, Lowell Papers, HA.

[28] Bartlett, *The League to Enforce Peace*, pp. v, 210.

late in 1916, that its officers resign from all other peace organizations.[29] Soon thereafter, Lowell and the secretary of the league,
William H. Short, began to worry about the presence of "extreme
pacifists" and "weak brothers" on the executive committee. Apparently they considered even such founders of the organization
as Hamilton Holt and John Bates Clark as falling into these cate-
gories. One officer began warning of "dangerous ones in our
midst" and referred to "a card index on us" in Berlin.[30]

Shortly after the United States entered the war, the league's
secretary concluded that the fate of the organization depended
upon its success in making itself "helpful to the Government in
the waging of the war." The word "enforce" would now take the
same dominant place in the league's title, he promised, that the
Allied armies were taking in the search for peace on the field of
battle. A league pamphlet declared that it would be "an imperti-
nence and a cause for offense" to hold any meetings to "talk merely about peace." The secretary of the league declared himself
eager to work "directly for the defeat of Germany" and described
himself, by analogy, as one of a great body of "liberty-loving citizens" who were rallying to the support of government to restore
law and order and put down an unruly mob. A league pamphlet
explained, with seeming relish, why "a man may be compelled at
times to thrash his neighbor." Certainly, the pamphlet made clear,
the league had no desire to be identified as a group that sought
"peace without victory." So enthusiastically did the league respond to American intervention that Frederick Lynch of the
Church Peace Union was remarking by July 1917 that it was "a
pity that the American League to Enforce Peace has got so possessed with carrying on the present war that it is losing sight of
the large constructive program. . . ."[31]

The league's increasing pugnaciousness culminated in May

[29] "In Re Conference with Preparedness Group," 1 Apr. 1916, "Minutes of the
Meeting of Committee on Management," 29 Nov. 1916, A. Lawrence Lowell to
William H. Short, 4 Dec. 1916 and Short to Lowell, 27 Dec. 1916, LEP Collection,
Lowell Papers, HA; W.H.P. Faunce to David Starr Jordan, 31 Oct. 1916, Jordan
Papers, HI; Hamilton Holt to George Nasmyth, 30 Dec. 1916, Box 1, George W.
Nasmyth Papers, SCPC; Kuehl, *Hamilton Holt*, p. 111.

[30] William H. Short to A. Lawrence Lowell, 3 Jan. 1917, Lowell to Short, 9 Feb.
1917, Charles Stewart Davison to Lowell, 11 Aug. 1917, LEP Collection, Lowell
Papers, HA.

[31] William H. Short to A. Lawrence Lowell, 2 July 1917, LEP Collection, Lowell
Papers, HA; Short to William I. Hull, 5 Nov. 1917, Frederick Lynch to Hull, 19
July 1917, and League to Enforce Peace, "The League's War-Time Program," Box
5, Hull Papers, FHL.

1918 in a "Win-the-War-for-Permanent-Peace" Convention intended, in the words of the league's secretary, "to burn in on the national mind that this League . . . will not be worth a passing thought unless we win this war." One active member of the league proclaimed that the United States was engaged "in the holiest war of history," a crusade in which "war is worship, war is prayer." Other speakers at the convention stressed Germany's perfidy and her plans for a "premature" peace.[32] Even President Lowell's hand-picked director of the World Peace Foundation complained that the league seemed to have forgotten its positive proposals. The convention's three-day program, he pointed out, "looks to me like a sandwich, composed of two thick slices of war bread and mustard, with a little potted peace pigeon in between."[33]

For all of its eventual participation in the nation's war enthusiasm, the League to Enforce Peace continued to manifest many of the characteristics of the "new peace movement" of the prewar decade. It drew its support from many of the same persons and groups and focused its attention on the same domestic and international goals: order and stability. In contrast to the postwar international programs of other contemporaneous peace organizations, the League to Enforce Peace said nothing about the need for economic or social change and offered no proposals for the abolition of secret diplomacy or the democratic control of foreign policy. The proposed league, according to one of the principal founders of the league, would accept as legitimate the territorial status quo (presumably after an Allied victory), and guarantee nations the right to restrict immigration, to safeguard "certain doctrines such as the Monroe Doctrine," and to retain spheres of influence.[34] The leaders of the league, as Sondra Herman has pointed out, conceived of international organization in terms of "polity" rather than of "community," as a matter of imposing po-

[32] "A Personal Talk by the Secretary of the League to Enforce Peace Concerning a WIN-THE-WAR-FOR-PERMANENT-PEACE CONVENTION, May 16-17-18, 1918," typed MS, LEP Collection, Lowell Papers, HA; Bartlett, *The League to Enforce Peace*, pp. 94-95.

[33] Edward Cummings to William H. Short, 23 Mar. 1918, WPF Collection, Lowell Papers, HA.

[34] For an outline and comparison of the programs of ten American and European organizations see *The Survey*, 35 (20 Nov. 1915), 186-87. Lowell privately opposed both democratic control and the abolition of secret diplomacy. Lowell to Charles Stewart Davison, 13 June 1918, Lowell to C. R. Ashbee, 1 June 1915, LEP Collection, Lowell Papers, HA; "From Theodore Marburg," 25 Jan. 1915, typed MS, p. 5, Box 1, Giddings Papers, CUL.

litical order rather than of developing social and economic integration.[35]

Gradually, the league's original vision of a cooperating council of nations gave way to the conception of a small group of "civilized nations," headed by the United States and Great Britain, imposing peace and justice upon the world. In 1916 leaders of the league had begun to conceive of the Allied nations as a league to enforce peace already called into existence to "discipline the lawbreaker." By 1917 the president and secretary of the league were both arguing that, by joining the Allies, the United States had become a member of a spontaneous league to enforce peace. "We should insist," the secretary wrote to Lowell, "that the war not end without a victory that will discourage further aggressors and conditions that will make the league permanent."[36] Thus the idea of a league of nations tended to become identified with ideas of a "league of democracies" or a "league of victorious allies." Senator Philander Knox carried this line of thought to its logical conclusion in 1918:

> We have now passed from a dangerous balance of power to a beneficent preponderance of power in the hands of the proved trustees of civilization. The English-speaking peoples and our principal allies formed a real league and they have enforced peace and saved civilization. . . . Power in the hands of the defenders of civilization holds the best promise of an ultimate international order founded upon justice and good will.[37]

From the outset, the leaders of the League to Enforce Peace had realized that to gain wide public support they must appeal to men more isolationist in sentiment than themselves. Even in their own proposals, they were disinclined to contemplate the need for curtailment of any aspect of American sovereignity and independence of decision. The mere existence of a league, they argued, would be sufficient to cow potential aggressors. The proposed league would "probably never be called upon to put its mil-

---

[35] Sondra R. Herman, *Eleven Against War: Studies in American Internationalist Thought, 1898-1921* (Stanford 1969), pp. 7, 77-78, 219-21, 224-25.

[36] Theodore Marburg to A. Lawrence Lowell, 28 Oct. 1916, William H. Short to Lowell, 3 July 1917, LEP Collection, Lowell Papers, HA; Short to William I. Hull, 5 Nov. 1917, Box 5, Hull Papers, FHL; William H. Taft, "The League to Enforce Peace," *National Conference of Social Work, 1917*, p. 42. For earlier statements by eventual League to Enforce Peace leaders foreshadowing the idea of an American or Anglo-American dominated league see Herman, *Eleven Against War*, p. 64.

[37] Theodore Marburg, ed., *Taft Papers on the League of Nations* (New York 1920), pp. 133, 142. Knox is quoted in F. M. Huntington Wilson, *Memoirs of an Ex-Diplomat* (Boston 1945), p. 364.

itary force into operation."[38] In suggesting the idea of a league of
victorious allies and in implying that no actual collective action
would be necessary, they further encouraged their more nationalistic supporters to assume that any eventual league would be so
thoroughly American that participation would involve no surrender of American freedom of action. It was thus not entirely inconsistent for many of the leaders of the League to Enforce Peace
to oppose the eventual proposal for a league of nations when it
reached the Senate. They had never really contemplated a commitment to possible collective action that would not be under effective American control; and their predominantly Republican
Party allegiances did nothing to ease their anxieties about a
league so closely identified with Woodrow Wilson.[39]

So thoroughly did the League to Enforce Peace absorb the
energies of the New York Peace Society and the funds of
the World Peace Foundation that those two prewar organizations
ceased to function as effective peace organizations after 1914. The
major officers of the New York Peace Society, including its energetic secretary, William H. Short, gave most of their attention to
the new organization. In the World Peace Foundation, the trustees largely abandoned their work among businessmen and within the colleges. No replacement was sought for Albert Bryant; his
work among businessmen's organizations was left to the National
Chamber of Commerce. The foundation's Committee of College
Presidents refused to encourage any activities in setting up new
international clubs in the colleges. Some faculty leaders in such
clubs had proved to be "indiscreet or dogmatic . . . causing at
times no little harm to the institution and to the principles of academic freedom."[40] The dissenting mood and more radical proposals of the 1914-1917 peace movement held no attractions for
either the New York Peace Society or the World Peace Foundation. Both dissociated themselves from peace activism and fas-

---

[38] "From Theodore Marburg," 25 Jan. 1915, typed MS, p. 5, Box 1, Giddings
Papers, CUL; A. Lawrence Lowell to Frank J. Goodnow, 26 July 1916, LEP Collection, Lowell Papers, HA; League to Enforce Peace, *Independence Hall Conference*
(Philadelphia 1915), pp. 17, 25, 41, and *Enforced Peace* (New York 1916), pp. 132,
138, 177.

[39] On the effect of party allegiances on leaders of the League to Enforce Peace
and their opposition to Wilson's league, see Bartlett, *The League to Enforce Peace*,
pp. 55-59, 108-10, 133, 166, 184-200. On the assumption of American dominance in
any prospective league and on divisions of opinion within the League to Enforce
Peace, see also Herman, *Eleven Against War*, pp. 48, 80-83.

[40] "Minutes of Special Meeting of Board of Trustees," 11 Oct. 1915 and 8 Jan.
1916, WPF Papers, SCPC; Peter Filene, "The World Peace Foundation and Progressivism: 1910-1918," *New England Quarterly*, 36 (Dec. 1963), 499; Patterson, "The
Travail of the American Peace Movement," pp. 394, 397-401.

tened their hopes for international order and stability on post-war programs.

In the Carnegie Endowment and the international law organizations, as in the peace societies, the outbreak of war evoked more embarrassment than action. Unlike the World Peace Foundation and the diffuse peace societies, however, the Carnegie Endowment had two well-developed lines of activity to fall back upon: scientific scholarship and international law. The directors and trustees of the Carnegie Endowment showed no more sympathy for "stop-the-war" schemes or conferences of neutrals than did the trustees of the World Peace Foundation, but their commitment to research provided them with a program that was relatively impervious to the dislocations of war. The scholarly program had never promised quick results. Elihu Root reminded the trustees in 1915 that the changes they sought were necessarily so gradual that they could "be produced only by persistent effort, running through generation after generation and century after century."[41] Given such a timetable, the outbreak of war was certainly no cause for despair, panic, or the hasty adoption of some premature scheme. The endowment could thus take the long view. The need for international law and the justification for continuing research would remain.

The Carnegie Endowment, however, could not entirely ignore the war. Its propaganda work in Europe might now involve it in unneutral behavior and the contents of some manuscripts awaiting publication "might tend to give rise to international controversy."[42] Despite the protests of the leaders of the Berne Peace Bureau and other European organizations, the directors quickly cut off support for European societies. All activity in Europe, the trustees quickly agreed at their next meeting, should be suspended to avoid impairing the future usefulness of the endowment.[43] Officers of the endowment also sought to preserve its neutrality and "constructive influence" by withholding from

[41] Carnegie Endowment for International Peace, *Year Book for 1915* (Washington, D.C. 1915), p. 20. "Our critics," James Brown Scott complained, "seem to labor under the delusion that the abolition of war . . . is the work of a single life time or of a single generation" (*Ibid.*, p. 105).

[42] *Ibid.*, p. 24.

[43] *Ibid.*, pp. 18, 21, 55; unsigned to Senator Henri LaFontaine, 22 Oct. 1914, "Report of the Acting Director of the Division of Intercourse and Education," 17 Mar. 1915, Division of Intercourse and Education, 1914 and 1915, and "Minutes of the Meeting of the Board of Trustees," 13 Nov. 1914, p. 13, Carnegie Endowment for International Peace Papers, CUL.

publication several potentially controversial completed works on armaments and on socialism. At a "hurried meeting" immediately after the outbreak of war, the endowment's officers decided to bury in safe deposit vaults a number of manuscripts which might "supply propaganda to the unrighteous as well as the righteous."[44] While outwardly concerned to maintain the organization's neutrality, the endowment's leaders were privately strongly pro-Allied. Root had long distrusted Germany as the main opponent of his program for an international court and James Brown Scott privately revealed his pro-British sympathies soon after the war began. Joseph Choate, an outspoken trustee, remarked that some members of the board would be delighted if the endowment were to seek peace by donating its entire income to the support of the Allied armies. Alvin Johnson, assistant to John Bates Clark, later recalled that "we were pretty sympathetic to the British. . . ." The endowment held documents which revealed French and British as well as German responsibility for the war. These had to be "pigeonholed," Johnson stated, because they "would have had a bad influence."[45]

In keeping with its policy of avoiding all controversial questions, the endowment refused to take any position on military expenditure, proposals to end the war, or even specific programs for a peace settlement. The trustees generally agreed that "the less said by us just now, so much the better." Carnegie agreed that under the circumstances, "wisdom is silence." Nearly every trustee who spoke at the meetings in 1914 and 1915 agreed that the endowment should cease "any advocacy of peace." President Eliot even underlined their revulsion against "peace propaganda" by praising school books that taught liberty and heroism through an emphasis on war. The trustees finally agreed upon public statements in early 1915 in which they ignored such issues as military preparedness and programs to end the war and confined themselves to observing that the war itself was "teaching the gospel of peace" and doing more to educate the public "than any argument or statistics." The war, they argued, "affords no just cause for dis-

[44] Alvin Johnson, *Pioneer's Progress: An Autobiography* (New York 1952), p. 229.
[45] Alvin Johnson, "The Reminiscences of Alvin Johnson," p. 88, Oral History Research Office, Columbia University; "Minutes of the Meeting of the Board of Trustees," 13 Nov. 1914, pp. 13, 22, 53 and 16 Apr. 1915, pp. 49-50, CEIP Papers, CUL. On Scott's sympathies see James Brown Scott to James Bryce, 10 Oct. 1914, Division of Intercourse and Education, 1914, CEIP Papers, CUL. On Root's long-standing view of German obstructionism, see Elihu Root to Andrew Carnegie, 3 Apr. 1909, Andrew Carnegie Papers, MS Div., Library of Congress.

couragement, no discredit to past efforts. . . ." Still, "to cast our weak protest now among the tremendous forces that are urging on the great conflict would be futile. . . ."[46]

President Nicholas Murray Butler of Columbia University, the acting director of the endowment's Division of Intercourse and Education, suggested in 1915 that the endowment should project no future course of action until the war had ended and the terms of peace had been determined. Meanwhile the endowment should conserve its resources. Butler himself had briefly joined the anti-preparedness forces in late 1914, but he quickly withdrew again from these activities and threw his support behind preparedness by the end of 1915.[47] His division did sponsor a campaign to organize international polity clubs in the colleges in late 1914 and a series of summer-school courses and lectures in 1915, but Butler warned the summer lecturers to avoid all "purely contentious questions" and any "special propaganda in reference to the unhappy conditions which now prevail. . . ." "There are no short-cuts to peace," he observed. George Nasmyth, one of the polity club organizers, emphasized that his group was seeking to engender scientific inquiry, in the Carnegie Endowment tradition, and was "not a group of peace hustlers." In late 1915, twenty-four out of twenty-eight trustees voted to omit any special meeting of the board, the trustees again concluding that "the less said about peace in these days the better."[48]

The Carnegie Endowment, however, did not merely practice and promote inaction during the years preceding American intervention. In its commitment to research it found not only a justification for looking beyond and away from the present crisis but also one basis for a constructive program. The pro-Allied biases of most of the endowment's officers and trustees and their preferences for sedate, conservative methods insured their opposition to ambitious and dramatic attempts to end the war. But merely

[46] Andrew Carnegie to William H. Short, 2 Nov. 1914, Box 3, NYPS Papers, SCPC; "Trustees' Statement" 16 Feb. 1915, Folder 1004, and "Minutes of Meeting of the Board of Trustees," 13 Nov. 1914, pp. 38, 41, 45, 50 and 16 Apr. 1915, pp. 20, 23-24, 27, 30, 34, 36, CEIP Papers, CUL; George A. Finch to Emmett J. Scott, 3 Dec. 1914, Division of Intercourse and Education, 1914, Vol. IV, CEIP Papers, CUL; "Carnegie Endowment for International Peace" (printed statement, 27 Jan. 1915), Box 395, Charles W. Eliot Papers, Harvard University Archives; James Brown Scott to Charles W. Eliot, 9 Oct. 1915, Box 396, Eliot Papers, HA.

[47] Carnegie Endowment, *Year Book for 1915*, p. 81; *New York Times*, 24 Sept. 1914, 10:5, 19 Dec. 1914, 4:3, and 19 Nov. 1915, 5:4.

[48] *Advocate of Peace*, 77 (Nov. 1915), 255; *New York Times*, 10 May 1915, 11:5; James Brown Scott to Charles W. Eliot, 26 Oct. 1915, Eliot to Scott, 11 Oct. 1915, Box 396, Eliot Papers, HA.

to study the war was another question. If diplomacy had failed, scholarship still might triumph.

Only in the United States, John Bates Clark began arguing in 1914, could a neutral and comprehensive history of the war be written. Through scholarship the endowment could continue to render a great service to the world. An economic history, composed by a team of scholars, could "record the effects of war" upon peoples and their economies without entering the dangerous "ethical region." With the scholar's enthusiasm Clark reported: "We are in a position to produce a monumental work."[49]

Clark did confess in the fall of 1914 that his Division of Economics and History was "a little discouraged" because the war had "rent asunder so remorselessly" the ties of economic interdependence which Clark and his scholars had intended to study as harbingers of an emerging "world state." But he also observed that "a division devoted mainly to investigation would naturally find a large opportunity in the tragic events of the war, which is so discouraging in a general way." In short, if the war was "discouraging in a general way," it was also stimulating in specific ways. It had "infused enormous value into previously selected topics." As Clark later observed: "The war is a terrifically costly laboratory for the study of war, but as a rich source of data for conclusions of inestimable value, it is simply incomparable." Here, in the scientific study of this war, lay an opportunity to apply "rigid methods of induction" and to demonstrate the feasibility of compiling a history that would be authoritative and impartial. Many of the individual studies involved would be "such that facts, statistical, historical, and descriptive, will constitute nearly the whole of their content." What was more, the endowment might thus transform the academic world by determining "to a large degree the direction of not one but most of the political and social sciences."[50]

Clark's elaborate plans for the expansion of the endowment's already substantial commitment to research gained strong support from Root and the other trustees. Root called for "thorough scientific investigation to take the place of balderdash and rhet-

---

[49] John Bates Clark to James Brown Scott, 3 Oct. 1914, John Bates Clark, "Project of a History of the European War," 22 Oct. 1914, Division of Economics and History, 1914, Vol. II, and Clark, "Project of a History of the European War," Division of Economics and History, 1915, CEIP Papers, CUL.

[50] Untitled Memorandum on the Need for a Scientific History of War, pp. 2-4, Division of Economics and History, 1914, and "Minutes of the Meeting of the Board of Trustees," 13 Nov. 1914, pp. 18-22 and 20 Apr. 1917, pp. 154-56, CEIP Papers, CUL.

oric," and Henry S. Pritchett and Charles W. Eliot characterized "these careful researches" as "probably the greatest contribution we will ever make." By 1917 the Division of Economics and History had received large increases in research funds.[51]

The Carnegie Endowment found a second basis for ongoing activity during the years 1914-1918 in the realm of international law. Like scholarly research, the program of the international lawyers had always entailed a slow, deliberate campaign against war and had never promised immediate results. In fact, scientific research and the development of international law, in the view of the endowment leaders, were mutually inseparable. The law which a true international court would administer would have to be discovered, in part, by full and scholarly investigation of historical precedent and current practice.

But before the Carnegie Endowment could comfortably and enthusiastically renew its efforts in developing international law, the prominent international lawyers among its officers had to overcome the consternation that both they and the international law organizations experienced immediately after the outbreak of the war. Those who had always been skeptical of the existence of international law had immediately pointed to the international anarchy created by the war as proof that the lawyers had been pursuing a chimera. How could it be claimed that there were international laws if in a crisis nations refused to recognize them? As George Grafton Wilson, professor of international law at Harvard, lamented: "Nearly every one who has been concerned with international law . . . has probably been greeted by friends with condolences of various sorts as to his possible future, as to whether he was planning to undertake some new form of occupation in view of the disappearance of international law."[52]

But the international lawyers had more than simply an occupational interest in upholding their position. Everything in their experience and training told them that only a recognized body of international law, applied by courts, could hope to replace the intolerable old system of devious diplomacy, international power politics, and inevitable war. To deny the possibility of the governance of international relations through law was to deny the

---

[51] "Minutes of the Meeting of the Board of Trustees," 21 Apr. 1916, p. 68 and 20 Apr. 1917, pp. 223, 270, CEIP Papers, CUL.

[52] *Proceedings of the Twelfth Annual Meeting of the American Society of International Law* (Washington, D.C. 1916), p. 104 (hereafter cited as ASIL, *Proceedings*, with appropriate date). Carnegie Endowment, *Year Book for 1915*, p. 103.

American position; it was to surrender the world to the dictates of amoral power and the depredations of anarchical confusion.

Most of the lawyers quickly rallied to a common position. The temporary eclipse of international law was merely the result of acts of outlawry against the sanctity of treaties and other recognized international rights. Although international law was sorely threatened by these lawless acts, it might ultimately triumph if the outlaws were thwarted in their aims. James Brown Scott remarked in 1915 that some of the belligerents were already discovering that "the greatest burden" they had to bear was "the charge that they have violated treaties and disregarded the rules of international law." Germany's sins, he suggested obliquely, could be traced directly to the fact that until very recently she had not seen fit to create a single academic chair "exclusively devoted to the teaching of international law." By 1916 several of the lawyers were contending that only by going to war against the principal outlaw, Germany, or at the least, severing relations, could America establish the validity of international law.[53] In 1917, the American Society of International Law offered its services to the government in the prosecution of a war "which is essentially one for the vindication of law." The following year its executive council decided to hold no annual meeting, since "the only great question of international law today is whether the law shall continue to exist," and this question would be answered on the battlefield, not through discussion.[54]

But if the fate of international law lay temporarily in the hands of the Allied armies, still there was the encouraging prospect that the defeat of the nations embodying international lawlessness might clear the way for a renaissance of international law and a rejuvenation of the world court plan. Thus, although Root confessed "a strong distaste for much talk" about problems of international law and Scott argued that public meetings for the discussion of international law would "hold us up to ridicule," anticipation of the needs of the postwar period stimulated quiet but active promotion of the lawyers' program for international relations throughout the period from 1914 to 1919.[55] In 1915 James Brown Scott had sufficiently recovered his optimism to comment confidently on the growth and "enlarged influence and impor-

[53] ASIL, *Proceedings, 1916*, pp. 5, 17, 18-50, 92-97; Carnegie Endowment, *Year Book for 1915*, p. 105.

[54] ASIL, *Proceedings, 1917*, p. 25; *ibid., 1918*, p. 14; "Minutes of the Meeting of the Board of Trustees," 19 Apr. 1917, pp. 59-61, 111, CEIP Papers, CUL.

[55] ASIL, *Proceedings, 1918*, pp. 15-16.

tance" of international law. If the work of the Division of International Law had been "somewhat checked in Europe," its work in the Western Hemisphere—in developing national societies in Latin America and a unifying American Institute of International Law—were moving ahead with increased speed.[56] Scott became chairman of the Joint State and Navy Neutrality Board, charged with advising the administration on matters of international law. Although this responsibility absorbed much of Scott's time, it served to give the division another concrete program to pursue in international law and tied the endowment even closer to the State Department. The endowment even provided the staff, officers, and meeting rooms for most of the Neutrality Board's work. Scott still found time to push forward such other projects as the publication of the text of the Hague Conventions, the implementation of the report of the Conference of Teachers of International Law, and the publication of treaties of arbitration and classics of international law.[57]

A few of the international lawyers were sufficiently shaken by the war to abandon their previous insistence upon nonentanglement, nonenforcement of arbitral or judicial decisions, and reliance upon public opinion alone as an international sanction. For this group the court-centered program of the League to Enforce Peace proved attractive. The majority of the international lawyers, however, were more likely to be attracted to the World's Court League which promoted a postwar program confined to an international court of justice and the codification of international law.[58] For many of the lawyers the program of the League to Enforce Peace, which rested upon the threat of organized military or economic coercion, remained an unacceptable one. The requirements of such a league would lead to the organization of the world on political rather than judicial lines. It would sacrifice

[56] Carnegie Endowment, *Year Book for 1915*, pp. 25, 103, 106.

[57] *Ibid.*, pp. 26, 31-32, 106-50.

[58] Thirteen of those I have included in the "international lawyers group" (see chap. two, p. 40) were on the provisional committee of one hundred for the organization of the League to Enforce Peace. Several of these, however, later withdrew from activity in the league or protested against the provision for coercion. See Bartlett, *The League to Enforce Peace*, pp. 37, 215-18 and John Bassett Moore to William Short, 3 July 1915, LEP Collection, Lowell Papers, HA. On the World's Court League, see Charles Herbert Levermore, *Samuel Train Dutton, A Biography* (New York 1922), pp. 166-70; John Hays Hammond, *The Autobiography of John Hays Hammond* (New York 1935), II, 617, 621-23; and Warren F. Kuehl, *Seeking World Order: The United States and International Organization to 1920* (Nashville 1969), pp. 196-97, 208-9, 248.

some of the main virtues of judicial organization—nonentanglement and complete national freedom of action.[59]

Under the leadership of lawyers Root and Scott, the Carnegie Endowment criticized the League to Enforce Peace and refused to support its efforts with endowment funds. George Kirchwey, one of the founders of the American Society of International Law, tried to prevent the league from adopting the provision calling for the use of force in its platform. Scott, the most active leader of the international lawyers, remarked privately that the league "seems to me to be nothing more than a Holy Alliance to use force, and to cut throats if need be, in the sacred cause of conciliation, arbitration and judicial decision." He freely denounced the "viciousness of the League" in threatening to destroy all the work that had gone into laying the groundwork for a self-executing world judicial system since the First Hague Conference. Other prominent leaders among the international lawyers such as John Bassett Moore, Joseph Choate, George Gray, and Simeon Baldwin joined Root and Scott in their refusal to support the League to Enforce Peace. By 1917 the Carnegie Endowment had cut off support for the New York Peace Society because its secretary, William H. Short, was working primarily for the League to Enforce Peace.[60]

Theodore Marburg, an early convert to sanctions, became one of the principal founders and leaders of the league. But in 1917

---

[59] For examples of resistance by leading international lawyers to the League to Enforce Peace Program see ASIL, *Proceedings, 1915*, pp. 5-6; *ibid., 1916*, p. 153; *ibid., 1917*, pp. 101-7; and James Brown Scott, *Peace Through Justice: Three Papers on International Justice and the Means of Attaining it* (New York 1917), pp. 51-53. See also Bartlett, *The League to Enforce Peace*, pp. 37, 43; Kuehl, *Seeking World Order*, pp. 206-13; and Herman, *Eleven Against War*, p. 47. On complaints by leaders of the League to Enforce Peace of the lawyers' opposition, see William H. Short to A. Lawrence Lowell, 7 July and 28 July 1915 and Lowell to Short, 13 July 1915, LEP Collection, Lowell Papers, HA.

[60] Kuehl, *Seeking World Order*, p. 205; *The Survey*, 34 (26 June 1915), 293; George W. Kirchwey, "The Inconsistency of Trying to Enforce Peace," *Mohonk Conference, 1916*, pp. 131-36; James Brown Scott to William I. Hull, 11 Feb. 1916, Box 3, Hull Papers, FHL; Arthur D. Call to Benjamin Trueblood, 1 Mar. 1916, Box 8, APS Papers, SCPC; Carnegie Endowment for International Peace, "Minutes of the Annual Meeting of the Board of Trustees," 20 Apr. 1917, p. 149, CEIP Papers, CUL. Within the Carnegie Endowment, Oscar Straus was the sole figure among the international lawyers to promote the League to Enforce Peace plan. Carnegie Endowment for International Peace, "Minutes of the Meeting of the Board of Trustees," 21 Apr. 1916, p. 56 and 19-20 Apr. 1917, pp. 38-43, 53-55, 237-44, CEIP Papers, CUL. For a survey of Elihu Root's views during the period see Martin David Dubin, "Elihu Root and the Advocacy of a League of Nations, 1914-1917," *Western Political Quarterly*, 19 (Sept. 1966), 439-55. Root never endorsed sanctions in any but the vaguest terms.

even Marburg began to reassert the lawyers' position. In private discussions he and several other international lawyers in the League to Enforce Peace drafted and presented a report that sacrificed nothing of the lawyers' prewar plans. The report called for a true Court of Justice, patterned upon the Supreme Court, determining its own jurisdiction, establishing law and precedent without relying on sanctions, and composed of judges nominated by national legal associations, appointed for life, and paid $50,000 per year.[61] Within the administration, Secretary of State Robert Lansing never abandoned his preference for an international judicial system based upon codified law. He sought to have State Department experts, among whom his adviser, James Brown Scott, would undoubtedly have been included, draft a postwar treaty plan. If Wilson had not cut short this project, refusing to allow the treaty planning to fall into the hands of the lawyers, the State Department might well have produced another version of the international lawyers' program.[62]

These refusals on the part of a number of international lawyers to depart from a purely judicial program carried over easily into opposition to Wilson's League of Nations. Many of them had strictly partisan reasons for opposing any league championed by Wilson, and the administration hardly placated the lawyers when it appointed none of the established leaders among the international lawyers to the International Law Division of the informal commission of experts preparing for the peace conference.[63] But the lawyers had ample reasons beyond Republican partisanship and personal pique for opposing the League of Nations. As Elihu Root complained, the treaty had barely mentioned international law and had treated the whole Hague system as "scrapped." Root appeared before the American Society of International Law in 1919 to propose amendments to the League of Nations charter that would reestablish the central position of a court at The Hague and provide for a general conference to determine the

---

61 "Résumé of Discussions at a Private Dinner held in the Century Club, New York City, on Invitation of Theodore Marburg," 8 June 1917, typed minutes, General Correspondence, LEP Collection, Lowell Papers, HA.

62 Daniel M. Smith, "Robert Lansing," in Norman A. Graebner, *An Uncertain Tradition: American Secretaries of State in the Twentieth Century* (New York 1961), pp. 121-22.

63 For the membership of the international law section of what came to be known as "The Inquiry" see Lawrence E. Gelfand, *The Inquiry: American Preparations for Peace, 1917-1919* (New Haven 1963), p. 341. At least two of the established participants in the American Society of International Law, Chandler P. Anderson and Alpheus H. Snow, were rejected as members of The Inquiry for reasons which included their having criticized the administration. See Gelfand, pp. 72-73.

principles and rules of international law. The majority of international lawyers continued to insist that only an international organization centered around a court and based upon law rather than political expediency was acceptable. Only such an international organization would build stability slowly and surely while guarding American freedom of action.[64]

The commitment to research and international law carried the Carnegie Endowment through the period of American neutrality by giving it relatively uncontroversial programs upon which to fasten its attention. With the decision for American intervention in 1917, the endowment threw itself headlong into the war activity which many of its trustees had impatiently awaited. There was no dissent among the trustees when Judge George Gray insisted that they must "associate themselves" with the "dominant spirit" and "patriotic impulses" of the country. James Brown Scott offered the services of the Division of International Law to the State Department as a new Bureau of International Law and reported that he had been requested by the State Department to prepare a "justification of the United States in entering this war. . . ." Elihu Root remarked that he took no interest in any discussions about international agreements and peace programs at the end of the war. He was interested only in the destruction of the German government. The trustees formalized their sentiments in a resolution which insisted that "the most effectual means of promoting durable international peace is to prosecute the war against the Imperial Government of Germany to final victory for democracy. . . ."[65]

These open expressions of belligerency by the Carnegie Endowment only reemphasized how far its course of action since 1914 had separated it from the active elements of the peace movement. In focusing its attention on research and international law the endowment had avoided all immediate issues of peace raised by the war and had maintained stability and composure during the critical years of 1914-1917. But in so doing it had also revealed itself as cowardly, irrelevant, and reactionary in the eyes of those who came forward to drive the peace movement in new directions after 1914.

If the leaders of the international law societies and the economists and lawyers of the Carnegie Endowment opted for the deliber-

---

[64] ASIL, *Proceedings, 1919*, pp. 45, 50; Herman, *Eleven Against War*, pp. 46, 48-49, 52-53, 77-78.

[65] "Minutes of the Meeting of the Board of Trustees," 21 Apr. 1916, pp. 28-30, 33-34, 19 Apr. 1917, pp. 12, 19, 26, 48, 56-57, 59-61 and 20 Apr. 1917, p. 177, CEIP Papers, CUL.

ate, long view and the other prewar organizations largely disengaged themselves from immediate peace activities, what role could the businessmen in the peace movement be expected to play? Recently the objects of special solicitation and recruitment efforts by the peace societies, they were the supposed generators of action and practicality within the movement. How would they respond when prewar abstractions about the interdependence of business and peace were put to the sterner test of actual wartime conditions? Suppose that war did bring the predicted dire effects upon commerce and business conditions. Would businessmen insist upon immediate action by the peace organizations to which they belonged? Would they promote special programs of their own to attempt to bring the war to an end?

The first reaction of the business community to the war, as reflected in the business journals, was to find the worst predictions of economic dislocations confirmed. With the stock exchange closed, gold flowing abroad, a crisis impending in the cotton market, and foreign trade disrupted, the economic costs of war seemed fully apparent. *The Commercial and Financial Chronicle* called the war "a peril the like of which has not been witnessed since the dawn of history," and *Bradstreet's* warned that the "economic waste of war" would be felt by all. The *Wall Street Journal*, equating "the age of business" with "the age of Peace" lamented the outbreak of world conflict just when finance and commerce "had begun to make their opposition to war effective." It recalled the waste of war and the economic burden of armaments and held up the present crisis as an "object lesson" to "economists who think a European war would stimulate business here. . . ." *The Banker's Magazine* described the war as a "total financial disaster" and a spokesman for J. P. Morgan & Co. remarked, "It is idle to say that America will not be hurt by a general European war."[66] But despite the financial chaos and economic recession of the summer of 1914, the business journals recovered their composure with amazing speed. Some even began to find cause for cautious optimism, and the reasoning behind this optimism did not lead toward any desire to bring the war to an early end.

Although foreign trade had always been depicted as the probable major casualty of war, it was in overseas trade opportunities that spokesmen for business found cause for consolation and even for enthusiasm. The position of the belligerents in international

[66] *The Commercial and Financial Chronicle*, 99 (1 Aug. 1914), 292-93; *Bradstreet's*, 42 (8 Aug. 1914), 508; *The Banker's Magazine*, 89 (Sept. 1914), 211; *Wall Street Journal*, 29 July 1914, 1:2, 30 July 1914, 1:2 and 1 Aug. 1914, 1:2, 2:3, 2:4.

trade had been weakened by the war. The Central Powers were almost entirely cut off from former overseas markets. Theories explaining how an economic injury to one was an injury to all had seemed true enough in abstract, before one knew *who* was going to be injured, but now that war was a reality it was time to calculate how general misfortune might yet be turned to American advantage. "This is not our trouble, it is our opportunity," advised the New York financier, A. Barton Hepburn. Hepburn called upon "merchants, manufacturers, bankers and statesmen" to cooperate to "take and hold" the former overseas trade of Germany which was now at the mercy of the first nation to move aggressively to obtain it. The *Wall Street Journal* quoted an unidentified young Wall Street banker as suggesting the possibility that war in Europe might bring a business boom and unprecedented prosperity in the United States. "War is a great evil," the *Journal* commented, "but an evil wind may sometimes blow good to somebody." The foreign manager of one New York firm proclaimed the advent of "the export opportunity of a lifetime" and painted for American businessmen an enticing picture of the opportunities of entering "waiting and eager markets . . . practically unopposed." *Bradstreet's* reassured its readers that it was "not unnatural" that there should be discussion of the economic advantages America might gain from Europe's disaster.[67]

Almost single-mindedly the business journals turned their attention to the new opportunities for the United States in the South American trade. *The Nation's Business* immediately pointed out the need to "reassure" the South American nations and to handle all their trade. In *Iron Age* the discussion of how to promote and finance greater South American trade became a weekly topic. *Iron Age* exhorted its business audience to take over the export and import trade and financing of South America and published a nation-by-nation survey of Latin American business conditions and opportunities. By the end of August 1914 *The Commercial and Financial Chronicle* was describing South America as "a fruitful field for exploitation." With Europe preoccupied and her shipping disrupted, the United States could gain a dominant position in the South American trade. United States' trade with South America had been increasing, *The Commercial and*

[67] *Wall Street Journal*, 1 Aug. 1914, 2:4, 7 Aug. 1914, 3:2; John Chapman (pseud.), "America's Trade Opportunity," *The System*, 26 (1914), 236-37; *Bradstreet's*, 42 (8 Aug. 1914), 508; 42 (15 Aug. 1914), 521. The statement by Hepburn is quoted in Robert Wiebe, *Businessmen and Reform: A Study of the Progressive Movement* (Cambridge, Mass. 1962), p. 145. See also *The Nation's Business*, 2 (15 Sept. 1914), 1 and *The Commercial and Financial Chronicle*, 99 (3 Oct. 1914), 922, 924.

Financial Chronicle acknowledged later, but there was no reason why the United States should not freeze out England entirely and capture it *all.* By mid-August, the *Wall Street Journal* was already giving space to those who considered it necessary to preach more conservative methods and a more systematic approach to partly counteract the "hysterical attempt on the part of American business men to plunge headlong into the Latin-American field." Certainly the *Journal* itself had been speculating freely and regularly on the opportunities in South America and the need for an expanded American merchant marine and the expansion of American overseas banking. By the time that the initial enthusiasm for heroic advances in the South American trade began to subside, trade opportunities in supplying the European belligerents had developed to sustain business optimism.[68]

Amid the growing enthusiasm for the exploitation of wartime advantages, American businessmen refused to weep over European misfortunes. There was nothing "callous or inhuman," wrote one business spokesman, "in our trying to meet and to profit by a situation not of our contriving and emphatically not of our desiring." Business had wished and worked for peace. It refused to take any responsibility for European madness. If America should prosper while European business and trade was suffering, that only served to add to the axiom that "war hurts business" the additional theorem that "avoidance of war helps business." Meanwhile Americans need feel no compunction about helping to teach Europe a very lengthy lesson in the economic effects of war by vigorously pursuing what E. L. Howe of Marshall Field called "a most remarkable opportunity" for American businessmen.[69] John Barrett, head of the Pan American Union, came to a similar conclusion but found it more comfortable to talk about expansion of American trade in Latin America in terms of duty rather than of opportunity: "While everybody must profoundly regret that a condition of war and the sufferings of European nations . . . should in any way be exploited for the selfish gain of the United States, its business interests have a duty and responsibility in this

---

68 *The Nation's Business,* 2 (15 Aug. 1914), 2; 2 (15 Sept. 1914), 1; 2 (15 Oct. 1914), 1, 3; *Iron Age,* 94 (6 Aug. 1914 to 15 Oct. 1915), 354-55, 405-6, 455-58, 473-76, 586, 587, 624-25, 692, 743, 798; *The Commercial and Financial Chronicle,* 99 (29 Aug. 1914), 566; 99 (31 Oct. 1914), 1258; 99 (7 Nov. 1914), 1340; *Wall Street Journal,* 3 Aug. 1914, 2:2; 8 Aug. 1914, 2:3; 10 Aug. 1914, 3:3; 12 Aug. 1914, 8:3; 13 Aug. 1914, 8:2; 14 Aug. 1914, 1:2, 2:4; 15 Aug. 1914, 3:3.

69 Chapman, "America's Trade Opportunity," 237; *The System,* 26 (1914), 349; *Iron Age,* 96 (5 Aug. 1915), 319; *The Commercial and Financial Chronicle,* 99 (15 Aug. 1914), 432-33; 99 (29 Aug. 1914), 564; 99 (19 Sept. 1914), 772.

crisis which must be met even if it may bring them vast material benefits."[70]

As the war continued some business spokesmen began to see foreign trade expansion as a race against time in which American business would benefit if the war was prolonged. In 1914 Joseph French Johnson, an economist, had implied that the threat of sudden peace made it advisable for businessmen to take quick profits and avoid long-range investments. But by late 1915 the war had clearly taken on a less ephemeral cast. Members of the International Trade Conference now denounced quick profits and urged that America take advantage of a "unique strategic position" with foreign customers "at our mercy." American business should establish lasting connections with satisfied customers and promote consolidation of its newly won "financial supremacy of the world." One speaker at the 1915 conference, exasperated with the nation's inept trade expansion, complained of having "lost already fifteen months," and another warned that the opportunity for extending American foreign trade "will not present itself again."[71] Many discussions of the advancement of United States' interests in world markets contained the implication that it would be best if the competitive advantages created by wartime conditions did not come to an early end. Business journals frequently predicted that a "trade war" would break out after the European war ended. The prospect of a postwar economic struggle in which the United States might relinquish wartime gains did not encourage American businessmen to hope for an early peace.[72]

With American foreign trade interests hopeful of capturing a larger share of neutral markets, especially in South America, and fearful of intensified trade competition from Europe after the war, their lack of interest in efforts to bring the war to an early end was not surprising. Nor did other American businessmen

[70] Pan American Union, "Special Memorandum: The South America-United States Situation as Affected by the European War," 8 Aug. 1914, Division of Intercourse and Education, 1914, CEIP Papers, CUL; *Wall Street Journal*, 8 Aug. 1914, 2:4.

[71] Joseph French Johnson, *The War and American Business* (New York 1914), pp. 12, 14; *Proceedings of the International Trade Conference* (New York 1915), pp. 163, 183, 215-17, 220, 229, 255, 306, 315-16, 324, 357-58.

[72] *Iron Age*, 94 (18 Mar. 1915), 616, 631-32; 95 (1 Apr. 1915), 746; 96 (5 Aug. 1915), 319; 96 (14 Oct. 1915), 884; 97 (1 Jan. 1916), 154-55; 98 (9 Nov. 1916), 1064; 98 (7 Dec. 1916), 1294; *The Commercial and Financial Chronicle*, 100 (20 Mar. 1915), 930; 103 (7 Oct. 1916), 1256-57; *The Nation's Business*, 5 (Jan. 1917), 7-9; 5 (Feb. 1917), 8-12. See also George W. Perkins, "We Are as Unprepared for Peace as We Are for War," pamphlet reprint of address to Bankers' Association, 12 Oct. 1915, pp. 4, 6-7.

play any significant role in organizations seeking peace overtures or neutral mediation. Henry Ford did make one dramatic attempt to stop the war through his promotion of an official conference to be publicized and set in motion by the sailing of a "peace ship," but his brief venture gained no support from other businessmen. Several business journals began to conclude as early as 1914 that the war in Europe would accentuate a "tendency toward conservatism" at home and reduce the domestic agitation against business interests. Indeed, one of the first reactions of the *Wall Street Journal* to the European war had been to recognize the "chance to dissipate the prejudices against Wall Street created by dishonest politicians," to assert that the American people were turning to Wall Street for leadership and rejecting the Pujo Committee and the reformers, and to insist that trade expansion and prosperity might come during the war only if there was "confidence that business would receive fair treatment."[73] Although certain individual business and trade interests were badly hurt, the general economic effects of the war upon America were salutary and the prospects of trade expansion promising. Under such circumstances the specific economic motives for a campaign by businessmen to shorten the war were clearly lacking.

Of course the businessmen who rose to influence in such peace organizations as the New York Peace Society or the Carnegie Endowment for International Peace were not motivated solely, or in many cases even primarily, by business considerations. But many of them shared the Anglophile sentiments of the other leading members of these societies, and nearly all held common assumptions about the impropriety and impracticality of radical actions and highly controversial positions. They found the methods, personnel, and programs of most of the emerging peace organizations of 1915 distastefully spectacular, dangerously radical, and clearly impractical. Except for lone mavericks like George Foster Peabody, or those with deep pro-German or anti-Russian sentiments like James Speyer and Jacob Schiff, the businessmen of the prewar peace movements did not join or support such new organizations as the American Union Against Milita-

[73] *Wall Street Journal*, 31 July 1914, 1:2; 1 Aug. 1914, 1:2, 2:4. On expectations of a more favorable public attitude toward business, see Harold C. Syrett, "The Business Press and American Neutrality, 1914-1917," *Mississippi Valley Historical Review*, 32 (Sept. 1945), 216-17. On Ford's efforts, see Louis P. Lochner, *America's Don Quixote* (London 1924) and Louis P. Lochner, *Always the Unexpected* (New York 1956). Of the delegates who sailed on Ford's ship none could be identified as businessmen.

rism, the American Neutral Conference Committee, or the Emergency Peace Federation.[74]

Despite the disinclination of businessmen in the prewar peace organizations to urge economic measures to end the war or to promote any particular program of their own, a few signs of a special business outlook toward peace did persist after 1914. For the most part these programs and organizations stressed the particular capabilities of business groups to deal with what they viewed as the most important international problems. Edward A. Filene, a leading Boston merchant and businessman-reformer, promoted through the Chamber of Commerce of the United States a referendum for a League of Nations. The program proposed in Filene's referendum differed from that of the League to Enforce Peace only in its emphasis upon "more comprehensive and better-defined sea law," its stress upon the role of businessmen in the peace movement thus far, its concern with the economic dangers to American business of an unsatisfactory postwar settlement, and its stress upon economic nonintercourse as a means of compelling nations to submit controversies to adjudication.[75]

Charles L. Bernheimer, another businessman and a member of the New York Peace Society, stressed the analogy between the businessman's principle of arbitrating commercial disputes and the need for mediation and arbitration of international crises. The peace conference, he argued, should be composed of businessmen and other representative persons, not just diplomats and military men. Roger Babson, the business statistician, sought to bring new effectiveness to the peace movement with an organization composed entirely of shippers and manufacturers. Another organization under Babson's leadership, the Society to Eliminate Economic Causes of War, brought together bankers, manufacturers,

[74] Of the 193 businessmen surveyed in the membership of the New York Peace Society in 1913-1914, only three could be discovered on the various lists of officers, advisory committees, and lists of members of these new, New York City-centered organizations. One poll of a wider segment of the business community, a survey of the chambers of commerce by *The Nation's Business*, reported votes of 970 to 8 for "general preparedness," 952 to 10 for "an adequate navy," and 889 to 56 for universal military training. Such sentiments hardly aligned them with the American Union Against Militarism or other similar antiwar organizations of 1916.

[75] "Referendum on the Report of the Special Committee on Economic Results of the War and American Business," *International Conciliation*, No. 97 (Dec. 1915), 3-17; *The Survey*, 35 (22 Jan. 1916), 473; Edward A. Filene to William H. Short, 29 Oct. 1915, LEP Collection, Lowell Papers, HA. On Filene's continuing view of the importance of businessmen in the movement for a league, see Edward A. Filene to A. Lawrence Lowell, 5 Sept. 1917, LEP Collection, Lowell Papers, HA and *The Nation's Business*, 5 (Jan. 1917), 7-9; 5 (Oct. 1917), 28-29.

and shippers in a campaign to internationalize and neutralize trade routes, establish international controls over immigration, and eliminate unfair tariff and trade barriers.[76]

None of these programs resulted in any continued and expanded role for businessmen in the peace movement. Leaders of the League to Enforce Peace at first opposed Filene's referendum because it emphasized economic sanctions and diverted attention from the league's own proposals for ultimate military sanctions. Later they decided, without enthusiasm, to support the referendum, but its passage never led to further business action.[77] Bernheimer's proposal never found organized support and Babson was later to reflect that his "hard-headed, practical businessmen" had not proved effective promoters of even limited economic proposals for peace. The businessmen, Babson recalled, had known that the principles of his society of bankers, shippers, and manufacturers were sound:

> They knew that the ideas of most pacifists were both impractical and dangerous. Therefore they rallied to my international program. . . . Unfortunately, however, the business of most of these men was definitely dependent upon tariffs, immigration restrictions, control of trade routes and various other things which we knew must be broken down before the world would ever enjoy peace. In their libraries they were wholehearted members of our little society, but in their business they were unconsciously traitors to our principles.[78]

But it was not only the specific economic interests of Babson's businessmen that dictated the quiescent or conservative role of American businessmen in the peace movement after 1914. Businessmen in the movement had never united behind a particular program of their own. Much of their support had been sincere but superficial enthusiasm for a respectable, morally satisfying cause based upon appealing but untested abstractions. Many a businessman had supported the movement more out of a sense of

[76] Charles L. Bernheimer, "Peace Proposal: A Business Man's Plan for Settling the War in Europe," enclosure in Charles L. Bernheimer to David Starr Jordan, 1 Apr. 1915, Box 3, Jordan Papers, HI; Bernheimer to Benjamin Trueblood, 19 Apr. 1915, Box 5, APS Papers, SCPC; Roger W. Babson, *Actions and Reactions* (New York 1935), pp. 190-91; Roger W. Babson to David Starr Jordan, 11 Jan. 1915, Box 3, Jordan Papers, HI.

[77] Samuel J. Elder to A. Lawrence Lowell, 16 Oct. 1915 and Lowell to Elder, 18 Oct. 1915, WPF Collection, Lowell Papers, HA; Lowell to William H. Short, 23 Nov. and 26 Nov. 1915, Short to Lowell, 22 Nov. 1915, LEP Collection, Lowell Papers, HA.

[78] Babson, *Actions and Reactions*, p. 197.

social responsibility and philanthropic self-satisfaction than out of economic considerations. After 1914 the American businessman in the peace movement found little reason to transform his earlier commitment into any radical antiwar position. Insofar as he looked upon the international situation through the narrow prism of his business interests he found no compelling reasons to seek to stop or limit the war by economic restrictions or neutral mediation. When he examined the international scene through the broader social, political, and cultural perspectives he shared with his fellow members of the prewar peace societies, he was likely to reach the same conclusions. His vaunted sense of practicality told him that nothing *could* be done about stopping the European war; and his sympathy with the Allied cause, or an adversion to controversial action, told him that nothing *should* be done.

The disinclination of businessmen who had joined the prewar peace societies to support the new antiwar organizations of 1915-1917 was no act of apostasy. Their goal had been economic and social stability based upon the absence of class antagonism and international disorder. They could hardly have been expected to sympathize with programs of peace predicated upon further domestic and international change, and proposed by those who had been leaders in disruptive social and political agitation at home.

Of course the responses of the various prewar peace societies and foundations, as organizations, or the general reactions of international lawyers and businessmen, as groups, do not account for all the courses of action taken by leaders of the prewar peace movement. In all organizations and groups there were exceptions. Even among those who fit the generalizations there were significant individual variations. Some members of prewar peace societies quietly or dramatically severed all connection with a cause they now believed totally discredited. A few sought and failed to lead their particular organization to a more active and dissenting position. Others, while maintaining their place in older organizations, drifted between November 1914 and February 1915 into such short-lived new organizations as the American League to Limit Armaments in New York and the Emergency Peace Federation in Chicago, which seemed to promise bolder immediate action. A few of the members of the latter groups assumed a more dissident stance by moving on into the more durable peace organizations that were to dominate the active part of the peace movement between 1915 and 1917.

Significant among those who followed the last alternative were a handful of men and women who proved flexible enough and independent enough to maintain at least tenuous relations with both the old peace organizations and those on the cutting edge of the transformed peace movement. Several dozen such figures could probably be discovered whose activities spanned the obvious and widening rifts within the peace movement. Among them would certainly be listed such leaders as Hamilton Holt, David Starr Jordan, Emily Balch, Louis Lochner, Frederick Lynch, Charles Macfarland, Sidney Gulick, Fannie Fern Andrews, Lucia Ames Mead, George Foster Peabody, Anna Garlin Spencer, George Kirchwey, and Oswald Garrison Villard.

Even within this unique group of individuals there were divergent patterns of action. A few, like Jordan, followed a largely independent course, associating themselves only intermittently with a number of organizations. Jordan himself voiced a more and more radical critique of American foreign policy as intervention loomed, thus cutting himself off from the older peace organizations. The trustees of the World Peace Foundation voted to remove him as a director in 1916.[79] Others, like O. G. Villard and George Foster Peabody, allowed their backgrounds of absolute pacifism to carry them further and further into association with social radicals in the peace movement. They, too, soon put themselves beyond the pale of the old peace organizations.[80]

Frederick Lynch, Charles Macfarland, and Sidney Gulick formed an effective triumvirate which held the interrelated Church Peace Union, the Federal Council of Churches, and the World Alliance of Churches upon a middle course in the peace movement during 1915 and part of 1916. The liberal influence of a moderate social gospel position enabled these organizations to remain in sympathetic contact with the more radical peace organizations, at least for a time. Lucia Ames Mead, Fannie Fern Andrews, and Anna Garlin Spencer found new and greater opportunities for leadership by women in the new peace organizations, only to conclude eventually that they must back away from the more radical expressions of dissent. George Kirchwey, who was named president of the American Peace Society late in 1916, had

[79] "Minutes of a Special Meeting of the Board of Trustees," 8 Jan. 1916, WPF Papers, SCPC; Filene, "The World Peace Foundation and Progressivism: 1910-1918," p. 501. On Jordan's activities between 1914 and 1917 see Charles Roland Marchand, "David Starr Jordan and the Peace Movement in America, 1913-1917," M.A. Thesis, Stanford University 1960, *passim.*

[80] For an example of this process, see the description of Villard's partial transformation in Michael Wreszin, *Oswald Garrison Villard: Pacifist at War* (Bloomington, Ind. 1965), esp. pp. 36-37, 75-80.

managed to participate both in active peace groups and organizations seeking only a postwar league. But his efforts to prevent war with Germany in early 1917 brought the violent disapproval of the officers of the Carnegie Endowment who eliminated him from the presidency of the American Peace Society by refusing to renew the society's annual subvention.[81]

The youthful Louis Lochner and the middle-aged Emily Balch were both radicalized by their experiences in the attempt, in the face of ridicule and condemnation, to put into action the idea of continuous mediation by an unofficial conference of neutrals. Hamilton Holt, although he gave his main sympathies and energies to the League to Enforce Peace, still attempted to keep a foot in the more pacifist camp by participating in the American Union Against Militarism and the American Neutral Conference Committee. But Holt's interest in the immediate action organizations had already dwindled before the League to Enforce Peace forced him to withdraw from all other peace organizations late in 1916. And Balch and Lochner were by then taking positions that were countenanced by none of the prewar peace organizations.[82]

A number of these men and women were to play important roles in the peace movement during the period of neutrality and American intervention. But so dramatic were the changes in the peace movement between 1914 and 1917 that very few, even of the most flexible of these figures, were able to bridge the widening gap that separated the prewar peace organizations from the more radical groups that began to take shape after 1914. The peace movement, so recently transformed into an affluent, prestigious, and "practical" reform, was now, in response to the war crisis, about to undergo another major transformation.

[81] George W. Kirchwey to Anna Garlin Spencer, 20 May 1917, Box 1, Anna Garlin Spencer Collection, SCPC. On the three women and the leaders of the Church Peace Union, see below, chaps. six and nine respectively.

[82] On Holt's activities, see Kuehl, *Hamilton Holt*, pp. 106-33. On Lochner and Balch, see below, chaps. six through eight. Lochner, one of the most active young officers in the American Peace Society, was forced out of the society in late 1915 when he led the drive for the Ford Peace Ship expedition and the campaign for continuous mediation. John Mez to David Starr Jordan, 9 Dec. 1915, Jordan Papers, HI; Louis P. Lochner to Arthur D. Call, 28 Nov. 1915, Box 8, APS Papers, SCPC.

CHAPTER SIX

The Maternal Instinct

O<small>N</small> 29 August 1914 fifteen hundred women in mourning dress marched silently down Fifth Avenue in New York City to the beat of muffled drums. Crowds interrupted their silence with applause as the leaders of the parade displayed their peace flag, a large white banner with a dove carrying an olive branch in the center. The women's funereal but dramatic protest against the war in Europe marked the beginning of a remarkable transformation of the peace movement in the United States.[1]

Within a year after the Woman's Peace Parade a multitude of new leaders and societies emerged to challenge the political and methodological biases of earlier peace organizations. Prewar leaders had viewed their peace campaign as a movement for stability, order, and the extension abroad of established American institutions; the new leaders after 1914 came to visualize the peace movement as a vehicle of change, of economic and political democratization. As their standard for the reform of international relations, these new leaders looked to social and political ideals that they insisted were still quite imperfectly embodied in present American institutions. While the older emphasis upon order and stability persisted vigorously in such organizations as the League to Enforce Peace, new groups explored the full range of possible connections between peace, particular domestic reforms, and political radicalism.

The Woman's Peace Parade, organized within less than a month after the outbreak of the war, actually gave only the slightest intimations of the changes in the peace movement that were soon to come. The impetus for the parade had stemmed not from the desire to promote a specific peace program, but from "an imperative necessity for expression."[2] The urgency of making a timely protest overrode attempts to formulate a set of policies. Most of the leaders of the Parade Committee were content to view the

[1] *New York Times*, 30 Aug. 1914, II, 11:3.

[2] "Minutes of the Peace Parade Committee," 12 Aug. 1914, p. 2, Fanny Garrison Villard Papers, Houghton Library, Harvard University.

parade as having three broad purposes: to express horror of war and sympathy with suffering in Europe; to emphasize the particular complaint of women against war; and to urge President Wilson to continue his efforts to offer mediation.[3] But despite the modesty of its proposals, the Woman's Peace Parade did mark a departure in style, and to a lesser extent in leadership and content, from the prewar peace organizations.

The Parade Committee's most apparent departure was in method. Several of the older organizations had made quiet protests through regular channels, but none had taken dramatic public action. The women, many of them veterans of woman suffrage, social reform, and labor organizations did not share the distrust of demonstrations and the fear of indiscreet action that inhibited leaders of older peace organizations. The new departures in style symbolized by the Peace Parade suggested also the possibility of changes in political philosophy. In these years the tactic of appealing for popular support through public demonstrations had been frequently adopted by labor and reform groups. Leaders of the older peace societies were apt to view such methods as demagogic and undignified. They sought to exert influence quietly and judiciously through official channels, an approach long preferred by promoters of more conservative causes.

Not only had the Parade Committee acted dramatically while the older peace societies remained relatively silent, but it had begun to enlist a new leadership. The chairman of the Parade Committee, Mrs. Henry Villard, the daughter of abolitionist William Lloyd Garrison and a discontented member of the New York Peace Society, proclaimed, "this is a time for a new peace movement."[4] Of the fourteen vice-chairmen of the committee, all from New York, only one was affiliated with the New York Peace Society; only nine of a committee of 121 supporting the parade belonged to that organization. Among the many women who were new to the peace movement were active social workers and settlement house residents, leaders of the Women's Trade Union League, presidents of women's clubs and veteran woman suffrage workers.[5] Some of the club and society women and the repre-

[3] *Ibid.*, pp. 2, 19-23, 25; "Rough draft of two-page memorandum of Woman's Peace Parade," F. G. Villard Papers, HL; *New York Times*, 7 Aug. 1914, 7:6 and 8 Aug. 1914, 4:2.

[4] "Minutes of the Peace Parade Committee," 12 Aug. 1914, p. 10, F. G. Villard Papers, HL. For Mrs. Villard's opinion of peace organizations like the New York Peace Society, see Mrs. Henry Villard, "A Real Peace Society," printed copy of address, 21 Sept. 1914, F. G. Villard Papers, HL.

[5] A list of parade supporters was derived by combining lists from "Woman's Peace Parade Committee," typed sheet, F. G. Villard Papers, HL and the *New York*

sentatives of women's patriotic societies who participated in the Peace Parade proved to be only momentary recruits to the peace movement, but those with reform backgrounds often became part of the continuing leadership of the new post-1914 organizations.

The Parade Committee's most radical innovation was its insistence upon the special mission of women. In confining their membership to women, the Peace Parade Committee and later the Woman's Peace Party tapped not only a source of energetic workers and leaders largely untouched by the older peace organizations, but also a source of potential radicalization. The committee drew upon women already active in public affairs, many of whose instincts for social and political agitation had been sharpened by the stimulation and frustrations of campaigns for woman suffrage, social reform programs, or labor legislation. Some of them deeply resented a political system and a government controlled exclusively by men. Many were hardened to political controversy and some may have acquired a positive taste for the advocacy of unpopular causes. Self-consciously part of an underprivileged group, these well-educated but underchallenged women displayed an affinity for egalitarian ideals and radical programs unknown in the earlier peace organizations.

The organizers were intent that the parade should be carried through as a "feminine achievement." In response to inquiries about the participation of men and men's organizations the women replied innocently that the parade idea had grown so rapidly that men had simply been overlooked. "The idea was originated by women," the committee noted, "and if it appears the men wish to make a protest they will have to organize a parade of their own."[6] But the men had not merely been overlooked; the logic of the women's protest demanded their exclusion. The parade and later the Woman's Peace Party based their protests on one primary article of faith—the solidarity of all women in an instinctive but rational opposition to war. The idea that women had a special

---

Times, 17 Aug. 1914, 5:6. The supporting committee was originally planned as a committee of 100 but later expanded. Among the leaders of the Woman's Peace Parade Committee were such figures as Lillian Wald, head of the Henry Street Settlement House; Melinda Scott, Leonora O'Reilly, Mary E. Dreier, and Rose Schneiderman of the Women's Trade Union League; Mrs. Kate Waller Barrett of the National Council of Women; Charlotte Perkins Gilman, radical philosopher of feminism; and suffragists Anna Howard Shaw, Carrie Chapman Catt, Harriot Stanton Blatch, and Mary Garrett Hay. Such names suggested a high level of reform activism. Other members of note included Lillian Russell, Mary Antin, Crystal Eastman, and Mary Beard.

6 Typed memorandum, n.d., folder 3993, Oswald Garrison Villard Papers, HL.

interest in peace, and thus a special contribution to offer to all mankind, inevitably led to the subsequent question of how this potential contribution could be made effective in actual political decisions. Thus, from the beginning, the women's peace organizations found themselves inextricably involved in the issue of women's political participation.

As an effective peace society, the Woman's Peace Parade Committee hardly outlasted its single demonstration of 29 August. Within five months, however, a new organization, the Woman's Peace Party, had emerged to become one of the most influential elements of the peace movement. While the emphasis of the Woman's Parade Committee on the particular concern of women for peace had been relatively spontaneous and uncalculated, the Woman's Peace Party took up the same idea with a clearer sense of its full implications.

The notion of special "women's causes" represented one of the means by which middle-class American women, while accepting much of the Victorian ideology of special feminine characteristics of domesticity, emotionalism, sentimentality and purity, nevertheless employed these alleged traits as justifications for public action. Beginning in the early nineteenth century, a growing vanguard of women had propelled themselves into reform organizations. In temperance and abolition societies, in antivice and purity leagues, in charity and friendly visiting associations, in organizations for the abolition of child labor and the protection of working women, they had waged public crusades in the name of purity, piety, the home, and the conservation of life. Toward the end of the nineteenth century, millions of other middle-class women, less committed to specific social and reform issues, had been led toward at least tacit sympathy with the growing cluster of "women's causes" through their participation in local and national women's clubs and federations. Only a small proportion of these club women were active in the suffrage movement; even among the "social feminists" of the prohibition, settlement house, child labor, and other social movements, the active suffrage workers were probably in a minority. But the suffragists, as William O'Neill remarks, were undismayed by the relative sparsity of their own forces. They were confident that activity by women in other "women's causes," even in the club movement, would work eventually to enlist them in the suffrage ranks.[7]

[7] William L. O'Neill, *The Woman Movement: Feminism in the United States and England* (London 1969), pp. 33, 49, 53. "For every active suffragist," O'Neill esti-

One of the women's causes of the era with the widest, although not the most imperative, appeal was the quest for international peace. Women were presumed to be particularly inclined, by instinct and temperament, to concern themselves with the nurture of children and, by extension, with the nurture of human life generally. "Conservation of life" ranked high among the standard, clichéd statements of purpose in a host of constitutions of women's organizations. "Protection of the home" was an equally common motto. But what other threat so directly endangered the home and the conservation of human life than war? Thus the persistence of international conflict called for a special organized reaction on the part of those invested with the "maternal instinct."

Since international relations still remained a somewhat distant concern to most Americans before World War I, the peace movement gained less attention from women's organizations than the temperance movement, antivice campaigns, child protection and antichild labor efforts, and various charity works. But it was not entirely neglected among the women's causes. The Woman's Christian Temperance Union, under Frances Willard's prodding, established a Peace and Arbitration Department in 1887. The superintendent of this new department, Quaker peace worker Hannah J. Bailey, spread the argument that work for peace was "especially adapted to women," since mothers were used to settling quarrels and maintaining peace in the family through their spiritual power. Peace work was certainly within the province of the WCTU, since that organization constituted "organized mother love." Before the end of the nineteenth century the National Council of Women had joined the WCTU in endorsing peace petitions and resolutions. The General Federation of Women's Clubs and a great variety of other women's organizations gave their support to petitions, resolutions, and appeals for peace and arbitration.[8]

---

mates, "there were a hundred women engaged in club work, education, charity and various reforms."

[8] Hannah J. Bailey, "The W.C.T.U. in Relation to Peace and Arbitration," n.d., "Woman's Place in the Peace Reform," n.d., and "Untitled Convention Address," n.d., in Boxes 1 and 2, Hannah J. Bailey Papers, Swarthmore College Peace Collection. See also Mary Earhart, *Frances Willard: From Prayers to Politics* (Chicago 1944), pp. 260-72; Mildred White Wells, *Unity in Diversity: The History of the General Federation of Women's Clubs* (Washington, D.C. 1953), pp. 234-35; Page Smith, *Daughters of the Promised Land: Women in American History* (Boston 1970), pp. 267-69; and Marie Louise Degen, *The History of the Woman's Peace Party* (Baltimore 1939), pp. 15-16, 39-40. The participation in and support of the peace movement by many of these women's organizations, however, was often merely pro forma and lacking in commitment. See, for example, Mrs. Elisabeth B.

Spokesmen for the woman suffrage movement itself often made claims of the potential contribution of women voters to world peace. By the turn of the twentieth century, the leaders of the suffrage movement had begun to shift their appeal away from predominant emphasis on the argument from "justice"—the appeal for the vote upon the basis of their rights as human beings—toward greater stress upon the argument from "expediency"—the appeal on the basis of the contributions that women voters could be expected to make to social and political conditions because of their special "feminine" interests, insights, and moral sensitivities.[9] As suffrage campaigns began to gain momentum about 1910, practical suffrage workers were even further tempted to stress various arguments from expediency at times and places where they might pick up extra votes or sympathy by suggesting the probability that women's votes would lead to prohibition, good government, or even world peace. But the use of arguments from expediency did not mean that the suffrage leaders were prepared to make any permanent or entangling alliances with other women's causes. In fact, the suffrage leaders were increasingly keeping a cool distance from their most recent allies, the temperance women.[10]

The woman suffrage movement had not always so cautiously eschewed close alliances with other causes. At one time its leadership had been unabashedly linked with that of the abolitionist crusade; at another, several of its foremost leaders had been outspoken advocates of a variety of radical social and feminist causes. In the later nineteenth century its leadership had been openly interlocked with that of the temperance movement. But the woman suffrage movement of the early twentieth century had come under a new, somewhat more conservative and clearly more practical and organizationally astute leadership. Best exemplified by Carrie Chapman Catt, this new cadre of leaders sought victory

---

Plummer to Lucia Ames Mead, 14 Dec. 1912, Box 6, Lucia Ames Mead Papers, SCPC.

[9] A valuable discussion of the relationship between the arguments from justice and those from expediency appears in Aileen S. Kraditor, *The Ideas of the Woman Suffrage Movement, 1890-1920* (New York 1965), pp. 43-72. The handy terms "justice" and "expediency" are Professor Kraditor's.

[10] *Ibid.*, pp. 57-59; Janet Giele, "Social Change in the Feminine Role: A Comparison of Woman's Suffrage and Woman's Temperance, 1870-1920," Ph.D. diss., Radcliffe College, 1961, esp. pp. 85, 285; Eleanor Flexner, *Century of Struggle: The Woman's Rights Movement in the United States* (Cambridge, Mass. 1959), pp. 184-85. An interesting reflection of the early signs of tension between the two movements appears in Frances Willard to Susan B. Anthony, 24 Nov. 1894, Ida Husted Harper Papers, Henry E. Huntington Library.

on the narrow question of suffrage, without complicating and distracting side issues. Mrs. Catt and the other leaders made pragmatic use of the arguments from expediency. They gave measured support to, and made cautious claims on behalf of, "women's causes." Finally sensing some hope for victory, but disciplined in political tactics and realities by frequent defeats in their state-by-state campaigns, these leaders increasingly made only temporary and expedient alliances with other movements.[11] But in the fall of 1914, with the nation awestruck at the outbreak of war in Europe, the suffrage leaders, for all their caution and narrowness of purpose, could hardly fail to see potential advantages in stressing the pacific and humanizing qualities of women. What a temptation to ally themselves with a popular and suddenly dramatic woman's cause that would help demonstrate the expediency of votes for women!

Thus, within the new Woman's Peace Party, it was the woman suffrage leaders who particularly emphasized the potential *contributions* of women in the search for peace. The war, according to the suffragists, revealed once again the follies and barbarisms that inevitably characterized male governments that refused political equality to women.[12] By organizing now to restore and preserve peace, women might offer their special contribution to mankind and prove conclusively the worth and necessity of political participation by women at the highest national and international levels.

The confused and complex origins of the Woman's Peace Party foreshadowed the organization's subsequent development. Delegates arrived at the organizing convention with what William L. O'Neill has characterized as a "mixture of caution, suspicion, enthusiasm, and confusion. . . ."[13] During the first weeks of agitation and organization emerged most of the political divisions,

11 On changes in the nature of the leadership of the woman suffrage movement see Kraditor, *Ideas of the Woman Suffrage Movement*, pp. xi, 12-13, 45-46, 52; O'Neill, *The Woman Movement*, pp. 71-72, 75, 77; and Flexner, *Century of Struggle*, pp. 235-37.

12 Carrie Catt, for instance, had already connected the war with male imperialism. "Our protest," she wrote to the *New York Times* on 5 Oct. 1914, "is against the imperialism which makes the Kaiser and the Czar hold that they have a divine right to rule over men in their respective realms and which in attenuated form persuades men as a whole to think they have a divine right to rule over women as a whole." Carrie C. Catt Papers, New York Public Library.

13 William L. O'Neill, *Everyone Was Brave: The Rise and Fall of Feminism in America* (Chicago 1969), p. 174.

conflicts between rival reform organizations, disputes over method, and personal incompatibilities and antagonisms that were to vex the party over the subsequent three years. A variety of separate initiatives contributed to the ultimate emergence of the Woman's Peace Party and behind these initiatives stood a number of prominent, tenacious, and often charismatic women who brought to the peace movement differing temperaments, ideas, and reform goals.

One of the most vigorous promoters of a permanent women's peace organization was seventy-year-old Fanny Garrison Villard who had marched down Fifth Avenue as the chairman of the Woman's Peace Parade in August. Fanny Villard had inherited all of her father's uncompromising militancy. She had joined a number of peace societies, but had never found one that met her standards of absolute nonresistance. All had proved "weak and ineffectual," she claimed, because they had compromised the true principles of peace to support "adequate armament" and defensive war.[14] During September and October of 1914 Mrs. Villard sought to revive the Parade Committee as "an organization totally different from the existing peace societies . . ." based upon the principle of "the inviolability and sacredness of human life under all circumstances." Men had tried the futile policies of compromise and expediency and had failed. The hope of the future lay in a new "moral movement" launched by women.[15]

In the course of her efforts, Mrs. Villard arrived at a new estimate of one prominent leader whom she had first counted among her main adversaries. Mrs. Carrie Chapman Catt, former president of the principal woman's suffrage association in the United States and now president of the International Woman Suffrage Alliance, had blunted the initial optimism of the Woman's Parade Committee by warning of the parade's probable ineffectiveness. A master of organization and tactics and a consummate politician, Mrs. Catt measured peace agitation, as all other issues, in terms of the probabilities of tangible success. Pessimistic of the ability of any power to end the war in advance of an unprecedented military cataclysm, she warned the Parade Committee that no single parade in a single city would make an impact on the warring nations. They were deluding themselves, she warned, if they thought that "a thousand, five thousand or a million women

14 Villard, "A Real Peace Society," p. 4 and Fanny G. Villard to Francis Garrison Villard, 1 Aug. 1914, F. G. Villard Papers, HL.
15 Villard, "A Real Peace Society," pp. 3-4, 7, F. G. Villard Papers, HL.

marching through the streets of New York or speaking upon the abstract subject of peace" would influence Europe.[16] The only hope of success, she implied, was in persistent and determined work through such international organizations as the Suffrage Alliance.

In a private letter Mrs. Villard at first described irritably how Mrs. Catt had "made light of the proposed attempt to influence public opinion."[17] But as Mrs. Villard continued to attend private peace meetings and plan committee sessions her opinion of Mrs. Catt changed. By mid-September she was claiming Mrs. Catt's support in her attempt to form a nonresistance society. In October Mrs. Villard ecstatically reported Mrs. Catt's "magnificent" address before the New York State Woman Suffrage Association Convention: "Never have I heard such a heart-felt and moving address from her. It was a great sermon against war."[18] While Mrs. Villard's nonresistance position was too radical to gain wide support, Mrs. Catt's new and outspoken interest in peace, coupled with her prestige as an effective organizer and leader, made her a focus for attempts to initiate a women's peace society with a broad and moderate program.

In her enthusiasm, Mrs. Villard had overestimated the extent of Mrs. Catt's conversion. Mrs. Catt had not become a nonresister nor had world peace become her dominant concern. Undoubtedly she had experienced a dramatic revulsion against the war, especially as she had observed the passions of war engulf the International Woman Suffrage Alliance that she had struggled so long to strengthen. At the outbreak of the war she had joined in the International Alliance's manifesto for peace and in September she had tentatively agreed to accompany Rosika Schwimmer, a leading figure in the International Woman Suffrage Alliance, to lay a petition before President Wilson urging him to lead the neutral nations in demanding an armistice and mediation. But it is dubious if she long remained, as Mrs. Villard expressed it, "more deeply moved by the war than anything else."[19] Despite all her activities for peace, Carrie Catt renewed her primary allegiance to the woman suffrage movement at home. Always a pragmatist, she never allowed her efforts in the peace

---

[16] "Minutes of the Peace Parade Committee," 12 Aug. 1914, pp. 11-12, F. G. Villard Papers, HL.

[17] Fanny G. Villard to Francis Garrison Villard, 12 Aug. 1914, F. G. Villard Papers, HL.

[18] *Ibid.*, 12 Sept. and 17 Oct. 1914, F. G. Villard Papers, HL.

[19] Mary Gray Peck, *Carrie Chapman Catt* (New York 1944), pp. 213, 220; Fanny G. Villard to Francis Garrison Villard, 2 Jan. 1915, F. G. Villard Papers, HL.

movement to detract from her effectiveness in forwarding woman suffrage, her chosen reform.

But dedication to woman suffrage did not, at least during the early months of the war, preclude nearly equal dedication to peace. On the contrary, Carrie Catt realized, this was just the time, while the nation recoiled with dismay from this reversion to barbarism, for suffragists to throw their energies into a great protest against war. The suffragists might gain new stature if women assumed leadership in so noble a cause. Since suffragists had long emphasized women's superior sensitivity to the sacredness of human life, they had no reason to be surprised that in forwarding the peace movement good suffrage tactics should coincide with unselfish humanitarianism. Mrs. Catt quickly initiated a campaign to obtain evidence of wartime atrocities against women, seeking documentation that would support both an appeal for peace and an argument for the necessity of giving women protection against the barbarism of war through full political participation.[20]

At the same time that she stressed women's protest against war in her suffrage speeches, Mrs. Catt also insisted that organized suffragists *not* become the "prime mover" in forming a women's peace organization.[21] Her political instincts warned her against too formal an alliance of the two reform causes. A protégée of Susan B. Anthony, Carrie Catt knew the history of the suffrage movement's decades of frustrations and tribulations arising from association with such other causes as abolitionism, sexual freedom, and religious unorthodoxy.[22] Since the turn of the century

---

20 Flora M. Denison to Carrie C. Catt, 24 Aug. 1914, Mary Sheepshanks to Rosika Schwimmer, 15 Dec. 1914, Rosika Schwimmer Papers, Hoover Institution on War, Revolution and Peace; Carrie C. Catt, "The Atrocities of War," mimeographed sheet, n.d. [Sept. 1914], Catt Papers, NYPL.

21 Carrie C. Catt to Jane Addams, 16 Dec. 1914, Carrie C. Catt Papers, MS Div., Library of Congress.

22 Some suffragists argued that the abolitionists had sold them out when Negroes but not women gained suffrage in 1865. In the 1870s Elizabeth Cady Stanton's association with Victoria Woodhull, a spiritualist and advocate of free love, had enabled critics of the woman suffrage movement to charge it with promoting ideas of sexual permissiveness, charges which Mrs. Catt found herself still forced to combat in 1915. Mrs. Stanton's indiscretions had also included the composition of a "Woman's Bible," a set of commentaries that ridiculed the Bible and its masculine bias and invited critics of woman suffrage to charge the movement with atheism. Susan B. Anthony found herself frequently forced to denounce the introduction of "side issues." "I don't care what men believe about prohibition, the *Bible* or anything," she wrote, "[just] so they believe in & vote for the W. S. Amendment." Susan B. Anthony to Clara Colby, 18 Dec. 1895, 13 Jan. and 29 Mar. 1896, Clara B. Colby Papers, HHL; Andrew Sinclair, *The Better Half: The Emancipation of the American Woman* (New York 1965), pp. 192, 200; Flexner, *Century of Struggle*, pp. 142-55;

both Carrie Catt and Anna Howard Shaw, as presidents of the National Woman Suffrage Association, had adopted a policy (occasionally violated when the local political situation so dictated) of refusing to give formal support to prohibition. Prohibition might be unpopular, they reasoned, among groups whose votes for woman suffrage they badly needed. Mrs. Catt warned her followers to remain "aloof from all entanglements," and to refuse to "promise what women will do with the vote." The woman suffrage movement, she wrote in 1914, "has no other plank in its platform than Votes for Women."[23]

Late in the fall of 1914, while Carrie Catt was still weighing the advantages in increased immediate stature that the suffrage movement might gain from taking a prominent lead in the peace movement against the dangers of allying her foremost cause with another reform, she received a call from Anna Garlin Spencer, ordained minister, reformer, and an officer in the New York Peace Society. Mrs. Spencer predictably had a peace program to promote, but she also had some views on the older peace organizations that caught Carrie Catt's attention. "If I have received the right impression from Mrs. Spencer," she wrote, ". . . the present management of the peace movement in this country is over-masculinized. . . ." The peace organizations had "as little use for women and their points of view" as the militarists.[24] Such a discovery could hardly fail to provoke a career suffragist to action. Mrs. Spencer had suggested simultaneous peace demonstrations in several major cities and Carrie Catt now proposed that such demonstrations be carried on by women alone.[25]

Peck, *Carrie Chapman Catt*, p. 87; Carrie C. Catt to Men and Women of New York, Oct. 1915, Catt Papers, NYPL. Susan Anthony's exasperation with side issues was strikingly expressed in a letter to Clara Colby in 1894: "As to your proposition to take the Indian baby to meetings with you—I say, 'No' most emphatically . . . you would distract the thought from the *one point* of woman's enfranchisement—and turn to adoption of Indian babies—the amalgamation of the races and all sorts of side thoughts. . . ." Anthony to Colby, 26 May 1894, Colby Papers, HHL.

[23] Giele, "Social Change in the Feminine Role," pp. 85, 285; Flexner, *Century of Struggle*, pp. 184-85; Carrie C. Catt, "The Suffrage Single Plank, 1915," speech manuscript, typescript copy, and Carrie C. Catt, "Statement," n.d., typescript copy, Catt Papers, NYPL. Anna Howard Shaw even refused to encourage a proposal in 1908 for a men's association to promote woman suffrage. Such an association might attract "pessimistic and discontented" men and "involve us in all sorts of isms." "We have more of them (isms) now than we can ward off," she wrote, "with some of our over-zealous women." Anna Howard Shaw to Oswald Garrison Villard, 6 Feb. 1908, O. G. Villard Papers, HL.

[24] Carrie C. Catt to Jane Addams, 16 Dec. 1914, Catt Papers, LC. See also Catt to O. G. Villard, 15 Dec. 1914, O. G. Villard Papers, HL.

[25] *Ibid.*

Persuaded by Mrs. Spencer to take some further part in promoting a women's peace movement, Mrs. Catt still approached the matter cautiously—gauging how she might participate without involving her suffrage forces in too formal an alliance and seeking to insure effective leadership for a new peace organization. She learned from Mrs. Spencer that Lucia Ames Mead (wife of Edwin Mead, the current director of the World Peace Foundation, and peace propagandist in her own right) had taken over Anna Garlin Spencer's idea and had already written a manifesto for the proposed demonstrations. Mrs. Mead's leadership, Carrie Catt decided, would prove disastrous. Lucia Ames Mead was a "very unpopular woman" she commented ("I confess that while I cannot name a single sensible reason for my feelings, I always want to run when I see her coming").[26] Since the Meads, after having been so prominent in the prewar peace movement, had taken no forceful action for over four months since the war began, others less discredited by old associations should take up the cause. In mid-December Carrie Catt appealed to Jane Addams of Hull House in Chicago: ". . . you are the one woman in the nation who ought to call such demonstrations. . . ." At the same time she offered to work circumspectly to find the right leaders for the New York City phase of the demonstrations.[27]

Carrie Catt's letter came to Jane Addams as the culmination of a host of appeals for her to take the initiative in forming a national women's peace organization. That the search for a leader should have focused upon Jane Addams was hardly surprising. Not only was she the nation's most prominent and respected woman, but she had undertaken several times during recent years to describe the intimate and necessary connections between international peace, domestic humanitarian reforms, and woman suffrage. In an address to the Second National Peace Congress in 1909 she had argued that the world stood in need of cooperative effort and that women, who had learned cooperative processes in constructive work rather than on the battlefield, were best trained for peacemaking. Earlier, in *Newer Ideals of Peace*, she had suggested that the experiences gained by immigrants and reformers in the urban slums might contribute to new conceptions and modes of cooperation on the international plane.[28] Pressure

---

[26] *Ibid.*　　　　　　　　　　[27] *Ibid.*

[28] Jane Addams, "Woman's Special Training for Peacemaking," *Proceedings of the Second National Peace Congress* (Chicago 1909), pp. 252-53; Jane Addams, *Newer Ideals of Peace* (New York 1907), pp. 11-18, 119, 202-6, 225. For extended discussions

for a women's peace organization came from former participants in the peace movement such as Fanny Garrison Villard, Anna Garlin Spencer, and Lucia Ames Mead, from promoters of social reform such as Lillian Wald, and from suffragists such as Carrie Catt. As a prominent figure in all of these movements—peace, social reform, and suffrage—Jane Addams became the logical focus of agitation for a national organization.

The mounting sentiment for a women's peace organization in November and December 1914 stemmed largely from the work of two European suffragists, Emmeline Pethick-Lawrence of England and Rosika Schwimmer of Hungary. Madame Schwimmer had been working in London in 1914 as a correspondent of European newspapers and as international press secretary of the International Woman Suffrage Alliance. Earlier in Hungary she had organized Hungary's first Women's Trade Union, helped found the Hungarian Council of Women, drafted legislation for child welfare, and represented Hungary in the International Neo-Malthusian League.[29]

When the war upstaged her suffrage efforts and plunged her nation into turmoil, Rosika Schwimmer reacted with passion and determination. After failing to gain support from the European leaders of the International Woman Suffrage Alliance for her plans, she embarked for the United States in late August on a mission to urge neutral mediation of the war. She went first to Mrs. Catt, who endorsed her peace mission but attempted also to utilize her talents in behalf of woman suffrage. Carrie Catt's letters to Rosika Schwimmer in the fall of 1914 dealt almost exclusively with woman suffrage activities. She even advised Madame Schwimmer not to talk peace at a German Bazaar and instead to continue her mission, as Mrs. Catt saw it, to "turn the Germans to thinking kindly of woman suffrage. . . ."[30]

But Rosika Schwimmer was not to be diverted from her peace

---

of Jane Addams' ideas on peace see Sondra Herman, *Eleven Against War: Studies in American Internationalist Thought, 1898-1921* (Stanford 1969), pp. 114-49; John C. Farrell, *Beloved Lady: A History of Jane Addams' Ideas on Reform and Peace* (Baltimore 1967), pp. 140-216; Merle Curti, "Jane Addams on Human Nature," *Journal of the History of Ideas*, 22 (Apr.-June 1961), 240-53; and Charles Roland Marchand, "The Ultimate Reform: World Peace in American Thought during the Progressive Era," Ph.D. diss., Stanford University, 1964, pp. 55-59, 157-66, 295-97.

[29] Degen, *Woman's Peace Party*, p. 26; "Rosika Schwimmer, World Patriot," pamphlet, 1947, O. G. Villard Papers, HL.

[30] Rosika Schwimmer to Carrie Catt, 22 Aug. 1914, Schwimmer to Aletta Jacobs, 21 Aug. 1914, Schwimmer Papers, HI; Catt to Schwimmer, 17 Sept., 24 Sept., 28 Oct., and 25 Nov. 1914, Catt Papers, LC.

mission. Suffragist Anna Howard Shaw once described her as "all force and fire, alive from her feet to her fingertips."[31] Rosika Schwimmer applied this "force and fire" to the passionate appeal for neutral mediation to end the war. She remained an ardent advocate of woman suffrage, identifying woman suffrage with peace and lecturing on suffrage to support herself. But by November 1914 her schedule listed four talks on peace to one on woman suffrage. In the Midwest, particularly, her depictions of the horrors of war and her appeals for peace brought an enthusiastic response. The secretary of the Chicago Peace Society bemoaned her excessive emotionalism, characterizing her as "evidently unstrung and nothing short of hysterical."[32] But although Madame Schwimmer's unreliability and predilection for melodrama were later to plague the advocates of mediation, in 1914 her flamboyant approach provided a needed spark to kindle sentiment for a women's organization.

While Madame Schwimmer was exciting demands for action in the Midwest and urging Jane Addams to call a national conference, Emmeline Pethick-Lawrence was busy in Washington. Mrs. Pethick-Lawrence had gained notoriety as the leading lieutenant of Emmeline Pankhurst, England's most prominent militant suffragist. She had led stone-throwing raids on government property and participated in hunger strikes, but had broken with Mrs. Pankhurst in 1911 and had refused to support arson and the destruction of private property. Despite her break with Mrs. Pankhurst, she was still identified when she came to the United States in the fall of 1914 as the erstwhile "terror of the London 'bobbies.'"[33] American suffragists who admired the more militant approach to woman suffrage had invited Mrs. Pethick-Lawrence to inaugurate a new suffrage campaign by speaking at a mass meeting at Carnegie Hall in October, an invitation deeply regretted by Carrie Catt who saw militancy as disruptive to the cause of suffrage internationally and detrimental to the reputation of the woman suffrage cause at home. In her Carnegie Hall address, however, Mrs. Pethick-Lawrence put forward a sug-

[31] Anna Howard Shaw, *The Story of a Pioneer* (New York 1915), p. 330.

[32] Josephine Simpson to Rosika Schwimmer, 20 Nov. 1914, Schwimmer to Harriet Upton, 25 Oct. 1914, Jane Addams to William Jennings Bryan, 13 Dec. 1914, Schwimmer Papers, HI; Louis P. Lochner to David Starr Jordan, 22 Dec. 1914, David Starr Jordan Papers, HI.

[33] George Dangerfield, *The Strange Death of Liberal England* (New York 1961), pp. 165, 183; Emmeline Pethick-Lawrence, *My Part in a Changing World* (London 1938), pp. 227-40, 278-85, 292-94; *Chicago American*, 25 Nov. 1914, 1:5, clipping, Schwimmer Papers, HI.

gestion similar to an earlier notion of Mrs. Catt's—that American women should enhance their political prestige by associating themselves with the effort to restore peace and reconciliation to the world.[34]

Mrs. Pethick-Lawrence had met with Rosika Schwimmer before the latter's departure from England and had strongly endorsed Madame Schwimmer's peace mission. "Women see in this devastating War," she wrote Madame Schwimmer in late August, "the utter failure to safeguard the human family, on the part of the male Governments of all the nations. . . ." "Perverted diplomacy" and "male statecraft" had ignored the bonds uniting women, workers, and common people throughout the world.[35] Once in the United States, Mrs. Pethick-Lawrence duplicated Rosika Schwimmer's conversion from emphasis on suffrage to emphasis on peace. Like Madame Schwimmer she began to discuss woman suffrage primarily as a necessary prerequisite for international peace. In private conferences she met with Anna Garlin Spencer and Fanny Villard who were already promoting a women's peace organization and with a number of social reformers and settlement house leaders, including Lillian Wald, Mary K. Simkhovitch, Irene and Alice Lewisohn, Crystal Eastman, and Madeline Doty, all of whom were soon to become active in peace organizations. During a speaking tour of the East, Mrs. Pethick-Lawrence concentrated increasingly on the issue of peace and organized local peace groups at the conclusion of her meetings. In one such meeting in Washington, D.C., in late November Mrs. Pethick-Lawrence proposed the consolidation of local groups into a national movement. Several of those present, including some leaders of the Congressional Union (a militant stepdaughter of the National American Woman Suffrage Association), seized upon the idea and set a date for a national conference in Washington on 10 January 1915. Meanwhile Crystal Eastman had suggested to Mrs. Pethick-Lawrence that she go to Chicago to see Jane Addams.[36]

34 Pethick-Lawrence, *Changing World*, p. 309.

35 *Ibid.*, p. 308; Emmeline Pethick-Lawrence to Rosika Schwimmer, 25 Aug. 1914, Schwimmer Papers, HI.

36 Pethick-Lawrence, *Changing World*, pp. 308-9; Fanny G. Villard to Francis Garrison Villard, 17 Oct. 1914, F. G. Villard Papers, HL. See also Carrie C. Catt to Jane Addams, 30 Dec. 1914, Catt Papers, LC and Catt to Addams, 4 Jan. 1915 and enclosure, Woman's Peace Party Correspondence, 1915-1919, Box 1, SCPC. (Hereafter the Woman's Peace Party Correspondence will be cited as WPP Correspondence to distinguish it from the organizational materials of the party which are boxed separately in the Swarthmore College Peace Collection as Woman's Peace Party [WPP] Papers.)

Emmeline Pethick-Lawrence's arrival in Chicago raised the campaign for a women's peace organization to a new peak of intensity. At Jane Addams' Hull House she met Rosika Schwimmer again. Together they pressed Jane Addams to take action and roused Chicago audiences with their combined fervor and militancy. Both appealed to the "motherhood instinct." Mrs. Pethick-Lawrence called for a "new force," a woman's movement to overcome the folly of male governments. Since the intrigues and ambitions of men had brought about the war, she argued, peace could only come through the enfranchisement of the "natural custodians of the human race"—the "mother-half of humanity."[37] By 8 December Jane Addams reported to Lillian Wald that she was under almost irresistible pressures to build a national organization to seek "immediate action looking toward a cessation of hostilities." The enthusiasm stirred up by Madame Schwimmer and Mrs. Pethick-Lawrence should not be wasted, she wrote. Perhaps a large number of women's organizations could be called together to meet with the conference that Mrs. Pethick-Lawrence had organized for January in Washington.[38]

A week later Carrie Catt's letter criticizing the old peace societies for inaction and neglect of women and calling for women's demonstrations for peace reached Jane Addams. "I quite agree with you as to the masculine management of the existing peace societies," Jane Addams replied. Although she preferred cooperation of men and women on public measures, on this issue the women were the "most eager for action."[39] Madame Schwimmer assured Jane Addams that Carrie Catt had requested that Miss Addams send out a call to other women's organizations to join in the meeting already scheduled in Washington. In response to what she now considered a spontaneous and widespread demand, Jane Addams, with "a certain sinking of the heart" at the thought of the problems ahead, now sent out a call for a meeting in Washington on 10 January signed by herself and Carrie Catt. Mrs. Catt assented to the call for a meeting and the use of her name.[40] The movement toward a national women's peace organization had nearly reached fruition.

[37] Pethick-Lawrence, *Changing World*, pp. 309-10; Jane Addams to Lillian Wald, 8 Dec. 1914, Lillian Wald Papers, NYPL. Emmeline Pethick-Lawrence, "Union of Women for Constructive Peace," *The Survey*, 33 (5 Dec. 1914), 230; Degen, *Woman's Peace Party*, pp. 31-34.

[38] Jane Addams to Lillian Wald, 8 Dec. and 21 Dec. 1914, Wald Papers, NYPL.

[39] Jane Addams to Carrie C. Catt, 21 Dec. 1914, Division of Intercourse and Education, Vol. IV, 1914, Carnegie Endowment for International Peace Papers, Columbia University Library.

[40] *Ibid.*; Carrie C. Catt to Jane Addams, 30 Dec. 1914 and 4 Jan. 1915, Catt Papers,

It was at this point that the emerging alliance between woman suffrage and peace first threatened to introduce divisiveness into the as yet unborn women's peace organization. The militant tactics of one segment of the woman suffrage movement in England had begun to influence American women. Alice Paul, an American who had served prison terms with the militants in London, had gained permission from the National Suffrage Association in the spring of 1913 to organize a suffrage parade at the presidential inaugural and obtained the chairmanship of the association's Congressional Committee. But Miss Paul and her militant allies quickly adopted tactics that Carrie Catt, Anna Howard Shaw, and other leaders of the National Suffrage Association feared as politically unwise and dangerously militant. In late 1913 Alice Paul was forced out of the National Association. She continued her work for suffrage as the head of her own organization, the Congressional Union, which now attracted most of the more militant and radical proponents of woman suffrage.

The Congressional Union adopted the British policy of holding the "party in power responsible." Since the Democrats controlled the presidency and Congress after the 1912 elections, the Congressional Union sought to force the Democratic Party to endorse a suffrage amendment by urging all women who were enfranchised in the western states to oppose all Democrats until the party took a favorable position. Mrs. Catt and other leaders of the National Association looked upon this tactic as a "stupendous stupidity" when the suffrage issue needed the help of favorable Democrats and when suffrage campaigns in a number of states stood in need of Democratic votes.[41]

Shortly after the call for the January meeting in Washington went out, Carrie Catt discovered that members of the rival and "distasteful" Congressional Union were in charge of the conference arrangements and had planned the peace meeting long in advance to coincide with the annual meeting of the Congressional Union. "I am caught in a Congressional Union and militant trap," she exploded to Jane Addams. She had known nothing of the prior arrangements for a national meeting by the Congressional Union group, she complained. She did not wish to be in the lead-

LC; Addams to various organizations, 28 Dec. 1914, Jane Addams Papers, SCPC; Addams to Catt, 21 Dec. 1914 and Catt to Addams (night letter), 23-24 Dec. 1914, Box 1, WPP Correspondence, SCPC.

41 Carrie C. Catt and Nettie R. Shuler, *Woman Suffrage and Politics* (New York 1923), pp. 245-48, 264; Flexner, *Century of Struggle*, pp. 263-70; Carrie C. Catt to Jane Addams, 4 Jan. 1915, Catt Papers, LC.

ership of the new peace organization. Madame Schwimmer, in her "emotional advocacy of peace" had "bungled things" in leading Jane Addams to believe that "I had requested you to call this meeting."[42] Carrie Catt made clear her primary commitment to the suffrage cause and her embarrassment at appearing as a leading initiator of a conference which the Congressional Union would control.

Woman suffrage was scheduled for a referendum in New York in 1915. As chairman of the New York Campaign Committee, Mrs. Catt explained to Jane Addams, she must avoid any association with the unpopular and "anti-democratic" militants. Moreover as president of the International Alliance she dare not "consort with militants who are extremely out of favor in the Alliance just now." Her prayer, she wrote, had been that she might "walk so straight a path" that she could pull the Alliance together again after the war. As it was, the leaders of the National Suffrage Association were attacking her for cooperating with the Congressional Union, and the "peace women" were angry at the usurpation of their field by the suffragists. Even greater dissension would result, she feared, when women "summoned to Washington supposedly to attend an unorganized conference" found the conference rigged and the platform already determined. Carrie Catt warned Jane Addams that she, too, had probably been used as "an unconscious tool."[43]

Despite her wish for "an honorable retreat" Carrie Catt did participate in the organizing meeting in January for what was to become the Woman's Peace Party. "I am coming down," she told Jane Addams, "because you may need a rescuing party." But she also warned that if the conference at Washington was in any way "confused with" the Congressional Union, she would have to "wiggle out."[44] Afterwards she declared herself pleasantly surprised at the way the conference had surmounted great difficulties and gained a fair degree of unanimity. But she had learned again the lesson of the dangers of alliances between reform movements. She accepted unenthusiastically a position as chairman of the Foreign Relations Committee of the new organization, but warned that she could give little time to its work. "Please regard me as a movable, elastic sort of figure," she wrote Jane

[42] Carrie C. Catt to Jane Addams, 30 Dec. 1914 and 4 Jan. 1915, Catt Papers, LC; Catt to Addams, 29 Dec. 1914, Box 1, WPP Correspondence, SCPC.

[43] Carrie C. Catt to Jane Addams, 4 Jan. 1915, Catt Papers, LC; Catt to Addams, 29 Dec. 1914, Box 1, WPP Correspondence, SCPC.

[44] *Ibid.*

Addams. "If my name is of any use to you in any way, use it; if not drop me out. I have no feelings in the matter." She still approved of a tactical association between suffrage and peace, but wished to maintain her own freedom of action in support of her principal reform cause. For leadership in the peace organization, she suggested, "someone a little on the outskirts of the suffrage cause" would be a wiser choice.[45]

Mrs. Catt was to assume leadership of the National Woman Suffrage Association in 1915 and lead it in its final drive toward victory. In her own mind she had already, by January 1915, prepared herself for breaking the temporary alliance between the causes of woman suffrage and peace (a shadowy alliance acknowledged far more frequently by leaders of the Woman's Peace Party than by woman suffrage workers) when the step should prove tactically advisable later on.

Other ardent woman suffragists, less strategy-minded than Mrs. Catt, did not share her reluctance to join wholeheartedly in the peace movement. Over the years many of them had come to realize how intimately the campaign for votes for women was linked with peace. Suffragists agreed that the Civil War had set back their cause for decades. Again in 1898 woman suffrage had seemed to suffer even from a brief conflict. "Women and their freedom," Susan B. Anthony had complained in 1898, "are always sacrificed to whatever else may come before the public."[46]

Just as aggravating to suffragists as the effects of wars themselves were the arguments of the antisuffragists based upon the probability of war. These opponents persistently reminded the woman suffragists that governments were based upon force and defended by force. Therefore only those who could actually bear arms in defense of the nation and its laws should be allowed to vote. The vote was "the 'insignia of actual power,' " Helen Kendrick Johnson wrote in a typical exposition of the antisuffrage case. This insignia should not be bestowed upon those "not physically fitted to maintain the obligations that may result from any vote or any legislative act." "Manhood strength," she warned, "is the natural and only defense of the state."[47] Suffrage leaders

---

[45] Carrie C. Catt to Jane Addams, 27 Jan. and 16 Mar. 1915, Box 1, WPP Correspondence, SCPC.

[46] Flexner, *Century of Struggle*, pp. 108-9; Catt and Shuler, *Woman Suffrage and Politics*, pp. 31, 160; Susan B. Anthony to Clara B. Colby, 20 Apr. 1898, Colby Papers, HHL.

[47] Helen Kendrick Johnson, *Woman and the Republic* (New York 1897), p. 55. For a sample of similar arguments see Lyman Abbott, "Why Women Do Not Wish

found themselves constantly challenged by the contention that those who could not fight should not vote. Anna Garlin Spencer complained that the "government is force" axiom was the "chief argument" of her antisuffrage opponents and Carrie Catt lamented in 1914 that "the anti-suffragists have always made the physical force theory their chief and loudest claim. . . ."[48]

Two arguments dominated the suffragists' attempt to refute the "bullets must support ballots" doctrine: the argument from changed conditions and the argument for ameliorative influence. The argument from changed conditions asserted bluntly that physical force no longer controlled human society. Since nations were no longer "essentially military organizations," Jane Addams argued, defense of the state was no longer the central duty of citizenship.

> As long as a state of preparedness against the ever-present danger of attack from outside foes formed the only stable foundation for national existence, it was quite fitting that military prowess should be regarded as the first of virtues, and the ability to bear arms the test of citizenship. But the entire structure of the modern world is built upon a groundwork of industry, and the problems that concern it are in the main those of industrial well-being, and of national, state and city housekeeping.[49]

With the rise of industry and the evolution of the basis of government from force to mutual consent, government had come more and more within the woman's sphere. It had become, in Jane Addams' phrase, "enlarged housekeeping," and the wisdom of the world's traditional housekeepers was needed to guide its action.[50]

---

the Suffrage," *The Atlantic Monthly*, 92 (Sept. 1903), 291-94, Mrs. Gilbert E. Jones, "Some Impediments to Woman Suffrage," *North American Review*, 190 (Aug. 1909), 160-61 and "The Stock Argument Against Woman Suffrage," *Harper's Weekly* 52 (11 Apr. 1908), 6.

[48] Anna Garlin Spencer, "Woman and the State," *The Forum*, 48 (Oct. 1912), 402 and *Woman's Share in Social Culture* (Philadelphia 1912), p. 291; Carrie C. Catt to Editor, *New York Times*, 23 Nov. 1914, Catt Papers, NYPL. According to one account, Carrie Catt's career as a suffragist began when, as a thirteen-year-old farm girl, she had disputed the contention by a male friend that women should not vote because they could not fight. Louise R. Noun, *Strong-Minded Women: The Emergence of the Woman-Suffrage Movement in Iowa* (Ames, Iowa 1969), p. 227.

[49] Jane Addams, "The Working Woman and the Ballot," *Woman's Home Companion*, 36 (Apr. 1908), 19.

[50] *Ibid.*; Jane Addams, "The Modern City and the Municipal Franchise for Women," *The Woman's Journal*, 37 (7 Apr. 1906), 54-55; Addams, *Newer Ideals of Peace*, pp. 180-85.

The argument for ameliorative influence reversed the sequence and viewed women's votes as a potential cause rather than a probable result of a decrease in warfare. Women embodied the "gentler traits of tenderness and mercy" and therefore had a special contribution to offer to government, this argument maintained. They could "best represent the human interests in government."[51] As wives and mothers, women could always be expected to vote against military measures and war. Destructive masculine ideas of physical force would only be overcome, militant suffragist Harriot Stanton Blatch argued, when the "mother viewpoint" forced its way into international diplomacy.[52] When the nation reacted with horror to the outbreak of World War I, suffragists redoubled their promises that women voters would always vote for peace.

The two arguments against the "physical force theory" even derived some sociological, anthropological, and biological underpinnings from the theories presented by Charlotte Perkins Gilman and Jane Addams. Mrs. Gilman, poet, novelist, and "philosopher" of American feminism, argued that the differences between male instincts toward aggression and female instincts toward preservation could be detected in differences between the initial sperm and germ cells. The germ cell, she wrote, "attracts, gathers, draws in," while the sperm cell "repels, scatters, pushes out." On the level of common observation, "sex-distinctions" between male and female were common among all animals:

The tendency to "sit" is a sex-distinction of the hen:
the tendency to strut is a sex-distinction of the cock.
The tendency to fight is a sex-distinction of males
in general: the tendency to protect and provide for,
is a sex-distinction of females in general.[53]

[51] Carrie C. Catt, "Evolution and Woman's Suffrage," typescript speech MS for speech delivered 18 May 1893, Catt Papers, NYPL; Lillian Wald, "Address at Columbia University," Oct. 1915, typescript copy, p. 17 and "Suffrage," typed MS for speech, Feb. 1914, Wald Papers, NYPL.

[52] Harriot Stanton Blatch and Alma Lutz, *Challenging Years, The Memoirs of Harriot Stanton Blatch* (New York 1940), pp. 251-52; Florence Kelley, "Women and Social Legislation in the United States" and Anna Howard Shaw, "Equal Suffrage—A Problem of Political Justice," *The Annals of the American Academy of Political and Social Science*, 56 (Nov. 1914), 62-63, 97-98. See also A. Elizabeth Taylor, *The Woman Suffrage Movement in Tennessee* (New York 1957) p. 66.

[53] Charlotte Perkins Gilman, *Our Man-Made World or Our Androcentric Culture* (New York 1911), p. 79; Charlotte Perkins Stetson [Gilman], *Women and Economics* (Boston 1898), p. 41. Mrs. Gilman is described as the philosopher of feminism in Carl Degler, "Charlotte Perkins Gilman on the Theory and Practice of Feminism," *American Quarterly*, 7 (Spring 1956), 21-22.

In human males, the tendencies to repel, scatter, strut, and fight had found their natural outlet in a long history of piracy, competition, and warfare. "In warfare, *per se*," Mrs. Gilman concluded, "we find maleness in its absurdest extremes. Here is . . . the whole gamut of basic masculinity, from the initial instinct of combat, through every form of glorious ostentation, with the loudest possible accompaniment of noise."[54]

The antidote for a male-dominated, war-oriented state of society was, of course, the utilization of the truly human instincts of women. The "mother instinct" was one of "unmixed devotion" of love and care with "no self-interest." "Mother-power" was the basis for the more human processes of industry. Man had, for long years, achieved no productive work at all, being merely a fighter and hunter. It was woman who had prompted the human race to labor, thus displaying the truly "human" instinct toward growth and mutual service. Male dominance had thus been a ghastly mistake from the beginning. Men had confused politics with warfare and had thus retarded the growth of industry and cooperation by utilizing the nation only as a fighting organization.[55]

Jane Addams, and later Carrie Catt, Lillian Wald, and many others, took up Mrs. Gilman's thesis (also elucidated by Thorstein Veblen and Olive Schreiner) that men were the military sex and women the industrial sex.[56] Jane Addams, like Veblen, postulated an initial human state of "peaceful savagery," a "matriarchal period" in which women had maintained a direct and vital connection with the state. Subsequently, however, during a "fighting era" the warriors had gained control and women had been excluded from the councils of war. Under male dominance, the state had forgotten its duty to nurture and protect life. As their traditional occupations had moved from the home into the factories, women had lacked a voice in governments based upon warfare and had been unable to extend protective and humanizing legislation over new industries and the cities they affected.

[54] Gilman, *Our Man-Made World*, pp. 182, 189, 211.

[55] *Ibid.*, pp. 36-37, 58, 98, 131, 224, 233, 238.

[56] For examples see Jane Addams, "If Men Were Seeking the Franchise," *Ladies' Home Journal*, 30 (June 1913), 21 and *Newer Ideals of Peace*, pp. 28, 180-84, 188-89, 197, 205; Lillian Wald, "Address at Columbia University," Oct. 1915, Wald Papers, NYPL; Carrie C. Catt, "Then and Now," typewritten ms, n.d., Catt Papers, NYPL. For further discussion of anthropological theories, see Kraditor, *The Ideas of the Woman Suffrage Movement*, p. 102. On Veblen and Schreiner, see Thorstein Veblen, *The Theory of the Leisure Class: An Economic Study of Institutions*, 2d ed. (New York 1919), pp. 4-5, 7-8, 13-14 and Olive Schreiner, *Woman and Labor* (New York 1911), 3d ed., pp. 27-34, 158-61.

Government had developed along the lines of men's interests, but the requirements of present statesmanship were for the restoration of a more "human" balance in which women's interests would receive attention and women's contributions would be utilized. The present need was for woman suffrage and political participation. The result would be a more peaceful, more humane world.[57]

This whole complex of attitudes and arguments about the relationship between war and woman suffrage underlay the discussion of a platform at the organizing convention of the Woman's Peace Party in January 1915. Those like Jane Addams, Carrie Chapman Catt, Charlotte Perkins Gilman, Anna Howard Shaw, Harriot Stanton Blatch, and Emmeline Pethick-Lawrence, who had most frequently theorized about the necessary connection between woman suffrage and peace played prominent roles at the convention. The delegates overwhelmingly approved a plank calling for woman suffrage as part of their peace platform. Anna Garlin Spencer had feared that the peace movement might be weakened by alienating the antisuffragists and Lucia Ames Mead and the other representatives of the peace movement in Boston opposed mixing the peace and suffrage issues. But they acquiesced in the suffrage plank, Mrs. Spencer reported, when it became clear that "a ground-swell movement, a great peace crusade" had burst forth among the suffragists.[58] Jane Addams, playing her usual role of harmonizer and unifier, kept the militant suffragists from entirely dominating the meeting. But she insisted herself that a suffrage plank was "absolutely fundamental to the undertaking." In international affairs as in domestic social legislation, governments would not meet their responsibilities until they were humanized by the active participation of women.[59]

Although ardent suffragists like Anna Howard Shaw outspokenly suggested that antisuffragists lacked the gumption to contribute any strength to the organization and invited them to

[57] Addams, "Woman and the State," 21; Carrie C. Catt, "Address to the Fifth Conference of the International Woman Suffrage Alliance, 1909," speech MS, p. 72, Catt Papers, NYPL.

[58] Anna Garlin Spencer to Rev. Marion Murdoch, 18 Jan. 1915, Box 1, Anna Garlin Spencer Papers, SCPC. For an indication of a brief organized attempt to prevent a suffrage plank and an expression of fears by veteran peace workers that combining peace and suffrage would "cripple" both movements, see Ruth H. Spray to Lucia Ames Mead, 7 Jan. 1915, Box 6, L. A. Mead Papers, SCPC.

[59] *Ibid.*; Jane Addams to Mrs. Hemenway, 30 Jan. 1915, Box 2, WPP Papers, SCPC, "Minutes of Organizational Meeting," 10 Jan. 1915, pp. 16-17, Box 1, WPP Papers, SCPC; Unsigned to Mrs. Frederic Cunningham, 4 Mar. 1915, Box 2, WPP Correspondence, SCPC.

form their own peace society, the Woman's Peace Party officially invited into membership any women who were "in substantial sympathy" with the party's central purpose, whether or not they could accept every plank in the platform.[60] The Massachusetts branch of the new party tried first to repeal the suffrage plank and then to ignore it. The Connecticut branch adopted its own platform which pointedly stated that the "Woman's Peace Party was *not* organized for suffrage propaganda."[61]

Such evasion, invited by the deliberate vagueness of the doctrinal requirements for membership and the considerable autonomy of the local branches of the Woman's Peace Party, served partially to blunt the potential divisiveness of the suffrage issue. A few women, incensed at the domination of the organizing convention by suffragists, made appeals for a new convention or for a reconsideration of the suffrage plank by the executive committee.[62] Others were content simply to observe that the new party would probably achieve more for woman suffrage than it would for peace. Anna Garlin Spencer concluded: "It gives a great practical aim to the woman suffragists which will unite and elevate them all." Mrs. Robert La Follette appeared to confirm such a conclusion when she wrote in February 1915: "There is nothing suffragists can do now to promote suffrage like working tooth and nail for peace."[63]

The suffrage plank continued to vex the Woman's Peace Party, provoking a renewed debate at the 1916 convention; but as a primary cause for division within the party it gradually gave way to the issue of radicalism. From the outset, several of the proposals of the Woman's Peace Party went beyond anything contemplated by most respectable and prominent prewar peace organizations. The women resented the discrimination against women

[60] "Woman's Peace Party" (printed pamphlet) and "Minutes of Organizational Meeting," 10 Jan. 1915, p. 27, Box 1, WPP Papers, SCPC.

[61] Unsigned letter, 4 Apr. 1916, Mrs. J. Malcolm Forbes Papers, SCPC; "Woman's Peace Party: Connecticut Branch" (printed pamphlet), Box 4, WPP Papers, SCPC. See also, "Minutes of the First Session of the First Annual Convention of the Woman's Peace Party," 1916, pp. 30-33, 40, 43-44, Box 1, WPP Papers, SCPC and Susan Fitzgerald to Jane Addams, 1 Feb. 1915, Box 1, WPP Correspondence, SCPC. A Maryland state branch even eliminated suffrage from its platform and required that the suffrage question not be introduced at any of its meetings. "Minutes of Meeting of the Summer Campaign Committee of the Washington Branch of the Woman's Peace Party," 23 June 1915, Box 4, WPP Papers, SCPC.

[62] Alice F. Post to Lucia Ames Mead, 16 July 1915, Box 2, WPP Papers, SCPC; Alice S. T. Ayres to Jane Addams, 25 Jan. 1915, Box 1, WPP Correspondence, SCPC.

[63] Anna Garlin Spencer to Jane Addams, 18 Jan. 1915, Box 1, Spencer Papers, SCPC; Memorandum entitled "Extract from a letter by Mrs. Robert La Follette," 21 Feb. 1915 (presumably addressed to Jane Addams), Box 1, WPP Correspondence, SCPC.

in the prewar peace movement, attacked the prewar organizations as "undemocratic," and called for a true democracy within
the movement and in the management of foreign affairs. Not only
should women be given the vote, the leaders of the Woman's
Peace Party argued, but they should serve on delegations to
peace conferences. The party's platform called for democratic
control of foreign policy, removal of the "economic causes of
war," and nationalization of armament manufacture. In a special
resolution, the organizing conference denounced "further preparedness for war" as a "menace to our civilization."[64] By later
standards this hardly constituted a radical program. But in contrast to the attitudes of prewar peace organizations, the emphasis
upon further democratization and popular control of foreign
policy and the implications of a need to control potential American aggressiveness represented a significant departure. The
trend toward the demand for a "people's peace" had begun.

At first the Woman's Peace Party seemed to have successfully
enlisted the support of a wide group of women's organizations
and to have compromised the differences between its activist
leaders. Among the charter members were several representatives of the WCTU, the Daughters of the American Revolution,
the National Federation of Settlements, the General Federation
of Women's Clubs, the National Council of Women, and even the
International Kindergarten Union. Jane Addams inevitably became president. Rosika Schwimmer and Emmeline Pethick-Lawrence were both awarded honorary memberships and Carrie
Catt became honorary president.[65] The suffrage militants in the

[64] Woman's Peace Party, "Preamble and Platform adopted at Washington," 10
Jan. 1915, "Addresses Given at the Organization Conference of the Woman's Peace
Party," pp. 5-15, and "Woman's Peace Party" (proof for pamphlet with penciled
heading "Corrections as made in Chicago & Washington"), Box 1, WPP Papers,
SCPC. On the continuing debate over the suffrage plank, see "Minutes of the First
Session of the First Annual Convention of the Woman's Peace Party," 1916, p. 28-33,
38-41, Box 1, WPP Papers, SCPC. In his account in *Everyone Was Brave*, William
O'Neill emphasizes the platform's call for a "Concert of Nations" rather than the
old "Balance of Power" and the endorsement of world law and an international
police. The cosmopolitanism of the woman movement, he suggests, "had accustomed
feminists to thinking and working in global terms," thus advancing beyond most
Americans in shedding "parochial nationalism" (O'Neill, *Everyone Was Brave*, p.
175). However, these planks were far from new in the peace movement. They had
been endorsed by some of the moe conservative segments of the prewar peace movement and were to characterize the very moderate League to Enforce Peace. The planks
on democratic control of foreign policy and economic causes of war had potentially
more radical implications.

[65] "Addresses Given at the Organization Conference of the Woman's Peace Party,"
pp. 2-3, Box 1, WPP Papers, SCPC.

Congressional Union gained control of the Committee for Congressional Action and Mrs. Villard was temporarily appeased with a reference to the "sacredness of human life" in the preamble to the platform and a place on the executive board. Anna Garlin Spencer had warned of Mrs. Villard's "obstructionist" tendencies but declared herself "glad that there is at last a Peace Society in which she can be happy, as she has had to leave all the others."[66]

The initial inclusion of representatives of the DAR, the women's clubs, and similar organizations had merely masked the Woman's Peace Party's potential for further movement in a radical direction. The officers of the national organization, in addition to Jane Addams, Mrs. Spencer, Mrs. Mead, and Mrs. Villard, included Mrs. John Jay White, a Congressional Union supporter, Mrs. Louis F. Post, a former editor of a single-tax journal, Miss Sophonisba Breckinridge, noted promoter of social legislation, Mrs. Glendower Evans, Congressional Union member and promoter of women's trade unions and minimum wage legislation, and Mrs. William I. Thomas, who later left to join the radical People's Council. Charlotte Gilman, noted for her outspoken feminism, and Florence Kelley, socialist and agitator for labor and social legislation, sat in at the first executive board meeting.[67] Soon Crystal Eastman, the vivacious and indefatigable sister of the editor of *The Masses*, Max Eastman, had attracted to the New York branch of the party a leadership of even more radical potential. By 1917 she had established herself and such other youthful radicals as Freda Kirchwey, Fola La Follette, Jessie Hughan, Rose Schneiderman, Anna Walling, Anne Herendeen, and Margaret Lane as the active leaders of the New York branch.

Although militancy in the suffrage cause was not synonymous with radicalism on other issues, and several of the leading American suffrage militants eschewed all other causes, there was a tendency for those who were backers of the Congressional Union to form the radical wing of the Woman's Peace Party as well. Often they carried the methods of the militant woman suffrage groups and their tolerance for public disapproval into the new peace organization. Such women, Mrs. Spencer noted with

[66] Anna Garlin Spencer to Jane Addams, 18 Jan. 1915, Box 1, Spencer Papers, SCPC; Woman's Peace Party, "Preamble and Platform," Box 1, WPP Papers, SCPC.

[67] Woman's Peace Party, "Preamble and Platform," Box 1, WPP Papers, SCPC; "Notes of First Meeting of the Executive Council of the Woman's Peace Party," 24 Jan. 1915, Box 2, WPP Papers, SCPC.

grudging admiration, brought to the party the "advantage of the enthusiasm and push of the radical wing."[68] In 1917, as the New York branch became the most active in the party, its radical methods and personnel began to worry other segments of the organization.

Long before the New York branch had begun to embarrass the more conservative women with its radical activities, the Woman's Peace Party had established itself within the vanguard of a new phase of the peace movement in America. The theory of women's particular propensities for peace, which became the rationale for the party, had found expression during the organizing convention in embittered denunciations of male governments, imputations of guilt for the war to men, and the unabashed glorification of women.[69] Often the speakers had revealed a deep sense of alienation that might foreshadow a willingness to play the role of critic. American foreign policies and American diplomacy, since they embodied masculine biases, might not escape such criticism.

Even the basic suppositions of the Woman's Peace Party—that the war was unpopular and could and ought to be brought to an early end, and that there existed a solidarity of all women on the issue of peace—led to an increasingly radical stance by the party as many Americans came to see mediation as utopian or as beneficial to Germany and her allies. As the women called first for official mediation and later for semiofficial or unofficial mediation their attacks upon the old diplomacy became more strident, their demands for a more democratic and representative diplomacy more experimental and egalitarian, and their criticisms of dominant elements in the American business and political leadership more frequent. As they courted workers and farmers in support of their campaigns against expanded military expenditures, for American initiatives toward mediation, and finally for the preservation of American neutrality they came to see themselves as leaders of a democratic coalition. Peace no longer represented, as it had for the leaders of the older peace societies and foundations, stability, restraint, and order. Rather it now connoted democratization, the preservation of social reform, and even the acceleration of social change.

These tendencies toward the radicalization of the peace move-

---

[68] Anna Garlin Spencer to Jane Addams, 18 Jan. 1915, Box 1, Spencer Papers, SCPC.

[69] "Addresses Given at the Organization Conference of the Woman's Peace Party," pp. 4, 7, 10-15, Box 1, WPP Papers, SCPC.

ment were to reach culmination in subsequent organizations far more radical than the Woman's Peace Party, but the women's theories led them into actions as early as 1915 that helped inaugurate the search for a new diplomacy. The International Woman Suffrage Alliance had scheduled its biennial meeting for Berlin in 1915. The war prevented any such meeting in Berlin and attempts to schedule it in Amsterdam were rejected by several of the belligerents. But several leaders of the International Alliance, including Aletta Jacobs of Holland and Rosika Schwimmer, insisted that women should take some action to display the solidarity of women against war. A group of individuals, all leaders of the international woman suffrage movement, called a conference for April 1915 at The Hague.[70]

The Woman's Peace Party responded to the call with a large and enthusiastic delegation. Here was an opportunity to illustrate dramatically the contrasts between the divisive and catastrophic diplomacy of men and the healing, unifying, informal diplomacy of women who could maintain their solidarity in behalf of peace even though war was raging. Jane Addams, the leader of the Woman's Peace Party's delegation, distrusted "a certain aspect of moral adventure" about the convention of women at The Hague, but hoped that women who were "willing to fail" might, by this experiment in international action, "break through that curious hypnotic spell" and the inhuman irrelevancies of traditional diplomacy that kept the belligerents from considering peace.[71]

Both the personnel and the program of the conference of women at The Hague demonstrated the extent of departure of the Woman's Peace Party from the conservative peace societies which by 1915 had rejected all attempts to end the war. The American delegation included a number of leading suffragists, four social workers, two leaders of women's labor unions, three members of the Women's Trade Union League, a prison reformer, a leader in the William Lloyd Garrison Equal Rights Association, a leading exponent of the single tax, and three Socialists including the wife of millionaire Socialist William Bross Lloyd. The European delegates were largely engaged in social work and suffrage agitation.[72] The convention called for the voiding of all secret treaties, the democratization of foreign policy, the na-

---

[70] Degen, *Woman's Peace Party*, pp. 64-68; *The Survey*, 35 (9 Oct. 1915), 46.

[71] Jane Addams to Lillian Wald, 26 Mar. 1915, Wald Papers, NYPL.

[72] "List of American Delegates to the Hague Conference," Box 15, Woman's Peace Party, New York Branch, Correspondence, SCPC; Mary Chamberlain "The Women at The Hague," *The Survey*, 34 (5 June 1915), 221.

tionalization of armament manufacturing, liberty of commerce and prohibition of government protection for overseas investments, the political enfranchisement of women, and representation of "the people" (including women representatives) at the eventual peace conference. In an effort to end the war promptly the convention sent its leaders to visit the heads of state of the main belligerent and neutral nations to seek expressions favorable to mediation by a conference of neutrals.[73]

With the sinking of the *Lusitania* fresh in the minds of Americans, and with Germany apparently holding the advantage territorially, the women's campaign to end the war through mediation subjected the Woman's Peace Party to widespread criticism. Although the leaders of the party continued to assume that they were expressing the desires of the mass of the American people for peace, they soon became conscious that in calling for American initiative in mediating the war they were moving against the tide of influential opinion and toward a minority position.

The Woman's Peace Party's gradual alienation from majority opinion in influential circles, particularly on the eastern seaboard, was aggravated by the party's informal connection with the Peace Ship adventure sponsored by Henry Ford in December of 1915. Since the visits of the women to the heads of state in the summer of 1915, the Woman's Peace Party had thrown its major energies behind the campaign for a conference of neutrals to mediate the war. The specific proposal for this conference was known as the "Wisconsin Plan," the idea having been formulated by Julia Grace Wales, an instructor at the University of Wisconsin. The plan had the backing of the Wisconsin state legislature and the endorsement of Wisconsin Senator Robert M. La Follette. A group of experts representing the neutral nations were to form a continuous mediating body which would continue submitting proposals to the belligerent powers until a mutually satisfactory solution was reached. The expert representatives would not commit the neutral nations to action; they would have only the "scientific" function of formulating proposals. Thus neutral nations could take the initiative in mediating the conflict without the risks of formal commitments.[74]

The leaders of the Woman's Peace Party had sought to per-

---

[73] *The Survey*, 34 (5 June 1915), 218; Degen, *Woman's Peace Party*, pp. 83-92.
[74] Degen, *Woman's Peace Party*, pp. 46-47, 128-29; Walter I. Trattner, "Julia Grace Wales and the Wisconsin Plan for Peace," *Wisconsin Magazine of History*, 44 (Spring 1961), 203-13.

suade President Wilson to call an official conference of neutrals. But as the likelihood of an official conference faded, many of the women, including Jane Addams, began to give attention to an alternative "unofficial" conference of neutrals in which representatives of the people instead of unrepresentative professional diplomats would confer. Prospects for an American-sponsored official conference had nearly vanished when suddenly, late in November 1915, word burst upon the peace movement that Rosika Schwimmer, the irrepressible Hungarian, had somehow persuaded Henry Ford to support a conference of neutrals. Here was firm financial backing for the Woman's Peace Party's central objective, but Madame Schwimmer's penchant for the dramatic and Ford's precipitous action soon brought the entire venture into public ridicule. Ford chartered a ship to carry the American delegates to an unofficial conference and he and other leaders began to speak of getting the boys out of the trenches by Christmas. Jane Addams felt she should support the Ford mission, since it had adopted the Woman's Peace Party's program for an unofficial conference, but she distrusted the leadership of the Ford mission and found the choice of delegates disappointing. She agreed to serve as a delegate, but illness kept her from sailing.[75]

Jane Addams had supported the Ford venture as an individual, but her acceptance of a position as a delegate and unauthorized statements by Madame Schwimmer were enough to link the Woman's Peace Party publicly with Ford's "shipload of pacifists." This tenuous connection brought upon the party another wave of ridicule and disapproval. At the party's annual convention in January 1916 several disgruntled members challenged Jane Addams to explain the party's relation to the Ford ship and urged her to publish a disavowal of any connection. Jane Addams denied any official connection and criticized the methods of the Ford enterprise; but she refused to make any statement that would imply criticism of the ship while it was still under ridi-

[75] Degen, *Woman's Peace Party*, pp. 127-39. Anna Garlin Spencer sent Jane Addams a detailed account of the shortcomings of the Ford mission some days before the ship sailed. See Anna Garlin Spencer to Jane Addams, 29 Nov. 1915, Box 1, Spencer Papers, SCPC. Jane Addams' own ambiguous attitude toward the venture was expressed concisely in a private letter several weeks later: "I am such a believer in the 'Counsel of Imperfection' that I am confident that something can be pulled off from this rather peculiar start." Jane Addams to William I. Hull, Box 4, William I. Hull Papers, Friends' Historical Library. The most detailed account of the Ford Peace Ship venture is Peter Guertin Tuttle, "The Ford Peace Ship: Volunteer Diplomacy in the Twentieth Century," Ph.D. diss., Yale University 1958.

cule.[76] By early 1916, Miss Addams and her fellow leaders were already finding their peace programs declining precipitously in popularity. The ability to withstand public disapproval was looming as a crucial test for the organization. Frustrated in international action, the Woman's Peace Party turned its major efforts during 1916 to the less unpopular domestic campaign to resist further military preparedness. Even in this effort, the women found themselves forced gradually back into a minority position.

The real test of the Woman's Peace Party's ability to retain its supporters came after the United States broke diplomatic relations with Germany in February 1917. In a nation expectantly on the verge of war, opposition to military preparations and demands for new peace initiatives and national forbearance evoked violent denunciations. What had once been an innocuous, even a commendable, reform movement now appeared a dangerous promoter of disunity and dissent. Organizations which had once found it advantageous to aid or ally themselves with the peace movement began to find identification with active peace organizations embarrassing. As its allies began to reevaluate their best interests, the Woman's Peace Party braced itself for defections.

The most dramatic defection was that of the National American Woman Suffrage Association. The alliance, never fully acknowledged, between the suffragists and the Woman's Peace Party had always been a fragile one. Of course the suffragists had demanded and been delighted with the party's inclusion of woman suffrage as a necessary part of a peace program. A few suffragists had even indulged briefly in 1914 in visions of the peace issue as the one on which women might demonstrate their competence at statesmanship. But the suffrage workers, no matter how sympathetic to the Woman's Peace Party, were hard at work in their own campaigns. Between 1915 and 1917 suffrage workers faced numerous crucial state referenda, including two campaigns in New York alone. Suffrage workers frequently reminded the leaders of the Woman's Peace Party that despite their interest in the peace movement, their energies were totally absorbed by the suffrage campaigns.[77] Not surprisingly, suffrage workers demon-

[76] "Minutes of the Fifth Session of the First Annual Convention of the Woman's Peace Party," 1916, pp. 37-41, Box 1, WPP Papers, SCPC; Degen, *Woman's Peace Party*, pp. 139-42.

[77] Laetetia Moon Conard to Eleanor Karsten, 10 May 1916, Box 2, WPP Correspondence, SCPC; Lucia Ames Mead to Jane Addams, 13 July 1915 and Mary Reid Cory to Addams, 26 Oct. [1915], Box 1, WPP Correspondence, SCPC; Laura Belknap to Margaret Lane, 17 Jan. 1917, Box 14, WPPNY Correspondence, SCPC. On the

strated their allegiance to woman suffrage by disavowing peace activities when, in 1917, these threatened to compromise the suffrage cause.

The shifting relationship between Carrie Chapman Catt, the president of the National American Woman Suffrage Association, and the Woman's Peace Party accurately reflected the widening breach between the two causes after early 1915. Mrs. Catt, despite her active participation in the calling of the organizing conference of the Woman's Peace Party, had never relinquished her primary concern with suffrage work. She had accepted the chairmanship of the New York state woman suffrage campaign committee in 1914 and refused to leave her suffrage work to organize the Woman's Peace Party in New York or to go to the Conference of Women at The Hague. The women of the warring countries had "literally gone mad," she had written Jane Addams early in 1915. She had decided then that to try to bring them together in an international meeting while the war continued "would be too much like trying to organize a peace society in an insane asylum." Her interest in the peace movement had reached a climax during a brief lull in the suffrage movement immediately after the beginning of the war when, as she recalled, "a spirit of reaction" against the suffrage movement had set in. But by March 1915 Mrs. Catt was convinced that "the pendulum of popular opinion" had swung back in the direction of woman suffrage again.[78]

From this point on Mrs. Catt gave her time entirely to the suffrage cause. She did not appear at the Woman's Peace Party's annual convention in 1916 and withdrew from her position as honorary chairman of the party. She declined also to serve on a committee of five to represent America on an International Council for Permanent Peace. Her postwar mission, she explained to Jane Addams, would be to pull the International Woman Suffrage Alliance together again. Too much peace activity might discredit her with some of the belligerents and impair her ability to bring about harmony. Besides, she pointed out, a pacifist who had recently gone to Canada to invite a new suffrage society into the International Alliance had been too outspoken in behalf of peace and had "queered her suffrage mission."[79] Mrs. Catt had already

---

suffrage campaigns of the period see Catt and Shuler, *Woman Suffrage and Politics*, pp. 250-99 and Flexner, *Century of Struggle*, pp. 270-82.

[78] Carrie C. Catt (chairman, Empire State Campaign Committee) to all Field Workers, 17 Mar. 1915 and to Campaign District Chairmen, 19 Mar. 1915, Catt Papers, NYPL; Catt to Jane Addams, 16 Jan. 1915, Box 1, WPP Correspondence, SCPC.

[79] Harriet P. Thomas to Jane Addams, 9 Feb. 1916, Box 1, WPP Correspondence,

returned to her old adage: don't compromise the suffrage movement by attaching it to other, more controversial, reforms.

Meanwhile, both Mrs. Catt and the leading suffrage periodical, the *Woman's Journal*, had been moving toward a new line of argument on the relationship of women to war. In 1914 and early 1915 they had emphasized the probable effects of votes for women in promoting peace. But this contention was gradually superseded by a new stress upon women's service to the nation in time of war. The *Woman's Journal* proclaimed that no nation could carry on the war without the help of women and insisted that those who shared such burdens should be allowed the vote. Mrs. Catt pointed out that women had always been "part of the so-called war power of a nation."[80] War was proving the economic value of women. After being called upon for service, they could never be overlooked in politics again. Mrs. Catt began praising the women who fought in the American Revolution and stressed the role of women as "war assets." She reviewed the history of women generals and soldiers and denied that women were "weaklings in war." Every woman suffrage association in Europe, Mrs. Catt announced proudly, had enlisted for war service. Suffragists now praised women less for their peaceful propensities than for their courage and their sacrificial support of their nations. Despite its "frightful price," Mrs. Catt concluded, the war might bring a final emancipation of women. Other suffragists sensed the possibility of earning the franchise through war service and rushed to form preparedness and war service organizations.[81]

In February 1917, while the Woman's Peace Party was seeking desperately to ally with other peace groups to forestall war, the suffrage workers moved firmly in the opposite direction. Mrs.

SCPC; Carrie C. Catt to Thomas, 27 Dec. 1915, and Unsigned [Thomas] to Catt, 31 Dec. 1915, Box 2, WPP Correspondence, SCPC; "Third Report of the Executive Session of the Woman's Peace Party," 13 Mar. 1915, p. 5, Box 2, WPP Papers, SCPC; Catt to Addams, 12 Nov. 1915, Catt Papers, LC; Catt to Addams, 15 Aug. 1915, Box 5, Addams Papers, SCPC.

80 For the gradual shift in emphasis in the *Woman's Journal* see the following sequence of editorial comments: 8 Aug. 1914, p. 230; 22 Aug. 1914, p. 242; 29 Aug. 1914, p. 246; 14 Nov. 1914, p. 300; 9 Jan. 1915, p. 12; 1 Jan. 1916, p. 6; 22 Jan. 1916, p. 28; 18 Mar. 1916, p. 92; 4 Nov. 1916, p. 354; 13 Jan. 1917, p. 8; and 10 Feb. 1917, p. 31. Carrie C. Catt, "Speech Manuscript," typewritten (1915), pp. 1-2, Catt Papers, NYPL.

81 Carrie C. Catt, "The Crisis" (typed copy of speech MS for Atlantic City Convention of NAWSA, 1916), pp. 4-8, 12, "Speech Manuscript" typewritten [1915], pp. 1-2, Carrie C. Catt et al., "An Appeal for Liberty," 6 July 1915, and Catt, "Woman and War," typed MS, n.d., Catt Papers, NYPL; Catt, untitled speech MS [1916], Catt Papers, LC; *Woman's Journal*, 48 (24 Feb. 1917), 45; Mrs. George A. Scott to Anna Garlin Spencer, 8 Mar. 1917, Box 1, Spencer Papers, SCPC.

Catt had noted in her presidential address to the national convention in September 1916 that three Canadian provinces had given their women the vote "in sheer generous appreciation of their war work."[82] The American suffragists, now enthusiastically embarked upon a redoubled national effort and sensing victory, had no intention of discrediting their cause by failing to join energetically in the great national effort that seemed imminent. On 10 February and again the following week the *Woman's Journal* announced that women would serve if war came. On 6 February the New York State Woman Suffrage Association offered its help to the governor in the event of war, and the New York City organization quickly followed suit. Mrs. Catt called a meeting of the National Council for 23 and 24 February to "decide upon the most effective service the members can render the nation in this time of stress." Despite the frantic protests of the leaders of the Woman's Peace Party, all of whom were members of the National American Woman Suffrage Association, the National Council offered its services to the federal government in case of war.[83]

As letters of protest from supporters of the Woman's Peace Party poured in, Mrs. Catt's own position hardened. Some critics accused Mrs. Catt of undemocratic action in pledging the total membership to service without a referendum. Others complained that she and other suffrage leaders were encouraging the war spirit by acting as though war was probable or even inevitable. Several charged that she had abandoned the principle of "simple suffrage" by endorsing another cause. An organization pledged to suffrage work, they argued, had no right to contribute its energies and funds to some other cause. *The Suffragist*, the organ of the militant suffragists, warned that the National Association was inviting a recurrence of the tragedy of the 1860s when woman suffrage had stood aside for the war and the Negro.[84]

But Carrie Catt and the other suffrage leaders were hardly

[82] Catt, "The Crisis," p. 8, Catt Papers, NYPL.

[83] *Woman's Journal*, 48 (10 Feb. 1917), 34; 48 (17 Feb. 1917), 37; "NY State Woman Suffrage Party," mimeographed sheets, unsigned, 1917, Wald Papers, NYPL; Anna Garlin Spencer to Carrie C. Catt, 17 Feb., 2 Mar., and 12 Mar. 1917, Box 1, Spencer Papers, SCPC; Executive Council of the Woman's Peace Party to Carrie C. Catt, 22 Feb. 1917, Box 6, Addams Papers, SCPC; Caroline Wagner to Miss M. G. Hay, City Chairman, Woman Suffrage Party, 23 Feb. 1917, Box 18, WPPNY Correspondence, SCPC; Mary McHenry Keith to Catt, 19 Mar. 1917, Alice L. Park Papers, Henry E. Huntington Library; Alice L. Park to Catt, 17 Feb. 1917, Alice L. Park Biography (unpublished), p. 47, Alice L. Park Papers, Hoover Institution on War, Revolution and Peace; "Statement by Mrs. Henry Villard," n.d., Emergency Peace Federation Papers, SCPC.

[84] *The Suffragist*, 5 (17 Feb. 1917), 7-8. See also letters cited in n. 83 above.

convinced that their pledge of service to the government was a mistake. The pacifists might have "lost their heads," Mrs. Catt replied, but the suffragists had not. An early pledge of support to the government, the suffrage leaders argued, was not only expedient; it had been absolutely necessary to satisfy the demands for such action by a majority of the suffrage association members. Mrs. Catt denounced one of her critics as disloyal to suffrage for attacking her publicly, and declared with satisfaction that since she had been "ousted" by the New York branch of the Woman's Peace Party she had "been receiving congratulations from all sides." When Crystal Eastman sought to persuade her that she need not leave the New York branch, Carrie Catt replied that she preferred to "stay ousted." The same day she cut off correspondence with one of her most persistent critics, Anna Garlin Spencer, by asserting that as a suffrage worker she was too busy seeking the vote to consider peace or war.[85]

During the spring of 1917 the militant suffragists pursued a course more congenial to those women who continued to work for peace. In early February the militant journal, *The Suffragist*, announced that the Congressional Union would refuse either to offer itself for war services or to turn itself "into a society for peace."[86] The militants would work for the single goal of suffrage and would continue to demand that the government consult women before taking actions that would directly affect their lives. They accused the National Association of abandoning the cause and denied that women needed war as a chance to prove their worth. Of the opportunities war offered women to prove their true value, one writer in *The Suffragist* remarked acidly: "Before the war women were only the mothers of men. They have now risen to the dizzy heights of makers of machine guns."[87]

In March, members of the National Woman's Party (the new militant body composed of the old Congressional Union and the Woman's Party) began picketing the White House on behalf of the suffrage amendment. The great issue of the moment, they insisted, was not peace or war, but self-government at home. They

[85] Carrie C. Catt to Anna Garlin Spencer, 19 Feb., 10 Mar., and 21 Mar. 1917, Box 1, Spencer Papers, SCPC; Vera Boardman Whitehouse to Lillian Wald, 23 Feb. 1917, Wald Papers, NYPL; unsigned [Crystal Eastman] to Catt, 12 Mar. 1917, and Catt to Eastman, 21 Mar. 1917, Box 14, WPPNY Correspondence, SCPC. Another statement in defense of abandonment of the peace movement for full and unhampered service to the suffrage cause appears in Josepha Whitney to Lucia Ames Mead, 20 Nov. 1917, Box 1, WPP Papers, SCPC.

[86] *The Suffragist*, 5 (6 Feb. 1917), 6.

[87] *Ibid.* (7 Feb. 1917), 6; 5 (24 Feb. 1917), 7; 5 (3 Mar. 1917), 4.

offered little assistance to the Woman's Peace Party, holding to their single purpose of suffrage, but their refusal to abandon their militant demands for suffrage despite the war crisis in effect aligned them with other critics of the administration. A number of the militant pickets eventually served jail sentences and acquired a degree of martyrdom. Interestingly, the most socially radical of the supporters of the militant suffrage movement found the increasing radicalism of the peace movement more attractive than militant suffrage activities and left the picketing for suffrage to those whose militancy was not as clearly tied to a vision of broad social transformation.

While the militant suffragists carried out what amounted to an obstructionist policy against the administration's war efforts, the National American Woman Suffrage Association became increasingly enthusiastic over the policy of ingratiating itself with the administration. Carrie Catt certainly continued to put suffrage first, but she was not, as she had written, too busy to consider matters of peace and war—especially as they bore upon suffrage tactics. Suffrage leaders pushed their program very cautiously, solicitously inquiring of President Wilson when it would be most convenient to resume agitation for their cause. Mrs. Catt publicly denounced the militant pickets for intruding upon Wilson's "peace of mind." She aided schemes to try to persuade the large press associations to impose a voluntary censorship against coverage of the picketing activities of the militants and quietly hoped that their opposition during the war crisis would discredit and ultimately silence them.[88]

Meanwhile Mrs. Catt and the moderate suffragists had completed the revision of their theory of the relationship of women to war. What they had sought all along was convincing evidence of the political indispensability of women. If in 1914 they had found it desirable to stress the indispensability of women in preserving peace, in 1917 they found it even more efficacious to stress their indispensability in making war. Mrs. Catt and other leaders began to refer constantly to the suffrage amendment as a "war measure," as an aid to internal morale and democratic propaganda. Suffrage for women, Mrs. Catt told the Congress, would mean "suffrage for the loyal forces, for those who know

[88] Woodrow Wilson to Carrie C. Catt, 8 May 1917, H. H. Gardener to Woodrow Wilson, 19 July 1917, Gardener to Mr. Brahang, 25 July 1917, unsigned [Maud Wood Park] to Gardener, 24 Nov. 1917, Catt Papers, NYPL; Ethel M. Smith to Catt, 26 June 1917, Women's Rights Collection, Arthur and Elizabeth Schlesinger Library, Radcliffe College; Flexner, *Century of Struggle*, pp. 283-84, 286.

what it means 'to fight to keep the world safe for democracy.' "[89] Mrs. Henry Wade Rogers reminded readers of *The Public* that the National Association had offered four lines of work to the government as early as February. They had *enlisted* in war, rather than waiting to be drafted. She and Anna Howard Shaw emphasized the efficient organizational machinery that the suffragists could put at the government's disposal. Carrie Catt pointed out that, unlike "the more sluggish of their sex," suffragists were alert and "tense for action." "It has been frankly acknowledged," she wrote, "that but for the suffrage movement in Great Britain, the massing of women for war service would not have been possible." She praised the work of women in the factories, fields, and munitions plants, accused the adversaries of suffrage of "trying to Kaiserize America," and called for every worker in the New York referendum campaign to match the "idealism of General Pershing."[90]

The suffrage associations immersed themselves in war activities. Some sold war bonds and savings stamps as they campaigned door to door for suffrage. Others helped take the military census or knitted for the Red Cross. The Woman Suffrage Party of New York was delighted to act as an employment agency for the United States Ordnance Department, but did not forget to keep a record of those the suffrage workers had recruited to serve the government.[91] Everywhere the suffrage workers now identified the suffrage cause with the nation's war aims. Believing themselves on the verge of final victory, they shunned any association with the increasingly disreputable peace movement. Despite their complaints about the nation's failure to grant them full rights, they now sensed that suffrage would surely come as a part of the worldwide advance of democracy that would result from an Al-

[89] Carrie C. Catt, "An Address to the Congress of the United States," pamphlet (1917), p. 18, Women's Rights Collection, SL and "Woman Suffrage as a War Measure," speech MS, 1918, Catt Papers, LC; Peck, *Carrie Chapman Catt*, pp. 273, 297.

[90] *The Public*, 20 (24 Aug. 1917), 813-17; Carrie C. Catt, "Votes and Patriotism," handwritten speech MS, n.d. [1917 or 1918], p. 18, "War Messages to the American People, no. 1, 'War Aims,'" speech MS, n.d. [1917], p. 9, Women's Rights Collection, SL; Catt, "Speech Delivered at the State Suffrage Convention in Saratoga," 30 Aug. 1917, p. 5, Catt Papers, NYPL. For a more extensive description of the wartime activities and attitudes of the NAWSA and a thoughtful analysis of the combination of political sagacity and moral flaccidity they embodied, see O'Neill, *Everyone Was Brave*, pp. 184-85, 198-206.

[91] New York State Woman Suffrage Party, "Address of Miss Mary Garrett Hay," 4 Feb. 1918, mimeographed; [New York] City Suffrage Party, *Weekly News Bulletin* (typed copy), 26 Feb. 1918, p. 3; Adelaide M. Balch to Lillian Wald, 22 Dec. 1917, Wald Papers, NYPL; Ronald Schaffer, "The New York City Woman Suffrage Party, 1909-1919," *New York History*, 43 (July 1962), 283.

lied victory in the war. Support for woman suffrage had never been necessarily related to movements for basic social reforms. As success approached, the suffrage workers found little reason to remain critical of American society, or to support a peace movement which had become a vehicle for the expression of social criticism and deep political alienation.

The defection of the suffrage forces, jarring though it was, still proved less disruptive to the Woman's Peace Party than the ripening issue of "radicalism." In a sense the two questions were related, for a choice of loyalty to suffrage rather than to the peace movement represented the choice of a reform of increasing respectability over one with growing implications of social radicalism. But it was not only the suffrage workers who feared that the more radical leaders of the Woman's Peace Party would lead it too far from the mainstream of American social and political opinion.

As early as 1915 several of the leaders of the party had begun to complain of the radical leadership of the New York branch. Mrs. Mead warned that Crystal Eastman was "such an extreme socialist that she cannot greatly help the movement . . ." and Mrs. Villard complained that Mrs. Glendower Evans was "manipulating matters" and had placed herself, Mrs. Amos Pinchot, and other apparent IWW sympathizers in strategic positions in the New York organization.[92] On nearly every issue from that of an uncompromising suffrage plank to uncompromising opposition to military preparations the New York group took the radical position while the New England members, led by the Massachusetts branch, pleaded for less controversial stands. By 1917 these two branches—New York and Massachusetts—had emerged as the only strong branches and their positions had become increasingly polarized. Anna Garlin Spencer was led to remark that Boston and New York seemed to represent "opposite ends of the moral universe."[93] The national party office tried to smooth over the differences. Jane Addams often admired the more dramatic, less quietist approach of the New York Branch, but she temperamentally preferred a more cautious, unprecipitate approach. She

[92] Lucia Ames Mead to Jane Addams, 13 July 1915, Box 1, WPP Correspondence, SCPC; Fanny G. Villard to Francis Garrison Villard, 7 Feb. 1915, F. G. Villard Papers, HL.

[93] Elizabeth G. Evans to [Harriet P. Thomas], 22 Oct. 1915 and 14 Nov. 1916, Box 3, WPP Correspondence, SCPC; Blanche Watson to Crystal Eastman, 30 Nov. [1917], Box 18, WPPNY Correspondence, SCPC; Anna Garlin Spencer to Lucia Ames Mead, n.d., Box 1, WPP Papers, SCPC.

hesitated to undermine her influence and make it difficult to gain assistance in carrying out her other responsibilities by discrediting herself through unseemingly radical actions. Thus she sought to steer a middle course not only out of expediency, but also out of conviction.

The New York branch took great pride in having built up the party from "a polite society affair into an active democratic, decisive organization." Late in 1916 it was eagerly encouraging the influx of authors and playwrights and other "rather interesting people," mostly of a radical or bohemian hue, into its membership. Even one of the branch's more radical members soon suggested that the group's new periodical might have adopted a "little too much of a Village prose." About the same time Crystal Eastman was suggesting revolutionist Jack Reed as a speaker for a branch meeting.[94] The process of radicalization continued until by late 1917 a secretary of the branch had to urge one of the officers to write a friend to the effect that "on thinking it over" she had "discovered a number of Board members who were not Socialists." For example, the secretary pointed out, one leading officer was no longer a Socialist, but merely a "philosophic anarchist."[95]

Meanwhile the Massachusetts branch was frantically plying its way back into the mainstream. Its members participated in various forms of war service and refused to criticize the administration's policies or urge peace initiatives upon it. Although the national office of the party remained silent, the Massachusetts members resented what they considered the overly critical and obstructionist policies of the New York branch and the reputation that this active branch was bringing to the whole organization. Lucia Ames Mead reported that Massachusetts members were disturbed over the appearance of a pamphlet by Randolph Bourne with a Woman's Peace Party stamp, and that they were "distressed" over the radicalism and flippancy of a New York branch publication entitled *The Fourlights*. Mrs. Mead warned that to prevent a defection of the Massachusetts branch, the party would have to be "more explicit" in its patriotism, more apprecia-

[94] Unsigned [Margaret Lane] to Crystal Eastman, 28 Apr. 1916 and Mary Ware Dennett to Lane, 16 Feb. 1917, Box 15, WPPNY Correspondence, SCPC; unsigned to Katherine Leckie, 17 Nov. 1916 and unsigned to Agnes B. Leach, 18 June 1917, Box 16, WPPNY Correspondence, SCPC; unsigned [Margaret Lane] to Agnes Warbasse, 20 Nov. 1916, Box 18, WPPNY Correspondence, SCPC.

[95] Unsigned to Mrs. Henry G. Leach, 20 Dec. 1917, Box 16, WPPNY Correspondence, SCPC.

tive of President Wilson's aims. It should declare that "there can be no peace until the military domination of Prussia is destroyed." It would be best, she argued, to keep Crystal Eastman off of the national executive board as she was "so conspicuous in more radical organizations."[96]

No reconciliation between the rival branches was effected. The national secretary, Mrs. William I. Thomas, had left to join the more radical People's Council and Jane Addams was devoting her efforts to humanitarian relief and to proposals for a conference of women after the war. Probably no reconciliation was feasible. Those who sympathized with the position of most leaders of the Massachusetts branch gravely distrusted the anarchistic or revolutionary implications of any opposition to the government policies during wartime, while the New York radicals had glimpsed the possibilities of the peace movement as a carrier of ideas of basic social reconstruction. One New York member who had previously worked for the Massachusetts branch referred to the "total lack of the democratic spirit" in that branch and characterized Mrs. Mead and another of its leaders as "women who are, always have been, and always will be reactionaries. . . ." A secretary of the New York branch reflected the new context in which her coworkers were beginning to view the peace movement when she remarked that she liked to think of the movement "as not simply an emotional anti-war cause but as part of the fight for freedom for the great masses of people."[97] While the New York branch turned toward political action, five leaders of the Massachusetts branch issued a statement calling for peace only after the defeat of Germany, opposing those (like the New York members) who were "continually rebuking the government," and declaring a willingness to undergo "a temporary curtailment of our freedom" because of the "necessity of a rigid regime" during wartime. In 1918 the Massachusetts branch changed its name and broke all ties with the national Woman's Peace Party.[98]

The Woman's Peace Party did survive, however, and emerged in 1919 as a section of the new Women's International League for

[96] Unsigned [Margaret Lane] to Mrs. Frederick Holt, 14 May 1917, Box 15, WPPNY Correspondence, SCPC; Lucia Ames Mead to Jane Addams, 5 Nov., 12 Nov., and 13 Nov. 1917, Mead to Alice Post, 17 Nov. 1917, Box 1, WPP Papers, SCPC; Mead to Anna Garlin Spencer, 13 Nov. 1917, Box 1, Spencer Papers, SCPC.

[97] Unsigned to Mrs. Frederick Holt, 16 July 1917, Box 15, WPPNY Correspondence, SCPC; Blanche Watson to Crystal Eastman, 30 Nov. [1917], Box 18, WPPNY Correspondence, SCPC.

[98] "An Expression of Views of Some Workers for a Durable Peace," printed pamphlet, 11 Dec. 1917, Box 18, WPPNY Correspondence, SCPC.

Peace and Freedom.[99] Both the Massachusetts conservatives and the New York radicals were largely absent from the revived organization. The short history of the Woman's Peace Party had revealed a process that other wartime peace organizations were also to experience—a process of gradual radicalization during which those seeking radical social and economic change at home were attracted by the democratic ideology and antiestablishment quality of the peace movement, while those of more conservative social views and those with other, more respectable, reform interests gradually moved away from a movement that was bringing them into dangerous and disreputable association with the political Left. The decisive division within the movement had occurred not so much over questions of world peace or the solidarity of women, abstractly considered, but over the implications of various international programs and appeals for peace initiatives for movements of social reform and of social revolution at home.

[99] For the subsequent history of the Women's International League for Peace and Freedom see Gertrude Bussey and Margaret Tims, *Women's International League for Peace and Freedom, 1915-1965: A Record of Fifty Years' Work* (London 1965); Dorothy Detzer, *Appointment on the Hill* (New York 1948); Jane Addams, *Peace and Bread in Time of War*, pp. 178-243; and Lawrence S. Wittner, *Rebels Against War: The American Peace Movement, 1941-1960* (New York 1969), pp. 11, 25-26, 33, 52-53.

CHAPTER SEVEN

Preserving the Social Fabric

WHILE Rosika Schwimmer and Emmeline Pethick-Lawrence frenetically toured the country in the fall of 1914 delivering emotion-laden appeals to American women to build a peace movement upon the "motherhood instinct," a small group of humanitarian social reformers met quietly at the Henry Street Settlement House in Manhattan's Lower East Side to consider the implications of war in Europe for social work and reform programs. On 22 September 1914 the nation's most revered settlement house leaders, Jane Addams and Lillian Wald, had jointly issued an invitation to a group of twenty-six prominent men and women associated with reform programs to attend a round-table meeting to ponder the "subtle reactions of war, inevitably disastrous to the humane instincts which had been asserting themselves in the social order." Since all others had failed to prevent the war or stem its ill effects, their letter implied, the time might well have come when "some of us who deal with the social fabric" would have to "act in concert."[1] Thus the settlement house workers and social reformers approached the perception, previously or simultaneously arrived at by the international lawyers, businessmen, woman suffragists, and clergymen, that the everyday professional or reform experiences of their particular group had afforded it with talents and insights essential to the proper reform of international relations.

Before 1914 the social workers had taken very little interest in foreign affairs. Preoccupied with internal social problems they had found foreign policy "something rather remote, rather arid."[2] Industrial conditions, labor relations, and urban living conditions had cried out so urgently for their attention that the peace movement had seemed more of a distraction than a worthy reform. Jane Addams, it was true, had sought to link international peace with the domestic reform ideas growing out of the settlement house movement and Edward T. Devine, director of the New

---

[1] Lillian Wald to William Dean Howells, 26 Sept. 1914 (form letter sent to 25 others), Box 5, Jane Addams Papers, Swarthmore College Peace Collection.

[2] Emily G. Balch, "A Week with War Books," *The Survey*, 37 (28 Oct. 1916), 93.

York School of Social Work, had defined the "Spirit of Social Work" as a comprehensive policy of "conservation" which offered "a new way of looking at all physical and human resources" and provided new principles for all social relations, including international relations.[3] But Devine never spelled out a new program for foreign affairs and most settlement and social workers found themselves too absorbed in immediate problems to give much attention to international diplomacy. The main periodical of the social workers, *The Survey*, devoted little attention to foreign policy before August 1914. Its editor, Paul Kellogg, later confessed that *The Survey*, "in common with most American social agencies," had "ignored the threat of war, ignored the movements to prevent it." "War was, of course, a nightmare . . ." he reflected, "but nothing which closely concerned us."[4]

But within six weeks of the outbreak of the war in Europe, Kellogg and other leading social reformers had begun to initiate a new peace movement of their own. The fact of war had shocked them into action. They saw already the social reform programs of the belligerent nations endangered or eclipsed. In America, overseas relief funds threatened to drain financial resources from domestic programs. If the United States should heed the mounting cry for increased military preparations, they feared, money would be withdrawn from social programs, militaristic practices would be imposed, and child labor laws and other labor legislation overturned. "Who . . . cares a fig about the social movement [now]?" John Haynes Holmes asked gloomily in a late September issue of *The Survey*. Even after the war, he warned, "social progress" would long be subordinated to the demands of "mere social survival."[5] If social reformers and social workers had largely ignored foreign policy before 1914, they now feared that the inter-

[3] Jane Addams, *Newer Ideals of Peace* (New York 1907), pp. vii, 11-18, 25-27, 202-35; Edward T. Devine, *The Spirit of Social Work* (New York 1911), p. 5. For fuller discussions of the development of Jane Addams' views on international relations, see Sondra R. Herman, *Eleven Against War: Studies in American Internationalist Thought, 1898-1921* (Stanford 1969), pp. 114-49; John C. Farrell, *Beloved Lady: A History of Jane Addams' Ideas on Reform and Peace* (Baltimore 1967), pp. 140-216; and Charles Roland Marchand, "The Ultimate Reform: World Peace in American Thought During the Progressive Era," Ph.D. diss., Stanford University, 1964, pp. 156-66.

[4] Paul Kellogg, "The Fighting Issues," *The Survey*, 37 (17 Feb. 1917), 572; "Annual Report for Year Ended 1914-1915," *ibid.*, 35 (13 Nov. 1915), 8. For an illustration of the low priority among reforms to which Kellogg relegated the prewar peace movement (as represented by the Carnegie Endowment), see Paul U. Kellogg, "Of Peace and Good Will," *American Magazine*, 71 (Apr. 1911), 739-745.

[5] John Haynes Holmes, "War and the Social Movement," *The Survey*, 32 (26 Sept. 1914), 629-30.

national crisis would have to be settled before any social reform could make progress again. Not only did the threat of war to social reform require social workers to lead a new movement for peace, but the entire world crisis revealed the need for "experts in social relations" to come forward to repair the failures in traditional international diplomacy.[6]

The small group that met at the Henry Street Nurses Settlement on 29 September to formulate a coordinated response to the war did not represent a new coalition of forces. The same group of social workers and social reformers had cooperated frequently in the past to promote various reform causes. They had formed ad hoc committees to promote labor legislation, assist strikers, and campaign for a federal children's bureau. As Allen Davis has pointed out, the group was strikingly similar to the one that had met in 1911 to initiate a campaign for an Industrial Relations Commission.[7] Twelve of the twenty participants at the Henry Street meeting had lived and worked in settlement houses. Eight had been members of the Committee on Industrial Relations.[8] Six of the participants were officers in the American Association for Labor Legislation; nine were officers or trustees of the National Child Labor Committee; and five had been among the sponsors of a petition to the president the previous year to make a special investigation of violations of constitutional rights during the Paterson strike. Ten were associates, editors, or contributing editors of *The Survey*.[9] Together the twenty participants comprised the

[6] "Minutes of the Henry Street Peace Committee," 29 Sept. 1914, pp. 4-5, Lillian Wald Papers, New York Public Library.

[7] Allen F. Davis, "The Campaign for the Industrial Relations Commission, 1911-1913," *Mid-America*, 45 (Oct. 1963), 228.

[8] The group of twenty included: Jane Addams, Felix Adler, Leo Arnstein, Emily G. Balch, Edward T. Devine, John P. Gavit, Mrs. John Glenn, John Haynes Holmes, Hamilton Holt, Frederic C. Howe, William I. Hull, Florence Kelley, Paul U. Kellogg, George Kirchwey, Julia Lathrop, Samuel McCune Lindsay, Owen Lovejoy, Julian W. Mack, Lillian Wald, and Mornay Williams. Of the twenty, only William Hull, a Quaker and professor of international relations at Swarthmore, had not participated actively in social work. Addams, Arnstein, Balch, Devine, Gavit, Holt, Howe, Kelley, Kellogg, Lathrop, Lovejoy, and Wald had all lived in settlement houses and Adler's ideas had strongly influenced the early settlements. Addams, Holmes, Kelley, Kellogg, Lindsay, and Wald had comprised six of the seven-member group which had first pushed the Industrial Relations Commission idea. The seventh had been Rabbi Stephen Wise, who was unable to attend the initial Henry Street Peace Meeting, but later became a regular member of the peace group. Devine and Lovejoy had played important roles in the drive for an Industrial Relations Commission. See Davis, "The Campaign for the Industrial Relations Commission," p. 211.

[9] Those serving on the various organizations listed were as follows: American Association for Labor Legislation: Addams, Arnstein, Devine, Kellogg, Lindsay, Lovejoy; National Child Labor Committee: Addams, Adler, Arnstein, Devine,

leaders of a cluster of interrelated reform and social welfare organizations that included the Consumers' League, the Immigrant's Protective League, the National Conference of Charities, the Russell Sage Foundation, the National Child Labor Committee, the New York Charity Organization Society, the New York School of Philanthropy, the Children's Bureau, the New York Prison Reform Commission, and the National Conference of Jewish Charities.

Paul Kellogg, editor of *The Survey* and a leader in promoting the conference on the war, confessed frankly that in breaking into the peace movement the little group was entering a "pretty thoroughly unexplored field." None of them, he wrote, could approach the problems of peacemaking with the firsthand knowledge that they could employ in questions of labor conditions, sanitation, or immigration.[10] But while they lacked the confidence of expertise that they had usually brought to new reform ventures, the band of social workers still began with a cohesive strength arising from strong personal ties and previous experiences in mutual cooperation. At the core of the group stood a handful of New York journalists, social workers, and reformers—including Kellogg, Edward T. Devine, Samuel McCune Lindsay, Owen Lovejoy, John Haynes Holmes, and Florence Kelley—who were famous for creating new reform organizations during informal get-togethers at the *Survey* offices.[11] As in previous reform campaigns this group looked immediately to the settlement houses and to previous allies in humanitarian reform causes for support. Thus the group that met at the Henry Street Settlement on 29 September shared a common fear of the threat of war to domestic social programs and a common background of reform cooperation. Although the social workers entered the peace movement with little previous experience in questions of foreign policy and international relations, they were united by personal friendships, common social goals, common settlement house and social reform experiences, and common fears. If they had shown little interest in foreign policy before, that inattention had quickly given way to a sharply focused concern now that their most cherished domestic goals were threatened.

Kelley, Lindsay, Lovejoy, Wald, Williams; Petition on Paterson strike: Howe, Kelley, Kellogg, Lovejoy, Wald; staff of *The Survey*: Addams, Devine, Holmes, Howe, Kelley, Kellogg, Lindsay, Lovejoy, Mack, Wald.

[10] Paul Kellogg to George Nasmyth, 24 Sept. 1914, Box 5, Addams Papers, SCPC.

[11] Josephine Goldmark, *Impatient Crusader: Florence Kelley's Life Story* (Urbana, Ill. 1953), pp. 68-69.

Jane Addams had at first proposed a program of joint action between the social workers and the established peace organizations. But she and the others quickly abandoned this plan. The events of the first two months of the war convinced the social workers that the leaders of the old peace societies, the directors of the Carnegie Endowment, and others "in the seats of the mighty" either could not, or would not act. Even before the war, John Haynes Holmes had attacked the old peace organizations for their "undemocratic atmosphere," their "high-priced dinners," and their hand-picked conferences at remote summer resorts."[12] Reformers and social democrats, he had strongly implied, could hardly expect to find useful guidance in questions of international relations from such conservative organizations. Edward Devine argued that "the more obvious peace people" should be excluded from whatever action the social workers took, in favor of those who would come to the Henry Street deliberations with "an open mind." The "conservative peace people," Kellogg pointed out, had not met the world crisis with any action or message that expressed the "youth and vision of America."[13]

As an alternative to cooperation with the established peace movement, Kellogg had proposed early in September that the close-knit group of social work leaders, plus a few others whose prominence would insure national attention, meet in a small conference, withdrawing to consult quietly with one another in the manner of an "old time retreat." From such a retreat, Kellogg hoped, the small hand-picked group of reform leaders would emerge to launch a national movement and proclaim a bolder program than that of the old peace societies, a program that would challenge commercialism and commercial exploitation, denounce armaments, and "breathe the spirit of democracy."[14] When President-emeritus Charles Eliot of Harvard University and Thomas A. Edison, who had been invited to give the group prestige and a more "representative" appearance, failed to attend, the conference clearly assumed the character of a social workers' and social reformers' reunion. True to Kellogg's expectations, the Henry Street Conference, and the organizations such as the Anti-Preparedness Committee and the American Union Against Militarism that eventually grew out of it, injected a new approach to

12 Paul Kellogg to Jane Addams, 11 Sept. 1914, Box 5, Addams Papers, SCPC; John Haynes Holmes to William Short, 27 Jan. 1914, Box 4, New York Peace Society Papers, SCPC.

13 Paul Kellogg to Jane Addams, 11 Sept. and 15 Sept. 1914, Box 5, Addams Papers, SCPC.

14 *Ibid.*

international relations into the peace movement. They broke sharply with the emphasis on order and stability of the old peace organizations and envisaged the search for an enduring international peace as integrally connected with the advance of liberal or radical social and political programs at home.

The rather loose terms "social workers" and "social reformers" have been employed thus far to refer to an identifiable group of figures including Jane Addams, Lillian Wald, Paul Kellogg, Edward T. Devine, Owen Lovejoy, Florence Kelley, John Haynes Holmes, Emily Balch, Sophonisba Breckinridge, Samuel McCune Lindsay, Frederic C. Howe, Julia Lathrop, Grace Abbott, Julian Mack, John L. Elliott, Graham Taylor, Mary K. Simkhovitch, Mary McDowell, Mornay Williams, Helena Dudley, and dozens of others of similar positions in the field of social work who began to take an active and organized part in the peace movement beginning in 1914 or early 1915. But although most of these men and women were engaged, as a vocation or avocation, in some phase of social work, they were by no means representative of the social work profession as a whole. The great majority of the leaders in social work did not become actively involved in the peace movement even after 1914. For instance, of the 284 persons who delivered addresses before the National Conference of Charities and Corrections between 1913 and 1916, only sixteen participated actively in the peace movement. Speakers before the conference during these years included thirty-two officers of public charitable organizations and institutions and thirty-seven officers of private charity organization societies and provident associations. Nineteen of these were officers of Children's Aid Societies, Humane Societies, Orphans' Homes and Child Welfare Bureaus. Not one of these officers, representing the public and private social welfare organizations of nearly every large city, assumed any role of leadership in the new post-1914 peace organizations.[15]

But if those who sought to lead and transform the peace movement represented only a small minority among the nation's social workers, they were a vocal, visible, and distinctive minority. Several qualities distinguished them from the majority of their colleagues. For the most part, those who concerned themselves with the peace movement were those within the social welfare field who had the widest national experience and the most varied

[15] These figures are based upon a survey of the *Proceedings of the National Conference of Charities and Corrections*, the principal national organization of social workers, for the years 1913 through 1916.

backgrounds and were the least specialized in their social concerns and least provincial in their outlooks. Many of them had served with national organizations or on committees with national reform goals. Others were engaged in the social welfare field primarily as teachers or journalists. In reporting and interpreting the tasks of social work and the results of social welfare efforts they had come to see the social welfare movement as a single entity, dependent upon the advance of a galaxy of interrelated reform programs. In seeking common principles and in attempting to place individual developments into a meaningful pattern, they had come to stress national issues and to concern themselves not merely with a favorite individual program or reform, but with the fortunes of "social progress" generally.

The tendency of those in the social welfare field who sought involvement in the peace movement to be "generalists" rather than "specialists" was related to another line of distinction within the social work field: the growing divergence between those who stressed social reform and those who emphasized individual casework. During the late nineteenth century a slight tension had already risen between those social workers, often with settlement house connections, who emphasized reform and the change of social and economic conditions and those, most often associated with charity organization societies, who rejected sentimental sympathy for the poor and looked to the reform of the individual rather than of social conditions.[16] But despite this tension, the social work profession at the turn of the twentieth century remained amorphous and undifferentiated. "It was a compound of casework, settlement work, institutional and agency administration, and social reform," Roy Lubove has written, "and anyone, paid or volunteer, who enlisted in the crusade to improve humanity's lot claimed the title of social worker."[17]

During the second decade of the century, however, as the percentage of paid workers and the degree of functional specialization increased, a majority within the emerging profession of social work came to emphasize professional technique rather than broad social reform. Those like Jane Addams and Lillian Wald who had looked upon themselves, in Allen Davis' phrase, as "the

[16] Roy Lubove, *The Professional Altruist: The Emergence of Social Work as a Career, 1880-1930* (Cambridge, Mass. 1965), p. 10; Allen F. Davis, *Spearheads for Reform: The Social Settlements and the Progressive Movement, 1890-1914* (New York 1967), pp. 17-19. I am much indebted to these two works for the ensuing discussion of changes in social work and social workers during the early twentieth century.

[17] Lubove, *The Professional Altruist*, p. 119.

general practitioners of social work," who had seen social work more as cause than function, more a matter of sentiment than technique, found that like general practitioners in other developing professions, they soon lost their central position within the field.[18] Gradually, despite their national prominence, they became a group apart from those social work leaders with aspirations to a more recognized professional status based upon scientific training and specialization. Individual casework, with increasing emphasis on psychology, upon "personality" rather than environment, characterized the approach of the new social work professionals. Those whose apolitical attitudes or functional position within the social work field inclined them toward this casework emphasis were less likely than the old social reformers and political activists to worry about the threat of war to social reform or to take an interest in developing new peace organizations. It was the old social reformers, the group that Allen Davis has termed the "social justice progressives," who brought attitudes arising from experiences in social work and social reform into the peace movement after 1914.[19]

Several other characteristics distinguished the social progressives who took up the cause of world peace after 1914 from the majority of their fellow workers in the social welfare field. Those who joined the peace movement tended to be located in the largest urban centers, such as New York and Chicago, where various peace organizations were active and, not surprisingly, where the major national social reform organizations had their headquarters. They were more likely to be theorists or propagandists and educators in the social work field than bureaucrats or practitioners and were typically those who placed more emphasis on academic training for social work than a more vocational training in specific social work skills.[20] Several of the peace groups restrict-

18 Davis, *Spearheads for Reform*, p. 234.

19 Lubove, *The Professional Altruist*, pp. 79-83, 86; Allen F. Davis, "Welfare, Reform and World War I," *American Quarterly* 19 (Fall 1967), 517, 533. In his "Reminiscences" Roger Baldwin, a social worker drawn temporarily into leadership in the main social workers' peace organization, has described accurately, from the viewpoint of a "social justice progressive," the growing divergence in concerns among social workers. At the National Conferences of Charities and Corrections, he recalls, "I was drawn most to those who occupied their professional obligations with a social philosophy and political crusading. They were not numerous. Most were preoccupied with techniques which I minimized or accepted as routine. The 'art of case work,' goal of so many social workers, left me cold or scoffing." "The Reminiscences of Roger Baldwin," p. 33, Oral History Research Office, Columbia University.

20 On the division among social workers over the role of academic emphasis in the training of social workers see Lubove, *The Professional Altruist*, p. 144.

ed their membership to picked executive and advisory committees; personal friendships and allegiances, often going back to
the settlement houses or reform organizations, frequently determined who was approached to join the peace committees and societies. Finally, those attracted to the peace movement tended, as
their reform proclivities would suggest, to have been those who
participated far more frequently in the discussions of "social legislation" and "standards of living and labor" during the National
Conferences of Charities and Corrections than in discussions of
questions of health, social hygiene, insanity, inebriety, or penal
corrections and probation.[21]

In theory, all those in the social welfare field should have
feared the adverse effects of war upon social conditions and social programs, and have been equally impelled into the peace
movement by that heightened feeling for the conservation of human life that social work, whether it be in the field of health, children's aid, corrections, or living and working conditions, presumably engendered. But, in fact, it was only those long imbued with
the reform spirit, those previously allied in "social progressive"
causes, and those inclined toward political action who sought to
meet the crisis with an organized response on behalf of those
"who deal with the social fabric."[22]

The peace meeting on 29 September at the Henry Street Settlement proved highly inconclusive in its results. The participants
organized themselves tentatively into an informal Peace Committee, but they drew up no common program and initiated no concerted course of action. The rambling and sometimes disjointed
discussions revealed agreement among the participants about the
dangers of war and militarism but considerable confusion and
disagreement about how these dangers might best be met and
countered. A few members reiterated support for such traditional
peace movement programs as the calling of another Hague Conference or the promotion of an international prolaw movement,
but John Haynes Holmes and Emily Balch pointed the direction
that the group would eventually take by blaming the war upon
a competitive and exploitative economic system and calling for

21 *Proceedings of the National Conference of Charities and Corrections, 1913-1916.*

22 The phrase appears first in Paul Kellogg to Jane Addams, 11 Sept. 1914, Box
5, Addams Papers, SCPC. Later it became part of the standard rhetoric of the peace
movement leaders among the social workers. See Lillian Wald to various persons,
22 Sept. 1914, Wald Papers, NYPL and "Towards the Peace That Shall Last," *The
Survey*, 33 (6 Mar. 1915), part II, 1.

an uncompromising new peace movement that would seek closer cooperation with the labor movement.[23]

Nearly all the participants agreed that the social workers had a special responsibility for taking the lead in efforts toward peace and that they could draw upon a valuable fund of experience in making such efforts. Jane Addams and Owen Lovejoy dwelt upon the ill effects that continued war would have upon child labor. Others added their own laments for endangered social reforms and agreed that unless the war was halted, "our causes" would certainly lose out. Most were confident that the Wilson administration would soon take positive action to seek an end to the war. The immediate need, therefore, was to help the president formulate plans and gain strong public support for them. The president's mind was "in bits," Frederic Howe told the group. Someone had to "think hard." "Groups of social workers have thought hard in the past," he reminded them, "and put over the Children's Bureau, Industrial Relations Commission, etc." Now they had the opportunity and responsibility to exert the same kind of influence in the present situation. Florence Kelley, drawing inspiration, as did Howe, from the victories of the social progressives in the recent past, reminded her fellow reformers that achievements like the protocol in the New York clothing strike had been won, not during peace and prosperity, but at the culmination of a period of conflict. Although the meeting adjourned on an inconclusive note, the members left with an understanding that when an appropriate line of action should become clear, when the time was ripe, they should be ready to make their indispensable contribution to the attainment of world peace.[24]

While the Henry Street Peace Committee remained inactive as a group, individual members aggressively broadcast the social workers' viewpoint toward the war during the fall of 1914. Jane Addams warned in interviews that "all the social gains of the past . . . all organized social welfare activities" would be set back for years. What interests could social workers expect the public to show in infant mortality rate, factory conditions, or old age pensions, she asked, when a million men were suffering in the

[23] "Minutes of the Henry Street Peace Committee," 29 Sept. 1914, *passim*, Wald Papers, NYPL.

[24] *Ibid.*, pp. 2-3, 17, 24, 26. The persistence and eventual self-deception of the Henry Street group's faith in Wilson, and their optimistic assumption that they could again assert the kind of decisive influence that they had on several recent social issues, appear as central themes in Blanche Wiesen Cook, "Woodrow Wilson and the Antimilitarists, 1914-1917," Ph.D. diss., The Johns Hopkins University, 1970.

trenches?[25] Lillian Wald championed the cause of the social progressives in December before the organizing meeting of the American League to Limit Armament, a short-lived organization headed by Oswald Garrison Villard, grandson of William Lloyd Garrison and publisher of the New York *Evening Post*, and Hollingsworth Wood, a prominent Quaker lawyer. Reviewing the short history of the Henry Street Committee, she reiterated the fears of the social workers of the social costs and political dangers of the war. The menace, she warned, "lies within our own boundaries. . . ." Behind the agitation for military preparations lay "an embryonic military party." Rather than turn to preparedness the United States should prohibit the export of all arms, explosives, and strategic raw materials and eliminate private profit from armament manufacture by making such manufacture a monopoly of the federal government. As a more positive response to the world crisis, Miss Wald urged, the United States should draw upon its experience in fusing diverse peoples and nationalities to instruct the world in the mutual relations necessary for a new world order.[26]

Meanwhile *The Survey*, under Kellogg's guidance, was vigorously seeking to focus the attention of its audience of social workers and social progressives upon the impact of the war. Early in September an editorial had warned of the "inevitable disaster" which war would bring to "the humane instincts which were asserting themselves in the social order," and avowed that *The Survey* would remain alert against attempts to reverse social reforms under the cover of preoccupation with the war. Reports and analyses of conditions in Europe included news of the destruction of the consumers' league in Belgium, of grave threats to programs of social insurance, of desperately overcrowded and understaffed hospitals, and of the collapse of YMCA work in Europe. The editors blamed unemployment in Chicago on the war and warned that appeals for war relief abroad would divert funds from domestic agencies and programs.[27] John Haynes Holmes offered premonitions of frustration and defeat in the battles for widow's pensions, child labor laws, and social insurance. Confronted with

25 New York *Evening Post*, 30 Sept. 1914 (clipping), Box 5, Addams Papers, SCPC.
26 Lillian Wald, "Meeting at the Railroad Club," 18 Dec. 1914, Wald Papers, NYPL. For a full account of the meeting see, "Organization Meeting of the American League to Limit Armament," Oswald Garrison Villard Papers, Houghton Library, Harvard University.
27 *The Survey*, 33 (3 Oct. 1914), 29; 33 (17 Oct. 1914), 59-60, 62, 73, 75; 33 (21 Nov. 1914), 198; 33 (26 Dec. 1914), 336.

such a prospect, he concluded, "every lover of civilization and servant of human kind—the social worker first among them all—must be a *peace fanatic*." In so doing, he must strike at the roots of commercialism and militarism, and reject the "dilettante, academic, pink-tea, high-brow" approach of the old organized peace movement.[28] Edward T. Devine employed his column in *The Survey* to warn of the threat of "reactionary currents" to international social movements and to call for an embargo on munitions. Kellogg, in a December editorial, warned of a "recrudescence of militarism" in America in the Colorado mining fields arising from the same imperialistic practices of absentee capitalism that had engendered the war in Europe.[29]

The early peace efforts of the social progressives culminated in March 1915 with the publication of a special two-part issue of *The Survey* which included a discussion of "War and Social Reconstruction" and a separate insert signed by eighteen members of the Henry Street Committee entitled "Towards the Peace That Shall Last." In this separate manifesto, the social justice progressives summarized the dangers, by now fully elaborated and documented in their articles and speeches, that the war posed for the whole social justice movement. War had destroyed their reforms, burdened them with additional responsibilities for relief and welfare, and undermined the sense of social conscience and individual responsibility essential for their causes. Attacked by war and threatened by militarism, they had a right and responsibility to counterattack: "By the unemployed of our water-fronts, and the augmented misery of our cities; by the financial depression which has curtailed our school building and crippled our works of goodwill; by the sluicing of human impulse among us from channels of social development to the back-eddies of salvage and relief—*we have a right to speak*."[30]

Their "right to speak," the manifesto continued, was reinforced by a special competence to do so. Experience with the problems of American industrial life had made them experts in conflict resolution and had reassured them that after strife, new and finer mutual relationships might be achieved. Rejecting by implication

28 Holmes, "War and the Social Movement," 630.

29 *The Survey* 33 (5 Dec. 1914), 261; 33 (2 Jan. 1915), 387; 33 (6 Feb. 1915), 518-19.

30 "Towards the Peace That Shall Last," *The Survey*, 33 (6 Mar. 1915), Part II, 3. Four additional names were subsequently added to the eighteen signers of the social workers' manifesto on peace, *The Survey*, 34 (17 Apr. 1915), 72. Of the twenty-two, seventeen had attended the initial Henry Street Meeting, and the others, including Graham Taylor, Rabbi Stephen Wise, and William Kent had been invited but unable to attend.

and omission the programs of the old peace societies, the social progressives called for a "cross-breeding" of cultures on the model of the blend of immigrant cultures in America and a replacement of the old diplomacy of secrecy and intrigue, of profit-takers and diplomats, with a new diplomacy controlled by the people.[31] Thus, by early 1915, in their attacks on commercial imperialism, private profit in armaments, military preparedness, the old established peace movement, and the old diplomacy and in their emphasis upon the incompatibility of war with the advance of social reform, the social reformers had formulated the ideas that were to guide their efforts in the peace movement down to, and in some cases, after the point of American intervention.

Despite the profusion of dire warnings and the actual evidence of declining funds and support for domestic programs, pessimism about the probable effects of the war was never unanimous among the social workers. Even among many of those who gravitated into the peace movement, ambiguous attitudes persisted. No one denied that there would be greater competition for contributions, that welfare programs would be severely overburdened, or that certain advances in social legislation would be endangered. But was it not still possible, as Graham Taylor, president of the National Conference of Charities and Corrections and founder of Chicago Commons, suggested in September 1914 that "even the darkest war clouds" might have some "silver linings"?[32] Even the most reform-minded among the social workers had sought certain goals beyond mere improvement in the living and working conditions of the lower classes, beyond specific items of social legislation. Most of them had sought to realize an ideal of a cooperative and socially responsible society in which class antagonisms were overcome, artificial divisions and alienations between ethnic and social groups eliminated, and a sense of community among all groups established. Gradually some of them began to wonder if the war, despite its awful devastation, might not engender some of the spiritual rejuvenation and social cohesiveness that they had sought to bring about through settlements and neighborhood work at home.

Graham Taylor, who joined in the social workers' peace movement and signed the March 1915 peace manifesto in *The Survey*, wrote several articles early in the war that revealed the ambiva-

[31] "Towards the Peace That Shall Last," pp. 7-8.

[32] Graham Taylor, "Social Measures Prompted by the War," *The Survey*, 32 (12 Sept. 1914), 587.

lence with which some social progressives came to view the relation between the war and social development. Although the war drained energies and resources from certain programs, the belligerents had also reacted to the war emergency by enacting advanced social legislation in the areas of relief, housing, and price controls. The first week in August, Taylor reported, had witnessed the greatest surge of constructive legislation in British history. The process of mobilization, and the rise of a "national consciousness" that went with it, offered a precedent and a model for mobilization in times of peace to meet problems of depression and unemployment. "In the very act of denying the right to live," Taylor wrote, "war is asserting the long and unjustly withheld right to work for a living."[33]

Other voices repeated and elaborated upon Taylor's message. As the war wore on through 1915 into 1916, positive evaluations of the effect of the war in *The Survey* came to be more frequently interspersed among the peace proposals and lamentations over the war's social toll. *The Survey*'s annual report in November 1914 drew solace from the thought that the war had destroyed complacency, offering hope for a new resurgence of "social reconstruction" after the war. Social progressives had sensed a conservative reaction during 1914 which coincided with the collapse of the Progressive Party. But if the war did create a period of flux and upheaval, or stimulate a new degree of social involvement, perhaps basic changes could be effected and a new era of reform initiated.[34]

Reports from abroad often sounded a positive note. Bruno Lasker reported that the pressure of common danger had solidified the cooperative movement in rural England. Graham Taylor observed a new surge of national cooperation in production and distribution in Europe. Class distinctions were decreasing. "Perhaps," he observed, "it was necessary that the people of each nation thus should be welded together . . . on the anvil of awful wrath, before Mazzini's dream of the 'association of the peoples' could be realized in European democracy." From the experience

[33] *Ibid.*, pp. 587-89; Graham Taylor, "Unemployment in War and Peace," *The Survey*, 33 (6 Feb. 1915), 516-17.

[34] "Annual Report," *The Survey*, 33 (28 Nov. 1914), 15; Edward T. Devine, "Through Good Will to Peace," *ibid.*, 35 (18 Dec. 1915), 337; Graham Taylor, "World Salvage," *ibid.*, 35 (29 Jan. 1916), 525-26; "Using Battlefields for Laboratories," *ibid.*, 33 (27 Mar. 1915), 683. On the onset of a "conservative reaction," see Irwin Yellowitz, *Labor and the Progressive Movement in New York State, 1897-1916* (Ithaca, N.Y. 1965), pp. 4, 119; Davis, "Welfare, Reform & World War I," 517, 532-33; and Louis Lee Athey, "The Consumers' Leagues and Social Reform, 1890-1923," Ph.D. Diss., University of Delaware, 1965, p. 238.

of the war, might not a "cooperative commonwealth" arise?[35] Reports from prominent Englishmen confirmed that the war was fostering internal social and political harmony and giving a stimulus to collective action. The cooperative movement was flourishing, housing was improved, unprecedented progress had been made on the "drink question," and class and caste attitudes were fading as a community feeling began to emerge. With distrust and internal antagonism submerged, England was extracting from the ordeal of war a "spiritual gain" and a "larger democracy."[36]

For some, like Graham Taylor, the new appreciation of the positive gains that might be salvaged from the war did not undermine the desire to bring about an early peace. A number of social workers, however, were inclined to find the promise of the regeneration of spiritual values and the restoration of social harmony worth all the sacrifices of war and thus to long more for the chance to share in the regenerative sacrifices of war than for the negotiation of an early peace. Some found an outlet in various relief organizations for their desire to participate in the sacrifices of war. Here they could satisfy the impulses to minister to human needs, to feel absorbed in the most poignant "realities" of human life that may initially have drawn them into social work. Others, often those most active in the prohibition and immigration restriction movements, also remained aloof from the peace movement and were eventually lured by the vision of war-engendered social cohesiveness and class harmony to seek American participation. Even for those vaguely committed to the peace movement, the desire to see an individualistic society achieve a wider social consciousness and responsibility and take concerted public action for social goals provided the basis for a resurgent optimism about the possible results of war when, in 1917, many of them abandoned agitation for peace as a hopeless cause.[37]

[35] Bruno Lasker, "Rural Cooperation in War Times," *The Survey*, 35 (18 Mar. 1916), 715-16; Graham Taylor, "World Salvage," 525-26.

[36] Percy Alden, "National Stress: A Stimulus to Social Action," *The Survey*, 37 (7 Oct. 1916), 23-26; B. Seebohm Rowntree, "The Co-operative Movement with Europe at Arms," *ibid.*, 34 (12 June 1915), 249; *ibid.*, 36 (3 Apr. 1916), 1-2; Dorothy Thurtle, "Government Intervention in Industry in War Times," *ibid.*, 34 (15 May 1915) 155.

[37] For salient examples of concern with sacrifices and regeneration see Edward T. Devine, "Ourselves and Europe," *The Survey*, 37 (4 Nov. 1916), 100; Graham Taylor, "Shattered Ideals—The War's Greatest Casualty," *ibid.*, 36 (3 June 1916), 267; and Joseph Lee, "What Substitute for War," *ibid.*, 33 (3 Oct. 1914), 31-32. Examples of those social workers most concerned about prohibition and immigration restriction that eschewed the peace movement would include Robert A. Woods, Frances A. Kellor, and Philip Davis among others.

During the spring and summer of 1915 the members of the Henry Street Peace Committee moved slowly toward a more formal peace organization and a more active program. While some of them acknowledged the social gains that might be salvaged from the war, those who continued to meet with the committee concluded that social losses from the war would far outweigh any social gains and that the human cost of war demanded that they oppose its continuation for any purposes. At first the committee found little cause to do more than meet informally to exchange views. Several other new peace organizations, including the American League to Limit Armament, the Woman's Peace Party, and the Emergency Peace Federation (Chicago), were already in the field by February 1915. The social workers could continue to meet and air their views without establishing another new organization to compete for members and support.

The first real impetus to greater organized activity by the Henry Street Peace Committee came in July 1915 when Jane Addams returned from the Conference of Women at The Hague and her journeys on behalf of mediation to the belligerent capitals of Europe. On 9 July she addressed an overflow crowd at New York City's Carnegie Hall, describing a popular revolt against war in Europe that would surely soon bring the belligerent governments to accept mediation by a conference of neutral nations. The idea for a conference of neutrals seemed to give hope of a focus for public agitation. Paul Kellogg and Lillian Wald immediately called together the Henry Street group to plan support for Jane Addams' proposals. In Chicago, Louis Lochner, an energetic young journalist and organizer who had graduated directly from the Cosmopolitan Club movement in the colleges into the organized peace movement, was busily planning a mass meeting to welcome Jane Addams and pass resolutions supporting her proposals for a conference of neutrals. The leaders of the Henry Street group urged Lochner to come east to meet with them and began to question whether a new national organization might be needed to carry the new program into action.[38]

On 20 July Jane Addams met with the Henry Street group and reaffirmed privately to her old friends and reform colleagues her judgment that an attempt at mediation which would bypass the formalized and unresponsive channels of the old diplomacy and

[38] Lillian Wald to Jane Addams, 14 July 1915, Wald Papers, NYPL; Paul Kellogg to Jane Addams, 15 July 1915, Box 1, Woman's Peace Party Correspondence, SCPC; Marie Louise Degen, *The History of the Woman's Peace Party* (Baltimore 1939), p. 111.

draw upon the desires of the belligerent peoples for peace would stand a good chance of success. The diplomats of Europe were discredited, she reported. The people of Europe were awaiting a "bold stroke," a "new deal." As negotiators and mediators, the nations needed not old fashioned diplomats and heads of state but "men of a different type" who were "experiencing the international life," participating in international cooperation, and living in "international" (i.e., multinational urban) areas.[39] Drawing upon the past experiences and triumphs of the social progressives, she suggested mediation by a small group of representatives "qualified by experience in great human and economic activities" who would "seek the cooperation of like-minded men from other nations" and act in a manner analogous to mediation committees during labor strikes.[40]

The Henry Street Committee responded to Jane Addams' plea with resolutions and a public statement. *The Survey* summarized her report on its cover. New figures such as philanthropist George Foster Peabody, editor Oswald Garrison Villard, Louis Brandeis, and Felix Frankfurter were drawn into temporary, and in the case of Villard, extended, cooperation with the group. But the brief flurry of activity ended abruptly after the end of July without plans for a further course of action. Most members and advisers of the group were reluctant to pressure the president to support an unofficial body of mediators and by late September the committee had neither an active secretary nor minimal funds. At a meeting "of information rather than action" at Henry Street in late September Lillian Wald lamented that they were still "all groping, and unhappy at doing nothing."[41]

Finally, several circumstances combined to bring the social workers into fully organized participation, and, for a time, into a position of leadership in the peace movement. On 4 November 1915 President Wilson had publicly called for support of a program of "reasonable" military preparedness which included a greatly expanded program of shipbuilding and the creation of a new reserve army of 400,000 men. Social progressives who had constantly assured themselves that Wilson was one of them, a

39 "Minutes of Meeting at Henry Street Settlement," 20 July 1915, pp. 3-4, Wald Papers, NYPL. See also the second set of minutes for same meeting, pp. 4-7 in Wald Papers, NYPL.

40 *Ibid.*

41 *Ibid.*; *The Survey*, 34 (17 July 1915), cover; Lillian Wald to Jane Addams, 23 July 1915, Addams to Wald, 29 July and 3 Aug. 1915, Wald Papers, NYPL; [Paul Kellogg] to Addams, 21 Sept. and "Memoranda on Henry Street Meeting," 27 Sept. 1915, Box 4a, Emily Greene Balch Papers, SCPC.

man who could be trusted to act wisely if only supported and given freedom to wait for the appropriate time, now concluded abruptly that their comrade in the White House had surrendered to the forces of militarism. If for no other reason, an effective organization was now necessary to coordinate opposition to the president's preparedness program. Moreover, the American League to Limit Armament, the major new organization already operating primarily in the antipreparedness field, had failed after almost a year of effort to attract an energetic president and was expiring through lack of leadership and diminution of funds.[42]

On 15 November the Henry Street group stepped into the vacuum left by the American League to Limit Armament and organized itself as the "Anti-Militarism Committee."[43] (In January 1916 the name was changed to "Anti-Preparedness Committee" and in April 1916 to "American Union Against Militarism." For clarity, I shall refer to the same group, during these and other subsequent name changes in 1917, as the "American Union.") At the crucial post of secretary the new American Union elected Crystal Eastman, a social worker with research experience as a part of the team which conducted the Pittsburgh Survey. The sister of socialist Max Eastman, the editor of *The Masses*, Crystal was young, beautiful, and by all accounts a stunning, "gorgeous creature." It was her enthusiasm, inventiveness, indefatigability, and instinct for the dramatic that were largely responsible for the primary influence that the new American Union came to have in the peace movement during 1916 and 1917.[44]

The initial structure and proposed methods of the American Union reflected the reform experiences of its organizers. Originally the union was envisioned as a small, tight-knit junta which

[42] Oswald Garrison Villard to Nicholas Murray Butler, 8 Jan. 1915, L. Hollingsworth Wood to Villard, 9 Oct. and 30 Dec. 1915, O. G. Villard Papers, HL. Wood even speculated that the previously upright Wilson had been corrupted by the influence of his new fiancée, Edith Galt. "His big armament policy seems to coincide with the waxing of her influence," Wood wrote. "I expect she is wrong on the Negro question too."

[43] "American Union Against Militarism" (MS history of the union), Box 1, American Union Against Militarism Papers, SCPC; "Minutes of Peace Meeting, Survey Library," 15 Nov. 1915, Wald Papers, NYPL.

[44] Crystal Eastman's personal qualities are attested to in John Haynes Holmes, *I Speak for Myself: The Autobiography of John Haynes Holmes* (New York 1959), p. 189, Roger Baldwin, "Reminiscences," p. 55, John Spargo, "The Reminiscences of John Spargo," p. 174, Oral History Research Office, Columbia University, and Max Eastman, *Love and Revolution* (New York 1964), p. 26. Her dominant role in the American Union Against Militarism is revealed in nearly every set of minutes of the organization. Her first significant participation as a member of the Henry Street group appears to have come during July 1915. See Lillian Wald to Jane Addams, 14 July 1915, Wald Papers, NYPL.

would provide information to and coordinate the activities of the various militant peace groups. Like the committee that brought about the establishment of a Federal Commission on Industrial Relations, the junta should limit its membership to a small devoted coterie. Like successful ventures in housing, pure food and drugs regulation, and similar reforms, it should build its program around the efforts of a few "high-class experts." Immediately it would launch a muckraking investigation into the special interests behind agitation for military preparedness. Hopefully a muckraker of the caliber of Samuel Hopkins Adams, who had exposed the drug frauds, would lead the muckraking campaign. Certainly the union should employ investigators of the quality of those who had unearthed the facts on the great insurance companies or on Secretary of the Interior Ballinger during the Pinchot-Ballinger controversy. A "prize agitator" from the woman suffrage or prohibition campaigns would be enlisted to carry out a propaganda program. Weekly meetings of a steering committee composed almost exclusively of New York City social reformers would keep the leaders in close personal touch with each other and flexible enough for rapid shifts of program.[45]

The composition of the new American Union and its initial program suggested the extent to which its policies would diverge from those of the prewar peace organizations. Several slightly variant lists of initial members, persons attending the organizing meetings, and persons suggested for a steering committee exist. Every list tells approximately the same story. Social workers continued to dominate the organization. Lillian Wald became chairman; Florence Kelley, vice-chairman; and Crystal Eastman, secretary. Alice Lewisohn, promoter of the dramatic arts at New York City settlements, joined and immediately donated $1,000 to help launch the organization. Max Eastman and Allan Benson, the Socialist Party's 1916 presidential candidate, became members and several of the more radical New York clergymen continued to give strong support. The union declared its intentions to "throw . . . a monkey wrench into the machinery of preparedness" and to

[45] "Minutes of Peace Meeting, Survey Library," 15 Nov. and "Minutes of Peace Committee, Survey Library," 24 Nov. 1915, Wald Papers, NYPL; "Minutes, Organization Meeting," 29 Nov. [1915], Box 1, AUAM Papers, SCPC; "Memorandum," Box 1, Anna Garlin Spencer Papers, SCPC. So influential was the muckraking tradition in the thinking of the social progressives that in 1917 Oswald Garrison Villard, then a leader in the American Union, even sought to persuade the noted expert on international law, John Bassett Moore, to muckrake the State Department, publishing the exposé anonymously. Villard to Moore, 27 Aug. 1917, O. G. Villard Papers, HL.

"stop the war" through a conference of neutrals—programs little favored by any of the prewar peace groups. Members of the union proposed calling for the nationalization of armament factories and pursuing peace through unofficial negotiators if efforts to persuade Wilson to call an official conference of neutrals failed. Although most members of the American Union shrank from the bizarre approach and, in their opinion, undistinguished and ill-chosen delegation that sailed on Henry Ford's Peace Ship in December 1915 they continued to support various means of bypassing the unresponsive channels of official diplomacy.[46]

Within weeks after its organization the American Union was already engaged in feverish activity. It quickly abandoned the idea of remaining merely a small local junta and decided to expand to include affiliated groups, develop local branches, and attract nationwide membership. Despite the success of its expansion, however, effective control and action continued to come entirely from the small group of faithful regulars who met weekly at Henry Street, at the *Survey* offices, or, more often, at a corner table in a nearby restaurant. The union planned for a "truth squad" to follow President Wilson on his "Swing Around the Circle" for preparedness. When Wilson challenged opponents of increased military preparations to hire their own halls and answer him, the American Union responded by organizing mass meetings against preparedness in eleven major cities. Artist Walter Fuller, Crystal Eastman's husband, prepared graphic antiwar displays including one featuring a papier-mâché dinosaur to suggest the futility of mere armament without intelligence. With the increased level of activity came an expansion of the union's goals. A new program in April 1916 added such objectives as a campaign to keep military training out of the schools, resistance to conscription, the imposition of income and inheritance taxes to meet the costs of any increased military expenditures, and reiteration of proposals for a democratic federation of the American Republics and a joint international commission to settle all outstanding issues with the Orient.[47]

[46] For lists of members see the minutes and memoranda cited in n. 45, above. At one point in 1916 Lillian Wald even proposed a new social work leader for membership with slight trepidation, concerned that some might think the union "overweighted with so-called social workers." Wald to Amos Pinchot, 30 June 1916, Amos Pinchot Papers, MS Div., Library of Congress. For the Union's early policy statements see "Minutes of Peace Meeting, Survey Library," 15 Nov. 1915, Wald Papers, NYPL and "Editorial Department, Anti-Militarism Committee," 21 Dec. [1915], Box 4, AUAM Papers, SCPC.

[47] Holmes, *I Speak for Myself*, p. 188; "American Union Against Militarism," "Minutes of Anti-Preparedness Committee," 14 Feb. 1916, "Minutes of Anti-Pre-

Encouraged by the sudden surge of their influence during the antipreparedness campaign, the leaders of the American Union moved on to achieve what seemed a major triumph during the war crisis with Mexico in June and July 1916. The union helped focus antiwar sentiment in America by countering the bellicose accounts in some newspapers of a clash between American and Mexican troops at Carrizal in June 1916. The union bought ads in influential papers and utilized the space to reprint an account by one of the American officers which revealed that the Americans had been the aggressors in the incident.[48] Meanwhile the union sponsored the establishment of an unofficial joint high commission of three American civilian leaders and three Mexican civilians to mediate the controversy. Unable to meet in El Paso as originally planned, the unofficial commission began sessions in New York early in July with Moorfield Storey, Paul Kellogg, and David Starr Jordan representing the United States. Later, when an official Mexican-American Commission was appointed by the two governments to ease the crisis and mediate the outstanding grievances, the American Union predictably claimed credit for preserving the peace and establishing the precedent for the official commission. As in so many other instances, it was Crystal Eastman who took the initiative and persuaded the others to stake everything on the seemingly quixotic scheme of an unofficial commission.[49]

The seeming success of unofficial diplomacy in the Mexican crisis heightened even further the hopes of the American Union's leaders for a "people's diplomacy." In her proposed program for the American Union for 1917, Crystal Eastman emphasized their Mexican triumph. "We must make it known to everybody," she exhorted, "that the *people* acting directly—not through their governments or diplomats or armies, stopped that war and can stop

paredness Committee," 28 Mar. 1916, "Statement Concerning the Anti-Militarism Committee," n.d. [May 1916], Box 1, AUAM Papers, SCPC; "Swinging Around the Circle Against Militarism," *The Survey*, 36 (22 Apr. 1916), 95; Donald Johnson, *The Challenge to American Freedoms: World War I and the Rise of the American Civil Liberties Union* (Lexington, Ky. 1963), pp. 4, 6-7; *American Union Against Militarism Bulletin* (mimeographed), No. 52 (12 June 1916), Box 4, AUAM Papers, SCPC.

48 Arthur S. Link, *Wilson: Confusions and Crises, 1915-1916* (Princeton 1964), pp. 315-16; Merle Curti, *Peace or War: The American Struggle, 1636-1936* (Boston 1936), pp. 247-48.

49 Curti, *Peace or War*, pp. 247-48; "The Mexican Crisis: Some Inside Information," *American Union Against Militarism Bulletin* (No. 53 mimeographed), (15 July 1916), Box 4, AUAM Papers, SCPC; "Special Conference of American Union Against Militarism," 21 June 1916, and "Minutes of the Inter American Peace Committee," Box 1, AUAM Papers, SCPC.

all wars if enough of them will act together and act quickly."[50]
In *The Survey*, Paul Kellogg of the American Union, who had
earlier attacked the "crust of inertia" and "bonds of red-tape" of
the old diplomacy, now warned that since governments continued
to fail to make peace through cautious conventional diplomacy,
the new peace movements would have to place their hope for
peace in the people back of the governments.[51]

Like the Woman's Peace Party and others of the new peace organizations, the American Union quickly arrogated the right to
speak on behalf of the masses. The union discovered sympathetic
forces among the farmers and among organized labor. If the common people of the nation (represented by the farmers, labor
unions, and the unorganized urban immigrant masses, for whom
the social work leaders now presumed to speak) opposed preparedness and sought a mediated end to the war, then a government that failed to take action in accordance with their desires
must be under the sway of special groups employing it against
majority interests. The extent of popular sentiment for preparedness sometimes challenged this logic and many of the social progressives remained reluctant to think ill of the Wilson administration. Still, among American Union members the idea continued
to grow that the old, familiar domestic battle between the people's interests and the entrenched special interests, in which they
had long participated, was now being reenacted in the struggle
over military preparedness and war.

Even while they were proclaiming the triumph of unofficial
diplomacy in the Mexican Crisis of June-July 1916, the leaders of
the American Union were chagrined to find that their central
campaign against preparedness had proved to be, at best, only a
partial success. Slowly the tide of sentiment in influential circles
had turned against them. As they fought to stem this tide and preserve their welfare and reform programs the social workers in the
peace movement came more and more to believe that they were
confronted by a "conspiracy of class and press." Everywhere,
they concluded, the campaign for preparedness had gained the
support of "hereditary wealth and influence," of the "masters of

---

[50] [Crystal Eastman] "Suggestions for 1916-1917," Box 1, AUAM Papers, SCPC;
AUAM, "Program for 1917" (typed MS), pp. 5, 7, subject file #15, Pinchot Papers,
LC.

[51] *The Survey*, 35 (4 Dec. 1915), 263-64 and 37 (16 Dec. 1916), 297. On the frequent expressions of disillusionment with traditional diplomacy and official governmental channels by members of the AUAM, see also Cook, "Woodrow Wilson and
the Antimilitarists," pp. 102, 111, 122-24.

privilege," of the "big employers and monopolists."[52] Amos Pinchot, a leading figure in the American Union by 1916, warned, "Such men are using the preparedness campaign as an excuse for preaching the sanctity of American industrial absolutism. They are telling us that we must aid and abet our monopolist buccaneers, so that our monopolist buccaneers will protect us from foreign aggression."[53]

It was no mere coincidence, the social workers concluded, that as the preparedness campaign became increasingly energetic, the attacks upon their social legislation and the diversion of funds from public needs also intensified. It was the old reactionary tactic of promoting foreign involvement, even foreign wars, in order to divert attention and funds from social reform at home. The preparedness forces, the American Union charged, were "menacing democracy" in America. Their object, warned Oswald Garrison Villard, Frederic Howe, Amos Pinchot, and others in the American Union, was to entrench themselves in the government, to reap huge profits, to check and then reverse the movements toward greater democracy and social reform.[54]

It was not only in demanding greater military preparedness that the old foes of the social progressives seemed to have extended their evil influence into international affairs. Social progressives had concerned themselves so deeply with domestic matters before 1914 that they had given little thought to the influence of their enemies, the privileged economic interests, in the realm of foreign policy. Socialist spokesmen and fervid antimonopolists had occasionally reiterated theories about the connections between big business expansionism, economic and political imperialism, and resulting military interventions and war crises. Now, in 1916, the social workers in the peace movement began to find such explanations not only plausible but alarmingly relevant.

Frederic Howe, who had only touched upon the international

52 Lillian Wald, "Seeing Red: When Militarism Comes in at the Door, Democracy Flies Out of the Window," MS dated 19 May 1916, Wald Papers, NYPL; A. A. Berle to Amos Pinchot, 28 Apr. 1916, Pinchot to Roy W. Howard, 23 May 1916, Pinchot Papers, LC; Michael Wreszin, Oswald Garrison Villard: Pacifist at War (Bloomington, Ind. 1965), p. 48.

53 Amos Pinchot, "America and Real Preparedness" (typewritten MS), p. 3, Box 1, AUAM Papers, SCPC.

54 Untitled pamphlet, Box 1, AUAM Papers, SCPC; Frederic C. Howe, "Democracy or Imperialism—the Alternative that Confronts Us," The Annals of the American Academy of Political and Social Science, 46 (July 1916), 250, 252; Frederic C. Howe, Why War? (New York 1916), pp. 311, 313; Wreszin, Villard, pp. 48, 68; Pinchot, "America and Real Preparedness," p. 31; Committee for Rational Preparedness, "Some Suggestions for Propaganda Material," Box 1, AUAM Papers, SCPC.

role of the monopolists and the "titans of finance" in his *Privilege and Democracy in America* in 1910, devoted an entire volume to the topic in 1916. "War and preparations for war," Howe warned, "are the international expression of the same struggle that has convulsed San Francisco, Cleveland, Chicago, Denver, or Toledo in the conflict of franchise corporations to protect their grants from the city; it is an expression of the same conflict over the resources of Alaska, of the seizure of the public lands of the nation, of the financial exploitation of the New Haven, Rock Island, and other railroads." Behind the preparedness campaign lay "the same merger of interests," the "same 'invisible government' which for the past twenty years has been waging war on democracy."[55]

Amos Pinchot reaffirmed Howe's conclusions and pressed them upon other members of the American Union. The American plutocracy, he argued, having crushed competition at home, was now "branching out to impose upon the rest of civilization and semi-civilization the same system of exploitation they have so successfully brought to perfection here."[56] A committee of the union warned President Wilson during an interview that any encouragement to aggressive action through greater preparedness should be avoided since the United States was "potentially more aggressive" than other nations because "our economic organizations are more active, more powerful, in reaching out and grasping for the world trade." The preparedness movement was thus a "dangerous expression of class and national aggression."[57]

Two methods of attacking this network of control by the special economic interests seemed to hold promise. One was to institute popular control over foreign affairs. "Diplomacy has always been the prerogative of the upper classes," Frederic Howe complained. Jane Addams, through the programs of the Woman's Peace Party, had been steadily mounting an attack on the regular diplomats as men who, in every nation, were "the least representative of modern social thought and the least responsive to changing

---

[55] Frederic C. Howe, *Privilege and Democracy in America* (New York 1910), p. 62 and *Why War?*, pp. viii, 307, 309, 317. Paul Kellogg stressed the same connection between the domestic struggle and foreign policy when he questioned sharply whether those "who are espousing the war in the name of liberalism in Europe are those from which we can expect leadership when democracy and privilege lock horns in municipality, state capital or Congress" (*The Survey*, 37 [17 Feb. 1917], 574). See also Oswald Garrison Villard to David Lawrence, 18 Apr. 1916, O. G. Villard Papers, HL and Cook, "Woodrow Wilson and the Antimilitarists," pp. 64, 72, 76.

[56] Amos Pinchot to Stephen S. Wise, 26 Apr. 1916, Pinchot Papers, LC.

[57] "The President interviewed by Committee of the American Union at the White House," 8 May 1916, pp. 2-5, Wald Papers, NYPL.

ideals." Emily Balch, a leader in the American Union, even came by 1917 to reject any attempt to revive the Hague Peace Conferences, since they were "so fundamentally involved with all the old war system and with the rotten type of predatory diplomacy. . . ." Howe agreed that the Hague Conferences had been a "chimera." They had represented privilege—with which democracy could not unite on a peace program. Even the relatively cautious Lillian Wald attacked the "old forms of intercourse between nations which have so often misrepresented the views of the plain peoples and led them to disaster."[58] Most members of the American Union concluded that an open diplomacy, conducted through true representatives of the people rather than a professional corps of diplomats, would undercut the power of the special economic interests to create international mischief through devious, interest-serving diplomacy.

The other likely avenue for an attack on the imperialistic economic interests was through their pocketbooks, the more radical American Union members concluded. Take the profits out of war and military preparedness, they argued, and the demands for great military expenditures would end. Certainly the enthusiasm for preparedness would subside markedly if the cost of armaments was to be met by taxes on income and on inheritances rather than by the usual bonds and taxes which placed the financial burden of war on the poor. Real preparedness, an antipreparedness conference asserted in mid-1916, would consist of a child labor bill, social insurance against sickness and accidents, federal acquisition of natural monopolies, sharply progressive taxes on large incomes and inheritances, and the termination of perpetual franchises. Such steps would insure the "social preparedness" needed during both peace and war.[59] But it seemed obvious to the social workers that as long as those great economic interests currently standing behind the preparedness campaign remained entrenched, programs for peace would be difficult to carry through to success. The only answer seemed to be a direct attack upon the citadels of privilege, even when this meant a vio-

58 Howe, *Why War?*, pp. ix, 49, 340; Jane Addams to [Emily Balch], 10 Jan. 1917, Balch Papers, SCPC; *The Survey*, 35 (15 Jan. 1916), 444; Degen, *Woman's Peace Party*, p. 161; Jane Addams, Emily G. Balch, and Alice Hamilton, *Women at the Hague: The International Congress of Women and Its Results* (New York 1916), pp. 129-33; Emily G. Balch to Fannie Fern Andrews, 31 July 1917, Box 30, Fannie Fern Andrews Papers, Arthur and Elizabeth Schlesinger Library, Radcliffe College; Lillian Wald *et al.*, to Woodrow Wilson, 24 Jan. 1917, Wald Papers, NYPL.

59 "A Prescription for 'Real Preparedness,'" *The Survey*, 36 (15 July 1916), 420; Pinchot, "America and Real Preparedness," p. 3.

lent attack upon those who had been supporters of the peace movement in times past. Frederic Howe described the task to his fellow social progressives in familiar terms: "We should strike at the privileges, profits, and immunities which the ruling classes enjoy. If we end profit from war and preparations for war, if we democratize all of the agencies of foreign relations, so that they may not be used by privileged interests, then we shall strike at the very foundations of privilege and shall tend to identify all classes with proposals for peace."[60]

During the fall of 1916 and January of 1917 the leaders of the American Union Against Militarism lapsed into a state of relative inaction. They had gradually lost ground in the struggle against preparedness and the war seemed little closer to a mediated end, but at least America did not appear close to intervention. Wilson's campaign for reelection on a program of "peace and progressivism" at least partly satisfied the social workers in the American Union. A delegation from the American Union had earlier interviewed Wilson's opponent, Charles Evans Hughes, in the hope that Hughes, as a former spokesman for the "interests of the people" against the insurance companies and other business interests, could be persuaded to share the social workers' opposition to preparedness as undemocratic. But Hughes failed to meet their expectations. Disappointed as they were over Wilson's support for preparedness and his relative inaction on recent social justice legislation, the leaders of the American Union still pinned their hopes on Wilson. It was true that, except during the Mexican crisis, Wilson had given little evidence of responding to their frequent interviews, petitions, and appeals. Still, they were convinced that Wilson shared their basic outlook; their previous experiences with his administration on domestic issues showed that his "instincts" were sound, and they continued to convince themselves that they retained sufficient personal influence with Wilson to gain his sympathetic attention at a crucial moment. Although their private discussions and public propaganda increasingly expressed disenchantment with unrepresentative and undemocratic aspects of official governmental and diplomatic action, they refused to abandon hope in the efficacy of their own influence in high circles of the administration. Many of them diverted part of their energies in the fall of 1916 to helping reassure Wilson's reelection. And although it formally endorsed neither candidate,

60 Howe, *Why War?*, p. 341.

the American Union was bold enough afterwards to claim that pacifist sentiment had carried the election for Wilson.[61] Wilson buoyed their spirits with his "Peace Without Victory" speech on 22 January 1917. Nine days later, however, Germany announced her intended resumption of unrestricted submarine warfare.

During the next seven weeks the social workers in the peace movement led the desperate propaganda campaign against American intervention. In this effort they found themselves increasingly alienated from "respectable" American opinion. They found themselves torn between the moral appeals for intervention on behalf of democracy and their own conviction that social reform depended upon peace, and worried lest their unpopular activities discredit the social causes for which they were also fighting. Alternately apprehensive and sanguine about the losses or gains in social welfare activity and legislation that war conditions might bring, the social workers who had formed the core of the American Union Against Militarism now faced a period of profound testing and self-questioning.

The war crisis brought a surge of peace movement activity. New organizations, most of them microscopic in active membership and radical in tendency, arose almost daily. The Committee for Democratic Control, for instance, consisted, in its entirety, of Amos Pinchot, Randolph Bourne, Max Eastman, and Winthrop D. Lane. The organization was simply an additional publicity arm of the American Union Against Militarism. Crystal Eastman's name sometimes appeared on the letterhead and Margaret Lane, secretary of the New York branch of the Woman's Peace Party and wife of one of the four members, served as secretary.[62] Another vociferous new group, the American Committee on War Finance, consisted basically of Amos Pinchot, John L. Elliott, ethical culturist and settlement house leader, and Owen Lovejoy of the National Child Labor Committee. All were also leaders in the American Union. The American Neutral Conference Committee, a slightly older organization, had a small active membership that largely duplicated that of the other active peace groups. The Emergency Peace Federation, headed by Louis Lochner, sought

61 Davis, "Welfare, Reform and World War I," 518; Arthur S. Link, *Wilson: Campaigns for Progressivism and Peace, 1916-1917* (Princeton 1965), pp. 39, 57-59, 124-25; Cook, "Woodrow Wilson and the Antimilitarists," pp. 153-55, 168, 240-41; *New York Times*, 15 Oct. 1916, I, 12:1, 17 Oct. 1916, 1:1, 13 Nov. 1916, 6:5.

62 Committee for Democratic Control, "Referendum," Box 4, AUAM Papers, SCPC; Joy Young to Amos Pinchot, 8 Apr. 1917, Pinchot Papers, LC; Max Eastman, *Love and Revolution*, p. 28. Winthrop D. Lane was a criminologist and regular contributor to *The Survey*.

simply, as its name implied, to federate and coordinate those groups still fervently opposing American intervention.[63]

Much of the work of these organizations consisted of appeals to the president, antiwar propaganda campaigns, and desperate attempts to devise alternative solutions to the crisis. The American Union, in keeping with the political progressivism its members had espoused for a decade or more, sought to promote a popular decision on the question of intervention through a referendum. While attempts to induce Congress to countenance such an idea quickly proved futile, the American Union pushed forward its own unofficial, postcard referendum, sending out postcard ballots on the question of intervention at its own expense to the constituents of selected congressmen and urging the recipients to return the cards with their "vote" to their representative in Congress.[64] The Emergency Peace Federation attempted to repeat the American Union's triumph during the Mexican crisis by promoting a Joint High Commission with Germany. Roger Baldwin, a leading St. Louis social worker, urged the American Union to organize mass protest meetings while Norman Thomas and Crystal Eastman sought to establish a continuous arm of the committee in Washington during the crisis. Various members of the American Union struggled manfully with the complex details of various plans for armed neutrality, limited hostilities, or defensive alliances of neutrals as concrete alternatives to propose to the president.[65] As pressure for American participation mounted and their position became more desperate, the active peace workers attacked their enemies with increasing virulence. Chancellor David Starr Jordan of Stanford University, a member of the American Union and one of the leading antiwar speakers during the

[63] No detailed account of the activities of these short-lived organizations has been written. Brief surveys of the activities of these and other peace organizations during the hectic months of February and March may be found in Curti, *Peace or War*, pp. 249-57; Degen, *Woman's Peace Party*, pp. 180-91; and Lella Secor Florence, "The Ford Peace Ship and After," in Julian Bell, ed., *We Did Not Fight: 1914-1918 Experiences of War Resisters* (London 1935), pp. 97-125.

[64] AUAM Executive Committee, "Minutes of Meeting" 5 Feb. 1917 and Committee for Democratic Control, "Do the People Want War" (broadside), subject file #15, Pinchot Papers, LC; AUAM Executive Committee, "Minutes of Meeting" 10 Feb. 1917, Box 1, AUAM Papers, SCPC; "Resolution proposed at the Joint Conference of Peace Societies, 22, 23 Feb. by the Executive Committee of the American Union Against Militarism," Box 4, AUAM Papers, SCPC.

[65] David Starr Jordan to Jessie Jordan, 17 Mar. 1917, David Starr Jordan Papers, Hoover Institution on War, Revolution and Peace; AUAM Executive Committee, "Minutes of Emergency Meeting" 9 Feb. 1917 and "Minutes of Emergency Meeting" 10 Feb. 1917, subject file #15, Pinchot Papers, LC; Paul Kellogg, "The Fighting Issues," *The Survey*, 37 (17 Feb. 1917), 572-77.

months of crisis, joined forces with Socialists and other radicals
he had previously avoided. He turned his attack upon the plutocracy, the "New York brokers" and "Boston tories," charging that
the war was a deliberate "backfire against democracy." "Peace,"
he wrote in defense of his new vehemence, "gains nothing by being mealy-mouthed."[66] The American Committee on War Finance
pointed its accusing finger at Wall Street, berating the "bankers,
stock brokers and other prominent citizens who mess at Delmoni-
co's, bivouac in club windows, . . . and are at all times willing to give to their country's service the last full measure of
conversation."[67]

During this period of crisis for the peace movement in early
1917, the social workers and the American Union continued to
provide much of the active leadership and most of the prominent
names that gave the movement the modicum of respectability it
still preserved. Jane Addams, Lillian Wald, Paul Kellogg, and
Emily Balch continued to play prominent roles. Mary Simkhovitch of Greenwich House, John Lovejoy Elliott of Hudson Guild,
Mary McDowell of the Stockyards Settlement in Chicago, Dr.
Alice Hamilton, expert on industrial conditions and former resi-
dent of Hull House, Alice Lewisohn, promoter of the arts in New
York settlement houses, and Elizabeth Glendower Evans, promoter of the Women's Trade Union League and other reform causes,
gave their support to eleventh-hour appeals, petitions, and antiwar rallies.[68]

But this did not mean that the ranks of the social workers, or
even of the old Henry Street group remained unbroken. Social
workers who had never joined the peace movement, and a number
of those who had given brief early support to it in 1914 and 1915

[66] David Starr Jordan to Jessie Jordan, 24, 25, 26 Mar. and 1 Apr. 1917, Jordan
Papers, HI; *Boston Evening Transcript*, 29 Mar. 1917, 11:3; *Boston Daily Globe*, 29
Mar. 1917, 5:3.

[67] Committee for Democratic Control, "'Do the People Want War," subject file
#15, Pinchot Papers, LC.

[68] Indications of the participation in peace efforts during this period by various
groups and individuals can be derived from a variety of sources such as organizational letterheads, petitions, signatures on open letters, and minutes of meetings
of the executive committees of the peace organizations involved. A sample of such
sources might include: Lella Faye Secor to H.W.L. Dana, 11 Apr. 1917 (Emergency
Peace Federation stationery), Box 1, Henry Wadsworth Longfellow Dana Collection,
SCPC; AUAM Executive Committee, "Minutes of Meeting" 10 Feb. 1917 and
"Minutes of Meeting" 28 May 1917, Box 1, AUAM Papers, SCPC; John Lovejoy
Elliott *et al.* to Woodrow Wilson, 1 Feb. 1917, Balch Papers, SCPC. See also Mercedes
M. Randall, *Improper Bostonian: Emily Greene Balch* (New York 1964), p. 230 and
Alice Hamilton, *Exploring the Dangerous Trades: The Autobiography of Alice
Hamilton, M.D.* (Boston 1943), p. 180.

were already moving toward a prowar position. Leading social workers in Baltimore denounced *The Survey* for its "pacifism" and a large group of social workers in Boston wired the president to pledge their "unswerving support" for immediate and forcible measures of defence."[69] Even Rabbi Stephen Wise, steadfast ally of the reform-minded New York social workers in the peace movement and other reform causes, wavered and then broke with the American Union during February and March 1917. During a meeting of the American Union which Emily Balch characterized as a struggle for a man's soul and in which the other officers of the union gave Wise a "roasting" until, as Villard remembered, "the sweat finally ran down his face in streams," Wise proclaimed his intention to declare himself for war and against "Prussianism" at his next appearance at the Free Synagogue. Paul Kellogg described the session during which Wise announced his "recantation" as "morally and spiritually . . . the most gripping experience I have ever been through."[70] But other social progressives in the American Union, including Kellogg himself, would soon find themselves forced to make agonizing, if less dramatic, decisions about how long to give full support to a peace movement that continued to move in a radical direction.

By March 1917 the trend Leftward among the new peace organizations had become apparent in the membership as well as in the ideas of such groups as the American Union Against Militarism. Norman Thomas, who was begining his transit from social gospeler to Socialist, had emerged as one of the most active members of the American Union's executive committee. Roger Baldwin, a St. Louis social worker deeply attracted to philosophical anarchism, came to New York in late March 1917 to aid the American Union and was immediately appointed associate director. When Crystal Eastman took a temporary leave of absence in March to give birth to her baby, Baldwin assumed virtual control of the organization. Meanwhile Crystal Eastman had proposed the addition to the union's executive committee of a group of six new members including poet, revolutionary, and war correspondent John Reed and Socialists Joseph Cannon, Frank Bohn, and Ar-

---

[69] *The Survey*, 37 (10 Mar. 1917), 659; 37 (24 Mar. 1917), 729-30. Members of *The Survey* Board sought to curb Paul Kellogg's antiwar policies in the periodical. See Lillian Wald to Jane Addams, n.d., Wald Papers, NYPL, Paul U. Kellogg to William I. Hull, 12 June 1917, Box 5, William I. Hull Papers, Friends' Historical Library, Swarthmore College, and Clarke A. Chambers, *Paul U. Kellogg and the Survey: Voices for Social Welfare and Social Justice* (Minneapolis, 1971), pp. 58-61.

[70] Paul Kellogg to Jane Addams, 9 Feb. 1917, Box 6, Addams Papers, SCPC; Oswald Garrison Villard to Max Eastman, 27 Aug. 1938, Villard Papers, HL.

thur LeSueur.[71] James Maurer, a prominent leader in the Socialist Party of America, was now serving on the American Union's executive committee and Scott Nearing, recently driven out of two universities for his radicalism, began to attend union policy-making meetings. Max Eastman, long a member, had begun to give more frequent attention to the activities of the union.

The United States' declaration of war on 6 April 1917 and the trend toward radicalism in the American Union precipitated a prolonged six-month crisis within the organization. An influential minority of the officers now sought a more "quiet" approach. Arguing that they would lose all opportunity for exerting influence in the country if they appeared to continue in opposition to American intervention, this group, which included many of the prominent social work leaders, preferred either to leave the peace movement or to work within it for such limited goals as democratic peace terms, no compulsory military training, and the preservation of industrial standards and labor laws.[72] A larger group of the active officers of the union, including Crystal Eastman and Roger Baldwin, while joining the others in protesting that "we are not a party of opposition . . . we are not, by habit or temperament, troublemakers," sought to pursue a more militant and inevitably a more unpopular course.[73] Torn by this conflict and weakened by the equivocal sentiments of a number of its major figures, the American Union became less and less the representative in the peace movement of the social progressives. It split, continued to convulse, split again, and then, ironically deserted by *both* major factions, slumped finally into desuetude.

The first wartime crisis within the American Union erupted as soon as the tendencies of Roger Baldwin's leadership became apparent. On 3 April 1917, three days before the actual declaration

[71] AUAM, Executive Committee, "Minutes of Meeting," 5 Mar. 1917, and "Minutes of Meeting" 27 Mar. 1917, subject file #15, Pinchot Papers, LC. See also Crystal Eastman's proposals for financing an expedition by John Reed to investigate American imperialism in the Caribbean, AUAM Executive Committee, "Minutes of Meeting," 27 Feb. 1917 and "Minutes of Meeting," 5 Mar. 1917, Box 1, AUAM Papers, SCPC. On Baldwin, see Johnson, *Challenge to American Freedoms*, pp. 9-14 and Baldwin, "Reminiscences," pp. 36-55.

[72] For expressions of this viewpoint, see George Foster Peabody to Emily Balch, 6 Apr. 1917, Balch Papers, SCPC; Henry R. Mussey to Crystal Eastman, 27 Sept. and 17 Oct. 1917, Frederick Lynch to Crystal Eastman, 26 Sept. 1917, Lillian Wald to Executive Committee, AUAM, 5 June and 13 Sept. 1917, AUAM Executive Committee, "Minutes of Meeting" 13 Sept. 1917, Box 3, AUAM Papers, SCPC; Kellogg, "Statement" (undated typed copy), Box 4, AUAM Papers, SCPC.

[73] AUAM, "Rough Draft of Possible Basis for Immediate Statement to the Press," 15 June 1917, Box 4, AUAM Papers, SCPC.

of war, Baldwin had submitted his recommendation for a wartime program for the union. The organization should conduct a campaign against conscription, he argued, organizing the conscientious objectors for mutual aid during the war and effective unity afterwards. On 4 April and again on 9 April, Baldwin reiterated his proposals for a national organization to fight conscription. In response to Baldwin's urgings, the union formed a committee to fight conscription on 9 April 1917. Out of this initial embryonic committee a distinct subgroup within the union, a "Civil Liberties Bureau" gradually took form. Baldwin's group, initially designated as the Bureau for Conscientious Objectors, included several of the more conservative leaders of the American Union but it was clearly dominated by the more radical and purely pacifist element, including Scott Nearing, Hollingsworth Wood, Edmund Evans, Norman Thomas, and Baldwin himself.[74] Since the campaign for a mediated settlement of the war had been eclipsed by American intervention and proposals for peace terms would be highly unpopular so soon after the war declaration, the tasks of defending civil rights and protecting conscientious objectors quickly usurped most of the energies of the union. Crystal Eastman's description of the new emphasis of the American Union, although written in September, would have been equally accurate in June: "The work of this Bureau [the Civil Liberties Bureau], as we anticipated, has come to be our chief war-work. A Union Against Militarism becomes, during war time, inevitably a Union for the Defense of Civil Liberty."[75]

But the new preoccupation of the American Union greatly disturbed some of the prominent social workers who had long been among its leaders. They wished, in the words of Paul Kellogg, to "distinguish between opposition to militarism and war and active opposition to this war."[76] Several of them wanted to confine the union's work to the promotion of a democratic peace and propaganda for an appropriate form of international organization after the war. An important part of their program, Lillian Wald

74 AUAM, "Minutes of Meeting of Executive Committee," 4 and 9 Apr. 1917, subject file #15, Pinchot Papers, LC; Roger Baldwin to members of the Executive Committee, AUAM, 3 Apr. 1917, Pinchot Papers, LC; Roger Baldwin to Dear Sir, 23 May 1917, Box 3, AUAM Papers, SCPC.

75 [Crystal Eastman], "Proposed Announcement for Press" (typewritten results of meeting of Executive Committee of AUAM, 24 Sept. 1917), Box 1, AUAM Papers, SCPC. For other confirmations of the dominant role of the Civil Liberties Bureau in the AUAM see Oswald Garrison Villard to Crystal Eastman, 27 Sept. 1917 and Frederick Lynch to Crystal Eastman, 26 Sept. 1917, Box 3, AUAM Papers, SCPC.

76 Paul Kellogg, untitled statement, n.d. [May-June 1917], Box 4, AUAM Papers, SCPC.

warned, entailed friendly relations with the government. They could not expect government cooperation if they allowed themselves to drift into a "party of opposition."[77] The aggressive defense of conscientious objectors seemed to border on deliberate efforts to interfere with the administration in its prosecution of the war. Baldwin's speeches to mass audiences, Kellogg charged, had become "an espousal of conscientious objection rather than a defense of the rights of conscientious objectors." Baldwin and Nearing, he suggested, were using the tactic of defense of conscientious objection, as well as other tactics, to attempt to stir up mass opposition to American participation in the war.[78] At a special meeting on 1 June 1917 Henry Mussey reported that he and several other leaders of the American Union—Lillian Wald, Jane Addams, Alice Lewisohn, and Paul Kellogg—had conferred and concluded that the Bureau for Conscientious Objectors should be established as a separate organization, outside of the American Union. Kellogg and Wald soon threatened to resign over the issue.[79]

Crystal Eastman, whose sympathies lay with the more radical faction, managed to heal the breach temporarily by persuading Baldwin and his group to operate under the wider and more respectable title of a "Civil Liberties Bureau" rather than as a "Conscientious Objectors Bureau" and by reminding the radicals that they needed Kellogg and Wald for their "balance," their influence, and their mediation between "the revolutionary and the non-resistant motives that make up our combination."[80] But the compromise had hardly been effected when the dispute between the two factions erupted again over a new but related issue.

[77] Lillian Wald is quoted in Crystal Eastman, "Statement," 14 June 1917, Box 3, AUAM Papers, SCPC. On the responses of several of the more conservative members to the Baldwin program see also Cook, "Woodrow Wilson and the Antimilitarists," pp. 210, 212, 217.

[78] Paul Kellogg, untitled statement, n.d. [May-June 1917], Box 4, AUAM Papers, SCPC.

[79] AUAM, "Minutes of Special Meeting of Executive Committee," 1 June 1917, subject file #15, Pinchot Papers, LC; Crystal Eastman, "Statement," 14 June 1917, Box 3, AUAM Papers, SCPC.

[80] Crystal Eastman, "Statement," 14 June 1917, Box 3, AUAM Papers, SCPC; Johnson, Challenge to American Freedoms, pp. 20-21. Although Crystal Eastman and Roger Baldwin did not always work easily together, her sympathies were unquestionably with a radical approach. "Can't we dash in and save the country from conscription?" she wrote to Amos Pinchot apparently shortly after giving birth to her child in March 1917. "I'm crazy to get back on the job, Amos. And I'm so afraid it will be over—the fight lost—nothing left for me to do" (Crystal Eastman to Amos Pinchot, n.d., Pinchot Papers, LC). On Baldwin and Eastman, see Baldwin, "Reminiscences," p. 55. On Crystal Eastman's eventual clear break with Lillian Wald on the issue, see Eastman to Wald, 24 Aug. 1917, Box 3, AUAM Papers, SCPC.

In the wake of American intervention in the war, radicals and socialists in New York City had planned a Conference on Democracy and the Terms of Peace as a kind of popular-front organization to continue agitation on the war issue. Roger Baldwin, apparently with Lillian Wald's consent, had devoted much of his time to the organization of this conference.[81] Other American Union officers, including Emily Balch, Norman Thomas, Crystal Eastman, Max Eastman, and James Maurer, had joined in promoting the conference. The American Union, despite the involvement of many of its members as individuals in the conference, at first decided not to give official support to it.[82] But when a new organization, the People's Council, emerged from the Conference on Democracy and Terms of Peace and when this council, which quickly gained a popular reputation as subversive and treasonous, called a convention for 1 September in Minneapolis, the American Union had to decide whether to dissociate itself from the new organization or to support it by sending delegates to its convention.

A majority of the officers of the union favored participating in the People's Council Convention. Even Charles Hallinan, one of the more conservative officers, pointed out that since the People's Council had "drawn together . . . nearly all the sincere, courageous anti-militarists" the American Union would write itself off as another of the pusillanimous peace societies if it declined to be represented.[83] But Lillian Wald, Paul Kellogg, and several other officers again protested heatedly against the union's proposed action. The American Union, Lillian Wald reminded her fellow officers, had "stood before the public as a group of reflective liberals." But the People's Council was neither reflective nor liberal. Its public image, she warned, was one of "impulsive radicalism." The American Union had suffered "irretrievable" losses in public influence and stature through its failure to keep aloof and independent, free from interlocking directors with other "so-called 'peace societies.' "[84] Miss Wald again threatened to resign as chairman. In a showdown vote among the officers on the question

[81] AUAM, "Minutes of Meeting of Executive Committee," 28 May 1917, Box 1, AUAM Papers, SCPC.

[82] Louis P. Lochner to Emily Balch, 12 May 1917, American Conference for Democracy and Terms of Peace Papers, SCPC.

[83] Charles T. Hallinan to Amos Pinchot, 29 Aug. 1917, Pinchot Papers, LC.

[84] Lillian D. Wald to Crystal Eastman, 28 Aug. 1917 and Wald to Executive Committee, AUAM, 13 Sept. 1917, Box 3, AUAM Papers, SCPC. See also Oswald Garrison Villard's statement of opposition to participation in the People's Council in Villard to Eastman, 29 Aug. 1917, Box 3, AUAM Papers, SCPC.

of relations with the People's Council and the retention within the American Union of the Civil Liberties Bureau the "radicals" triumphed 18-5.[85]

At this point the American Union entered the final stages of disintegration. The more active radicals sought to preserve the union as a liberal ally by offering to leave. Crystal Eastman hoped to refurbish the union's respectability by disengaging its officers from interlocking directorates with more radical groups and stressing the less controversial parts of the old American Union program.[86] But Wald, Kellogg, Alice Lewisohn, and several others had already departed and no new liberals sought to join. Every day seemed to bring new threats to the respectability and public influence of liberals who might continue to adhere to the American Union. The press hurled epithets at it. On the lobby walls of the building in which it was housed a handwritten scrawl announced each arrival's entrance into "Treason's Twilight Zone." Perhaps in defiance, the occupants allowed the intended slur to remain. As Roger Baldwin later remarked of the group, "We all lived in a spirit of heresy to the times."[87]

Crystal Eastman, while trying to placate the less radical members of the union, nevertheless continued to propose aggressive and potentially disruptive programs to test civil liberties. In a plan similar to that undertaken by the Congress of Racial Equality to test desegregation of public transportation facilities in the freedom rides of 1961, she proposed that the union defy local authorities by attempting to hold public meetings for the discussion of a negotiated peace or "some other controversial subject" to test rights of free speech in areas where attempts to hold anti-war meetings had been denied. Either free speech would be vindicated, she argued, or a case for an appeal to the courts would

[85] Lillian D. Wald to Crystal Eastman, 28 Aug. 1917 and Wald to Executive Committee, AUAM, 13 Sept. 1917, Box 3, AUAM Papers; AUAM, "Minutes of Meeting of Executive Committee," 30 Aug. 1917, Box 1, AUAM Papers, SCPC; Crystal Eastman to Amos Pinchot, 27 Aug. 1917, Pinchot Papers, LC.

[86] AUAM, "Minutes of Meeting of Executive Committee," 13 Sept. and 9 Oct. 1917, subject file #15, Pinchot Papers, LC; Amos Pinchot to Roger Baldwin, 6 Oct. 1917, Pinchot to John A. McSparran, 11 Oct. 1917, [Pinchot] to Alice Lewisohn, 11 Oct. 1917, Pinchot Papers, LC; L. Hollingsworth Wood to Pinchot, 2 Oct. 1917, Box 3, AUAM Papers, SCPC. See also Crystal Eastman's recommendations in AUAM "Minutes of Meeting of Executive Committee," 9 Oct. 1917 and "Proposed Statement of our Relation to People's Council to be Agreed upon by both Executive Committees and sent out confidentially in answer to Inquiries," Box 1, AUAM Papers, SCPC.

[87] Frances Witherspoon and Tracy D. Mygatt, "The Reminiscences of Frances Witherspoon and Tracy D. Mygatt," pp. 7-8, Oral History Research Office, Columbia University; Baldwin, "Reminiscences," p. 306.

be established. What she did not say was that such attempts would almost certainly evoke violent, perhaps riotous reprisals, and that such an attitude of defiance would further mark the union as an agent of opposition and dissension.[88]

With the resignation of Wald, Kellogg, and the others, influential participation of the social workers in the peace movement came to an end. Mary Simkhovitch, Florence Kelley, Elizabeth Glendower Evans, Julia Lathrop, Alice Hamilton, and Grace Abbott had already abandoned the movement for other activities. Jane Addams did not yet resign, but she took no active part in the subsequent, declining activities of the union. In the face of increasing public condemnation and federal actions against seditious publications, the American Union staggered on into the fall of 1917. In November the remaining members of the executive committee announced that the union had "suspended activity" and simultaneously sought to rejuvenate their cause by reorganizing under a new name, The American Union for a Democratic Peace. But even this attempt to look ahead toward the peace settlement did not remove the cloud of opprobrium under which they now operated. Within two weeks after the reorganization, a tired and pessimistic Crystal Eastman recommended that they sell the furniture, transfer their assets to the Civil Liberties Bureau, and remain in contact only through informal gatherings. The Civil Liberties Bureau steadily expanded its activities and emerged in 1920 as the American Civil Liberties Union and Villard, Hallinan, and several others revived the American Union Against Militarism in 1918 to wage a narrower anticonscription battle that extended feebly into the early 1920s.[89] But the old American Union, and with it the social justice progressives' crusade to save the social fabric from the ravages of war, had come to an end.

The time had come, many of the social progressives concluded, when it was necessary to measure the good that one might accomplish through an uncompromising antiwar stand against the good one might accomplish as a social worker or reformer by preserving at least a modicum of public influence and devoting

---

[88] [Crystal Eastman], "Secretary's Recommendations," [24 Sept. 1917], Box 1, AUAM Papers, SCPC.

[89] "Minutes of Meeting of Executive Committee," 29 Oct. and 26 Nov. 1917, 31 Jan. 1918, and 10 Feb. 1919, untitled typed MS dated 12 Nov. 1917, Box 1, AUAM Papers, SCPC; Crystal Eastman to Oswald Garrison Villard, 16 Nov. 1917, Box 3, AUAM Papers, SCPC; Charles T. Hallinan to Villard, 1 Dec. 1917, 13 May 1918, Villard to Hallinan, 3 Dec. 1917, O. G. Villard Papers, HL; *New York Times*, 13 Nov. 1917, 4:6; Johnson, *Challenge to American Freedoms*, pp. 24-25, 145-48.

one's energies to pressing social tasks. And the social tasks *were* pressing. There were working conditions at munitions factories to be investigated, a child labor amendment to be upheld and enforced, welfare needs and problems of dislocation in the settlement neighborhoods to be met, labor standards to be set and enforced for companies working on military contracts, women and children to be protected from overwork during wartime. For many of the reform-minded social workers, the decision to withdraw from the radical peace organizations did not come easily. Like Jane Addams and Lillian Wald they withdrew reluctantly, still convinced that war entailed irreparable losses to social welfare and social reform programs. But they believed that, even at the expense of appearing less courageous than their more radical friends, they must eschew a cause that promised only futility in order to conserve their energies and influence for more constructive work.

In the end, as Lillian Wald later commented, it was the "free lances," those without responsibilities for existing social welfare institutions such as settlement houses, national reform organizations, government bureaus, or established schools and journals, who carried on with the radical peace movement. Such "free lances" were not "disciplined by the torture-chamber method" of having the very survival of institutions that represented their life work and central social concern threatened by loss of financial support from those who objected to the radical peace activities.[90] Alice Hamilton recalled that although both she and Julia Lathrop were pacifists, "neither of us took a conspicuous anti-war stand, for the same reason—we were deeply attached to our jobs and feared to lose them." Then she added, "I have never been sure I was right in this. Perhaps it would have been better to make an open protest, but I knew I was not influential enough to have that protest count for much, while my work in the war industries counted for a good deal."[91]

All of those engaged in on-going programs of social services, and those who had committed themselves deeply to the accomplishment of a specific reform program faced the same question: should they work for immediate, visible goals in support or de-

---

[90] Lillian D. Wald, *Windows on Henry Street* (Boston 1934), pp. 307-8. For an example of the threats to which she referred see J. Horace Harding to Lillian Wald, 4 Aug. 1917, Wald Papers, NYPL. Jacob Schiff, head of Kuhn, Loeb & Co., a personal friend of Lillian Wald and long a generous supporter of her settlement work, had by mid-1917 shifted from an antiwar to a prowar position and this undoubtedly placed pressure on Miss Wald to eschew radical peace organizations.

[91] Hamilton, *Exploring the Dangerous Trades*, p. 192.

fense of long-treasured social welfare programs, or should they endanger their ability to meet such immediate needs by working for the more revolutionary but less tangible goals of the radical peace organizations. With rare exceptions the answer was the same: a continuing sympathy with the ideals and goals of the peace organizations, but a practical abandonment of those groups for social work programs that met immediate needs and which often contributed to the nation's war effort.

There was another reason, too, for the ostensibly ignominious desire on the part of influential social progressives to preserve their public respectability—a reason that even the more radical adherents of the peace movement could occasionally appreciate. Influence in high places was needed in order to provide needed protections and assistance to the more unpopular activities of the radicals. Lillian Wald had earlier warned about the need to be able "to get before the powers that be." Intervention through such strategically placed friends of the social workers as Secretary of War Newton Baker, and Frederick Keppel, also influential in the War Department, brought informal arrangements and favorable decisions in cases of conscientious objectors. Sympathetic liberals who remained on good terms with the administration might also be able to help save radical periodicals from post-office censorship.[92] Even those who remained with the radical organizations occasionally found reason to reject ties with those of even less public repute. Roger Baldwin, for instance, found himself forced to reject the support of his old friend Emma Goldman and other anarchists despite their common opposition to the war and the draft. Baldwin later related, ". . . I saw that their support compromised the rest of us, who carried no such heavy burden of public hostility. . . ." Emma Goldman, he added, "was indignant that I opposed their participation in mass meetings, regarding me as a compromiser, willing to sell out my principles for the little respectability we might gain." But all of his colleagues in the Civil Liberties Bureau, Baldwin reported, were of the same

[92] Lillian Wald to Executive Committee, AUAM, 5 June 1917, Crystal Eastman, "Statement," 14 June 1917, Box 3, AUAM Papers, SCPC; Oswald Garrison Villard to Joseph P. Tumulty, 26 Sept. 1917, Baldwin to Villard, 20 Nov. 1917, and Baldwin, "Memorandum for the Directing Committee of the Civil Liberties Union," 31 May 1918, O. G. Villard Papers, HL; "Memorandum for Mr. Tumulty" (to accompany letter from Mr. Villard, Sept. 1917), typewritten copy, Wald Papers, NYPL; Baldwin, "Reminiscences," pp. 58-61; L. Hollingsworth Wood to H.W.L. Dana, 6 June 1918, Box 1, Dana Papers, SCPC. On the desire of the Civil Liberties Bureau "radicals" to retain organizational ties to the respected liberals of the AUAM see also Cook, "Woodrow Wilson and the Antimilitarists," p. 212.

opinion. Even among the radicals, those who sought immediate social goals short of revolution found that some degree of public repute was necessary for effective action.[93]

During 1915 and 1916 many of the reform-minded social workers had looked upon the peace movement as a logical extension of, or at least a necessary mode of protection for, the various social welfare measures and social reforms to which each was personally committed. In 1917, however, as the nation became absorbed in the process of mobilizing for war, they often found that the circumstances of national emergency offered opportunities for unprecedented advances in many of their social programs. Allen Davis has described in some detail the way in which wartime conditions stimulated such movements as those for urban housing, social insurance, public health and health insurance, improved labor standards, women's rights, and prohibition.[94] In *The Survey* many social work leaders seemed bent upon surpassing each other in their paeans to the possibilities of the war. Frederic Almy predicted that war would help lessen poverty. Others celebrated the new enthusiasm for prohibition and for public health. A letter to the editor warned social workers "not to lose the chance to cooperate with the newly aroused ardor of the heretofore indifferent." One article quoted a speaker at the National Conference of Social Work: "God has given it to us as a priceless heritage to live in these great times."[95]

Some social workers had long denounced all manifestations of class antagonisms and had taken as their mission the restoration of social homogeneity and national unity. Often these social workers found deep satisfactions in war work that emphasized rigid social control. Philip Davis volunteered to recruit immigrant workers for the shipyards and to keep them contented with their work. He rejoiced that the war had forced the nation "to unify its diverse nationalities under a common flag." The perception of this need he termed a "Great Awakening."[96] Robert Woods called for "The Regimentation of the Free," and took satisfaction in the way in which the relations established by his settlement house in Boston had facilitated the organizing of the people for war service. He and others delighted in the stimulus which the war

93 Baldwin, "Reminiscences," p. 268.
94 Davis, "Welfare, Reform & World War I," 518-32.
95 *The Survey*, 38 (5 May 1917), 111-12; 38 (21 Apr. 1917), 77; 38 (16 June 1917), 254-56, 258.
96 Philip Davis, *And Crown Thy Good* (New York 1952), pp. 209-11, 219.

gave to Americanization campaigns.[97] Bruno Lasker of *The Survey* asked settlement house leaders in a questionnaire on war activities whether they would advocate "a new and hastened process of Americanization by introduction of the compulsory use of the English language at all gatherings held in or in connection with the settlement," whether they should provide "frequent opportunities for demonstrations of patriotism and loyalty. . . ," and whether they should participate in recruiting campaigns. Even Lillian Wald, who shared none of the enthusiasm for the war crisis, noted that settlements had become the logical organizations for handling problems of fuel and food, for spreading propaganda, and for the "awakening of a sense of civic and national responsibility in the foreign population and among the tenement house dwellers in general. . . ."[98]

Social work leaders like Lillian Wald, who had strongly supported the peace movement, found themselves serving on national committees and commissions and absorbed in the processes of war mobilization. Grace Abbott, Lillian Wald, Pauline Goldmark, and numerous other social work and social reform leaders were appointed to committees of the Council of National Defense. Grace Abbott and Julia Lathrop served as consultants to the War Labor Policies Board and Florence Kelley became secretary of the Board of Control of Labor Standards for Army Clothing.[99] Judge Julian Mack, an early member of the American Union, was commissioned by the Council of National Defense to draw up a program for compensation, pensions, and separation allowances for soldiers. Edward Devine, another early member, took up overseas relief work and editorialized on the importance of social work as a part of "the organizing and training of a nation for

[97] Eleanor H. Woods, *Robert A. Woods, Champion of Democracy* (Boston 1929), pp. 317-18.

[98] Bruno Lasker to Lillian Wald, 14 Apr. 1917, [Lillian Wald], "Replies to Questionnaire for the Survey," typed MS, 19 Apr. 1917, Lillian Wald, "Settlements," typed MS, 1917, Wald Papers, NYPL; R. L. Duffus, *Lillian Wald, Neighbor and Crusader* (New York 1938), p. 199; Wald, *Windows on Henry Street*, pp. 7-8. On the wartime role of settlements see also Mary Kingsbury Simkhovitch, *Neighborhood: My Story of Greenwich House* (New York 1938), pp. 187-93 and Cook, "Woodrow Wilson and the Antimilitarists," p. 13.

[99] Athey, "Consumers' Leagues and Social Reform," pp. 240-41; Duffus, *Lillian Wald*, p. 197; Mary Chamberlain, "Women and War Work," *The Survey*, 38 (19 May 1917), 153-54; Edith Abbott, "Grace Abbott," *Social Service Review*, 13 (Sept. 1939), 383. For an example of continuing sympathy for the peace organizations by social workers but refusal to devote their energies to any but their immediate social causes see Florence Kelley to Margaret Lane, 8 Aug., 27 Aug., and 1 Sept. 1917 and Kelley to Crystal Eastman, 15 Jan. 1918, Woman's Peace Party, New York Branch, Correspondence, SCPC.

war." Other social workers were absorbed into a variety of relief and service organizations, at home and overseas, under the Red Cross, the YMCA, or the federal government.[100] Some of these social workers attained positions of considerable influence and power; others found themselves fully taxed, but also personally fulfilled in responding to the pressing immediate needs of crisis conditions. In either case they were likely to find their energies too fully absorbed to allow for further work in the peace movement and their immediate responsibilities too grave to risk discrediting themselves by further association with the radical peace organizations.

Thus ended the brief interval during which the reform-minded social workers had strengthened the peace movement with their leadership and imbued it with their ideas. During the period from late 1914 until mid-1917 in which they shared the leadership of the movement, it had cast off its alliance with genteel reform, self-interested business philanthrophy, and conservative legalism. The American Union Against Militarism and the other active peace organizations influenced by its policies had reacted to the outbreak of war in Europe by transforming the conception of a movement for world peace. Under their influence the movement's purpose had been converted from an attempt to insure stability and order by circumscribing potential sources of disorder and upheaval with legal and moral sanctions to an attempt to preserve and advance goals of social and political reform by democratizing and humanizing international relations. In the process, the social workers had increasingly characterized the foes of international peace—the aristocratic professional diplomats, the politicians unrepresentative of basic human and popular interests, and the monopolists of big business and finance—as allied with, or identical to the traditional enemies of the social reformers at home. So compelling did their vision of the interrelatedness of foreign policy and internal social issues become, in fact, that some social progressives came to see the peace movement as inseparable from an attack on the whole established social order. "The situation is at once so confused and interwoven," Norman Thomas wrote to Crystal Eastman in September 1917, "that one cannot take hold of any aspect of the problem without finding himself dealing with the whole question of the wrong organization of society; capitalistic exploitation, milita-

[100] *The Survey*, 38 (7 July 1917), 316-17, 321, 336; Lillian Wald to Tom Barry, 7 Dec. 1917, Wald Papers, NYPL; Davis, "Welfare, Reform & World War I," pp. 519-528; Chambers, *Paul U. Kellogg*, pp. 62-67.

rism, contempt of civil liberties . . . these are all aspects of the wrong basis of our social life."[101]

The radical implications of Thomas' vision led directly into the programs and ideas of active remnants of the radical peace movement in 1917 and 1918—the People's Council and the Fellowship of Reconciliation. But social workers took little part in these organizations. Those social work leaders who had joined the peace movement had represented a rapidly diminishing minority of reformers, of "generalists," of "amateurs" within a rapidly developing profession. The new dominant majority in the social work profession, those who emphasized what Clarke Chambers has called the "retail phase" of social work, the concern with individual casework, had never shown any particular interest in the peace movement.[102] Among the distinct group of reform-minded social workers, the peace movement had seemed the temporary means toward their reform goals. When American intervention drove them to devote all their energies to their long-cherished social programs, either out of the necessity to protect old achievements or the opportunity to make new gains, they retreated from the increasing radicalism that they had helped engender in the peace movement and recommitted themselves to their old concerns. Many continued to think of themselves as allies of the peace movement, although they could not identify thoroughly with the methods or ideas of the new radical organizations. Many also retained their interest in foreign policy to the extent of organizing to support a democratic peace settlement and call for a liberal league of nations. A few like Jane Addams continued longer than most to question whether she should not continue to work with the People's Council.[103] But in the end the social progressives, like many groups before them, put the peace movement aside when it no longer seemed to lead toward fulfillment of their

101 Norman Thomas to Crystal Eastman, 27 Sept. 1917, AUAM Papers, SCPC.

102 Clarke A. Chambers, "Social Service and Social Reform—A Historical Essay," *Social Service Review*, 37 (Mar. 1963), 80. See also discussion above, pp. 228-31.

103 Jane Addams to Mary Rozet Smith, 2 Sept. 1917, Box 6, Addams Papers, SCPC; Addams to Lillian Wald, 4 June and 23 Aug. 1917, Lillian Wald to Roger Baldwin, 12 Oct. 1917, Wald Papers, NYPL; Clayton Lusk, ed., *Revolutionary Radicalism: Report of the Joint Legislative Committee of the State of New York* (Albany 1920), Part I, Vol. I, p. 1120. The continued interest in foreign policy manifested itself in the formation of a "Committee on Nothing at All" in 1918 with the nucleus of the original American Union Against Militarism. After the war this committee emerged from its semi-underground status to become the League of Free Nations Association and later to form the basis for the Foreign Policy Association. Wald, *Windows on Henry Street*, pp. 311-15.

most important goals. Leadership would next be taken up by those who envisioned in the increasingly revolutionary implications of the movement a fulfillment of, or a vehicle for, their particular domestic goals and concerns.

CHAPTER EIGHT

The Workingman's Burden

THE American declaration of war against Germany on 6 April 1917 nearly destroyed the surviving peace organizations. The leaders of the Woman's Peace Party and the American Union Against Militarism had come to the peace movement through their initial and dominant concerns with various domestic reforms. After the spring of 1917, they found that energetic work for peace severely jeopardized their influence and public acceptability, and thus their ability to defend or push forward their domestic reform programs. Gradually they drew back from the struggle to reverse or substantially alter the government's apparently irreversible course of action.

As the reformers and social workers withdrew, however, a few of their more radical and "unattached" colleagues carried forward the peace movement to a new and culminating phase of its early twentieth century development. Drawing into temporary alliance a group of single-taxers, antiwar Socialists, deeply alienated intellectuals, and leaders of radical, immigrant-dominated unions, these leaders created a new focal peace organization and carried the American peace movement to the most extreme expression of its newly discovered revolutionary potential.

The new vehicle of the peace movement was the People's Council of America for Democracy and Peace, first publicly proposed and tentatively organized on 30 May 1917 and finally and officially established over three months later amid turmoil, public denunciation, and armed repression. In seeking to establish a kind of popular front, the People's Council brought together indigenous and immigrant radicals, labor leaders, and intellectuals in a manner reminiscent of the coalition that formed behind Henry George in the New York mayorality campaign of 1886. By 1917 such a coalition could look to the added strength of a vastly expanded body of newly arrived, radically oriented immigrant laborers at the center of organizational activity, New York City, and a potential ally in the rising organization of disgruntled farmers in the Nonpartisan League. Perceptions of the poten-

tiality of the war for major social disruption and the example of
the Russian Revolution gave leaders of the People's Council encouragement to think in terms of imminent, though hopefully
peaceful, revolution. Supported actively by leading Socialists and
by the heads of the largest New York City unions, the new
organization not only promised a radical potential; it also appeared finally to have tapped a source of support long discussed
within the peace movement but rarely drawn upon—the workingman.

The notion of the workingman as the particular victim of war
—in military service, in taxes, and in depressed living standards
—was hardly new in 1917. Those who presumed to speak for
the workingman, whether trade union leaders, Socialists, reformers, or single-taxers, had long insisted that the workingman
despised war, recognized it as a conspiracy against his interests,
and from the very nature of his economic position, sought brotherhood and cooperation with all other workingmen. But while
those who sought to articulate the feelings of labor could be
counted upon to proclaim the abstract interest of workingmen in
international peace on ceremonial occasions, labor spokesmen
had not, on that account, become major integral forces within
the various peace organizations.

On the contrary, both trade union leaders and Socialists in
America gave no more than formal and infrequent lip service to
the peace societies and gave relatively little attention to the whole
subject of foreign relations. In practice, their commitment to
peace was qualified by tactical considerations and by a conviction
that the advance of their own parties or unions, rather than the
success of the peace organizations, was the true key to improved
international relations. Thus some account of the nature of the
commitment of labor spokesmen to peace, in ideology and in
practice, during the two decades prior to 1917 is necessary to an
understanding of how portions of labor came at last to involve
themselves significantly in a major peace organization. Such a
backward glance also helps to explain how the People's Council
came to reflect and deepen the divisions already present among
labor spokesmen on other than international issues.

Of all those who presumed to speak for American workingmen
the Socialists were traditionally the most uncompromising in their
antiwar declarations and the least interested in peace societies.
During the prewar decade the Socialists, European and American, had adopted antiwar resolutions, debated the use of the

general strike as an antiwar tactic, and warned ominously but obscurely that they might utilize capitalist-inspired wars to promote internal revolution. But by and large, international relations had not commanded their primary attention. This was particularly true of the American Socialists who concerned themselves before 1914 almost entirely with domestic issues. The major Socialist organization in the United States after 1901, the Socialist Party of America, perfunctorily passed antiwar resolutions and joined in the antiwar proclamations of the Second International. But not one of the party platforms from 1904 through 1912 contained a single proposal for international affairs, although one contained as many as thirty-three specific demands for other political and industrial reforms. Although Socialist theoretician John Spargo bragged that Socialist bodies had adopted "several ringing resolutions" against war, the gravest attention the Socialist Party of America appears to have given to international affairs at its national conventions was to bicker over how many delegates it could afford to send to the next international congress.[1]

The leading Socialist theoreticians in America clearly manifested this relative unconcern with international affairs in their major early twentieth century works. Morris Hillquit's *Socialism in Theory and Practice* devoted less than six pages to war and international relations; John Spargo's numerous treatises hardly touched upon the subject. Spargo's textbook, *Elements of Socialism*, gave less than one page to international relations. William English Walling displayed the same unconcern in three books published between 1912 and 1914.[2] Charles Edward Russell gave international problems a short chapter in *Why I Am a Socialist*, but the only complete book to discuss problems of war and peace from a Socialist viewpoint during the period was *War—What For?* by George R. Kirkpatrick, a little-known party member

[1] *Proceedings of the National Convention of the Socialist Party* (Chicago 1904), pp. 229-35, 306-9; *ibid.* (1908), pp. 320-23; *ibid.* (1912), pp. 196-98. On each occasion from 1904 through 1914 the International Secretary's report was adopted with only perfunctory discussion. Spargo is quoted in Ira Kipnis, *The American Socialist Movement 1897-1912* (New York 1952), p. 298.

[2] Morris Hillquit, *Socialism in Theory and Practice* (New York 1909), pp. 296-302; John Spargo, *Socialism* (New York 1906), *The Socialists, Who They Are and What They Stand For* (Chicago 1906), *The Common Sense of Socialism* (Chicago 1908), and *Applied Socialism* (New York 1912); John Spargo and George Louis Arner, *Elements of Socialism* (New York 1912), p. 219; William English Walling, *Socialism As It Is: A Survey of the World-Wide Revolutionary Movement* (New York 1912), *The Larger Aspects of Socialism* (New York 1913), and *Progressivism and After* (New York 1914). On the American Socialists' disinterest in the theoretical analysis of war see also Gerald Friedberg, "Marxism in the United States: John Spargo and the Socialist Party of America," Ph.D. diss., Harvard University, 1965, pp. xix, 161.

who emerged as the vice-presidential candidate in 1916 on the strength of his vehement antiwar position. Despite his virulent attacks on the "grinning, well-fed, silk-lined, lily-fingered, decorated 'great' men" who cause wars, and his threats to keep a list of those who favored war for future front-line duty, Kirkpatrick could produce nothing more positive than a running sequence of insults and vague threats, a call for increased Socialist antiwar propaganda, and a demand for the abolition of capitalism by Socialist victory at the polls.[3]

While Kirkpatrick's diatribe was atypical of the concerns and the style of most Socialist leaders in the prewar period, his expectation that international peace would come through the victory of socialism rather than the efforts of peace societies reflected a universal judgment among party leaders. How could peace societies, led by men who perfectly represented the forces of competitive and exploitative capitalism, be expected to eliminate wars which were the inevitable result of capitalistic competition? Morris Hillquit argued that Socialists must avoid such movements as those headed by Andrew Carnegie and men with similar interests. "The classes and men who cause wars and thrive on them," he warned, could not be expected "to intelligently and honestly combat them."[4] In the wake of the outbreak of war in 1914 another Socialist sneered, "Peace societies are nothing more or less than schemes whereby certain parasites of the present system amuse themselves or gain a livelihood." Charles Edward Russell attacked the Hague Conferences and the peace societies which backed them. How could war be abolished, he asked, by this "trifle of tinkering" by men who had "resolutely shut their eyes to the existence of poverty, misery and insufficiency in the world"?[5]

The conservative prewar peace organizations did not solicit Socialist cooperation; predictably Socialist leaders rarely joined or supported them.[6] On the one occasion when a National Peace

[3] Charles Edward Russell, *Why I Am a Socialist* (New York 1910), pp. 108-17; George R. Kirkpatrick, *War—What For?* (West LaFayette, Ohio 1910), pp. 25-28, 201, 204, 229, 272, 293, 304; David A. Shannon, *The Socialist Party of America* (New York 1955), p. 91.

[4] Morris Hillquit to W. H. Short (executive secretary, New York Peace Society), 12 June 1911, quoted in Robert W. Iverson, "Morris Hillquit, American Social Democrat," Ph.D. diss., State University of Iowa, 1951, p. 158.

[5] The first of these charges is quoted in Shannon, *The Socialist Party of America*, pp. 87-88; Russell's charge appears in *Why I Am a Socialist*, p. 110.

[6] The rare exceptions to this rule included Socialist Congressman Meyer London who was briefly a member of the New York Peace Society in 1913-14 and Socialist John Kennedy who was listed as a member of the Chicago Peace Society in 1914.

Congress did invite a spokesman for socialism, the speaker, Carl D. Thompson of the Municipal Ownership League, insisted that war would end only when Socialists captured the parliaments of the world. Until socialism triumphed, he implied, the achievement of peace might actually be a victory for reaction. "We cannot have peace on earth," he argued, "until we shall have established justice, industrial, economic and world-wide. And we ought not to try to secure one without the other."[7]

Although some American Socialists reiterated a number of the antiwar complaints and arbitration proposals of the peace societies, they continued to distrust the motives of these capitalist-oriented organizations and to deny their ability to bring about a just or lasting peace. Lacking other specific peace proposals of their own to promote, they satisfied themselves with calling upon their followers to strike a blow for international peace by simply voting the Socialist ticket.[8]

In proclaiming the primacy, even the indispensability, of their own movement in the search for international peace, the American Socialists drew upon an inconsistent, unstable, and relatively undeveloped segment of Socialist doctrine. Marx and Engels had laid down no clear or consistent body of doctrine on the question of war. Both had supported "defensive" wars by "progressive" nations, and both, at one time, had been willing to look upon wars positively as "engines of social progress." Later they both came to fear a general European war, although Engels again introduced ambiguities by prophesying in 1892 that such a war would result in the "immediate victory of Socialism," or, at the least, in the acceleration of the social revolution.[9] But by the late 1870s, Marx and Engels had begun generally to describe wars as byproducts of imperialism, breeders of chauvinism, and threats to socialism. It was this viewpoint, developed by the second generation of Socialist leaders and proclaimed steadily by the Second International after 1896, that characterized the declared

[7] Carl D. Thompson, "International Socialism as a Peace Force," *Proceedings of the Second National Peace Congress* (Chicago 1909), pp. 170-73 (hereafter cited as Chicago Peace Congress, 1909). For similar statements see Charles Edward Russell, *Why I Am a Socialist* (New York 1915 [New and rev. ed.]), pp. xx-xxi, and Hillquit's views in William English Walling, ed., *The Socialists and the War* (New York 1915), p. 23. Eugene Debs assured his followers that when the "bread and butter problem" was solved there would be no further dread of war. Eugene Debs, "Socialist Ideals," *The Arena*, 40 (Nov. 1908), 433.

[8] Allan L. Benson, *The Truth About Socialism* (New York 1913), pp. 118-19; Kirkpatrick, *War—What For?*, pp. 49, 56, 104, 159, 203, 287, 304.

[9] Theodore Draper, *The Roots of American Communism* (New York 1957), pp. 50-51; Walling, *The Socialists and the War*, pp. 10-14.

but infrequently discussed opposition to war by the American Socialists prior to 1914.[10]

The basic elements of the socialists' theoretical opposition to war can be simply stated. Modern wars were an integral and inevitable part of the capitalist system. Under capitalism the worker was unable to command in wages the full value of his labor. The concomitant unequal distribution of income meant that capitalists would accumulate more profits than they could profitably invest at home and produce more goods than the workers could afford to buy. Thus surplus capital sought more profitable investment abroad and surplus goods sought foreign markets. The result was intensified competition between the industrialized nations for empires and spheres of influence which would serve as new investment and marketing areas.[11]

But when the competitive struggles of capitalists for markets and colonies broke into war, it was the workingmen, not the capitalists, who were called upon to make the economic sacrifices in higher taxes and to do the fighting. Eugene Debs later summed up this class selectivity of warfare in classic Socialist prose: "The master class has always declared the wars, the subject class has always fought the battles."[12] Even rumors of war brought armament races, increases in the military forces, and cutbacks in inadequate social welfare programs. The expanded armies justified by such war scares not only provided military support for overseas expansion; they also served as a standing reserve force for strike-breaking and political repression. So advantageous, in fact, were wars and war scares in increasing profits, expanding armies, undercutting organization by the working class, and distracting the people from internal grievances, that the great capitalists and their political pawns welcomed them and even deliberately provoked them.[13]

10 Draper, *The Roots of American Communism*, p. 51; Walling, *The Socialists and the War*, pp. 14-24; James Joll, *The Second International, 1889-1914* (London 1955), pp. 46, 70; Howard Quint, "The American Socialists and the Spanish-American War," *American Quarterly* (Summer 1958), p. 131.

11 The basic argument appears in nearly every early twentieth century discussion of the problem of war. For typical examples see Walling, *The Socialists and the War*, pp. 22-23; Russell, *Why I Am A Socialist*, p. 122, and Kirkpatrick, *War—What For?*, pp. 32, 40, 137, 287.

12 Arthur M. Schlesinger, Jr., ed., *Writings and Speeches of Eugene V. Debs* (New York 1948), p. 425.

13 Thompson, "International Socialism as a Peace Force," pp. 175-76; Joseph R. Buchanan, "Remarks," *Proceedings of the National Arbitration and Peace Congress* (New York 1907), p. 223; Kirkpatrick, *War—What For?*, pp. 9, 11-12, 32, 37, 45, 128, 165, 171, 287, 312; Benson, *The Truth About Socialism*, pp. 104, 115-16; Upton Sinclair, *Socialism and War* (London [1913]), (pamphlet), pp. 2-3; Mary

Such an analysis underlined the importance of international peace to the working class. There was only one war in which the working class had any interest, the Socialists argued. This was the class war against the bourgeoisie. All other wars were distractions from this central struggle and threats to the international solidarity and brotherhood of labor. Demonstrations of such international solidarity among workingmen were actually the most effective deterrents to war. Socialist spokesmen boasted loudly of how demonstrations of working class opposition had prevented incipient wars in Europe between 1905 and 1913.[14] In moments of despair, or within the extreme left wing of socialism, some Socialists still conjured up visions of the triumph of the cause through the cataclysm of war. But most Socialist leaders were sufficiently intoxicated by the promise of imminent success through parliamentary means to conclude that their triumph in the domestic struggle could only be thwarted by some international "distraction."[15]

In the United States the hope of reformist success had been kindled by more than a decade of apparently steady advances in Socialist political fortunes since the founding of the Socialist Party of America in 1901. In the election of 1912, despite the competition of two "progressives," Woodrow Wilson and Theodore Roosevelt, the Socialist Party candidate Eugene Debs had gained nearly a million votes. In 1911 the Socialists had obtained the support of nearly 30 percent of the delegates to the AFL Convention in an attempt to force the AFL leadership to end its participation in the business-dominated National Civic Federation. In 1912 Max Hayes, the Socialist candidate against Gompers for president of the AFL, polled over 5,000 votes against Gompers' nearly 12,000. To optimists among the moderate and right-wing Socialists, socialism "seemed to be sweeping the trade union movement."[16] Increasingly hopeful of success through peaceful, parliamentary reform, the reformist leaders of the Socialist Party

---

E. Marcy, "The World-Wide Revolt," *International Socialist Review*, 22 (Nov. 1911), 263; Anon., "A Rich Man's War," *International Socialist Review*, 14 (June 1914), 751.

[14] George Allan England, "Fiat Pax," *International Conciliation*, No. 81 (Aug. 1914), 3, 9-11; George Allan England, "International Socialism as a Political Force," *The American Review of Reviews*, 37 (May 1908), 578; Morris Hillquit, *Socialism Summed Up* (New York 1912), p. 92.

[15] Sinclair, *Socialism and War*, pp. 6-7; Friedberg, "Marxism in the United States," pp. 167, 170.

[16] Bernard Mandel, *Samuel Gompers* (Yellow Springs, Ohio 1963), p. 326; Friedberg, "Marxism in the United States," p. 157; Marc Karson, *American Labor Unions and Politics, 1900-1918* (Carbondale, Ill. 1958), 126-28, 130.

after 1912, the so-called "Hillquit-Berger axis," could look upon the upheaval of war only as a threat to their continued progress. Upton Sinclair warned in 1913 that war was socialism's "enemy of enemies." So long as peace prevailed, he argued, socialism would advance. "Irresistibly the light is spreading, the people are awakening, and our movement grows hour by hour. It is only when the frenzy of war is permitted to seize the people that it is possible for reaction to make any headway."[17]

Despite the clear antiwar implications of prevailing Socialist doctrine and their perception of war as a threat to continued Socialist advances, the American Socialists failed to establish a vigorous or consistent record of action on behalf of peace during the two decades preceding 1914. One opportunity for establishing a precedent by action during crisis—the Spanish-American War in 1898—passed without any semblance of a unified antiwar stand by the badly fragmented American Socialists. Fabian Socialist W. J. Ghent endorsed American intervention in Cuba in 1898 as did the leading organ of Jewish socialists, the Yiddish-language *Daily Forward*. America's leading Marxian theoretician, Daniel DeLeon, attacked the war and warned that the new army would soon be utilized against strikers, but he failed to induce his Socialist Labor Party to take an unequivocal antiwar stand. No clear plans for antiwar activity emerged from Socialist thinking during the crisis, and no call for a general strike to prevent war was sounded.[18]

During the next decade and a half, the American Socialists moved no closer to agreement on an effective program for war prevention. Even the European-dominated Second International, which devoted most of its attention after 1904 to the question of war, arrived at no viable solution despite its more active concern. Most European Socialists apparently satisfied themselves with the belief that the mere existence of the Second International would prevent war until the triumph of socialism eliminated its basic causes.[19] The general strike as an antiwar tactic was frequently debated at congresses of the Second International but never endorsed. American delegates to the International sup-

[17] Sinclair, *Socialism and War*, p. 7. The phrase "Hillquit-Berger axis" is taken from Shannon, *The Socialist Party of America*, p. 79.

[18] Daniel Bell, "Marxian Socialism in the United States," in Egbert *et al.*, *Socialism and American Life* (Princeton 1952), I, 266; Howard Quint, "American Socialists and the Spanish-American War," pp. 134-40.

[19] Joll, *The Second International*, pp. 46, 70, 126, 135, 157; Walling, *The Socialists and the War*, pp. 26-42; Lewis L. Lorwin, *Labor and Internationalism* (New York 1929), pp. 89-92.

ported the vague antiwar resolution of the 1907 Stuttgart Congress, but in 1910 at Copenhagen they voted six to one against the left-wing proposal for adoption of the general strike.[20] The lone American dissenter at Copenhagen, "Big Bill" Haywood of the Industrial Workers of the World (IWW), also sought unsuccessfully to commit the Socialist Party of America to the general strike as a means of preventing war with Mexico. But the moderate Socialist leaders opposed such a stand as impractical for the present state of Socialist strength and organization. The party convention in 1912 satisfied itself with the pronouncement that Socialists should prevent war by the "most efficacious" means.[21]

Until August 1914, nothing occurred to disrupt this satisfaction of the American Socialists with an approach to the problem of war that combined vague antiwar pronouncements with massive unconcern. The Basel Congress of 1912, which Socialists claimed had prevented the outbreak of a European war, seemed to confirm the notion that a mere demonstration of solidarity would deter any national leaders bent upon war.[22] In the United States, as Socialist leaders sought to woo trade union members and press the campaign of "boring from within" to capture the trade unions for socialism, even the facade of international solidarity was occasionally dropped on behalf of positions attractive to union members. Thus in frequent debates culminating in 1910 the party moved toward support for the restriction of immigration. Later, Victor Berger even acknowledged the need of great military preparedness to protect policies of restrictive immigration that would protect the white worker.[23] Except for brief, optimistic articles by Upton Sinclair in 1913 and George Allan England in 1914, the American Socialists maintained their habitual silence on the problem of war. The national committee even neglected in May 1914 to instruct its delegates to the Vienna Congress of the Second International what stand to take on the central issue for that Congress, the general strike to prevent war. There can be little quarrel with the conclusions of most students of American socialism that the Socialist Party of America, absorbed in domestic problems and still confident of gradual and

---

[20] Friedberg, "Marxism in the United States," p. 164; Walling, *The Socialists and the War*, p. 25; Shannon, *The Socialist Party of America*, p. 89.

[21] Shannon, *The Socialist Party of America*, p. 89; Kipnis, *The American Socialist Movement*, pp. 297-98; Friedberg, "Marxism in the United States," pp. 153, 165.

[22] England, "Fiat Pax," pp. 11-12; Joll, *The Second International*, p. 157.

[23] Kipnis, *The American Socialist Movement*, pp. 276-88; Mandel, *Samuel Gompers*, p. 323; Draper, *The Roots of American Communism*, p. 58.

peaceful success, "was poorly prepared for the outbreak of war."[24]

The right of the Socialists to speak for the American working-man on any subject was emphatically denied by most leaders of the American Federation of Labor. But the protests against war which AFL leaders voiced in behalf of workingmen before 1914 differed little from the socialist representations. Samuel Gompers and other AFL officers often surpassed the Socialists in bemoaning the burdens which war always placed upon the workingman. Repetitive but infrequent editorials in the AFL organ, the *American Federationist*, warned that the financial burdens of war and standing armies fell "most heavily upon the working people," that it was the workers who fought the wars, and that war interrupted "natural progress" and diverted money away from "social uplift."[25]

Although the AFL leaders gave a far more sympathetic hearing to the programs of the peace societies for peace through international arbitration, they usually concluded, as did the Socialists, that the international solidarity of workingmen was the best avenue toward peace. Gompers envisioned the development of such solidarity through an International Federation of Trade Unions rather than through international socialism; but he rivaled the Socialists in his descriptions of how the workers would refuse to take up arms once labor solidarity was attained. When that day arrived, he threatened, "those who may want to provoke wars will find themselves . . . [without] soldiers."[26] The AFL,

---

[24] England, "Fiat Pax"; Sinclair, *Socialism and War*; Friedberg, "Marxism in the United States," p. 166; Michael E. B. Bassett, "The Socialist Party of America, 1912-1919: Years of Decline," Ph.D. diss., Duke University, 1964, pp. 69, 77-78. For further evidence of the unconcern of Socialists and other radicals with international war and foreign policy generally, see Milton Cantor, "The Radical Confrontation with Foreign Policy: War and Revolution, 1914-1920," in Alfred F. Young, ed., *Dissent: Explorations in the History of American Radicalism* (DeKalb, Ill. 1968), pp. 217-19. The concluding quote is from Shannon, *The Socialist Party of America*, p. 81.

[25] *American Federationist*, 11 (Dec. 1904), 1081; 14 (May 1907), 328; 18 (March 1911), 222; 18 (Sept. 1911), 710; 20 (Oct. 1913), 863. For similar expressions by other trade union leaders see the "Symposium" in *American Federationist*, 14 (May 1907), 321-27. For all the idealism of their declamations on peace, however, the trade union leaders were no pacifists. They recognized the analogies between strikes and wars, and however much they bemoaned the violence and waste of strikes, they had no intention of abandoning their foremost weapon in return for compulsory arbitration. W. B. Wilson of the United Mine Workers summarized the more realistic trade union position: "I do not believe in 'peace at any cost' in international affairs any more than I do in the trade union movement" *ibid.*, pp. 321-22.

[26] Samuel Gompers, "Address," *Official Report of the Thirteenth Universal Peace*

upon joining the International Secretariat of National Trade Union Centers in 1909, had opposed the French policy of "anti-patriotism, anti-militarism, . . . and the general strike." Nevertheless, on the question of war, as on other issues that remained relatively abstract, Gompers and other AFL leaders often displayed a penchant for revolutionary phrases that belied their more conservative course of action. Thus Gompers, while utterly dismissing the left-wing Socialist tactic of the general strike against war in practice, was still willing to intimate that the working people of all countries would "stop work simultaneously" if profit-mongers tried to start a war.[27]

Samuel Gompers later described himself as having been a "doctrinaire pacifist" in the years before 1914.[28] His actual course of action during the two decades before the war, however, was characterized far more by expediency than by "pacifism." It was true that he periodically reiterated a standard set of clichés about the advantages of peace to workingmen and the creation of international brotherhood through the federation of unions. Undoubtedly he sincerely believed that, as a spokesman for trade unionism, he was constantly promoting world peace. But the concrete stands that he and the AFL took on specific international issues reflected more clearly the immediate domestic goals of AFL unions and their underlying biases and fears on such issues as immigration restriction, standing armies, foreign competition, and alliances with nations despised by powerful ethnic groups within the unions than they did any direct concern for international peace. Gompers and his lieutenants spoke as idealists on international peace. Some even convinced themselves that they were pacifists. But in practice, they never forget their primary concern with the domestic fortunes of trade unionism.

By 1914 Gompers could point to a long record of at least superficial effort on behalf of international peace. As early as 1887 he had brought the British labor leader and peace propagandist, Randal Cremer, to address the AFL. At the same time he had declared his own faith in arbitration and a federation of

---

Congress (Boston 1904), p. 136; Seventy Years of Life and Labor: An Autobiography (New York 1925), II, 329; "Humanity's Growth Towards Peace," Proceedings of the National Arbitration and Peace Congress (New York 1907), p. 245, and President's Report to the 25th Annual Convention of the A. F. of L. (Pittsburgh 1905), pp. 8-9; American Federationist, 18 (Sept. 1911), 709-10.

27 Samuel Gompers, American Labor and the War (New York 1919), p. 106; Philip Taft, The A. F. of L. in the Time of Gompers (New York 1957), p. 424.

28 Gompers, Seventy Years, II, 331 and American Labor and the War, p. 106.

the world. He had opposed war over the Venezuela Boundary question in 1895, had urged McKinley to resist demands for war in April of 1898, had opposed the annexation of Hawaii, and had become a leading anti-imperialist during 1898 and 1899. He had consistently supported the arbitration treaties proposed in 1904, 1907, and 1911. Moreover, he had taken the initiative in prodding the provincial AFL to take a greater interest in international affairs.[29]

But such a record of words and action on behalf of peace had not been inspired wholly by motives of international idealism. Gompers and the AFL had wavered several times on the question of Cuba, advocating American intervention during 1896 and 1897. Competition from nonunionized Cuban cigarmakers threatened American cigarmakers, and Gompers, as a former officer of the Cigarmakers Union had hoped to soften the competition by spreading the "gospel of unionism" in Cuba, a mission "practically impossible under Spanish rule."[30] A different set of problems concerning competition by cheap labor set the context for Gompers' opposition to Hawaiian annexation. John C. Appel concludes that the "relationship of American labor to the annexation of Hawaii can be summarized as 'pure and simple unionism' at work."[31] Behind Gompers fervent post-1898 anti-imperialism lay the same concern that stimulated his increasing support for immigration restriction: the fear of undercutting the wages and living standards of American labor by including, by immigration or annexation, large elements of cheap foreign labor within the national labor market.[32]

Similarly, Gompers' participation in the programs of various peace societies and peace congresses evinced as much a desire to establish the social respectability of organized labor as it did an attempt to fulfill his "dream" of an "international parliament of man." A significant step in labor's ambition "to win acceptance as a 'legitimate social group', . . . as an established institution of American life," as Daniel Bell has pointed out, was the AFL's

[29] Gompers, *Seventy Years*, II, 322-29; Delber Lee McKee, "The American Federation of Labor and American Foreign Policy, 1886-1912," Ph.D. diss., Stanford University, 1952, pp. 19-23, 40-51, 63-76, 213; Mandel, *Samuel Gompers*, pp. 199-206, 212-14.

[30] Horace B. Davis, "American Labor and Imperialism," *Science and Society*, 27 (Winter 1963), 70; Mandel, *Samuel Gompers*, pp. 201-3.

[31] John C. Appel, "American Labor and the Annexation of Hawaii: A Study in Logic and Economic Interest," *Pacific Historical Review*, 23 (Feb. 1954), 17.

[32] Mandel, *Samuel Gompers*, pp. 203, 206, 214; Davis, "American Labor and Imperialism," 73.

participation in the National Civic Federation.[33] At Civic Federation meetings and dinners, Gompers and his lieutenants came into direct contact with Andrew Carnegie, Nicholas Murray Butler, Seth Low, August Belmont, George W. Perkins, and other business and civic leaders who were promoting the New York Peace Society and other aspects of the new, practical, post-1905 peace movement. One of the Civic Federation's "largest and most significant conferences" was its 1907 "peace evening" at Carnegie's spacious Fifth Avenue residence. Four hundred federation members, including over a hundred labor leaders, listened while Belmont, Carnegie, Gompers, and others reviewed the "striking analogies" between international warfare and industrial disputes. Belmont and Nicholas Murray Butler extolled the virtues of industrial peace and industrial arbitration while Carnegie reminded his guests that "peace like charity begins at home." It was through the Civic Federation, and through invitations from peace movement leaders in it that Gompers came to make many of his public pronouncements on labor's attitude toward international peace and arbitration.[34]

Thus Gompers' interest in the peace movement can be explained partly in the same terms in which Gompers later explained his objective in entering the Civic Federation: "It helped to establish the practice of accepting labor unions as an integral social element and logically of including their representatives in groups to discuss policies."[35] In his speeches before audiences of the influential and respectable at peace congresses, Gompers never forgot his primary concern with the promotion of the proper image of organized labor. Nor did he neglect to devote much of his time to explanations of how the organization of labor promoted industrial peace and stability and how the unions deplored strikes and violence. Other AFL spokesmen before the peace congresses followed much the same pattern. Commitments to peace societies and peace programs were never allowed to interfere with the hard realities of labor movement politics. In 1911 Gompers abruptly canceled a scheduled address before a

[33] Gompers, Seventy Years, I, 331; Bell, "Marxian Socialism in the United States," p. 254. The National Civic Federation was formed in 1900 primarily for the purpose of bringing together labor and management under the pressure and encouragement of public opinion for the prevention or peaceful settlement of industrial disputes. On the employers side, it was supported by the new cadre of "civic-minded" businessmen. See James Weinstein, The Corporate Ideal in the Liberal State, 1900-1918 (Boston 1968), pp. 3-39.

[34] New York Times, 6 Apr. 1907, 1:7; The National Civic Federation Review, 3 (Sept. 1907), 1-3.

[35] Gompers, Seventy Years, II, 105.

meeting sponsored by the New York Peace Society at the Cooper Union when the Central Federated Union, deferring to its German and Irish members, complained that his presence at the meeting might imply labor support for the recently announced proposal for a more comprehensive arbitration treaty with Great Britain.[36]

If Gompers and other AFL officers found peace congresses a useful forum in which to express the idealism of their movement and enhance its public image, the leaders of these congresses and of such organizations as the New York Peace Society found that speaking invitations to Gompers and his lieutenants enabled them to satisfy themselves that they were fulfilling the often-discussed but rarely implemented task of attracting workingmen to the peace movement. Occasional musings about the need to tap the potential support of labor for the peace movement had amounted to nothing in the earliest years of the century. Genteel reformers found it difficult to reach out to organized labor, or to discover a labor leader whom they considered appropriate to invite to the Lake Mohonk resort. Henry Demarest Lloyd told the Mohonk Conference in 1901 that he would like to hear the topic of the session, "Industrialism and Peace," discussed by "accredited representatives of labor." The actual spokesman for labor on that occasion was a clergyman who declared himself glad to speak on the subject "because the industrial classes are not here to speak for themselves." Despite other suggestions of the need for support by labor and despite the very active solicitation of participation by businessmen, the Lake Mohonk Conference never did hear from the "industrial classes." Although Gompers occasionally spoke at national peace congresses, most peace societies remained isolated from spokesmen for the workingman until the New York Peace Society, impressed with the success of the Civic Federation in bringing together labor, business, and the public on industrial matters, began in 1911 to experiment with a similar, token cooperation with organized labor on the issue of international peace.[37]

[36] On the 1911 incident, see Samuel Gompers to William Short, 15 Apr. 1911, and [William Short], untitled typed memorandum, [1911], Box 4, New York Peace Society Papers, Swarthmore College Peace Collection. For typical examples of the stress AFL spokesmen placed on the positive role of labor unions in promoting industrial peace, see Gompers, "Organized Labor and Peace," *Chicago Peace Congress, 1909*, pp. 159-62 and John Lennon, "Labor's Interest in World Peace," *American Federationist*, 27 (June 1910), 492-97.

[37] *Report of the Seventh Annual Meeting of the Lake Mohonk Conference on International Arbitration* (Lake Mohonk, N.Y., 1901), pp. 62-66; [Short], untitled

The early attempts to solicit cooperation from organized labor, however, proved meager and unproductive. George Kirchwey, Dean of the Columbia Law School, complained early in 1912 that the New York Peace Society was "weakest where it should be strongest, namely in the formulation and pursuit of a definite policy of bringing the working classes and especially organized labor wholeheartedly and aggressively into the peace movement."[38] The society did attempt that year to renew old efforts to seek cooperation from Gompers, John Mitchell, and other AFL leaders in promoting the peace society programs. It even appointed an "influential committee" to confer with labor leaders. But the effort apparently accomplished little: neither the AFL nor the New York Peace Society was *vitally* interested in cooperation on the peace issue. Andrew Carnegie continued to urge his foundation to publish a pamphlet by Gompers, who could "reach" organized labor for them, but Gompers eventually drew back from the project as tactically unsound. Effective cooperation never resulted.[39] By 1914 so little continuing communication between trade union leaders and peace organizations had been established that the executive secretary of the New York Peace Society, the organization which had given the most thought to enlisting the support of workingmen, was still soliciting ideas "as to the best method of procedure" for reaching organized labor.[40]

Thus the peace societies of the prewar period failed to bring about any significant degree of active participation in their work by workingmen or labor spokesmen. Some of the peace societies apparently saw no important role for labor to play. Others may

---

memorandum, [1911] and Gompers to Short, 15 Apr. 1911, Box 4, NYPS Papers, SCPC.

[38] George W. Kirchwey to Frederick Lynch, 27 Mar. 1912, Box 5, NYPS Papers, SCPC.

[39] William Short to Samuel Gompers, May 29, 1912, Box 4, NYPS Papers, SCPC; New York Peace Society, *Yearbook, 1912*, pp. 7, 15, 26; James Brown Scott to Andrew Carnegie, 21 Apr. and 16 May 1914, Carnegie to Scott, 14 May 1914, Vol. IV, Division of Intercourse and Education Correspondence, 1914, Carnegie Endowment for International Peace Papers, Columbia University Library. About the same time the World Peace Foundation experienced some evanescent flutterings of interest in "the matter of coming into closer touch in some wise way with the great labor interests of the country . . ." but quickly buried the question by referring it to a standing committee. "Minutes of the Annual Meeting of the Board of Trustees of the World Peace Foundation," 26 Nov. 1912, p. 45, Box 1A, World Peace Foundation Papers, SCPC. On the awkward and futile attempts on the part of prewar peace societies to establish contact with organized labor see also David Sands Patterson, "The Travail of the American Peace Movement, 1887-1914," Ph.D. diss., University of California, Berkeley, 1968, pp. 264, 272-73.

[40] William H. Short to John Bates Clark, 6 Apr. and 9 Apr. 1914, Box 3, NYPS Papers, SCPC.

have accepted, in abstract, the idea of the importance of labor in the peace movement, but found the social distance between themselves and representatives of labor too great to bridge comfortably. Intermittent contacts by such organizations as the New York Peace Society and the officers of the national peace congresses resulted in no continuing pattern of cooperation. The staff of the Carnegie Endowment went so far as to collect over 300 letters on the subject of peace and international arbitration by leaders of labor organizations, only to have a leading secretary of the endowment successfully oppose the printing of them in an appendix to a study on American Labor and War because they were, in his view, "foolish," "worthless," and "commonplace, without novelty or intrinsic value."[41]

For their part, the AFL leaders approached the peace movement with occasional verbal enthusiasm tempered by a great deal of practical caution and a preoccupation with domestic issues. Except for reprinting the usual paragraph on international peace in Gompers' annual address to the AFL annual convention, the *American Federationist* gave major attention to the issue of international peace in only five issues during the decade preceding 1914. Gompers, John Lennon, John Mitchell, and others promoted the AFL's social respectability by stressing organized labor's idealism and sense of social responsibility at peace congresses. But their support for specific treaties, legislation, and programs depended heavily on how the proposed action might affect questions of immigration, increases in the army and militia, or the welfare of the Democratic Party, to which the AFL had recently given its temporary and provisional support.

The stand taken by the AFL on such issues as the militia and the threat of war with Mexico indicate how strictly it tailored its positions on specific issues of foreign policy to domestic concerns. On the issue of intervention in Mexico, Gompers appears to have been guided by two primary motives: a determination to protect American workers against competition from Mexican workers, and a desire to avoid embarrassing the Wilson administration, under which the AFL was enjoying unprecedented political influence and public respectability. So unwilling was Gompers to embarrass the Wilson administration that he forced the AFL convention in 1913 to withdraw part of a resolution that opposed armed intervention in Mexico by the United States. The following

[41] S.N.D. North to J. B. Clark, 30 Nov. 1914, North to Alvin S. Johnson, 7 Dec. 1914, Vol. II, Division of Economics and History Correspondence, 1914, CEIP Papers, CUL.

May, shortly after the Vera Cruz incident, Gompers even began to back away from publishing some antiwar speeches through the Carnegie Endowment, arguing "that when he suggested that they be published, there was apparently no danger of intervention in Mexico." Although Gompers continued to work for a peaceful settlement of the Mexican crisis, he remained primarily concerned with the material self-interests of organized American labor and extremely wary of espousing any potentially unpopular cause.[42]

The increasing public respectability of the AFL during the second decade of the twentieth century even worked to moderate its long-standing opposition to increases in the army or militia. Like the Socialists, the AFL leaders had long distrusted all military forces as tools in the hands of the business classes for the suppression of labor. In 1892 the AFL had demanded that state legislatures enact laws providing more democratic controls over the calling out of state militia. If such laws were not enacted, unions should forbid their members to join the militia. In 1896 unions were asked to discourage enlistment of their members in the national guard. Meanwhile, in 1895, Gompers had charged that the Venezuela dispute was simply a diversion being employed as an excuse for building up the military. In the wake of the Spanish-American War, the AFL had warned that an enlargement of the army was one of the most probable and pernicious results of imperialism. Several secretaries of war, the federation pointed out, had previously urged that the army be increased to deal with internal social and industrial strife. Overseas expansion was simply a welcome excuse to increase the army, "and to use such increased army, as in time past . . . to further subjugate the working people."[43]

As the AFL became more powerful and secure, however, its position on the military became less rigid. The AFL executive council refused to condemn the Dick Military Law of 1903 which reorganized the state militia system to conform more closely to the pattern of the regular army, and Samuel Gompers increasingly emphasized the impossibility of disarmament and the virtues of a small standing army "supplemented by a volunteer citizen soldiery." In 1906, the AFL convention firmly rejected a

---

[42] Mandel, *Samuel Gompers*, pp. 336-45; James Brown Scott to Andrew Carnegie, 16 May 1914, Vol. IV, Division of Intercourse and Education Correspondence, 1914, CEIP Papers, CUL.

[43] AFL, *American Federation of Labor: History, Encyclopedia, Reference Book* (Washington, D.C. 1919), pp. 290-91; McKee, "The A.F. of L. and American Foreign Policy," p. 40; Mandel, *Samuel Gompers*, p. 212.

resolution forbidding union men to join the militia until a Swiss militia system was adopted. Gompers continued, intermittently, to warn of attempts "to foist militarism upon the people of our free country" and of "the use of armed men to defeat the labor movement." But fear of an expanded military establishment had come to play little part in Gompers' attitudes toward foreign policy. By 1916 he had come to endorse a full program of military "preparedness."[44]

Gompers' change in attitude, and that of the AFL generally, represented no major reevaluation of international affairs or of the relation of armies to world peace. What it did reflect, once again, was the subordination of the AFL's attitudes on international affairs to the immediate concerns of domestic trade unionism. As the growing power and security of the AFL made it less fearful of the militia on the domestic front and as support for military preparedness came to promise tactical advantages and a better public image, the AFL commitment to "antimilitarism" faded. When specific issues related to war and international affairs arose, considerations of practical advantages for trade unionism rather than rhetorical declamations about war as the "workingman's burden" determined the AFL's degree of "pacifism."

Thus, in spite of all the idealistic and pacifistic rhetoric of the AFL and in spite of Gompers' willingness to lecture the peace societies on the brotherhood of all workingmen and their aversion to bearing the burdens of war, there was little to indicate that the AFL would throw its weight behind any concrete peace efforts that did not also meet the practical exigencies of AFL trade unionism. Just as the Socialists had concluded that the triumph of socialism and the inauguration of world peace were synonymous, so Gompers and his lieutenants remained convinced that the success of the trade union movement held the greatest promise of achieving international peace. When the test of all the peace pronouncements and resolutions came after 1914, both the Socialists and the AFL trade unionists were forced to redefine their positions. The logic of their political position and their weakness within organized labor drove a number of Socialists to move toward more active participation in an increasingly radi-

44 Gompers, *American Labor and the War*, pp. 59-64; Samuel Gompers, "Militarism Must Not Prevail," *American Federationist*, 20 (Oct. 1913), 862-63 and "Editorial," *American Federationist*, 31 (Aug. 1914), 636; Mandel, *Samuel Gompers*, p. 214; AFL, *History, Encyclopedia, Reference Book*, pp. 201-2, 291; Samuel Gompers to W. L. Amthor, quoted in *The National Civic Federation Review*, 3 (15 Feb. 1912), 14.

calized peace movement. The AFL, meanwhile, discovered during the crisis that its true philosophy, in international as in domestic affairs, was expediency rather than pacifism.

During the period of American neutrality from 1914 to 1917, the AFL moved fitfully from neutrality to interventionism. Samuel Gompers, an early and vociferous convert, first to military preparedness and then to support for American participation, pulled and prodded the federation toward a culminating declaration of loyalty and support for the administration in March 1917, several weeks before Wilson's war message. However, Gompers did not swing the federation away from its former antimilitarism without bitter opposition. National unions with Socialist leadership opposed his attitude toward the war, as did German-dominated unions. Labor organizations which had recently been at odds with the AFL leadership such as the United Hebrew Trades (UHT) of New York City, the Amalgamated Clothing Workers of America (ACWA), and the International Ladies Garment Workers Union (ILGWU) predictably clashed with Gompers on the war issue. Despite such opposition—and the private protests of several prominent union leaders—Gompers was able to obtain unanimous support for his pledge to the government from a full conference of the officers of all but about a dozen of the federation's affiliated unions.[45]

For all of his inflated sermons on labor and peace, Gompers had been quick to abandon his "pacifism." When the war broke out in Europe, the Carnegie Endowment for International Peace had been preparing to publish some of Gompers' speeches on peace. Gompers "immediately went to the printer," he later recalled, "and got hold of that damn-fool stuff and took it back."[46] Although Gompers publicly supported Wilson's policy of neutrality during 1914 and 1915, his biographer Bernard Mandel argues that Gompers was in favor of American intervention on the side of the Allies from the very beginning. Certainly Gompers gave no support after 1914 to peace organizations seeking to end the war by mediation. By 1915 he was rejecting invitations to speak at peace meetings and by early 1916 he had renounced

[45] Mandel, *Samuel Gompers*, pp. 355-63; Taft, *The A.F. of L. in the Time of Gompers*, pp. 343-44; Louis L. Lorwin, *The American Federation of Labor* (Washington, D.C. 1933), pp. 142-44; Karson, *American Labor Unions and Politics*, pp. 94-95. On internal AFL opposition to Gompers' early declaration of wartime support, see also Ronald Radosh, *American Labor and United States Foreign Policy* (New York 1969), pp. 9-10.

[46] Gompers, *American Labor and the War*, p. 142 and *Seventy Years*, II, 331.

entirely his earlier "pacifism." His evolving prointerventionism represented an amalgam of tactical opportunities, a recently intensified nationalism, and a deep personal desire for social acceptance.[47]

Gompers' devotion to nationalism had been intensifying since 1909 when he had made a tour of Europe and returned thoroughly convinced of European backwardness and American superiority. "The Old World," he concluded, "is not our world."[48] After 1914, as the possibility of American intervention loomed larger, expressions of such sentiments of nationalism, particularly in the form of support for increased national defense, began to coincide with opportunities for elevated position and prestige. In 1916 Gompers was appointed to the Advisory Commission of the Council of National Defense. Constantly thereafter Gompers served on what he considered the inner councils of the national wartime administration. His new associates, he later reminisced, were suspicious of him at first but soon accepted him completely. His actions in insuring the loyalty of labor behind the war effort won him accolades from the leading newspapers and the "unstinted praise of the nation's leaders."[49] Long frustrated by public distrust of the unions and such exceptional incidents as that in which he had been accused of stamping upon the American flag, Gompers now fairly fell into the arms of the most strident patriots. "Delirious with patriotic feeling," he was overjoyed to find himself treated with such solicitude and respect, courted by the powerful and influential, and united in common and harmonious effort with so many. As Mandel remarks, Gompers could now demand that he be recognized by the public not as an "agitator" or "demagogue" but as a "statesman of labor."[50]

Gompers did not carry the trade unionists into a prewar declaration of wartime support of the administration without protests and defections. As early as mid-1915 several union leaders formed the Labor's National Peace Council in an attempt to bring union influence to bear against military preparedness and intervention

[47] Melvyn Dubofsky, "New York City Labor in the Progressive Era, 1910-1918: A Study of Organized Labor in an Era of Reform," Ph.D. diss., University of Rochester, 1960, pp. 370-71; Mandel, *Samuel Gompers*, pp. 351-57; Gompers, *Seventy Years*, II, 338-39; Gompers, *American Labor and the War*, pp. 52-53; *American Federationist*, 33 (Mar. 1916), 173-80; Lorwin, *The American Federation of Labor*, pp. 138-41; Karson, *American Labor Unions and Politics*, pp. 92-96.

[48] Samuel Gompers, *Labor in Europe and America* (New York 1910), p. 286.

[49] Taft, *The A.F. of L. in the Time of Gompers*, p. 343; Gompers, *Seventy Years*, II, 361; Mandel, *Samuel Gompers*, pp. 354, 371.

[50] *The National Civic Federation Review*, III (Feb. 1912), 13-15, 25; Gompers, *Seventy Years*, II, 361-62, 376; Mandel, *Samuel Gompers*, pp. 354, 387, 406, 410.

and to marshal support for an arms embargo. As Gompers threw his weight behind the preparedness campaign in early 1916, AFL Treasurer John Lennon, James Maurer of the Pennsylvania Federation of Labor, and officers of the United Mine Workers (UMW) appeared before the Senate Committee on Military Affairs to plead the opposite cause. The executive board of the Chicago Federation of Labor adopted a report condemning any increases in the army. The greatest danger to the American workingman, declared the Chicago Federation, was not from foreign attack but from foreign immigration.[51] Ernest Bohm of the Central Federated Union of New York City denounced a mid-1916 preparedness parade as "too much like a business proposition" and Benjamin Schlesinger, president of the ILGWU, refused to have anything to do with preparedness demonstrations backed by the employers of his union members. The UHT and the ACWA, embroiled in disputes with the AFL, gave no support to preparedness or intervention. The officials of eleven national AFL unions declined to attend the 12 March 1917 conference at which Gompers forced through his declaration of loyalty and cooperation with the government in case of war. A number of these dissenting unions, including the International Typographical Union (ITU), the UMW, and the ILGWU, had supported the Socialist candidate against Gompers at the 1912 AFL convention.[52] Thus the division within the trade unions over the issue of intervention began to reflect and reinforce lines of conflict over domestic and internal issues already well established within the AFL.

Gompers' argument for an early declaration of wartime support in 1917 was basically simple. For all his inflated sense of patriotism and desire for social respectability, he was still acting in accordance with a thoroughly plausible policy of labor opportunism. Having concluded that preparedness, and then intervention, were inevitable, he characterized labor's choice as twofold: it could give early support to the government, thus gaining a voice in the direction of wartime labor programs, or it could "withhold its cooperation and be whipped into line." English

[51] *New York Times*, 24 June 1915, 4:5, 30 June 1915, 4:1; Louis P. Lochner to David Starr Jordan, 8 July 1915, Box 4, David Starr Jordan Papers, Hoover Institution on War, Revolution and Peace; Anti-Preparedness Committee News Release, 7 Feb. 1916, Box 1, American Union Against Militarism Papers, SCPC; "Report of the Executive Board of the Chicago Federation of Labor on 'preparedness,'" 6 Feb. 1916, folder 193, Leonora O'Reilly Papers, Arthur and Elizabeth Schlesinger Library, Radcliffe College; James Hudson Maurer, *It Can Be Done: The Autobiography of James Hudson Maurer* (New York 1938), pp. 211-12.

[52] *The Survey*, 36 (20 May 1916), 108; Mandel, *Samuel Gompers*, pp. 360-62; Taft, *The A.F. of L. in the Time of Gompers*, p. 255.

workers had made the wrong decision, Gompers believed, and they had gained nothing during the war emergency. He did not intend for the AFL to make the same mistake.[53]

"In no previous war," the AFL observed, "has the organized labor movement taken a directing part." Gompers was determined to change this position—to gain some control and recognition through an early declaration of loyalty, and later through what verged upon a no-strike agreement, and then to demand the "justice" that such loyalty had earned. The wisdom of such a policy, even on the grounds of expediency alone, has been questioned.[54] But Gompers' view of the proper tactics of opportunism was shared by most other AFL leaders, and it coincided perfectly with emotional dedication to America's war crusade. Equally important, the policy of cooperation promised significant immediate gains for organized labor, gains which were largely realized, at least during the wartime period. Once embarked fully upon this pragmatic course of action, Gompers abandoned most of his clichés about workingmen and peace. All peace organizations became, in his view, pro-German and treasonous. Gompers was intent upon making labor a powerful and influential partner in the war effort and in the industrial policies required by the war. He was determined to block any new effort of the peace movement to bring any segment of American labor into a new, radical peace coalition.[55]

The outbreak of World War I forced upon American Socialists an agony of reappraisal and inner turmoil far greater than that undergone by the leadership of the AFL. While the AFL had only to reevaluate the very vague remarks of Gompers and a few other leaders about what workingmen would do to prevent war, the Socialists were publicly committed to a far more specific antiwar stance. American Socialists had contributed little to the Second International's frequent discussions of the proper means of preventing war, but they clearly expected their European fel-

[53] Mandel, *Samuel Gompers*, pp. 357, 360; Taft, *The A.F. of L. in the Time of Gompers*, p. 344; Radosh, *American Labor and United States Foreign Policy*, pp. 8-12.

[54] *AFL, History, Encyclopedia, Reference Book*, p. 66; Karson, *American Labor Unions and Politics*, pp. 94-97; Mandel, *Samuel Gompers*, pp. 354, 369. Those who have suggested, directly or indirectly, that Gompers might more wisely or more responsibly have opted for a different course include Radosh, *American Labor and United States Foreign Policy*, p. 23; John Steuben, *Labor in Wartime* (New York 1940), pp. 25ff.; and Mandel, *Samuel Gompers*, pp. 367-72, 386-87.

[55] Mandel, *Samuel Gompers*, pp. 361, 388-89; Lorwin, *The American Federation of Labor*, pp. 142-45, 169-72; Karson, *American Labor Unions and Politics*, pp. 100-103.

low Socialists to offer militant resistance against any course of action leading to war. Probably few expected that anything approximating a general strike would take place. But American Socialists were astounded to see French Socialists substitute national patriotism for class loyalty with such alacrity, and especially to see the German Socialists vote overwhelmingly for war credits and throw their support behind the "defense" of the fatherland. Germany had been the nation in which international socialism had gained its most conspicuous power and success. Many leaders of American socialism had taken the Socialists of Germany as their model. For a brief period some American Socialists refused to acknowledge that their German counterparts had deserted the antiwar position and insisted that, despite reports to the contrary, the German Socialists had fought the government's war policy to the bitter end.[56]

Eventually, of course, the defection of the European Socialists from the Socialist antiwar policies had to be accepted and explained.[57] But the attempts to do this, involved as they inevitably were with invidious distinctions between the actions and positions of the various belligerents, served to exacerbate the internal dissention already present within the Socialist Party of America. Whether they defended or criticized European Socialists for their actions, American Socialists suffered acute embarrassment from the inconsistency of doctrine and action by their European counterparts. In the course of trying to explain away the failure of the more powerful Socialist parties of Europe to prevent war many must have quietly vowed never to allow themselves to be distracted during crises by appeals to national patriotism and never to allow themselves to be trapped into such a degrading abandonment of principle.

At first American Socialists responded to the war crisis with a flurry of action. A Committee on Immediate Action was established, and a cable dispatched to the Socialist parties of ten nations to "exert every influence" on their governments to accept mediation by the United States. Proposals for relief funds, an export embargo, and a reconstitution of the Second International through an international Socialist conference in Washington were

---

[56] Bassett, "The Socialist Party of America," pp. 73-74; Shannon, *The Socialist Party of America*, pp. 81-83; Nathan Fine, *Labor and Farmer Parties in the United States 1828-1928* (New York 1928), pp. 301-2.

[57] For some sample explanations see Walling, *The Socialists and the War*, pp. 3-8, 378-92, 406, and Alexander Trachtenberg, ed., *The American Socialists and the War* (New York 1917), pp. 3-7, 10-12.

explored.[58] Morris Hillquit and other leaders of the Socialist Party sought to seize the initiative in reconstituting international socialism as a powerful force for peace. "We have been placed in the position of the main, if not the sole guardian of human civilization," Hillquit told his party members. "We must exert every atom of power that is within us to bring about a speedy and lasting peace between the nations."[59] But European Socialists were in no mood for early negotiations or mediation. Any attempt to bring together the Second International seemed certain to destroy it forever. American Socialists became pessimistic about an early peace, cautious about unrepresentative mediation efforts by neutral Socialist parties, and internally confused about policy and priorities. Disillusioned with the International Bureau, the American party refused to pay its 1914 and 1915 dues and thus cut its ties with the Second International.[60] Gradually the leaders of American socialism again turned their attention inward. In so doing, however, they escaped one set of dilemmas only to face another. For a decline in the party's political and financial fortunes since 1912 was now exacerbating long-standing internal divisions.

As questions of war, military expansion, and disarmament came to dominate internal Socialist Party debate, several lines of antagonism appeared. A pro-Ally *versus* pro-German division arose. Victor Berger and the Wisconsin Socialists led the pro-German, proembargo forces. Russian-Jewish segments of the party, violently anti-Czarist, were often inclined to sympathize with the pro-German faction and were particularly vehement in their opposition to any preparations looking to intervention on the side of Russia. Another division, coinciding only partly with the pro-German, pro-Ally split was the dispute over unilateral disarmament. Charles Edward Russell, one of the pro-Ally faction, took the logical position of upholding military preparedness as a precaution for defense or intervention against the antiliberal forces of German militarism. But other pro-Ally Socialists like John Spargo, A. J. Simons, and Allan Benson spoke out against preparedness. Nor did the dispute over military preparedness coincide entirely with long-standing ideological divisions within the party. Henry Slobodin of the left wing of the party supported

[58] Trachtenberg, ed., *The American Socialists and the War*, pp. 8-13; Walling, *The Socialists and the War*, 405-8; Bassett, "The Socialist Party of America," pp. 76-78, 86, 89.

[59] Hillquit's remarks, published in the *American Socialist*, are quoted in Bassett, "The Socialist Party of America," pp. 74-75.

[60] *Ibid.*, pp. 73-74, 80-85, 90-91, 93-98; Shannon, *The Socialist Party of America*, p. 86.

preparedness, but so did Berger, Russell, and W. J. Ghent of the right wing. Finally, party leaders disagreed over the underlying question of whether Socialists ought to throw their efforts behind peace initiatives that did not clearly lead to a triumph of socialism.[61]

Never during the period before American intervention did the Socialist Party give open and explicit support to the organized peace movement. Although the national chairman, Morris Hillquit, hoped that the party would take "a leading place in the anti-war movement of the nation," he also warned against too close a cooperation with the bourgeois peace advocates. Other party leaders lashed out vituperously against all peace societies as parasitic capitalist organizations, either consciously hypocritical or naively and ludicrously futile.[62] The Socialist Party of America was struggling to maintain its own identity in these years. Wilson's New Freedom had erased much of the distinctiveness of the party's domestic reform program. When even moderate, reformist leaders like Hillquit could worry about a loss of separate Socialist identity on the war issue, through too much cooperation with non-Socialist reformers, the party's left wing certainly was going to show no inclination to call for participation in non-Socialist peace organizations. Even to moderates, the war issue appeared to be one on which the party could reassert its separate identity once again.[63]

But for all the Socialists' determination to take the initiative on the war issue and carve out their own uncompromising position, their councils remained confused, their leadership and membership uncertain and disunited, and their programs largely indistinguishable from those of the active peace organizations. Hillquit and Eugene Debs led a party deputation in December 1915 to ask President Wilson to call a conference of neutral nations to mediate between the belligerents, a scheme developed and backed by

[61] For accounts of the internal divisions and alignments within the Socialist Party on the war issue see Bassett, "The Socialist Party of America," pp. 93-100, 148-61, 195-99; James Oneal, "The Socialists in the War," *The American Mercury*, 10 (Apr. 1927), 418-22; Freidberg, "Marxism in the United States," pp. 180-200; Shannon, *The Socialist Party of America*, pp. 83-85, 89; Draper, *The Roots of American Communism*, pp. 56-57; and James Weinstein, *The Decline of Socialism in America, 1912-1925* (New York 1967), pp. 121-33.

[62] Bassett, "The Socialist Party of America," pp. 90, 101; Charles Edward Russell, *Why I Am a Socialist* (New and rev. ed., New York 1915), p. xxi; Shannon, *The Socialist Party of America*, pp. 87-88.

[63] On the effects of Wilson's reform program on the Socialist Party see Bassett, "The Socialist Party of America," pp. iv, 22, 120-23, 138, 193, and Freidberg, "Marxism in the United States," pp. 194-95.

the leading peace organizations. Another Socialist delegation led by Hillquit and James Maurer made a smiliar plea early in 1916. The lone Socialist congressman, Meyer London, called for implementation of a continuous mediation scheme—the program sponsored by Henry Ford's nonsocialist Peace Ship venture. Allan Benson's 1916 campaign proposal for a national referendum on war, an extension of the direct democracy enthusiasm of Populism and Progressivism which the Socialists had long emphasized in internal party affairs, was hardly exclusively Socialist in conception or implication. Benson was one of the first to place primary emphasis on this issue, but non-Socialist peace leaders endorsed the idea and the American Union Against Militarism attempted to implement it on a small scale during the crisis months of early 1917. Moreover, a number of Socialist Party leaders were contemptuous of this scheme. Hillquit referred to it as "perfectly wild."[64]

David Shannon has noted that all but one paragraph of the Socialist Party's first proclamation on the European war "might have been written by any peace group."[65] The same observation is only slightly less accurate for the various party pronouncements, programs, and manifestos throughout 1915 and 1916. Not only did the party diverge very little from the more radical peace organizations in its antiwar programs, but its members often cooperated quietly with the peace organizations that its leaders were wont to denounce. Nine Socialist representatives, including national officers Carl Thompson, Walter Lanfersik, and May Wood-Simons, participated in the Emergency Peace Committee Meeting in Chicago in December 1914. Others joined the campaigns of the American Union Against Militarism and the Emergency Peace Federation early in 1917.[66] By that time the programs of the more radical peace organizations and those of the moderate Socialists were hardly distinguishable.

The stage was thus set for the difficult decision faced by the Socialist Party at its emergency national convention in St. Louis on 7 April 1917, the day after the official American war declaration. The moderate but antiwar Socialists found themselves in the most

[64] Shannon, *The Socialist Party of America*, p. 90; Bassett, "The Socialist Party of America," pp. 95, 161; Maurer, *It Can Be Done*, pp. 215-16.

[65] Shannon, *The Socialist Party of America*, p. 82.

[66] "Minutes of the Emergency Peace Committee Meeting, Held at the City Club," 19 Dec. 1912, Rosika Schwimmer Papers, HI; "Minutes of the Meeting," 27 Feb. [1917], Box 1, AUAM Papers, SCPC. For an account of one leading socialist's continuing cooperation with such peace organizations as the American Union Against Militarism see Maurer, *It Can Be Done*, pp. 215-20.

difficult position. On the one hand they wanted desperately to hold to their antiwar principles and avoid the disgrace of European socialism in 1914. Wilsonian reform had driven them to feel the necessity of staking out distinct Socialist positions on the issues still available to them. On the other hand, as gradualists and reformists, they hesitated to alienate themselves too far from their potential liberal allies and involve themselves in revolutionary tactics that would undermine all hope of gradualist advance. In the end, ethnic allegiances, the desire for consistency, and the pressure from the Left carried the day for an antiwar proclamation.

The majority report, written by the moderate Hillquit but supported by most of the left-wing leaders as well, condemned the war and proclaimed the Socialist Party's "unalterable opposition." In wording that even the Socialist *New York Call* found extreme, the report called for "continuous, active and public opposition to the war, through demonstrations, mass petitions, and all other means within our power." Workers of all countries were advised to "refuse support to their governments in their wars."[67] John Spargo's minority report accepted the war, called for sacrifices to insure a speedy victory, and sought to direct attention to the possibilities of gains for Socialist domestic programs during the war emergency. It was soundly defeated. How extreme an antiwar position the Socialist Party had taken in St. Louis becomes apparent when one realizes that even the militant national leadership of the Industrial Workers of the World refrained from dramatic proclamations of opposition to the war. Big Bill Haywood now rejected suggestions for an antiwar general strike. He and other IWW leaders continued to shun any involvement in the peace movement. Although much persecuted for their "pro-Germanism" and antiwar sympathies, the IWW members, as Melvyn Dubofsky has shown, chose to avoid "squandering precious resources" in "rhetorical opposition to America's involvement." They sought, instead, to concentrate on industrial organization at home.[68]

After the rejection of his minority report at St. Louis, John Spargo joined the exodus from the party of such pro-Ally, pro-interventionist Socialists as William English Walling, Algie Simons, W. J. Ghent, Charles Edward Russell, Allan Benson, J. G.

[67] Fine, *Labor and Farmer Parties in the United States*, pp. 311, 313; Bassett, "The Socialist Party of America," p. 216.

[68] Melvyn Dubofsky, *We Shall Be All: A History of the Industrial Workers of the World* (Chicago 1969), pp. 351-58.

Phelps Stokes, Gustavus Myers, Upton Sinclair, W. R. Gaylord, Robert Rives LaMonte, J. Stitt Wilson, Robert Hunter, Henry Slobodin, Frank Bohn, and William Edlin.[69] The defections, as has often been observed, did not follow traditional ideological lines. Simons, Walling, Phelps Stokes, Slobodin, and LaMonte were clearly of the left wing, while Ghent, Benson, Russell, and Hunter had adhered to the reformist, right-wing segment of the party. Those who left the party over the war issue have usually, and reasonably accurately, been characterized as the intellectuals of the party, although clearly not all of the Socialist intellectuals deserted.[70] An additional, and perhaps related characteristic of those who rejected the party's antiwar stance was that they were party leaders who had no continuing constituency—no ethnic minority, no local political organization—to which they felt responsible.

Those whose reactions to the St. Louis antiwar position were more important for the next phase of the peace movement were the moderates within the Socialist Party. Firmly wedded to an antiwar position in early 1917 for reasons of ideological consistency, national and ethnic partisanship, or mere reaction against the conservative forces dominating the prowar drive, they were nevertheless uncomfortable with the militancy of the language and program of the St. Louis report. Job Harriman, a moderate who had supported the majority report, still feared that it might be "exceedingly unwise and extremely dangerous." Victor Berger worried about the power that the "impossibilist" left wing of the party had gained during the emergency convention.[71] On other issues than the war, the left wing had also demonstrated new strength, a development which had encouraged Hillquit and the moderates to seek a compromise with the Left through a militant antiwar statement. The result was "the strongest depreciation of parliamentary political action the Socialist Party had ever entertained."[72]

[69] Fine, *Labor and Farmer Parties in the United States*, pp. 315-16; Shannon, *The Socialist Party of America*, pp. 99-102; Friedberg, "Marxism in the United States," pp. 201, 216; Bell, "Marxian Socialism in the United States," I, 312-13.

[70] For characterizations of the defectors as the intellectuals of the party see Shannon, *The Socialist Party of America*, p. 99 and Bell, "Marxian Socialism in the United States," I, 309. James Oneal, who did not leave the party on this issue, preferred another term. "We had always considered most of them gas-bags," he reminisced, "and were glad to be rid of them" ("The Socialists in the War," p. 419). James Weinstein uses the term "socialist muckrakers" to characterize many of those who later became part of the prowar group. Weinstein, *The Decline of Socialism in America*, pp. 76-79, 84.

[71] Bassett, "The Socialist Party of America," pp. 215-16, 220.

[72] Friedberg, "Marxism in the United States," pp. 205, 212-13.

Michael Bassett has called the St. Louis report a "product of desperation." The moderates, in deference to the growing strength of the Left had supported language in the St. Louis report that was, in Hillquit's later appraisal, "aggressive, defiant and provocative in tone." After such a compromise with the Left, many of the moderate Socialists were eager for antiwar action that would be less militant than that suggested by the St. Louis report and that might reestablish their credence among potential liberal and radical allies.[73] Conditions were ripe for a new peace organization that would bring the Socialist Right, and other militantly antiwar Socialists, into cooperation with the radical remnants of the preintervention peace organizations.

The People's Council of America for Democracy and Peace, tentatively formed at the end of May 1917 and formally constituted in September 1917, represented the culmination of the steady trend toward social and political radicalism that had taken place in the American peace movement since 1914. One segment of the pre-1914 peace movement, now headed by the League to Enforce Peace, had, by 1915, abandoned all agitation for immediate peace and had given its entire attention to schemes for postwar international organization. The newer peace organizations such as the Woman's Peace Party, the American Neutral Conference Committee, and the American Union Against Militarism, which had replaced the older organizations in the continuing agitation for a mediated peace and against American intervention, had brought a more politically liberal and socially activist leadership into the peace movement. Even these organizations had lost the less radical elements of their support as the nation had swung toward enthusiasm for American military involvement. By April of 1917 the remaining leaders of these organizations—and of other affiliated, ad hoc peace organizations that appeared during the early months of 1917—found themselves increasingly isolated from respectable and influential leaders of opinion.

The United States' decision to enter the war in early April 1917 ushered in a brief period of pessimism, acute frustration, and confusion of purpose for nearly all of the preintervention peace organizations. Many of their members, liberal and radical, had been persons whose activities and connections bridged two worlds: the world of institutional and organizational connections with the nation's political and social establishment that allowed them to

[73] Bassett, "The Socialist Party of America," pp. 212, 214, 235-36; Hillquit, *Loose Leaves from a Busy Life*, p. 167.

work as respectable reformers from within the system; and the world of radical dissent in which they operated as knowledgeable critics and occasional allies of those bent upon more revolutionary methods of change. Between March and August of 1917 the overwhelming majority of these men and women resigned from the remaining peace organizations or ceased to participate and allowed their organizations to atrophy. Few of them were prospective candidates for leadership or participation in a new, necessarily more radical, peace organization. Their connections with other reform or professional organizations that retained some power of action and influence during wartime helped persuade some of them that the war emergency could be manipulated for useful social purposes.[74] It was those who had no significant connections with established and respectable organizations and institutions, who had little access to means of applying social and political leverage during the war, and who had no continuing responsibilities to organized groups—no constituency of fellow workers in ongoing causes—who reacted to the frustrations and confused purposes of April and May 1917 by seeking to create a new, broader, antiwar coalition.[75]

The People's Council of America, which began to take form in late May, derived its impetus from the cooperation of several leading Socialists with the "free-lance" liberals and radicals of the preintervention peace organizations. But its composition was more complex and inclusive than such a description would indicate. During its early and most vital months of existence, it drew strength from a number of identifiable factions, cliques, and political constituencies and sought to extend its base to include several others.

[74] Allen F. Davis, "Welfare, Reform and World War I," *American Quarterly*, 19 (Fall 1967), 519-33. See also chap. seven, pp. 258-64. The most famous contemporary critiques of this reform optimism were Randolph Bourne's essays reprinted in his *Untimely Papers* (New York 1919).

[75] The tendency of the liberals who were responsible to constituent groups or ongoing institutions to eschew further organized antiwar action presents a striking contrast to the tendency, among Socialist Party members, for the "attached" members with constituencies to hold to an antiwar position. The answer to this apparent paradox, of course, is that the constituencies greatly differed. Certain ethnic groups and labor bodies provided at least temporary support for an antiwar position by their Socialist leaders, while the institutions and organizations in which liberals felt continuing responsibilities often subsisted only with governmental favor, broad middle-class support or munificent private donations. Even the immigrant and worker groups served by such liberal institutions often required services and political actions that, it seemed to liberals, only those with access to favor in high places could provide. The "constituencies" upon which these liberals had to draw for support often vehemently opposed further antiwar activities of any kind.

From the outset, national leaders of the Socialist Party of America, primarily moderates, played a crucial role in the organization of the People's Council. Morris Hillquit, national chairman of the party, Algernon Lee, Socialist candidate for governor of New York in 1916, and James Maurer, candidate for the party's presidential nomination in 1916, took part in the small group that began preliminary planning for a conference in May in New York City. In Chicago, John C. Kennedy and Adolph Germer participated in roughly parallel activities. Victor Berger, Eugene Debs, Arthur LeSueur, James Oneal, Harry Laidler, George H. Goebel, Julius Gerber, Job Harriman, Charles W. Ervin, Irwin St. John Tucker, Patrick Nagel, and Joseph Cannon were announced as early supporters of the new movement. Representing the New York City Socialist aesthetes, generally to the Left of the Socialist Party national leadership and often at odds with Hillquit and the party leaders, were Max Eastman, editor of *The Masses*, and John Reed, poet, revolutionist, and war correspondent.

Other New York City artists and intellectuals, some non-Socialists but long involved in radical causes, gave varying degrees of support to the emerging People's Council. Randolph Bourne served in several capacities during the organizing period. Art Young, cartoonist for *The Masses*, was appointed to the People's Council "Committee on Timely Literature," along with Max Eastman, John Reed, historian Charles A. Beard, and others. The names of Sara Bard Field, James Waldo Fawcett, Charles Rann Kennedy, Edith Wynne Matthieson, Rose and Ann Strunsky, and Fola La Follette, daughter of Senator La Follette, added cultural and artistic dimension to the People's Council. Active participation in the People's Council leadership by Max Eastman, A. W. Ricker, editor of *Pearson's Magazine*, and members of the staff of the *New York Call* and the *Appeal to Reason* assured the new organization of favorable coverage in portions of the radical press.[76]

[76] Information on participation in the People's Council and its temporary organizational form, the American Conference for Democracy and Terms of Peace, was derived from correspondence, pamphlets, letterheads, and memoranda in the People's Council of America Papers in the SCPC, the Tamiment Library, and the HI. Subsequent sections linking various individuals with the People's Council rely upon the same or similar sources. Particularly useful were the following: "Who's Who in the People's Council" (pamphlet), Box 1, PC Papers, SCPC and PC Papers, HI; "Members of the Organizing Committee Thus Far Elected" (memorandum), PC Papers, SCPC; Penciled four-page list, untitled, American Conference for Democracy and Terms of Peace Papers, SCPC; People's Council organizing committee minutes of meetings, Box 1, PC Papers, SCPC; *Report of the First American Conference for Democracy and Terms of Peace held at Madison Square Garden*, New York City, 30 and 31 May 1917 (booklet), PC Papers, TL and ACDTP Papers, SCPC; "Program, First American Conference for Democracy and Terms of Peace"

More numerous than the Socialist Party officers or socialist aesthetes within the early leadership of the People's Council, although not more influential in the inner circles of policy planning, were the labor union leaders of Socialist persuasion. The initial organizers of the People's Council were determined to avoid one common failing of all previous peace organizations—the lack of a base of support among organized workers. During the summer of 1917 it seemed that they had made great strides in correcting the middle-class provincialism of earlier phases of the peace movement. The council gained at least temporary support from a number of powerful labor groups, particularly those centered in New York City. Twelve of the fifty People's Council leaders listed in the organization's pamphlet, "Who's Who in the People's Council," were representatives of labor organizations. The Philadelphia Branch claimed support from the Cloakmakers, Bakers, Waist and Dressmakers, Upholsters, and Capmakers, and the national organizations included such diverse labor representatives as the president of the ILGWU, the president of the Big Six Typographical Union in New York, the chairman of the 60,000-member Workmen's Circle, the head of the New York City teachers' union, and members of locals of such peripheral unions as the Inside Iron and Brass Workers and the International Shingle Workers. Several leaders were active workers in the Women's Trade Union League. The Cigarmakers, Iron Moulders, Machinists, Carpenters and Joiners, Teamsters, United Mine Workers, and several city and state federations were also represented in the early People's Council leadership.[77]

Thus, compared with the feeble efforts of earlier peace organizations, the People's Council had marshaled impressive support from organized labor. The great majority of AFL trade union leaders shunned the organization, of course, and later followed Gompers' lead in mounting a formidable attack upon it.[78] But

---

(leaflet), ACDTP Papers, SCPC. See also Clayton R. Lusk, ed., *Revolutionary Radicalism: Report of the Joint Legislative Committee of the State of New York* (Albany 1920), Part I, Vol. I, pp. 1028-32, and Tracy Mygatt to Emily Balch, 17 Aug. 1917, and Emily Balch *et al.*, form letter, n.d. for American Conference for Democracy and Terms of Peace, Emily Greene Balch Papers, SCPC.

[77] "Who's Who in the People's Council," and "Partial List of Organizations Making up the People's Council for Democracy and Peace, Philadelphia Branch" (memorandum), Box 1, PC Papers, SCPC; *The Social Preparation*, 55 (Oct. 1917), 11, in Box 1, PC Papers, SCPC.

[78] On the attitudes and efforts of Gompers and most AFL leaders, see Frank L. Grubbs, Jr., *The Struggle for Labor Loyalty: Gompers, the A. F. of L. and the Pacifists, 1917-1920* (Durham, N.C. 1968), pp. 35ff. and Radosh, *American Labor and United States Foreign Policy*, pp. 54-71.

prominent leaders in at least three large national unions and representatives from a variety of locals gave brief but active support to the People's Council. Occasionally, as in the case of Duncan McDonald and Adolph Germer of the Mine Workers, participation in the People's Council became one more phase in a continuing Socialist opposition to Gompers and the conservative majority within the American trade union movement. Far more frequently, however, labor support for the People's Council came from those whose opposition to conservative unionism was as much an expression of their Jewish consciousness as it was of their Socialist bias.

The largest segment of union support for the People's Council came from the major national unions in the garment industry—the ILGWU, the ACWA, and the United Cloth Hat and Cap Makers Union. All three of these unions were composed primarily of East European Jewish immigrants and all were generally Socialist in outlook. All were semi-industrial unions which had come into at least momentary conflict with older unions or AFL policies because of their drives for more inclusive membership, their attacks on conservative leadership, and their tendencies toward organizational unity along ethnic lines through the UHT. The ACWA had been in constant conflict with the AFL since its secession from the United Garment Workers of America in 1914. The ILGWU, under Socialist leadership since 1914, had recently proved a thorn in the side of the AFL leadership and had militantly pushed the cause of the ACWA at AFL conventions. The Cap Makers, long opponents of Gompers, were to walk out of the AFL later in 1917.[79]

Leaders in these garment unions were often also leaders in specifically Jewish organizations and enterprises such as the UHT, the influential Yiddish journal *Forward (Vorwarts)*, the Jewish Socialist Federation and the Workmen's Circle *(Arbeiter Ring)*, a workers' mutual aid association. The People's Council drew support from a number of these organizations, particularly the UHT and the Workmen's Circle. Max Pine and Abraham Shiplacoff, active figures in the early planning of the People's Council, were both officers in the UHT, while the Workmen's Circle was represented on the People's Council by its chairman, two of its three vice-chairmen, its treasurer, secretary, executive secretary, recording secretary, and three additional members of its executive

[79] Melech Epstein, *Jewish Labor in U.S.A., 1914-1952: An Industrial, Political and Cultural History of the Jewish Labor Movement* (New York 1953), pp. 11-49; Dubofsky, "New York City Labor in the Progressive Era," pp. 292-99, 307.

committee. Jacob Panken, an early and active leader in the People's Council, acted as attorney for the ACWA, the UHT, and the Ladies' Waist Makers Union, as well as serving as chairman of the Workmen's Circle. Max Pine and Benjamin Schlesinger were former members of the staff of the *Forward* and J. B. Salutsky, prominently listed among the People's Council leaders, was secretary of the Jewish Socialist Federation and editor of its journal, *Naye Velt*.[80]

These Jewish labor organizations drew their temporary fervor for peace from an intense combination of anti-Czarist and anti-capitalist sentiments. Since 1914 many of these groups had consistently opposed the war, supported an embargo and other efforts to restrict American aid to the Allies, and sympathized with Germany in their hope for a crushing defeat for Czarist Russia. The membership of the Jewish workers' organizations and the garment unions included large numbers of recent immigrants. Many had fled from the pogroms and from other forms of restriction and persecution. They were often artisans or merchants who had undergone a process of "proletarianization" as part of their immigration experience. Many who emerged as leaders of immigrant-dominated unions and other workers' organizations in America had been leaders in radical movements in Russia before and during the 1905 revolution. Some had been anarchists, some Labor Zionists, some members of the Bund. Compared to earlier Jewish immigrants, they brought with them "a more militant conception of a labor movement and a keener regard for Jewish cultural values."[81] They combined a deep attachment to communal ties and communal responsibility with a "spiritual restlessness," a yearning for an apocalyptic end to the tumult and suffering of the present and the creation of a cooperative commonwealth or a Jewish national state. The labor movement became for them, in Moses Rischin's words, "a folk mission"; their dedication to socialism, according to Will Herberg, "not so much a social ideology or political creed as a '*moral cement. . . .*' "[82] For a brief moment in

[80] Joseph Rappaport, "Jewish Immigrants and World War I: A Study of American Yiddish Press Reactions," Ph.D. diss., Columbia University, 1951, pp. 261-63, 286, 300-301, 309-10. For 1917 officers of the Workmen's Circle, see J. B. Salutsky to Amos Pinchot, 23 Oct. 1917, Amos Pinchot Papers, MS Div., Library of Congress.

[81] Epstein, *Jewish Labor in the U.S.A., 1914-1952*, pp. 1-2, 6; Rappaport, "Jewish Immigrants," pp. 42, 47, 78, 85-86, 145-49; Melech Epstein, *Jewish Labor in the U.S.A., 1882-1914* (New York 1950), pp. 301-10.

[82] Will Herberg, "Jewish Labor Movement in the United States: Early Years to World War I," *Industrial and Labor Relations Review*, 5 (July 1952), 504, 510; Moses Rischin, *The Promised City: New York's Jews, 1870-1914* (Cambridge, Mass. 1962), p. 193; Moses Rischin, "The Jewish Labor Movement in America: A Social

1917, many of them found in the peace movement the expression, concurrently, of their hatred of the Czar, their enthusiasm for the New Russia of the revolution, their anticapitalist contempt for the "war profiteering" of the alien American establishment, their long-standing antagonism against Gompers and the conservative unionists in the AFL, and their idealistic longings for a world transformed.

It was not only the leaders of Jewish labor organizations that saw in the People's Council a possible expression of immigrant Jewish aspirations toward communitarianism and nationalism. Much of the early impetus behind the formation of the People's Council came from Dr. Judah L. Magnes, of Temple Emanu-El in New York City, a reform rabbi with conservative leanings, a conservative congregation, and a strong sense of identification with such leaders of Conservative Judaism as Solomon Schechter. Magnes had long felt himself called to the mission of uniting New York City's Jews into a community and leading that community to a spiritual and national reawakening. Like the Jewish labor leaders he did not find his way into the organized peace movement until 1917. But for several years he had been exploring various avenues of bridging the gap between the immigrant Jewish masses and the established, earlier Jewish immigrants of largely German origin.[83]

In 1905 Magnes had taken the lead in establishing a Jewish Defense Association in America, a popular organization to raise funds for the defense of Russian ghettos, to engender a sense of Jewish pride, and to support forceful resistance to persecution. Later he had replied on behalf of New York's Jews to sensational charges of Jewish criminality. He proposed and established a Kehillah (communal council) to bring together the various segments of New York's Jewish community and sought constantly, although unsuccessfully, to identify himself with the Jewish masses. Having successfully brought the prominent, assimilationist, and generally conservative leaders of the American Jewish Committee into affiliation with his Kehillah movement, Magnes had

Interpretation," *Labor History*, 4 (Fall 1963), 234-36, 240; Rappaport, "Jewish Immigrants," pp. 6-7; Melvyn Dubofsky, *When Workers Organize: New York City in the Progressive Era* (Amherst, Mass. 1968), pp. 32-37.

[83] Norman Bentwich, *For Zion's Sake: A Biography of Judah L. Magnes* (Philadelphia 1954), pp. 27, 37-38, 40, 44, 48, 80, 90; Arthur A. Goren, *New York Jews and the Quest for Community: The Kehillah Experiment, 1908-1922* (New York 1970), pp. 23, 37-39, 57-59, 231; Rischin, *The Promised City*, p. 243; Oscar Handlin, *Adventure in Freedom: Three Hundred Years of Jewish Life in America* (New York 1954), p. 167.

thrown his energies into labor mediation and other activities on behalf of the recent immigrants in an effort to make the Kehillah a truly representative communal body by gaining the support of the Socialist and workers' organizations. But he never gained more than intermittent and suspicious cooperation from the Jewish labor movement. Then, in 1915 and 1916, his whole Kehillah movement had been gravely endangered by the tensions within the Jewish community over war issues and the open struggle between conservatives and democratic Zionists over the calling of an American Jewish Congress. As Arthur Goren points out, Magnes, who had been until now the "mediator par excellence" and the "most popular figure in Jewish public life," was caught, along with his whole Kehillah movement, "in the crossfire of a struggle between a patrician Old Guard and a rising immigrant community."[84]

It was at this point, during the last weeks of 1916, that Magnes first began to take an interest in the peace movement. By February 1917, he had involved himself with the Emergency Peace Federation and in April of 1917, inspired by the promise of a new world that he saw in the implications of the Russian Revolution, he threw himself into the peace movement with great energy. He refused to support American intervention and argued that the attachment of Zionism to the allied war aims would undermine the spiritual nature of the Zionist movement.

Exactly why Magnes suddenly cast his lot with the peace movement is difficult to explain. The possibility still existed of reviving the Kehillah movement, which he still headed, as an expression of unified Jewish loyalty and war service. Certainly Magnes' dissenting position imposed new burdens on the struggling Kehillah. The major historian of the Kehillah movement, Arthur Goren, discovers no other explanation for Magnes' new enthusiasm for peace than the "dictates of conscience." Perhaps Magnes was also influenced by the recent frustrations and declining fortunes of the Kehillah and irritated by the rigid and intransigent position of the "Old Guard" which had thwarted the Kehillah's attempt to serve as mediator in the Jewish community. Perhaps, also, he suddenly saw in the peace movement, particularly as embodied in the People's Council idea, a possible vehicle for finally bridging the gap between himself and the Jewish masses. As a leader of the People's Council, he associated himself with the radical visions of the new Russia, the immigrant's distrust of conscription, and the

[84] Goren, *New York Jews and the Quest for Community*, pp. 44-56, 186-230, 249-50; Bentwich, *For Zion's Sake*, pp. 39, 55, 63, 69, 72, 76, 91, 105; Rischin, *The Promised City*, p. 243.

spiritual idealism of Zionist utopianism. But certainly he must have realized very early that his peace activities were not helping unite the community behind the Kehillah. His further adherence to the People's Council reflected not expediency, but an apparent combination of conscience, consistency, and either a despair of attaining his old goals or a new, radical democratic vision.[85]

Not all of the radical support for the People's Council came from the Jewish organizations or even from within the Socialist camp. Single-taxers, including Bolton Hall, Daniel Kiefer, Mary Ware Dennett, Edward Hartman, S. A. Stockwell, Western Starr, Amy Mali Hicks, Lindley Keasbey, and Frank and Donald Stephens played a large role in the organization throughout its brief career. Kiefer, Dennett, Hartman, Starr, Keasbey, Hicks, and Donald Stephens all served on the crucial organizing committee. Other radicals, both prominent and obscure, temporarily entered the peace movement as part of the People's Council coalition. Gertrude B. Kelly, a leader in the Irish freedom campaign, was a regular participant, as was Charles Kruse, president of the "Hobo Union" (James Eads How's International Brotherhood Welfare Association). Radical clergymen such as Jenkin Lloyd Jones of Chicago, Richard Hogue of Baltimore, Herbert J. Bigelow of Cincinnati, and J. Howard Melish of Brooklyn became members.[86] Although such leaders of the new Socialist left wing as Leon Trotsky and Louis Fraina shunned the People's Council as gradualist and class collaborationist, several subsequent Communists, including Benjamin Gitlow, Juliet Poyntz, and Elizabeth Gurley Flynn, played brief roles in this, the most radical phase of the early twentieth century peace movement. At one point anarchists Alexander Berkman and Emma Goldman emerged as probable delegates to the People's Council Constituent Assembly. Apparently they were privately dissuaded from standing for election as delegates by People's Council leaders who feared that connections with radicals as notorious as Berkman and Goldman would

[85] Goren, *New York Jews and the Quest for Community*, pp. 231-35; Bentwich, *For Zion's Sake*, pp. 105, 108.

[86] Information on participation in the People's Council is derived from a variety of sources. See above, n. 76. Joseph Freeman suggested the "popular front" character of the People's Council when he reflected on "socialists, wobblies, anarchists, liberals and pacifists of every kind" that crowded the Madison Square Garden organizing convention. As young radicals, he and his brother found in the People's Council convention, "representing all shades of radical and liberal opinion, . . . the world to which we properly belonged" (Joseph Freeman, *An American Testament: A Narrative of Rebels and Romantics* [New York 1936], pp. 100, 103). On the variety of radicals loosely associated in this and other causes during 1917 see also Louis Lochner, *Always the Unexpected* (New York 1956), p. 73.

cut them off from any sympathies from liberals whom they still hoped to include in their antiwar coalition.[87]

But for all the numerical strength of the Socialists, Jewish labor organizations, single-taxers, and other radicals within the People's Council coalition, the new organization was still basically a peace organization, an integral part of the continuing but rapidly changing peace movement in America. Undaunted bitter-enders from derelict preintervention peace organizations like the Emergency Peace Federation and the American Neutral Conference Committee provided the People's Council with some continuity of leadership from the preintervention peace movement. Several members of the radical New York branch of the Woman's Peace Party joined the new antiwar coalition. The popular support for the organized peace movement now came temporarily from the Socialist and other labor groups that were well represented on People's Council committees, but much of the organizational work and policy formulation was carried out by men and women whose participation in the peace movement went back as far as 1915. The People's Council's major staff positions—executive secretary, organizing secretary, and financial secretary—were held, respectively, by Louis P. Lochner, Lella Faye Secor, and Rebecca Shelly, all members of the Henry Ford Peace Ship venture of December 1915, and all leading staff members of the Emergency Peace Federation. Miss Secor and Miss Shelly had also been the driving forces behind the American Neutral Conference Committee. Other major participants in earlier peace organizations such as Emily Balch, H.W.L. Dana, Crystal Eastman, and Norman Thomas also became officers in the new organization.

Thus, despite its more radical appeal to a new antiwar constituency, the People's Council was in one sense simply a new phase in a rapidly evolving peace movement. Reflecting back on the period, Emily Balch was impressed by the continuity of leadership between the preintervention organizations—the Emergency Peace Federation and the American Neutral Conference Committee—and the postintervention People's Council. It was all the same movement, she recalled, merely taking on different organizational names at different times.[88] While properly stressing the

[87] James Waldo Fawcett to Louis Lochner, Aug. 1917; Lochner to Fawcett 17 Aug. 1917; Lusk, *Revolutionary Radicalism*, Part I, Vol. I, pp. 1067, 1070; Draper, *The Roots of American Communism*, p. 112; Weinstein, *The Decline of Socialism in America*, pp. 188-89.

[88] Emily Greene Balch Memorandum, 8 June 1940, Box 1, PC Papers, SCPC. Lella Faye Secor described the organizational transmutations of the Spring of 1917 in similar terms. She and Rebecca Shelly had summoned the Executive Committee

continued influence of experienced peace workers in the People's Council, Emily Balch's description failed to suggest just how much more had changed with the People's Council than the name. Leadership of the peace movement, as never before, was now shared with Socialist and radical leaders. Finding the potential antiwar following further and further to the political Left, the peace workers phrased their objections to war in more strident anticapitalistic slogans. Their alienation from the nation's political establishment became more complete, their fulminations against big business more frequent, their enthusiasm for revolutionary language more pronounced.

One established peace organization that might have been expected to throw its support to the new People's Council peace coalition in the spring of 1917 was the American Union Against Militarism. The American Union was still relatively vigorous and growing more radical. But personal suspicions and the desire of several of its leaders to remain firmly within the liberal fold prevented official American Union participation in the early planning of the People's Council. Lillian Wald, Roger Baldwin, Norman Thomas, Crystal and Max Eastman, and several other American Union members did attend early meetings leading to the planning for the eventual People's Council. But Miss Wald, and several other American Union leaders, including John Haynes Holmes, Paul Kellogg, and O. G. Villard, decided in mid-May that the American Union should maintain its separate, liberal identity and not endanger its reputation or freedom of action by too close an association with the emerging radical peace group.[89]

---

of the "dignified" American Neutral Conference Committee to a meeting in Feb. 1917, immediately after the United States had severed diplomatic relations with Germany. "Most of the members promptly resigned," she later recalled, "leaving the meagre machinery to us. So the American Neutral Conference Committee was reborn as a militant peace organization, and christened the Emergency Peace Federation." The transformation from the Emergency Peace Federation to the People's Council she described simply as a "further reorganization." Lella Secor Florence, "The Ford Peace Ship and After," in Julian Bell, ed., *We Did Not Fight, 1914-1918 Experiences of War Resisters* (London 1935), pp. 119, 123. See also Lella Faye Secor to Dear Friends, n.d., and Tracy D. Mygatt to William I. Hull, 20 June 1917, Box 5, William I. Hull Papers, Friends' Historical Library, Swarthmore College.

[89] For a more complete discussion of the debate over the People's Council within the AUAM see chap. seven, pp. 256-57. See also Donald Johnson, *The Challenge to American Freedoms: World War I and the Rise of the American Civil Liberties Union* (Lexington, Ky. 1968), pp. 19-25; Grubbs, *The Struggle for Labor Loyalty*, p. 22; Blanche Wiesen Cook, "Woodrow Wilson and the Antimilitarists, 1914-1917," Ph.D. diss., The Johns Hopkins University, 1970, pp. 220-21; and H.W.L. Dana to Rebecca Shelly, 22 Mar. 1917, Box 1, Henry Wadsworth Longfellow Dana Papers, SCPC.

Distrust of several of the potential leaders of the new coalition also played a role in the American Union's decision. Several American Union leaders considered Lochner too immature and too frequently involved in quixotic causes in the recent past. Villard referred to Secor and Shelly as "the most trying people to work with I have ever known, being as destitute of judgment in political matters as March hares."[90] After momentary indecision, the American Union Against Militarism refused to affiliate with the new group and most of its leaders refused to allow their names to be used in the call to the organizing conference. Despite this rejection of official support for the emerging People's Council, however, peace workers from the ranks of the American Union did lend individual assistance. Norman Thomas, H.W.L. Dana, Emily Balch, and Crystal and Max Eastman became members of the People's Council organizing committee and Amos Pinchot and Roger Baldwin gave individual support and advice despite their refusal to lend their names to the new enterprise.[91]

Some of those who migrated from the earlier peace organizations into the People's Council were thorough-going pacifists; but a majority were driven by a mixture of motives. Some seem to have been spurred by the excitement of their rapid radicalization to further adventures that would bring them into even more intimate contact with working class and bohemian radicalism. Others had found a satisfying sense of community in the comradeship of "that faithful little regiment which stood the test—stood firm when the whole world shook. . . ." "The loyalty, enthusiasm and devotion of those workers created an atmosphere which cannot be described," Lella Secor later reminisced. "I have never lived through such a vivid and buoyant emotional experience."[92]

Margaret Lane, an early promoter of the postintervention, radical peace coalition, spoke for a number of nonpacifist peaceworkers who continued their efforts through the People's Council when she related her peace activities to her more general "revolt

[90] Lusk, *Revolutionary Radicalism*, Part I, Vol. I, p. 1022; Oswald Garrison Villard to Roger Baldwin, 12 Apr. 1917, Box 3, AUAM Papers, SCPC.

[91] Louis P. Lochner to Emily Balch, 9 May and 12 May 1917, ACDTP Papers, SCPC; Amos Pinchot to Lochner, 9 May 1917 and W. W. Williams to Pinchot, 15 June 1917, Amos Pinchot Papers, MS Div., LC; Max Eastman, *Love and Revolution: My Journey Through an Epoch* (New York 1964), pp. 49-57; Crystal Eastman to H.W.L. Dana, 15 Aug. 1917, Box 1, Dana Papers, SCPC; Roger Baldwin to Lochner, 21 Aug. 1917, in Lusk, *Revolutionary Radicalism*, Part I, Vol. I, p. 1057.

[92] Lella Faye Secor to H.W.L. Dana, 25 June 1917. Box 1, Dana Papers, SCPC; Florence, "The Ford Peace Ship and After," p. 122. See also Lochner, *Always the Unexpected*, pp. 228-29.

against everything grayhaired and respectable."[93] Like earlier organizations in the peace movement, then, the People's Council was not the formal embodiment of unmixed motives of pacifism. Most conscientious objectors, and probably most uncompromising pacifists, were not, and never had been, participants in the organized peace movement.[94] A few uncompromising pacifists took roles of leadership in the People's Council just as they had participated in earlier peace organizations. But like earlier peace societies, the People's Council drew its overwhelming support from those for whom the appeal for immediate peace and a reform of international diplomacy coincided with other, more immediate interests. The attraction of the People's Council was the way in which it merged domestic radicalism with agitation for peace. Even among the more experienced peace workers, its appeal was not so much its pacifistic message as the way in which current events in Russia enabled it to combine ostensible pacifism with a vision of a new American revolution.

The People's Council of America for Democracy and Peace took its first formal shape with the American Conference for Democracy and Terms of Peace at Madison Square Garden in New York City on 30-31 May 1917. During the next four months, the period of its most vigorous activity, the Council drew its major inspiration from the Russian Revolution and its major model from the Petrograd Soviet. At first, the direction of the eventual council had been unclear. It had begun with small private meetings during late April and early May as the remaining peace workers sought a new organizational framework and some new line of action during wartime. Simultaneously Socialist leaders in New York City had begun to explore the possibility of an opening to the Right through cooperation with antiwar liberals in order to blunt the separatist thrust of their St. Louis proclamation.

Rabbi Magnes took the initiative in the search for a new peace coalition, at first raising only "a rather shabby little group" and then, with a second effort, bringing together leaders in the surviving peace organizations with Morris Hillquit, Joseph Cannon, a Socialist and former organizer for the International Mine, Mill and Smelter Workers, and Edward Cassidy, a Socialist leader of

[93] Unsigned [Margaret Lane] to Anne Herendeen, 18 Jan. 1916, Box 15, Woman's Peace Party, New York Branch, Correspondence, SCPC.

[94] Most conscientious objectors came from the traditional peace sects and churches, some of which rejected all forms of political involvement. For an attempt to categorize the various types of conscientious objectors in World War I, see Norman Thomas, *The Conscientious Objector in America* (New York 1923), pp. 30-55, 64-74.

the typographical workers. After small meetings at the headquarters of the New York branch of the Woman's Peace Party, the group launched a more ambitious organizing conference at the Hotel Astor on 2 May. Although some of the more conservative members of the American Union Against Militarism participated, control quickly passed to those who sought "a new amalgamation of forces" and who had come to view the American Union as too compromising and too incapable of reaching "the radical element."[95]

The enthusiasts for a new antiwar "amalgamation" set to work at the Hotel Astor meeting to formulate the program they would present at the public conference at Madison Square Garden at the end of the month. The tentative outline was a moderate one, going little beyond the proposals of the more radical previous peace organizations. A "speedy and universal peace" was demanded, based upon "general principles outlined by the President of the United States and endorsed by the revolutionary government of Russia, the Social Democratic organizations of France, Italy, Germany and Austria and liberal and democratic forces of England." The peace should involve no annexation of territory, no punitive indemnities, and a reorganization of international affairs. Diplomacy should be democratized and popular referenda held on alliances and declarations of war. The proposed resolutions for the conference opposed compulsory military training, conscription, the suspension of labor laws, the lowering of living standards of the working class, and any curtailment of the rights of workers to organize. They called for high taxes on war profits, a steeply progressive income tax, and public control of the production and distribution of food and the transportation of food and war supplies.[96]

Such a program was hardly unprecedented within the peace movement, although it did devote more attention to the specific concerns of labor than had earlier, preintervention proposals. What was new was the way in which the Petrograd Soviet came to serve as the source of a peace program for the council, and ultimately as a model for domestic political reconstruction. The

[95] Unsigned [Margaret Lane] to Jessie Wallace Hughan, 27 Apr. 1917, Box 15, WPPNY Correspondence, SCPC; unsigned [Margaret Lane] to Mr. George Beaver, 27 Apr. 1917, Box 14, WPPNY Correspondence, SCPC; Donald Stephens, to H.W.L. Dana, 27 Apr. 1917, Dana to Rebecca Shelly, 22 Mar. 1917, Box 1, Dana Papers, SCPC; Emily G. Balch, Judah L. Magnes, Edward F. Cassidy, Morris Hillquit, and John Haynes Holmes to William I. Hull, 27 Apr. 1917, Box 5, Hull Papers, FHL.

[96] Conference Committee at Hotel Astor, 2 May 1917, "Tentative Outline of Program" (memorandum), ACDTP Papers, SCPC.

name "council" was a deliberate attempt at direct translation of the Russian term "Soviet." The name "People's Council" had been chosen, Judah Magnes told the Madison Square Garden conference, because its leaders believed they spoke for the American people and because "that name is now a new and glorious word in the vocabulary of all free and liberty loving men the world over—because the word Council is the word that has been given to their Council by the free Russian people."[97] As early as mid-May, Rebecca Shelly was writing that the program and plan of action of the new organization would "undoubtedly be in thorough accord with that of the Russian Council of Workmen and Soldiers." At the 30-31 May public conference she was to make the nature of the inspiration from Russia even more explicit.[98]

Rebecca Shelly, young, zealous, and a veteran of the Ford Peace Ship and several subsequent peace organizations, quickly emerged as a major architect of the council's program and doctrine. Morris Hillquit later referred to her as the "Maid of Orleans of the People's Council" and described how her speech to the American Conference for Democracy and Terms of Peace at Madison Square Garden had galvanized the unfocused antiwar sentiments of the conference into a specific program for organizational action. Actually, other supporters of the new coalition had already proposed a nationwide organizing effort and Miss Shelly had helped formulate earlier the plans for action adopted by the Madison Square Garden Conference.[99] But her speech at the conference clearly did act as a kind of catalyst uniting various antiwar elements in a new and purposeful organizational compound. It also made clear the revolutionary implications of the People's Council idea.

"Congress as now constituted," Rebecca Shelly charged, "does not represent the American People." Just as a Council of Workmen's and Soldiers' Delegates had come forward in Russia to contest against an unrepresentative government and seek peace, so

[97] People's Council of America for Democracy and Peace, *Report of the First American Conference for Democracy and Terms of Peace* (New York 1917), p. 80 (hereafter cited as *First American Conference*).

[98] Rebecca Shelly to Dr. D. F. Taylor, 19 May 1917, in Lusk, *Revolutionary Radicalism*, Part 1, Vol. I, p. 1027; *First American Conference*, p. 77; Rebecca Shelly, "The People's Council for Democracy and Peace: How Shall it Be Organized? What Shall It Do?" (pamphlet, reprint from *First American Conference*), pp. 2-3, Box 1, PC Papers, SCPC.

[99] Hillquit, *Loose Leaves*, p. 171; Alexander Trachtenberg, ed., *The American Labor Year Book, 1919-1920* (New York 1920), p. 80; Frank L. Grubbs, Jr., "The Struggle for the Mind of American Labor 1917-1919," Ph.D. diss., University of Virginia, 1963, pp. 45-46.

should the People's Council play an analogous role in the United States. The People's Council should represent "the productive working classes." Religious, humanitarian, social, political, educational, and geographical groups should be represented, as should the "live" peace organizations. "But the majority of delegates should come from the progressive trade union locals, the single taxers, the vigorous socialist locals, the Granges, the Farmers' Co-operative Union and other agricultural organizations." At its first official session, it should "consider ways and means of re-establishing representative government in America. . . ." "While Congress is in session, and especially in times of crisis, the Council should sit in Washington as the authoritative spokesman for the American People."[100]

In its full implications, this was an ambitious and revolutionary proposal: the creation of a separate political structure paralleling that of the existing government with the notion that it, like the Council of Workmen's and Soldiers' Delegates in Russia, might aspire to assume sovereign power during the next national crisis. "In war time," the People's Council charged, "the government is apt to assume that its extraordinary authority extends even to the question of ending the war, of deciding upon what issues it shall be fought, and what shall be the terms of peace." Such an assumption, however, usurped authority that "belongs absolutely to the people." Therefore, the People's Council would now "give the American PEOPLE (sic) an instrument through which their will may be more directly expressed than through a government organized for the conduct of war."[101]

Most leaders of the emerging People's Council probably did not subscribe to all the implications of this proposal, but there was widespread concurrence in the appropriateness of the Russian model. Jacob Pankin, speaking before the Madison Square Garden Conference, declared that although he could not predict "whether it will exercise the power and influence that the Council of Soldiers' and Workmen's Delegates of Petrograd does in Russia," he foresaw in the People's Council "the beginning of democracy in the United States."[102] The organizing committee of the People's Council, formed at the Madison Square Garden Confer-

[100] Shelly, "The People's Council for Democracy and Peace," pp. 2-3.

[101] "A Call to Action to Men and Women Everywhere Who Are Allies of Real Democracy," enclosure to Lella Faye Secor to William I. Hull, 23 June 1917, Box 5, Hull Papers, FHL.

[102] *Verbatim Report of Addresses delivered at Convention of the American Conference for Democracy and Terms of Peace, Madison Square Garden, 30, 31 May 1917,* p. 55, ACDTP Papers, SCPC.

ence, went on to print the bulletins of the Petrograd Soviet in its own *Bulletin* and to call for the final creation of a "People's Council of America" as a "response to this message from Russia." The organizing committee sought to establish regular contacts with the Petrograd Soviet and the English Workmen's Council, and invited Ramsay MacDonald, Phillip Snowden, and Bertrand Russell to attend the People's Council's first constituent assembly.[103] One People's Council manuscript described the new organization as a "great pendulum of 'people's power,'" as a mouthpiece "through which the will of the people may be expressed, even as the voice of the Russian people is now being heard through the Council of Workmen and Soldiers." Another broadside of unidentified origin among the People's Council papers exhorted: "Fellow workers of the United States . . . why don't you do the same thing here that your brother-workers are doing in Russia?"[104]

This emphasis upon the model of the "new Russia" continued throughout the history of the People's Council, but it was only one expression of a more common theme that characterized almost every statement by People's Council leaders. This theme was the insistence that lasting international peace could only be obtained through the internal democratization of political life, especially in the United States. Nearly every speaker at the Madison Square Garden Conference stressed the connection between war and domestic tyranny. "Democratization of diplomacy will not come until we have democratized our state," Lindley Keasbey warned. Leonora O'Reilly of the Women's Trade Union League proclaimed that with the founding of the People's Council, the few people who had maneuvered America into the war would "now get their first lesson in real democracy." Other speakers laid full blame for the war upon "industrial plutocracy" and the "undemocratic action of the official government."[105] Emily Balch clearly summarized the theme when she asked: "Is not the lesson of this war that the problem is all one—that the economic and social problem at home is part of the war problem, and the war prob-

---

[103] *Bulletin* of the organizing committee of the People's Council of America, 1 (7 Aug. 1917), 2-3 (hereafter cited as *Bulletin*); Minutes of the Organizing Committee of the People's Council, Ninth meeting (21 June 1917) and Thirteenth meeting (19 July 1917), Box 1, PC Papers, SCPC; Crystal Eastman to H.W.L. Dana, 15 Aug. 1917, Box 1, Dana Papers, SCPC.

[104] "To Men and Women Everywhere who are Allies of True Democracy" (typewritten MS) and "Workers of America, Will you Answer the Call of President Wilson?" (broadside), Box 1, PC Papers, SCPC.

[105] *First American Conference*, pp. 3, 41, 59-60, 86.

lem is part of the economic and social problem that faces us in our domestic affairs?"[106]

In September, James Maurer reiterated her thoughts in more specific terms: "The very same interests which in the past corrupted our courts, denuded our forests, polluted our streams, robbed us of our lands and mineral deposits, exploited, oppressed, deported, imprisoned, starved and in industrial disputes unhesitatingly murdered the toilers—these are the people who are opposing the People's and Workmen's Councils. . . ."[107] The resolutions of the Madison Square Garden Conference underlined the theme: "Industrial plutocracy makes for war—industrial democracy for peace." And a subsequent broadside by the People's Council spotlighted the contrast between the council's position and the official war ideology: "The President has said that it is our purpose to help make the world safe for democracy. We would like to make democracy safe in our own country!"[108]

The "new Russia" became a symbol and a beacon of hope for those convinced of the impossibility of establishing peace without the overthrow of the "industrial plutocracy" in America. Those who sought a revolution in America could take hope in the emergence of the People's Council, implied Alexander Trachtenberg, a former Russian revolutionist, because the Russian Revolution had been born in an antiwar movement. There was hope too, said Louis Lochner, in the fact that the peace movement was now no longer "largely owned by the Carnegie Peace Trust."[109] The People's Council called constantly for a joining of hands with the "new democracy of Russia" and reverence for the "great vision" the new Russia offered. It urged its followers to "throw off the yoke of your semi-autocratic regime as the Russian people did. . . ."[110]

But the ideal represented by the new Russia was itself, according to People's Council leaders, simply a restatement of an old, but forgotten, American ideal. People's Council publications called for an indigenous "fresh creative impulse springing from

106 *Ibid.*, p. 44.

107 James H. Maurer, "Maintenance of Labor Standards" (pamphlet reprint of address to People's Council Convention, Chicago, 2 Sept. 1917), Box 1, PC Papers, SCPC.

108 "Resolutions of the First American Conference for Democracy and Terms of Peace" (pamphlet), p. 7 and "To Men and Women Everywhere who are Allies of True Democracy," Box 1, PC Papers, SCPC.

109 *First American Conference*, pp. 27-28, 30.

110 "A Call to Action" (printed letter), "People's Council of America for Democracy and Peace" (broadside), *Bulletin*, 1 (7 Aug. 1917), 2-3, Box 1, PC Papers, SCPC.

the people" and envisaged the People's Council as "rising phoenix-like out of the ashes of American democracy." "The movement represented by the People's Council of America," the first *Bulletin* of the People's Council concluded, "is plain, genuine democracy and those who oppose it are reactionary and un-American."[111]

Having made democracy its theme and having charged that the American Congress was unrepresentative, the organizing committee of the People's Council set out to establish its own claim to represent "the people." Its major efforts were directed toward de-emphasizing the heavy pacifist and Socialist composition of its working leadership and stressing its grass roots support from farmers' and workers' organizations.[112] Expanding upon the tentative efforts of the American Union Against Militarism and the Emergency Peace Federation, the leaders of the People's Council sought to enlist wide support from the Grange, Farmers' Co-operative Unions, and the Nonpartisan League. A. C. Townley, president of the Nonpartisan League, was appointed to one of seven select positions on the organizing committee and Pat Nagle, editor of the *Tenant Farmer*, became a member of a subsequent, expanded organizing committee.[113]

At least some local councils gained strong support from farmers, but relations with the Grange broke down and the link with the Nonpartisan League proved a weak one. Townley's organization was concerned almost entirely with internal problems. The Nonpartisan League's only interest in the war, as Charles Edward Russell later put it, was to see that it did not obscure their case against the railroads and other exploiters. The League's official organ announced prior to American intervention that it was "absolutely neutral on the war—except on the war against grain gam-

[111] "People's Council of America for Democracy and Peace," (separate typed description added to broadside), *Facts* (12 July 1917), 5, *Bulletin*, 1 (7 Aug. 1917), 3, Box 1, PC Papers, SCPC.

[112] On the de-emphasis of Socialist and "pacifist" roles in the Council see "Minutes of the Organizing Committee of the People's Council, Ninth Meeting," 21 June 1917, Box 1, PC Papers, SCPC; Roger Baldwin to Louis Lochner, 21 Aug. 1917, in Lusk, *Revolutionary Radicalism*, Part I, Vol. I, p. 1057; Lola Maverick Lloyd to Emily Balch, 13 May 1917, ACDTP Papers, SCPC; and Louis P. Lochner to William I. Hull, 28 June 1917, Box 5, Hull Papers, FHL.

[113] For examples of the interest of People's Council leaders in eliciting the support of farmers see "Suggestions for Organizers" (pamphlet) and "Appendix to Minutes of Meeting of the Organizing Committee of the People's Council, Seventh Meeting," 13 June 1917, Box 1, PC Papers, SCPC; Rebecca Shelly to Lella Faye Secor, 17, 23, and 25 Feb. 1917, Roger Baldwin to Louis Lochner, 21 Aug. 1917, and Harriet Thomas to Louis Lochner, 25 Aug. 1917, in Lusk, *Revolutionary Radicalism*, Part I, Vol. I, pp. 1004, 1057, 1066; and Grubbs, "The Struggle for the Mind of American Labor," p. 73.

blers and loan sharks." Although Townley and others made statements and endorsed platforms much like those espoused by the People's Council, the League officially declared its support for the Wilson administration. Despite its refusal to oppose the war, the Nonpartisan League found itself under severe attack on the loyalty issue and never gave direct support to the increasingly "disreputable" People's Council.[114]

The campaign to obtain "grass roots" support gained far greater success among organized workers than within farmers' organizations. A Conference for the Maintenance of Workers' Rights and Standards at the end of June resulted in the establishment of a Workmen's Council as the radical labor wing of the People's Council. The UHT, the ACWA, the ILGWU, the Cloth Hat and Cap Makers, and the Fur Workers constituted the main support for the Workmen's Council and provided all the members of its executive committee. The ACWA even founded a committee to raise funds for the People's Council. Jacob Panken, chairman of the Workmen's Council, announced plans to establish branches in every major American city. Benjamin Schlesinger, president of the ILGWU, gave the People's Council his endorsement and Joseph Schlossberg, secretary of the ACWA, declared his union's intention to "work hand in hand" with the People's Council to gain acceptance of the Russian peace formula.[115]

The People's Council organizing committee, meanwhile, had appointed Alexander Trachtenberg to serve as a link between it and the Workmen's Council. Workmen's Councils soon appeared in Boston and Philadelphia. In Chicago they announced elaborate plans. *The Survey* observed perceptively that the unions which joined the Workmen's Council are those "which have consistently fought the leadership of Mr. Gompers as head of the A.F. of L."[116] Internal antagonisms within the labor movement thus gave the People's Council a strong initial source of allies among organized

114 Charles Edward Russell, *The Story of the Nonpartisan League* (New York 1920), pp. 232-33; Robert L. Morlan, *Political Prairie Fire: The Nonpartisan League, 1915-1922* (Minneapolis 1955), 110-11, 133, 136-39, 152, 156; Carol Elizabeth Jenson, "Agrarian Pioneer in Civil Liberties: The Nonpartisan League in Minnesota During World War I," Ph.D. diss., University of Minnesota, 1958, pp. 23-24, 49-50, 61-62. The League's organ is quoted in *ibid.*, p. 24.

115 Dubofsky, "New York City Labor in the Progressive Era," pp. 381, 384-85; *The Survey*, 38 (4 Aug. 1917), 411.

116 *The Survey*, 38 (4 Aug. 1917), 412; "Minutes of the Organizing Committee of the People's Council, Seventh meeting," 13 June 1917, Box 1, PC Papers, SCPC; James H. Dolsen to Dear Sir, 25 Sept. 1917, ACDTP Papers, SCPC. According to one account, the New York Council specifically set up a committee to "fight against 'Gomperism'" (Rappaport, "Jewish Immigrants," p. 302).

workers. Amidst all the talk of labor standards and peace programs at the Conference for the Maintenance of Workers' Rights and Standards, no single utterance, according to the *New York Times*, received so much applause as a denunciation in Yiddish of Samuel Gompers.[117]

The People's Council sought to extend its influence and broaden its base in other directions as well. It sought to interest leaders of other segments of the labor movement such as Frank Hayes of the United Mine Workers and A. B. Garretson of the Railroad Conductors. Council leaders attempted to obtain regular representation in the council by a Negro leader and lodged at least one protest against racial discrimination among laborers in military camps. But at the same time, they discussed the race-baiting Tom Watson of Georgia, the former Populist leader, as a potential powerful ally.[118]

In actuality, the base of support for the People's Council narrowed rather than broadened after the first few months. Scott Nearing confessed in September that "all of our recent efforts to reach the American people have been hampered" because the council could not seem to discover "the natural leaders of liberal public opinion in the various localities." He appealed to loyal supporters for funds to make a survey and compile a list of "liberal people, organizations and publications. . . ." By October the executive committee was still seeking to interest "a Negro, a farmer, a miner, and a person in railroad circles" in joining the committee.[119] The passion for identification with "the people" remained, but, as Max Eastman later reflected, the People's Council, "like most things supposedly deriving from 'the people,' was operated by less than a dozen of these unusual beings. . . ."[120]

The "grass roots" support behind these working leaders of the People's Council had begun to erode even before the People's

[117] *New York Times*, 1 July 1917, I, 12:3.

[118] "Minutes of the Organizing Committee of the People's Council, Seventh meeting," 13 June and Twelfth meeting, 12 July 1917, "Report of the Organizing Secretary for Week ending July 26, 1917," Box 1, PC Papers, SCPC; "Minutes of First Executive Meeting of People's Council of America," Second Session, 15 Sept. 1917, and Louis P. Lochner to secretaries of war and the navy, 10 Nov. 1917, PC Papers, HI.

[119] "Minutes of the Third Regular Meeting of the Executive Committee of the People's Council of America," 16 Oct. 1917, Box 1, PC Papers, SCPC; Scott Nearing to William I. Hull, Box 5, Hull Papers, FHL.

[120] Eastman, *Love and Revolution*, p. 49. On the desire to identify with "the people" see Lella Faye Secor to Delegates to the People's Council for Democracy and Peace, n.d. [circa 31 Aug. 1917], Box 1, PC Papers, SCPC; Roger Baldwin, "The Individual and the State," p. 8, Box 1, AUAM Papers, SCPC, "Our Slogan: A Letter A Day" and Rebecca Shelly to Dear Friend, 11 Aug. 1917, Box 5, Hull Papers, FHL.

Council of America for Democracy and Peace had been formally constituted. An organizing committee had been established at the Madison Square Garden Conference at the end of May and it had immediately begun the work of propaganda, of establishing Workmen's Councils, and of seeking financial support. But to build a representative, democratic, nationwide organization of constitutent local councils was no easy task, particularly with talk of peace increasingly suspect and local and national authorities extremely unsympathetic. The organizing committee, after several delays, sent out a call for a national constituent assembly for 1 September in Minneapolis to formally establish the People's Council. But even such isolationist territory proved inhospitable to the People's Council. The assembly was prevented from meeting in Minneapolis and feelers for meeting sites in North Dakota and Wisconsin were rebuffed. The assembly finally had to draw up a permanent organization during a hurried session in Chicago before troops arrived to break up the meeting.[121]

Although arrangements were completed at subsequent secret meetings and the constitution was revised by a permanent executive committee, the debacle at Minneapolis and Chicago revealed fully the atmosphere of public distrust and official harassment in which the People's Council would have to operate.[122] Groups that had already begun to reconsider their war position now began the process of disentangling themselves from an increasingly futile peace effort. Once again, other immediate considerations deflected temporary allies away from the campaign for an early peace.

By early September 1917, when the People's Council held its fugitive constituent convention, it was already under direct frontal attack from a new propaganda organization—the American Alliance for Labor and Democracy. Led by Samuel Gompers and several prowar Socialists and largely financed by the federal government through George Creel's Committee on Public Information, the American Alliance directly contested the People's Council's bid for labor support. Gompers launched his campaign

121 For accounts of the tribulations of the People's Council's constituent assembly see Grubbs, *The Struggle for Labor Loyalty*, pp. 58-64 and Louis Lochner, *Always the Unexpected* (New York 1956), pp. 68-70.

122 "What Was Done By the Executive Committee At Chicago," Box 1, PC Papers, SCPC; "First Executive Meeting of People's Council of America, Minutes," 16 Sept. 1917, PC Papers, HI. For appraisals of the futility of People's Council efforts after the Chicago Convention see Eastman, *Love and Revolution*, p. 57, Hillquit, *Loose Leaves*, p. 179, and Florence, "The Ford Peace Ship and After," p. 124.

against the People's Council on 29 June with a speech before the Central Federated Union of New York City, which had been hovering on the verge of cooperation with the People's Council. Gompers' appearance reinforced the efforts of some of the CFU leaders to disentangle their organization entirely from the antiwar forces. With the help of John Spargo, Robert Maisel, William Edlin, Chester Wright, Charles Edward Russell, William English Walling, and other prowar Socialists, Gompers built the American Alliance into an effective propaganda organization that stressed the benefits labor was gaining from the war—the advantageous war contracts, high wages, reduced unemployment. "This is Labor's War," proclaimed the American Alliance. "Labor must prove its merits to play a principal role in the human drama of tomorrow," another item of its propaganda avowed. "Out of the war will arise the golden days for the men who toil. Autocracy in industry will be just as much annihilated as will autocracy in government. The winning of this war means better wages, better hours, better shop conditions, better opportunities, a fuller life, more leisure. . . ."[123]

The American Alliance for Labor and Democracy undertook a dual mission. On the one hand it sought to impress the public with labor's loyalty through patriotic utterances and full participation in patriotic programs. Concurrently, it sought to *insure* the loyalty of labor and stimulate enthusiastic labor support for the war. Both goals required the crushing of the People's Council. Gompers sought to use the American Alliance to undermine the position of recalcitrant, dissident, and secessionist unions while John Spargo and other Socialists tried to use it as a vehicle for launching a new, prowar, radical political party. The platform of the Alliance was aimed directly at wooing workingmen away from the Workmen's Councils. It stressed the protection of labor standards and called for the "conscription of wealth," the taxation of excess profits, government control of industries to maintain production, control of speculation, and the taxation of "idle land in private possession on its full rental value" (an appeal to single-taxers). Robert Maisel, writing to Gompers during the earliest stages of planning for the American Alliance, declared that the

---

123 Mandel, *Samuel Gompers*, pp. 388-92; Karson, *American Labor Unions and Politics*, pp. 102-5; Grubbs, *The Struggle for Labor Loyalty*, pp. 35ff. The quotations are taken from Grubbs, "The Struggle for the Mind of American Labor," pp. 242, 244. The secrecy that shrouded the transfer of federal funds to the AALD has prompted Ronald Radosh to describe the Alliance as an "Administration 'labor front' meant to drum up support for a pro-war policy among workers" (*American Labor and United States Foreign Policy*, p. 59).

struggle against the People's Council for influence over labor must be a "fight to the finish." By 1 September 1917, when it held its successful convention in St. Paul while the People's Council desperately searched for a city which would allow it to convene, the American Alliance had proved itself a powerful antagonist to the People's Council.[124]

But for all the propaganda and the pressure that Gompers was able to bring to bear through his influence in governmental circles, the People's Council lost labor support less from such frontal attacks than it did from the direct effects of the wartime economy upon certain unions and the changing attitudes within New York City's Jewish community. As production boomed and as government contracts became critically important in the clothing industry, practical economic motives began to dictate cooperation with the federal government. And as the possibilities of Allied support for a Jewish state increased, radical Zionist opposition to the Allied cause disappeared.

The process of labor defection from the People's Council can be seen very clearly in the case of the ACWA. The ACWA, denounced by the AFL since its inception in 1914 as an illegitimate dual union, was led by two men of very divergent backgrounds and viewpoints. Joseph Schlossberg, the general secretary, was an "old-timer," a fervent speaker and writer on behalf of the missionary socialism of immigrants of bundist backgrounds, an early supporter of the People's Council, and probably the author of the "revolutionary" preamble of the ACWA's original constitution. Sidney Hillman, the president, was "a graduate of Hull-House," a "protégé of the reformers," and closely associated with Jane Addams and Lillian Wald. Hillman, the practical reformer, "spoke about wages and conditions," writes the historian of Jewish labor, Melech Epstein. Schlossberg, the former Socialist Labor Party leader, proclaimed "the higher aims of the labor movement."[125]

In the late spring and early summer of 1917, business was slack in the clothing industry. Schlossberg, drawing upon the anti-AFL feeling in the union and its traditional radicalism, brought it into outspoken support of the People's Council. Hillman acquiesced in such a position, but devoted his energies to obtaining favorable

---

124 "Platform of the American Alliance for Labor and Democracy" (typewritten copy), Box 1, PC Papers, SCPC; Grubbs, *The Struggle for Labor Loyalty*, pp. 36-46; Grubbs, "The Struggle for the Mind of American Labor," p. 57.

125 Epstein, *Jewish Labor in the U.S.A., 1914-1952*, pp. 46-47; Matthew Josephson, *Sidney Hillman, Statesman of American Labor* (Garden City, N.Y. 1952), pp. 105, 109, 136, 138; Benjamin Stolberg, *Tailor's Progress: The Story of a Famous Union and the Men Who Made It* (New York 1944), p. 87.

federal control over labor conditions in the clothing industry and the awarding of government uniform contracts only to union shops. Hillman gained a highly favorable directive from Secretary of War Baker in August 1917. Soon the ACWA began a period of spectacular growth as the federal government became the clothing industry's largest customer.[126] When antiunion forces began to attack the ACWA as disloyal for its association with the People's Council and when Schlossberg's articles in the union paper, *The Advance*, provoked concern by the postmaster general, Hillman moved to solidify his union's practical position by first persuading the ACWA to rule out any editorial criticisms of the government and then by declaring publicly that the ACWA was not affiliated with the People's Council.[127] Times were simply too good economically, and good relations with the federal government were too advantageous materially for the ACWA to continue to indulge in its early inclinations toward participation in the peace movement. By 1918 the ACWA was pledging $500,000 of union funds to the third Liberty Loan campaign, and its executive board was referring to the war in terms of the "releasing of vast democratic forces" and the "coming emancipation of mankind."[128]

Wartime prosperity, tactical considerations, and, finally, the Balfour declaration in support of a Jewish nation in the Holy Land and the treaty of Brest-Litovsk further eroded union support for the People's Council. The United Cloth Hat and Cap Makers acknowledged at their 1917 convention that the war had "turned into a war for democracy. . . ."[129] The ILGWU never took an extreme antiwar position and constantly sought cooperation with the government. By spring of 1918, nearly every union once associated with the People's Council was making prowar pronouncements, repudiating the St. Louis resolution of the Socialist Party, and taking part in war bond campaigns.[130]

The slackening of union support for the People's Council was closely related to, and sometimes identical with, the gradual defection of Socialist leaders and Jewish organizations. The Jewish community had long been subject to warnings from Jewish civic

---

[126] Josephson, *Sidney Hillman*, pp. 165-70; Epstein, *Jewish Labor in the U.S.A., 1914-1952*, p. 53; Stolberg, *Tailor's Progress*, p. 96.

[127] Josephson, *Sidney Hillman*, pp. 161, 168; Radosh, *American Labor and United States Foreign Policy*, pp. 17-18.

[128] Rappaport, "Jewish Immigrants," pp. 351-53.

[129] *Ibid.*, p. 288.

[130] *Ibid.*, p. 351; Dubofsky, "New York City Labor in the Progressive Era," pp. 390-91.

leaders that antiwar activities by Jewish organizations would provoke reactions of anti-Semitism.[131] Nevertheless, most Jewish radicals had continued to oppose the war throughout the summer of 1917. But the Bolshevik takeover in November persuaded some that the defeat of Germany would help preserve the Russian Revolution, and the Balfour declaration of a few days before enlisted full support of the left-wing Zionists in America for the Allied cause. Even Joseph Schlossberg now spoke on behalf of "the war for freedom and the emancipation of nationalities," and the Workmen's Circle, an early leader in antiwar sentiment, endorsed the war and Zionism.[132]

Meanwhile, the Socialist Party leaders had thrown their energies behind the campaign of Morris Hillquit for mayor of New York City in the fall elections. Energies that had previously been devoted to the work of the People's Council were now rechanneled into a political campaign that was only partly concerned with the peace movement. The same unions that had briefly devoted their political energies to the Workmen's Councils now expended their efforts on the election. Judah Magnes, Lella Faye Secor, Mary Ware Dennett, Rebecca Shelly, Daniel Kiefer, Frank Stephens, and Crystal Eastman, all central figures in the working staff of the People's Council, joined the Hillquit campaign.[133] Not only did the Hillquit campaign divert energies from the more direct peace activities of the People's Council, but the more moderate Socialist Party leadership in New York was gradually moving away from the St. Louis resolution. In December of 1917 the Socialist Party ruled out an antiwar meeting for Madison Square Garden and declined to consider other peace meetings. Those moderates who had supported the St. Louis resolution as a backfire against a more radical program gradually emerged from their antiwar position. The seven Socialist aldermen of New York City announced their support of the third Liberty Loan drive in the spring of 1918 as did Socialist Congressman Meyer London.[134]

Thus the People's Council had hardly been formally constituted, when, in the early fall of 1917, it began to founder. Direct repres-

[131] Morris Schappes, "The Attitude of Jewish Labor to World War I, 1917-1918," *Jewish Life*, 9 (Mar. 1955), 21; Rappaport, "Jewish Immigrants," p. 319.

[132] Rappaport, "Jewish Immigrants," pp. 325, 331-32.

[133] Mary Ware Dennett to Amos Pinchot, 30 Oct. 1917, Pinchot Papers, LC; Dubofsky, "New York City Labor in the Progressive Era," pp. 354-55; Epstein, *Jewish Labor in the U.S.A., 1914-1952*, p. 79.

[134] Dubofsky, "New York City Labor in the Progressive Era," p. 389; Schappes, "The Attitude of Jewish Labor to World War I," p. 24; Draper, *The Roots of American Communism*, p. 94.

sion hindered its attempts at large meetings and some of its potential support was undoubtedly discouraged by fear of repression of the kind already being felt by the IWW, several Socialist
Party leaders, and the editors of antiwar publications. Tactical
considerations, wartime prosperity, and loyalty to other causes
distracted its early supporters. Evicted from its New York office,
its base of support undermined, and its financial condition pre-
carious, the council increasingly projected a mood of futility and
desperation.[135] Its pronouncements became not so much more
radical as more shrill. It did pursue its democratic theme with a
very modest campaign to choose by referendum a delegation for
an eventual peace conference that would be directly representative of the people. The names of those receiving the most votes
would be submitted to President Wilson with the suggestion that
he appoint one or more of them to the peace delegation.[136]

An endless chain letter campaign to bring People's Council
ideas to the president was attempted and the establishment of a
"people's lay congress" discussed. But the major work of the council became the publication and circulation of the fulminations of
its president, Scott Nearing, and its executive secretary, Louis
Lochner. Nearing's warnings about "all the forces of reaction . . .
arrayed against us" and his attacks upon big business, profiteers,
and plutocrats increased in vituperativeness until he was eventually brought under federal indictment. Lochner, equally de-
nunciatory of the "sinister forces" opposing the People's Council,
but disturbed by Nearing's increasingly doctrinaire socialism,
tried to keep the focus on international relations and away from
Nearing's fixation on the "brutal" American ruling class and its

135 A financial report on 14 Sept. 1917 showed the People's Council nearly $9,000
in the red. By October Fannie Witherspoon was referring to the Council as "bank-
rupt" ("Financial Statement of the People's Council," 14 Sept. 1917, PC Papers, TL
and Fannie Witherspoon to Lucile Davidson, 4 Oct. 1917, Box 16, WPPNY Correspondence, SCPC). See also Scott Nearing to Delegates to Minneapolis-Chicago
Conference, 8 Oct. 1917, and Louis Lochner, to members of People's Council, 27
Aug. 1918, Box 1, PC Papers, SCPC; and Scott Nearing to Fellow Members, 21
Nov. 1917, PC Papers, HI.

136 In *Opponents of War*, Peterson and Fite argue that the People's Council "fell
into the hands of Radicals" by Sept. 1917, citing the presence of Maurer, Hillquit,
and Nearing on the executive committee by September as evidence (Horace C.
Peterson and Gilbert C. Fite, *Opponents of War, 1917-1918* [Madison, Wis. 1957],
p. 74). But the working leadership of the council had changed very little. Maurer
and Hillquit had been among the council's leadership since May, and Nearing
nearly as long. On the referendum, see "Who Shall Represent the Plain People,"
Bulletin, 1 (10 Oct. 1917) and "A Referendum to the Men and Women of America
From the People's Council of America," PC Papers, TL. Winners in the council
referendum were Judah Magnes, Jane Addams, ex-Senator John D. Works, James
Maurer, and Victor Berger (*Bulletin*, 1 [15 Jan. 1918]).

"iron heel" of "industrial tyranny."[137] People's Council publications continued to trumpet forth the Soviet message and instruct readers in Soviet diplomacy and internal politics. But with funds failing, public support nearly nonexistent, and government action against them a constant danger, the leaders of the People's Council found it hard to maintain an optimistic front. "Did you expect the People's Council to succeed in less than one year?" snapped one California leader.[138]

Nothing could hide the fact that this last, most radical of the wartime peace organizations was disintegrating. "The peace movement is not dead," the organizing secretary of the People's Council wrote to her coworkers at the end of 1917 in a desperate plea for funds. But her very assertion bespoke the fact that, in the absence of impassioned claims to the contrary, the council's own members might reasonably conclude that the peace movement had expired.[139] The AFL had long ceased to view this war as the "workingman's burden," and the moderate Socialists and radical Jewish labor organizations were now finding their interests more compatible with support for the war effort than support for a peace organization. Eventually even Nearing, the president of the council, "wash[ed] his hands of all peace activities, excepting through the S[ocialist] P[arty]."[140] Once again the peace movement had momentarily drawn its support from groups who embraced the movement when the call for peace coincided with their search for other objectives, but who abandoned it when peace agitation no longer served to advance their more treasured goals. "Somehow it made me a bit sad," reminisced Elizabeth Freeman, the organizing secretary of the People's Council, "to see [the peace movement] . . . cast adrift for some group who have not cared one jot for the Cause, to just take our trust and possibly use it for a vastly different purpose than the one we intended. . . ."[141]

But that had been the history of the peace movement. Elizabeth Freeman was no less responsible for seeking to accomplish her own purposes through the peace movement than were the others. As various groups, at first liberal and then radical, had come to

[137] Rebecca Shelly to "Dear Members and Contributors," 23 Aug. 1917, Scott Nearing to "Fellow Members," 21 Nov. 1917, Louis P. Lochner to "Dear Friend," 2 Apr. 1918, PC Papers, HI; Scott Nearing, "Open Letters to Profiteers: Arraignment of Big Business in Its Relation to the War" (pamphlet, letters originally addressed to the *New York Times*), Box 1, PC Papers, SCPC; "War: Who Gets the Profits?" PC Papers, TL; Grubbs, "The Struggle for the Mind of American Labor," p. 132.

[138] William Short to "Dear Fellow Member," 2 Apr. 1918, PC Papers, HI.

[139] Elizabeth Freeman to Dear Co-worker, 20 Dec. 1917, Box 1, PC Papers, SCPC.

[140] Elizabeth Freeman to H.W.L. Dana, 15 Oct. 1918, Box 1, Dana Papers, SCPC.

[141] *Ibid.*

associate themselves with the peace movement since 1914, the movement had taken on their political coloring. Now the People's Council had become so nearly an adjunct of the Socialist Party that its president apparently concluded that a separate peace organization or peace movement had no purpose. It would remain for one final wartime organization to search for another redefinition of the peace movement in terms of a religious quest for a just and peaceful world. Such a search would bring the peace movement as close as it would ever come in the early twentieth century to a position of "pacifism."

CHAPTER NINE

Peace, Church Unity, and the Social Gospel

O F the various professional groups represented among participants in the early twentieth century peace movement, the clergy, by its continued presence, seemed most to lend the movement a semblance of continuity. But even in the realm of clerical participation, the tide of internal revolution that surged through the peace movement between 1898 and 1918 produced ample waves of change. Since clerical interest in peace expressed itself, somewhat uniquely, in active but dissimilar peace organizations both before and after 1915, the story of evolving clerical attitudes can best be recounted by retracing the several phases of the peace movement already chronicled in the preceding eight chapters. An account of the clergymen and their peace organizations may thus serve not only to delineate the interrelationships between the peace movement and the more immediate interests of various factions of clergymen, but also to provide a résumé, from a new perspective, of the peace movement's transformations and tribulations.

Even for the clergy, participation in the new peace movement of the twentieth century often involved a sense of discovery, a consciousness of having seized upon a suddenly relevant reform. Although Protestant clergymen and leading laymen had provided much support for the struggling peace societies in the United States for nearly a century, their organized participation in the peace movement after 1910 represented a new realization of how this cause might relate to current problems and movements within the churches. It is true that the clergy did not enter the peace movement in so dramatic a way as did the woman suffragists, the social workers, or the Socialists. In contrast to these groups the clergy's participation during the two decades after 1898 appears at first to have been more constant, and therefore, perhaps, less affected by considerations of tactics and expediency. But the appearance of continuity of support and participation by the clergy is, to some extent, a deceptive one. For it was not the same clergymen or the same factions of the clergy who were most deeply involved in each successive phase of the peace movement between 1898 and 1918.

The new, organized attention which the clergy gave to the peace movement after 1910, particularly through the Church Peace Union and the Commission on Peace and Arbitration of the Federal Council of Churches of Christ in America, should more accurately be termed a "rediscovery." The earliest peace societies in the United States, established in the wake of the War of 1812, had been explicitly "Christian" in character. The New York Peace Society of that early period had required, for membership on the executive committee, the belief that war is inconsistent with Christianity and had demanded that new members of the society be "members in good standing of evangelical churches." The Massachusetts Peace Society of the same era had included "an imposing array of ministers of religion." The two major early leaders, David Low Dodge and Noah Worcester were, respectively, an elder in the Presbyterian Church and a Unitarian minister. Most of the second echelon of early leaders had been clergymen.[1]

Clergymen had continued to play a prominent role in the leadership of peace organizations throughout the nineteenth century. At the turn of the twentieth century, over a third of the vice-presidents and almost half of the directors of the largest peace society, the American Peace Society, were clergymen. Many of the non-clergymen were prominent and devout laymen. The Lake Mohonk Conferences on International Arbitration, instituted by a Quaker layman in 1895, were dominated in the early years by clergymen and editors of religious journals. Card playing, dancing, and drinking were forbidden at the hotel which housed the conference. Morning prayers and services were an integral part of the annual meetings.[2] By about 1905 the proportion of clergy-

---

[1] Peter Brock, *Pacifism in the United States: From the Colonial Era to the First World War* (Princeton 1968), pp. 450-52, 459-69, 472; Merle E. Curti, *The American Peace Crusade, 1815-1860* (Durham, N.C. 1929), pp. 8-9, 12-13, 21-23.

[2] Ira V. Brown, *Lyman Abbott, Christian Evolutionist: A Study in Religious Liberalism* (Cambridge, Mass. 1953), p. 89. Between 1895 and 1900, over seventy clergymen participated in the Mohonk Conferences, some attending three or four times during the period. Participants included a number of editors of religious journals and journals recently heavily religious in nature including: *Christian Work, The Outlook, The Examiner, The Independent, The Standard, The New World, The American Friend, The Watchman, The Evangelist, Friends' Intelligencer and Journal, Light and Life, The Observer,* and *Christian Endeavor World.* See *Report of the First-Sixth Annual Meetings of the Lake Mohonk Conference on International Arbitration* (Lake Mohonk, N.Y. 1895-1900) in "Members of Conference" sections (hereafter cited as *Mohonk Conference,* with appropriate date). For clergymen in the American Peace Society see the list of officers at the end of each issue of the *Advocate of Peace.*

men among the leaders of peace organizations had begun to decline, but clerical participation continued on a somewhat reduced level in the New York Peace Society, the World Peace Foundation, the American Union Against Militarism, the American Neutral Conference Committee, and even the People's Council. Ministers, former ministers, and influential church laymen such as William Short and Samuel T. Dutton of the New York Peace Society, Edward Cummings of the World Peace Foundation, and John Bates Clark of the Carnegie Endowment often held influential positions in the newer organizations.

Thus there was continuity of clerical participation in the peace movement; but it was not the same clergymen who participated during different phases of the movement between 1900 and 1918, nor did clerical enthusiasm for the movement during the various phases stem from the same attitudes and impulses. The clergymen who served most prominently with the Church Peace Union and the Federal Council's Commission on Peace and Arbitration between 1912 and 1915 were not usually those who had been prominent in the American Peace Society or at the Mohonk Conferences.[3] Those who joined the American Union Against Militarism were not the same as those leading the Church Peace Union. And those who participated in the Fellowship of Reconciliation, first established in the United States in 1915, were rarely those who had been prominent in the peace movement before the war began. Of the scores of clergymen who held offices in the American Peace Society in the two decades before 1917, only one minister, Jenkin Lloyd Jones, joined either the Fellowship of Reconciliation or the People's Council. Of over 100 clergymen who spoke at the Mohonk Conferences in the decade from 1906 through 1915, only Jenkin Lloyd Jones became associated with the People's Council and only Frederick Lynch and Charles Jefferson participated actively in the American Union Against Militarism. Hundreds of ministers had associated themselves with the work of the American Peace Society, the New York Peace Society, and the Mohonk Conferences, but of these hundreds only the Quaker leader Rufus Jones was active in the major organization

[3] Of the thirty initial appointees to positions as trustees and officers of the Church Peace Union, for instance, only eight had previously been officers in the American Peace Society. Similarly, only five out of the twenty-two initial members of the Federal Council's Commission on Peace and Arbitration were former officers in the American Peace Society. Data for these and the following comparisons were derived from a variety of published and unpublished reports, letterheads, and lists of members in organizational periodicals and manuscript collections for the various organizations involved.

for the expression of Christian pacifism, the Fellowship of Reconciliation, by 1917. The Federal Council of Churches' Commission on Peace and Arbitration numbered 105 members in the spring of 1914. Not one of these members joined the People's Council and only two were active in the Fellowship of Reconciliation after the spring of 1917.[4]

Such abrupt discontinuities between the clergymen active in one phase of the peace movement and those prominent in subsequent stages were far from fortuitous. At each stage in its progress, the peace movement attracted clergymen with different attitudes and purposes. As the movement after 1900 moved first toward a secular and practical emphasis, and later toward association with basic social reform, its clerical membership changed correspondingly. The ideas and purposes which brought individual clergymen into participation in the peace movement at various times after 1900—particularly into such organizations as the Church Peace Union, the Commission on Peace and Arbitration, and the Fellowship of Reconciliation—were deeply intertwined with internal issues and movements that were stirring and sometimes dividing Protestant clergymen during the early years of the twentieth century.

Like other groups that entered the peace movement more suddenly or dramatically, various factions of the clergy were attracted to successive phases of the peace movement partly by perceptions of how it might affect or promote their more immediate professional and reform interests. To demonstrate how these interests became interconnected with the goals of the peace movement, it is necessary first to describe the assumptions and ideas which clergymen found attractive in the peace movement of 1895-1905 and then to suggest how clerical participation in the peace movement of the next decade was affected by the dynamic forces at work within American Protestantism: theological modernism, church unity, and the social gospel.

With rare exceptions, the clergymen who participated in the major peace organizations at the turn of the century were not pacifists.[5] Some were anti-imperialists, but a considerable minor-

<hr>

[4] The list of 105 members of the Commission on Peace and Arbitration is taken from the extended list of members on the printed letterhead of the stationery used for the commission's statement on the Mexican crisis, dated 21 Apr. 1914, in the William I. Hull Papers, Box 2, Friends' Historical Library, Swarthmore College. The other data is derived from a variety of manuscript sources.

[5] Most of them were peace advocates, in the sense of desiring some ultimate abolition of war, but few would have been willing to renounce the resort to war

ity were proponents of American imperialism. All were vociferous champions of American nationalism and the expansion of American influence by moral means. In this respect they differed little from their secular colleagues. What they contributed to the movement was not an independent critique of the moral issues of international relations, but rather a style, a tone, an intensification of the movement's aura of righteous purpose. Clergymen reinforced the peace movement's tendency to ignore social, economic, and to some extent, political, analysis and to stress the dangers arising from the unrestrained, uncivilized, un-Christian character of nations insufficiently evangelized. In so doing, they also nurtured the nationalism of the peace movement and suggested the identity of interests between it and the crusade for foreign missions.

Clergymen who participated in the peace movement at the turn of the century appear to have had little quarrel with the assumptions about American destiny endorsed by the great majority of the Protestant clergy during the period. They recognized in the United States the eventual, if not already realized, locus of the Kingdom of God. The United States, because of its geographical position, Anglo-Saxon racial predominance, and Christian principles and policy, had a "unique destiny and responsibility." Its mission was to evangelize and civilize the world, thus bringing world peace.[6]

The exact method by which the United States should accomplish this civilizing mission, however, did become an issue among clergymen at the Lake Mohonk Conferences between 1898 and 1900. Some followed Lyman Abbott, editor of the formerly religious journal *The Outlook*, in interpreting the peace movement as perfectly consonant with all means of promoting Anglo-Saxon

---

under the present conditions of the world. Much of their "quasi-pacifism" stemmed from what Norman Thomas has called "a sentimental rationalization and moralization of our fortunate geographical position" (*The Conscientious Objector in America* [New York 1923], p. 65). Succinct discussions of the changes in the meaning of the word "pacifism" appear in Charles Chatfield, *For Peace and Justice: Pacifism in America, 1914-1941* (Knoxville 1971), p. 4 and John K. Nelson, *The Peace Prophets: American Pacifist Thought, 1919-1941* (Chapel Hill 1967), pp. 3-5. I have sought to hold to the more rigid definition of pacifism as the persistent and principled refusal to sanction all organized warfare.

[6] John Edwin Smylie, "Protestant Clergymen and America's World Role, 1865-1900: A Study of Christianity, Nationality and International Relations," Th.D. diss., Princeton Theological Seminary, 1959, pp. 81-121, 190-93. See also John Edwin Smylie, "Protestant Clergymen and American Destiny: II, Prelude to Imperialism, 1865-1900," *Harvard Theological Review*, 56 (Oct. 1963), 297-311 for a summary of Smylie's major conclusions. On the views of two specific clergymen, see Jacob Henry Dorn, *Washington Gladden, Prophet of the Social Gospel* (Columbus, Ohio 1966), pp. 403, 406-14 and Brown, *Lyman Abbott*, pp. 161-78.

power and solidarity. Abbott enthusiastically endorsed the Spanish-American War and American retention of Cuba and the Philippines, expectantly looking forward to the day when England and the United States would "enwrap the world with liberty and fill it with peace." He lectured his 1899 Mohonk audience on the instances in which "war is or may be right" and described the wonders of General Wood's work in uplifting Cuba. At the same conference the Reverend W. S. Crowe proclaimed, "We are here to meddle with other people's affairs" and rejoiced that after American commerce and missionaries had "gone everywhere," now "through war and peace, our politics is going everywhere."[7]

Staunchly anti-imperialist clergymen such as Charles F. Dole, Benjamin Trueblood, and Theodore Cuyler, however, denounced any extension of American influence by military means. America should take a new, commanding role in world affairs, but her role should be that of peacemaker and evangelist. As the events of 1898-1900 gradually receded from the forefront of public controversy, this call for an "imperialism of righteousness," a call also sounded by those who had favored political expansion as well, served to reunite clergymen behind what Albert Weinberg has characterized as a resurgence of the ideal of international moral leadership. The brief division between imperialists and anti-imperialists among the clergymen was soon forgotten in the verbiage of righteous and patronizing beneficence with which they both proclaimed the necessity for expanding the influence of their own "Christian Nation." Neither faction had cause to dissent when the Reverend Edward Everett Hale reminded the 1901 Mohonk Conference that "The United States of America is the greatest Peace Society that God's sun ever shone upon."[8]

---

[7] Brown, *Lyman Abbott*, p. 163; *Mohonk Conference, 1899*, pp. 80-81, 83. Leading clergymen in the American Peace Society, such as Philip Moxom and Scott Hershey, also publicly declared their full support for war in 1898 and Robert S. MacArthur, a frequent participant at Lake Mohonk, called for retention of the Philippines. According to one story, Abbott fully endorsed his wife's desire to obtain "one of the popular sofa pillows covered with an American flag and embroidered with '1898,'" as expressing "a true feeling of patriotism" (Smylie, "Protestant Clergymen and America's World Role," pp. 413, 433, 439, 446, 468, 500, 503; Brown, *Lyman Abbott*, p. 168).

[8] *Mohonk Conference, 1899*, pp. 85-86; *ibid., 1900*, p. 67; *ibid., 1901*, p. 102; Albert K. Weinberg, *Manifest Destiny: A Study of Nationalist Expansion in American History* (Baltimore 1935), pp. 460-63, 478; William Warren Sweet, *The Story of Religion in America* (New York 1939), p. 515; Smylie, "Protestant Clergymen and American Destiny," pp. 301, 308 and "Protestant Clergymen and America's World Role," pp. 81, 91, 93, 193. One indication of the relative unimportance of the distinction between "imperialist" and "anti-imperialist" clergymen is that both groups endorsed what Smylie has called "the doctrine of the two Englands." This doctrine,

The war of 1898 and its aftermath did serve to stimulate increased interest in international affairs, and with this increased interest came a new appreciation of the possible interconnections of the peace movement with one of the Protestant clergy's most vital concerns: foreign missions. Expansion of America's role in the world intensified both the expectations and the fears of clergymen involved in promoting the peace movement and foreign missions. The excitement of gaining new access to areas in need of evangelizing and civilizing took on an added quality of anxiety when peace or missions advocates reflected on the decreasing isolation of the United States. The possibility now loomed that uncivilized and un-Christian peoples might threaten civilization with outbursts of international barbarism if their conversion to peaceable and pious ways was not quickly effected.[9]

Valentin H. Rabe's perceptive analysis of the supporters of Protestant foreign missions at the turn of the century reveals many parallels between clerical interest in the peace movement and clerical enthusiasm for the foreign missions crusades. Both movements drew upon an "unconscious nationalism" that did not distinguish between the goals of the churches and the national mission. Both exuded confidence and optimism. The sanguine predictions of the leaders of the peace movement found their echo in the motto of the Student Volunteer Movement: "the evangelization of the world in this generation."[10] Clergymen in both movements appear to have acted out of similar motives: a sense of noblesse oblige; the desire to participate in widely acclaimed and socially prestigious philanthropies and perhaps thereby gain new positions in church hierarchies; the desire to participate in

---

never carefully analyzed by its proponents for obvious reasons, held that England had been wicked in her methods of gaining imperial possessions but exemplary in her governance of them. Clergymen found it difficult to condemn the *results* of English imperialism, which had been to establish order and open paths for Christian missions (Smylie, "Protestant Clergymen and America's World Role," pp. 294, 303, 310-14).

[9] John R. Mott, *The Present World Situation* (New York 1914), pp. 3-5, 8-9; Valentin Hanno Rabe, "Protestant Foreign Missions, 1880-1920," Ph.D. diss., Harvard University, 1964, pp. 77, 675, 813. I am much indebted to Professor Rabe's thorough analysis of the foreign missions movement as a basis for the comparison between this movement and the peace movement in the paragraphs which follow.

[10] Rabe, "Protestant Foreign Missions," pp. 8, 649. Rabe uses the term "unconscious nationalism" to suggest that supporters of the foreign missions movement were so absorbed in their vision of an expanding empire of Christian moral influence that they were able to support national expansion without ever considering it as more than an incidental step toward a much larger and self-justifying goal. For an elaboration of the motto of the Student Volunteer Movement, see John R. Mott's *The Evangelization of the World in this Generation* (New York 1905).

great causes—to "do great things"; and the need to find safe and conservative outlets for activist zeal. The peace organizations, even before 1905, were less dominated by clergymen inclined toward social and theological conservatism than were the various boards of commissioners for foreign missions. But the peace movement, even through the early months of World War I, offered some of the same attractions to conservative and moderate activists that Rabe attributes to the foreign missions organizations. The peace movement, too, could serve as an outlet for "social service" and good works for clergymen who preferred less controversial forms of social service than those which radical proponents of the social gospel proposed.[11]

Some of the interconnections, in both ideas and personnel, between the peace movement and the domestic supporters of foreign missions were even more apparent. Promoters of foreign missions were sometimes apt to insist that their own missionaries constituted the world's most efficacious peace movement. "Every onward step for Christ's conquest of the world," wrote one advocate of foreign missions, "is an onward step for universal peace." Samuel Capen, a leader in both the foreign missions and peace movements, argued that the missionary boards with sufficient financial resources could themselves bring peace to the world. Missions might also serve as a moral equivalent for war.[12]

But the supporters of missions also acknowledged that the progress of international arbitration, a central goal of the peace organizations, was critically important to their own missionary work. Violent methods of extending the territorial holdings of the great nations often created fears and antagonisms that hampered their progress. Converts to Christianity could be won more easily

11 On the motives of foreign missions supporters and their relation to the social gospel, see Rabe, "Protestant Foreign Mission," pp. 108-9, 166-68, 320-23, 509, 515-16, 729, 740, 856. On theological conservatism among foreign missions supporters, see Rabe, pp. 60-62, 133 and Paul A. Varg, "Motives in Protestant Missions, 1890-1917," Church History, 23 (Mar. 1954), 70.

12 Caroline Atwater Mason, World Missions and World Peace (West Medford, Mass. 1916), p. 247; Rabe, "Protestant Foreign Missions," pp. 77, 92, 320, 811; Samuel B. Capen, "Foreign Missions and World Peace," World Peace Foundation Pamphlet Series, No. 7, Part III (Oct. 1912), pp. 12-14; Sidney L. Gulick, The White Peril in the Far East (New York 1905), p. 170; Sidney L. Gulick, The American-Japanese Problem (New York 1914), pp. 208-9, 271-72. Occasionally, as in Capen's address, a single sentence would reveal the intermingling of sentiments in favor of peace, missionary work, the building of a Christian Empire, and the expansion of American power: "In this struggle for world peace our missionaries have a great asset in the influence of the United States as a world power" (Capen, p. 14). See also "American World Peace and American Missions in 1913," The Outlook, 106 (24 Jan. 1914), 154-55.

and potential converts rendered less skeptical if the supposedly Christian nations would forsake barbaric warfare for the more Christian methods of arbitration.[13] Leading clergymen and laymen on the missions boards, such as Samuel B. Capen, Philip Moxom, Nehemiah Boynton, Robert E. Speer, Arthur Judson Brown, George N. Boardman, George Dana Boardman, Francis E. Clark, Charles F. Thwing, W.H.P. Faunce, David J. Brewer, William E. Barton, John R. Mott, and numerous others, also participated actively in the peace movement. They, and others in each of the two movements, stressed the common goals of foreign missions and peace organizations and celebrated the common ideal of a "Pax Christiana."[14]

Despite certain similarities between the two movements in aims and attitudes, however, the relationship between the peace movement and promoters of foreign missions remained a tenuous one. For all the logic of their concern for international peace, missionary agencies could display equal enthusiasm for opportunities for proselytizing created by war. The American Board of Commissioners for Foreign Missions, for instance, dismissed the interference of the Russo-Japanese War with mission work as "largely temporary" and "far outweighted by the benefits . . . arising from the war." In 1914, the report of the same board of commissioners elatedly reported instances in which missionaries had found it easier to preach the gospel under war-bred conditions of in-

[13] Mason, *World Missions*, pp. 247-48, 252; *Advocate of Peace*, 62 (June 1900), 124; Smylie, "Protestant Clergymen and America's World Role," p. 386; Capen, "Foreign Missions and World Peace," pp. 3-4, 7, 15-16; Mott, *The Evangelization of the World*, p. 32; Rabe, "Protestant Foreign Missions," p. 810. A striking instance of the possible ambivalent attitudes toward aggressive foreign action is found in Mott's book. After attacking such actions as the forcing of treaty rights and the extension of protectorates for increasing the "difficulty of evangelizing the inhabitants of all these regions . . . ," he remarks with obvious satisfaction that "within a generation Africa has been parcelled out among the nations of Western Europe. Aggressive missionary operations are now carried on in all the great divisions of that continent" (Mott, pp. 32, 46-47). Reactions to the outbreak of World War I continued to reveal ambivalent views of war as both a handicap and a creator of opportunities. See *The Missionary Review of the World*, 37 (Nov. 1914), pp. 801-2, 843.

[14] Rabe, "Protestant Foreign Missions," pp. 593-95; Capen, "Foreign Missions and World Peace," pp. 14, 21-23. Samuel Capen, who served as president of the American Board of Commissioners for Foreign Missions and later as chairman of the executive committee of the Layman's Missionary Movement was a vice-president of the American Peace Society and an active leader in the peace movement. Barton, Clark, G.D. Boardman, G. N. Boardman, and Moxom were all officers in the society. Faunce was a trustee of the World Peace Foundation and a frequent participant at Lake Mohonk. Mott, Brown, Speer, Clark, and Faunce all later served as trustees of the Church Peace Union. Boynton spoke at Mohonk and later served on the World Alliance.

creased poverty, suffering, and desolation.[15] Although they bemoaned the burdens imposed by war, missionary agencies were invariably ready to make the best of any conditions. Whatever their involvement in the peace movement, staunch supporters of foreign missions might thus find ample reasons during wartime to decide to capitalize on wartime experiences of sacrifice and suffering rather than to bend their utmost efforts to the reestablishment of peace.

One final point of similarity between the interests of clergymen in the peace movement and those in foreign missions agencies lay in their common advocacy of interdenominational cooperation. William Warren Sweet has called the cause of missions the most influential single factor in the development of interdenominational cooperation, and Valentin Rabe has described the origins of the ecumenical movement in the United States as "inseparable from the mission movement."[16] A combination of grandiose plans and limited resources had early turned the attention of supporters of foreign missions to the efficiencies of interdenominational cooperation. But cooperation was not merely the result of the practical needs created by foreign missions. The impulse toward united efforts also stemmed from those basic concerns of Protestant clergymen in the late nineteenth century that had themselves stimulated the foreign missions crusades. The clergy of the period presented the world a countenance of unabashed and expansive optimism, occasionally clouded by troubled self-examination. It was alarmed by increasing industrial strife and the loss of church influence among the urban working classes and dismayed by the erosion of the clergy's role in the moral guidance of the community and nation on public issues. But it also found considerable relief from such anxieties in an expectant contemplation of the inevitable world triumph of Christianity.[17]

In the 1880s Josiah Strong, who served as secretary of one of

[15] *One Hundred and Fourth Annual Report of the American Board of Commissioners for Foreign Missions, 1914* (Boston 1914), pp. 76, 212, 214; *Annual Report of the American Board of Commissioners for Foreign Missions, 1904-1905* (Boston 1905), pp. 114-15. See also John R. Mott's comments on the Christianizing effect of the Russo-Japanese War upon the Koreans in his *Decisive Hour of Christian Missions* (London 1910), p. 259.

[16] Sweet, *The Story of Religion in America*, p. 516; Rabe, "Protestant Foreign Missions," p. 51.

[17] The paradoxical picture of a clergy both uneasy and supremely confident can be pieced together from scattered suggestions in Rabe, pp. 99-101, 108, 166, 509, 729, 750, 856. See also William R. Hutchison's assessment of the interwoven strains of "clerical complaints about the decline of religion" and their constant expressions of "progressive optimism" in his "Cultural Strain and Protestant Liberalism," *American Historical Review*, 76 (Apr. 1971), 390-93.

the major early expressions of the search for Protestant unity, the Evangelical Alliance, had given somewhat exaggerated expression to this amalgam of domestic anxiety and international optimism in his famous *Our Country*. Other leading Protestant clergymen of the next two decades expressed themselves similarly, if less dramatically. The best defense against the danger of a loss of ecclesiastical dynamism at home, as Rabe suggests, might well be a strong, revitalizing offense abroad. Similarly, the best defense against any decline in public influence by the clergy might lie in movements toward denominational cooperation and unity through which the church could regain initiative by pronouncing on broad public issues with a single, authoritative voice.[18]

The 1905 conference which laid the plans for the Federal Council of Churches of Christ in America announced just such a goal—"to secure a larger combined influence for the Churches of Christ in all matters affecting the moral and social condition of the people. . . ."[19] During the early years of the twentieth century, both the foreign missions crusade and the peace movement offered avenues through which the moderate leaders of the Protestant clergy might simultaneously promote church unity, avoid the dangers of too deep an involvement in domestic industrial issues, and seek to reassert their role as public leaders by taking an initiative in defining the nation's proper new destiny in the international arena.

Between 1900 and the outbreak of World War I the nature of the clergy's participation in the peace movement changed slowly, but perceptibly. In the process, the complicated relationship between the peace movement and such religious movements as theological liberalism, the social gospel, and church unity were gradually defined. As the peace movement became more widely accepted and endorsed by the nation's political and social elite, it also attracted wider participation from the nation's most prominent clergymen. And as the peace movement came to stress practicality, political activity on behalf of arbitration treaties, and concrete planning for a world judicial system it gained attention from those clergymen who were most anxious to keep the church at the forefront of national life, even if doing so meant far greater involvement in

---

[18] Josiah Strong, *Our Country* (New York 1885), *passim*; Rabe, "Protestant Foreign Missions," pp. 99-103.

[19] Quoted in John A. Hutchison, *We Are Not Divided: A Critical and Historical Study of the Federal Council of the Churches of Christ in America* (New York 1941), p. 36.

secular activities. By late 1911, when the fledgling Federal Council of Churches established its Commission on Peace and Arbitration, the peace movement had won a temporary place as one of the principal official concerns of organized American Protestantism.

The story of changing motives and modes in clerical participation in the early twentieth century peace movement is primarily the story of a segment of the Protestant clergy from the major Protestant denominations. Religious leaders of the smaller pacifist sects, although gradually emerging from purely sectarian concerns, played no significant part in the organized peace movement. Jewish and Catholic clergymen participated in some phases of the peace movement, but took no active part in any of the three major organizations which were specifically religious in composition and approach. Catholic prelates were intent upon establishing the American character of the Catholic Church and the full compatibility of the church with American political institutions. Most of them followed the pattern set by Cardinal Gibbons—i.e., ceremonial and sometimes effusive support for the peace movement while it enjoyed the support of most American political leaders; immediate dissociation from the cause once it represented even the slightest hint of disloyalty or criticism of American leaders or policies. A few, like Archbishop John Ireland, frankly glorified war and gave the peace movement no sympathy whatsoever.[20] Jewish rabbis, although they did not join the specifically religious peace organizations, did play a more continuous role in the peace movement and followed the Protestant pattern of a perceptible increase of interest after 1905 by those with social reformist tendencies. Reform Rabbis Stephen Wise and Emil Hirsch took an active part in secular peace organizations, seeking through the peace movement and other reform activities to reestablish the relevancy and leadership of the rabbinate. Judah Magnes became a leading figure in the People's Council. But the

[20] Dorothy Dohen, *Nationalism and American Catholicism* (New York 1967), pp. 101, 105, 134, 143-44, 147-48. For a sample of Cardinal Gibbons' prewar peace orations, most of which praised the record of the church, see *The Independent*, 76 (25 Dec. 1913), 586; *The North American Review*, 185 (7 June 1907), 252-54; *Mohonk Conference, 1906*, pp. 62-63; and *Cardinal Gibbons on the Arbitration Treaties* (World Peace Foundation pamphlet, Boston 1911), pp. 2-3. Archbishop John Farley acknowledged a lack of deep interest in the peace movement by American Catholics, but excused this apathy because the Holy See had been excluded from playing a leading role in international arbitration. See *Proceedings of the National Arbitration and Peace Congress* (New York 1907), p. 25. Archbishop John J. Glennon participated in the Peace Congress of 1913 and Archbishop Edward Hanna in the Congress of 1915, but no Catholic prelate was active in any of the antiwar or antipreparedness organizations after 1915.

total number of rabbis involved was very small. Specifically religious approaches to the peace movement remained the province of the major Protestant denominations.

One of the dynamic forces within American Protestantism that bore some relationship to the changing clerical participation in the peace movement was the movement toward theological liberalism. First gaining strength in America in the 1870s, theological liberalism or "modernism" had become the dominant strain of thought in many of the larger Protestant denominations by the early twentieth century. Theological liberals edited many of the religious periodicals, dominated the hierarchies of several denominations, and held full control of most interdenominational organizations.[21]

The ascendancy of theological liberalism was partly reflected in clerical participation in the peace movement. Like other secular reform activities, the peace movement had never been compatible with extreme religious conservatism. Moderately conservative clergymen, however, had regularly participated. But after about 1905 the number of theological conservatives in the peace movement declined noticeably. Between 1895 and 1905 the proportion of prominent conservative clergymen attending the Mohonk Arbitration Conferences had kept pace with the proportion of prominent liberal clergymen. But as the liberals increased their participation, the leading conservatives gradually departed, appearing at Mohonk for the last time in the years 1907 to 1911. Two conservatives were appointed to the Federal Council's Commission on Peace and Arbitration, but one of these, Bishop E. R. Hendrix of the Methodist Episcopal Church South, had played no previous role in the peace movement. Hendrix was also the only conservative Protestant selected as a trustee of the Church Peace Union. In each case Hendrix's appointment was made in the interests of church unity, not in recognition of service to the peace movement. By 1912, with few exceptions, the clergymen in the peace organizations were almost entirely of liberal persuasion.[22]

21 William R. Hutchison, ed., *American Protestant Thought: The Liberal Era* (New York 1968), pp. 3-4.

22 I am indebted to Professor William Hutchison of the Harvard Divinity School for the opportunity to make use of unpublished data compiled for his study of theological liberals and conservatives in America between 1875 and 1915, the first results of which appeared in "Cultural Strain and Protestant Liberalism," pp. 386-411. I have checked his lists of 33 most prominent liberals, 93 other liberals from the DAB, 32 well-known liberals not listed in the DAB and 100 conservatives against lists of officers and data on participants of all the major peace organizations from 1900 to 1917. The results do not yield conclusive evidence on the relation of theological liberalism to the various peace organizations since the majority of clergymen,

One reason for the increasing predominance of theological liberals among the clergymen in the peace movement was that the peace movement, particularly as it became more and more an "establishment reform" with support from political and social leaders, drew into its orbit those ministers who held or aspired to high position within denominational hierarchies. As liberals gained control of denominational bodies and rose to positions of spokesmanship for their denominations, they also assumed the civic duties of their positions as members of metropolitan and national elites. The peace movement was a respectable reform. It had clear moral implications and, by 1910 or so, impressive backing from the socially and politically prominent. A highly-placed clergyman, whatever his theological views, might well find that at least token participation in the peace movement had become a natural part of his required responsibilities for civic and philanthropic leadership on behalf of the church.

Similarly, if a clergyman held an important editorial post on a religious journal, he was likely to find himself called upon to propound to his readers on the religious and moral implications of current national and international issues. Whatever his theological preferences, he might find membership in a peace organization useful simply to keep himself current and informed, especially now that American overseas involvements had awakened greater interest in international problems and the Hague Confer-

---

both conservative and liberal, on Hutchison's lists did not participate actively in any of the peace organizations. Of those who did, however, the trend toward increased liberal participation and declining conservative activity in the peace movement is clear. At the Lake Mohonk Conference, for instance, nine of the liberals on Hutchison's lists and seven of the conservatives participated between 1895 and 1905. During the following decade, however, the conservatives were represented by only four men, three of whom did not attend again after 1909. The number of liberals attending had meanwhile increased to thirteen.

The fact that relatively few of the clergymen on Hutchison's lists were active in the peace movement may be due, in part, to the extremely sectional nature of the major peace organizations which drew their members primarily from Massachusetts and New York. The relatively low representation from among the various lists of liberals may suggest that participants in the peace movement, although increasingly drawn from the ranks of theological liberalism, were likely to be men who associated themselves more fully with movements for Protestant church unity or a moderate social gospel than they did with theological liberalism itself. Many liberal clergymen who participated in the peace movement were simply not prominent enough as *spokesmen* for theological liberalism to merit inclusion on the lists Hutchison has employed. Short of an independent study of the theological views of all clergymen in the peace movement, the test against Hutchison's findings seemed the best available. Bishop Hendrix was a frequent defender of extreme nationalism and the military virtues. But his election to high office in the Federal Council was crucial in insuring the adherence of the southern branch of the Methodist Church to the more liberal Federal Council.

ences had stimulated thought about the reform of international relations. As liberals came increasingly to occupy more editorships and more prominent ecclesiastical positions in the Protestant denominations, they almost inevitably became candidates for participation in the peace movement.

But it was not only the occupation of crucial ecclesiastical positions that drew theological modernists toward the peace movement. There was also a clear logical connection between the tenets of theological liberalism and advocacy of peace activities. The modernists' rejection of Old Testament literalism and otherworldliness, and their call for the establishment of the Kingdom of God on earth, meshed well with the aspirations of the peace movement. In contrast, a conservative acceptance of the divine authority and literal truth of every word in the Old Testament, as Washington Gladden pointed out, might allow militaristic nations to "furnish themselves with conceptions of God and religion which harmonize perfectly with the most unscrupulous and predacious policies."[23] The Old Testament had always been called upon, George Gilbert complained, whenever there was a war "to promote or defend." Thus the rejection of the literal truth of each passage of the Old Testament would serve to emancipate the church from the "elements of tribal and egoistic imperialism" in certain passages which seemed to glorify war.[24] A rejection of biblical literalism might also bring emancipation from an older theology that had obscured Christ's true message of universal brotherhood by stressing God's hatred and everlasting punishment of the unbaptized, the nonelect, and the unregenerate. "What is the use of telling men to love their enemies," Washington Gladden exclaimed, "when they know that God is going to plunge all his enemies into a fiery pit and watch them burning there eternally? Do you expect men to be better than God?"[25]

To the extent that modernist theology undercut the validity of Old Testament justifications for war, discouraged other-worldly

[23] Washington Gladden, *The Forks of the Road* (New York 1916), p. 118.

[24] *Ibid.*, pp. 130-31; George Holley Gilbert, *The Bible and International Peace* (New York 1914), pp. 193, 199.

[25] Gladden, *The Forks of the Road*, pp. 127-28, 133. The connection between modernism and the peace movement was not entirely a new phenomenon of the twentieth century. As early as 1847 the organ of the American Peace Society, the *Advocate of Peace*, had published a debate in which peace promoters had attempted to undermine prowar arguments based on seeming sanctions of war by the God of the Old Testament. Employing a "modernist" argument, they had claimed that no valid conclusions could be based on writings of which exact knowledge was lacking. See Amos Arnold Hovey, "A History of the Religious Phase of the American Movement for International Peace to the Year 1914," Ph.D. diss., University of Chicago, 1930, p. 82.

and after-worldly concerns, and emphasized Christ's teaching of brotherhood, it encouraged sympathy for the peace movement. But the logical connections between modernism and peace did not, in themselves, insure that liberal clergymen would join the peace movement. In fact, of the thirty-three most prominent theological liberals in America between 1875 and 1915, only two participated regularly in the peace movement before 1915. Several others, like Gladden and Walter Rauschenbusch, subsequently took part in peace organizations, but their participation appears to have stemmed as much from the social activism that they incorporated into their social gospel as it did from any sense of logical consistency within theological modernism.[26]

Thus the clergymen who joined the peace movement before 1914 were most often *not* those who were actively exploring and propounding the new theology. Instead, they were usually those who accepted a largely unexamined theological liberalism more or less as a matter of course because they found such a theology compatible with the secular activities to which they felt themselves drawn. "The hallmark of modernism," William Hutchison has written, "is the insistence that theology must adopt a sympathetic attitude toward secular culture and must consciously strive to come to terms with it."[27] The clergymen who were moving into positions of metropolitan prominence and national leadership in the Protestant denominations in the early twentieth century were determined to maintain the church's prestige and moral authority by bringing its influence to bear upon the great national and international issues of the day. They accepted theological liberalism as an integral part of the effort to keep the church relevant and vital. It was in much the same spirit that they also accepted the opportunity to participate in the peace movement and similar popular reforms.

One of the primary means by which the Protestant clergy was attempting to establish the church's contemporary relevance in

[26] See above, n. 22 on source of data. The two consistent supporters of the peace movement among the 33 most prominent liberals were Lyman Abbott and William Adams Brown. Abbott, despite his frequent participation, was deeply distrusted for his militaristic views by many peace movement leaders. Abbott denounced the peace movement after 1914. William Adams Brown did not remain active after 1914 and apparently applied pressure to oust Norman Thomas from his ministerial position in 1917 when Thomas' peace activities began to weaken the financial position of Brown's home missions operations. See Harry Fleischman, *Norman Thomas, A Biography* (New York 1964), pp. 63-64.
[27] Hutchison, *American Protestant Thought*, p. 4.

the early twentieth century was, of course, the social gospel movement. To this movement, too, clerical participation in the peace movement was clearly, although not unambiguously, related. Proponents of the social gospel rejected the "individualistic interpretation of Christianity" which recognized the salvation of the individual soul as the church's only duty. They called for "social salvation" through social reform action and envisaged the Kingdom of God, not as a future other-worldly state to be sought by the individual soul, but as a perfected national and international social order, to be created "in this world here and now."[28] If the social gospel, as it is commonly defined, sought to create the Kingdom of God on earth through the application of the teachings of Jesus to the social order, and if central among those regenerative teachings was the doctrine of the brotherhood of man, then efforts to establish lasting peace among nations would seem to exemplify perfectly the social gospel impulse. If conflict and disharmony among men were to be replaced by love through Christian-inspired social action, then what would better test the power of love in the social order than attempts to eliminate the massive disharmonies and murderous conflicts of international war? Surely world peace would seem to be a crucial element in any vision of an evolving Kingdom of God on earth.

But such potential affinity for the peace movement found meager expression in the social gospel literature before 1915. One searches vainly through its main expositions for any suggestion that the peace movement constituted a part of its program. Few of the social gospel works published between 1900 and 1915 even mentioned world peace. The rest treated international relations only perfunctorily. None attempted to relate the peace movement in any meaningful way to the message of the social gospel. Washington Gladden's *Social Salvation* contained chapters on the poor, the unemployed, prisons, social vices, public education, and the redemption of the city, but made no mention of war or peace. John Haynes Holmes' *The Revolutionary Function of the Modern Church* devoted sections to poverty, disease, criminality, and prostitution, but none to war. Chapters entitled "Human Sacrifice," in Scott Nearing's *Social Religion* and "Is It Peace or War?" in Washington Gladden's *Applied Christianity* dealt entirely with

---

28 The quotations are from Sidney Gulick, "Constructive Methods for Promoting International Peace," in Frederick Lynch, *Through Europe on the Eve of War* (New York 1914), p. 116. The term "social salvation" was popularized in Washington Gladden, *Social Salvation* (New York 1902).

industrial accidents and labor problems. Neither work contained any discussion of international affairs.[29]

The leading theoretician of the social gospel, Walter Rauschenbusch, did devote about two pages to international problems in each of his major works during the prewar period, *Christianity and the Social Crisis* and *Christianizing the Social Order*. But even this slight attention to world affairs served largely to establish the connection between capitalism and war, and thus to add another charge to Rauschenbusch's general indictment of capitalism.[30] The works of Francis Peabody did not touch the problem of world peace at all, nor did those of such prominent social gospelers as George Hodges and Samuel Zane Batten. Shailer Mathews did not mention the peace movement in either *The Social Teaching of Jesus* or *The Church and the Changing Order*, nor did Charles Stelzle in *American Social and Religious Conditions*.[31] Charles H. Hopkins, in his study of the social gospel in American Protestantism, has listed at least eleven major concerns of the social gospel in the twentieth century without including in the list any aspect of the reform of international relations. Perhaps the most conclusive evidence that the peace movement was not considered a part of the social gospel program is the fact that neither "The Social Creed of the Churches," adopted as a general statement of the social goals of unified Protestantism by the Federal Council in 1908, nor the revision of that creed in 1912, contained a single mention of international peace or arbitration.[32]

Not only did the peace movement receive no recognition as an accepted part of the social gospel, but it failed to attract some of the most thorough-going practitioners of the social gospel into its ranks. Walter Rauschenbusch did not take an active role until well after 1914. Washington Gladden gave the prewar peace

[29] Gladden, *Social Salvation*; John Haynes Holmes, *The Revolutionary Function of the Modern Church* (New York 1912); Scott Nearing, *Social Religion* (New York 1913); Washington Gladden, *Applied Christianity* (Boston 1886), all *passim*.

[30] Walter Rauschenbusch, *Christianity and the Social Crisis* (New York 1907), pp. 350, 378-79 and *Christianizing the Social Order* (New York 1912), pp. 278-79.

[31] Francis Greenwood Peabody, *Jesus Christ and the Social Question* (New York 1902) and *The Approach to the Social Question* (New York 1912); Samuel Zane Batten, *The Social Task of Christianity* (New York 1911); George Hodges, *Faith and Social Service* (New York 1896); Shailer Mathews, *The Social Teaching of Jesus* (New York 1902) and *The Church and the Changing Order* (New York 1907); Charles Stelzle, *American Social and Religious Conditions* (New York 1912).

[32] Charles Howard Hopkins, *The Rise of the Social Gospel in American Protestantism, 1865-1915* (New Haven, Conn. 1940), pp. 245, 319. For the text of the creed and its revision, see Harry F. Ward, *The Social Creed of the Churches* (New York 1914), pp. 6-7.

movement only slight attention. Charles Stelzle, Leighton Williams, Harry F. Ward, Samuel Zane Batten, John Howard Melish, and Scott Nearing were not among the participants in prewar peace organizations. Those like Norman Thomas, A. J. Muste, and Willard Sperry, who were later to integrate world peace with other social gospel concerns, took no part in the organized peace movement until after the war began.

How can this discrepancy between the logical implications of the social gospel for international affairs and the apparent indifference of many of the leading social gospelers toward the peace movement be explained? One answer lies in the nature of the prewar peace movement. Dominated, particularly after 1910, by the new foundations and by such conservative figures as Elihu Root, Andrew Carnegie, and Nicholas Murray Butler, the peace movement had become associated with the nation's political, economic, social, and educational elite. The more radical practitioners of the social gospel were not likely to be attracted to zealous participation in a movement under such leadership. Another answer lies in the perceived priorities of the social gospelers. Awakened to the need for a practical social application of Christianity by the labor upheavals and social unrest of the late nineteenth and early twentieth centuries and by the effect of urban social disorder in frustrating the work of evangelism, the social gospelers naturally devoted their energies to what seemed to them to be the more immediate, more socially significant problems of industrial conflict and deteriorating urban conditions. The more radical social gospel leaders undoubtedly viewed the peace movement as a "safe" reform that promised no immediate social amelioration.[33]

This did not mean, however, that activity in the peace movement by clergymen was totally unrelated to social gospel proclivities. A long list of clergymen, including Graham Taylor, Philip Moxom, George Hodges, Luther B. Wilson, Charles S. Macfarland, Frederick Lynch, Newell D. Hillis, Frank Mason North, Sidney Gulick, and numerous others, actively supported both the peace movement and some form of social gospel action. No hard

[33] Even such exceptions among the more radical exponents of the social gospel as John Haynes Holmes, who did lend his name to one of the prewar peace organizations, did not view war as a pressing problem and "preferred to spend time on another front." Holmes reflected later that he had felt no inclination toward pacifism before the war and had "never thought the question through" prior to 1914 (Kenneth Jackson Smith, "John Haynes Holmes: Opponent of War," B.D. diss., University of Chicago, 1949, pp. 38, 42-46). See also John Haynes Holmes to Kenneth Jackson Smith, 22 Mar. 1949 in *ibid.*, p. 130.

and fast line of distinction can be drawn between the social gospel proponents who joined actively in the prewar peace movement and those who did not. But those clergymen who combined support for the peace movement and some form of social gospel action were usually not the most thoroughly involved or the most radical proponents of the social gospel. Rather, they were those leading clergymen who were more moderate in their support of social reform and who embraced the social gospel as part of a more general drive to maintain church leadership in the public arena.

A third major development in American Protestantism during the early twentieth century was the drive toward church unity. This movement, related closely to both theological liberalism and the ascendancy of the social gospel, influenced clerical participation in the peace movement more directly than either of the other two. Both the Commission on Peace and Arbitration of the Federal Council of Churches and the Church Peace Union owed their existence as much to efforts to promote church unity as they did to the quest for world peace. While the social gospel movement and the growth of theological liberalism both progressed steadily without any assistance whatsoever from the peace movement, the drive for church unity early discovered that cooperative activity on behalf of peace might help the fledgling unity movement through a period of hard times. Thus clerical leaders in the church unity movement found themselves attracted to the peace movement for practical and opportunistic reasons as well as by the more abstract considerations of the common cooperative goals of religious unity and world peace.

The movement for unity among Protestant leaders in the United States had begun haltingly and spasmodically in the nineteenth century with cooperative action in foreign missions and in such supradenominational organizations as the Evangelical Alliance, the YMCA, The Young People's Society of Christian Endeavor, and the Student Volunteer Movement.[34] In 1894 a more specific movement toward tentative federation began to take shape with the founding of the Open and Institutional Church League. In 1901 this league provided the nucleus for the National Federation of Churches and Christian Workers. By 1905 a new, more concrete federation had been projected—the Federal Council of Churches of Christ in America. After three more years of

---

[34] Robert Lee, *The Social Sources of Church Unity, An Interpretation of Unitive Movements in American Protestantism* (New York 1960), p. 77.

planning and conferences, the Federal Council was officially launched in 1908.[35]

The leaders in this movement for Protestant federation came largely from three segments of the clergy: pastors of urban, institutional churches; editors of religious journals; and secretaries of denominational and interdenominational boards and commissions. Most of them had spent some part of their careers in religious journalism.[36] Their experiences in these areas of the ministry had made them particularly conscious of some of the weaknesses of American Protestantism, and had alerted them to the challenges that secularism presented to the church's traditional moral authority and to its influence over a wide range of public issues. Their work as secretaries of boards with national, or even international, jurisdiction and responsibility and their experiences as editors in assessing a variety of broad concerns of the church had made them acutely aware of the church's opportunities and failings on matters that affected all denominations. Having, by virtue of their experience, stood at vantage points where they could survey the church's whole theater of action, they became authorities on the perils and opportunities facing the church and students of grand strategy through efficient cooperation. They were ambitious men—ambitious for themselves and ambitious for the advancement of the church. Frank Mason North expressed their aspirations when he asserted, "The twentieth century pastor will be something more than a preacher or controversialist in theological discussions; he will be a leader in the world."[37]

But despite this bold prophecy, the leaders of American Protestantism in the early twentieth century worried that their profession was falling short of this ministerial ideal. Charles Macfarland, later to become general secretary of the Federal Council and one of the prime leaders of its peace activities, confessed in 1909 that the Christian ministry had come to be judged unattractive to strong men. Fewer men sought a career in the ministry, he suggested, because the minister was too confined "to a limited round of relatively small functions" and was "shut off from the

[35] A detailed but often tiresome account of the history of the early organizations leading up to the Federal Council is available in Elias B. Sanford, *Origin and History of the Federal Council of the Churches of Christ in America* (Hartford, Conn. 1916). For a more concise summary, see Hutchison, *We Are Not Divided*, pp. 18-53.

[36] At least a dozen of the foremost leaders in the church unity movement, including Elias Sanford, Charles Macfarland, Charles Thompson, William Ward, Frederick Lynch, Frank Mason North, Amory Bradford, Amos Wells, John B. Calvert, and Francis E. Clark had been editors of religious journals. See also Hutchison, *We Are Not Divided*, pp. 22-23.

[37] Quoted in Sanford, *Origin and History of the Federal Council*, p. 69.

great movements of mankind." At the founding conference of the Federal Council, Newell Dwight Hillis recounted unhappily the list of traditional functions in fields such as education and social leadership that secular agencies had appropriated from the church.[38]

But what could be done to resist the inroads of secularism and restore vitality to American Protestantism? Charles Macfarland acknowledged that "in some ways the church has lost her place and power . . . ," but he spoke for most of his fellow clergymen when he offset such concerns with an expansive optimism. The church would rejuvenate itself through an eager response to the unprecedented opportunities to make itself "a place of directing power and influence," a "mover and . . . moulder" of the social order. "Get power," he told an audience of Yale Divinity Students. A modern minister should make his church a center of power "from which his wider influence must radiate," a platform "from which to speak to the more distant and uncertain multitudes." He should discard petty functions and throw himself into the great movements of the day, making himself "a vital factor in his city, a man to be reckoned with in every great movement. . . ." Macfarland reaffirmed the old New England conception of the ministry. "In those days," he reminded his listeners, "the minister and his church dominated the public life. In these latter days most of this authority has been temporarily relinquished, but we must gain it again."[39]

[38] Charles S. Macfarland, ed., *The Christian Ministry and the Social Order* (New Haven, Conn. 1909), p. 6; Hutchison, *We Are Not Divided*, p. 41. For other observations on the declining moral authority and stature of the ministry in the face of an advancing secularism, see Lee, *Social Sources of Church Unity*, p. 81; Henry F. May, *Protestant Churches and Industrial America* (New York 1949), pp. 125, 204; Aaron Ignatius Abell, *The Urban Impact on American Protestantism 1865-1900* (London 1952), pp. 225-27; Richard Hofstadter, *The Age of Reform: From Bryan to F.D.R.* (New York 1955), pp. 150-52; Robert S. Michaelsen, "The Protestant Ministry in America: 1850 to the Present," in H. Richard Neibuhr and Daniel D. Williams, eds., *The Ministry in Historical Perspective* (New York 1956), p. 277; Hopkins, *The Rise of the Social Gospel*, p. 302; and Hutchison, *We Are Not Divided*, pp. 17-18, 21, 39. One must guard, of course, against too uncritical an acceptance of the objective validity of the ministerial complaints. In the most thorough analysis of the question of ministerial status in this period William R. Hutchison concludes that there is no clear evidence of objective decline, or even of widespread clerical pessimism. See Hutchison, "Cultural Strain and Protestant Liberalism," 390-93. Church unity leaders often exemplified a seemingly inconsistent position, the possibility of which is suggested in Hutchison's article. They combined intermittent jeremiads about the loss of moral authority and status by the clergy with a "progressive optimism" in ultimate Protestant triumph.

[39] Macfarland, *The Christian Ministry and the Social Order*, pp. 5-6, 13-15, 21, 39, 42-43, 115-17. In several ways Macfarland's ideas and activities exemplified Robert T. Handy's description of an "aggressive, dynamic" Protestantism which, in

The church unity movement seemed to offer one avenue toward the expansion of ministerial power and influence. "We believe," stated the letter of invitation to the 1905 planning conference for the Federal Council, "that the great Christian bodies in our country should stand together and lead in the discussion of and give an impulse to all great movements that 'make for righteousness.' "[40] Among these "great movements" the social gospel received early recognition, closely followed by world peace. Several clergymen argued that if the church was undivided and exerting its proper influence in the world, there would have been no need for such things as child labor committees and peace societies.[41] A revitalized and united church should resume initiative and authority in such public questions again. A united Protestantism, one that eschewed sectarian squabbling and that did not squander its resources on competing programs and overlapping organizations, might reassert its authority over public issues and thwart the advance of secularism. Visions of the possibilities of church unity buoyed clerical optimism and contributed to reassuring escapism. The decline in the church's authority had been largely the result of inefficient and debilitating inner conflict and division, it was confidently assumed. Once effective federation was achieved, all losses would be regained.

But church unity among the major Protestant denominations, even in the form of a loose federation, was not easily achieved. It was not a "grass roots" movement, but was strictly the vision of a group of ambitious denominational leaders characterized by a "moderate liberalism." The movement's principal financial support through the early years came not from the denominations but from wealthy individuals and foundations. Not only were the participants of the Federal Council theologically and socially more liberal than the denominations they represented, but such subsections as the Commission on the Church and Social Service were dominated by a few of the most activist members and were

---

its crusade to confront and evangelize American life, moved toward "partial envelopment" by "secularized culture." See Robert T. Handy, "The Protestant Quest for a Christian America, 1830-1930," *Church History*, 22 (Mar. 1953), 10, 12, 15-17.

[40] Quoted in Hutchison. *We Are Not Divided*, p. 33. Viewing the church unity movement in long perspective, Robert Lee (*Social Sources of Church Unity*, p. 81) concludes that "one of the continuing strands in the drive toward church unity is the concerted effort of churches to *make an effective impact upon the secular world*" (Emphasis mine).

[41] Peter Ainslie, *Christ or Napoleon—Which?* (New York 1915), pp. 43-44; Frederick Lynch, *The Peace Problem* (New York 1911), pp. 59-62, 96; Carl Herman Voss, *Rabbi and Minister: The Friendship of Stephen S. Wise and John Haynes Holmes* (New York 1964), p. 112.

engaged in work far more radical than the member denominations were inclined to support.[42] With so flimsy a popular base, the leaders of the new Federal Council had to proceed cautiously, seeking issues to pursue which would reinforce rather than undermine the tenuous unity already achieved.

Although the promotion of the social gospel provided one motive for unity, it was a rather mild and uncontroversial form of social gospel that came to characterize the early work of the Federal Council.[43] The leaders delegated to carry on the work of the incipient council between 1905 and 1908 gave their primary attention to such issues as atrocities in the Congo, race-track gambling, a more stringent divorce law in North Dakota, and temperance. The 1908 conference endorsed a progressive "Social Creed" with surprisingly little dissent, but many preferred to interpret social action simply as more effective home missions work. "These men were not radicals," John Hutchison quite accurately concludes.[44] They were interested in the general extension of church influence, not in radical social action. Almost instinctively they seized upon those issues that would keep the churches abreast of popular current movements and give the council something to do without alarming its constituent bodies. A mild form of social gospel action and the peace movement conveniently met these specifications in the years before 1914.

The proposal of activity within the peace movement was brought before the leaders of the church federation movement as early as 1905 by Justice David Brewer of the Supreme Court. In

---

[42] Hutchison, *We Are Not Divided*, pp. 22, 34, 57, 59-60; Charles S. Macfarland, *Christian Unity in the Making* (New York 1948), pp. 57, 98. Elias Sanford recounted the "disappointments that early convinced me that the laity . . . were indifferent to the course of Christian unity" (*Origin and History of the Federal Council*, pp. 303-4). See also John Franklin Piper, Jr., "The Social Policy of the Churches of Christ in America During World War I," Ph.D. diss., Duke University, 1965, pp. vii, 38, 68.

[43] The social gospel is characterized as the essential ingredient in the making of the Federal Council by Hopkins in *The Rise of the Social Gospel*, p. 302; by Hutchison in *We Are Not Divided*, pp. 22, 25, 39, 99; and by Macfarland himself in *Christian Unity in the Making*, p. 46. But on the mildness, vagueness, and occasional conservatism of the social gospel views expressed by the majority of the Federal Council spokesmen and supporters and the Council's concern for avoiding "controversial political and social matters which might hamper union," see Hutchison, pp. 30, 42, 46-49, 100.

[44] Hutchison, *We Are Not Divided*, pp. 37, 48; Sanford, *Origin and History of the Federal Council*, pp. 254-58. For an overview of the Council's early activities, see *Church Federation: First Annual Report of the Executive Committee of the Inter-Church Conference on Federation* (New York, 1906), pp. 7-14 and *Church Federation: The Second Annual Report of the Executive Committee having charge of Work and Arrangements for the First Meeting of the Federal Council of the Churches of Christ in America* (New York 1907), pp. 3-13.

1908, another promoter of the international lawyers' ideas, Dean Henry Wade Rogers of the Yale Law School, brought the issue before the Federal Council again. The 1908 conference adopted a resolution calling for a "Peace Sunday" and two officers of the council, Frank Mason North and Elias B. Sanford, journeyed to Mohonk to promote the new Federal Council and affirm its interest in peace.[45] But the Federal Council did not really "discover" the peace movement until 1911 when a crisis in the fortunes of the council coincided with a drive by the secular peace organizations in support of President Taft's general arbitration treaties with France and Great Britain.

The year 1911 began as a dismal one for the Federal Council of Churches. Its first major project, the attempt to establish local branches, had collapsed. Its only full-time, salaried official, Corresponding Secretary Elias Sanford, was in poor health. The council had found no program of action around which to rally enthusiasm and financial support. The denominations ignored the council and failed to meet their financial pledges. The mood of optimism of the years before 1908 had given way to a sense of frustration. In 1910 a colleague warned Charles Macfarland, who was soon to assume leadership in the Federal Council, that the organization had two more years of life at the most.[46] The only clear sign of vitality came from the council's one permanent commission, the Commission on the Church and Social Service, which had filled one "void" left by the churches and which showed promise of obtaining sufficient independent financial support for its social gospel activities. One other ray of hope, at first unrecognized, lay in the council's nationwide distribution of a statement to ministers in support of the current arbitration treaties. The expenses of this work were paid by the Carnegie Peace Endowment.[47]

It was at this point in its uncertain development that Charles Macfarland assumed the direction of the Federal Council. In the spring of 1911 he accepted a position as secretary of the Commis-

---

[45] Hutchison, *We Are Not Divided*, pp. 163-64.

[46] *Ibid.*, pp. 59, 61; Macfarland, *Christian Unity in the Making*, pp. 51-54, 60; Sanford, *Origin and History of the Federal Council*, pp. 303, 305; Charles S. Macfarland, *Across the Years* (New York 1936), pp. 89-92.

[47] *Church Federation: Third Annual Report of the Executive Committee of the Federal Council of the Churches of Christ in America* (New York 1911), pp. 17-19, 32-40; Macfarland, *Christian Unity in the Making*, pp. 46, 55, 62, 64, 98; Junius B. Remensynder, "Report of the Commission on Peace and Arbitration" (1912), pp. 2-3, Box 3, Federal Council of Churches of Christ in America Papers, Swarthmore College Peace Collection.

sion on the Church and Social Service and in October became the council's first general secretary. Coming from a poor Boston family, Macfarland had found the ministry an avenue of upward social mobility. He had progressed from a brief business career as bookkeeper and commission merchant to YMCA secretary, to Yale Divinity School, to the ministry and religious journalism, and finally to a parish in Connecticut where he championed a moderate social gospel, developed a Sunday Evening Institute, and demonstrated a "flair for administrative and promotional work."[48]

As soon as he took control of the Federal Council, Macfarland began a campaign of promotional work, attending denominational assemblies and extending the reputation of the Federal Council by participating in the congresses and conventions of a variety of organizations. He moved to reduce internal friction and to strengthen the council among its member denominations by throwing its energies into areas where the individual denominations lacked organizations and programs. He joined flourishing movements like the Men and Religion Forward movement and then worked to bring them under the wing of the Federal Council in order to capture their vitality and support for the council itself. To rescue the council from financial disaster, he proposed to seek supplementary financial support from individuals and organizations who were interested in projects that the council might be willing to undertake.[49] Under such a policy, he and the council were naturally apt to adopt those programs which were likely to attract outside financing.

Macfarland and the other leaders of the council were anxiously "looking for a program on which the churches might unite" in 1911 when the possibility of tapping Carnegie money through activity in the peace movement suddenly arose.[50] The Reverend Frederick Lynch, a close friend of Macfarland's at Yale Divinity School, had long been seeking to convince Andrew Carnegie of the potential role of the churches in the peace movement. A visit to the Mohonk Conference in 1910 by leading German and British clergymen had stimulated some interest in the idea of clerical leadership in the building of a peace coalition of the great powers. Such an entente had been a pet idea of Carnegie's in recent years. In 1911 the Taft arbitration treaties with Britain and

[48] Macfarland, *Across the Years*, pp. 10-11, 17-18, 24, 26, 38, 60-61, 63-64, 66, 87; Hutchison, *We Are Not Divided*, p. 61.

[49] Hutchison, *We Are Not Divided*, pp. 61, 64; Macfarland, *Christian Unity in the Making*, pp. 62, 64, 66-67.

[50] Charles S. Macfarland, *Pioneers for Peace Through Religion* (New York 1946), p. 35.

France, a potential first link in a great-power coalition for peace, came before the Senate. Carnegie was anxious to support any promising agency that might propagandize effectively for the treaties. He gave Lynch "a large sum of money" to "line up the churches to help put these treaties through," and arranged, probably with Lynch's prodding, for the Carnegie Endowment to finance the Federal Council of Churches in distributing a nation-wide message to ministers in support of the treaties.[51]

Macfarland and his associates saw their opportunity. Here, in the peace movement, was an unobjectionable and increasingly popular cause with moral implications. It had already proved a momentary source of funds and activity for the becalmed and disregarded Federal Council and might likely prove a source of revitalizing funds again. Macfarland recalled later that by 1912 "we had already been approached by an individual who was likely to make a substantial contribution in the interest of international peace."[52] If the Federal Council could organize itself for effective work in the peace movement it might develop the kind of unifying program it had been seeking and bolster its sagging finances in the bargain.

Macfarland and Lynch set to work at once. Macfarland called for "the immediate development of the Commission on Peace and Arbitration for which financial support had already been pledged, with some promise of later enlargement."[53] Frederick Lynch became secretary of the new commission. Lynch had been participating in the peace movement for nearly a decade and had been ingratiating himself with Andrew Carnegie for several years. In 1911 he had published a book entitled *The Peace Problem*, for which Carnegie had written an introduction and which appears to have been directed, at least partly, toward Carnegie himself. In the book, Lynch extolled the new practicality of the peace

[51] Frederick Lynch to Reverend David H. Greer, 18 Feb. 1914 ("Confidential History of the Church Peace Union"), Church Peace Union Papers, Council on Religion and International Affairs, New York City; Macfarland, *Pioneers for Peace*, pp. 34-35; Macfarland, *Across the Years*, p. 38. On Carnegie's idea of a peace-enforcing entente of three or four great powers, see chap. four, pp. 116-18.

[52] Macfarland, *Christian Unity in the Making*, p. 67.

[53] *Ibid.*, p. 68. As early as 1912 the Federal Council was able to report that the commissions on Social Service and International Peace "have not only met the expenses of their own work, and by it increased an interest in the Council, but have also contributed a surplus to the general budget in addition." From 1909 to 1912 the council's income from denominations had increased only from $9,180 to $14,586 while its income from individuals (among whom Carnegie figured most prominently) had jumped from $4,195 to $18,404. *Report of Proceedings, The Second Quadrennial Council of the Federal Council of the Churches of Christ in America* (Chicago 1912), pp. 67, 84-85.

movement, praised those important "men of affairs" (among whom Carnegie was most prominently mentioned) who had given a new impulse to the movement, and commented favorably upon several of Carnegie's favorite schemes including the "league of peace" plan which Carnegie had urged upon former President Roosevelt.[54]

Lynch had already obtained Carnegie's financial assistance in buying the *Christian Work* and had obtained a $1,000 a year pledge from Carnegie for peace work. By his own account, he now continued to see Carnegie nearly every week, "walked and talked" with him, and "kept him thoroughly in touch" with the peace work of the churches. He explored schemes that might excite Carnegie and engineered the establishment of a "Church Peace League of America" to back a judicially oriented peace program that might catch Carnegie's fancy. "Confidentially . . . ," Lynch wrote later, "Mr. Carnegie first became interested in this alignment of the churches through the monthly reports with which I submerged him of what the Peace Commission of the Council and the Church Peace League were doing."[55]

In 1913, Lynch decided to approach Carnegie directly. Evidently he gained some partly unintended support from several peace workers who were beginning to convince Carnegie that his Peace Endowment was proceeding too academically and dispassionately and was failing to exploit the moral argument against war.[56] When the endowment officers resisted Carnegie's suggestion that they set aside funds for work by the churches, Lynch pressed his case for a separate endowment of $10 million. Carnegie brought Lynch and his associates to the house of his most trusted adviser on international affairs, Elihu Root, in order, according to Root's interpretation, to get him to defend Carnegie against their "assaults." At this point the accounts of the course of events by Root and Lynch diverge, but Root, who was contemptuous of the whole proposal, was clearly instrumental in insuring that Lynch came away with only $2 million. Lynch and his

54 Lynch, *The Peace Problem*, pp. 82-83, 87, 89, 116-17; Frederick Lynch to Andrew Carnegie, 23 Jan. 1909 and 4 July 1910, Andrew Carnegie Papers, MS Div., Library of Congress. On Carnegie's peace league schemes see chap. four.

55 Frederick Lynch to David H. Greer, 18 Feb. 1914, CPU Papers, CRIA; Frederick Lynch, *Personal Recollections of Andrew Carnegie* (New York 1920), pp. 111-13; Lynch to Edwin D. Mead, 2 May 1912, Box 3, World Peace Foundation Papers, SCPC; Samuel T. Dutton to R. A. Franks, May 1909, Carnegie Papers, LC; Lynch to Benjamin Trueblood, 16 Dec. 1911, Box 6, American Peace Society Papers, SCPC; Lynch to William I. Hull, 19 Feb. 1914, Box 2, Hull Papers, FHL.

56 Frederick Lynch to Benjamin Trueblood, 31 Mar. 1913 and Samuel T. Dutton to Trueblood, 11 Apr. 1913, Box 6, APS Papers, SCPC.

friends never forgave Root for his intercession. Still, they had obtained an endowment of $2 million for a new peace organization, the Church Peace Union.[57]

Conveniently for Macfarland and the Federal Council, Carnegie happened also to be an advocate of church unity. An agnostic himself, and occasionally a stern critic of the churches, Carnegie nevertheless loved to see himself as the organizer and manipulator of great movements for the moral benefit of mankind. The subject of church unity called forth his characteristic optimism: "If Christians were all one, in one Church, of one mind, and all the power now used in rivalry with each other unitedly directed against the evils of world, intemperance, war, poverty, ignorance, superstition and disease—they could all soon be banished."[58]

According to Lynch, Carnegie was intrigued by the idea that a donation by him for peace work through the churches might bring together as his trustees "twenty-five of the biggest men of all the denominations. . . ."[59] Even after the Church Peace Union was established, Lynch recalls, Carnegie ". . . was as much pleased over the success in securing leaders from the different branches of the Church to serve on the same board as he was over the prospect of the service it might render to the cause of universal peace. He would ask me two or three times a week if there was any other board working solely among the churches on which Catholics, Protestants and Jews were serving together."[60] When Lynch, in January of 1914, suggested that the prospective new organization should more appropriately be called a "foundation" rather than a "union," Carnegie replied sharply, "Your preference for 'Foundation' has little foundation! UNION is the word!"[61]

The all-inclusiveness of Carnegie's idea of "Christian union" presented a few problems for the Federal Council. Carnegie insisted that Catholics and Jews were to be included among the

[57] Root's account appears in "Annual Meeting of the Board of Trustees," 21 Apr. 1916, pp. 67-68, Carnegie Endowment for International Peace Papers, Columbia University Library. Lynch's version is recorded in Lynch to David H. Greer, 18 Feb. 1914 and in unsigned [Trustees of the Church Peace Union] to Andrew Carnegie, 15 Oct. 1914, CPU Papers, CRIA. The idea of an endowed church peace organization found little sympathy among the Carnegie Endowment trustees. One trustee scoffed, "They have had two thousand years to show what they can do" ("Minutes of the Meeting of the Board of Trustees," 14 Nov. 1913, pp. 72-79, 129, CEIP Papers, CUL).

[58] Quoted in Lynch, *Recollections of Carnegie*, p. 74.

[59] Macfarland, *Pioneers for Peace*, p. 36.

[60] Lynch, *Recollections of Carnegie*, p. 161.

[61] Andrew Carnegie to Frederick Lynch, 4 Feb. 1914, CPU Papers, CRIA.

trustees. He even passed on to Lynch a letter noting that the Christian Scientists had not received representation on the Church Peace Union with the penciled notation, "Who is to blame."[62] Here was a far more extreme notion of church unity than the Federal Council could endorse, but Macfarland and Lynch proceeded nonetheless with their manuevers to insure that the Federal Council would tap the energies and financial resources of the new Church Peace Union.

Once Carnegie had committed himself to the new $2 million endowment, Lynch began a campaign to convince Carnegie that the directors of the Church Peace League, puppet organization of the Federal Council's Commission on Peace and Arbitration, would be perfect—in fact, indispensable—as trustees for Carnegie's new organization. "It would be a great mistake," he wrote Carnegie, "to approach the churches through any organization not composed of the men who compose this League since they are the heads and leaders of the denominations."[63] Lynch was largely successful in this effort, although Carnegie's visions of Christian unity required the additional appointment of two Catholic clergymen, one rabbi, a Jewish and a Catholic layman, a Universalist, and a Unitarian. Two other laymen received appointments for Carnegie's "reasons of personal friendship."[64] But Lynch was appointed secretary of the new Carnegie philanthropy, and staunch supporters of the Federal Council comprised a large majority of those trustees who would give the greatest attention to the new Church Peace Union's affairs.

No sooner had the union been publicly launched in February 1914 than Macfarland, with Lynch's support and connivance, presented a "plan of mutual action for the Church Peace Union and the Federal Council." The essence of the plan was that the Federal Council serve as the Church Peace Union's operating agent— that the Church Peace Union pay the Federal Council to carry on much of its work. About the same time, Lynch received a letter from a director of the Russell Sage Foundation, which had become involved in the financial support of the Federal Council, suggesting that Church Peace Union funds be used to increase

---

[62] H. J. Cure to Andrew Carnegie, 31 Jan. 1914 and Carnegie to Frederick Lynch, n.d., CPU Papers, CRIA.

[63] Unsigned [Frederick Lynch] to Andrew Carnegie, n.d. [Jan. 1914], rough draft and J. A. Poynton to Lynch, 9 Jan. 1914, CPU Papers, CRIA. See also Lynch to William I. Hull, 19 Feb. 1914, Box 2, Hull Papers, FHL.

[64] Lynch, *Recollections of Carnegie*, p. 159; "Minutes of the First Meeting of the Church Peace Union," p. 2, CPU Papers, CRIA.

Macfarland's salary, since the Federal Council would be assuming responsibility for carrying on part of the union's work.[65] Macfarland persuaded an intermediary to correspond with Bishop Greer, the president of the new union, "urging that the Church Peace Union do its work as far as possible through the Federal Council. . . ." "I should judge by Bishop Greer's letter," Macfarland confided to Lynch, "that it was more or less a new thought to him. Perhaps it might be well to put the matter in his hands and get him to propose it to the Executive Committee of the Church Peace Union, and let him think that he did it all by himself."[66]

The Federal Council did not manage to bend the new Church Peace Union to its own purposes without opposition. Several of the trustees including Edwin Mead, director of the World Peace Foundation, concluded that because of "misunderstandings and limitations within the Federal Council of Churches" the Church Peace Union should remain independent. In March 1914 Mead wrote to another trustee that "the function of the Federal Council of Churches has clearly got to be cut down very considerably from that outlined by Mr. Macfarland. . . ." Mead had already sought to link the prospective church peace endowment with his own World Peace Foundation. Perhaps he still harbored hopes of such an arrangement.[67] But Lynch aggressively defended his right to control the Carnegie grant and Macfarland carefully lined up votes for his proposition. By mid-March he was able to report to Lynch that ten trustees, besides himself and Lynch, had expressed themselves "as believing that the Church Peace Union

[65] Frederick Lynch to Charles S. Macfarland, 20 Feb. 1914, Macfarland to Lynch, 16 Mar. and 6 Apr. 1914, Macfarland to John R. Mott, 6 Apr. 1914, John M. Glenn to Lynch, 13 Feb. 1914, CPU Papers, CRIA. Since Lynch had been secretary of both the Church Peace League and the Federal Council's Commission on Peace and Arbitration it came as little surprise that he suggested that the union "utilize the existing agencies in the Federal Council. . . ." He hardly needed to add his conjecture that "the Federal Council would not object to the closest supervision of their work by the Secretary of the Peace Union" (Lynch to William I. Hull, 19 Feb. 1914, Box 2, Hull Papers, FHL).

[66] Charles S. Macfarland to Frederick Lynch, 5 Mar. 1914, CPU Papers, CRIA.

[67] William I. Hull to Edwin D. Mead, 12 Mar. 1914, Mead to Hull, 16 Mar. 1914, and Frederick Lynch to Hull, 19 Feb. 1914, Box 2, Hull Papers, FHL; [Lynch] to Andrew Carnegie, n.d. [Jan. 1914], rough draft, and Lynch to David H. Greer, 18 Feb. 1914, CPU Papers, CRIA. According to Lynch, Carnegie had first offered the position of secretary of the new organization to Mead, but Mead had felt a loyalty to Edwin Ginn and the World Peace Foundation and had declined. Perhaps he still hoped to channel the funds through the foundation. On previous relations between the foundation and Carnegie, see Mead to Carnegie, 13 Dec. 1913, Box 5, WPF Papers, SCPC, and chap. four, pp. 102-4, 107-10.

should adjust its work to the Federal Council." Four others were generally in favor of cooperation.[68] Those few who opposed full cooperation, he later argued, were mainly those from small denominations "practically unknown 100 miles away from Boston" (a reference to Mead, a Unitarian) and those lacking "acquaintanceship with the churches at large." Macfarland assured Lynch that his own position would not be diminished by the channeling of Church Peace Union funds and projects through the Federal Council. "I am sure we can shape the matter up," he wrote Lynch, "so that the Federal Council can be used by the Church Peace Union in such a way as to magnify the work of the Church Peace Union rather than otherwise."[69]

Within a few months of the founding of the Church Peace Union, Macfarland had accomplished his purpose. The Federal Council had become the major agency for carrying on the work of the union. Very quickly it diverted a sizable portion of the Church Peace Union's yearly income to the support of a new Asiatic Commission of the Federal Council which merged peace work with the more traditional Asian missions concerns of American Protestantism. "The relationship in this matter between the two bodies, the Church Peace Union and the Federal Council of Churches, was easily and effectively established," Macfarland later recalled. "The entire scope of the Federal Council was at once enlarged, and the Church Peace Union had a large, if not a major, part during the critical year of 1914, in the effective establishment of the Council."[70]

The problem of reconciling the wider conception of "Christian unity" represented by the Church Peace Union with the cautious approach toward "federation" of the Federal Council proved less difficult than might have been anticipated. The non-Protestant clergymen—Rabbi Hirsch, Cardinal Gibbons, and Archbishop

[68] [Frederick Lynch] to Andrew Carnegie, n.d. [Jan. 1914], rough draft, Lynch to Charles S. Macfarland, 20 Feb. 1914 and Macfarland to Lynch, 16 Mar. 1914, CPU Papers, CRIA; Lynch to William I. Hull, 19 Feb. 1914, Box 2, Hull Papers, FHL.

[69] Charles S. Macfarland to Frederick Lynch, 16 Mar. and 6 Apr. 1914, CPU Papers, CRIA.

[70] "Minutes of the Meeting of the Executive Committee of the Church Peace Union," 1 May 1914 and Frederick Lynch to Charles Macfarland, 25 Mar. 1914, CPU Papers, CRIA; Macfarland, *Pioneers for Peace*, p. 39. Macfarland, in *Christian Unity in the Making*, implies that Carnegie had agreed at the outset to work through the Federal Council. But the CPU Papers indicate that whatever Carnegie's informal promises, Macfarland and Lynch worked actively to *insure* that the Federal Council would be the main beneficiary of the Carnegie grant. The Church Peace Union had not, as Macfarland later put it, merely "invited" the Federal Council to implement its program. Macfarland, pp. 89, 93.

Glennon—did not appear at any of the Church Peace Union's regular meetings. Neither Lynch nor Macfarland apparently felt called upon to consult them and Lynch had to plead with Archbishop Glennon not to resign, even though he could not attend meetings, because the union needed his name. At least one critic pointed out Lynch's "failure to understand the Catholic view point . . ." and noted that "the majority of the Catholic clergy are very reluctant to work with organizations that do not employ Catholics. . . ." Of the non-Protestant trustees, only Dr. James Walsh, a Catholic layman, regularly participated in the union's direction. A small group of eight or nine Protestant clergymen and laymen comprised the participants in most of the union's meetings.[71]

For all practical purposes the union was soon identical with the Federal Council's Commission on Peace and Arbitration. While participation by non-Protestants faded, Macfarland supplied Lynch with ideas on how to persuade Carnegie that the Federal Council was still promoting "actual union" as well as "mere federation."[72] In October 1914 the trustees even petitioned Carnegie to increase the endowment to the originally requested $10 million so that he, who had "brought the churches of America into union" might become "the one to create the 'United Churches of the World,'" ushering in "that one church . . . for which the Prince of Peace himself prayed."[73] Carnegie was flattered, but declined.

The Church Peace Union's first major undertaking was an International Peace Conference of the Churches on 1 August 1914 at Constance, Switzerland, attended primarily by Protestant ministers and laymen. It was to be followed a week later by a similar conference of Catholic clergymen in Liège, Belgium. Ironically, and perhaps symbolically, it was literally the first guns of war that disrupted this expression of the momentary coalescence of the causes of world peace and church union.

Despite its disruption by the outbreak of war, the International Conference at Constance did leave a legacy. The delegates had to flee Constance on 2 August, but a Continuation Committee, carrying out the mandate of the conference, met several days

---

[71] "Minutes of the Meetings of the Executive Committee and Board of Trustees of the Church Peace Union for the Years 1914-1918," Frederick Lynch to Rev. J. J. Glennon, n.d. [1914], CPU Papers, CRIA; A. W. Kliefoth to William I. Hull, 12 Nov. 1915, Box 3, Hull Papers, FHL.

[72] Charles S. Macfarland to Frederick Lynch, 30 Sept. 1914, CPU Papers, CRIA.

[73] Unsigned [Board of Trustees] to Andrew Carnegie, 15 Oct. 1914, CPU Papers, CRIA.

later in London and formed what came to be known as the "World Alliance for International Friendship Through the Churches." In most respects, the new World Alliance was impossible to distinguish from either the Church Peace Union or the Federal Council's Commission on Peace and Arbitration. It received nearly all of its funds from the Church Peace Union and was directed by the same secretary, Frederick Lynch. The executive committee of the American branch of the World Alliance included sixteen trustees of the Church Peace Union among its twenty-one members. One of the five executive committee members not on the Church Peace Union was Andrew Carnegie's private secretary.[74] The World Alliance's relationship with the Federal Council was equally close. Sidney Gulick, a leading figure in the World Alliance and the Federal Council subsequently commented, ". . . from the standpoint of the Federal Council this World Alliance is identical with the Commission on Peace and Arbitration." The new name, he continued, offered opportunities to bring denominations that were not members of the Federal Council into the projects of the "World Alliance."[75]

The Church Peace Union and the Federal Council responded uncertainly and largely unimaginatively to the crisis of war in 1914. The Federal Council prevailed upon President Wilson to set aside a day of prayer and dispatched an appeal to the churches of the nations at war urging that their members write their relatives in the army to act individually to reduce the horrors of war. The Church Peace Union continued its essay contests and its efforts to get peace sermons preached. As late as December 1914 Lynch referred to his attempts to promote peace sermons as "about the most valuable work we do."[76] Both the Federal Council and the Church Peace Union seem to have been largely preoccupied with the initiation of a campaign for improved relations with Japan. Sidney Gulick, the son of missionary parents and himself a missionary to Japan for twenty-six years, had returned to the United States in 1913 gravely concerned about deteriorating American-Japanese relations. His appeals for Federal Council attention to this matter reinforced a traditional

---

[74] Carnegie Endowment for International Peace, *A Manual of the Public Benefactions of Andrew Carnegie* (Washington, D.C. 1919), pp. 263-64; Macfarland, *Pioneers for Peace*, pp. 46, 49.

[75] Sidney Gulick to Charles P. Watson, 19 May 1916, CPU Papers, CRIA.

[76] *New York Times*, 9 Sept. 1914, 4:5 and 13 Sept. 1914, II, 4:8; Macfarland, *Christian Unity in the Making*, pp. 92, 94; "Report of the Secretary to the Trustees of the Church Peace Union for the Year 1914," pp. 4-5, 11, CPU Papers, CRIA; Frederick Lynch to William I. Hull, 12 Dec. 1914, Box 2, Hull Papers, FHL.

Protestant interest in Asian missions. While action regarding the European war languished, the Federal Council established a new, special commission on Japan and the Church Peace Union diverted at least $10,000 to Gulick's campaign. Such were the Church Peace Union's main signs of activity at a time when, acacording to Lynch himself, it was "receiving many letters daily inquiring whether the church is going to have anything to say or not in this crisis."[77]

By the end of 1914, however, the Church Peace Union had begun to align itself with one side of a domestic issue intimately connected with the European War. In December of 1914 the National Security League had been founded to promote the expansion of the nation's military forces. In response, Oswald Garrison Villard, the editor of *The Nation*, and Hollingsworth Wood, a Quaker lawyer, had organized the American League to Limit Armaments. The organized public controversy over military preparedness had begun. The prewar peace organizations had fallen into silence and inaction. Macfarland and Bishop Greer threw the financial weight of the Church Peace Union on the side of Villard's antipreparedness organization. Bishop Greer enthusiastically committed himself to diverting $10,000 of Church Peace Union funds to what promised to be an active and controversial new peace group and even sought, unsuccessfully, to persuade John R. Mott, the dynamic international organizer of the YMCA and a Church Peace Union trustee, to be president of the league.[78]

Some of the Church Peace Union trustees, particularly those of basically conservative views, opposed such antipreparedness activity. But Lynch, Macfarland, and several other Church Peace Union leaders had, as promoters of moderate social gospel activity on behalf of the Federal Council, found themselves in frequent and cooperative contact with many of the New York humanitarian reformers who were now gravitating toward the peace movement as an expression of social liberalism. The Church Peace Union officers, until now frustrated in their search for a stand that the union might take, apparently concluded that resist-

[77] Frederick Lynch to William I. Hull, 24 Nov. 1914, Box 2, Hull Papers, FHL; "Report of the Secretary to the Trustees of the Church Peace Union for the Year 1914," p. 5, CPU Papers, CRIA; Macfarland, *Christian Unity in the Making*, pp. 87, 89-91; Sidney Gulick to Frederick Lynch, 1 July 1914 and Lynch to Gulick, 3 July 1914, CPU Papers, CRIA.

[78] Oswald Garrison Villard to Francis Jackson Garrison, 22 Dec. 1914, Villard to Lillian Wald, 17 Dec. 1914, David H. Greer to Villard, 22 Dec. 1914, John R. Mott to Villard, 18 Dec. 1914, Villard to Mott, 19 Dec. 1914, and L. Hollingsworth Wood to Villard, 9 Oct. 1915, Oswald Garrison Villard Papers, Houghton Library, Harvard University; Hutchison, *We Are Not Divided*, p. 171.

ance to "militarism" at home represented the clearest mandate for an organization charged with expressing the peace sentiment of the nation's churches. Such a stand would keep the church federation leaders in working alliance with those whose social reform efforts they were backing as part of their social gospel programs. Lynch immediately fired off 10,000 questionnaires to test the sentiments of the nation's clergy on this and related questions.[79]

The results of this questionnaire and his personal contacts with members of the American League to Limit Armaments, the American Union Against Militarism, the American Neutral Conference Committee, and the Woman's Peace Party sustained Lynch in at least a moderate program of antipreparedness work until mid-1916. Throughout 1915, Lynch maintained a great enthusiasm for the "big fight" to save the United States from its own militarists. He began to begrudge the union's overseas financial commitments and cut them back in order to conserve money for use in combating militarism at home. "We are backing the women, we are getting behind the anti-armament leagues," he wrote excitedly.[80] Later he recounted immodestly how peace organizations and peace movement leaders, including Jane Addams and Lillian Wald, had held conferences with him and sought his advice. The Church Peace Union issued messages and appeals calling for moderation and opposed the "present clamor for armament." Even after President Wilson began his own campaign on behalf of preparedness, the Church Peace Union appealed to the public to resist armament increases and set aside $3,000 for use by the American Union Against Militarism to finance a tour by several clergymen in support of its antipreparedness campaign.[81]

[79] *New York Times*, 18 Jan. 1915, 3:4; "Report of the Secretary to the Trustees of the Church Peace Union for the Year 1915," CPU Papers, CRIA.

[80] Frederick Lynch to Benjamin F. Battin, 23 June, 24 July and 28 July 1915, Lynch to Dr. Siegmund-Schultze, 17 July 1915, CPU Papers, CRIA; *New York Times*, 2 July 1915, 10:7 and 17 Dec. 1915, 8:1. See also "Address of the Church Peace Union to the Churches and the People," n.d. and Frederick Lynch to William I. Hull, 23 Feb. 1915, Box 3, Hull Papers, FHL.

[81] "Report of the Secretary to the Trustees of the Church Peace Union for the Year 1915" and "Minutes of the Special Meeting of the Executive Committee of the Church Peace Union," 18 Feb. 1916, CPU Papers, CRIA; "The American Churches and the European War: A Message from the Church Peace Union" (8 Feb. 1915), Division of Intercourse and Education, 1915, CEIP Papers, CUL; Jacob Henry Dorn, *Washington Gladden*, p. 425. Elihu Root, who as head of the Carnegie Endowment had opposed any endowment for a Church Peace Union at the outset, now complained privately to his colleagues in the endowment that the union "has talked more nonsense and done more harm than any organization that I know of in this

But as the campaign for moderate preparedness gained headway, Lynch's opponents within the Church Peace Union and the World Alliance stepped up their efforts to curtail the union's antiarmament agitation. In mid-February 1916 the issue came to a head in connection with an open antipreparedness letter by clergymen to President Wilson. Several signers of the letter, which was sponsored by the union, claimed that after receiving their signatures, it had been altered in such a way as to misrepresent their position. George William Douglas, a leader in the World Alliance, used this incident to rally opposition to Lynch's policies in general.

Many of the trustees of the Church Peace Union, Douglas complained, feared that the union was on the verge of making a "disastrous mistake" by publishing statements representing the views of only one wing of the organization. The union, he insisted, should "not undertake to oppose reasonable preparedness or to meddle with politics." An organization seeking union should not alienate any members unnecessarily and should avoid controversial stands. Particularly, it should be wary of the bad reputation it received by locating its offices near those of the Woman's Peace Party, from which antipreparedness demonstrations were launched. Douglas quickly obtained at least partial support for his complaints from Bishop Hendrix, John R. Mott, William Pierson Merrill, Francis L. Stetson, and George Plimpton of the Church Peace Union, and from several members of the executive committee of the World Alliance. Douglas concentrated his efforts on Sidney Gulick, now a leader in shaping World Alliance policies. Gulick had already been questioning whether it might not be better if the war continued until Germany had been taught a lesson. He was also, despite his new prominence in the overall peace activities of the Federal Council, still primarily concerned with plans for changes in American immigration policies that would lead to better relations with Japan. He was unwilling to make any unnecessary enemies for his Asian programs by taking controversial stands on other issues, and was thus inclined to compromise with Douglas and the foes of antipreparedness.[82]

country, and we are being cursed for it." It was an embarrassment for any organization carrying the Carnegie name to oppose military preparedness. "Minutes of the Annual Meeting of the Board of Trustees," 21 Apr. 1916, CEIP Papers, CUL.

[82] Canon George William Douglas to Sidney Gulick, 26 Jan., 2 Feb., 28 Feb., and 9 Mar. 1916, Nehemiah Boynton to Douglas, 25 Feb. 1916, Eugene Russell Hendrix to Douglas, 4 Mar. 1916, John R. Mott to Douglas, 8 Mar. 1916, Douglas to William Pierson Merrill, 28 Feb. 1916, Gulick to Charles S. Macfarland, 6 Dec. 1915, and unsigned [Gulick] to Douglas, 4 Mar. 1916, CPU Papers, CRIA.

The growing resistance to Lynch's cooperation with the more radical peace and antiarmament organizations coincided with the failure of Macfarland's most ambitious peace undertaking. Throughout most of 1915, the Federal Council had contented itself with the initiation of a war relief program, a message of sympathy to church bodies in Europe, the preparation of a Sunday School course on international peace, and some unfocused musings about an international conference of church bodies after the war.[83] In December 1915, however, Macfarland had embarked on a visit to the church leaders of Europe to reaffirm spiritual ties, obtain information to prepare the American churches for the eventual task of reconstruction and reconciliation, and, hopefully, to engage in a little unofficial diplomacy and initiate steps toward mediation through the churches. He returned with personal conclusions unconducive to further cooperation with the more radical peace organizations. "The present moment is not the time for any definite, concrete, political or semi-political or even nonpolitical overtures for peace," he declared. "A mistaken movement at just this time might work incalculable harm and delay."[84]

The disappointments of Macfarland's mission and the dissension within the Church Peace Union coincided in early 1916 to usher in a period of quiescence in the peace activities of the union and the World Alliance. Since the connection between the churches and the peace movement had been established within the context of the church unity movement and the specific institutional structure of Protestant federation, the requirements of unity and harmony now set limitations on activism in the cause of peace. Peace work must be unifying, not divisive. Macfarland proposed to the Federal Council that "we should restrain the impatience of our various organizations" and should "act quietly and unofficially." He began to talk about "rising above the conflict . . . into a higher spiritual atmosphere."[85]

[83] Macfarland, *Christian Unity in the Making*, pp. 101-3, 105-6; Norman E. Richardson, "International Peace: A Study in Christian Fraternity (A Course of Thirteen Lessons Prepared for the Commission on Christian Education of the Federal Council of the Churches of Christ in America, Cooperating with the Church Peace Union)," Box 59, Fannie Fern Andrews Papers, Arthur and Elizabeth Schlesinger Library, Radcliffe College; "The Church and Permanent Peace; A Summary Report of the First Annual Conference of the National Council of the World Alliance for Promoting International Friendship Through the Churches," 25-27 Apr. 1916, pp. 28-29, Box 3, CPU Papers, SCPC.

[84] Macfarland, *Christian Unity in the Making*, pp. 109-11; Macfarland, *Across the Years*, pp. 101, 107; Hutchison, *We Are Not Divided*, pp. 173-74; "Report of Mission to Europe," Dec. 1915-Jan. 1916, by Charles S. Macfarland, Box 1, FC Papers, SCPC.

[85] Macfarland, *Across the Years*, p. 109; "Report of Mission to Europe," Box 1, FC Papers, SCPC.

At the annual conference of the World Alliance in April 1916 one speaker announced: "How to stop the war we do not inquire. We do not want the war stopped until peace can be established on a basis of justice." Several others called for preparedness or questioned the desirability of peace. Sidney Gulick of the World Alliance denied any opposition to "suitable military equipment" for national defense and privately explained to one correspondent that the best way of stemming preparedness was "not by attacking it and by becoming identified with the anti-preparedness program" but by "setting up a big, positive, constructive Christian program." Such a tactic would unite both sides of the preparedness controversy and eliminate any "virus" in the preparedness agitation "by emphasizing international righteousness and good will." Gulick launched a campaign to establish "Peace Makers Committees" in all the churches and asked the Church Peace Union to set aside fifteen to twenty thousand dollars for this project. Such committees would study Gulick's book on peace and promote cooperation and goodwill. In the thinking of Federal Council leaders, according to Franklin Piper Jr., "peace was now primarily understood to be the period *after* the war, not something to be regained by immediate cessation of hostilities. Arbitration . . . was spoken of mainly as the way to prevent *another* war."[86]

With activity on behalf of antipreparedness or an early peace fading as an instrument for promoting church unity and clerical leadership on popular issues, some of the more enduring concerns of the Federal Council and its agencies reasserted themselves again. Gulick emphasized that his goal for the World Alliance was a program on which "all can and will unite." "Righteousness, good will and the Golden Rule in international affairs" would lie at the heart of such a program. He protested that whatever his

---

[86] "The Church and Permanent Peace" (summary report of annual conference of the World Alliance, 25-27 Apr. 1916), pp. 9-11, Box 2, World Alliance for International Friendship Through the Churches (American Council) Papers, SCPC; Piper, "The Social Policy of the Federal Council," pp. 59-61. Significantly, the Federal Council in Dec. 1916, changed the name of its Commission on Peace and Arbitration to that of Commission on International Justice and Goodwill. On Gulick's ideas and proposals see Sidney L. Gulick to Frederick Lynch, 25 Oct. and 9 Dec. 1915, Gulick to Manley O. Hudson, 13 Nov. 1915, unsigned [Gulick] to E. Guy Talbot, 11 Feb. 1916, unsigned [Gulick] to Dorothy Baldwin, 3 Apr. 1916, Gulick to Mrs. Henry W. Peabody, 8 May 1916, unsigned [Gulick] to John B. Clark, 20 Nov. 1916, CPU Papers, CRIA, and *New York Times*, 9 June 1916, 12:7. In his *Fight for Peace* (New York 1915), Gulick rejected "Tolstoian" pacifism and stressed the common goals of such "juridical pacifists" as Elihu Root and such "military pacifists" as Theodore Roosevelt. The book reflected Gulick's equivocal stand on preparedness; see esp. pp. 36, 38, 175, 178, 180.

sympathies with the antipreparedness groups, he must keep himself "free from the possibility of identification with radical utterances," since his identification with antipreparedness movements might cause "the larger movement for which the World Alliance stands" to suffer.[87] Similarly, John R. Mott, although agreeing with one peace statement proposed for the Federal Council, deemed it "inexpedient and unwise, for the sake of our future influence with the Christians in the countries now at war, to let this document go forth in the name of the American churches." With his eye on the future of international Christian movements, he opposed any peace action which might "cause irritation and offence and . . . handicap our future efforts. . . ."[88] So great was the dissension within the Church Peace Union and so great the desire in all the church peace organizations to maintain internal unity and avoid offense, that Lynch, by fall 1916, abandoned the effort to obtain support for a peace statement "which will mean anything."[89]

As the Federal Council, the Church Peace Union, and the World Alliance backed away from active peace efforts, several of their spokesmen began to dwell upon the theme of the religious value of suffering and sacrifice—a theme that would provide a rising crescendo of enthusiasm for war by 1917. "Self-sacrifice," Canon George William Douglas had written earlier, "is the raw stuff of Christianity—the soil in which to plant Christ's seed. . . ."[90] Frustrated in their search for unifying and acceptable programs for peace, the Federal Council leaders began to discuss with greater appreciation the redeeming values of war. Both Charles Macfarland and John R. Mott expressed fears in the summer of 1916 that the war was having adverse moral effects upon Americans because they were failing "to enter sufficiently into fellowship with the sufferings . . . of our brothers and sisters in Europe," and because Americans, as neutrals, experienced only the

---

[87] Unsigned [Sidney Gulick] to Dorothy Baldwin, 3 Apr. 1916, Gulick to Margaret L. Thomas, 1 July 1916, Gulick to Nellie M. Smith, 1 July 1916, CPU Papers, CRIA.

[88] John R. Mott to Charles S. Macfarland, 19 Oct. 1916, CPU Papers, CRIA.

[89] Frederick Lynch to Sidney Gulick, 11 Sept. 1916, CPU Papers, CRIA. It had also become apparent that in opposing preparedness the Church Peace Union no longer represented the clergy generally. See Ray H. Abrams, *Preachers Present Arms* (New York 1933), pp. 33-37.

[90] George William Douglas, "Christianity and the War" (typed MS, 4 Nov. 1914), p. 11, CPU Papers, CRIA. On the prominence of the themes of suffering and self-sacrifice in clerical discussions of American participation in the war see the speeches at the Federal Council convention of May 1917 in Charles S. Macfarland, ed., *The Churches of Christ in Time of War* (New York 1917), pp. 15, 17, 49, 53, 73, 112-13, 115-16.

commercial effects of the war without the "compensatory influences" of opportunities for "bravery, self-sacrifice, patriotic devotion, and Christian resignation. . . ."[91] This was "not the time to argue with Europe," John R. Mott insisted. It was not the time to criticize the belligerents or attempt peace efforts. Rather, it was a time of "boundless opportunity to serve and to sympathize with men." The trenches, training camps, and prisoner-of-war camps had created favorable conditions for Christian ministry— an opportunity "the like of which we will never again confront."[92]

Such observations on the spiritual values of participation in Europe's sufferings coincided with a rapid expansion of the Federal Council's role in war relief. In 1916 the Federal Council operated on a budget of $84,000. It raised and handled an additional $59,000 of war relief funds. The administration of relief funds was coming to constitute a larger and larger part of the council's activity, and war relief, as an unqualifiedly popular philanthropy, provided a program upon which all denominations and all factions could unite. A speaker at the annual conference of the World Alliance in 1916 characterized relief as "our one clear duty." Whereas peace advocacy and antipreparedness activities threatened to divide and weaken the World Alliance, the "clear duty" of relief would "greatly strengthen our position and influence. . . ." Macfarland, although he later cooperated in a perfunctory bit of private diplomacy with the League to Enforce Peace, gradually shifted his efforts from support of peace organizations to involvement with war relief. A new spirit of unselfishness and self-sacrifice might be awakened, he wrote, by transfusing the war relief movement with "a spiritual light." War relief, he proclaimed, would be "a means of lifting our nation out of its economic and industrial confusion to a higher idealism which shall make us a moral power in the world."[93]

Under Lynch's direction the Church Peace Union had sought, despite sharp differences of opinion among the trustees, to maintain some continuing role in the peace movement. But the ever-widening gulf between the radical and conservative peace organizations made this task increasingly difficult. In the fall of 1916, while the public tension over the issues of preparedness and in-

[91] Charles S. Macfarland, "Is Ours a Moratorium of Christian Faith," *The Survey*, 36 (15 July 1916), 409; John R. Mott to Sidney Gulick, 29 May 1916 and to "Dear Friend," 3 Aug. 1916, CPU Papers, CRIA.

[92] John R. Mott to "Dear Friend," 3 Aug. 1916, CPU Papers, CRIA.

[93] Macfarland, "Is Ours a Moratorium of Christian Faith?" p. 411; Hutchison, *We Are Not Divided*, pp. 57, 172; Piper, "The Social Policy of the Federal Council," pp. 57-58; "The Church and Permanent Peace," p. 13, Box 2, WA Papers, SCPC.

tervention eased, the Church Peace Union made a final attempt to exert leadership within the peace movement. In late October the Church Peace Union financed a "Conference of Peaceworkers" which sought to bring together representatives of such disparate organizations as the Woman's Peace Party of New York, the American Peace Society, the League to Enforce Peace, the Carnegie Endowment, the American Neutral Conference Committee, the World Peace Foundation, and the American Union Against Militarism, and to unite the "peaceworkers" in all these organizations behind a single, unified platform. The Church Peace Union was probably as well suited as any group to attempt such a reconciliation and unification. As nearly as any peace organization, it spanned the political distance between social conservatives, such as Francis Lynde Stetson, J. P. Morgan's lawyer, who now considered all peace activities radical and unwise, and social liberals, like Frederick Lynch, who shared many of the attitudes of the leaders of the American Union Against Militarism, including their identification of the peace movement with social reform.

But the fissure within the peace movement, related as it was to so many other social, political, and occupational attitudes and interests, was simply too wide to be bridged. The conference could agree only on a mild resolution that concerned itself with postwar proposals and peripheral issues. Frederick Lynch and Sidney Gulick, by virtue of their sponsorship of the conference, were appointed to a continuation committee that again sought to discover common ground through a "peace questionnaire" submitted to all those who had been invited to the conference. Less than half replied, and again, even among these "peaceworkers," agreement could be reached only on relatively abstract issues. Questions concerning the desirability of an American initiative in the calling of a neutral conference and of a protest against economic warfare after the present war elicited confused and divergent responses, as did a question that seemed to summarize the proposals of the League to Enforce Peace. A second conference was attempted in early 1917; but by then the Church Peace Union was receiving resignations from several trustees in protest against Lynch's continuing connections with the peace movement. Lynch and Gulick quickly lost enthusiasm for what had already proved a futile endeavor.[94]

94 "Minutes of Conference of Peaceworkers," 26 and 27 Oct. 1916, Box 14, Woman's Peace Party, New York Branch, Correspondence, SCPC; "Minutes of the First Meeting of the Continuation Committee of the Conference of Peaceworkers held at

Frederick Lynch's annual report to the board of trustees of the Church Peace Union in 1917 made little effort to conceal his deep sense of frustration and malaise. This well-financed organization, envisaged by Lynch as an instrument for furthering world peace and church unity and for reestablishing the moral leadership of the clergy on great national issues, had lost its dynamic qualities. Far from exerting leadership in the peace movement, it had succumbed to internal dissension and fallen into inaction.

At the last meeting, he reminded the trustees, they had expressed "almost every shade of opinion" and had divided so evenly on several issues that it had been impossible to frame statements of Church Peace Union attitudes toward the Pope's recent plea for peace or on the threats of war to democracy and free speech. United action was an "utter impossibility." So strictly had the board limited the right of any trustee to speak for the union that Lynch had felt constrained to refuse all interviews from the press and to send out only letters that solicited opinions without expressing any viewpoints on behalf of the union. Lynch suggested some "quiet work" for the organization, but acknowledged that no extensive program was possible "except that of education for the future." He consoled himself with passing reflections on the problems of other peace organizations and their similar rifts among officers, directors, and trustees, but he obviously remained unreconciled to the union's present, imposed state of inaction. He denied that the clergy had become "full of the war spirit" but acknowledged that they saw no alternative now but to prosecute the war to a successful conclusion and plan for a new, postwar world order.[95]

While Lynch pondered the shortcomings of the union's work in the peace movement and waited hopefully for the appearance of new lines of action, the Federal Council had begun to flourish on wartime activity and support. "The war presented the Federal Council with its big opportunity," concludes John A. Hutchison. "It entered the war as a small, obscure organization and it emerged as perhaps the most influential organization in American Protestantism. . . ."[96] The council added a new Commission on

---

the Broadway Tabernacle," 1 Nov. 1916, Conference of Peaceworkers, "Resolution," and "A Peace Questionaire (sic)," Boxes 1 and 2, CPU Papers, SCPC; "Minutes of the Meeting of the Board of Trustees of the Church Peace Union," 5 Oct. 1916 and 1 Mar. 1917, CPU Papers, CRIA; Macfarland, *Pioneers for Peace*, pp. 48-49.

[95] "Report of the Secretary to the Board of Trustees of the Church Peace Union for the Year 1917," pp. 2-16, CPU Papers, CRIA; Frederick Lynch to William I. Hull, 19 July 1917, Box 5, Hull Papers, FHL.

[96] Hutchison, *We Are Not Divided*, p. 175.

Army and Navy Chaplains, administered steadily mounting war relief funds, more than doubled its own budget, and initiated its own *Bulletin* and research department. With the federal government's blessing, it established a "General War-Time Commission of the Churches" to coordinate the war work of the various Protestant denominations and improve moral conditions at home and abroad. As the representative of nearly all the major Protestant denominations, it found itself in demand by the federal government as the most convenient agency through which to reach the various religious groups with messages and appeals.[97]

The council now had a popular and important task to perform on behalf of its member bodies. Its coordination of their war activities solidified its formerly insecure position. When it met in May to "pledge both support and allegiance in unstinted measure," it also announced a war program that embodied many of its continuing concerns. It reaffirmed its moderate social gospel position by warning against the lowering of labor standards during wartime and calling for prohibition as a war measure beneficial to workingmen. It looked toward evangelism in the army and in the training camps and began its campaign to obtain control over the appointment of chaplains.[98]

With the Federal Council enthusiastically throwing itself into wartime programs and the Church Peace Union searching for new avenues through which to exert moral leadership, both were receptive to the federal government's proposal that they assist in the government's wartime propaganda campaign. George Creel's Committee on Public Information proposed to the Church Peace Union that it act as the CPI's agency in carrying on education among the churches in "the moral aims of the war." The federal authorities were impressed, Lynch reported, by "the fact that we had the machinery for bringing together large groups of clergymen and could get ready access to the Churches. . . ."[99]

The League to Enforce Peace, always in search of funds to help finance its campaign, worked through Hamilton Holt, a leader of the league and also a trustee of the Church Peace Union, to secure the opportunity to join in the educational campaign. By the

[97] *Ibid.*, pp. 57, 62-63; Lee, *Social Sources of Church Unity*, pp. 80-81; William Adams Brown, *A Teacher and His Times* (New York 1940), pp. 232, 238-39, 243.

[98] "The Duty of the Church in this Hour of National Need: A Message from the Federal Council of the Churches of Christ in America," 9 May 1917, Box 29, Andrews Papers, SL; *New York Times*, 9 May 1917, 4:3.

[99] "Report of the Secretary to the Board of Trustees of the Church Peace Union for the Year 1917," pp. 28-30, CPU Papers, CRIA.

end of 1917 a new organization had been formed—the National Committee on the Churches and the Moral Aims of the War— with an executive committee composed of five trustees of the Church Peace Union, five members of the League to Enforce Peace, Charles Macfarland representing the Federal Council and Sidney Gulick representing the World Alliance. The Federal Council and World Alliance put their "machinery and resources" at the disposal of the new organization and the Church Peace Union borrowed from its prospective income through 1919 in order to appropriate $65,000 for the wartime educational campaign.[100]

Frederick Lynch did not guide the Church Peace Union into the government's campaign without some misgivings. He had worried earlier that the League to Enforce Peace, with which the Church Peace Union was now allied, had become "so possessed with carrying on the present war that it is losing sight of the large constructive program. . . ." According to one trustee, William Hull, Lynch had actually worked to try to prevent the Church Peace Union from "being tied up first with the League to Enforce Peace and then with a government committee . . . for the sole purpose of 'whooping up the war,' " But the frustrations of trying to continue to formulate peace programs when half of the trustees opposed negotiation in any form and rejected any avenue toward peace except the "thorough thrashing of the Germans," finally convinced Lynch that the only hope for the exercise of moral leadership in international relations by the churches lay in looking beyond the war, not in seeking to end it. Eventually he convinced himself that by working with the government, the Church Peace Union would not only avoid the stigma now attached to all "peace" groups, but also gain the stature and influence necessary to bring church leaders into an influential moral role in the peace settlement and postwar international relations. Noting that "our message might at times be shaped to assist our government in the prosecution of its immediate task . . . ," Lynch nevertheless concluded that acting as the "agent" of the federal government was the Church Peace Union's "greatest opportunity." By November 1917 he had convinced himself that "it is practically the Govern-

---

100 National Committee on the Churches and the Moral Aims of the War, "Announcement," Box 29, Andrews Papers, SL; Carnegie Endowment for International Peace, *Manual of the Carnegie Benefactions*, pp. 265-66; "Minutes of the Annual Meeting of the Church Peace Union," 5 Dec. 1918, pp. 2-3, CPU Papers, CRIA; Warren F. Kuehl, *Hamilton Holt: Journalist, Internationalist, Educator* (Gainesville, Fla. 1960), p. 131.

ment endorsing our program," giving the Church Peace Union "increased effectiveness" as well as "official standing."[101]

The purpose of the campaign of the new National Committee on the Churches and the Moral Aims of the War, in its own words, was "to quicken the spirit of America in support of the President's policies in prosecuting the war for Democracy, International Justice and a League of Nations." Leaders of the committee described their work as "emphatically a war campaign." They promised to give the government every assistance in the prosecution of the war. As part of its "message," the committee endorsed Hamilton Holt's argument that the Allies had been fighting a morally righteous war from the beginning and that the United States had entered the war, not mainly over the issue of neutral rights, but because Russia's collapse threatened defeat for the forces of righteousness. The committee had no intention of advocating a "premature peace"—that is, a peace negotiated before the complete defeat of Germany.[102]

It has been argued, with justification, that the General War-Time Commission of the Churches and the National Committee on the Churches and the Moral Aims of the War acted as moderating forces upon the churches, stressing the most elevated goals of the war and decrying excessive hatred and glorification of war at a time when many clergymen were indulging themselves in ecstacies of war enthusiasm. But despite their relative restraint, these church organizations maintained no standpoint of independent perspective or judgment. John Hutchison reports that he was unable to discover "a single instance in which a voice of criticism was raised against any aspect of the government's conduct." The Federal Council, Hutchison concludes, "simply accepted what the government did and interpreted it in religious terms to the people of the churches."[103]

[101] Frederick Lynch to William I. Hull, 19 July 1917, 26 Sept. 1917, Hull to Jenkin Lloyd Jones, 28 Nov. 1917, Lynch to "Dear Sir," 12 Nov. 1917, Box 5, Hull Papers, FHL.

[102] National Committee on the Churches, "Announcement," Box 29, Andrews Papers, SL; Macfarland, *Pioneers for Peace*, p. 68.

[103] Hutchison, *We Are Not Divided*, pp. 178, 181-82. The most elaborate defense of the moderation of the Federal Council and its agencies during the wartime period is Piper's "The Social Policy of the Federal Council," pp. 89-90, 108-10, 118-19, 158-68, 182-200, 225, 297, 347, 403-4. Despite Piper's often convincing demonstrations of the relative moderation of several Federal Council leaders, his study does not uncover any instances in which the Federal Council or the General War-Time Commission made any public criticism of, or protest against, any policies of the government. Even the infrequent private protests to the War Department appear to have been either extremely mild or concerned with such narrow and limited concerns as the training and appointment of chaplains. See Piper, pp. 264-66, 346-47. Hutchison's con-

The activities of the Committee on the Moral Aims of the War and of the General War-Time Commission of the Churches may have contributed little to the protection of dissent and freedom of conscience or to the maintenance of an independent Christian critique of the state. But they did greatly expand the influence and prestige of the Federal Council and the movement for church unity. The federal government found the Federal Council and the Church Peace Union convenient and efficient agencies through which to transmit its messages to individual Protestant churches and through which to promulgate its policy with the proper moral and spiritual tone; the Federal Council found that the responsibility delegated to it and its adjuncts by the federal government vastly increased its influence among its member denominations and gave it important and unifying projects to administer among the churches. Whereas the church unity leaders had earlier found the peace movement both a source of funds and unifying activity and an expression of the gospel of Jesus, they now found in sanctification of the war for democracy an equally satisfying expression of the Christian virtues of sacrifice and suffering for a righteous cause and an even more promising avenue of advance for the fortunes of the Federal Council. "I believe we have an almost providential opportunity," Frederick Lynch reported to his trustees in 1917.[104]

Of course the programs of the Federal Council, and to some extent those of the Church Peace Union, represented not only the specific impulses of their leaders toward expanded activity, influence, and unity, but also the interests and sentiments of their constituent denominations and individual churches and clergymen. But the pressure from below only enhanced the enthusiasm for war activity. Everywhere the war had shown promise of elevating the stature and influence of the clergy. Church attendance had been increasing and the clergymen felt more deeply needed in communities that were giving increasing attention to war relief, and which were now sending husbands and sons to war. "What a temptation war is to a minister," Harry Emerson Fosdick later

---

clusions would seem to stand. See also William Adams Brown, *The Church in America: A Study of the Present Condition and Future Prospects of American Protestantism* (New York 1922), p. 97 and *A Teacher and His Times*, pp. 223-47.

104 "Report of the Secretary to the Board of Trustees for the Church Peace Union for the Year 1917," pp. 30-31, CPU Papers, CRIA; Piper, "The Social Policy of the Federal Council," p. viii. On the Federal Council's gains in public repute and self-esteem as a result of its wartime activities, see Piper, "The Social Policy of the Federal Council," p. vii; Abrams, *Preachers Present Arms*, p. 79; and Hutchison, *We Are Not Divided*, pp. 62-63, 175.

reflected. The war provided the preacher with "attentive audiences." It created "a medium of deeply stirred and well-nigh unanimous emotion in which the preacher's work can become thrilling." If "self-sacrifice" was truly the "raw stuff of Christianity," then the war might prove the instrument for that rejuvenation of Christian spirit for which leading clergymen had been praying. Protestant leaders spoke in breathless tones of the "priceless opportunities" and the unprecedented possibilities for evangelism. The Federal Council only solidified its position with its constituents by pursuing a vigorous wartime program.[105]

The positive attractions of embarking upon nationalistic, wartime programs encouraged the Federal Council and the Church Peace Union to cut all ties with the increasingly radical peace organizations. Macfarland refused to cooperate with the Civil Liberties Bureau of the American Union Against Militarism in efforts on behalf of conscientious objectors, noting that the council had "to act in a representative capacity" and "had to be very careful to consider the psychology of the people."[106] Frederick Lynch refused to sign his name to the call for the First American Conference on Democracy and Terms of Peace, arguing that by keeping himself free from radical associations he could best preserve the "high potency of good" present in the organizations to which he owed his primary allegiance—the World Alliance and the Church Peace Union.[107] By the spring of 1917 active participation in the peace movement of a specifically religious nature had devolved on a small and hitherto relatively quiet organization that had come increasingly to view the peace movement as integrally related to a Christian-inspired, radical social reconstruction. This new organization was the Fellowship of Reconciliation.

The origins of the Fellowship of Reconciliation in the United States were quiet, unobtrusive, and deliberately informal. An organization of the same name had been founded in Britain in December 1914 by pacifists who found compliance with the Conscription Acts incompatible with their understanding of the Christian ethic. Although the British Fellowship of Reconciliation

[105] Lee, *Social Sources of Church Unity*, p. 80; Hutchison, *We Are Not Divided*, pp. 62-63; Harry Emerson Fosdick, *The Living of These Days: An Autobiography* (New York 1956), p. 121; Brown, *The Church in America*, pp. 26, 65-66; Macfarland, ed., *The Churches of Christ in Time of War*, pp. 15, 17, 27, 32, 49, 68-69, 80-81.

[106] Hutchison, *We Are Not Divided*, p. 184.

[107] Frederick Lynch to Louis P. Lochner, 10 May 1917, in Clayton R. Lusk, ed., *Revolutionary Radicalism: Report of the Joint Legislative Committee of the State of New York* (Albany 1920), Part I, Vol. I, pp. 992-93.

regarded compromises of the Christian ethic as the source of "all social disorder" its members concerned themselves primarily with the immediate issue of conscientious objection to service in war. Some segments of American opinion were inclined to be quite sympathetic to conscientious objectors in England during the first years of the war, and the leader of the British Fellowship, Henry Hodgkin, found considerable interest in his work in some Christian circles in the United States when he visited in 1915.[108]

Hodgkin's visit culminated in a two-day conference at Garden City, Long Island, at which an American version of the Fellowship of Reconciliation was formed. The conference, according to Frederick Lynch's analysis, drew primarily upon three distinguishable groups: "Y.M.C.A. leaders, Quakers, and non-Quaker social workers, reformers and philanthropists." Several influential figures in American Protestantism attended, including John R. Mott, prominent evangelist, General Secretary of the American YMCA, and master organizer of international Christian movements. Mott had already been instrumental in arranging Hodgkin's visit. At least eight of the trustees of the Church Peace Union were invited to attend.[109]

The members of the conference appear to have been drawn toward participation in the new organization by a variety of motives. Many were Quakers, like Hodgkin himself, who had involved themselves deeply in secular activities and the secular peace movement. Such men and women now sought to find mutual support for a more uncompromising stand on the peace issue than the secular peace organizations were taking, a stand more in keeping with the traditional Quaker testimony. Others, distressed by what they considered the shallow and inert Christianity of the present churches, foresaw in the founding of a Fellowship of Reconciliation in America an opportunity "to enter into the fellowship of the sufferings of the world," to share in Europe's sorrows, and thus to engender a "spiritual awakening." Many participants, as the conference's printed statement expressed it, were

---

[108] "The Fellowship of Reconciliation," *The Nation*, 103 (21 Dec. 1916), 585; Lilian Stevenson, *Towards a Christian International: The Story of the International Fellowship of Reconciliation*, new and enlarged ed. (London 1941), p. 3; Norman Thomas, *The Conscientious Objector in America* (New York 1923), pp. 58-59; "The Fellowship of Reconciliation: Some General Considerations" (typed draft of statement), Box 22, Fellowship of Reconciliation Papers, SCPC.

[109] E. Charles Chatfield, Jr., "Pacifism and American Life, 1914 to 1941," Ph.D. diss., Vanderbilt University, 1965, pp. 70, 124; "Names of Persons Invited to Conference" and "Names of Persons Who Have Accepted Invitation (*sic*) to Garden City Conference," Box 1, FOR Papers, SCPC; John R. Mott to William I. Hull, 7 Aug. 1915, Box 3, Hull Papers, FHL.

"profoundly disturbed by the confused utterance of the Christian Churches concerning the war and other great social questions." They sought to "explore together the religious ethic" and to re-establish a solid moral basis for private affirmations and public action in time of crisis.[110]

Discussions at the founding conference at Garden City ranged broadly and revealed wide differences of opinion. Some advocated supporting the League to Enforce Peace; others called for a commitment to the abolition of the competitive economic system. But the dominant group expressed views that were specifically concerned with the application of uncompromising religious principles to the question of participation in war. Gilbert Beaver, a prominent Quaker and YMCA worker who became the first chairman of the Fellowship of Reconciliation, pointed out that men had come to take the Sermon on the Mount "on a sliding scale," carrying out its principles only to the extent that public opinion approved. The time had come, he contended, "for some to go the whole way." Others insisted upon an uncompromising application of the principles of Christian love, whatever the consequences. The conference ultimately adopted a set of principles uncompromising enough that only forty-one of the approximately seventy persons present found themselves able to give complete assent and accept full membership in the new Fellowship of Reconciliation.[111]

The members of the new organization declared themselves "unable to take part in war." They proclaimed that love, "as revealed and interpreted in the life and death of Jesus Christ" was the "only power by which evil can be overcome." Since war involved not the attempt to overcome evil by converting it to righteousness, but rather the attempt to overcome evil with evil, it could never succeed. Members regarded themselves as called upon to undertake "a quest after an order of society in accordance with the mind of Christ." Christians were "forbidden to wage war" but obliged to seek a world order in which all relations would be based upon love.[112] An aura of traditional Quaker pacifism, although

110 *The Survey*, 35 (18 Dec. 1915), 331; "Minutes of the Garden City Conference of the Fellowship of Reconciliation," pp. 2, 4, 6, Box 1, FOR Papers, SCPC; Charles Chatfield, *For Peace and Justice: Pacifism in America, 1914-1941* (Knoxville 1971), pp. 38-41.

111 "Minutes of the Garden City Conference of the Fellowship of Reconciliation," pp. 3-5, 7-8.

112 "Principles Agreed to at the Conference Which Gave Rise to the Fellowship of Reconciliation" (printed sheet), Box 1, FOR Papers, SCPC; *The Survey*, 35 (18 Dec. 1915), 331; "The Fellowship of Reconciliation" (printed statement, n.d.), Box 22, FOR Papers, SCPC.

not of an extremely narrow or literal quality, dominated the early statements of the fellowship. All the major offices were held by Quakers, and Quakers dominated the early meetings of the guiding "Fellowship Committee." But non-Quakers, and even non-Christians eventually came to play a larger and larger role in the Fellowship of Reconciliation.

At the outset, the fellowship deliberately shunned formal organization. The group emphasized that it was a "fellowship," not a league, society, or association. "We are not an organization with a platform for the purpose of pushing particular propaganda," wrote one of the officers, "but a group of persons who find the need of fellowship in expressing the ideals to which we are committed."[113] A memorandum for the organizing conference had warned at the outset against certain "dangers to be avoided." Among these were overorganization, a "paper membership," becoming too middle-class, and becoming a political organization. The Garden City conference sought no publicity. A fellowship statement on "The Nature of Our Task" stressed the desire "to avoid formalism," and Dr. Rufus Jones, the Quaker editor and writer, reminded the members that "the movement is so essentially a thing of the spirit that when the spirit is lost the organization is dead."[114]

Even with its uncompromising moral vision, the fellowship sought to set forth no more than the most tentative of programs. Hodgkin had warned after the initial conference, "Big visions are very dangerous, unless we start at once to work them out in little things. Day by day we are to be finding out what the Fellowship means." Thus the fellowship could be no "ordinary organization of the modern type." It could adopt "no definite and complete program" since its dynamic lay in its individual members. It could only sustain "fearless individual thinking and cautious social experiment" and gradually discover what it might become.[115]

By mid-1916 the Fellowship of Reconciliation had already be-

113 Secretary pro tem. of the Fellowship of Reconciliation to [unaddressed], n.d., Box 22, FOR Papers, SCPC; Thomas, *The Conscientious Objector*, p. 54; the *News Sheet* of the Fellowship of Reconciliation, U.S.A., No. 1 (Oct. 1916), p. 4, Box 29, FOR Papers, SCPC (hereafter cited as *News Sheet*).

114 "Memoranda for Garden City Conference" (mimeographed sheet, n.d. [1915], Box 22, FOR Papers, SCPC; "From the Council of the Fellowship of Reconciliation: The Nature of Our Task," n.d., and "Minutes of the Garden City Conference of the Fellowship of Reconciliation," 11 and 12 Nov. 1915, p. 7, Box 1, FOR Papers, SCPC.

115 Henry Hodgkin to Members of the Fellowship of Reconciliation in America, 19 Nov. 1915 and "From the Council of the Fellowship of Reconciliation: The Nature of Our Task," n.d., pp. 3-4, 12, Box 1, FOR Papers, SCPC.

gun to give evidence of discovering its "natural," and eventually irresistible, direction of development. Fellowship leaders had insisted at the beginning that they viewed war "not as an isolated phenomenon but as only one out of many unhappy consequences of the spiritual poverty of society."[116] But if war and other social evils were the results of a common spiritual failing in the ordering of society, the inescapable conclusion was that the whole basis of society, in social and industrial matters as well as in international relations, should be radically reconstructed along the lines of the proper spiritual principles of Christian love. Rufus Jones expressed this broadening of the fellowship's initially rather narrow pacifism into wider social concerns in a paragraph he proposed for insertion into a fellowship statement of "General Considerations":

> It must not for a moment be supposed that war is the only form of evil which is inconsistent with the spirit of the kingdom. It happens at this crisis that war stands out in all its horror as a violation of the way of love and our minds are of necessity occupied with this one tragedy to the obliteration of other forms of social wrongs. But we can not stop the ministry of reconciliation until we have applied the remedial force of love to every feature of the social life which works wrong and injustice to any of our fellowmen, or to any groups of them, anywhere.[117]

Another fellowship paper declared that the war was "disclosing the spirit of anti-Christ in sordid commercialism, industrial strife and social injustice." The fellowship began to consider such topics as penal reform, race relations, and industrial conflict. It invited radical social gospel exponents such as Walter Rauschenbusch and Willard Sperry to address the 1916 conference, and soon added Norman Thomas of the American Union Against Militarism to its staff. Its recommendation to the members for preparatory reading for its 1916 conference included works by Henry George, Walter Rauschenbusch, George Herron, and Jane Addams. The entire fellowship was clearly drifting toward increased involvement in issues of domestic social reform and many of its members were "integrating their pacifism with the demand for drastic social reorganization."[118]

116 Quoted in Chatfield, "Pacifism and American Life," p. 123. See also "From the Council of the Fellowship of Reconciliation: The Nature of Our Task," n.d., p. 11, Box 1, FOR Papers, SCPC.

117 Rufus M. Jones to Edward Evans, 3 Aug. 1916, Box 1, FOR Papers, SCPC.

118 "Minutes of the Meeting of the Central Committee of the Fellowship of Reconciliation," 13 Oct. 1916, "Minutes of the Meeting of the Council of the Fellowship of

The approach of American intervention in the war served only to accelerate the fellowship's movement toward a broader, more radical social gospel position. New members such as Norman Thomas, Walter Rauschenbusch, Bishop Paul Jones, and Harry F. Ward, and fuller participation by Helena Dudley, a settlement-house worker, Jessie Wallace Hughan, a socialist, and John Haynes Holmes of the American Union Against Militarism reinforced the fellowship's tendencies toward support of fundamental social reconstruction. A *News Sheet* was established late in 1916 to increase cohesion and intercommunication within the fellowship, now an organization of some 240 members. Social radicals such as Jessie Hughan and Helena Dudley employed the pages of the *News Sheet* to evoke sympathy for striking workers, to call for a new appreciation of socialism and an identification with workingmen, and to demonstrate how closely the "roots of war" were "bound in with business expansion." Willard Sperry discussed "The Seeds of War in the Social Order," and Norman Thomas placed war within the context of the multiple evils of a ruthless, competitive social order.[119]

In February 1917, with war imminent, the Fellowship of Reconciliation published an open letter warning that war would "arrest social progress for untold years" and ultimately defeat its own ends. The signers of the letter argued that evil could only be overcome with good and urged that the nation risk the application of love to the international crisis. Mankind, they argued, could draw upon "inexhaustible resources of love and good will" which had hitherto been little trusted in the resolution of conflicts in "social, industrial and international relations."[120] As war approached, pressures for cooperation with other active peace organizations increased. Norman Thomas, Emily Balch, Hollingsworth Wood, John Haynes Holmes, Jane Addams, and others provided links between the fellowship and the Woman's Peace Party

Reconciliation," 20-21 Oct. 1916, "Outline of Partial Program Tentatively Suggested by the Fellowship Committee," 19 Feb. 1916, "Books Suggested for Fellowship of Reconciliation Conference at Ocean Grove, N.J.," 13-16 Apr. 1916, "Fellowship Papers" (typed sheet dated 1916), and E. W. Evans to Members of the Fellowship Committee, 11 Apr. 1916, Boxes 1 and 22, FOR Papers, SCPC; Chatfield, "Pacifism and American Life," p. 223.

119 *News Sheet*, No. 1 (Oct. 1916), pp. 6-10; "The Fellowship of Reconciliation: Outline of Personnel and Functions of Committees" (typed copy from Minutes of the Fellowship Committee meeting, 13 Apr. 1917), and Norman Thomas to Members and Friends of the Fellowship, 24 Mar. 1917, Box 22, FOR Papers, SCPC; Edward W. Evans to Margaret Lane, 15 June 1916, WPPNY, Correspondence, SCPC; Chatfield, "Pacifism and American Life," pp. 207-11.

120 The Fellowship of Reconciliation to Men and Women of Good Will Throughout the United States, 10 Feb. 1917, *The Survey*, 37 (3 Mar. 1917), 620-21.

and the American Union Against Militarism. Gilbert Beaver, the chairman of the fellowship, became a delegate to the First American Conference on Democracy and Terms of Peace while Darwin Messerole, Emily Balch, Paul Jones, Sidney Strong, Helena Dudley, and Norman Thomas served simultaneously on the Fellowship of Reconciliation and on organizations involved in the planning for the People's Council. The fellowship was to serve for some of its members as a refuge in which to seek mutual support for private antiwar affirmations. But its leaders were also beginning to open avenues along which other previously apolitical pacifists might move toward social action.[121]

With American intervention and the establishment of military conscription, the Fellowship of Reconciliation embarked upon a dual wartime program: activity on behalf of conscientious objectors and elaboration of a radical social gospel philosophy of which pacifism was now an integral component. Edward W. Evans, the fellowship's national secretary, who adhered to a less socially activist and more traditional Quaker pacifism, worried about presentations of radicalism "in an inflamatory, bitter or purely obstructionist way" and purely economic critiques of capitalism. But despite such hesitancies, the organization increasingly embraced the goals of the radical social gospel. The Fellowship Committee recommended in May 1917 that the fellowship take out membership in the Child Labor Association, the Consumers' League, and the American Association for Labor Legislation. The November 1917 News Sheet proclaimed, "One of our most important lines of work is to make known our fundamental message and ideas to the working class on whom the church is losing its hold." It called for members "to establish points of contact with class conscious workers" and recommended several works by Socialist spokesmen.[122]

At the same time, Norman Thomas and Hollingsworth Wood moved to place the radical labor issue at the focus of the 1917 annual conference of the fellowship. As a result of their efforts the program included the Reverend Harry F. Ward, an increasingly radical exponent of the social gospel, Joseph D. Cannon, organizer for the Mine, Mill and Smelter Workers, and Elizabeth Gurley Flynn, speaking on behalf of the IWW. Arturo Giovannitti of

---

121 For an example of Fellowship of Reconciliation encouragement of cooperation with radical peace organizations see News Sheet, No. 2 (May 1917), p. 4.

122 News Sheet, No. 4 (Nov. 1917), p. 4; Edward W. Evans to Norman Thomas, 15 Nov. 1917, Evans to Gilbert Beaver, 24 Jan. 1918, and "Minutes of Meeting of Fellowship Committee of the Fellowship of Reconciliation," 17 May 1917, Boxes 1 and 2, FOR Papers, SCPC.

the IWW was apparently also invited to speak. Edmund Chaffee reported on a meeting of the New York Branch of the fellowship in the People's House, a center for the discussion of "liberal ideas" set up by radical groups in New York City, where the committee "felt they could best learn the point of view of the working classes." The topic was "Christianity and the Class-conscious Worker." Harry F. Ward and a Socialist spokesman shared the platform.[123]

Meanwhile Norman Thomas, Harry F. Ward, Willard Sperry, and others sought to explore the full implications of the interconnection between uncompromising pacifism and a radical social gospel in the fellowship's new organ, *The New World*. The first issue, in January 1918, featured Willard Sperry's "The Seeds of War in the Social Order," in which he followed the pattern of the postintervention, radical peace movement by turning the cutting edge of his criticism inward upon American society. The enemies of the American Christian, he warned, "are not those of another race or state. They are those of his own household. . . ." The "spirit of Anti-Christ," as manifested in the war, was not merely "a European phenomenon":

> If the apostles of Anti-Christ are marching back and forth across modern Europe . . . the same spirit is also sitting in our counting houses, stock exchanges . . . mills, mines, slums. . . . This evil genius of an un-Christian attitude toward life is the same in the Colorado mines and the New England mills and on the New York curb that it is in Belgium. . . . It can kill a man as dead with a starvation wage as with a piece of shrapnel shell. It can mutilate childhood as effectively with a loom as with a bayonet. . . . It is not, therefore, Anti-Christ in Europe which concerns the sober American half so much as Anti-Christ in his own country and his own city. . . .[124]

The "spirit of Anti-Christ" that manifested itself both in war and social injustice, according to Sperry, was simply the spirit of competition, "unconsciously latent and operative in our whole social order." Norman Thomas and others drew the obvious conclusion that "War will not be eliminated from the world while the spirit of war remains in our economic and industrial systems." They called for the "one untried remedy" to America's "funda-

---

123 *News Sheet*, No. 4 (Nov. 1917), pp. 1, 3; No. 5 (Mar. 1918), p. 2; Edward Evans to Norman Thomas, 15 Nov. 1917, Box 1, FOR Papers, SCPC.

124 *The New World*, 1 (Jan. 1918), 2, 14-16. The periodical was later retitled *The World Tomorrow*.

mentally unchristian" industrial order: "root-and-branch" application of the Christian gospel. The churches themselves had failed to see this, had allied themselves with the government and the "industrial status quo." The churches had so occupied themselves with promoting devotion to the state, that they had maintained no independent moral position from which to launch the needed Christianizing of the social order. Only groups that combined allegiance to the teachings of Jesus with a radical social vision could point the way toward the new order that was soon to come. That was the kind of organization the Fellowship of Reconciliation was now becoming. "We must have *this* revolution," Thomas warned, "or accept a revolution of another kind."[125]

Initially, the Fellowship of Reconciliation had attracted "the interest and even the allegiance of some who were leaders in the religious life of the country." Even then, it had embodied an implied criticism of such organizations as the Federal Council and the Church Peace Union which had contributed to the "confused utterances of the Christian churches on the war and other great social questions." Although increasingly critical of the major church organizations, the Fellowship had later sought, with little success, to persuade the Federal Council and the Church Peace Union to take up the cause of conscientious objection. It would be "unfortunate for religion," Norman Thomas warned, if the major church organizations allowed the struggle for freedom of conscience to "pass over largely to those who avow themselves the foes of all organized religion. . . ."[126] By 1918 the fellowship had clearly rejected any semblance of a role as a peace organization of the established churches. Norman Thomas, for instance, remarked early in 1918 that he had "no desire to make any defense of 'Christianity' but a very eager one to see what we can do to try to apply the spirit of Jesus to the problems of our day." Several of the fellowship's major leaders—Thomas, A. J. Muste, and Harry F. Ward—were already in the process of transformation into leaders of social and political radicalism. Others of devout and evangelical backgrounds, including those such as Kirby Page, Sherwood Eddy, and Harold Gray (whom Charles Chatfield categorizes as the "Y secretaries"), were finding the Fellowship of

---

[125] *The New World*, 1 (Jan. 1918), 4-6, 15; 1 (Feb. 1918), 30, 42-43; 1 (Mar. 1918), 57.

[126] *The Survey*, 35 (18 Dec. 1915), 331; Norman Thomas to Frederick Lynch, 23 June 1917, Box 5, Hull Papers, FHL; Thomas, *The Conscientious Objector*, p. 55; Chatfield, *For Peace and Justice*, p. 57.

Reconciliation a way station on the passage from religious pacifism to broader social concerns.[127]

Except for Quakers, no leading clergymen of power and influence in their denominations remained active in the fellowship by 1918. New members were more likely to be little-known young clergymen like William Fincke, a Presbyterian minister forced out of his church because of his opposition to the war. Fincke, like a number of others in the fellowship, moved from simple pacifism to a more general social radicalism and eventually became director of the Presbyterian Labor Temple in New York and a prominent figure in strike support and radical political action. A. J. Muste, in Boston, followed a similar pattern of conversion—first to pacifism and the Fellowship of Reconciliation, and then to strike support and radical political action.[128]

The Fellowship of Reconciliation had served to encourage the realization by some narrowly religious pacifists of the "social implications of war" and what Chatfield calls "the positive obligations of their 'non-resistant' faith."[129] In the process it had substituted a radical social vision for the milder, more compromising social gospel of the Federal Council. As Norman Thomas had observed, the fellowship would "not amount to much" unless its members thought out the implications of their position in industrial as well as international affairs. As they did so, they came "to view war as an integral part of an unjust social order." While such organizations as the Federal Council concluded optimistically that they could preserve and extend justice and democracy through the violence of a "defensive" war, the fellowship insisted that pacifism must become an integral part of the method for reforming a competitive, exploitative, and therefore war-creating economic and social system.[130]

Other peace organizations had discovered important interrela-

[127] Norman Thomas to H.W.L. Dana, 9 Jan. 1918, Box 1, H.W.L. Dana Papers, SCPC; J. Neal Hughley, *Trends in Protestant Social Idealism* (New York 1948), pp. 89-90; A. J. Muste, "Sketches for an Autobiography," in Nat Hentoff, ed., *The Essays of A. J. Muste* (Indianapolis 1967), pp. 46-86; Harry Fleischman, *Norman Thomas: A Biography* (New York 1964), pp. 54-64; Chatfield, *For Peace and Justice*, pp. 43-55 and "Pacifism and American Life," pp. 139, 146-47, 149, 458.

[128] Chatfield, *For Peace and Justice*, pp. 49-50; Muste, "Sketches for an Autobiography," pp. 46-86.

[129] Chatfield, "Pacifism and American Life," pp. 110, 149, 152.

[130] Norman Thomas to William I. Hull, 25 May 1917, Box 5, Hull Papers, FHL; Chatfield, *For Peace and Justice*, p. 66; *The Survey*, 37 (3 Mar. 1917), 620-21; "The Fellowship of Reconciliation," *The Nation*, 103 (21 Dec. 1916), 585; Stevenson, *Christian International*, p. 2.

tionships, some of them merely tactical and temporary, between the peace movement and their other social, political, and occupational concerns. But the Fellowship of Reconciliation went beyond them in envisaging the peace movement as a central expression of what it believed to be the only eternally moral, valid, and effective means of social reform: the method of nonviolence, which alone employed means that would not distort the end of a peaceful and reconciled social order. In the 1930s the impulse of the fellowship leaders to "far-reaching reform" would come into "conflict with their refusal to sanction violence in any cause."[131] But the fellowship's initial commitment to pacifism under all circumstances, and its fusion of that commitment with a radical social vision, proved one of the most enduring legacies of the early twentieth century peace movement. Its influence was to reappear in the reform philosophies of a later generation.

[131] Chatfield, *For Peace and Justice*, pp. 191-97.

CHAPTER TEN

Conclusion

THE brief ascendancy of the People's Council in 1917 and the maturing of the Fellowship of Reconciliation early in 1918 conveniently mark the conclusion of the early twentieth century phase of the peace movement in the United States. Activity by these and other organizations continued and the struggle over the League of Nations lay ahead, but by the beginning of 1918 the possibilities of the peace movement's recent course of development had been thoroughly explored.

The peace movement had gained an impetus during the opening years of the twentieth century from America's increased international involvements. Commercial growth, the Spanish-American War, territorial expansion, a ripening crusade for foreign missions, and prospects for an Anglo-American diplomatic rapprochement had all contributed to increased interest in international relations. The peace movement, now self-consciously "practical" in its programs for a world court and international arbitration and uncritically nationalistic in its vision of a world order reshaped in the American image, had begun increasingly after 1905 to win the support of America's social and political elite. For a decade after 1905 it had remained a highly respectable and uncontroversial reform movement, enlisting the energies of such professional groups as the international lawyers and attracting businessmen who sought to bolster their images as civic leaders by participating in "forward-looking" philanthropies. Generously endowed by Edwin Ginn and Andrew Carnegie, the new peace foundations attracted the solicitations of scholars with research programs and of church unity leaders who identified world peace with their own particular goals.

Although a great variety of groups had lent at least perfunctory support to the peace movement before 1914, the dominant bias of the movement had been toward the association of peace with stability. To many Americans their nation's increasing international involvements not only promised economic benefits and the psychic satisfactions of "world leadership"; they also awakened

381

fluttering anxieties about American entanglement in a world still insufficiently civilized and self-restrained. The peace movement expressed optimistic expectations of surmounting the dangers of international instability by reforming the world's international relations and institutions to conform with American models. Peace, in Robert Wiebe's succinct summary, "connoted order and stability, the absence of violence, the supremacy of reason and law."[1] The identification of peace with order was not unrelated to the predominance of conservatives and moderates in the peace movement in the prewar years. Conservatives occasionally carried the precepts of the peace movement back into their discussions of industrial conflicts, their encomiums of judges and the domestic judicial system, and their general defenses of constitutionalism and legalism. The more radical social reformers of the period, by contrast, were inclined to ignore the prewar peace movement, finding it too abstract, too far removed from pressing internal problems, and too much the province of groups unsympathetic to fundamental social reform.

With the outbreak of World War I, the peace movement in the United States began a process of transmutation. Most of the prewar peace organizations, continuing to associate peace with order, stability, and the absence of disruptive change, looked ahead to the postwar establishment of a court or league that would accomplish such ends. Nationalistic in temper and pro-Allied in sympathies, they remained uncritical of American policies and institutions. Many of them yearned more intently for Germany's total defeat than they did for an early, mediated end to the war. Meanwhile, however, new groups such as the social workers, the woman suffragists, and a few of the social gospelers had come to fear war and military preparedness as threats to the progress of their favored social reforms. Convinced that prolongation of the war and the diversion of funds and public attention to military expansion would undermine their social programs and create a political atmosphere uncongenial to the promotion of their reforms, these groups created new peace organizations that associated peace with social change, reform, and the progress of "democratization." By 1915 and 1916 major peace organizations, for the first time in the twentieth century, were calling for the reform of *American* institutions and *American* foreign policy.

By 1918 the full implications of the new association of peace with fundamental social reform had been explored by such new organizations as the Fellowship of Reconciliation and the People's

[1] Robert H. Wiebe, *The Search for Order, 1877-1920* (New York 1967), p. 260.

Council. The People's Council had structured its organization so as to provide a popular instrument through which to achieve peaceful overthrow of the present, "unrepresentative" federal government. It unabashedly linked agitation for peace with admiration for the Russian Revolution. The Fellowship of Reconciliation, while finding inadequacies in the "philosophy" of the People's Council, still associated peace with a new social order in which the war-breeding competitiveness of the old order would be eliminated through social reorganization. Many of those who had entered the fellowship as "simple pacifists" soon concluded that war could only be ended by a domestic social revolution that would eliminate "the seeds of war in the social order."[2] For the old peace organizations and their successor, the League to Enforce Peace, the peace movement remained largely a search for order and stability. But for the antipreparedness, antiwar groups after 1915, peace came to connote, not "order and stability," but movement, reform, even revolution.

Thus the peace movement had thoroughly transformed itself between 1905 and 1917. Few other reform movements had experienced such discontinuities of leadership and support. For obvious reasons, those who led organizations that opposed war in 1905 or 1910 did not become leaders in the organizations that opposed war in 1917. Of the forty-five leading international lawyers in the American Society of International Law and the American Society for Judicial Settlement of International Disputes, not one became a member of the People's Council or the Fellowship of Reconciliation. None of the scholars from the Carnegie Endowment or the businessmen from the New York Peace Society joined either of these radical antiwar organizations. Only one of the trustees of the Church Peace Union remained active in the Fellowship of Reconciliation after April 1917. Of the 218 men and women who served as officers of the American Peace Society between 1900 and 1917, only fifteen associated themselves with either the American Union Against Militarism, the American Neutral Conference Committee, or the Woman's Peace Party, and only five participated after April 1917 in either the People's Council or the Fellowship of Reconciliation.[3]

[2] On the Fellowship of Reconciliation's view of Scott Nearing, head of the People's Council, see *The New World*, 1 (Apr. 1918), 86. The phrase "the seeds of war in the social order," is taken from Willard Sperry's article of the same title in *ibid.* (Jan. 1918), 14-16. See also E. Charles Chatfield, Jr., "Pacifism and American Life 1914 to 1941," Ph.D. diss., Vanderbilt University, 1965, pp. 110, 129-52, 458.

[3] Information on participation in the various organizations is derived from the sources on each organization listed in the footnotes of the chapter in which that

Changes in the personnel of major peace organizations in New York City and Chicago provide one of the best measures of short-term discontinuities in the leadership of the peace movement. In November 1914, three months after the war began, the Chicago Peace Society listed 409 individuals as members. Of this group, only fifteen persons subsequently became members in 1917 of the Chicago Conference Committee on Terms of Peace, an adjunct of the American Conference for Democracy and Terms of Peace and one of the precursors of the People's Council.[4] In New York City, out of more than eight hundred regular members of the New York Peace Society during 1913-1914, only two persons, less than one-quarter of one percent of the membership, participated in 1917 in the planning and organization of the People's Council. Similarly, only two of the earlier New York Peace Society members maintained a continuing relationship with the Fellowship of Reconciliation after the spring of 1917. Less than two percent of the New York Peace Society's 1913-1914 members had even given active support to the antipreparedness work of the American Union Against Militarism in 1915-1916.[5]

Such radical discontinuities in leadership and participation in the peace movement make it impossible even to suggest a profile of the typical "peace advocate" or "peace worker" or member of the peace movement during this period. During this era of progressive reform, the peace movement at various times attracted such diverse "progressives" as Jane Addams and Lyman Abbott, Scott Nearing and Austen G. Fox, Amos Pinchot and George W. Perkins, S. S. McClure and John Reed, Max Eastman and Theodore Marburg. But even the great diversities within progressivism do not begin to suggest the range of political and social view-

organization is initially analyzed. The one trustee of the Church Peace Union who apparently continued participating in the Fellowship of Reconciliation after early 1917 was Peter Ainslie. Of the American Peace Society officers, only Jane Addams, Louis Lochner, William I. Hull, Jenkin Lloyd Jones, and May Wright Sewall appear to have taken part in either the People's Council or the Fellowship of Reconciliation. Among the most active and dedicated peace workers of the prewar peace movement, only Lochner and Hull continued on into these radical peace organizations.

4 Chicago Peace Society, "Members" (mimeographed sheets), 16 Nov. 1914, Box 5, Jane Addams Papers, Swarthmore College Peace Collection; "Members of the Chicago Conference Committee on Terms of Peace" (mimeographed sheets [1917]), and "Chicago Permanent Conference Committee on Terms of Peace" (typed sheets [1917]), American Conference for Democracy and Terms of Peace Papers, SCPC.

5 On sources of data see above, n. 3. Of the New York Peace Society members, only Alfred Boulton and Judah Magnes joined the People's Council and only Hollingsworth Wood and John Haynes Holmes remained active in the Fellowship of Reconciliation.

points held by those who participated in one phase or another of the peace movement between 1900 and 1917. Conservatives such as Elihu Root, William Howard Taft, Joseph Choate, Justice David J. Brewer, Justice Melville Fuller, Simeon Baldwin, Francis Lynde Stetson, and John Hays Hammond played leading roles in the movement. Yet during later phases of the movement, the place of such conservatives in organizations actively agitating for peace was taken by such representatives of the American Left as Norman Thomas, Scott Nearing, Morris Hillquit, Max Eastman, Joseph Schlossberg, Roger Baldwin, Alexander Trachtenberg, Harry F. Ward, and Elizabeth Gurley Flynn.

Those whose activity did span several phases of the peace movement—in particular, those who joined the movement in 1915 or earlier and remained active through mid-1917—underwent a process of "radicalization." Whether they were already social reformers like Jane Addams and Roger Baldwin, young clergymen with inchoate social views like Norman Thomas and A. J. Muste, or naive young apostles of international friendship like Louis Lochner, they all moved toward the Left politically and they all believed they had attained new insights into the interconnections between the domestic social and economic system and international affairs. Louis Lochner and Lella Faye Secor have described in retrospect the process of their transformation, through leadership in the peace movement, from naive idealism to economic radicalism. In some cases the wartime crisis may have simply pushed further to the Left those who had already developed a habit of vociferous dissent on prewar domestic issues. Others, after finding themselves widely denounced for actions they had naively considered meritorious, may have suddenly discovered a temperamental affinity for living "in a spirit of heresy to the times."[6]

Jane Addams, who took no joy in belonging to a "persecuted minority," and who stopped short of formal participation in the People's Council, nevertheless experienced her own transformation:

[6] For some accounts of "radicalization" through participation in the peace movement see Louis P. Lochner, *Always the Unexpected: A Book of Reminiscences* (New York 1956), esp. pp. 228-29; Lella Secor Florence, "The Ford Peace Ship and After," in Julian Bell, ed., *We Did Not Fight: 1914-1918, Experiences of War Resisters* (London 1935), pp. 97-125; Roger Baldwin, "Reminiscences," I, 1, and *passim*, Oral History Research Project, Columbia University; A. J. Muste, "Sketches for an Autobiography," in Nat Hentoff, ed., *The Essays of A. J. Muste* (Indianapolis 1967), pp. 44-57; and Harry Fleischman, *Norman Thomas, A Biography* (New York 1964), pp. 54-64. The concluding quotation is from Baldwin, "Reminiscences," I, 306.

My temperament and habit had always kept me rather in the middle of the road; in politics as well as in social reform I had been for "the best possible." But now I was pushed far toward the left on the subject of the war and I became gradually convinced that in order to make the position of the pacifist clear it was perhaps necessary that at least a small number of us should be forced into an unequivocal position.[7]

Several dozen others, including Oswald Garrison Villard, Hollingsworth Wood, Norman Thomas, Roger Baldwin, John Haynes Holmes, A. J. Muste, Emily Balch, Rebecca Shelly, Scott Nearing, Edward Evans, Helena Dudley, and Margaret Lane found themselves "radicalized," in varying degrees, as a result of continuing participation in the peace movement.

Superficially, despite the discontinuities of leadership and participation in the peace movement between 1900 and 1917, the ideas of the movement often seem to have remained relatively unchanged. Any reader who surveys the thousands of speeches, pamphlets, books, and manifestos of the peace organizations is likely to be impressed initially by the frequency and tediousness with which spokesmen for peace organizations repeated the same clichés, examples, statistics, and vague sentimentalities. Again and again, during every phase of the movement between 1900 and 1917, its leaders called for the democratization of diplomacy, the abolition of secret treaties, the triumph of reason over emotion, and the fostering of international brotherhood. They applauded the increase of peaceful international contacts, and proposed the development of mediating institutions and "cooling-off" procedures. They called for the exercise of power by enlightened public opinion and prayed for the demise of sensationalist segments of the press.

But even in ideas, appearances of continuity within the early twentieth century peace movement are often deceiving. The same words, phrases, and arguments can often come to mean quite dif-

[7] Jane Addams, *Peace and Bread in Time of War* (New York 1922), p. 133; Alice Hamilton, *Exploring the Dangerous Trades: The Autobiography of Alice Hamilton, M.D.* (Boston 1943), p. 66. On Jane Addams' sympathy with, but reservations about, the People's Council, see Jane Addams to Mary Rozet Smith, 2 Sept. 1917, Box 6, Addams Papers, SCPC; Jane Addams to Emily G. Balch, 1 Feb. 1918, Box 1, Emily Greene Balch Papers, SCPC; Jane Addams to Lillian Wald, 24 Aug. 1917, Lillian Wald Papers, New York Public Library; Lola M. Lloyd to Louis P. Lochner, 12 Aug. 1917, in Clayton Lusk, ed., *Revolutionary Radicalism: Report of the Joint Legislative Committee of the State of New York* (Albany 1920), Part I, Vol. I, 992-93.

ferent things when expressed at different times, under different conditions, by persons who present them in a new context and give them different overtones and emphases. The call for greater democratization of diplomacy, for instance, contained one meaning for prewar peace movement leaders who voiced it with the "aristocratic" diplomacy of the European powers in mind, and quite another meaning when members of the People's Council or even the American Union Against Militarism directed it against the privileged interests (including international lawyers and peace society businessmen) who were shaping American foreign policy. Appeals for international brotherhood or international mediation did not carry the same implications in 1916 and 1917 that they had in 1913. Reason, in the prewar period, was often regarded as the particular attribute of the nation's elite, and emotionalism the characteristic of the unenlightened masses. Leaders of the peace movement after 1916 were apt to reverse these characterizations. Although each recognizable group that entered the peace movement accepted some of the accumulated complex of ideas and arguments from previous phases of the movement, it soon molded these ideas and arguments to its own purposes. Each new group or organization, having come to the peace movement out of a realization of how the reform of international affairs might now coincide with its own concerns, added new ideas derived from its previous occupational and reform interests and restated the clichéd phrases of the peace movement to fit its own circumstances and conceptions.

I have stressed the subordination of the peace movement, in the minds of many of its participants, to other, more immediate concerns. It was, indeed, a protean reform, assuming successively the various ideological and methodological shapes to which its new groups of adherents molded it. I have not intended to imply that the interest of any of these groups in the peace movement, as they understood it, was not sincere. To argue that their interest in the movement was temporary or expedient is not to suggest that their participation was hypocritical. The woman suffragists, the international lawyers, the promoters of church unity, and the social workers, for instance, found participation in the peace movement temporarily expedient; but they were sincere in their belief that the peace movement, as they envisaged it, was another expression of the general goals which they had sought through their particular reform efforts in other fields. Since the peace movement appeared to them to coincide with their larger goals, fervent advocacy of specific peace programs required no feigned sentiments, no dissembling.

Neither do I intend to suggest any single source of motivation among various peace advocates. Leaders of the Federal Council of the Churches of Christ in America were not attracted to the peace movement *only* by the desire to promote church unity, nor were international lawyers motivated solely by a desire either to enhance the standing of their profession or to promote conservative legalism. These and other groups, and the individuals who composed them, were driven by a variety of motives including, for most of them, the natural desire to exercise influence and control over events and the ultimate vision of a world untorn by violence and unscarred by war. Still, thousands of other Americans who did not join peace organizations undoubtedly felt the same desires and glimpsed the same visions. It was not the widely shared and rather generalized longing for a world at peace that brought most men and women into the organized peace movement during this period, but rather the activation of these sentiments by other, more specific, motives and interests.

Despite the increased international involvements of the 1890s and early 1900s, Americans of the progressive era still focused their attention on domestic problems. Only when proposals for peace and the reform of international relations could be seen as expressing or fulfilling the domestic and occupational aspirations and needs of various groups did they engender new surges of participation in the peace movement. The peace movement contained few uncompromising pacifists and few men and women who pursued the rather abstract goal of world peace as a single, isolated reform objective. But it included a great number of men and women who found themselves drawn into a socially and politically congenial phase of the movement through their efforts to promote their own social prestige and sense of civic leadership, the status of their profession, or the progress of their favorite reform.

The massive defections from the peace movement between 1914 and 1917 have variously been interpreted as acts of apostasy by traitors to the pacifist cause, or as the gravitation of moralists and idealists toward support for a "moral" war and an even higher idealism. But a glimpse at the variety of motives that brought men and women into the peace movement before 1917 suggests the possibility of additional, or perhaps alternative, explanations. Those who envisaged the peace movement as part of a wider campaign for domestic and international order and stability were entirely consistent in abandoning the movement when it took on implications of social upheaval and reform. Men who found in the prewar peace movement an expression of nationalistic and anglophilic sentiments were likewise consistent in rejecting the movement when it became critical of American foreign policy and seemingly overeager to mediate an end to a war in which Germany temporarily held the upper hand. And those who were attracted to the peace movement because it had become a necessary or likely adjunct to their own programs for church unity or woman suffrage or social welfare—or to their personal aspirations for social prestige and civic recognition—might very naturally be expected to have retired from the movement when association with it might endanger the prospects of their primary reform cause or their own social repute.

Men and women joined the peace movement when it expressed conceptions of world politics and the social order that coincided with their most immediate social and professional biases, their political prejudices, and their conceptions of appropriate means. When new peace organizations arose that expressed different conceptions of methods and goals, different visions of the ultimate world order, or when older organizations in taking antiwar actions supported such new conceptions, former participants in the peace movement naturally looked elsewhere for the expression of their "ideals." What is perhaps most surprising is not that many "defected," but that some did linger on.

Despite the culmination of the process of radicalization in the peace movement by 1918, and the demise or quiescence of the resulting radical peace organizations, the twentieth century peace movement was not dead. Nor had the recent evolution of the peace movement from a conservative to a liberal to a radical movement established an irreversible pattern of development. Several of the conservative and moderate foundations—the Carnegie Endowment, the World Peace Foundation, and the Church Peace Union—extended their influence into the postwar years and beyond. New organizations espousing peace programs that associated world peace with domestic conservatism would once again emerge. The Woman's Peace Party became the Women's International League for Peace and Freedom, carrying into later decades its liberal-radical outlook and its conception of the particular relation between the interests of women and world peace. Both the lawyers' program for peace through international courts and the People's Council's vision of the interconnection between international peace and domestic radicalism received organized expression within the peace movement of the 1920s and 1930s.[8]

But by 1918 the peace movement had undergone so thorough a process of successive transmutations that it had explored essentially all of the basic ideas, methods, and notions of interrelationships between international affairs and domestic reform that were to recur within the peace movement of the next two decades. It had served as the agency through which many leading figures of the era had explored the interrelationships between foreign policy and domestic programs and through which they had refined their political philosophies and reevaluated, sometimes with great agony, their social priorities.

The peace movement, despite its lively and varied career over the intervening years, remained in 1918 what it had been at the turn of the century—a kind of "second-class" reform, subordinated by most of its adherents to more pressing and immediate concerns. But it was not, for that reason, any less revealing than other contemporary reform movements of the processes by which important groups in the nation became conscious of the extension of the prestige and power contexts in which they operated to national and international levels. Some Americans were coming to perceive that social stability, or women's rights, or Christian influence, or social reform might prove elusive if pursued too narrowly and provincially. The peace movement became part of their efforts to prevent their ideas and programs from being eclipsed by war, and thus to gain for their political conceptions or social programs, an international "place in the sun."

[8] On the various facets of the peace movement in the 1920s and 1930s, see Lawrence Wittner, *Rebels Against War: The American Peace Movement 1941-1960* (New York 1969); Gertrude Bussey and Margaret Timms, *The Women's International League for Peace and Freedom, 1915-1965* (London 1965); John E. Stoner, *S. O. Levinson and the Pact of Paris: A Study in the Techniques of Influence* (Chicago 1942); Robert H. Ferrell, *Peace in Their Time: The Origins of the Kellogg-Briand Pact* (New Haven, Conn. 1952); Charles S. Macfarland, *Pioneers for Peace Through Religion* (New York 1946); Chatfield, "Pacifism and American Life"; Charles Chatfield, *For Peace and Justice: Pacifism in America, 1914-1941* (Knoxville 1971); John K. Nelson, *The Peace Prophets: American Pacifist Thought, 1919-1941* (Chapel Hill 1967). See also the bibliographical essay in Chatfield, *For Peace and Justice.*

Bibliography

I. UNPUBLISHED MATERIALS

A. Manuscript Collections

Jane Addams Papers, Swarthmore College Peace Collection.

American Conference for Democracy and Terms of Peace Papers, Swarthmore College Peace Collection.

American Peace Society Papers, Swarthmore College Peace Collection.

American Union Against Militarism Papers, Swarthmore College Peace Collection.

Fannie Fern Andrews Papers, Arthur and Elizabeth Schlesinger Library, Radcliffe College.

Hannah J. Bailey Papers, Swarthmore College Peace Collection.

Emily Greene Balch Papers, Swarthmore College Peace Collection.

Andrew Carnegie Papers, Manuscript Division, Library of Congress.

Carnegie Endowment for International Peace Papers, Columbia University Library.

Carrie C. Catt Papers, Manuscript Division, Library of Congress.

Carrie C. Catt Papers, New York Public Library.

Church Peace Union Papers, Council on Religion and International Affairs, New York City.

Church Peace Union Papers, Swarthmore College Peace Collection.

Clara B. Colby Papers, Henry E. Huntington Library, San Marino, California.

Henry Wadsworth Longfellow Dana Papers, Swarthmore College Peace Collection.

Charles W. Eliot Papers, Harvard University Archives.

Emergency Peace Federation Papers, Swarthmore College Peace Collection.

Federal Council of the Churches of Christ in America Papers, Swarthmore College Peace Collection.

Fellowship of Reconciliation Papers, Swarthmore College Peace Collection.

391

Mrs. J. Malcolm Forbes Papers, Swarthmore College Peace Collection.

Franklin Giddings Papers, Columbia University Library.

Ida Husted Harper Papers, Henry E. Huntington Library, San Marino, California.

Hamilton Holt Papers, Rollins College, Winter Park, Florida.

William I. Hull Papers, Friends' Historical Library, Swarthmore College.

David Starr Jordan Papers, Hoover Institution on War, Revolution and Peace, Stanford, California.

League to Enforce Peace Collection, A. Lawrence Lowell Papers, Harvard University Archives.

Edwin D. Mead Papers, Swarthmore College Peace Collection.

Lucia Ames Mead Papers, Swarthmore College Peace Collection.

George W. Nasmyth Papers, Swarthmore College Peace Collection.

New York Peace Society Papers, Swarthmore College Peace Collection.

Leonora O'Reilly Papers, Arthur and Elizabeth Schlesinger Library, Radcliffe College.

Alice L. Park Papers, Hoover Institution on War, Revolution and Peace, Stanford, California.

Alice L. Park Papers, Henry E. Huntington Library, San Marino, California.

People's Council of America Papers, Hoover Institution on War, Revolution and Peace, Stanford, California.

People's Council of America Papers, Swarthmore College Peace Collection.

People's Council of America Papers, Tamiment Institute and Library, New York City.

Amos Pinchot Papers, Manuscript Division, Library of Congress.

Elihu Root Papers, Manuscript Division, Library of Congress.

Rosika Schwimmer Papers, Hoover Institution on War, Revolution and Peace, Stanford, California.

Anna Garlin Spencer Papers, Swarthmore College Peace Collection.

Fanny Garrison Villard Papers, Houghton Library, Harvard University.

Oswald Garrison Villard Papers, Houghton Library, Harvard University.

Lillian Wald Papers, New York Public Library.

Woman's Peace Party Correspondence, Swarthmore College Peace Collection.

Woman's Peace Party, New York Branch, Correspondence, Swarthmore College Peace Collection.

Woman's Peace Party Papers, Swarthmore College Peace Collection.

Women's Rights Collection, Arthur and Elizabeth Schlesinger Library, Radcliffe College.

World Alliance for International Friendship Through the Churches (American Council) Papers, Swarthmore College Peace Collection.

World Peace Foundation Collection, A. Lawrence Lowell Papers, Harvard University Archives.

World Peace Foundation Papers, Swarthmore College Peace Collection.

B. Materials from Oral History Project, Columbia University

Angell, Norman. "The Reminiscences of Norman Angell."

Baldwin, Roger. "The Reminiscences of Roger Baldwin."

Johnson, Alvin. "The Reminiscences of Alvin Johnson."

Mygatt, Tracy D. and Frances Witherspoon. "The Reminiscences of Tracy D. Mygatt and Frances Witherspoon."

Spargo, John. "The Reminiscences of John Spargo."

Thomas, Norman. "The Reminiscences of Norman Thomas."

C. Dissertations and Theses

Athey, Louis Lee. "The Consumers' Leagues and Social Reform, 1890-1923," Ph.D. dissertation, University of Delaware, 1965.

Bassett, Michael Edward Rainton. "The Socialist Party of America, 1912-1919: Years of Decline," Ph.D. dissertation, Duke University, 1964.

Beisner, Robert L. "The Anti-imperialist Impulse: The Mugwumps and the Republicans, 1898-1900," Ph.D. dissertation, University of Chicago, 1965.

Chatfield, E. Charles, Jr. "Pacifism and American Life, 1914 to 1941," Ph.D. dissertation, Vanderbilt University, 1965.

Cook, Blanche Wiesen. "Woodrow Wilson and the Antimilitarists, 1914-1917," Ph.D. dissertation, The Johns Hopkins University, 1970.

Doherty, R. W. "Alfred Love and the Universal Peace Union," Ph.D. dissertation, University of Pennsylvania, 1962.

Dubin, Martin David. "The Development of the Idea of Collective Security in the American Peace Movement, 1899-1917," Ph.D. dissertation, Indiana University, 1960.

Dubofsky, Melvyn. "New York City Labor in the Progressive Era, 1910-1918: A Study of Organized Labor in an Era of Reform," Ph.D. dissertation, University of Rochester, 1960.

Friedberg, Gerald. "Marxism in the United States: John Spargo and the Socialist Party of America," Ph.D. dissertation, Harvard University, 1965.

Giele, Janet. "Social Change in the Feminine Role: A Comparison of Woman's Suffrage and Woman's Temperance, 1870-1920," Ph.D. dissertation, Radcliffe College, 1961.

Grubbs, Frank L., Jr. "The Struggle for the Mind of American Labor 1917-1919," Ph.D. dissertation, University of Minnesota, 1968.

Hovey, Amos Arnold. "A History of the Religious Phase of the American Movement for International Peace to the Year 1914," Ph.D. dissertation, University of Chicago, 1930.

Iverson, Robert W. "Morris Hillquit, American Social Democrat," Ph.D. dissertation, State University of Iowa, 1951.

Jensen, Gordon Maurice. "The National Civic Federation: American Business in an Age of Social Change and Social Reform, 1900-1910," Ph.D. dissertation, Princeton University, 1956.

Jenson, Carol Elizabeth. "Agrarian Pioneer in Civil Liberties: The Nonpartisan League in Minnesota During World War I," Ph.D. dissertation, University of Minnesota, 1968.

Katz, Joseph. "The Legal Profession, 1890-1915, The Lawyer's Role in Society: A Study in Attitudes," M.A. thesis, Columbia University, 1953.

Lutzker, Michael Arnold. "The 'Practical' Peace Advocates: An Interpretation of the American Peace Movement, 1898-1917," Ph.D. dissertation, Rutgers University, 1969.

McKee, Delber Lee. "The American Federation of Labor and American Foreign Policy, 1886-1912," Ph.D. dissertation, Stanford University, 1952.

Marchand, Charles Roland. "David Starr Jordan and the Peace Movement in America, 1913-1917," M.A. thesis, Stanford University, 1961.

Marchand, Charles Roland. "The Ultimate Reform: World Peace in American Thought During the Progressive Era," Ph.D. dissertation, Stanford University, 1964.

Patterson, David Sands. "The Travail of the American Peace Movement, 1887-1914," Ph.D. dissertation, University of California, Berkeley, 1968.

Piper, John Franklin, Jr. "The Social Policy of the Churches of

Christ in America During World War I," Ph.D. dissertation, Duke University, 1965.

Rabe, Valentin Hanno. "Protestant Foreign Missions, 1880-1920," Ph.D. dissertation, Harvard University, 1964.

Rappaport, Joseph. "Jewish Immigrants and World War I: A Study of American Yiddish Press Reactions," Ph.D. dissertation, Columbia University, 1951.

Rutherford, W. Louise. "The Influence of the American Bar Association On Public Opinion and Legislation," Ph.D. dissertation, University of Pennsylvania, 1937.

Smith, Kenneth Jackson. "John Haynes Holmes: Opponent of War," B.D. dissertation, University of Chicago, 1949.

Smylie, John Edwin. "Protestant Clergymen and America's World Role, 1865-1900: A Study of Christianity, Nationality and International Relations," Th.D. dissertation, Princeton Theological Seminary, 1959.

Steidle, Barbara C. "Conservative Progressives: A Study of the Attitudes and Role of Bar and Bench, 1905-1912," Ph.D. dissertation, Rutgers University, 1969.

Tompkins, Edwin Berkeley. "The Great Debate: Anti-imperialism in the United States, 1890-1920," Ph.D. dissertation, University of Pennsylvania, 1963.

Tuttle, Peter Guertin. "The Ford Peace Ship: Volunteer Diplomacy in the Twentieth Century," Ph.D. dissertation, Yale University, 1958.

II. Essay on Sources

Since the peace movement in the United States between 1898 and 1918 underwent a series of transforming changes, no single set of sources provides an adequate basis for understanding the movement during its profoundly dissimilar phases. Moreover, the derivative character of most of the ideas and attitudes expressed in peace societies, foundations, unions, councils, and committees makes an understanding of those organizations dependent upon a study of the respective domestic, professional, and reform contexts from which successive leadership groups in the peace movement drew their assumptions and derived their compelling motivations. I have decided, therefore, to provide brief chapter-by-chapter selective bibliographical essays, preceded by a short general bibliographical review of the historiography of the peace movement during the progressive era. I hope that this arrangement may serve the reader better than an extended list of all the books, articles, and pamphlets consulted, a list in which items dealing exclusively with such diverse topics as legal education, socialism, the history of church federation, nineteenth-century New England reform, Jewish immigration to New York City, the ideas of the woman suffrage movement, the ideology of the business community, and the development of professionalism in social work would be neatly arranged in alphabetical order but in conceptual and topical chaos. The essays make no attempt to achieve comprehensive coverage, or even to list all sources previously cited in the footnotes. They seek only to suggest those sources most directly pertinent to the approach attempted in each particular chapter.

The Peace Movement, 1898-1918, General Works

Any study of the American peace movement in this period builds on the base provided over three decades ago by Merle Curti in *Peace or War: The American Struggle, 1636-1936* (New York 1936). Although the immense scope of Curti's coverage precluded a detailed analysis of each of the shifts of ideology and organization in the peace movement in this important transitional period, the balanced coverage of his study still provides the framework of chronology and interpretation with which most of the new studies have begun. Perhaps the major weakness of Curti's ambitious survey was his tendency to view the peace movement as a single movement, characterizing nearly all members of peace organizations as "peace advocates," "friends of peace," or "champions of peace." Newer studies, many of them taking advantage of the manuscript sources more recently available and the interpretive sophistication possible in more intensive investigation of narrowly delineated periods and segments of the movement, have generally moved toward an appreciation of the divisions within the peace movement and the variations of meaning and intent expressed by the various "advocates of peace."

Although Curti's work has long stood as the primary scholarly survey of the American peace movement, other related or more specialized scholarly studies and several less scholarly but often perceptive accounts by participants in the movement have been available. Of the histories to come from within the peace movement itself, Devere Allen's diffuse *The Fight for Peace* (New York 1930) is probably the most highly interpretive. An amalgam of argument and narrative, Allen's book dissects the previous career of the movement from the standpoint of social radicalism and uncompromising pacifism. Jane Addams' *Peace and Bread in Time of War* (New York 1922); William I. Hull's *The New Peace Movement* (Boston 1912); and Charles S. Macfarland's *Pioneers for Peace Through Religion* (New York 1946) all offer accounts of specific aspects of the peace movement of the early twentieth century from the perspective of participants. Julius Moritzen, *The Peace Movement of America* (New York 1912) and Edson L. Whitney, *The American Peace Society: A Centennial History* (Washington, D.C. 1928) are both dull and uninterpretive "court histories" that provide some useful factual details in the course of their uncritical eulogies. Of the relatively few scholarly treatments of specific aspects of the peace movement that had appeared before 1960, the most valuable are Marie Louise Degen, *History of the Woman's Peace Party* (Baltimore 1939); Ruhl J. Bartlett, *The League to Enforce Peace* (Chapel Hill, N.C. 1944); Merze Tate, *The Disarmament Illusion: The Movement for a Limitation of Armaments to 1907* (New York 1942); Ray H. Abrams, *Preachers Present Arms* (New York 1933); and Merle Eugene Curti, *Bryan and World Peace* (Northampton, Mass. 1931).

With the 1960s there came a new surge of interest in the history of the peace movement in the United States, much of it undoubtedly stimulated by the intensification and frustrations of a contemporary peace movement opposing American involvement in the Vietnam war. Very little of this new work, however, could be characterized as part of a superficial and "presentist" effort to remake the past in the name of current expediency. On the whole it has been thorough, painstakingly scholarly, and careful and balanced in interpretation. Rather than seeking the simplified "truths" which might enhance present peace propaganda, newer historians of the peace movement have gradually reached toward more and more complex and sophisticated interpretations.

Of six book-length studies of segments of the peace movement in the twentieth century which have been published since 1967, four deal significantly with portions of the period 1898-1918. Lawrence S. Wittner's *Rebels Against War: The American Peace Movement, 1941-1960* (New York 1969) and John K. Nelson's *The Peace Prophets: American Pacifist Thought, 1919-1941* (Chapel Hill, N.C. 1967), deal exclusively with subsequent periods and do not carry their analyses back into the period before 1918. But Charles Chatfield's account of pacifism between the two world wars in *For Peace and Justice: Pacifism in America, 1914-1941* (Knoxville 1971) offers important insights into the 1914-1918 period and Peter Brock's monumental *Pacifism in the United States:*

From the Colonial Era to the First World War (Princeton 1968) carries his thorough and readable history of sectarian and non-sectarian pacifism into the early twentieth century. Warren F. Kuehl, in *Seeking World Order: The United States and International Organization to 1920* (Nashville 1969), traces the step-by-step development of American ideas for international federations, leagues, courts, legislatures, and a variety of other simple and complex plans for international organization in far greater detail than has been attempted before. Finally, Sondra R. Herman's *Eleven Against War: Studies in American International Thought, 1898-1921* (Stanford 1969), although largely confined to an intellectual history approach, introduces a new quality of interpretive imaginativeness in her contrast of the ideals of "community" and "polity" in the thinking of leaders of peace organizations.

In spite of this recent outpouring of scholarly studies of the early twentieth century peace movement, much of the best recent work is yet to be published. David Sands Patterson's "The Travail of the American Peace Movement, 1887-1914," Ph.D. dissertation, University of California, Berkeley, 1968, despite its lack of an explicit overall interpretive theme, achieves a new level of sophistication in dealing with the pre-World War I peace movement and neatly links diplomatic events with peace movement initiatives and reactions. Michael Arnold Lutzker's exceptionally readable "The 'Practical' Peace Advocates: An Interpretation of the American Peace Movement, 1898-1917," Ph.D. dissertation, Rutgers University, 1969, presents an interpretation of the peace foundations and their leaders that largely coincides with my own. Lutzker's analysis of the peace movement, although extended through the neutrality period of World War I, gives little attention to the vital new peace organizations that appeared after 1914. One of the most important of these organizations, the American Union Against Militarism, is interpreted, however, in Blanche Wiesen Cook's "Woodrow Wilson and the Antimilitarists, 1914-1917," Ph.D. dissertation, The Johns Hopkins University, 1970, an account which rests on impressive work in a variety of manuscript collections. My own dissertation, "The Ultimate Reform: World Peace in American Thought During the Progressive Era," Ph.D. dissertation, Stanford University, 1964, suffers from too abstract an approach to the intellectual history of the peace movement but contains much material not touched upon in the present work.

Several scholarly articles in recent years have reflected the beginning of new inquiry into the early twentieth century peace movement in the United States. Notable among these are: Charles Chatfield, "World War I and the Liberal Pacifist in the United States," *American Historical Review*, 75 (Dec. 1970), 1920-1937; Peter Filene, "The World Peace Foundation and Progressivism: 1910-1918," *New England Quarterly*, 36 (Dec. 1963), 478-501; and Milton Cantor, "The Radical Confrontation with Foreign Policy: War and Revolution, 1914-1920," in Alfred F. Young, ed., *Dissent: Explorations in the History of American Radicalism* (DeKalb, Ill. 1969), pp. 217-49.

This general essay has sought to deal in a selective manner with only the more general works on substantial phases of the peace movement in the 1898-1918 period. More specialized studies, and those dealing with specific aspects of the peace movement or with tangential ideas, events, and movements, are included in the chapter-by-chapter essays. Any student of the peace movement in this period will, of course, find himself dependent upon the major interpretations of foreign policy and political leadership during the period in works by Arthur S. Link, Arno Mayer, Robert E. Osgood, Thomas A. Bailey, Howard K. Beale, Ernest R. May, Charles S. Forcey, Daniel M. Smith, Lawrence E. Gelfand and numerous others. I have made no attempt to list each of these works here. They may be found in any recent bibliography of American foreign policy in the early twentieth century.

Chapter One. *Up from Sentimentalism*

The two major peace organizations of the turn of the twentieth century offer obvious opportunities to the researcher in their own voluminous publications. The *Advocate of Peace*, the monthly organ of the American Peace Society, had become by the 1890s, under Benjamin Trueblood's vigorous and scholarly editorship, an important, comprehensive source of information about nearly every aspect of the American peace movement and a revealing chronicle of the society's own character and ideas. The annual conference on arbitration at Lake Mohonk was reported in entirety in the yearly *Report of the Annual Meeting of the Lake Mohonk Conference on International Arbitration* (Lake Mohonk, N.Y. 1895-1916). Collected papers for each of these organizations are available in the Swarthmore College Peace Collection, but the diffuseness of these collections and the abundance of published material make research in these manuscript collections for the 1898-1905 period relatively unfruitful. The declining fortunes of the Universal Peace Union can be assessed from items in the *Advocate of Peace*, from the union's organ, *The Peacemaker*, and from the Benjamin Trueblood Correspondence in the APS Papers. On the Universal Peace Union, see also R. W. Doherty, "Alfred H. Love and the Universal Peace Union," Ph.D. dissertation, University of Pennsylvania, 1962, and the major surveys by Merle Curti and Peter Brock discussed above.

The nineteenth century backgrounds of the American peace movement are best reviewed in such early accounts as Christina Phelps, *The Anglo-American Peace Movement in the Mid-Nineteenth Century* (New York 1930) and Merle Curti, *The American Peace Crusade* (Durham, N.C. 1929) and in Peter Brock's thorough account of one major aspect of the movement in *Pacifism in the United States*. No adequate recent history of the movement as an international phenomenon exists, but Arthur Charles Frederick Beales, *The History of Peace: A Short Account of the Organized Movement for International Peace* (New York 1931) sketches in the broad outlines for the period before 1914. A number of varying scholarly approaches to the politics and culture of late nineteenth-century Boston help establish the context of reform ideas and legacies for the American Peace Society at the turn of the century. Those I found most helpful were Barbara Miller Solomon, *Ancestors and Immigrants: A Changing New England Tradition* (Cambridge, Mass. 1956); Arthur Mann, *Yankee Reformers in the Urban Age: Social Reform in Boston, 1880-1900* (Cambridge, Mass. 1954); Martin Green, *The Problem of Boston: Some Readings in Cultural History* (New York 1966); and Geoffrey Blodgett, *The Gentle Reformers: Massachusetts Democrats in the Cleveland Era* (Cambridge, Mass. 1966).

The anti-imperialist movement, with which the peace movement was briefly intertwined, has recently been more fully analyzed by Robert L. Beisner in *Twelve Against Empire: The Anti-Imperialists, 1898-1900* (New York 1968) and E. Berkeley Tompkins, *Anti-Imperialism in the United States: The Great Debate, 1890-1920* (Philadelphia 1970). I have also been influenced in varying degrees by the discussions of imperialism, expansionism, and anti-imperialism in Walter LaFeber, *The New Empire: An Interpretation of American Expansion, 1860-1898* (Ithaca, N.Y. 1963); Ernest R. May, "American Imperialism: A Reinterpretation," *Perspectives in American History*, 1 (1967), 123-283—subsequently published as *American Imperialism: A Speculative Essay* (New York 1968); and Blodgett, *The Gentle Reformers*, listed above.

The ideology of Anglo-Saxonism, adopted in its more "benevolent" forms by the major peace organizations, is discussed directly or tangentially in a multitude of works. Particularly pertinent to the discussion here are Richard Hofstadter, *Social Darwinism in American Thought*, rev. ed. (Boston 1955); Milton Berman, *John Fiske, The Evolution of a Popularizer* (Cambridge, Mass. 1961) ; Edward Saveth, *American Historians and European Immigrants, 1875-1927* (New York 1948); and the works by LaFeber, Solomon, and Green above. The backgrounds, activities, and results of the First Hague Peace Conference are reviewed in Merze Tate, *The Disarmament Illusion: The Movement for a Limitation of Armaments to 1907* (New York 1942) and elaborated more fully in Calvin DeArmond Davis, *The United States and the First Hague Peace Conference* (Ithaca, N.Y. 1962). Warren F. Kuehl provides a good summary of the appearance of new ideas and societies for international organization in his *Seeking World Order: The United States and International Organization to 1920* (Nashville 1969). Evidence of the sense of "newness" and the rising ideal of "practicality" in the peace movement can be found in the periodical literature of the movement, the annual reports and congress proceedings, the records of the New York Peace Society, the book-length contemporary accounts such as Frederick Lynch, *The Peace Problem: The Task of the Twentieth Century* (New York 1911) and William I. Hull, *The New Peace Movement* (Swarthmore, Pa. 1909), and in such autobiographical and biographical works as Nicholas Murray Butler, *Across the Busy Years* (New York 1935); Charles Herbert Levermore, *Samuel Train Dutton: A Biography* (New York 1922); and Warren F. Kuehl, *Hamilton Holt: Journalist, Internationalist, Educator* (Gainesville, Fla. 1960).

The major organizations of the peace movement in these early years of the twentieth century are discussed at length in the two recent dissertations by Thomas Patterson and Michael Lutzker listed above. Their sources and arguments at a number of points have corroborated and reinforced my own. These should be consulted for divergences of interpretation from the account in this chapter and for expanded and provocative discussions of events and intellectual influences that I have only touched upon.

Chapter Two. *Courts, Judges, and the Rule of Law*

The best sources on the ideas and programs of the international lawyers are the publications of the two new lawyers' organizations that served as partial adjuncts to the peace movement: the American Society of International Law and the American Society for the Judicial Settlement of International Disputes. The *Ameri-*

can Journal of International Law established a forum for the broad scholarly discussion of issues of international law and the extremely useful *Proceedings* of the annual meetings of the ASIL provide a year-by-year record of the ideas and preoccupations of the society's most influential participants. After 1910 the annual *Proceedings* of the ASJSID provide an equally important source of information about the more specialized concerns of this organization and the attitudes of its dominant officer, James Brown Scott.

The views of leading figures among the international lawyers can also be explored in their reports and addresses to other peace organizations, their articles in major law reviews and in their own treatises, monographs, and collected works. Of particular importance among these are: John Bassett Moore, *The Collected Papers of John Bassett Moore*, 7 vols. (New Haven 1944); Elihu Root, *Addresses on International Subjects*, collected and edited by Robert Bacon and James Brown Scott (Cambridge, Mass. 1916); Elihu Root, *Miscellaneous Addresses*, collected and edited by Robert Bacon and James Brown Scott (Cambridge, Mass. 1917); Joseph H. Choate, *The Two Hague Conferences* (Princeton 1913); James Brown Scott, *Peace Through Justice: Three Papers on International Justice and the Means of Attaining It* (New York 1917); David Jayne Hill, *World Organization as Affected by the Nature of the Modern State* (New York 1911); Theodore Marburg, *League of Nations*, 2 vols. (New York 1918); and James Brown Scott, *The Hague Peace Conferences of 1899 and 1907* (Baltimore 1909).

The broad professional context in which the international lawyers operated and the changes in the training, ideas, and self-image of the legal profession are best derived from Willard Hurst's excellent *The Growth of American Law: The Law Makers* (Boston 1950). Of supplementary value are Roscoe Pound, *The Lawyer: From Antiquity to Modern Times* (St. Paul 1953); Alfred Z. Reed, *Training for the Public Profession of the Law* (New York 1921); and Charles Warren, *A History of the American Bar* (New York 1911). A more general examination of the nature and growth of "professionalism" is introduced in Everett Cherrington Hughes, *Men and Their Work* (Glencoe, Ill. 1958). Other introductions to the sociology of professions are included in the essay on sources for chapter seven. The specific constitutional issues and domestic political concerns which preoccupied much of the legal profession and the judiciary during the late nineteenth and early twentieth century are discussed in Arnold N. Paul, *Conservative Crisis and the Rule of Law: Attitudes of Bar and Bench, 1887-1895* (Ithaca, N.Y. 1960) and Barbara C. Steidle, "Conservative Progressives: A Study of the Attitudes and Role of Bar and Bench, 1905-1912," Ph.D. dissertation, Rutgers University, 1969. The shifting concerns of the bar are also apparent in the *Reports of the American Bar Association*. Each of these sources reveals the fluctuating but continuing interest in the defense of judicial supremacy at home, an interest which was reflected in the lawyers' programs for international institutions.

No adequate account has yet appeared of the internal politics and tensions within the State Department during this period. The most useful general description of the internal structure of the department is Graham H. Stuart, *The Department of State: A History of its Organization, Procedure and Personnel* (New York 1949). Biographies of the individual secretaries of state usually do not explore the internal divisions within the department or the creation of effective policy at levels below that of the secretary himself. But Waldo H. Heinrichs, Jr.'s *American Ambassador: Joseph C. Grew and the Development of the United States Diplomatic Tradition* (Boston 1966) and Warren Frederick Ilchman, *Professional Diplomacy in the United States, 1779-1939* (Chicago 1961) attempt to analyze the growth of professionalism among diplomatic officers and suggest the strains within the department that such new professionalism created. More direct evidence of the muted conflict between diplomats and international lawyers appears in various memoirs, including F. M. Huntington Wilson, *Memoirs of an Ex-Diplomat* (Boston 1945); William Phillips, *Ventures in Diplomacy* (Portland, Me. 1952); and Lloyd C. Griscom, *Diplomatically Speaking* (Boston 1940); and in F. M. Huntington Wilson's heavy-handed but revealing anonymous play, *Stultitia: A Nightmare and an Awakening* (New York 1913).

The development of increasingly complex plans for world federation, of which the lawyers' plans for a court were a part, is surveyed in Warren F. Kuehl, *Seeking World Order: The United States and World Organization to 1920* (Nashville 1969). The context of ideas and organizations in the peace movement within which the international lawyers operated is provided in varying degrees in the works by Curti, Herman, Patterson, and Lutzker cited in the essay on general sources.

Chapter Three. *Businessmen and Practicality*

Since businessmen did not form their own separate peace organizations, evidence of their role in the peace movement must be gleaned from the published literature and manuscript materials of the American Peace Society, the Mohonk Conferences, the New York Peace Society, and other peace organizations. The richest sources of ideas about the relationship between business and peace, expressed both by businessmen and for the benefit of businessmen, are the *Annual Reports* of the Lake Mohonk Conference on International Arbitration; the *Official Report of the Thirteenth Universal Peace Congress* (Boston 1904); and the *Proceedings* (variously titled) of the first through fourth National Peace and Arbitration Congresses of 1907, 1909, 1911, and 1913.

The more specific analysis of the role of businessmen in the New York Peace Society, an organization which epitomized the rage for practicality and the enlistment of the elite of the "new" peace movement of 1905-1914, rests upon the variety of annual reports and membership lists of clubs, philanthropic organizations, cultural associations, and business groups in New York City indicated in the chapter footnotes. Additional information on individual businessmen was derived from the *Dictionary of American Biography, Who's Who in New York, 1914, New York Times* obituaries, and other biographical sources. The annual *Yearbook* of the New York Peace Society includes not only the list of officers and members but also useful reports on the society's goals and activities. Additional information on the internal history of the New York Peace Society is available in the NYPS Papers, SCPC, and in the Andrew Carnegie Papers, MS Div., Library of Congress.

Several recent works provide helpful analyses of businessmen as reformers during the progressive era. Robert Wiebe's *Businessmen and Reform: A Study of the Progressive Movement* (Cambridge, Mass. 1962) describes the "types" of businessmen engaged in a variety of business-related progressive reforms. Gordon M. Jensen's "The National Civic Federation: American Business in an Age of Social Change and Social Reform, 1900-1910," Ph.D. dissertation, Princeton University, 1956, invites a comparison of businessmen in the Civic Federation and the New York Peace Society because of his detailed information on the characteristics of businessmen who joined the former organization. James Weinstein's *The Corporate Ideal in the Liberal State, 1900-1918* (Boston 1968) draws heavily upon Jensen's study in bringing the National Civic Federation into sharper interpretive focus. Among the many other works which assess the ideas of businessmen of this era and the structure and changes in business leadership, I found most useful Edward C. Kirkland, *Dream and Thought in the Business Community, 1860-1890* (Ithaca, N.Y.

1956); John A. Garraty, *Right-Hand Man: The Life of George W. Perkins* (New York 1957); Barry E. Supple, "A Business Elite: German Jewish Financiers in Nineteenth-Century New York," *Business History Review*, 31 (Summer 1957), 143-177; and Morrell Heald, *The Social Responsibilities of Business: Company and Community, 1900-1960* (Cleveland 1970).

The several attempts during the period to construct a more elaborate theory of the incompatibility of war and business probably had more influence on others in the peace movement than they did upon business participants. The most celebrated of these treatises were Ivan Stanislavovich Bloch (Jean de Bloch), *The Future of War in its Technical, Economic and Political Relations* (Boston 1899) and Norman Angell, *The Great Illusion: A Study of the Relation of Military Power in Nations to Their Economic and Social Advantage* (New York 1910). Some of these ideas were popularized even further in David Starr Jordan, *War and Waste: A Series of Discussions of War and War Accessories* (New York 1913).

Chapter Four. *Peace Through Research: The Great Foundations*

Whatever else they accomplished, the peace foundations introduced a greater degree of system and order into the peace movement. Those qualities have provided subsequent historians with a wealth of printed and manuscript data on the foundations themselves and the movement to which they sought to give direction. The massive Carnegie Endowment for International Peace Papers at the Columbia University Library tell the "public" history of the endowment and reveal much of the private, internal history as well. The Andrew Carnegie Papers, MS Div., Library of Congress, are invaluable for the origins and background of the endowment and for Carnegie's relationships with a variety of leaders in the peace movement. Important supplementary materials on the Carnegie Endowment and its leadership can be gleaned from the Charles W. Eliot Papers, Harvard University Archives, The World Peace Foundation Papers, SCPC, and the Elihu Root Papers, MS Div., LC.

The relationship between the wealthy and bemused endowment and the bedazzled, benumbed, and manipulated American Peace Society can be deduced from portions of the Benjamin Trueblood Correspondence in the APS Papers, SCPC, together with the CEIP Papers themselves. Useful material on Carnegie's gradual involvement in the peace movement and related projects can be gained from Carnegie's *Autobiography* (Boston 1920) and from Burton J. Hendrick's flattering *The Life of Andrew Carnegie*, 2 vols. (Garden City, N.Y. 1932). Warren F. Kuehl's *Hamilton Holt: Journalist, Internationalist, Educator* (Gainesville, Fla. 1960), gives a description of the founding of the endowment. Undoubtedly further supplementary material lies in the Nicholas Murray Butler Papers, Columbia University Library, which I did not find time to explore. Butler's own correspondence is heavily represented in the Carnegie, Eliot, CEIP, and APS Papers listed above.

Significant holdings of the papers of the World Peace Foundation can be found in two repositories: the SCPC and the A. Lawrence Lowell Papers, HA. The WPF Papers at Swarthmore are most useful for the earlier, prewar years; those in the Lowell Papers are richest for the 1914-1915 period and merge, for most practical purposes, into the League to Enforce Peace Papers, also contained in the Lowell Papers, for the period after 1915. Thus the World Peace Foundation's effective assimilation by the League to Enforce Peace can be followed through the papers of the major architect of that *coup de grâce*. A particularly valuable additional source of information on the World Peace Foundation is the papers of one of its directors, David Starr Jordan, in the Hoover Institution on War, Revolution and Peace. The papers of the other major director, Edwin Mead, in the SCPC, contain relatively little of value on the World Peace Foundation. The Carnegie Papers, the APS Papers, and the William I. Hull Papers, Friends' Historical Library, Swarthmore College, contain some items of relevance to the World Peace Foundation.

Only recently have the peace foundations begun to attract scholarly attention. Peter A. Filene's "The World Peace Foundation and Progressivism: 1910-1918," *The New England Quarterly*, 36 (Dec. 1963), 478-501, the only published study, offers a useful interpretation, but is limited by the single question it poses. Sondra Herman provides some indirect insights on the Carnegie Endowment through her studies of Elihu Root and Nicholas Murray Butler in *Eleven Against War: Studies in American Internationalist Thought, 1898-1921* (Stanford 1969). Thomas Sands Patterson reviews the policies and activities of both foundations in his "The Travail of the American Peace Movement, 1887-1914," Ph.D. dissertation, University of California, Berkeley, 1968, and Michael Lutzker sharpens the focus considerably in his "The 'Practical' Peace Advocates: An Interpretation of the American Peace Movement, 1898-1917," Ph.D. dissertation, Rutgers University, 1969. A

general, comparative analysis of the rise of the early twentieth
century research and philanthropic foundations is still needed.

Chapter Five. *Responses to the War Crisis*

Manuscript materials revealing the responses of the established
peace organizations to the European war, the "preparedness"
movement, and the events leading to American intervention de-
rive largely from the same collections utilized in tracing the earlier history of these societies and foundations in chapters one
through four. Of particular importance for the 1914-1918 period
are the World Peace Foundation Collection and the League to
Enforce Peace Collection in the A. Lawrence Lowell Papers, Harvard University Archives; the Carnegie Endowment for International Peace Papers, Columbia University Library; and the American Peace Society Papers, Swarthmore College Peace Collection.
Collections of supplementary value include the William I. Hull
Papers, Friends' Historical Library, Swarthmore College; the David Starr Jordan Papers, Hoover Institution on War, Revolution
and Peace; the Franklin Giddings Papers, CUL; the Charles W.
Eliot Papers, HA; and the New York Peace Society Papers, SCPC.

The origins, philosophy, and influence of the League to Enforce
Peace have now been described and analyzed in a number of
scholarly studies. The fullest historical accounts of the development of the league appear in Ruhl J. Bartlett's solid monograph,
The League to Enforce Peace (Chapel Hill, N.C. 1944), and in
Martin David Dubin's detailed analysis of the league in terms of
the debate over emerging ideas of collective security in "The Development of the Idea of Collective Security in the American
Peace Movement, 1899-1917," Ph.D. dissertation, Indiana University, 1960. A description of the origins of the league also appears
in Warren F. Kuehl, *Hamilton Holt: Journalist, Internationalist,
Educator* (Gainesville, Fla. 1960). Warren F. Kuehl's *Seeking
World Order: The United States and International Organization
to 1920* (Nashville 1969), devotes considerable attention to the
League to Enforce Peace, attempting to place it in the context of
a process of development of increasingly sophisticated plans for
world organization. A more critical view of the policies and ideas
of the league can be found in Sondra Herman, *Eleven Against
War: Studies in American Internationalist Thought, 1898-1921*
(Stanford 1969) and in Michael Arnold Lutzker, "The 'Practical'
Peace Advocates: An Interpretation of the American Peace Move-
ment, 1898-1917," Ph.D. dissertation, Rutgers University, 1969.
Excellent printed sources on the ideas and programs of the league

are available in the *Reports* (variously titled) of the annual conventions of the league for 1915 through 1918 and in its numerous pamphlets and broadsides which appear in a number of the manuscript collections.

The older organizations have generally received less attention during the wartime period, an understandable neglect in view of their withdrawal into hesitant or calculated inactivity. Peter Filene's "The World Peace Foundation and Progressivism: 1910-1918," *New England Quarterly*, 36 (Dec. 1963), 478-501 gives sparse attention to the period after 1914. Thomas Sands Patterson, "The Travail of the American Peace Movement, 1887-1914," Ph.D. dissertation, University of California, Berkeley, 1968, describes briefly the quiescence of the World Peace Foundation after 1914 and relates more fully the story of the American Peace Society's gravitation away from the active peace movement. Michael Lutzker's "The 'Practical' Peace Advocates" gives some attention to the Carnegie Endowment in the post-1914 period. Alvin Johnson's *Pioneer's Progress: An Autobiography* (New York 1952) and "The Reminiscences of Alvin Johnson," Oral History Research Office, Columbia University, provide brief but revealing glimpses of the endowment's initial reaction to the European war. For each of the prewar organizations, the yearbooks, annual reports, and ongoing periodicals for 1914-1918 constitute important sources of information. Thus, for this, as for the earlier period, one should consult the *Advocate of Peace*, the annual *Year Book* of the Carnegie Endowment and the New York Peace Society, the *American Journal of International Law*, and the *Proceedings* of the Lake Mohonk Conference (to its termination in 1916), of the American Society of International Law and of the American Society for the Judicial Settlement of International Disputes. Pamphlets and proceedings of the World's Court League appear frequently in the Hull Papers, FHL; the CEIP Papers, CUL; and the APS Papers, SCPC.

The best guide to business attitudes during the period after 1914 is Harold C. Syrett, "The Business Press and American Neutrality, 1914-1917," *Mississippi Valley Historical Review*, 32 (Sept. 1945), 215-30. I supplemented Syrett's findings with my own study of the changes in business participation in several peace organizations during the period and a selective study of the business press which included, among other journals, the *Commercial and Financial Chronicle*, the *Wall Street Journal*, *Iron Age*, *The Nation's Business*, *Bradstreet's*, *The Banker's Magazine*, and *The System*. Descriptions of the rare and abortive attempts to establish busi-

nessmen's peace initiatives after 1914 can be found in Roger W.
Babson, *Actions and Reactions* (New York 1935); in the Filene
correspondence in the LEP Collection, Lowell Papers, HA; and
in Charles L. Bernheimer, "Peace Proposal: A Business Man's
Plan for Settling the War in Europe," Box 3, Jordan Papers, HI.

Chapter Six. *The Maternal Instinct*

Any analysis of the role of women in the wartime peace movement begins with the advantage of a sound, although not highly
interpretive, monograph to build upon. Marie Louise Degen's
The History of the Woman's Peace Party (Baltimore 1939) provides a full, detailed account of the development and activities of
this organization based on a variety of newspaper and periodical
sources, Jane Addams' own writings, and the correspondence and
pamphlets in the Jane Addams Papers, Swarthmore College
Peace Collection. A brief, but more interpretive account of the
women in the peace movement, which explores newer manuscript
sources, is William L. O'Neill's chapter on "The Woman Movement and the War," in his *Everyone Was Brave: The Rise and
Fall of Feminism in America* (Chicago 1969), pp. 169-224. O'Neill
includes an excellent analysis of the role and ideas of organized
women's groups during the period after American intervention.

Further accounts of the women's role in the peace movement
can now draw upon a rich variety of manuscript sources. Primary
among these are the extensive Woman's Peace Party Papers (including subcollections on the New York and other branches of the
party) in the SCPC. Invaluable for a study of the origins of the
Woman's Peace Party and its interrelationship with the woman
suffrage forces are the Fanny Garrison Villard Papers, Houghton
Library, Harvard University; the Carrie C. Catt Papers, MS Div.,
Library of Congress; and the Carrie C. Catt Papers, New York
Public Library. The Anna Garlin Spencer Papers, SCPC, contain
several important pieces of correspondence on the founding of
the party and the Rosika Schwimmer Papers, Hoover Institution
on War, Revolution and Peace and the Lillian Wald Papers,
NYPL, contain valuable material on the interaction between Jane
Addams and Madame Schwimmer and other leaders in the party.
Of peripheral usefulness are certain segments of the Oswald Gar-
rison Villard Papers, HL; the Alice L. Park Papers, HI; the Hannah J. Bailey Papers, SCPC; and the Clara B. Colby Papers,
Henry E. Huntington Library, San Marino, Calif.

Several autobiographical and contemporary accounts by participants in the Woman's Peace Party provide helpful perspec-

tives and essential information. The best of these is Jane Addams, *Peace and Bread in Time of War,* originally published in 1922 and now available in a new edition (New York 1971). The story of the International Congress of Women at The Hague is documented in *Report of the International Congress of Women* (The Hague 1915) and described more broadly, including the subsequent visits to world statesmen, in Jane Addams, Emily G. Balch, and Alice Hamilton, *Women at the Hague* (New York 1915). Important biographical and autobiographical accounts of prominent participants in the Woman's Peace Party include Emmeline Pethick-Lawrence, *My Part in a Changing World* (London 1938); Mercedes M. Randall, *Improper Bostonian: Emily Greene Balch* (New York 1964); Mary Gray Peck, *Carrie Chapman Catt* (New York 1944); and Jane Addams, *The Second Twenty Years at Hull-House* (New York 1930).

Jane Addams' ideas on peace and pacifism are interpreted in terms of her attitudes toward democracy and culture in John C. Farrell's *Beloved Lady: A History of Jane Addams' Ideas on Reform and Peace* (Baltimore 1967), in terms of a "Gemeinschaft" mode of thought in Sondra Herman, *Eleven Against War: Studies in American Internatinalist Thought, 1898-1921* (Stanford 1969) pp. 114-49, and in terms of her use of analogies from immigrant cosmopolitanism in Charles Roland Marchand, "The Ultimate Reform: World Peace in American Thought during the Progressive Era," Ph.D. dissertation, Stanford University, 1964, pp. 55-59, 157-66, 295-97. Other discussions of Jane Addams' basic ideas and motives appear in James Weber Linn, *Jane Addams: A Biography* (New York 1937); Merle Curti, "Jane Addams on Human Nature," *Journal of the History of Ideas,* 22 (Apr.-June 1961), 240-53; Daniel Levine, *Varieties of Reform Thought* (Madison, Wis. 1964); and Christopher Lasch, *The New Radicalism in America, 1889-1963: The Intellectual As a Social Type* (New York 1965).

The background of the "woman's movement" of these years has now been described and interpreted in a number of recent works including Eleanor Flexner, *Century of Struggle: The Woman's Rights Movement in the United States* (Cambridge, Mass. 1959); Page Smith, *Daughters of the Promised Land: Women in American History* (Boston 1970); William L. O'Neill, *The Woman Movement: Feminism in England and the United States* (London 1969); Andrew Sinclair, *The Better Half: The Emancipation of the American Woman* (New York 1965); and O'Neill, *Everyone Was Brave.* The relationship between the woman suffrage movement and the temperance movement is explored extensively in

Janet Giele, "Social Change in the Feminine Role: A Comparison of Woman's Suffrage and Woman's Temperance, 1870-1920," Ph.D. dissertation, Radcliffe College, 1961, and more briefly in Aileen S. Kraditor, *The Ideas of the Woman Suffrage Movement, 1890-1920* (New York 1965) and Mary Earhart, *Frances Willard: From Prayers to Politics* (Chicago 1944). Earhart also discusses the role of the WCTU in the peace movement.

The ideology of woman suffrage is provocatively explored in Professor Kraditor's *The Ideas of the Woman Suffrage Movement*. Among the many early twentieth century analyses of the relationship of women to war and peace, Jane Addams' *Newer Ideals of Peace* (New York 1907) and Charlotte Perkins Gilman, *Our Man-Made World or Our Androcentric Culture* (New York 1911) are the most interesting. Still useful, despite the flood of recent literature, is Carl Degler's earlier "Charlotte Perkins Gilman on the Theory and Practice of Feminism," *American Quarterly*, 7 (Spring 1956), 21-39.

The details of the suffrage campaigns and the story of antagonisms among and within the suffrage organizations can be explored from the participants' view in Carrie C. Catt and Nettie R. Shuler, *Woman Suffrage and Politics* (New York 1923) and Doris Stevens, *Jailed for Freedom* (New York 1920) as well as in the accounts by Flexner, Kraditor, O'Neill, Sinclair, and Smith. Responses to the crisis of American intervention are most easily followed in the two major woman suffrage periodicals of the time, the *Woman's Journal* and *The Suffragist*.

Chapter Seven. *Preserving the Social Fabric*

The single most important collection of materials on the activity of the social reformers in the peace movement of the neutrality period is the American Union Against Militarism Papers in the Swarthmore College Peace Collection. The rich AUAM Papers can be usefully supplemented with manuscript collections of several of the leading figures in the union: the Amos Pinchot Papers, MS Div., Library of Congress; the Jane Addams Papers, SCPC; the Emily Greene Balch Papers, SCPC; the Oswald Garrison Villard Papers, Houghton Library, Harvard University; and the Lillian Wald Papers, New York Public Library. An additional collection of Lillian Wald Papers, which I was not able to examine, is now available in the Columbia University Library. Other collections of potential usefulness are the Paul Kellogg Papers, University of Minnesota; the Norman Thomas Papers, NYPL; and the Louis P. Lochner Papers, State Historical Society of Wisconsin.

The unpublished "Reminiscences," of Roger Baldwin in the Oral History Research Office, Columbia University, are lively, readable and highly informative. Other manuscript collections of secondary usefulness are the H.W.L. Dana Papers, SCPC; the David Starr Jordan Papers, Hoover Institution on War, Revolution and Peace; and the Woman's Peace Party Correspondence, SCPC.

In printed sources, the history of the social reformers and social workers in the peace movement is best revealed in the issues of *The Survey* between 1914 and 1918. This was the central organ of the social workers and humanitarian social reformers of the era. No published monographs attempt to deal in detail with the American Union Against Militarism, but Blanche Wiesen Cook's dissertation, "Woodrow Wilson and the Antimilitarists, 1914-1917," The Johns Hopkins University, 1970, provides a detailed account of the union's origins, lobbying efforts, and internal divisions. Professor Cook places particular emphasis upon its almost unshakeable confidence in Wilson. Donald Johnson discusses the union briefly as the progenitor of the American Civil Liberties Union in his *The Challenge to American Freedoms: World War I and the Rise of the American Civil Liberties Union* (Lexington, Ky. 1963) and Allen W. Davis discusses the reactions of the social reformers to the war with passing mention of the American Union in "Welfare, Reform and World War I," *American Quarterly*, 19 (Fall 1967), 516-33 and in *Spearheads of Reform: The Social Settlements and the Progressive Movement, 1890-1914* (New York 1967). Charles Chatfield probes intermittently into the ideas and assumptions of the American Union in "World War I and the Liberal Pacifist in the United States," *American Historical Review*, 75 (Dec. 1970), 1920-37.

Numerous autobiographies and biographies offer personal glimpses of the reactions of reformers and social workers to the wartime challenges. Of particular value are Lillian Wald, *Windows on Henry Street* (Boston 1934); Michael Wreszin, *Oswald Garrison Villard: Pacifist at War* (Bloomington, Ind. 1965); John Haynes Holmes, *I Speak for Myself: The Autobiography of John Haynes Holmes* (New York 1959); Mercedes M. Randall, *Improper Bostonian: Emily Greene Balch* (New York 1964); Milton Cantor, *Max Eastman* (New York 1970); Clarke A. Chambers, *Paul U. Kellogg and the* Survey: *Voices for Social Welfare and Social Justice* (Minneapolis 1971); and Jane Addams, *Peace and Bread in Time of War* (New York 1922). Other useful personal insights from the perspective of individual participants can be gleaned from Jane Addams, *The Second Twenty Years at Hull-House* (New York 1930); Josephine Goldmark, *Impatient Crusader: Florence Kelley's Life Story* (Urbana, Ill. 1953); Max Eastman, *Love and Revolution* (New York 1964); Alice Hamilton, *Exploring the Dangerous Trades: The Autobiography of Alice Hamilton, M.D.* (Boston 1943); and Frances Witherspoon and Tracy D. Mygatt, "The Reminiscences of Frances Witherspoon and Tracy D. Mygatt," Oral History Research Project, Columbia University.

The ideas that came to animate the American Union are best explored in the numerous pamphlets and broadsides in the American Union Papers and in articles by its leaders in such periodicals as *The Survey*. The fullest early expression of the social reformers' ideas came in "Towards the Peace that Shall Last," *The Survey*, 33 (6 Mar. 1915), Part II. Some of these ideas received contemporary expression in larger published works including Frederick Howe, *Why War?* (New York 1916); John Haynes Holmes, *New Wars For Old* (New York 1916); and Emily Greene Balch, *Approaches to the Great Settlement* (New York 1918).

In attempting to suggest the connections between participation in the peace movement and changes in the situation of social reformers and social workers, I found two studies invaluable: Roy Lubove, *The Professional Altruist: The Emergence of Social Work as a Career, 1880-1930* (Cambridge, Mass. 1965) and Allen F. Davis, *Spearheads for Reform: The Social Settlements and the Progressive Movement, 1890-1914* (New York 1967). Allen F. Davis, "The Campaign for the Industrial Relations Commission, 1911-1913," *Mid-America*, 45 (Oct. 1963), 211-28 helped me to see the continuity in certain informal coalitions of social reformers. Clarke A. Chambers, "Social Service and Social Reform—A Historical Essay," *Social Science Review*, 37 (Mar. 1963), 76-90 provided a useful overview of trends in social work.

The best introduction to the wider issues of professionalization and professionalism is Everett Cherrington Hughes, *Men and Their Work* (Glencoe, Ill. 1958). Also useful are the first two chapters in Kenneth Lynn, ed., *The Professions in America* (Boston 1965). For brief introductions, respectively, to the functional and "process" approaches to the sociology of professions see William J. Goode, "Community within a Community: The Professions," *American Sociological Review*, 22 (Apr. 1957), 194-200 and Rue Bucher and Anselm Strauss, "Professions in Process," *American Journal of Sociology*, 66 (Jan. 1961), 325-34.

Chapter Eight. *The Workingman's Burden*

For all the clichéd discussions of war as the workingman's burden, no authentic peace organization controlled by actual workingmen appeared during the early twentieth century. Several peace societies made intermittent overtures to labor leaders and many peace organizations of the post-1914 years, despite their middle class leadership, claimed the support of workers and of "the masses." The closest the peace movement came to effective contact with groups of organized workers occurred during the few months immediately after American intervention. Not only did the major peace organization of those months, the People's Council of America for Democracy and Peace, make pronouncements on behalf of workers, but it actually established temporary links with Socialist segments of the labor movement.

The People's Council, the most radical of the secular peace organizations of the World War I era, can be examined through the use of several manuscript collections. Its papers in the Swarthmore College Peace Collection contain the fullest selection of pamphlets, correspondence, and organizational records. The council papers at the Hoover Institution on War, Revolution and Peace are very limited in size but contain some good materials on the organization during its period of decline. The People's Council papers at the Tamiment Institute are largely confined to printed materials and, in most instances, duplicate items available in other collections. Other manuscript collections with significant amounts of material bearing directly upon the council are the Amos Pinchot Papers, MS Div., Library of Congress; the Emily Greene Balch Papers, SCPC; the American Council for Democracy and Terms of Peace Papers, SCPC; the H.W.L. Dana Papers, SCPC; and certain segments of the papers of the American Union Against Militarism and the Woman's Peace Party, New York Branch, in the SCPC. Other potentially useful manuscript sources which I lacked time or opportunity to examine include the Louis P. Lochner Papers, State Historical Society of Wisconsin, and the papers of the American Alliance for Labor and Democracy in the Samuel Gompers Papers, American Federation of Labor Archives, Washington, D.C. Several important letters are reproduced in Clayton R. Lusk, ed. *Revolutionary Radicalism: Report of the Joint Legislative Committee of the State of New York* (Albany 1920).

Secondary accounts of the history of the People's Council are relatively few. The fullest account appears in Frank L. Grubbs,

Jr., *The Struggle for Labor Loyalty: Gompers, the A.F. of L. and the Pacifists, 1917-1920* (Durham, N.C. 1968), a monograph which emphasizes the career of the antagonist of the People's Council, the American Alliance for Labor and Democracy more than that of the People's Council, and which is concerned far more with the conflict between these two organizations than with the place of the council in the evolving peace movement. Useful materials also appear in Grubbs' "The Struggle for the Mind of American Labor, 1917-1919," Ph.D. dissertation, University of Virginia, 1963, which are not included in the published version. Brief accounts of the People's Council can be found in H. C. Peterson and Gilbert C. Fite, *Opponents of War, 1917-1918* (Madison, Wis. 1957); in Ronald Radosh, *American Labor and United States Foreign Policy* (New York 1969), pp. 54-57; in Melvyn Dubofsky, "New York City Labor in the Progressive Era, 1910-1918: A Study of Organized Labor in an Era of Reform," Ph.D. dissertation, University of Rochester, 1960; and in Milton Cantor's rather unfocused essay "The Radical Confrontation with Foreign Policy: War and Revolution, 1914-1920," in Alfred F. Young, ed., *Dissent: Explorations in the History of American Radicalism* (DeKalb, Ill. 1968), pp. 217-49. A contemporary account appears in "Rival War-Time Labor Bodies," *The Survey*, 38 (4 Aug. 1917), 410-12. Memoirs and autobiographies by participants in the council are disappointingly cursory in their treatment of this organization. The most useful of these are: Morris Hillquit, *Loose Leaves From a Busy Life* (New York 1934); James Maurer, *It Can Be Done: The Autobiography of James Hudson Maurer* (New York 1938); Louis P. Lochner, *Always the Unexpected: A Book of Reminiscences* (New York 1956); Max Eastman, *Love and Revolution: My Journey Through an Epoch* (New York 1964); and Lella Secor Florence, "The Ford Peace Ship and After," in Julian Bell, ed., *We Did Not Fight, 1914-1918 Experiences of War Resisters* (London 1935), pp. 97-125. Joseph Freeman's *An American Testament: A Narrative of Rebels and Romantics* (New York 1936) offers some brief views from a sympathetic young radical of the period.

The effort of the People's Council to give organized expression to the workingman's alleged complaint against war must be seen against the background of earlier attitudes toward war expressed by contenders for the role of spokesman for the laboring man. The evolution of the Socialist Party and its preoccupation with domestic issues can be traced in a number of the many studies of early twentieth century socialism in the United States. Among these I found most valuable David A. Shannon's *The Socialist Party of America: A History* (New York 1955); Ira Kipnis' *The American Socialist Movement, 1897-1912* (New York 1952); James Weinstein's *The Decline of Socialism in America, 1912-1925* (New York 1967); Theodore Draper's *The Roots of American Communism* (New York 1957); and Howard Quint's "The American Socialists and the Spanish-American War," *American Quarterly*, 10 (Summer 1958), 131-41. Two unpublished studies were particularly helpful: Gerald Friedberg, "Marxism in the United States: John Spargo and the Socialist Party of America," Ph.D. dissertation, Harvard University, 1965 and Michael E. B. Bassett, "The Socialist Party of America, 1912-1919: Years of Decline," Ph.D. dissertation, Duke University, 1964.

The Socialist attitudes toward war and a variety of international issues can be traced through the *Proceedings* of the party conventions, the party platforms, and the relatively infrequent (at least until 1915) extended Socialist treatises and compilations of documents on war. Among the latter, the most notable are: George R. Kirkpatrick, *War—What For?* (West LaFayette, Ohio 1910); Allan Louis Benson, *A Way to Prevent War* (Girard, Kans. 1915); William English Walling, ed., *The Socialists and the War* (New York 1915); Alexander Trachtenberg, ed., *The American Socialists and the War* (New York 1917); and Louis B. Boudin, *Socialism and War* (New York 1916). Important briefer statements on war from a Socialist perspective occur in Charles Edward Russell, *Why I Am a Socialist* (New York 1910) and its new and revised edition (New York 1915); Carl D. Thompson, "International Socialism as a Peace Force," *Proceedings of the Second National Peace Congress* (Chicago 1909); Upton Sinclair, *Socialism and War* (London [1913]); George Allan England, "Fiat Pax," *International Conciliation*, No. 81 (Aug. 1914); and James Oneal, "The Socialists in the War," *American Mercury*, 10 (Apr. 1927), 418-27. The theories and policies of the European Socialists and the Second International are conveniently surveyed in James Joll, *The Second International, 1889-1914* (London 1955) and in Lewis L. Lorwin, *Labor and Internationalism* (New York 1929).

The evolving attitudes toward war of the AFL and its president, Samuel Gompers, are largely documented in the issues of the *American Federationist*. A number of the AFL stands and policies are reviewed in the *American Federation of Labor: History, Encyclopedia, Reference Book* (Washington, D.C. 1919). Samuel Gompers' own views and his subsequent interpretation of his position appear in his *American Labor and the War* (New

York 1919) and his *Seventy Years of Life and Labor: An Auto-biography*, 2 vols. (New York 1925). Bernard Mandel views Gompers' actions and motivations from a more critical angle in his *Samuel Gompers* (Yellow Springs, Ohio 1963). Additional insights on the connections between domestic issues and attitudes toward international relations in the AFL can be derived from Marc Karson, *American Labor Unions and Politics, 1900-1918* (Carbondale, Ill. 1958) and Philip Taft, *The A. F. of L. in the Time of Gompers* (New York 1957).

A wealth of scholarly studies of the labor movement in New York City and of the Jewish immigrant community provide the context for understanding the prominent participation of Jewish labor unions in the People's Council. Melech Epstein's *Jewish Labor in the U. S. A., 1914-1952: An Industrial, Political and Cultural History of the Jewish Labor Movement* (New York 1953) provides an excellent survey which I supplemented, on specific issues, with Moses Rischin, *The Promised City: New York's Jews, 1870-1914* (Cambridge, Mass. 1962); Joseph Rappaport, "Jewish Immigrants and World War I: A Study of American Yiddish Press Reactions," Ph.D. dissertation, Columbia University, 1951; Matthew Josephson, *Sidney Hillman, Statesman of American Labor* (Garden City, N.Y. 1952); Benjamin Stolberg, *Tailor's Progress: the Story of a Famous Union and the Men Who Made It* (New York 1944); and Morris Schappes, "The Attitude of Jewish Labor to World War I, 1917-1918," *Jewish Life*, 9 (Mar. 1955), 21-24. Frequently helpful on this and other aspects of labor in New York City is Melvyn Dubofsky's "New York City Labor in the Progressive Era, 1910-1918: A Study of Organized Labor in an Era of Reform," Ph.D. dissertation, University of Rochester, 1960, which is broader in scope than his published account, *When Workers Organize: New York City in the Progressive Era* (Amherst, Mass. 1968). On the unique role of Judah Magnes in the People's Council I turned to Norman Bentwich, *For Zion's Sake: A Biography of Judah L. Magnes* (Philadelphia 1954) and Arthur A. Goren, *New York Jews and the Quest for Community: The Kehillah Experiment, 1908-1922* (New York 1970).

Various aspects of the radical approach to foreign policy suggested by the People's Council, and the reactions to the Russian Revolution which it expressed, can be explored in works which treat these issues in a wider international perspective and in works which treat American reactions to Russian policies and programs in the post-World War I era. Several of the most provocative of these are Arno J. Mayer, *Political Origins of the New*

Diplomacy (New Haven, Conn. 1959); Peter G. Filene, *Americans and the Soviet Experiment, 1917-1933* (Cambridge, Mass. 1967); Ronald Radosh, *American Labor and United States Foreign Policy* (New York 1969); Christopher Lasch, *The American Liberals and the Russian Revolution* (New York 1962); and N. Gordon Levin, Jr., *Woodrow Wilson and World Politics: America's Response to War and Revolution* (New York 1968).

Chapter Nine. *Peace, Church Unity, and the Social Gospel*

Of the various manuscript sources bearing upon the role of the churches in the early twentieth century peace movement, one of the most valuable, despite its limited size, is the collection of Church Peace Union Papers held by the union's successor organization, the Council on Religion and International Affairs, 170 E. 64th Street, New York City. The collection includes a small amount of important correspondence and nearly all of the minutes of the early years of the Church Peace Union. Another good collection of Church Peace Union papers is located in the Swarthmore College Peace Collection. The most important single manuscript collection for the early history of the Fellowship of Reconciliation in the United States is the Fellowship of Reconciliation Papers, SCPC. It contains good collections of FOR publications, minutes, and conference records but is relatively weak in correspondence. Of supplemental value are the Fannie Fern Andrews Papers, Arthur and Elizabeth Schlesinger Library, Radcliffe College, which contain large amounts of materials on peace distributed by the Federal Council and the World Alliance, and the Federal Council of the Churches of Christ Papers, The World Alliance for International Friendship Through the Churches Papers, and the William I. Hull Papers, all in the SCPC.

Evidence on the participation of clergymen in the American Peace Society and in the Mohonk Conferences in the prewar period can be readily derived from the issues of the *Advocate of Peace* and the *Annual Reports* of the Lake Mohonk Conference on International Arbitration. Particularly useful in comparing the peace movement to the foreign missions activities of the Protestant churches is Valentin Hanno Rabe, "Protestant Foreign Missions, 1880-1920," Ph.D. dissertation, Harvard University, 1964, a very thorough analysis and interpretation. For clerical attitudes toward foreign affairs it can be supplemented with John Edwin Smylie, "Protestant Clergymen and American Destiny: II, Prelude to Imperialism, 1865-1890," *Harvard Theological Review*, 56 (Oct. 1963), 297-311 which summarizes the major conclusions from Smylie's dissertation listed above, and Paul A. Varg, "Motives in Protestant Missions, 1890-1917," *Church History*, 23 (Mar. 1954), 68-82. Suggestions of the relationship between the peace movement and the foreign missions movement can also be derived from numerous contemporary sources including John R. Mott, *The Evangelization of the World in This Generation* (New York 1905); Caroline Atwater Mason, *World Missions and World Peace* (West Medford, Mass. 1916); Samuel B. Capen, "Foreign Missions and World Peace," *World Peace Foundation Pamphlet Series*, No. 7, Part III (Oct. 1912); and the *Annual Report* of the American Board of Commissioners for Foreign Missions.

The best data available for exploring the relationship between Protestant theological liberalism and the peace movement is contained in the unpublished materials of Professor William R. Hutchison of the Harvard Divinity School, the first conclusions from which have appeared in his "Cultural Strain and Protestant Liberalism," *American Historical Review*, 76 (Apr. 1971), 386-411. I am indebted to Professor Hutchison for the opportunity to examine portions of his raw materials. A convenient brief bibliography of materials on liberal theological thought in the late nineteenth century appears in William R. Hutchison, ed., *American Protestant Thought: The Liberal Era* (New York 1968), pp. 14-16. Useful contemporary works include Washington Gladden, *The Forks of the Road* (New York 1916) and George Holley Gilbert, *The Bible and International Peace* (New York 1914).

The history of the social gospel movement in American Protestantism in the late nineteenth and early twentieth centuries is recounted in C. Howard Hopkins, *The Rise of the Social Gospel in American Protestantism, 1865-1915* (New Haven, Conn. 1940); Henry F. May, *Protestant Churches and Industrial America* (New York 1949); and Aaron Ignatius Abell, *The Urban Impact on American Protestantism 1865-1900* (Cambridge, Mass. 1943). For the changing relationships with the peace movement of two prominent, moderate social gospel leaders see Jacob Henry Dorn, *Washington Gladden, Prophet of the Social Gospel* (Columbus, Ohio 1966), pp. 402-33 and Ira V. Brown, *Lyman Abbott, Christian Evolutionist: A Study in Religious Liberalism* (Cambridge, Mass. 1953), pp. 161-79, 184-87, 214-28.

On the interconnections between the peace movement and the church unity movement, the best secondary account is John A. Hutchison's interpretive *We Are Not Divided: A Critical and Historical Study of the Federal Council of the Churches of Christ in America* (New York 1941). Robert Lee's broader approach in

The Social Sources of Church Unity: An Interpretation of Unitive Movements in American Protestantism (New York 1960), is less specific. Elias B. Sanford's *Origin and History of the Federal Council of the Churches of Christ in America* (Hartford, Conn. 1916) contains much valuable information despite its dreary style and eulogistic approach. Charles S. Macfarland's own accounts of his roles in the church unity and peace movements in *Christian Unity in the Making* (New York 1948), *Across the Years* (New York 1936), and *Pioneers for Peace Through Religion* (New York 1946) rely heavily on the materials in the *Annual Reports* of the Federal Council and the Church Peace Union and are essentially official histories. Frederick Lynch's *The Peace Problem* (New York 1911) and *Personal Recollections of Andrew Carnegie* (New York 1920) are only partially revealing of Lynch's ideas and activities in his rise to a leading position within the peace movement and should be read in conjunction with Lynch's correspondence on behalf of the Church Peace Union.

For the role of the Federal Council and the Church Peace Union during the neutrality and wartime periods, Ray H. Abrams' indictment of the clergy in his muckraking *Preachers Present Arms* (New York 1933) should be balanced against Hutchison's *We Are Not Divided* and John Franklin Piper Jr.'s "The Social Policy of the Churches of Christ in America During World War I," Ph.D. dissertation, Duke University, 1965. Further materials on the wartime period are available in Charles S. Macfarland, ed., *The Churches of Christ in Time of War* (New York 1917); Frederick Lynch, *The Christian in War Time* (New York 1917); William Adams Brown, *A Teacher and His Times: A Story of Two Worlds* (New York 1940); Macfarland, *Pioneers for Peace Through Religion*; and in the broadsides, pamphlets, and other ephemera in the manuscript collections listed above.

The most thorough scholarly study of the Fellowship of Reconciliation appears in Charles Chatfield's recent *For Peace and Justice: Pacifism in America, 1914-1941* (Knoxville 1971) which devotes primary attention to the fellowship in the interwar years. Chatfield's "Pacifism and American Life, 1914 to 1941," Ph.D. dissertation, Vanderbilt University, 1965, contains additional information. Earlier accounts which give relatively little attention to the American branch of the fellowship and its early years are Lilian Stevenson, *Towards a Christian International: The Story of the International Fellowship of Reconciliation*, new and enlarged edition (London 1941) and Vera Brittain, *The Rebel Passion: A Short History of Some Pioneer Peace-Makers* (New

York 1964). John Nevin Sayre, *The Story of the Fellowship of Reconciliation, 1915-1935* (New York 1935) also contains little detailed information. Charles Chatfield, "World War I and the Liberal Pacifist in the United States," *American Historical Review*, 75 (Dec. 1970), 1920-1937 summarizes a few of his findings on the Fellowship of Reconciliation and suggests additional manuscript collections of value.

The activities of the fellowship in the postwar years are discussed in the context of the peace movement in Chatfield, *For Peace and Justice* and in the context of the social gospel movement in Donald B. Meyer, *The Protestant Search for Political Realism, 1919-1941* (Berkeley 1960) and Robert Moats Miller, *American Protestantism and Social Issues, 1919-1939* (Chapel Hill 1958). The backgrounds of religious pacifism in the United States before World War I are skillfully and comprehensively presented in Peter Brock, *Pacifism in the United States: From the Colonial Era to the First World War* (Princeton 1968). Earlier studies of sectarian pacifism include Margaret E. Hirst, *The Quakers in Peace and War: An Account of their Peace Principles and Practice* (New York 1923), pp. 517-21 and Rufus D. Bowman, *The Church of the Brethren and War* (Elgin, Ill. 1944), pp. 161-233. Brief views of the role of the fellowship from the perspective of early participants include Norman Thomas, *The Conscientious Objector in America* (New York 1963); A. J. Muste, "Sketches for an Autobiography," in Nat Hentoff, ed., *The Essays of A. J. Muste* (Indianapolis 1967); and in Harry Fleischman, *Norman Thomas: A Biography* (New York 1964).

Chapter Ten. *Conclusion*

Except for the materials on the Chicago Peace Society and the Chicago Conference Committee on Terms of Peace located in the Jane Addams Papers and the American Conference for Democracy and Terms of Peace Papers, Swarthmore College Peace Collection, the conclusion draws only upon materials already cited in the essays for specific chapters. Perhaps several works should be cited here, however, that treat the responses of various groups of politicians, intellectuals, and reformers to the first World War from a different standpoint or with different emphases than those I have chosen. The rapid transformation of the peace movement in this period should be viewed in relationship to the cultural and intellectual changes discussed in Henry F. May, *The End of American Innocence: A Study of the First Years of Our Own Time, 1912-1917* (New York 1959); Christopher Lasch, *The New*

Radicalism in America, 1889-1963: The Intellectual as a Social Type (New York 1965); Charles Forcey, *The Crossroads of Liberalism: Croly, Weyl, Lippmann and the Progressive Era 1900-1925* (New York 1961); and David W. Noble, *The Paradox of Progressive Thought* (Minneapolis 1958). Robert H. Wiebe's *The Search for Order, 1877-1920* (New York 1967) provides an excellent interpretive framework for the understanding of foreign policy during the early twentieth century. Useful shorter essays which deal with reactions of specific groups to the war situation are: Walter I. Trattner, "Progressivism and World War I: A Reappraisal," *Mid-America*, 44 (July 1962), 131-45; Charles Hirshfeld, "Nationalist Progressivism and World War I," *Mid-America*, 45 (July 1963); 139-56; David W. Noble, "The *New Republic* and the Idea of Progress, 1914-1920," *Mississippi Valley Historical Review*, 38 (Dec. 1951), 387-402; Allen F. Davis, "Welfare, Reform and World War I," *American Quarterly*, 19 (Fall 1967), 516-33; Sidney Kaplan, "Social Engineers as Saviors: Effects of World War I on Some American Liberals," *Journal of the History of Ideas*, 17 (June 1956), 347-69; and Stanley Shapiro, "The Great War and Reform: Liberals and Labor, 1917-19," *Labor History*, 12 (Summer 1971), 323-44.

Index

Abbott, Grace, 228, 258, 262

Abbott, Lyman, 11, 27-28, 36, 328n, 338n, 384; and "Christian imperialism," 28, 327-28

abolitionist movement: and peace movement, 4-7, 13; and woman suffrage movement, 185, 187, 191, 191n

academicians, 102, 106-7, 110-12, 120; and scholarly approach to peace, 162, 165

Academy of International Law, 47

Adams, Henry, 31

Adams, Herbert Baxter, 31

Addams, Jane, 148, 317, 320n, 358, 374-75, 384-85, 386n; and American Peace Society, 11, 12n; and origins of Woman's Peace Party, 193, 195-200; on physical force and woman suffrage, 201-4; leadership in WPP, 206-7, 209, 212-13; and Conference of Women at The Hague, 209-10, 238; and neutral conference plan and Ford peace ship, 210-11, 238-39; as critic of traditional diplomacy, 211, 246; faces conflict between peace activism and social reform responsibilities, 219-21, 258-59, 264; and Henry Street Committee, 223, 225n, 226n, 227-28; and social work, 229-30; on war and social conditions, 232; and model of immigrant cosmopolitanism, 239; and American Union Against Militarism, 251, 255, 258-59; and People's Council, 264

Adee, Alvey, 70

Adler, Felix, 225n

Advance, The, 318

Advocate of Peace, 8, 13-15, 20, 132, 146-50, 152, 337n; on Spanish-American War, 24-26; and anti-imperialism, 27; on First Hague Conference, 30; and Anglo-Saxonism, 34; and nationalism, 35-36

Ainslie, Peter, 384n

Alabama claims arbitration, 42, 46, 82

Alaska boundary tribunal, 46

Alcott, Bronson, 6

Algeciras Conference, 61

aliens: and federal protection, 29; and California antialien laws, 141

Almy, Frederic, 261

Amalgamated Clothing Workers of America (ACWA), 284, 286; and People's Council, 298-99, 313, 317-18

American Alliance for Labor and Democracy, 315-17

American Association for International Conciliation, 38, 122n

American Association for Labor Legislation, 225, 225n, 376

American Bar Association, 49, 63

American Board of Commissioners for Foreign Missions, 12, 27, 331, 331n

American Christian Missionary Society, 91

American Civil Liberties Union, 258. *See also* Civil Liberties Bureau

American Committee on War Finance, 249, 251

American Conference for Democracy and Terms of Peace (ACDTP), 256, 306, 308, 370, 376, 384. *See also* People's Council

American Federationist, 275, 281

American Federation of Labor (AFL), 272, 275-87, 298, 317, 321; on war and international issues before 1914, 275-78, 281-83; and peace societies, 275, 280-81; and public respectability, 278, 281-82; and neutrality period, 284; and wartime support, 284, 286-87; divisions within, 286

American Humane Education Society, 14

American Institute of International Law, 65, 168

American institutions, as models for international application, xii-xiv, 23-24, 28-29, 32-33, 35-37, 59, 382

American Jewish Congress, 301

American Journal of International Law, 41, 48